Modeling Derivatives Applications in Matlab, C++, and Excel

FINANCIAL TIMES

In an increasingly competitive world, it is quality
of thinking that gives an edge—an idea that opens new
doors, a technique that solves a problem, or an insight
that simply helps make sense of it all.

We work with leading authors in the various arenas
of business and finance to bring cutting-edge thinking
and best-learning practices to a global market.

It is our goal to create world-class print publications
and electronic products that give readers
knowledge and understanding that can then be
applied, whether studying or at work.

To find out more about our business
products, you can visit us at www.ftpress.com.

Modeling Derivatives Applications in Matlab, C++, and Excel

Justin London

An Imprint of PEARSON EDUCATION
Upper Saddle River, NJ • New York • London • San Francisco • Toronto • Sydney
Tokyo • Singapore • Hong Kong • Cape Town • Madrid
Paris • Milan • Munich • Amsterdam

Vice President, Editor-in-Chief: Tim Moore
Executive Editor: Jim Boyd
Editorial Assistant: Susie Abraham
Development Editor: Russ Hall
Associate Editor-in-Chief and Director of Marketing: Amy Neidlinger
Cover Designer: Chuti Prasertsith
Managing Editor: Gina Kanouse
Senior Project Editor: Lori Lyons
Copy Editor: Water Crest Publishing
Indexer: Christine Karpeles
Compositor: Lori Hughes
Manufacturing Buyer: Dan Uhrig

© 2007 by Pearson Education, Inc.
Publishing as FT Press
Upper Saddle River, New Jersey 07458

FT Press offers excellent discounts on this book when ordered in quantity for bulk purchases or special sales. For more information, please contact U.S. Corporate and Government Sales, 1-800- 382-3419, corpsales@pearsontechgroup.com. For sales outside the U.S., please contact International Sales at international@pearsoned.com.

Printed in the United States of America
First Printing December, 2006

ISBN: 0-13-196259-0

Pearson Education LTD.
Pearson Education Australia PTY, Limited.
Pearson Education Singapore, Pte. Ltd.
Pearson Education North Asia, Ltd.
Pearson Education Canada, Ltd.
Pearson Educatión de Mexico, S.A. de C.V.
Pearson Education—Japan
Pearson Education Malaysia, Pte. Ltd.

Library of Congress Cataloging-in-Publication Data

London, Justin, 1968-
    Modeling Derivatives Applications in Matlab, C++, and Excel / Justin London.
        p. cm.
    ISBN 0-13-196259-0 (hardback : alk. paper)
    1. Modeling Credit Derivatives. 2. Pricing Models in Matlab, C++, and Excel.   I. Title.
    HF5548.4.L692E45 2006
    005.5'7–dc22
                                        2006023492

*To the memory of my grandparents, Milton and Evelyn London;
my parents, Leon and Leslie; and my sister, Joanna.*

CONTENTS

PREFACE

Given the explosive growth in new financial derivatives such as credit derivatives, hundreds of financial institutions now market these complex instruments and employ thousands of financial and technical professionals needed to model them accurately and effectively. Moreover, the implementation of these models in C++ and Matlab (two widely used languages for implementing and building derivatives models) has made programming skills in these languages important for practitioners to have. In addition, the use of Excel is also important as many trading desks use Excel as a front-end trading application.

Modeling Derivatives Applications in Matlab, C++, and Excel is the first book to cover in detail important derivatives pricing models for credit derivatives (for example, credit default swaps and credit-linked notes), collateralized-debt obligations (CDOs), mortgage-backed securities (MBSs), asset-backed securities (ABSs), swaps, fixed income securities, and increasingly important weather, power, and energy derivatives using Matlab, C++, and Excel. Readers will benefit from both the mathematical derivations of the models, the theory underlying the models, as well as the code implementations.

Throughout this book, numerous examples are given using Matlab, C++, and Excel. Examples using actual real-time Bloomberg data show how these models work in practice. The purpose of the book is to teach readers how to properly develop and implement derivatives applications so that they can adapt the code for their own use as they develop their own applications. The best way to learn is to follow the examples and run the code. The chapters cover the following topics:

- Chapter 1: Swaps and fixed income securities

- Chapter 2: Copulas and copula methodologies

- Chapter 3: Mortgage-backed securities

- Chapter 4: Collateralized-debt obligations

- Chapter 5: Credit derivatives

- Chapter 6: Weather derivatives

- Chapter 7: Energy and power derivatives

- Chapter 8: Also covers model implementations for energy derivatives using Matlab, but is written and based on the proprietary work of its author, Craig Pirrong, professor of finance and director of the Global Energy Management Institute at the University of Houston.

- Chapter 9: Commercial real-estate backed securities (a type of asset-backed security), which is written and is based on the proprietary work of its author, Tien-Foo Sing, professor in the Department of Real Estate Finance at the National University of Singapore.

In order to provide different perspectives to readers and provide as much useful information as possible, the work and models developed and written by various leading practitioners and experts for certain topics are provided and incorporated throughout the book. Thus, not only does this book cover complex derivatives models and provide all of the code (which can be downloaded using a secure ID code from the companion Web site at *www.ftpress.com/title/0131962590*), but it also incorporates important work contributions from leading practitioners in the industry. For instance, the work of Galiani (2003) is discussed in the chapter on copulas and credit derivatives. The work of Picone (2004) is discussed in the chapter on collateralized-debt obligations. The work of Johnson (2004) is discussed in the chapters on fixed-income instruments and mortgage-backed securities. The valuable work for energy derivatives of Doerr (2002), Xiang (2004), and Xu (2004) is given. In Chapter 8, Craig Pirrong discusses the Pirrong-Jermayakan model, a two-dimensional alternating implicit difference (ADI) finite difference scheme for pricing energy derivatives. In Chapter 9, Tien-Foo Sing discusses using Monte Carlo to price asset-based securities. Moreover, numerous individuals named in the acknowledgments contributed useful code throughout the book.

The book emphasizes how to implement and code complex models for pricing, trading, and hedging using C++, Matlab, and Excel. The book does not focus on design patterns or best coding practices (these issues may be discussed in subsequent editions of the book.) Efficiency and modularity are important design goals in building robust object-oriented code. In some cases in this book, the C++ code provided could perhaps be more modular as with some of the routines in building interest rate trees. The emphasis throughout the book has been to provide working implementations for the reader to adapt. However, the book does provide some discussions and helpful tips for building efficient models. For instance, memory allocation for data structures is always an issue when developing a model that requires use and storage of multi-dimensional data. Use of a predefined two-dimensional array, for instance, is not the most efficient way to allocate memory since it is fixed in size. A lot of memory may be unutilized and wasted if you do not know how large the structure needs to be to store the actual data. On the other hand, the predefined array sizes may turn out not to be large enough.

Although two-dimensional arrays are easy to define, use of array template classes (that can handle multiple dimensions) and vectors (of vectors) in the Standard Template Library in C++ are more efficient because they are dynamic and only use as much memory as is needed. Such structures are used in the book, although some two-dimensional arrays are used as well. Matlab, a matrix manipulation language, provides automatic memory allocation of memory as data is used if no array sizes are predefined. All data in Matlab are treated as matrix objects; e.g., a single number is treated as a 1 x 1 array. Data can be added or removed from an object and the object will dynamically expand or reduce the amount of memory space as needed.

While every effort has been made to catch all typos and errors in the book, inevitably in a book of this length and complexity, there may still be a few. Any corrections will be posted on the Web site.

Hopefully, this book will give you the foundation to develop, build, and test your own models while saving you a great deal of development time through use of pre-tested robust code.

SUPPLEMENTAL FILES ON THE WEB SITE

To download the code in this book, you must first register online. You will need a valid email address and the access code that is printed inside the envelope located at the back of the book.

To register online, go to *www.ftpress.com/title/0131962590* and follow the on-screen instructions.

If you have any questions about online registration or downloading the code, please send us an inquiry via the Contact Us page at *http://www.ftpress.com/about/contact_us/*.

NOTE: The code files are Copyrighted © 2006 by Justin London and the contributors thereof. Unauthorized reproduction or distribution is prohibited. All rights reserved.

ACKNOWLEDGMENTS

Special thanks to the following people for their code and work contributions to this book:
Ahsan Amin
Sean Campbell
Francis Diebold
Uwe Doerr
Stefano Galiani
Michael Gibson
Stafford Johnson
Jochen Meyer
Dominic Picone
Craig Pirrong
Eduardo Schwartz
Tien Foo Sing
Liuren Wu
Lei Xiong
James Xu

ABOUT THE AUTHOR

Justin London has developed fixed-income and equity models for trading companies and his own quantitative consulting firm. He has analyzed and managed bank corporate loan portfolios using credit derivatives in the Asset Portfolio Group of a large bank in Chicago, Illinois, as well as advised several banks in their implementation of derivative trading systems. London is the founder of a global online trading and financial technology company. A graduate of the University of Michigan, London holds a B.A. in economics and mathematics, an M.A. in applied economics, and an M.S. in financial engineering, computer science, and mathematics, respectively.

SWAPS AND FIXED INCOME INSTRUMENTS

SECTIONS

Swaps are often used to hedge interest rate risk exposure to balance sheets as well as for bond and loan portfolios. By matching the durations of balance sheet fixed income assets and liabilities (e.g., bond or loan instruments), swaps can immunize the balance sheet from interest rate risk. Ideally, the hedge should match both the duration and timing of cash flows of the fixed income portfolio with that of the swap as closely as possible. For instance, if a bank has a portfolio of floating-rate loans that have a duration of five years, the bank can enter a swap with a duration of five years (the duration of the swap is the difference between the fixed- and floating-leg durations of the swap) to receive the fixed rate and to pay floating (effectively changing the characterization of the loan from floating to fixed and thereby locking in a fixed rate of return.) Although in general, basis risk exists because there is not an exact match between the cash flows—e.g., interest rate payments on the loans and those of the swap do not match—the bank has reduced its exposure to shifts in the yield curve. Moreover, institutional money managers can also use a combination

1

of Chicago Board of Trade (CBOT) Treasury note futures and swap futures to structure hedges to protect a portfolio of corporate and Treasury securities from a rise in interest rates. Due to the liquidity and standardization of swap futures, swap futures are becoming a cheaper and more efficient way to hedge a fixed income portfolio than entering a swap.[1] This chapter discusses the details of hedging interest rate risk and bond portfolios using swaps and fixed income instruments (e.g., futures).

In §1.1, we discuss using Eurodollar futures to compute LIBOR swap rates. In §1.2, we discuss Treasury bills and Treasury bonds, including how they are quoted and priced. In §1.3, we discuss bootstrapping the yield curve to compute discount swap rates. In §1.4, we discuss hedging debt positions and interest rate movements using fixed income instruments. In §1.5, we discuss bond duration, modified duration, and DV01 (dollar value of a one-basis-point move) calculations, which are necessary for computing swap durations and modified durations because a fixed-for-floating interest rate swap is composed of two legs that are equivalent to a fixed-rate bond and a floating-rate bond. In §1.6, we discuss term structure of rates, and in §1.7, we discuss how to numerically bootstrap the yield curve. In §1.8, we discuss bootstrapping in Matlab and provide examples, while in §1.9, we discuss bootstrapping using Excel. In §1.10, we discuss general swap pricing in Matlab using the Black-Derman-Toy (BDT) and Heath-Jarrow-Morton (HJM) interest rate models, and in §1.11, we discuss swap pricing using term structures like the forward curve built from zero-coupon and coupon-bearing bond cash flows. In §1.12, we implement and price fixed-for-floating swaps, including calculations for duration and risk measures, using C++. Finally, in §1.13, a Bermudan swaption pricing implementation in Matlab is provided.

1.1   EURODOLLAR FUTURES

Eurodollar futures[2] contracts maturing in March, June, September, and December are sometimes used to calculate the LIBOR swap zero rates for swap maturities greater than one year. The Eurodollar futures interest rate can be used to compute forward rates for long-dated maturities. In the United States, spot LIBOR rates are usually used to define the LIBOR zero curve for maturities up to one year. Eurodollar futures are typically then used for maturities between one and two years and sometimes for maturities up to five, seven, and ten years. In addition, swap rates, which define par yield bonds, are used to calculate the zero curve for maturities longer than a year. Using a combination of spot LIBOR rates, Eurodollar futures, and swap rates, the LIBOR/swap zero curve can be generated using a bootstrap method procedure.

Typically, a convexity adjustment is made to convert Eurodollar futures rates into forward interest rates. For short maturities (up to one year), the Eurodollar futures interest rate can be assumed to be the same as the corresponding forward interest rate. But for longer maturities, the difference between futures and forward contracts becomes important when interest rates vary unpredictably.[3]

Suppose the quoted Eurodollar futures price is P; then the cash contract price is

$$10000 \left(100 - 0.25(100 - P)\right) \tag{1.1}$$

which is equivalent to 10,000 times the cash futures price of $100 - 0.25(100 - P)$. Suppose $P = 96.7$; then the contract price is

$$10000\left(100 - 0.25(100 - 96.7)\right) = \$991,750$$

A Eurodollar contract is like a Treasury bill contract, but with some important differences. Both the Eurodollar and T-bill contracts have an underlying face value amount of $1 million. However, for a T-bill, the contract price converges at maturity to the price of a 91-day $1 million face-value Treasury bill, and if the contract held to maturity, this is the instrument delivered.[4] A Eurodollar futures contract is cash settled on the second London business day before the third Wednesday of the month.[5] The final marking to market sets the contract price equal to

$$f_0 = (\$1,000,000)\left(\frac{100 - 0.25R}{100}\right) = 10,000(100 - 0.25R)$$

where R is the quoted LIBOR Eurodollar rate at that time.[6] This quoted Eurodollar rate is the actual 90-day rate on Eurodollar deposits with quarterly compounding.[7] It is not a discount rate. As Hull states, "the Eurodollar futures contract is therefore a futures contract on an interest rate, whereas the Treasury bill futures contract is a futures contract on the price of a Treasury bill or a discount rate."[8]

1.2   TREASURY BILLS AND BONDS

Treasury bills are short-term discount securities issued by the U.S. Treasury. At the time of sale, a percentage discount is applied to the face value. Treasury bill prices are quotes as a discount rate on a face value of $100. At maturity, the holder redeems the bill for full face value. The basis (or day counting convention) for the interest accrual is actual/360 so that interest accrues on the actual number of elapsed days between purchase and maturity, assuming each year has 360 days. The Treasury price quote is the annualized dollar return provided by the Treasury bill in 360 days expressed as a percentage of the face value

$$\frac{360}{n}(100 - P) \tag{1.2}$$

where P is the cash price of a Treasury bill that has a face value of $100 and n days to maturity.[9] The discount rate is not the rate of return earned on the Treasury bill. If the cash price of a 90-day Treasury bill is 99, the quoted price would be 1.00. The *rate of return* would be 1/99, or 1.01%, per 90 days. This is translates to

$$\frac{1}{99} \times \frac{360}{90} = 0.0404$$

or 4.04% per annum on an actual/360 basis. Alternatively, it is

$$\frac{1}{99} \times \frac{365}{90} = 0.04096$$

or approximately 4.10% per annum on an actual/365 basis. Both of these rates are expressed with a quarterly compounding period of 90 days. In order to directly compare Treasury yields with yields quoted on Treasury bonds, often semiannual compounding (a compounding period of 180 days) is used on an actual/365 basis. The computed rate is known as the *bond equivalent yield*. In this case, the bond equivalent yield is

$$\frac{1}{99} \times \frac{365}{180} = 0.02048.$$

For short-term Treasury bills (fewer than 182 days to maturity), the *money-market yield* can be computed as 360/365 of the bond equivalent yield. In this example, it is 2.02%.

T-bill futures call for the delivery or purchase of a T-bill with a maturity of 91 days and a face value of $1,000,000. They are used for speculating and hedging short-term rates. Prices of T-bill futures are quoted in terms of the interbank money market (IMM) index or discount yield R_d:

$$\text{IMM} = 100 - R_d$$

Theoretical T-bill pricing is done with a carrying cost model

$$f_0 = S_0^M (1 + R_f)^T \tag{1.3}$$

where

$$f_0 = \text{price of T-bill futures}$$
$$T = \text{time to expiration on futures}$$
$$S_0^M = \text{price on spot T-bill with maturity of } M = 91 + T$$
$$R_f = \text{risk-free or repo rate}$$

Following Johnson (2004),[10] suppose the rate on a 161-day spot T-bill is 5.7% and the repo rate (or risk-free rate) for 70 days is 6.38%; then the price on a T-bill futures contract with an expiration of 70 days would be

$$f_0 = (97.5844)(1.0638)^{70/365} = 98.7487$$

where

$$S_0^{161} = \frac{100}{(1.057)^{161/365}} = 97.5844.$$

The future price is governed by arbitrage considerations. If the futures market price is above f^*, arbitrageurs would short the futures contract and go long the spot T-bill. For example, suppose the futures market price is $f^{M=70/365} = 99$. An arbitrageur would go short in the futures, agreeing to sell a 91-day T-bill at 99, 70 days later, and would go long the spot, borrowing 97.5844 at 6.38% for 70 days to finance the purchase of the 161-day T-bill that is trading at 97.5844. Seventy days later at expiration, the arbitrageur would sell the T-bill (which would now have a maturity of 91 days) on the futures for $f^{M=70/365} = 99$ and pay off his financing debt of $f^* = 98.74875$, realizing a cash flow (CF_T) of $2,513:

$$CF_T = f_0^M - f_0^*$$
$$= f_0^M - S_0^M (1 + R_f)^T$$
$$= 99 - 97.5844(1.0638)^{70/365}$$
$$= 99 - 98.7487 = 0.2513$$

so that the cash flow or profit is

$$CF_T = (\$1,000,000)\left(\frac{0.2513}{100}\right) = \$2,513.$$

Note that if $f^M = 99$, a money market manager planning to invest for 70 days in T-bills at 6.38% could earn a greater return by buying a 161-day bill and going short the 70-day T-bill futures to lock in the selling price. For example, using the preceding numbers, if a money manager was planning to invest 97.5844 for 70 days, she could buy a 161-day bill for that amount and go short in the futures at 99. Her return would be 7.8%, compared to only 6.38% from the 70-day T-bill:

$$R = \left(\frac{99}{97.5844}\right)^{365/70} - 1 = 0.078$$

If the market price is below f^*, then arbitrageurs would go long in the futures and short in the spot. Suppose $f^M = 98$. An arbitrageur would go long in the futures, agreeing to buy a 91-day T-bill for 98 seventy days later and would go short in the spot, borrowing the 161-day T-Bill, selling it for 97.5844 and investing the proceeds at 6.38% for 70 days. Seventy days later (expiration), the arbitrageur would buy the bill (which now would have a maturity of 91 days) on the futures for 98 (fm), use the bill to close his short position, and collect 98.74875 (f^*) from his investment, realizing a cash flow of $7487.

$$\begin{aligned} CF_T &= f_0^* - f_0^M \\ &= S_0^M(1 + R_f)^T - f_0^M \\ &= 97.5844(1.0638)^{70/365} - 98 \\ &= 98.7487 - 98 = 0.2513 = 0.7487 \end{aligned}$$

so that the cash flow or profit is

$$CF_T = (\$1,000,000)\left(\frac{0.7487}{100}\right) = \$7,487$$

If the carrying-cost model holds, then the spot rate on a 70-day bill (repo rate) will be equal to the synthetic rate (implied repo rate) formed by buying the 161-day bill and going short in the 70-day futures:

Buy 161-day T-bill $S_0^{161} = 97.5844$.

Short position in T-bill futures at $f_0^M = f_0^* = 98.74875$.

$$R = \left(\frac{98.74875}{97.5844}\right)^{365/70} - 1 = 0.0638.$$

Furthermore, if the carrying-model holds, then the yield-to-maturity, *YTM*, of the futures will be equal to the implied forward rate F. Locking in the 91-day investment to be made 70 days from now, as follows:

1. Short 70-day T-bill at $S_0^{70} = 98.821$.

2. Buy $n = \frac{S_0^{70}}{S_0^{161}} = \frac{98.821}{97.5844} = 1.01267$ of 161-day bill at 97.5844.

3. End of 70 days, cover short bill for 100.

4. 90 days later, collect on the investment in the original 161-day bill: $1.01267(100) = 101.267$.

$$R = \left(\frac{101.267}{100}\right)^{365/91} - 1 = 0.0518 = F_{91,70}$$

which is equal to

$$YTM_f = \left(\frac{100}{98.74875}\right)^{365/91} - 1 = 0.0518.$$

Hedging with T-Bill Futures

T-bill futures are often used for hedging by money managers. Suppose a money manager is expecting a \$5 million cash flow in June, which she plans to invest in a 91-day T-bill. With June T-bill futures trading at IMM of 91 (*June IMM* $= 91$ or $R_D = 9\%$), the manager could lock in a 9.56% rate by going long 5.115 June T-bill contracts:

$$f_0^{June} = (\$1,000,000)\left(\frac{100 - (9)(0.25)}{100}\right) = \$977,500$$

$$YTM_f = \left(\frac{\$1,000,000}{\$977,500}\right)^{365/91} - 1 = 0.0956$$

$$n_f = \frac{CF_T}{f_0} = \frac{\$5,000,000}{\$977,500} = 5.115 \text{ long contracts}$$

Suppose in June, the spot 91-day T-bill rate is at 8%. The manager would find T-bill prices higher at \$980,995, but would realize a profit of \$17,877 from closing the futures position. Combining the profit with the \$5 million cash flow, the manager would be able to buy 5.115 T-bills[11] and earn a rate off the \$5 million investment of 9.56%:

At June contract maturity, rate on T-bill $= 8\%$.

$$\text{spot rate} = S_T^{91} = \frac{\$1,000,000}{(1.08)^{91/365}} = \$980,995.$$

$$\text{profit} = \pi_f = [\$980,995 - \$997,500](5.115) = \$17,877.$$

$$\text{hedge ratio} = n_{TB} = \frac{CF + \pi_f}{S_T^{91}} = \frac{(\$5,000,000 + \$17,877)}{\$980,995} = 5.115.$$

$$\text{contract price} = f_0^{June} = (\$1,000,000)\left(\frac{100 - (9)(0.25)}{100}\right) = \$977,500.$$

$$\text{rate of return} = R = \left[\frac{(\$1,000,000)(5.115)}{\$5,000,000}\right]^{365/91} - 1 = 0.956 = 9.56\%.$$

Suppose instead that in June, the spot 91-day T-bill rate is at 10%. The manager would find T-bill prices lower at $976,518, but would realize a loss of $5,025 from closing the futures position. After paying the clearing house $5,025, the manager would still be able to buy 5.115 T-bills given the lower T-bill prices, earning a rate of return from the $5 million investment at 9.56%:

At June contract maturity, rate on T-bill $= 10\%$.

$$S_T^{91} = \frac{\$1,000,000}{(1.10)^{91/365}} = \$976,518.$$

$$\pi_f = [\$976,518 - \$997,500](5.115) = -\$5,025.$$

$$n_{TB} = \frac{CF + \pi_f}{S_T^{91}} = \frac{(\$5,000,000 - \$5,025)}{\$976,518} = 5.115.$$

$$f_0^{June} = (\$1,000,000)\left(\frac{100 - (9)(0.25)}{100}\right) = \$977,500.$$

$$R = \left[\frac{(\$1,000,000)(5.115)}{\$5,000,000}\right]^{365/91} - 1 = 0.956 = 9.56\%.$$

Note that at any rate, the money market manager earns a rate of return of 9.56%.

Long Futures Hedge: Hedging Synthetic Futures on 182-Day T-Bill

Suppose a money market manager is expecting a $5 million cash flow in June, which she plans to invest in a 182-day T-bill. Because the T-bill underlying a futures contract has a maturity of 91 days, the manager would need to go long in both June T-bill futures and a September T-bill futures (note that there are approximately 91 days between the contract) in order to lock in a return on a 182-day T-bill instrument. If June T-bill futures were trading at IMM of 91 and September futures were trading at IMM of 91.4, then the manager could lock in a 9.3% rate on an instrument in 182-day T-bills by going long in 5.115 June T-bill futures and 5.11 September contracts:

June IMM $= 91$ or $R_D = 9\%$

Sept IMM $= 91.4$ or $R_D = 8.6\%$

$$f_0^{June} = (\$1,000,000)\left(\frac{100 - (9)(0.25)}{100}\right) = \$977,500$$

$$f_0^{Sept} = (\$1,000,000)\left(\frac{100 - (8.6)(0.25)}{100}\right) = \$978,500$$

$$YTM_f^{June} = \left[\frac{\$1,000,000}{\$977,500}\right]^{365/91} - 1 = 0.0956$$

$$YTM_f^{Sept} = \left[\frac{\$1,000,000}{\$978,500}\right]^{365/91} - 1 = 0.091$$

$$n_f^{June} = \frac{CF_T}{f_0} = \frac{\$5,000,000}{\$977,500} = 5.115 \text{ long contracts}$$

$$n_f^{Sept} = \frac{CF_T}{f_0} = \frac{\$5,000,000}{\$978,500} = 5.112 \text{ long contracts}$$

so that the return is

$$YTM_f^{182} = \left[(1.0956)^{91/35}(1.091)^{91/365}\right]^{365/182} - 1 = 0.093.$$

Suppose in June, the 91-day T-bill rate is at 8% and the spot 182-day T-bill rate is at 8.25%. At these rates, the price on the 91-day spot T-bill would be

$$S_T^{91} = \frac{\$1,000,000}{(1.08)^{91/365}} = \$980,995$$

and the price on the 182-day spot T-bill would be

$$S_T^{182} = \frac{\$1,000,000}{(1.08)^{182/365}} = \$961,245.$$

If the carrying-cost model holds, then the price on the September futures at the June date is

$$f_0^{Sept} = S_0^{182}(1 + R_f)^T = \$961,245(1.08)^{91/365} = \$979,865.$$

At these prices, the manager would be able to earn futures profits of

$$\text{June } \pi_f = [\$980,995 - \$977,500]5.115 = \$17,877$$
$$\text{Sept } \pi = [\$979,865 - \$978,500]5.11 = \$6,975$$

for a total profit of $24,852 from closing both futures contract (which offsets the higher T-bill futures prices) and would be able to buy

$$n_{TB} = \frac{\$5,000,000 + \$24,852}{\$961,245} = 5.227$$

182-day T-bills, yielding a rate of return of

$$R = \left[\frac{(5.227)(\$1,000,000)}{\$5,000,000}\right]^{365/182} - 1 = 0.093$$

or 9.3% from a $5 million investment. Readers can verify for themselves that the rate of return will still be 9.3% if the 91-day and 182-day T-bill spot rates rise. Thus, Treasury bond futures contracts call for the delivery or purchase of a T-bond with a face value of $100,000. The contract allows for the delivery of a number of T-bonds; there is a conversion factor used to determine the actual price of the futures given the bond that is delivered. In actuality, the cheapest-to-deliver T-bond is delivered. T-bond futures are quoted in terms of a T-bond with an 8% coupon, semiannual payments, maturity of 15 years, and face value of $100.

In Matlab, one can make Treasury bills directly comparable to Treasury notes and bonds by restating U.S. Treasury bill market parameters in U.S. Treasury bond form as zero-coupon bonds via the following function:

```
[TBondMatrix, Settle] = tbl2bond(TBillMatrix)
```

TBillMatrix are the Treasury bill parameters. An N-by-5 matrix is where each row describes a Treasury bill. N is the number of Treasury bills. Columns are [Maturity DaysMaturity Bid Asked AskYield], as described in Table 1.1.

Table 1.1

Maturity	Maturity date, as a serial date number. Use datenum to convert date strings to serial date numbers.
DaysMaturity	Days to maturity, as an integer. Days to maturity is quoted on a skip-day basis; the actual number of days from settlement to maturity is DaysMaturity + 1.
Bid	Bid bank-discount rate: the percentage discount from face value at which the bill could be bought, annualized on a simple-interest basis. A decimal fraction.
Asked	Asked bank-discount rate, as a decimal fraction.
AskYield	Asked yield: the bond-equivalent yield from holding the bill to maturity, annualized on a simple-interest basis and assuming a 365-day year. A decimal fraction.

The output consists of the Treasury bond parameters given in **TBondMatrix**, an N-by-5 matrix where each row describes an equivalent Treasury (zero-coupon) bond. Columns are [CouponRate Maturity Bid Asked AskYield], as described in Table 1.2

Table 1.2

CouponRate	Coupon rate, which is always 0.
Maturity	Maturity date, as a serial date number. This date is the same as the Treasury bill Maturity date.
Bid	Bid price based on $100 face value.
Asked	Asked price based on $100 face value.
AskYield	Asked yield to maturity: the effective return from holding the bond to maturity, annualized on a compound-interest basis.

Example 1

Given published Treasury bill market parameters for December 22, 1997:

```
TBill = [datenum('jan 02 1998') 10 0.0526 0.0522 0.0530
         datenum('feb 05 1998') 44 0.0537 0.0533 0.0544
         datenum('mar 05 1998') 72 0.0529 0.0527 0.0540];
```

Execute the function:

```
TBond = tbl2bond(TBill)

TBond =
            0 729760 99.854 99.855 0.053
            0 729790 99.344 99.349 0.0544
            0 729820 98.942 98.946 0.054
```

1.3 COMPUTING TREASURY BILL PRICES AND YIELDS IN MATLAB

In Matlab, you can specify T-bills yield as money-market or bond-equivalent yield.

Matlab Treasury bill functions all assume a face value of $100 for each Treasury bill. The price of a T-bill can be computed using the function

```
Price = prtbill(Settle, Maturity, Face, Discount)
```

where the arguments are as listed in Table 1.3.

Table 1.3

Settle	Enter as serial date number or date string. Settle must be earlier than or equal to Maturity.
Maturity	Enter as serial date number or date string.
Face	Redemption (par, face) value.
Discount	Discount rate of the Treasury bill. Enter as decimal fraction.

Example 2

```
Settle = '2/10/2005';
Maturity = '8/7/2005';
Face = 1000;
Discount = 0.0379;
Price = prtbill(Settle, Maturity, Face, Discount);

Price =
     981.2606
```

The yield to maturity of the T-bill can be calculated using the yldtbill function:

```
Yield = yldtbill(Settle, Maturity, Face, Price)
```

The yield of the T-bill in this example is:

```
Yield = 0.0386
```

The bond equivalent yield of the T-bill is

```
BEYield = beytbill(Settle, Maturity, Discount)
```

where `Discount` is the discount rate of the T-bill, which can be computed from the `discrate` function:

```
Discount = discrate(Settle, Maturity, Face, Price, Basis)
```

In this example, Basis = 2 (Actual/360 day-count convention) so that

```
Discount = 0.0379
```

as expected (as initially given) so that the bond equivalent yield is as follows:

```
BEYield = 0.0392
```

1.4   HEDGING DEBT POSITIONS

Hedging a Future 91-Day T-Bill Investment with T-Bill Call

Following Johnson (2004), suppose a treasurer expects higher short-term rates in June but is still concerned about the possibility of lower rates. To be able to gain from the higher rates and yet still hedge against lower rates, the treasurer could buy a June call option on a spot T-bill or a June option on a T-bill futures. For example, suppose there was a June T-bill futures option with an exercise price of 90 (strike price $X = 975,000$), price of 1.25 ($C = \$3,125$), and June expiration (on both underlying futures and option) occurring at the same time a \$5,000,000 cash inflow is to be received. To hedge the 91-day investment with this call, the treasurer would need to buy 5.128205 calls (assume divisibility) at a cost of \$16,025.64:

$$n_c = \frac{CF_T}{X} = \frac{\$5,000,000}{\$975,000} = 5.128205 \text{ contracts}$$

$$Cost = (5.128205)(\$3,125) = \$16,025.64$$

$$\pi_c = 5.1282085[Max(S_T - \$975,000, 0) - \$3,125]$$

If T-bill rates were lower at the June expiration, then the treasurer would profit from the calls that she could use to defray part of the cost of the higher priced T-bills. As shown in Table 1.4, if the spot discount rate on T-bills is 10% or less, the treasurer could buy 5.112 91-day spot T-bills with the \$5 million cash inflow and profit from the calls, locking in a YTM of 9.3% on the \$5 million investment. On the other hand, if T-bill rates were higher, then the treasurer would benefit from lower spot prices, while the losses on the call would be limited to just the \$16,025.64 cost of the calls. In this case, for spot discount rates above 10%, the treasurer could buy more T-bills the higher the rates, resulting in higher yields as rates increase. Thus, for the cost of the call options, the treasurer can lock in a minimum YTM on the \$5 million June investment of 9.3%, with the chance to earn a higher rate if short-term rates increase.

Table 1.4 Hedging $5M *CF* in June with June T-Bill Futures Call

Call: X = 90 (975,000), C = 1.25 ($3,125), n = 5.1282051				
1	2	3	4	5
Spot Rate: R	Spot Price	Profit/Loss	nTB	YTM
8	980000	9615.38456	5.112	0.093
8.5	978750	3205.12819	5.112	0.093
9	977500	-3205.1282	5.112	0.093
9.5	976250	-9615.3846	5.112	0.093
9.75	975625	-12820.513	5.112	0.093
10	975000	-16025.641	5.112	0.093
10.25	974375	-16025.641	5.115	0.096
10.5	973750	-16025.641	5.118	0.098
10.75	973125	-16025.641	5.122	0.101
11	972500	-16025.641	5.125	0.104
11.25	971875	-16025.641	5.128	0.107

Source: Johnson, S. (2004)

Note that if the treasurer wanted to hedge a 182-day investment instead of 91-days with calls, then similar to the futures hedge, she would need to buy both June and September T-bill futures calls. At the June expiration, the manager would then close both positions and invest the $5,000,000 inflow plus (minus) the call profits (losses) in 182-day spot T-bills.

Short Hedge: Managing the Maturity Gap

Short hedges are used when corporations, municipal governments, financial institutions, dealers, and underwriters are planning to sell bonds or borrow funds at some future date and want to lock in the rate. The converse of the preceding example would be a money market manager who, instead of buying T-bills, was planning to sell her holdings of T-bills in June when the current bills would have maturities of 91 days or 182 days. To lock in a given revenue, the manager would go short in June T-bill futures (if she plans to sell 91-day bills) or June and September futures (if she planned to sell 182-day bills). If short-term rates increase (decrease), causing T-bill prices to decrease (increase), the money manager would receive less (more) revenue from selling the bills, but would gain (lose) when she closed the T-bill futures contracts by going long in the expiring June (and September) contract.

Another important use of short hedges is in locking in the rates on future debt positions. As an example, consider the case of a small bank with a maturity gap problem in which its short-term loan portfolio has an average maturity greater than the maturity of the CDs that it is using to finance the loans. Specifically, suppose in June, the bank makes loans of $1 million, all with maturities of 180 days. To finance the loan, though, suppose the bank's customers prefer 90-day CDs to 180-day, and as a result, the bank has to sell $1 million worth of 90-day CDs at a rate equal to the current LIBOR of 8.258%. Ninety days later (in September) the bank would owe $1,019,758 = ($1,000,000)(1.08258)^{90/365}$; to finance this debt, the bank would have to sell $1,019,758 worth of 90-day CDs at the LIBOR at that time. In the absence of a hedge, the bank would be subject to market risk. If short-term rates increase, the bank would have to pay higher interest on its planned September CD sale, lowering the interest spread it earns (the rate from $1 million 180-day loans minus interest paid on CDs to finance them); if rates decrease, the bank would increase its spread.

Suppose the bank is fearful of higher rates in September and decides to minimize its exposure to market risk by hedging its $1,019,758 CD sale in September with a September Eurodollar futures contract trading at IMM = 92.1. To hedge the liability, the bank would need to go short in 1.03951 September Eurodollar futures (assume perfect divisibility):

$$f_0^{Sept} = \frac{100 - (7.9)(0.25)}{100}(\$1,000,000) = \$981,000$$

$$n_f = \frac{\$1,019,758}{\$981,000} = 1.03951 \text{ Short Eurodollar Contracts}$$

At a futures price of $981,000, the bank would be able to lock in a rate on its September CDs of 8.1%.

$$YTM_f^{Sept} = \left(\frac{\$1,000,000}{\$981,000}\right)^{365/91} - 1 = 0.081$$

$$YTM_{182} = \left[(1.0825)^{90/365}(1.081)^{90/36}\right]^{365/180} - 1 = 0.0817.$$

With this rate and the 8.25% rate it pays on its first CDs, the bank would pays 8.17% on its CDs over the 180-day period: That is, when the first CDs mature in September, the bank will issue new 90-day CDs at the prevailing LIBOR to finance the $1,019,758 first CD debt plus (minus) any loss (profit) from closing its September Eurodollar futures position. If the LIBOR in September has increased, the bank will have to pay a greater interest on the new CDs, but it will realize a profit from its futures that, in turn, will lower the amount of funds it needs to finance at the higher rate. On the other hand, if the LIBOR is lower, the bank will have lower interest payments on its new CDs, but it will also incur a loss on its futures position and therefore will have more funds that need to be financed at the lower rates. The impact that rates have on the amount of funds needed to be financed and the rate paid on them will exactly offset each other, leaving the bank with a fixed debt amount when the September CDs mature in December. As Table 1.5 shows, where the bank's December

Table 1.5

Sept LIBOR (R)	0.075	0.085
(2) $S_T^{CD} = f_T^{Sept} = \$1M/(1+R)^{90/365}$	$982,236	$979,640
(3) $\pi_t = [981,000 - f_T]1.0391$	-$1,378	$1,413
(4) Debt on June CD	$1,019,758	$1,019,758
(5) Total Funds to finance for next 90 days: Row (4) − Row (3)	$1,021,136	$1,018,345
(6) Debt at end of next 90 days: Row (5) $(1+R)^{90/365}$	$1,039,509	$1,039,509
(7) Rate for 180-day period: $R_{CD}^{180} = [\$1,039,509/\$1,000,000]^{365/180} - 1$	8.17%	8.17%

Source: Johnson, R.S.

liability (the liability at the end of the initial 180-day period) is shown to be $1,039,509 given September LIBOR rate scenarios of 7.5% and 8.7% (this will be true at any rate).

Note that the debt at the end of 180 days of $1,039,509 equates to a September 90-day rate of 8.1% and a 180-day rate for the period of 8.17%:

$$YTM_f^{Sept} = \left[\frac{\$1,039,509}{\$1,019,758}\right]^{365/90} - 1 = 0.081$$

$$R_{CD180} = \left[\frac{\$1,039,509}{\$1,000,000}\right]^{365/180} - 1 = 0.0817$$

Maturity Gap and the Carrying Cost Model

In the preceding example, we assumed the bank's maturity gap was created as a result of the bank's borrowers wanting 180-day loans and its investors/depositors wanting 90-day CDs. Suppose, though, that the bank does not have a maturity gap problem; that is, it can easily sell 180-day CDs to finance its 180-day loan assets and 90-day CDs to finance its 90-day loans. However, suppose that the September Eurodollar futures price was above its carrying cost value. In this case, the bank would find that instead of financing with a 180-day spot CD, it would be cheaper if it financed its 180-day June loans with synthetic 180-day CDs formed by selling 90-day June CDs rolled over three months later with 90-day September CDs, with the September CD rate locked in with a short position in the September Eurodollar futures contract. For example, if the June spot 180-day CDs were trading 96 to yield 8.63%, then the carrying cost value on the September Eurodollar contract would be 97.897 ($97.897 = 96(1.08258)^{90/365}$). If the September futures price were 98.1, then the bank would find it cheaper to finance the 180-day loans with synthetic 180-days CDs with an implied futures rate of 8.17% than with 180-day spot CDs at a rate of 8.63%. On the other hand, if the futures price is less than the carrying cost value, then the rate on the synthetic 180-day CDs would exceed the spot 180-day CD rate, and the bank would obtain a lower financing rate with the spot CDs. Finally, if the carrying cost model governing Eurodollar futures prices holds, then the rate of the synthetic will be equal to rate on the spot; in this case, the bank would be indifferent to its choice of financing.

Managing the Maturity Gap with Eurodollar Put

Instead of hedging its future CD sale with Eurodollar futures, the bank could alternatively buy put options on either a Eurodollar or T-bill or put options on a Eurodollar futures or T-bill futures. In the preceding case, suppose the bank decides to hedge its September CD sale by buying a September T-bill futures put with an expiration coinciding with the maturity of its June CD, an exercise price of 90 ($X = \$975,000$), and a premium of .5 ($C = \$1,250$). With the September debt from the June CD of $1,019,758, the bank would need to buy 1.046 September T-bill futures puts at a total cost of $1,307 to hedge the rate it pays on its September CD:

$$n_p = \frac{CF_T}{X} = \frac{\$1,019,758}{\$975,000} = 1.0459056 \text{ puts}$$

$$Cost = (1.046)(\$1,250) = \$1,307$$

If rates at the September expiration are higher such that the discount rate on T-bills is greater than 10%, then the bank will profit from the puts. This profit would serve to reduce part of the $1,019,750 funds it would need to finance the maturing June CD that, in turn, would help to negate the higher rate it would have to pay on its September CD. As shown in Table 1.6, if the T-bill discount yield is 10% or higher and the bank's 90-day CD rate is 0.25% more than the yield on T-bills, then the bank would be able to lock in a debt obligation 90 days later of $1,047,500, for an effective 180-day rate of 9.876%.

On the other hand, if rates decrease such that the discount rate on a spot T-bill is less than 10%, then the bank would be able to finance its $1,047,500 debt at lower rates, while its losses on its T-bill futures puts would be limited to the premium of $1,307. As a result, for lower rates, the bank would realize a lower debt obligation 90 days later and therefore a lower rate paid over the 180-day period. Thus, for the cost of the puts, hedging the maturity gap with puts allows the bank to lock in a maximum rate paid on debt obligations with the possibility of paying lower rates if interest rates decrease.

Table 1.6

Maturity Gap Hedged with T-Bill Puts

(1) R_D	(2) S_Y	(3) $Rate_{CD}$	(4) π_P	(5) Debt on CD	(6) Funds Needed (5) - (4)	(7) Debt 90 Days Later $(6)[1+(3)]^{90/345}$	(8) Rate $[(7)/1M]^{365/180}$
7%	$982,500	.07588	−1307	1,019,750	1,021,065	1,039,646	8.203%
8%	$980,000	.08690	−1307	1,019,750	1,021,065	1,042,262	8.756%
9%	$977,500	.09807	−1307	1,019,750	1,021,065	1,044,893	9.313%
10%	$975,000	.10940	−1307	1,019,750	1,021,065	1,047,500	9.867%
11%	$972,500	.12080	1307	1,019,750	1,018,451	1,047,500	9.867%
12%	$970,000	.13240	3922	1,019,750	1,015,836	1,047,500	9.867%

Assume 90-day CD rate is .25% greater than T-bill rate:

$$Rate_{CD} = \left[\frac{\$1M}{S_T}\right]^{365/91} + .0025 - 1$$

$$\pi_P = 1.4059056[Max[\$975,000 - S_r, 0] - \$1307$$

Source: Johnson, R.S. (2004)

Short Hedge: Hedging a Variable-Rate Loan

As a second example of a short naive hedge, consider the case of a corporation obtaining a one-year, $1 million variable-rate loan from a bank. In the loan agreement, suppose the loan starts on date 9/20 at a rate of 9.5% and then is reset on 12/20, 3/20, and 6/20 to equal the spot LIBOR (annual) plus 150 basis points (.015 or 1.5%) divided by four: (LIBOR + .015)/4.

To the bank, this loan represents a variable-rate asset, which it can hedge against interest rate changes by issuing 90-day CDs each quarter that are tied to the LIBOR. To the corporation, though, the loan subjects them to interest rate risk (unless they are using the loan to finance a variable-rate asset). To hedge this variable-rate loan, though, the corporation could go short in a series of Eurodollar futures contracts—Eurodollar strip. For this case, suppose the company goes short in contracts expiring at 12/20, 3/20, and 6/20 and trading at the prices shown in Table 1.7.

Table 1.7

T	12/20	3/20	6/20
IMM Index	91.5	91.75	92
f_0(per $100 Par)	97.875	97.9375	98

The locked-in rates obtained using Eurodollar futures contracts are equal to 100 minus the IMM index plus the basis points on the loans:

$$Locked\text{-}in\ Rate = [100 - IMM] + [BP/100]$$
$$12/20 : R_{12/20} = [100 - 91.5] + 1.5\% = 10\%$$
$$3/20 : R_{3/20} = [100 - 91.75] + 1.5\% = 9.75\%$$
$$6/20 : R_{6/20} = [100 - 92] + 1.5\% = 9.5\%$$

For example, suppose on date 12/20, the assumed spot LIBOR is 9%, yielding a settlement IMM index price of 91 and a closing futures price of 97.75 per $100 face value. At that rate, the corporation would realize a profit of $1,250 from having it short position on the 12/20 futures contract. That is:

$$f_0 = \frac{(100 - (100 - 91.5))(0.25)}{100}(\$1,000,000) = \$978,750$$
$$f_T = \frac{(100 - (100 - 91))(0.25)}{100}(\$1,000,000) = \$977,500$$
$$\text{Profit on 12/20 contract} = \$978,750 - \$977,500 = \$1,250$$

At the 12/20 date, though, the new interest that the corporation would have to pay for the next quarter would be set at $26,250:

$$12/20\ \text{Interest} = [(\text{LIBOR} + .015)/4](\$1,000,000)$$
$$12/20\ \text{Interest} = [(.09 + .015)/4](\$1,000,000)$$
$$12/20\ \text{Interest} = \$26,250$$

Subtracting the futures profit from the $26,250 interest payment (and ignoring the time value factor), the corporation's hedged interest payment for the next quarter is $25,000. On an annualized basis, this equates to a 10% interest on a $1 million loan, the same rate as the locked-in rate:

$$\text{Hedged Rate} = R^A = \frac{4(\$25,000)}{\$1,000,000} = 0.10$$

On the other hand, if the 12/20 LIBOR were 8%, then the quarterly interest payment would be only $23,750((.08+.015)/4)(\$1,000,000) = \$23,750)$. This gain to the corporation, though, would be offset by a \$1,250 loss on the futures contract (i.e., at 8%, $f_T = \$980,000$, therefore, profit on the 12/20 contract is $\$978,750 - \$980,000 = -\$1,250$). As a result, the total quarterly debt of the company again would be $\$25,000(\$23,750 + \$1,250)$. Ignoring the time value factor, the annualized hedged rate the company pays would again be 10%. Thus, the corporation's short position in the 12/20 Eurodollar futures contract at 91.5 enables it to lock-in a quarterly debt obligation of \$25,000 and 10% annualized borrowing rate. If the LIBOR is at 9% on date 12/20, the company will have to pay \$26,250 on its loan the next quarter, but it will also have a profit on its 12/20 Eurodollar futures of \$1,250, which it can use to defray part of the interest expenses, yielding an effective hedged rate of 10%. The interest payments, futures profits, and effective interests are summarized:

$$12/20 : LIBOR = 9\%$$
$$\text{Futures:}$$
$$\text{Settlementprice: } S_T = 100 - LIBOR$$
$$S_T = 100 - 9(.25) = 97.75$$
$$\pi_f = \frac{97.875 - 97.75}{100}(\$1M) = \$1,250$$
$$\text{Interest} = \frac{LIBOR + 150BP}{4}(\$1M)$$
$$= \frac{.09 + .015}{4}(\$1M) = \$26,250$$
$$\text{EffectiveInterest} = \$26,250 - \$1,250 = \$25,000$$
$$\text{EffectiveRate} = R^A = \frac{4(\$25,000)}{\$1M} = .10$$

If the LIBOR is at 6% on date 12/20, the company will have to pay only \$18,750 on its loan the next quarter, but it will also have to cover a loss on its 12/20 Eurodollar futures of \$6,250. The payment of interest and the loss on the futures yields an effective hedged rate of 10%:

$$12/20 : LIBOR = 6\%$$
$$\text{Futures:}$$
$$\text{Settlementprice : } S_T = 100 - LIBOR$$
$$S_T = 100 - 6(.25) = 98.5$$
$$\pi_f = \frac{97.875 - 98.5}{100}(\$1M) = -\$6,250$$
$$\text{Interest} = \frac{LIBOR + 150BP}{4}(\$1M)$$
$$= \frac{.06 + .015}{4}(\$1M) = \$18,750$$

$$\text{EffectiveInterest} = \$18,750 + \$6,250 = \$25,000$$

$$\text{EffectiveRate} = R^A = \frac{4(\$25,000)}{\$1M} = .10$$

Given the other locked-in rates, the one-year fixed rate for the corporation on its variable-rate loan hedged with the Eurodollar futures contracts would therefore be 9.6873%:

$$\textit{Loan Rate} = \left[(1.095)^{.25}(1.10)^{.25}(1.0975)^{.25}(1.095)^{.25}\right]^1 - 1 = .096873.$$

Note, in practice, the corporation could have obtained a one-year fixed-rate loan. With futures contracts, though, the company now has a choice of taking either a fixed-rate loan or a synthetic fixed-rate loan formed with a variable-rate loan and short position in a Eurodollar futures contract, whichever is cheaper. Also, note that the corporation could have used a series of Eurodollar puts or futures puts to hedge its variable-rate loan. With a put hedge, each quarter the company would be able to lock in a maximum rate on its loan with the possibility of a lower rate if interest rates decrease.

1.5   BOND AND SWAP DURATION, MODIFIED DURATION, AND DV01

Duration (also known as Macauley's duration) is the present-value-weighted average time (in years) to maturity of the cash flow payments of a fixed income security. If C_i is the total cash flow payment at time t_i, then duration is computed as

$$\textit{Duration} = \frac{\sum_{i=1}^{n} \frac{t_i C_i}{(1+y_i)^{t_i}}}{B} \tag{1.4}$$

where n = number of cash flows, t = time to cash flow (in years), y_i is the simple-compound discount yield at time t_i, and $B = \sum_{i=1}^{n} \frac{C_i}{(1+y_i)^{t_i}}$ is the bond price.[12] At maturity, the cash flow includes both the principal face value and coupon payment. Yield modified duration[13] divides the duration number by $(1+1/YTM)$, where YTM is the yield to maturity of the bond. However, the YTM used to calculate the yield modified duration of a swap is the par swap rate (e.g., the swap rate that makes the present value of the swap zero).

To calculate the duration (modified duration) of a swap, we compute the modified duration of the long leg minus the modified duration of the short leg. Duration for the fixed leg is the present-value-weighted average maturity of the cash flows, whereas duration of the floating leg is the time to the next reset for the floating leg. The duration calculations (for both sides) divided by $1/(1 + YTM)$ is the modified duration for each side. The modified duration of an interest rate swap leg can be calculated like a bond

$$MD = \frac{\textit{Leg DV01}}{\textit{Leg PV}} * 10,000 \tag{1.5}$$

where DV01 (sometimes denoted PV01 in the literature) is the dollar value of a basis point change of the leg[14] and PV is the present value of the leg. This calculation should always be positive. An alternative, but equivalent, calculation to compute modified duration for each leg is to compute

$$MD = \frac{Leg\ DV01}{(Notional\ Value + Market\ Value)} * 10,000 \tag{1.6}$$

where the Market Value is the leg PV. This alternative computation is appropriate if the leg PV does not include the final exchange of principal. However, the leg DV01 must include the notional exchange to give a bond-like duration, so the leg DV01 must also include notional.

The difference between the modified durations of both legs, the net PV, is then taken to compute the modified duration of the swap:

$$\text{Swap MD} = \text{MD of Receive Leg} - \text{MD of Pay Leg} \tag{1.7}$$

Note that if the market value (leg PV) of the swap is zero, then duration is computed. Thus, for a par swap where the market value is zero, the duration (referred to as *deal risk* in Bloomberg) is equal to the modified duration.

For forward-starting swaps—e.g., a 10-year swap that starts in 7 years—typically a discounted swap modified duration is computed by adjusting equation (1.7) by a factor that is very close to the discount factor for the start date of the swap. An excellent approximation for this discount factor is provided by the NPV of the floating leg (including the final notional exchange), divided by the notional of the trade:

$$\text{Discounted Swap MD} = \text{Swap MD} \times \text{Floating Leg PV/Notional} \tag{1.8}$$

Note that quantitative differences arise between the yield modified duration (which assumes a flat discount rate) and the DV01 formulation in (1.5) or (1.6), based on various factors such as a sloping yield curve, instrument valuations away from par, instruments with long tenors, and forward-starting instruments. With an upward-sloping discount curve, the PV of the largest cash flow (at maturity) affects duration the most. Because the yield is lower than the discount rate at maturity, the value of the yield MD is higher than the value of the DV01 MD. The effect of the upward-sloping curve is amplified with a longer tenor, because the largest cash flow at maturity is even more different when discounted using the curve for DV01 MD and using the yield for yield MD; thus, the yield MD is greater than the DV01 MD. A downward-sloping discount curve has the opposite affect because the yield is higher than the discount rate at maturity.

Large NPVs during a tenor with an upward-sloping yield curve result from a coupon much different from the discount rate. The present value of the coupon cash flows have a larger weight in the bond price (PV). For DV01 MD, the PV of coupons in the long end decreases more when the curve is shifted by one basis point, compared to yield MD where coupons at the end are discounted at a lower rate (the yield) and are less sensitive to interest rate changes. Also, the DV01 MD is calculated by dividing by a higher value of bond PV so that the yield MD is greater than the DV01 MD. For a forward starting swap with an upward-sloping yield curve, yield MD is calculated as the sum of the yield MDs of two bonds with opposite signs—a long position in a bond starting today and maturing in T_2 years, and a short position in bond starting today and maturity in T_1 years, where

$0 < T_1 < T_2$. The cash flows affecting yield are those between $T_1 + 1$ and T_2 years, which are discounted at a yield lower than the discount rates at the long end of the curve. As a result, yield MD is higher than the DV01 MD.

Hedging Bond Portfolios

Consider the following bond portfolio example shown in Table 1.8.[15]

Of the Treasury bonds in the portfolio, the 5% of August 2011 was the current on-the-run 10-year, while the 6.5% of February 2010 became the cheapest-to-deliver (CTD) for the CBOT 10-year Treasury note futures when the data was recorded. The 5.625% of May 08 had recently been CTD. The coupons of the 11 corporate bonds in Table 1.8 range from a high of 9.375% to a low of 6.15% and have maturities from August 2007 to August 2011. With the exception of American Standard, all of these issues are investment grade credits where the credit ratings range from the S&P AA- of the Transamerica issue to the BBB- of the News America Holdings and Litton Industries issue. American Standard is a BB+ credit.

Table 1.8 shows weighted average durations for the two sectors and for the portfolio as a whole. The Treasury sector shows that this $262.34 million holding has a duration of 6.56 years. The $436.25 million corporate sector holding has a duration of 5.39 years, and the $698.59 million portfolio has a duration of 5.83 years.

Fixed income securities with different coupons and maturities respond differently to yield changes. This price sensitivity to yield change can be captured in terms of the dollar value of a basis point (DV01) for a given security. To find the DV01 for an individual fixed income security, given a modified duration and a full price, solve the following:

Table 1.8

Issuer	Coupon	Maturity	YTM	Modified Duration (years)	DV01 ($)	Par Amount ($ millions)	Full Price ($000s)	S&P Credit Rating
Treasury	6.5	2/15/10	4.55	6.56	0.0748	67	76,387	
Treasury	5.625	5/15/08	4.64	5.48	0.0588	92	98,762	
Treasury	5	8/15/11	4.57	7.77	0.0807	84	87,192	
Treasury Sector				6.56			262,341	
Time Warner Enterprises	8.18	8/15/07	5.47	4.72	0.0540	82	93,710	BBB+
Texas Utilities	6.375	1/1/08	6.19	5.06	0.0517	30	30,678	BBB
Rockwell International	6.15	1/15/08	6.14	5.13	0.0521	52	52,837	A
Transamerica Corporation	9.375	3/1/08	6.34	4.93	0.0573	15	17,445	AA-
Coastal Corporation	6.5	6/1/08	6.76	5.25	0.0528	30	30,153	BBB
United Airlines	6.831	9/1/08	5.99	5.51	0.0579	38	39,949	A-
Burlington Northern Santa Fe	7.34	9/24/08	5.67	5.36	0.0606	3	3,390	A+
News America Holdings	7.375	10/17/08	6.56	5.34	0.0575	30	32,292	BBB-
Litton Industries	8	10/15/09	5.70	5.81	0.0647	63	66,834	BBB-
American Standard Inc.	7.625	2/15/10	7.59	6.10	0.0615	41	41,332	BB+
Caterpillar Inc.	9.375	8/15/11	6.01	6.79	0.0853	22	27,628	A+
Corporate Sector				5.39			436,248	
Portfolio				5.83			698,589	

$$DV01 = \frac{(Duration/100) * Full\ \text{Price}}{100}$$

For instance, using this formula with the price and duration date in Table 1.8, we see that a \$98,762,000 position in the Treasury 5.625% of May 08, with its 5.48 duration, has a DV01 of \$54,122, while an \$87,192,000 position in the Treasury 5% of August 11, with its 7.77 duration, has a \$67,748 DV01. These DV01s predict that 1 basis point rise in yield would drive the value of the 5.625% of May 08 down \$54,122, while the same yield change would drive the value of the smaller holding in the 5% of August 11 down \$67,748. Clearly, the 5% of August 11 is more sensitive to yield changes than the 5.625% of May 08 is.

The portfolio is subject to inflation, interest rate, and credit risk that could sharply erode the value of the holdings and make it difficult to liquidate them at acceptable prices. The structuring of hedge positions then requires that the futures position be ratioed to the positions, and then requires that the futures position be ratioed to the position in the security being hedged in order that the two positions will respond equally to a given yield change. Given that the DV01 of the 10-year Treasury note futures contract was \$72.50 on the day these dates were recorded (the 10-year swap futures has a \$77.00 DV01), we can solve for the optimal hedge ratio to see that it would take 747 contracts to hedge the 5.625% of May 08 and 934 contracts to hedge the 5% of August 11:

$$\frac{5.625\%\ \text{of May 08 DV01}}{\text{futures DV01}} = \frac{54,122}{72.50} = 747\ \text{contracts}$$

$$\frac{5\%\ \text{of August 11 DV01}}{\text{futures DV01}} = \frac{67,748}{72.50} = 934\ \text{contracts}$$

To structure a portfolio hedge, we can use a weighted average duration for the Treasury sector, the corporate sector, or the entire holding, and then use the total full price of the relevant sectors to find DV01s. Table 1.9 shows that, based on the data in Table 1.8, the Treasury sector has a \$172,096 DV01, the corporate segment has a \$235,138 DV01, and

Table 1.9

		DV01 ($)
Treasury Sector		172,096
Corporate Sector		235,138
Portfolio		402,277
10-year Treasury Futures		72.50
10-year Swap Futures		77.00
Hedge Ratios		
	To Hedge	*Hedge Ratio*
1	Full portfolio with 10-yr. T-note futures	5,618
2	Full portfolio with swap futures	5,289
3	Treasury sector with 10-yr. T-note futures	2,374
4	Corporate sector with swap futures	3,054

the entire portfolio has a \$407,277 DV01 (note that the portfolio DV01 does not equal the sum of the two sector DV01s due to rounding error).

Plugging in these DV01s into the hedge ratio formulas yields the optimal hedge ratios. Hedging the entire portfolio with Treasury futures requires a short position in 5,618 contracts:

$$\frac{\text{Portfolio DV01 } 407,277}{\text{10-year Treasury Futures DV01 } 72.50} = 5,618 \text{ contracts}$$

Similarly, hedging the entire portfolio with swap futures requires a short position of 5,289 10-year swap futures contracts:

$$\frac{\text{Portfolio DV01 } 407,277}{\text{10-year Swap Futures DV01 } 77.00} = 5,289 \text{ contracts}$$

Finally, an optimal hedging strategy where the Treasury sector is hedged with Treasury futures and the corporate sector is hedged with swap futures requires a short position in 2,375 10-year Treasury futures contracts and a short position in 3,054 10-year swap futures contracts:

$$\frac{\text{Treasury Sector DV01 } 172,096}{\text{10-year Treasury Futures DV01 } 72.50} = 2,375 \text{ contracts}$$

$$\frac{\text{Corporate Sector DV01 } 235,138}{\text{10-year Swap Futures DV01 } 72.50} = 3,054 \text{ contracts}$$

It is important to note that these hedges are static in nature—they only apply at a given point in time based on current market data. Because Treasury, corporate yields, and swap rate cause shifts in the DV01s, these hedges should be monitored constantly and rebalanced based on the changes in interest rates and thus amount of risk exposure.

Hedging and portfolio performance can be measured by scenario and prediction analysis of yield shifts. During the summer of 2001, the 10-year Treasury-swap rate credit spread increased 40 basis points. Corporate yields generally followed the direction of the swap rate. Should that occur again where the swap rate and corporate yields rise 60 bps while Treasury yields rise only 20 bps, the underlying portfolio will incur an approximate \$17.55 million loss. Table 1.10 shows that the sector DV01s predict that \$3,441,920 of the loss will come from the Treasury sector and \$14,108,280 of it will come from the corporate sector. The Treasury futures hedge (according to the prediction of \$72.50 DV01) will respond to the 20 bp change in the Treasury yield and generate an \$8,146,000 gain (see Table 1.10, Scenario 1). Based on this scenario, a hedge mismatch loss of \$9,404,100 is incurred as a result of the fact that the Treasury futures hedge can be expected to offset less than half the portfolio loss.

Alternatively, swap futures can be used to hedge the entire portfolio. This strategy has the advantage of responding to the larger change in the swap rate and corporate yields. However, as Table 1.10 Scenario 2 shows, the relevant DV01s predict that this hedge will generate a futures gain much larger than the loss the underlying portfolio will incur. As Table 1.10, Scenario 3 shows, the relevant DV01s predict that these two hedge positions will generate a total futures gain of \$17,551,780. Thus, Scenario 3 appears far more promising

Table 1.10

Underlying Portfolio Result

Sector	DV01 ($)	Yield Change (bps)	Number of Contracts	Gain/Loss ($)
Treasury	172,096	20		-3,441,920
Corporate	235,138	60		-14,108,280
Portfolio				-17,550,200

Scenario 1 - Hedge Entire Portfolio with Treasury Futures

Sector	DV01 ($)	Yield Change (bps)	Number of Contracts	Gain/Loss ($)
10-year T-note	72.50	20	5,618	8,146,100
Portfolio				-17,550,200
Hedge Mistatch				-9,404,100

Scenario 2 - Hedge Entire Portfolio with Swap Futures

Sector	DV01 ($)	Yield Change (bps)	Number of Contracts	Gain/Loss ($)
10-year swap	77.00	60	5,289	24,435,180
Portfolio				-17,550,200
Hedge Mistatch				6,884,980

Scenario 3 - Hedge Treasury Sector with Treasury Futures, Hedge Corporate Sector with Swap Futures

Sector	DV01 ($)	Yield Change (bps)	Number of Contracts	Gain/Loss ($)
10-year T-note	72.50	20	2,374	3,442,300
10-year swap	77.00	60	3,054	14,109,480
Total Hedge Result				17,550,780
Portfolio				-17,550,200
Portfolio Mismatch				1,380
Treasury to 10-year T-note Mismatch				380
Corporate to Swap Mismatch				1,200

than either of the first two hedges given the minimal hedge mismatch of $1,580 (which represents less than a basis point and is far less than normal bid-ask spreads, and so for practical purposes represents a good offset). It highlights the importance of using exact or like (highly correlated) sector hedges to hedge underlying sectors: hedge the Treasury sector with 10-year Treasury note futures and the corporate sector with 10-year swap futures.

The large variation in Scenario 1 and Scenario 2, compared with the small hedge mismatch in Scenario 3, can be explained by the impact of basis risk that cannot be captured by single sector hedges of an entire underlying fixed income portfolio with multiple sectors. A 10-year Treasury futures is not as correlated with the corporate sector as the 10-year swap futures. In other words, swaps correlate more closely with corporates than Treasuries do. For example, consider a corporate-swap and corporate-Treasury regression using the TransAmerica Corp. 9.375% March 2008 corporate bond in Table 1.8. The corporate-swap correlation regression coefficient R^2 is 0.9134, while the corporate-Treasury R^2 is 0.7966, as shown in Figure 1.1.

The 0.9134 R^2 of the corporate-swap regression suggests that the variability of the swap rate accounts for 91.34% of the variability in the corporate yield. In contrast, the 0.7966

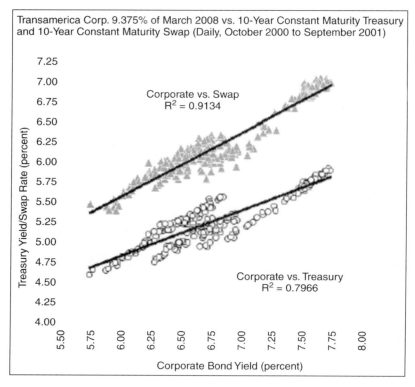

Figure 1.1 *Reprinted by permission of the Board of Trade of the City of Chicago, Inc., © 2001. All Rights Reserved.*

R^2 of the corporate-Treasury regression suggests that the variability of the Treasury yield accounts for slightly less than 80% of the variability of the yield of the corporate bond.

1.6 TERM STRUCTURE OF RATES

Term structure modeling is essential for valuation of fixed income securities and derivatives as a means for quantifying the relationship between either price or yield among a set of securities that differ only in the timing of their cash flows or their term until maturity. Term structure models describe the evolution of interest rates over time. The relationship expressed by the term structure is traditionally the par-coupon yield relationship, though in general, the term structure could be the discount function, the spot-yield curve, or some other price-yield relationship.

The set of securities that define a term structure is known as the *reference set*, which may be a set of U.S. Treasuries, agency debentures, off-the-run Treasury issues, interest rate swaps, or single-A rated corporate bonds, for instance. The n-year zero coupon yield, also known as the n-year spot rate, is the interest rate on an investment that is earned for a period of time starting today and lasting for n years. There is widespread usage of the par yield curve for the Treasury market so that many market sectors are defined from a reference set derived from the Treasury market;[16] for example, "the reference set that defines the agency debenture market is a set of yield spreads on the on-the-run Treasuries, so that the five-year debenture issued by an agency may be priced at par to yield 15 basis points more than the current five-year Treasury issue."[17] Other important yield curves include the forward rate curve and swap curve. Forward interest rates (future spot rates) are the rates of interest implied by current spot rates for periods of time in the future. The swap curve shows the fixed rate that is to be paid for receiving a floating rate such as three-month Libor, for a given swap maturity.

There are typically three types of term structures. The (coupon) yield curve is the yield-to-maturity structure of coupon bonds. The zero-coupon yield or spot-rate curve is the term structure of discount rates of zero-coupon bonds. The forward rate curve is the term structure of forward rates implicit in zero-coupon discount rates.

1.7   BOOTSTRAP METHOD

To construct the zero-coupon yield curve when spot rates cannot be observed directly, use the *bootstrap method* to extract it from observable coupon-bearing bond (cash) prices, swap rates, and interest rate futures. The bootstrap method, an iterative numerical method for extracting spot rates from previously computed spot rates and observable bond prices, can be used to construct the discount rate curve. Denote y_n as the yield to maturity of an n-period bond of maturity and d_n as the spot (discount) rate of the n-period maturity bond. The method is based on the idea that a coupon bond can be decomposed into the sum of zero-coupon bonds:

$$
\begin{aligned}
P_n &= \frac{c/m}{1+y_n/2} + \frac{c/m}{(1+y_n/2)^2} + \ldots + \frac{F+c/m}{(1+y_n/2)^n} \\
&= \frac{c/m}{1+d_n/2} + \frac{c/m}{(1+d_n/2)^2} + \ldots + \frac{F+c/m}{(1+d_n/2)^n} \\
&= Z_1 + Z_2 + \ldots + Z_n
\end{aligned}
$$

The standard procedure for bootstrapping the Treasury yield curve, known as *recursive stripping*, is as follows:

1. Obtain the current price of U.S. Treasuries (and/or Eurodollar futures).

2. Solve for the yield on the one-period zero-coupon bond, z_1.

3. Solve for z_2, given the price of the two-period bond and z_1 calculated in step 2.

4. Solve for z_3, given the price of the three-period bond and z_1 and z_2.

5. Continue until all the spot rates have been calculated.

Bootstrapping is a process whereby one starts with known data points and then solves for unknown data points using an underlying arbitrage theory. Every coupon bond can be valued as a package of zero-coupon bonds that mimic its cash flow and risk characteristics.

By mapping yields-to-maturity for each theoretical zero-coupon bond, to the dates spanning the investment horizon, one can create a theoretical zero-rate curve.

The zero spot rates are typically quoted on a bond equivalent basis.

One can use the bootstrap method to extract the zero coupon curve, which can, in turn, be used to construct a discount rate curve to discount cash flows. The generation of these curves typically starts with a series of on-the-run and selected off-the-run issues as input. All cash flows are used to construct the spot curve, and rates between maturities (for these coupons) are linearly interpolated.

For each bond maturity, we solve for the current yield that equates the current bond maturity with the sum of its discounted cash flows based on the determination of the yields of all the shorter maturity bonds. For instance, to determine the short rate yield on a bond that matures in n-years, we need to solve for d_n, which can be achieved only if all the yields for bonds maturing at periods $i = 1, ..., n - 1$ are determined. The method is called the bootstrap method because it determines yields (and thus the short rate curve) by building on top or "bootstrapping" from all previously determined yields:

$$P_n = \sum_{i=1}^{n-1} \frac{C_n}{(1 + d_i)^i} + \frac{C_n + FV}{(1 + d_n/2)^n}$$

For a zero-coupon bond, one can compute the (continuously computed) discount rate d_c from a discount spot rate with compounding n times per annum[18] via the following equation:

$$d_c = n \ln \left(1 + \frac{c_n}{n}\right)$$

Consider the Treasury bills and bonds listed in Table 1.11. We assume bond prices that mature every six months are available out to five years.

When computing the spot rates, on-the-run treasuries are typically used as they are more liquid and normally trade close to par, thereby mitigating any tax-biases associated with discount or premium bonds. Unfortunately, on-the-run securities are available only at 0.5-, 1-, 2-, 3-, 5-, and 10-year maturities. Of the methods used to obtain spot rates between

Table 1.11

Bond Price	Annual Coupon	Semiannual Period	Maturity (Years)	Period Coupon
102.2969	6.125	1	0.5	3.0625
104.0469	6.25	2	1.0	3.125
104.0000	5.25	3	1.5	2.625
103.5469	4.75	4	2.0	2.375
109.5156	7.25	5	2.5	3.625
111.1719	7.5	6	3.0	3.750
122.4844	10.75	7	3.5	5.375
119.6094	9.375	8	4.0	4.687
111.3281	7.0	9	4.5	3.500
108.7031	6.25	10	5.0	3.125

these values, exponential cubic splines[19] is the most common. However, recursive stripping is also common. We assume the maturity face value is 100.

To bootstrap the curve, we start by computing the discount spot rate that equates the cash flows to the 0.5-year maturity bond price of 102.27:

$$102.27 = \frac{(3.0625 + 100)}{(1 + d_1/2)}$$

or solving for d_1:

$$d_1 = (103.0625/102.27 - 1) * 2 = 0.014968$$

We compute the discount sum for semiannual period 1:

$$DiscountSum1 = 1/(1 + d_1) = 1/(1.04968) = 0.9853$$

We next solve for the one-year spot rate that gives the bond price at semiannual period 2:

$$104.05 = \frac{3.125}{(1 + d_1)} + \frac{103.125}{(1 + d_2/2)^2}$$
$$= 3.125 * DiscountSum1 + 103.125/(1 + d_2/2)^2$$
$$= 2 * \left(\left(\frac{PeriodCoupon2 + FaceValue}{BondPrice2 - PeriodCoupon2 * DiscountSum1} \right)^{1/2} - 1 \right)$$

so that

$$d_2 = 2.1250\%.$$

We compute the discount sum for semiannual period 2:

$$DiscountSum2 = DiscountSum1 + 1/(1 + d_2)^2$$
$$= 0.9853 + 1/(1.02125)^2$$
$$= 1.94407$$

We next solve for the sport rate that equates the cash flows to the 1.5-year maturity bond price (third semiannual period):

$$104 = 2.625 * DiscountSum2 + \frac{102.625}{(1 + d_3/2)^3}$$

or solving

$$d_3 = 2 * \left(\left(\frac{PeriodCoupon3 + FaceValue}{BondPrice3 - PeriodCoupon3 * DiscountSum2} \right)^{1/3} - 1 \right)$$
$$= 2.4822\%.$$

So that, in general, the bootstrapped spot rate for semiannual period n is given by

$$d_n = 2 * \left(\left(\frac{PeriodCoupon(n) + FaceValue}{BondPrice(n) - PeriodCoupon(n) * DiscountSum(n-1)} \right)^{1/n} - 1 \right)$$

where

$$DiscountSum(n-1) = DiscountSum(n-2) + 1/(1+d_2)^{n-1}.$$

If we continue the process, we find the discount sums and spot rates shown in Table 1.12, which yield the term structure of rates shown in Figure 1.2.

In practice, bootstrapping requires the input of T-bills, Treasury bond, Treasury note futures, Eurodollar futures, or coupon-bearing bond prices. One must interpolate the spot rate yields for specific maturities not available from the available market prices. For instance, some bond tables list net yields for bonds in a sequence of one, three, and five years. Interpolation would be used to determine the yield for the second and fourth year. In effect, interpolation is a process of trial and error utilizing a numerical method like the Newton-Raphson method. What complicates the procedure is that day count conventions need to be taken into account for computing accrued interest on coupon-bearing bonds.

Table 1.12

Period	Discount Sum	Spot Rate
1	0.985252547	1.4968%
2	1.944068996	2.1250%
3	2.87315116	2.4822%
4	3.76649457	2.8597%
5	4.623301565	3.1391%
6	5.442647715	3.3766%
7	6.227073953	3.5295%
8	6.975043088	3.6966%
9	7.682592791	3.9187%
10	8.359670683	3.9767%

1.8   BOOTSTRAPPING IN MATLAB

There are three ways to import data into Matlab: (1) loading the data as a "flat file" in ASCII format and then converting it to a numerical matrix; (2) loading the data first into Excel and then using ExcelLink to pass numeric matrices to the Matlab workspace; or (3) using the Matlab Database Toolbox to pull the data from an ODBC-compliant database.

Matlab, via the Financial Toolbox, provides two bootstrapping functions: `zbtprice`, which bootstraps the zero curve from coupon-bond data-given prices and `zbtyield`, which bootstraps the zero curve from coupon-bond data-given yields. Suppose we want to bootstrap the yield curve in Matlab using the corporate bond data in Figure 1.1 to get the zero rates at the maturity rates of the bonds. Assume the settlement date is January 2, 2006.

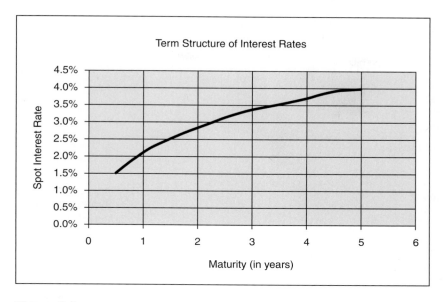

Figure 1.2 Term structure of rates

```
% Bonds = [Maturity CouponRate FaceValue]
Bonds = [datenum('15-Aug-2007')   0.08180    100;
         datenum('01-Jan-2008')   0.06375    100;
         datenum('15-Jan-2008')   0.06150    100;
         datenum('01-Mar-2008')   0.09375    100;
         datenum('01-Jun-2008')   0.06500    100;
         datenum('01-Sep-2008')   0.06831    100;
         datenum('24-Sep-2008')   0.07340    100;
         datenum('17-Oct-2008')   0.07375    100;
         datenum('15-Oct-2009')   0.08000    100;
         datenum('15-Feb-2010')   0.07625    100;
         datenum('15-Aug-2011')   0.09375    100];

Yields = [0.0547; 0.0619; 0.0604; 0.0634; 0.0676; 0.0599; 0.0567;
          0.0656; 0.0670; 0.0750; 0.0601];

Prices = [114.28; 102.26; 101.61; 116.30; 100.51; 105.13; 113.00;
          107.64; 111.39; 100.81; 125.58];

Settle = datenum('02-Jan-2006');

[ZeroRates, CurveDates] = zbtyield(Bonds,Yields,Settle)

ZeroRates =

    0.0547
    0.0623
```

```
    0.0607
    0.0641
    0.0683
    0.0600
    0.0565
    0.0661
    0.0676
    0.0769
    0.0586

datestr(CurveDates) =

15-Aug-2007
01-Jan-2008
15-Jan-2008
01-Mar-2008
01-Jun-2008
01-Sep-2008
24-Sep-2008
17-Oct-2008
15-Oct-2009
15-Feb-2010
15-Aug-2011
```

We could also bootstrap using the bond prices:

```
    [ZeroRates] = zbtprices(Bonds,Prices,Settle);

ZeroRates =

    0.0251
    0.0581
    0.0582
    0.0400
    0.0665
    0.0554
    0.0362
    0.0533
    0.0548
    0.0810
    0.0469
```

It should be noted that these zero rates are not risk-free discount rates because the coupon bonds are not risk free. To compute risk-free zero-rates, T-bills, Treasury notes, and Treasury bonds should be used.

1.9 BOOTSTRAPPING IN EXCEL

Consider the Excel spreadsheet[20] (ZC.xls) shown in Figure 1.3 with a worksheet called "Bootstrap," which takes zero coupon rates as input and interpolates between maturity dates. To view the Visual Basic code, click on Tools > Macro > Visual Basic Editor.

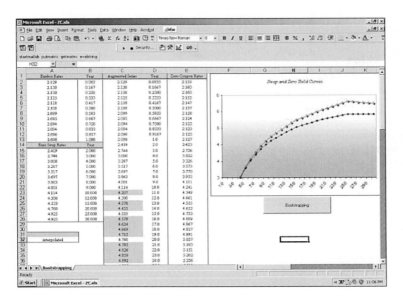

Figure 1.3 Interpolating zero coupon rates between maturity dates

```
Public ZC(1 To 100) As Double          // stores zero coupon rates
Public swaprate(1 To 100) As Double    // stores swap rates
Public dataswap(1 To 100) As Double
```

VB code in ZC.xls: Sub_interpolation_swap

```
Sub interpolation_swap()

  ReadRates_over10y  'Load swap rates over 10 years

  For i = 1 To 12
    Sheets("Bootstrapping").Cells(i + 1, 3) =
      Sheets("Bootstrapping").Cells(i + 1, 1)
    Sheets("Bootstrapping").Cells(i + 1, 4) =
      Sheets("Bootstrapping").Cells(i + 1, 2)
  Next i

  For i = 1 To 9
    Sheets("Bootstrapping").Cells(i + 13, 3) =
      Sheets("Bootstrapping").Cells(i + 14, 1)
    Sheets("Bootstrapping").Cells(i + 13, 4) =
      Sheets("Bootstrapping").Cells(i + 14, 2)

  Next i

  Sheets("Bootstrapping").Cells(24, 3) = swaprate(12)
  Sheets("Bootstrapping").Cells(27, 3) = swaprate(15)
  Sheets("Bootstrapping").Cells(32, 3) = swaprate(20)
  Sheets("Bootstrapping").Cells(37, 3) = swaprate(25)
```

```
Sheets("Bootstrapping").Cells(42, 3) = swaprate(30)

'Start the interpolation procedure for each knot

swaprate(11) = (swaprate(10) + swaprate(12)) * 0.5
Sheets("Bootstrapping").Cells(23, 3) = swaprate(11)


For i = 13 To 14
   swaprate(i) = swaprate(12) + ((swaprate(15) - swaprate(12)) *
     ((i - dataswap(2)) / (dataswap(3)
- dataswap(2))))
   Sheets("Bootstrapping").Cells(i + 12, 3) = swaprate(i)
Next i


For i = 16 To 19
swaprate(i) = swaprate(15) + ((swaprate(20) - swaprate(15)) *
  ((i - dataswap(3)) / (dataswap(4) - dataswap(3))))
   Sheets("Bootstrapping").Cells(i + 12, 3) = swaprate(i)
Next i


For i = 21 To 24
   swaprate(i) = swaprate(20) + ((swaprate(25) - swaprate(20)) *
     ((i - dataswap(4)) / (dataswap(5)
- dataswap(4))))
   Sheets("Bootstrapping").Cells(i + 12, 3) = swaprate(i)
Next i


For i = 26 To 29
swaprate(i) = swaprate(25) + ((swaprate(30) - swaprate(25)) *
  ((i - dataswap(5)) / (dataswap(6)
- dataswap(5))))
   Sheets("Bootstrapping").Cells(i + 12, 3) = swaprate(i)
Next i

End Sub

Sub ReadRates_over10y()

Dim i As Integer
Dim j As Integer
Sheets("Bootstrapping").Select

For i = 1 To 6
  dataswap(i) = Sheets("Bootstrapping").Cells(i + 22, 2)
  swaprate(dataswap(i)) = Sheets("Bootstrapping").Cells(i + 22, 1)
Next i

End Sub

Sub ZC_Rates()

Rates_Load
```

```
' Uniform the day-count convention between spot and swap rates
  (both 30/360)

For i = 1 To 12

  ZC(i) = Sheets("Bootstrapping").Cells(i + 1, 3) * 365 / 360

Next i

For j = 13 To 41

dummy_sum = 0

  For i = 1 To j - 12
        dummy_sum = dummy_sum + (swaprate(j) / 100) /
              ((1 + (ZC(11 + i) / 100)) ^ dataswap(11 + i))
  Next i

  ZC(j) = ((((1 + (swaprate(j) / 100)) / (1 - dummy_sum)) ^
    (1 / (dataswap(11 + i)))) - 1) * 100

Next j

For i = 1 To 41
  Sheets("Bootstrapping").Cells(i + 1, 5) = ZC(i)
Next i

End Sub

Sub Rates_Load()

  Dim i As Integer

  For i = 1 To 41
    dataswap(i) = Sheets("Bootstrapping").Cells(i + 1, 4)
            swaprate(i) = Sheets("Bootstrapping").Cells(i + 1, 3)
  Next i

End Sub
```

1.10   GENERAL SWAP PRICING IN MATLAB

The Matlab Fixed-Income Toolbox[21] contains functions that perform swap pricing and portfolio hedging. The Fixed-Income Toolbox contains the function **liborfloat2fixed**, which computes a fixed-rate par yield that equates the floating-rate side of a swap to the fixed-rate side. The solver sets the present value of the fixed side to the present value of the floating side without having to line up and compare fixed and floating periods.

The following assumptions are used for floating-rate input:

- LIBOR rates are quarterly—for example, that of Eurodollar futures.

- Effective date is the first third Wednesday after the settlement date.

- All delivery dates are spaced three months apart.

- All periods start on the third Wednesday of delivery months.

- All periods end on the same dates of delivery months, three months after the start dates.

- Accrual basis of floating rates is actual/360.

- Applicable forward rates are estimated by interpolation in months when forward-rate data in not available.

The following assumptions are used for floating-rate output:

- Design allows you to create a bond of any coupon, basis, or frequency, based upon the floating-rate input.

- The start date is a valuation date—that is, a date when an agreement to enter into a contract by the settlement date is made.

- Settlement can be on or after the start date. If it is after, a forward fixed-rate contract results.

- Effective date is assumed to be the first third Wednesday after settlement—the same date as that of the floating rate.

- The end date of the bond is a designated number of years away, on the same day and month as the effective date.

- Coupon payments occur on anniversary dates. The frequency is determined by the period of the bond.

- Fixed rates are not interpolated. A fixed-rate bond of the same present value as that of the floating-rate payments is created.

To compute par fixed-rate of swap given three-month LIBOR data, the following function is used:

```
[FixedSpec, ForwardDates, ForwardRates] =
      liborfloat2fixed(ThreeMonthRates, Settle, Tenor, StartDate,
      Interpolation, ConvexAdj, RateParam, InArrears, Sigma,
      FixedCompound, FixedBasis)
```

The input arguments are shown in Table 1.13.
The output is as follows:

FixedBasis computes forward rates, dates, and the swap fixed rate.
FixedSpec specifies the structure of the fixed-rate side of the swap:

- **Coupon**: Par-swap rate.

- **Settle**: Start date.

- **Maturity**: End date.

Table 1.13

`ThreeMonthRates`	Three-month Eurodollar futures data or forward rate agreement data. (A forward rate agreement stipulates that a certain interest rate applies to a certain principal amount for a given future time period.) An n-by-3 matrix in the form of `[month year IMMQuote]`. The floating rate is assumed to compound quarterly and to accrue on an actual/360 basis.
`Settle`	Settlement date of swap. Scalar.
`Tenor`	Life of the swap. Scalar.
`StartDate`	(Optional) Scalar value to denote reference date for valuation of (forward) swap. This in effect allows forward swap valuation. Default = `Settle`.
`Interpolation`	(Optional) Interpolation method to determine applicable forward rate for months when no Eurodollar data is available. Default is `'linear'` or 1. Other possible values are `'Nearest'` or 0, and `'Cubic'` or 2.
`ConvexAdj`	(Optional) Default = 0 (off). 1 = on. Denotes whether futures/forward convexity adjustment is required. Pertains to forward rate adjustments when those rates are taken from Eurodollar futures data.
`RateParam`	(Optional) Short-rate model's parameters (Hull-White) `[a S]`, where the short-rate process is: $dr = [\theta(t) - ar]dt + Sdz$ Default = `[0.05  0.015]`.
`InArrears`	(Optional) Default = 0 (off). Set to 1 for on. If on, the routine does an automatic convexity adjustment to forward rates.
`Sigma`	(Optional) Overall annual volatility of caplets.
`FixedCompound`	(Optional) Scalar value. Compounding or frequency of payment on the fixed side. Also, the reset frequency. Default = 4 (quarterly). Other values are 1, 2, and 12.
`FixedBasis`	(Optional). Scalar value. Basis of the fixed side. 0 = actual/actual, 1 = 30/360 (SIA, default), 2 = actual/360, 3 = actual/365, 4 = 30/360 (PSA), 5 = 30/360 (ISDA), 6 = 30/360 (European), 7 = act/365 (Japanese).

- `Period`: Frequency of payment.

- `Basis`: Accrual basis.

`ForwardDates` are dates corresponding to `ForwardRates` (all third Wednesdays of the month, spread three months apart). The first element is the third Wednesday immediately after `Settle`.

`ForwardRates` are forward rates corresponding to the forward dates, quarterly compounded, and on the actual/360 basis. To preserve input integrity, tenor is rounded upward to the closest integer. Currently traded tenors are 2, 5, and 10 years. The function assumes that floating-rate observations occur quarterly on the third Wednesday of a delivery month. The first delivery month is the month of the first third Wednesday after `Settle`. Floating-side payments occur on the third-month anniversaries of observation dates.

Example 3

Use the supplied `EDdata.xls` file as input to a `liborfloat2fixed` computation.

```
[EDFutData, textdata] = xlsread('EDdata.xls');
Settle                = datenum('15-Oct-2002');
Tenor                 = 2;

[FixedSpec, ForwardDates, ForwardRates] = ...
liborfloat2fixed(EDFutData, Settle, Tenor)

FixedSpec =

        Coupon: 0.0222
        Settle: '16-Oct-2002'
      Maturity: '16-Oct-2004'
        Period: 4
         Basis: 1

ForwardDates =

        731505  (16-Oct-2002)
        731596  (15-Jan-2003)
        731687  (16-Apr-2003)
        731778  (16-Jul-2003)
        731869  (15-Oct-2003)
        731967  (21-Jan-2004)
        732058  (21-Apr-2004)
        732149  (21-Jul-2004)

ForwardRates =

      0.0177
      0.0166
      0.0170
      0.0188
      0.0214
      0.0248
      0.0279
      0.0305
```

Table 1.14 shows Eurodollar data on Friday 11, 2002 that we will used for bootstrapping the yield curve and for computing swap rates in MATLAB.

Using this data, you can compute 1-, 2-, 3-, 4-, 5-, 7-, and 10-year swap rates with the toolbox function `liborfloat2fixed`. The function requires you to input only Eurodollar data, the settlement date, and tenor of the swap. Matlab then performs the required computations.

To illustrate how this function works, first load the data contained in the supplied Excel worksheet, `EDdata.xls`.

Table 1.14

Eurodollar Data on Friday 11, 2002						
Month	Year	Settle	Month	Year	Settle
10	2002	98.21	6	2007	94.88
11	2002	98.26	9	2007	94.74
12	2002	98.3	12	2007	94.595
1	2003	98.3	3	2008	94.48
2	2003	98.31	6	2008	94.375
3	2003	98.275	9	2008	94.28
6	2003	98.12	12	2008	94.185
9	2003	97.87	3	2009	94.1
12	2003	97.575	6	2009	94.005
3	2004	97.26	9	2009	93.925
6	2004	96.98	12	2009	93.865
9	2004	96.745	3	2010	93.82
12	2004	96.515	6	2010	93.755
3	2005	96.33	9	2010	93.7
6	2005	96.135	12	2010	93.645
9	2005	95.955	3	2011	93.61
12	2005	95.78	6	2011	93.56
3	2006	95.63	9	2011	93.515
6	2006	95.465	12	2011	93.47
9	2006	95.315	3	2012	93.445
12	2006	95.16	6	2012	93.41
3	2007	95.025	9	2012	93.39

Source: Matlab

```
[EDRawData, textdata] = xlsread('EDdata.xls');
```

Extract the month from the first column and the year from the second column. The rate used as proxy is the arithmetic average of rates on opening and closing.

```
Month = EDRawData(:,1);
Year = EDRawData(:,2);
IMMData = (EDRawData(:,3);
EDFutData = [Month, Year, IMMData];
```

Next, input the current date.

```
Settle = datenum('11-Oct-2002');
```

To compute for the two-year swap rate, set the tenor to 2.

```
Tenor = 2;
```

Finally, compute the swap rate with `liborfloat2fixed`.

```
[FixedSpec, ForwardDates, ForwardRates] =...
     liborfloat2fixed(EDFutData, Settle, Tenor)
```

Matlab returns a par-swap rate of 2.23% using the default setting (quarterly compounding and 30/360 accrual), and forward dates and rates data (quarterly compounded), comparable to 2.17% of Friday's average broker data in Table H15 of *Federal Reserve Statistical Release* (http://www.federalreserve.gov/releases/h15/update/).

```
FixedSpec =

      Coupon: 0.0223
      Settle: '16-Oct-2002'
    Maturity: '16-Oct-2004'
      Period: 4
       Basis: 1

datestr(ForwardDates) =

      731505   (16-Oct-2002)
      731596   (15-Jan-2003)
      731687   (16-Apr-2003)
      731778   (16-Jul-2003)
      731869   (15-Oct-2003)
      731967   (21-Jan-2004)
      732058   (21-Apr-2004)
      732149   (21-Jul-2004)

ForwardRates =

     0.0179
     0.0170
     0.0177
     0.0196
     0.0222
     0.0255
     0.0285
     0.0311
```

In the `FixedSpec` output, note that the swap rate actually goes forward from the third Wednesday of October 2002 (October 16, 2002), five days after the original `Settle` input (October 11, 2002). This, however, is still the best proxy for the swap rate on `Settle`, as the assumption merely starts the swap's effective period and does not affect its valuation method or its length.

The correction suggested by Hull and White improves the result by turning on convexity adjustment as part of the input to `liborfloat2fixed`. (See Hull, J., *Options, Futures, and Other Derivatives*, 4th Edition, Prentice Hall, 2000.) For a long swap—e.g., five years or more—this correction could prove to be substantial.

The adjustment requires additional parameters:

- StartDate, which you make the same as Settle (the default) by providing an empty matrix [ ] as input.

- ConvexAdj to tell liborfloat2fixed to perform the adjustment.

- RateParam, which provides the parameters a and S as input to the Hull-White short-rate process.

- Optional parameters InArrears and Sigma, for which you can use empty matrices [ ] to accept the Matlab defaults.

- FixedCompound, with which you can facilitate comparison with values cited in Table H15 of *Federal Reserve Statistical Release* by turning the default quarterly compounding into semiannual compounding, with the (default) basis of 30/360.

```
StartDate = [];
Interpolation = [];
ConvexAdj = 1;
RateParam = [0.03; 0.017];
FixedCompound = 2;
[FixedSpec, ForwardDates, ForwardRates] =...
liborfloat2fixed(EDFutData, Settle, Tenor, StartDate, Interpolation,
ConvexAdj, RateParam, [], [], FixedCompound)
```

This returns 2.21% as the two-year swap rate, quite close to the reported swap rate for that date. Analogously, Table 1.15 summarizes the solutions for 1-, 3-, 5-, 7-, and 10-year swap rates (convexity-adjusted and unadjusted).

Table 1.15

Calculated and Market Average Data of Swap Rates on Friday, October 11, 2002				
Swap Length (Years)	**Unadjusted**	**Adjusted**	**Table H15**	**Adjusted Error (Basis Points)**
1	1.80%	1.79%	1.80%	-1
2	2.24%	2.21%	2.22%	-1
3	2.70%	2.66%	2.66%	0
4	3.12%	3.03%	3.04%	-1
5	3.50%	3.37%	3.36%	+1
7	4.16%	3.92%	3.89%	+3
10	4.87%	4.42%	4.39%	+3

Source: Matlab

To compute the duration of a LIBOR-based interest rate swap, we use the **liborduration** function:

```
[PayFixDuration GetFixDuration] = liborduration(SwapFixRate, Tenor,
Settle)
```

The input arguments are shown in Table 1.16.

Table 1.16

SwapFixRate	Scalar or column vector of swap fixed rates in decimal.
Tenor	Scalar or column vector indicating life of the swap in years. Fractional numbers are rounded upward.
Settle	Scalar or column vector of settlement dates.

The output arguments are as follows:

- PayFixDuration is the modified duration, in years, realized when entering pay-fix side of the swap.

- GetFixDuration is the modified duration, in years, realized when entering receive-fix side of the swap.

Example 4

Given the following data

```
SwapFixRate = 0.0383;
Tenor = 7;
Settle = datenum('11-Oct-2002');
```

compute the swap durations.

```
[PayFixDuration GetFixDuration] = liborduration(SwapFixRate,...
    Tenor, Settle)

PayFixDuration =

  -4.7567

GetFixDuration =

   4.7567
```

A swap can be valued in Matlab using a Black-Derman-Toy (BDT) tree or an HJM tree. The syntax is as follows:

```
[Price, PriceTree, CFTree, SwapRate] = swapbybdt(BDTTree, LegRate,
    Settle, Maturity, LegReset, Basis, Principal, LegType, Options)
```

The input arguments are shown Table 1.17.
The outputs are as follows:

- Price is the number of instruments (NINST)-by-1 expected prices of the swap at time 0.

- PriceTree is the tree structure with a vector of the swap values at each node.

- `CFTree` is the tree structure with a vector of the swap cash flows at each node.

- `SwapRate` is a NINST-by-1 vector of rates applicable to the fixed leg such that the swaps' values are zero at time 0. This rate is used in calculating the swaps' prices when the rate specified for the fixed leg in `LegRate` is NaN. `SwapRate` is padded with NaN for those instruments in which `CouponRate` is not set to NaN.

Table 1.17

`BDTTree`	Interest rate tree structure created by `bdttree`.
`LegRate`	Number of instruments (NINST)-by-2 matrix, with each row defined as: `[CouponRate Spread]` or `[Spread CouponRate]` `CouponRate` is the decimal annual rate. `Spread` is the number of basis points over the reference rate. The first column represents the receiving leg, while the second column represents the paying leg.
`Settle`	Settlement date. NINST-by-1 vector of serial date numbers or date strings. `Settle` must be earlier than or equal to `Maturity`.
`Maturity`	Maturity date. NINST-by-1 vector of dates representing the maturity date for each swap.
`LegReset`	(Optional) NINST-by-2 matrix representing the reset frequency per year for each swap. Default = `[1 1]`.
`Basis`	(Optional) NINST-by-1 vector representing the basis used when annualizing the input forward rate tree. Default = 0 (actual/actual).
`Principal`	(Optional) NINST-by-1 vector of the notional principal amounts. Default = 100.
`LegType`	(Optional) NINST-by-2 matrix. Each row represents an instrument. Each column indicates if the corresponding leg is fixed (1) or floating (0). This matrix defines the interpretation of the values entered in `LegRate`. Default is `[1 0]` for each instrument.
`Options`	(Optional) Derivatives pricing options structure created with `derivset`.

Example 5

To price an interest rate swap with a fixed receiving leg and a floating paying leg, payments are made once a year, and the notional principal amount is \$1,000,000. The values for the remaining parameters are as follows:

- Coupon rate for fixed leg: 0.15 (15%)

- Spread for floating leg: 10 basis points

- Swap settlement date: Jan. 01, 2000

- Swap maturity date: Jan. 01, 2003

Based on the preceding information, set the required parameters and build the `LegRate`, `LegType`, and `LegReset` matrices.

```
Settle = '01-Jan-2000';
Maturity = '01-Jan-2003';
Basis = 0;
Principal = 1000000;
LegRate = [0.15 10]; % [CouponRate Spread]
LegType = [1 0]; % [Fixed Float]
LegReset = [1 1]; % Payments once per year
```

We price the swap using the `BDTTree` included in the MAT-file `deriv.mat`. `BDTTree` contains the time and forward rate information needed to price the instrument.

```
load deriv;
```

Use `swapbybdt` to compute the price of the swap.

```
Price = swapbybdt(BDTTree, LegRate, Settle, Maturity,...
    LegReset, Basis, Principal, LegType)

Price = 73032
```

Example 6

Using the previous data, calculate the swap rate, the coupon rate for the fixed leg such that the swap price at time 0 is zero.

```
LegRate = [NaN 20];

[Price, PriceTree, CFTree, SwapRate] = swapbybdt(BDTTree,...
    LegRate, Settle, Maturity, LegReset, Basis, Principal, LegType)

Price =

 -2.8422e-014

PriceTree =

    FinObj: 'BDTPriceTree'
     tObs: [0 1 2 3 4]
    PTree: {1x5 cell}

CFTree =

    FinObj: 'BDTCFTree'
     tObs: [0 1 2 3 4]
    CFTree: {1x5 cell}

SwapRate =
            0.1210
```

A swap can also be valued using an HJM tree.

```
[Price, PriceTree, CFTree, SwapRate] = swapbyhjm(HJMTree, LegRate,
    Settle, Maturity, LegReset, Basis, Principal, LegType, Options)
```

Table 1.18

HJMTree	Forward rate tree structure created by hjmtree.
LegRate	Number of instruments (NINST)-by-2 matrix, with each row defined as: [CouponRate Spread] or [Spread CouponRate] CouponRate is the decimal annual rate. Spread is the number of basis points over the reference rate. The first column represents the receiving leg, while the second column represents the paying leg.
Settle	Settlement date. NINST-by-1 vector of serial date numbers or date strings. Settle must be earlier than or equal to Maturity.
Maturity	Maturity date. NINST-by-1 vector of dates representing the maturity date for each swap.
LegReset	(Optional) NINST-by-2 matrix representing the reset frequency per year for each swap. Default = [1 1].
Basis	(Optional) NINST-by-1 vector representing the basis used when annualizing the input forward rate tree. Default = 0 (actual/actual).
Principal	(Optional) NINST-by-1 vector of the notional principal amounts. Default = 100.
LegType	(Optional) NINST-by-2 matrix. Each row represents an instrument. Each column indicates if the corresponding leg is fixed (1) or floating (0). This matrix defines the interpretation of the values entered in LegRate. Default is [1 0] for each instrument.
Options	(Optional) Derivatives pricing options structure created with derivset.

The arguments of the swapbyhjm function are shown in Table 1.18.

The Settle date for every swap is set to the ValuationDate of the HJM tree. The swap argument Settle is ignored. This function also calculates the SwapRate (fixed rate) so that the value of the swap is initially zero. To do this, enter CouponRate as NaN.

Description

[Price, PriceTree, CFTree, SwapRate] = swapbyhjm(HJMTree, LegRate, Settle, Maturity, LegReset, Basis, Principal, LegType) computes the price of a swap instrument from an HJM interest rate tree.

Price	The number of instruments (NINST)-by-1 expected prices of the swap at time 0.
PriceTree	The tree structure with a vector of the swap values at each node.
CFTree	The tree structure with a vector of the swap cash flows at each node.
SwapRate	A NINST-by-1 vector of rates applicable to the fixed leg such that the swaps' values are zero at time 0. This rate is used in calculating the swaps' prices when the rate specified for the fixed leg in LegRate is NaN. SwapRate is padded with NaN for those instruments in which CouponRate is not set to NaN.

Example 7

Price an interest rate swap with a fixed receiving leg and a floating paying leg. Payments are made once a year, and the notional principal amount is $100. The values for the remaining parameters are as follows:

- Coupon rate for fixed leg: 0.06 (6%)

- Spread for floating leg: 20 basis points

- Swap settlement date: Jan. 01, 2000

- Swap maturity date: Jan. 01, 2003

Based on the preceding information, set the required parameters and build the `LegRate`, `LegType`, and `LegReset` matrices.

```
Settle = '01-Jan-2000';
Maturity = '01-Jan-2003';
Basis = 0;
Principal = 100;
LegRate = [0.06 20]; % [CouponRate Spread]
LegType = [1 0]; % [Fixed Float]
LegReset = [1 1]; % Payments once per year
```

Price the swap using the `HJMTree` included in the MAT-file `deriv.mat`. `HJMTree` contains the time and forward rate information needed to price the instrument.

```
load deriv;
```

Use `swapbyhjm` to compute the price of the swap.

```
[Price, PriceTree, CFTree] = swapbyhjm(HJMTree, LegRate,...
    Settle, Maturity, LegReset, Basis, Principal, LegType)

Price =

   3.6923

PriceTree =

    FinObj: 'HJMPriceTree'
      tObs: [0 1 2 3 4]
     PBush: {1x5 cell}

CFTree =

    FinObj: 'HJMCFTree'
      tObs: [0 1 2 3 4]
    CFBush: {[0] [1x1x2 double] [1x2x2 double] ... [1x8 double]}
```

1.11   SWAP PRICING IN MATLAB USING TERM STRUCTURE ANALYSIS

This example illustrates some of the term structure analysis functions found in the Financial Toolbox. Specifically, it illustrates how to derive implied zero (*spot*) and forward curves from the observed market prices of coupon-bearing bonds. The zero and forward curves implied from the market data are then used to price an interest rate swap agreement. In an interest rate swap, two parties agree to a periodic exchange of cash flows. One of the cash flows is based on a fixed interest rate held constant throughout the life of the swap. The other cash flow stream is tied to some variable index rate. Pricing a swap at inception amounts to finding the fixed rate of the swap agreement. This fixed rate, appropriately scaled by the notional principal of the swap agreement, determines the periodic sequence of fixed cash flows. In general, interest rate swaps are priced from the forward curve such that the variable cash flows implied from the series of forward rates and the periodic sequence of fixed-rate cash flows have the same present value. Thus, interest rate swap pricing and term structure analysis are closely related.

Step 1. Specify values for the settlement date, maturity dates, coupon rates, and market prices for 10 U.S. Treasury bonds. This data allows us to price a five-year swap with net cash flow payments exchanged every six months. For simplicity, accept default values for the end-of-month payment rule (rule in effect) and day-count basis (actual/actual). To avoid issues of accrued interest, assume that all Treasury bonds pay semiannual coupons and that settlement occurs on a coupon payment date.

```
Settle = datenum('15-Jan-1999');

BondData = {'15-Jul-1999'  0.06000 99.93
            '15-Jan-2000'  0.06125 99.72
            '15-Jul-2000'  0.06375 99.70
            '15-Jan-2001'  0.06500 99.40
            '15-Jul-2001'  0.06875 99.73
            '15-Jan-2002'  0.07000 99.42
            '15-Jul-2002'  0.07250 99.32
            '15-Jan-2003'  0.07375 98.45
            '15-Jul-2003'  0.07500 97.71
            '15-Jan-2004'  0.08000 98.15};
```

`BondData` is an instance of a Matlab *cell array*, indicated by the curly braces {}.

Next, assign the date stored in the cell array to `Maturity`, `CouponRate`, and `Prices` vectors for further processing.

```
Maturity   = datenum(strvcat(BondData{:,1}));
CouponRate = [BondData{:,2}]';
Prices     = [BondData{:,3}]';
Period     = 2; % semiannual coupons
```

Step 2. Now that the data has been specified, use the term structure function **zbtprice** to bootstrap the zero curve implied from the prices of the coupon-bearing bonds. This implied zero curve represents the series of zero-coupon Treasury rates consistent with the prices of the coupon-bearing bonds such that arbitrage opportunities will not exist.

```
ZeroRates = zbtprice([Maturity CouponRate], Prices, Settle);
```

The zero curve, stored in `ZeroRates`, is quoted on a semiannual bond basis (the periodic, six-month, interest rate is simply doubled to annualize). The first element of `ZeroRates` is the annualized rate over the next six months, the second element is the annualized rate over the next 12 months, and so on.

Step 3. From the implied zero curve, find the corresponding series of implied forward rates using the term structure function **zero2fwd**.

```
ForwardRates = zero2fwd(ZeroRates, Maturity, Settle);
```

The forward curve, stored in `ForwardRates`, is also quoted on a semiannual bond basis. The first element of `ForwardRates` is the annualized rate applied to the interval between settlement and 6 months after settlement, the second element is the annualized rate applied to the interval from 6 months to 12 months after settlement, and so on. This implied forward curve is also consistent with the observed market prices such that arbitrage activities will be unprofitable. Because the first forward rate is also a zero rate, the first element of `ZeroRates` and `ForwardRates` are the same.

Step 4. Now that you have derived the zero curve, convert it to a sequence of discount factors with the term structure function **zero2disc**.

```
DiscountFactors = zero2disc(ZeroRates, Maturity, Settle);
```

Step 5. From the discount factors, compute the present value of the variable cash flows derived from the implied forward rates. For plain interest rate swaps, the notional principal remains constant for each payment date and cancels out of each side of the present value equation. The next line assumes unit notional principal.

```
PresentValue = sum((ForwardRates/Period) .* DiscountFactors);
```

Step 6. Compute the swap's price (the fixed rate) by equating the present value of the fixed cash flows with the present value of the cash flows derived from the implied forward rates. Again, because the notional principal cancels out of each side of the equation, it is simply assumed to be 1.

```
SwapFixedRate = Period * PresentValue / sum(DiscountFactors);
```

The output would be as follows:

```
Zero Rates Forward Rates
   0.0614      0.0614
   0.0642      0.0670
   0.0660      0.0695
   0.0684      0.0758
   0.0702      0.0774
   0.0726      0.0846
   0.0754      0.0925
   0.0795      0.1077
```

```
    0.0827      0.1089
    0.0868      0.1239

Swap Price (Fixed Rate) = 0.0845
```

All rates are in decimal format. The swap price, 8.45%, would likely be the midpoint between a market-maker's bid/ask quotes.

Example 8

Consider a nine-year fixed for floating swap with a notional of $3.3 million and fixed coupon rate of 3.969%, a floating rate based on three-month T-bill, with a start date of March 28, 2004, effective date of March 29, 2004, and a maturity of March 28, 2013. Assume the fixed side is on a 30/360 day count while the floating leg is on an actual/360 day count with quarterly resets. Figure 1.4 displays the Bloomberg screen with the swap data terms.

Figures 1.5–1.7 show the swap cash flow payments and payment schedule. Figures 1.8 provides the swap curve. Figure 1.9, shows the risk measures, DV01, and duration, for both the pay and receive legs.

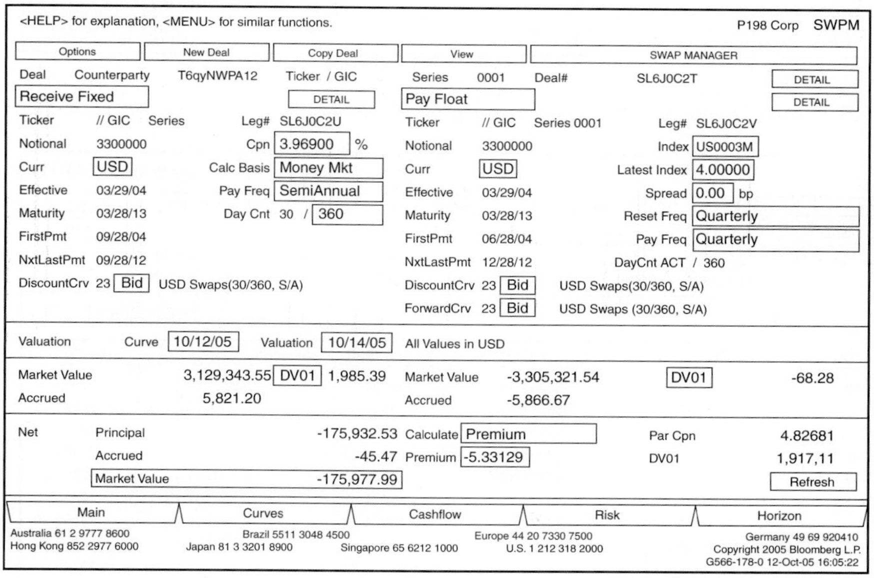

Figure 1.4   *Source: Reproduced with permission from Bloomberg.*

<HELP> for explanation.   P235 Corp SWPM

Options	New Deal	Copy Deal	View	SWAP MANAGER	

Deal   Counterparty T6qyNWPA12 Ticker / GIC Series 0001 Deal# SL6J0C2T DETAIL

REC FIXED Coupon 3.96900   Frequency S Curr USD Notional 3300000
PAY FLOAT Latest Index 4.00000 + 0.00 bp   Reset/Pmnt FreqQ/Q Curr USD Notional 3300000

Net   Cashflo Currency USD   EXPORT TO EXCEL

Payment Dates	Payments(Rcv)	Payments(Pay)	Net Payments	Discount	Net PV
12/28/2005	0.00	-33366.67	-33366.67	0.991587	-33085.94
03/28/2006	65488.50	-36550.57	28937.93	0.980724	28380.12
06/28/2006	0.00	-38758.48	-38758.48	0.969339	-37570.12
09/28/2006	65488.50	-39287.93	26200.57	0.957935	25098.43
12/28/2006	0.00	-38326.13	-38326.13	0.946937	-36292.42
03/28/2007	65488.50	-38039.88	27448.62	0.936146	25695.90
06/28/2007	0.00	-39213.28	-39213.28	0.925152	-36278.26
09/28/2007	65488.50	-39523.30	25965.20	0.914203	23737.47
12/28/2007	0.00	-39297.44	-39297.44	0.903445	-35503.06
03/28/2008	65488.50	-39531.82	25956.68	0.892750	23172.83
06/30/2008	0.00	-41091.95	-41091.95	0.881770	-36233.66
09/29/2008	65852.32	-39999.08	25853.25	0.871210	22523.61
12/29/2008	0.00	-39094.19	-39094.19	0.861010	-33660.49
TOTAL					-176149.58

Main	Curves	Cashflow	Risk	Horizon

Australia 61 2 9777 8600 Brazil 5511 3048 4500 Europe 44 20 7330 7500 Germany 49 69 920410
Hong Kong 852 2977 6000 Japan 81 3 3201 8900 Singapore 65 6212 1000 U.S. 1 212 318 2000 Copyright 2005 Bloomberg L.P.
G566-178-0 18-Nov-05 15:08:34

Figure 1.5 *Source: Reproduced with permission from Bloomberg.*

<HELP> for explanation.   P235 Corp SWPM

Options	New Deal	Copy Deal	View	SWAP MANAGER	

Deal   Counterparty T6qyNWPA12 Ticker / GIC Series 0001 Deal# SL6J0C2T DETAIL

REC FIXED Coupon 3.96900   Frequency S Curr USD Notional 3300000
PAY FLOAT Latest Index 4.00000 + 0.00 bp   Reset/Pmnt FreqQ/Q Curr USD Notional 3300000

Net   Cashflo Currency USD   EXPORT TO EXCEL

Payment Dates	Payments(Rcv)	Payments(Pay)	Net Payments	Discount	Net PV
12/29/2008	0.00	-39094.19	-39094.19	0.861010	-33660.49
03/30/2009	65852.32	-38911.34	26940.99	0.850976	22926.13
06/29/2009	0.00	-38927.60	-38927.60	0.841055	-32740.24
09/28/2009	64760.85	-38938.01	25822.84	0.831247	21465.15
12/28/2009	0.00	-39881.18	-39881.18	0.821321	-32755.23
03/29/2010	65852.32	-40177.71	25674.62	0.811441	20833.45
06/28/2010	0.00	-40274.03	-40274.03	0.801658	-32285.99
09/28/2010	65124.68	-40807.77	24316.91	0.791866	19255.72
12/28/2010	0.00	-40583.21	-40583.21	0.782245	-31746.04
03/28/2011	65488.50	-40243.83	25244.67	0.772821	19509.61
06/28/2011	0.00	-41217.01	-41217.01	0.763287	-31460.42
09/28/2011	65488.50	-41282.22	24206.28	0.753857	18248.07
12/28/2011	0.00	-40707.37	-40707.37	0.744671	-30313.59
TOTAL					-176149.58

Main	Curves	Cashflow	Risk	Horizon

Australia 61 2 9777 8600 Brazil 5511 3048 4500 Europe 44 20 7330 7500 Germany 49 69 920410
Hong Kong 852 2977 6000 Japan 81 3 3201 8900 Singapore 65 6212 1000 U.S. 1 212 318 2000 Copyright 2005 Bloomberg L.P.
G566-178-0 18-Nov-05 15:09:10

Figure 1.6 *Source: Reproduced with permission from Bloomberg.*

<HELP> for explanation.					P235 Corp **SWPM**

Options	New Deal	Copy Deal	View	SWAP MANAGER	
Deal Counterparty T6qyNWPA12		Ticker / GIC	Series 0001 Deal#	SL6J0C2T	DETAIL

REC FIXED Coupon   3.96900   Frequency   S   Curr USD Notional 3300000
PAY FLOAT Latest Index 4.00000 + 0.00 bp   Reset/Pmnt FreqQ/Q Curr USD Notional 3300000

Net	Cashflo Currency USD				EXPORT TO EXCEL

Payment Dates	Payments(Rcv)	Payments(Pay)	Net Payments	Discount	Net PV
03/29/2010	65852.32	-40177.71	25674.62	0.811441	20833.45
06/28/2010	0.00	-40274.03	-40274.03	0.801658	-32285.99
09/28/2010	65124.68	-40807.77	24316.91	0.791866	19255.72
12/28/2010	0.00	-40583.21	-40583.21	0.782245	-31746.04
03/28/2011	65488.50	-40243.83	25244.67	0.772821	19509.61
06/28/2011	0.00	-41217.01	-41217.01	0.763287	-31460.42
09/28/2011	65488.50	-41282.22	24206.28	0.753857	18248.07
12/28/2011	0.00	-40707.37	-40707.37	0.744671	-30313.59
03/28/2012	65488.50	-40705.47	24783.03	0.735597	18230.33
06/28/2012	0.00	-41183.89	-41183.89	0.726530	-29921.34
09/28/2012	65488.50	-41205.10	24283.40	0.717570	17425.05
12/28/2012	0.00	-41725.89	-41725.89	0.708611	-29567.41
03/28/2013	3365488.50	-3341534.93	23953.57	0.699803	16762.77
TOTAL					-176149.58

Main	Curves	Cashflow	Risk	Horizon

Australia 61 2 9777 8600   Brazil 5511 3048 4500   Europe 44 20 7330 7500   Germany 49 69 920410
Hong Kong 852 2977 6000   Japan 81 3 3201 8900   Singapore 65 6212 1000   U.S. 1 212 318 2000   Copyright 2005 Bloomberg L.P.
                                                                                                                                                                    G566-178-0 18-Nov-05 15:09:39

Figure 1.7 *Source: Reproduced with permission from Bloomberg.*

<HELP> for explanation.					P198 Corp **SWPM**

Options	New Deal	Copy Deal	View	SWAP MANAGER	
Deal Counterparty T6qyNWPA12		Ticker / GIC	Series 0001 Deal#	SL6J0C2T	DETAIL

Curve #23	USD Swaps (30/360,S/A)				

	Current Market		6 Month −50bp		6 Month +0bp		6 Month +50bp	
#	Mty/Term	Rate	#	Mty/Term	Rate	#	Mty/Term	Rate	#	Mty/Term	Rate

#	Mty/Term	Rate	#	Mty/Term	Rate	#	Mty/Term	Rate	#	Mty/Term	Rate
1	1 DY	3.50000	1	1 DY	3.00000	1	1 DY	3.50000	1	1 DY	4.00000
2	2 DY	3.80000	2	2 DY	3.30000	2	2 DY	3.80000	2	2 DY	4.30000
3	1 WK	3.81688	3	1 WK	3.31688	3	1 WK	3.81688	3	1 WK	4.31688
4	2 WK	3.82000	4	2 WK	3.32000	4	2 WK	3.82000	4	2 WK	4.32000
5	3 WK	3.86000	5	3 WK	3.36000	5	3 WK	3.86000	5	3 WK	4.36000
6	1 MO	3.94563	6	1 MO	3.44563	6	1 MO	3.94563	6	1 MO	4.44563
7	2 MO	4.02563	7	2 MO	3.52563	7	2 MO	4.02563	7	2 MO	4.52563
8	3 MO	4.14000	8	3 MO	3.64000	8	3 MO	4.14000	8	3 MO	4.64000
9	4 MO	4.20000	9	4 MO	3.70000	9	4 MO	4.20000	9	4 MO	4.70000
10	5 MO	4.26000	10	5 MO	3.76000	10	5 MO	4.26000	10	5 MO	4.46000
11	6 MO	4.32875	11	6 MO	3.82875	11	6 MO	4.32875	11	6 MO	4.82875
12	7 MO	4.37025	12	7 MO	3.87025	12	7 MO	4.37025	12	7 MO	4.87025

Horizon Curve Date	10/12/05	Horizon Curve Date	04/12/06	Horizon Curve Date	04/12/06	Horizon Curve Date	04/12/06
Horizon Settle Date	10/14/05	Horizon Settle Date	04/18/06	Horizon Settle Date	04/18/06	Horizon Settle Date	04/18/06

GLOBAL CHANGE FIELDS	------	From 1 To 34	Shift 0.00	From 1 To 34	Shift 0.00	From 1 To 34	Shift 0.00
Pay Leg PV	-3,305,321.54	Pay Leg PV	-3,331,694.62	Pay Leg PV	-3,308,454.83	Pay Leg PV	-3,305,221.38
Receive Leg PV	3,128,009.55	Receive Leg PV	3,239,101.26	Receive Leg PV	3,143,640.16	Receive Leg PV	3,051,445.05
Net PV	-177,311.99	Net PV	-72,593.36	Net PV	-164,814.67	Net PV	-253,776.32

Main	Curves	Cashflow	Risk	Horizon

Australia 61 2 9777 8600   Brazil 5511 3048 4500   Europe 44 20 7330 7500   Germany 49 69 920410
Hong Kong 852 2977 6000   Japan 81 3 3201 8900   Singapore 65 6212 1000   U.S. 1 212 318 2000   Copyright 2005 Bloomberg L.P.
                                                                                                                                                                    G566-178-0 12-Oct-05 15:48:54

Figure 1.8 *Source: Reproduced with permission from Bloomberg.*

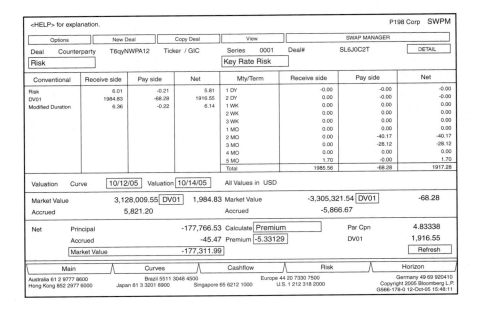

Figure 1.9   *Source: Reproduced with permission from Bloomberg.*

1.12   SWAP VALUATION IN C++

To price a vanilla fixed-for-floating swap in C++, we define a *Swap* class. The *Swap* class is composed of two legs—a *FloatingLeg* class, floatLeg, and a *FixedLeg* class, fixed-Leg, which represent the two sides of the swap. Because the calculation of payment dates based on the start date, effective date, and maturity date is required, the *Swap* class utilizes a *Date* class[22] that contains methods for computing date operations. The *Date* class is defined in the "datecl.h" file and will be used throughout this book to compute payment dates.

The *Swap* class contains the following *Date* data members:

```
Date maturity_;            // swap maturity date
Date fixedAccruedDate_;    // fixed interest accrual date
Date floatAccruedDate_;    // floating interest accrual date
Date effectiveDate_;       // effective date
Date settlementDate_;      // settlement date
Date valuationDate_;       // valuation date
```

The *Date* methods are defined in the "datecl.cpp" source file. The *Swap* class is defined with various inline methods to add in the computation of the swap payments, netting, and pricing:

```
double getNotional()        // return notional amount
double calcDV01()           // compute swap DV01
void netPayments()          // net fixed and floating payments
void calcPayDates(Date tradeDate, Date endDate, Date valuation)
```

```
   // calculate pay dates
void setDiscountRates(std::map<double,double> rate)   // set discount rates
```

The *Swap* class utilizes the *floatLeg* and *fixedLeg* data class members to perform many of the operations in these methods. The *Swap* class contains overloaded constructors to receive and store important data for pricing: the maturity date, effective date, settlement date, valuation date, floating (libor) rates, discount rates, fixed swap rate, and valuation type (receive fixed-pay floating or receive floating-pay fixed). The *Swap* class definition is:

SWAP.h

```cpp
#ifndef _SWAP_H__
#define _SWAP_H__

#include "TNT\TNT.h"
#include "datecl.h"
#include <string>
#include <vector>
#include <map>
#define NUM_DATES          100
#define THIRTY              30
#define THREE_SIXTY        360
#define THREE_SIXTY_FIVE   365
#define NOTIONAL          1000000

static std::vector<Date> payDates_;

static double interpolate(double rate1, double rate2, double t1, double t2,
  double x) {
  double dy = rate2 - rate1;
  double dt = t2 - t1;
  double slope = dy/dt;

  return rate1 + slope*x;
}

class FloatingLeg
{
  public:
    FloatingLeg(std::map<double,double> floatLegRate, double floatLegBasis,
      int payFrequency)
                  : floatLegRate_(floatLegRate),floatLegBasis_(floatLegBasis),
                    payFrequency_(payFrequency) {}
    FloatingLeg() {}
    virtual ~FloatingLeg() {}
    inline double calcDuration() {
      double duration = 0.0;
      duration = (double) (payDates_[0] -
        valuationDate_ + 1)/THREE_SIXTY_FIVE;
      return duration;
    }
    inline void setEffectiveDate(Date date) { startDate_ = date; }
    inline void setValuationDate(Date date) { valuationDate_ = date; }
    inline void setNotional(double notional) { notional_ = notional; }
    inline Date getEffectiveDate() { return startDate_; }
```

```cpp
inline void setFrequency(int frequency) { payFrequency_ = frequency; }
inline void setMaturityDate(Date mat) { maturityDate_ = mat; }
inline std::vector<double> getPayFloat() { return floatRates; }
inline void setFloatValue(double value) { value_ = value; }
inline double getFloatValue() {
    return value_;
}
inline void setFloatRate(std::map<double,double> rate) {
      floatLegRate_ = rate;
}
inline double calcDV01() {

      double duration = calcDuration();
      double val = getFloatValue();
      double DV = 0.0;

      DV = -(duration*notional_)*((double)1/10000);
      cout << "float DV01 = " << DV << endl;

      return -DV;
}
inline double calcModifiedDuration() {

      double val = calcDV01();
      double marketValue = getFloatValue();
      double MD = (val/(notional_ + marketValue))*10000;

      cout << "float modified duration = " << MD << endl;

      return MD;
}
inline void calcPayFloat() {

      std::vector<Date>::iterator iter;
      double val = 0;
      double diff = 0.0;
      int diff1 = 0.0;
      int d = 0.0;
      int d1 = 0.0;
      Date dateDiff;
      int cnt = 0;
      double floatVal = 0.0;

      for (iter = payDates_.begin(); iter != payDates_.end(); iter++)
      {
        d = payDates_[cnt+1] - payDates_[0] + 1;
        d1 = payDates_[cnt+1] - payDates_[cnt] + 1;

        diff = payDates_[cnt+1] - payDates_[0]+1;
        diff = (double) diff/THREE_SIXTY_FIVE;
        floatVal = interpolate(floatLegRate_[floor(diff)],
          floatLegRate_[ceil(diff)],floor(diff),ceil(diff),diff);

        if (payFrequency_ == 1)
              val = notional_*(THIRTY/THREE_SIXTY)*floatVal;
        else
              val = notional_*((double)d1/THREE_SIXTY_FIVE)*floatVal;
```

```
                       floatRates.push_back(val);
                       cnt++;
                   }
        }
    private:
       double floatLegBasis_;
            std::vector<double> floatRates;
            std::map<double,double> floatLegRate_;
            std::map<double,double> payfloatLeg_;
            Date startDate_;
            Date maturityDate_;
            Date valuationDate_;
            double value_;
            double spread_;
            double notional_;
            double duration_;
            double accrual_;
            int payFrequency_;
};

class FixedLeg
{
    public:
            FixedLeg(double payfixedLeg, double fixedLegRate,
               double fixedLegBasis, int payFrequency)
          : payfixedLeg_(payfixedLeg), fixedLegRate_(fixedLegRate),
            fixedLegBasis_(fixedLegBasis),
                    payFrequency_(payFrequency) {}
            FixedLeg() {}
            virtual ~FixedLeg() {}
            inline double calcDV01() {

                double duration = calcDuration();
                double val = getFixedValue();
                double DV = 0.0;

                DV = (duration*notional_)*((double)1/10000);
                cout << "fixed DV01 = " << DV << endl;

                return DV;
            }
            inline void setEffectiveDate(Date date) { effectiveDate_ = date; }
            inline double calcDuration() {

                double sum = 0;
                double val = getFixedValue();
                double duration = 0.0;
                double dis = 0.0;

                for (int i = 0; i < payfixedLeg_.size(); i++)
                   sum = sum + payfixedLeg_[i]*((double)(payDates_[i+1] -
                      valuationDate_ + 1)/
                        (maturityDate_ - valuationDate_ + 1));

                   sum = sum + notional_;
                   duration = sum/val;
```

```
            cout << "fixed duration = " << duration << endl;

            return duration;
        }
        inline double calcModifiedDuration() {

            double val = calcDV01();
            double marketValue = getFixedValue();
            double MD = (val/(notional_ + marketValue))*10000;

            return MD;
        }
        inline void setFixedValue(double val) { value_ = val; }
        inline void setValuationDate(Date date) { valuationDate_ = date; }
        inline double getFixedValue() {
            return value_;
        }
        inline void setNotional(double notional) { notional_ = notional; }
        inline void setFrequency(int frequency) { payFrequency_ =
          frequency; }
        inline void setFixedRate(double rate) { fixedLegRate_ = rate; }
        inline void setMaturityDate(Date mat) { maturityDate_ = mat; }
        std::vector<double> getPayFixed() { return payfixedLeg_; }
        inline void calcPayFixed()
        {
          std::vector<Date>::iterator iter;
          double val = 0;
          int diff = 0;
          Date dateDiff;
          int cnt = 0;

          for (iter = payDates_.begin(); iter != payDates_.end(); iter++)
          {
            if (payFrequency_ == 1)
            {
                if (cnt <= payDates_.size())
                {
                    if (cnt + payFrequency_ < payDates_.size())
                       diff = payDates_[cnt+payFrequency_] -
                          payDates_[cnt]+1;
                    else
                       diff = 0;

                    if ((cnt != 0) && (cnt % payFrequency_ == 0))
                       val = notional_*(THIRTY/THREE_SIXTY)*
                          fixedLegRate_;
                    else
                       val = 0;
                }
                else
                   val = notional_*(THIRTY/THREE_SIXTY)*fixedLegRate_;
            }
            else
            {
                if (cnt <= payDates_.size())
                {
                    if (cnt + payFrequency_ <= payDates_.size())
```

```
                                    {
                                // subtract five because there are 5 less days in a
                                // 360 day year
                                    diff = (payDates_[cnt+payFrequency_] -
                                        payDates_[cnt] + 1) - 5;
                                    }
                            else
                              diff = 0;

                            if ((cnt > 0) && ((cnt-1) % payFrequency_ == 0))
                              val = notional_*((double)diff/THREE_SIXTY)*
                                 fixedLegRate_;
                            else
                              val = 0;
                              }
                            else
                            {
                              val = 0;
                            }
                        }
                  cnt++;
                  payfixedLeg_.push_back(val);
              } // for
          }
  private:
        std::vector<double> payfixedLeg_;
        double fixedLegRate_;
        double fixedLegBasis_;
        double duration_;
        double value_;
        double accrual_;
        double notional_;
        double basis_;
    int payFrequency_;
        Date effectiveDate_;
        Date maturityDate_;
        Date valuationDate_;
};

class Swap
{
  public:
        Swap() : notional_(NOTIONAL), maturity_("12/31/2010"),
          swapType(0) {}
        Swap(double notional, Date maturity, Date effectiveDate,
          Date settlementDate, Date valuation,
        std::map<double,double> liborRate, std::map<double,double> disc,
          double fixedRate, int type)
            : notional_(notional), maturity_(maturity),
              effectiveDate_(effectiveDate), settlementDate_(settlementDate),
                valuationDate_(valuation), floatRates_(liborRate),
                fixedRate_(fixedRate), swapType(type)
        {
          getNotional();
          calcPayDates(effectiveDate_,maturity_,valuationDate_);
          fixedLeg.setNotional(notional_);
          fixedLeg.setValuationDate(valuationDate_);
```

```
      fixedLeg.setFrequency(2);
      fixedLeg.setFixedRate(fixedRate);
      fixedLeg.setMaturityDate(maturity);
      fixedLeg.calcPayFixed();
      fixedLeg.setEffectiveDate(effectiveDate_);
      floatLeg.setMaturityDate(maturity);
      floatLeg.setFrequency(4);
      floatLeg.setNotional(notional_);
      floatLeg.setFloatRate(liborRate);
      floatLeg.setValuationDate(valuationDate_);
      setDiscountRates(disc);
      floatLeg.calcPayFloat();
      netPayments();
      calcDV01();
}
virtual ~Swap() {}
inline double getNotional() {
        return notional_;
}
inline void setDiscountRates(std::map<double,double> rate) {
   discRates_ = rate;
}
inline double calcDV01() {

   double val = 0;

   if (swapType == 0)
        val = fixedLeg.calcDV01() - floatLeg.calcDV01();
   else
        val = floatLeg.calcDV01() - fixedLeg.calcDV01();

   cout << "Swap DV01 = " << val << endl << endl;

   return val;
}
inline void calcPayDates(Date tradeDate, Date endDate,
   Date valuation)
{
   effectiveDate_ = tradeDate-1;

   if (effectiveDate_ == Date::SATURDAY)
        effectiveDate_ = effectiveDate_ + 2;
   else if (effectiveDate_ == Date::SUNDAY)
        effectiveDate_ = effectiveDate_ + 1;

   Date currDate = effectiveDate_;
     int cnt = 0;

   while (currDate <= endDate)
   {
        currDate.AddMonths(3);
        while (currDate.day > effectiveDate_.day)
     currDate = currDate - 1;

        if (currDate <= valuation)
        {
           if (currDate.day_of_week == Date::SATURDAY)
```

```
                                     currDate = currDate + 2;
                          else if (currDate.day_of_week == Date::SUNDAY)
                             currDate = currDate + 1;
                          else if (currDate ==
                             currDate.ChristmasDay(currDate.year))
                             currDate = currDate + 1;

                          fixedAccruedDate_ = currDate;
                  }
                  if ((currDate <= endDate) && (currDate >= valuation))
                  {
                          if (currDate.day_of_week == Date::SATURDAY)
                             currDate = currDate + 2;
                          else if (currDate.day_of_week == Date::SUNDAY)
                             currDate = currDate + 1;
                          else if (currDate ==
                             currDate.ChristmasDay(currDate.year))
                             currDate = currDate + 1;

                          payDates_.push_back(currDate);
                          cnt++;
                  }
          }
  }
  inline void netPayments()
  {
    double val = 0.0;
    double y = 0.0;
    std::vector<double> fixed = fixedLeg.getPayFixed();
    std::vector<double> fl = floatLeg.getPayFloat();
    double x = 0;
    double sum = 0.0;
    double sumfix = 0.0;
    double sumfloat = 0.0;

    if (swapType == 0)
    {
      fixedAccrued_ =  notional_*fixedRate_*((valuationDate_ -
        fixedAccruedDate_))/THREE_SIXTY;
          floatAccrued_ = -notional_*floatRates_[0]*
            ((valuationDate_ - fixedAccruedDate_))/THREE_SIXTY_FIVE;
    }
    else
    {
          fixedAccrued_ = -notional_*fixedRate_*((valuationDate_ -
            fixedAccruedDate_))/THREE_SIXTY;
          floatAccrued_ =  notional_*floatRates_[0]*
            ((valuationDate_ - fixedAccruedDate_))/THREE_SIXTY_FIVE;
    }

    int cnt = 0;
    for (int i = 0; i < payDates_.size(); i++)
    {
          x = (double) (payDates_[i+1] - payDates_[0] +
            1)/THREE_SIXTY_FIVE;
          y = interpolate(discRates_[floor(x)],discRates_[ceil(x)],
            floor(x),ceil(x),x);
```

```
                  if (swapType == 0)
                  {
                    val = (fixed[i] - fl[i])*y;
                    sumfix = sumfix + fixed[i]*y;
                    sumfloat = sumfloat - fl[i]*y;
                  }
                  else
                  {
                    val = (fl[i] - fixed[i])*y;
                    sumfix = sumfix - fixed[i]*y;
                    sumfloat = sumfloat + fl[i]*y;
                  }
                  sum = sum + val;
              }
          fixedLeg.setFixedValue(sumfix);
          floatLeg.setFloatValue(sumfloat);

          cout << "Fixed Accrued = " << fixedAccrued_ << endl;
          cout << "Float Accrued = " << floatAccrued_ << endl;
          cout << "Accrued = " << fixedAccrued_ + floatAccrued_ << endl;
          cout << "Principal = " << sum << endl;
          cout << "Market Value = " << sum + (fixedAccrued_ + floatAccrued_)
             << endl;
      }
  private:
        int swapType;
        double notional_;
        double fixedAccrued_;
        double floatAccrued_;
        double fixedRate_;
        FloatingLeg floatLeg;
        FixedLeg fixedLeg;
        Date maturity_;
        Date fixedAccruedDate_;
        Date floatAccruedDate_;
        Date effectiveDate_;
        Date settlementDate_;
        Date valuationDate_;
        std::string index;
        std::map<double,double> discRates_;
        std::map<double,double> floatRates_;
        double value;
};

#endif _SWAP_H__
```

Consider the preceding swap with the following characteristics:

```
Notional = $3,300,000
Maturity = March 28, 2013
Effective Date = March 29, 2004
Valuation Date = October 14, 2005
Swap Rate = 3.969%
Floating Rate = 3 Mo. T-Bill
Basis Spread = 0.00
```

We read the following (Table 1.19) in the 3-Mo T-Bill data from a file (taken from Bloomberg).

Table 1.19

Maturity	3-Mo T-Bill	Discount	Maturity	3-Mo T-Bill	Discount
1 DY	0.0400000	0.999708	9 MO	0.0445188	0.967342
2 DY 0000	0.0380000	0.999708	10 MO	0.0448525	0.963507
1 WK	0.0381688	0.999258	11 MO	0.0451725	0.959660
2 WK	0.0382000	0.999258	1 YR	0.0454563	0.955712
3 WK	0.0386000	0.998517	2 YR	0.0463900	0.912185
1 MO	0.0394583	0.996614	3 YR	0.0471200	0.869450
2 MO	0.0402583	0.993225	4 YR	0.0472200	0.829536
3 MO	0.0414000	0.989193	5 YR	0.0475900	0.790131
4 MO	0.0420000	0.985853	6 YR	0.0479100	0.752230
5 MO	0.0426000	0.982445	7 YR	0.0481800	0.715816
6 MO	0.0432875	0.978239	8 YR	0.0486000	0.679864
7 MO	0.0437025	0.974794	9 YR	0.0487000	0.647234
8 MO	0.0441225	0.971079	10 YR	0.0490200	0.614542

To discount the cash flows on the scheduled payment dates, the floating (3-Mo T-Bill) and discount rates are linearly interpolated using the following globally defined function:

```cpp
static double interpolate(double rate1, double rate2, double t1, double t2, double x)
{
    double dy = rate2 - rate1;
    double dt = t2 - t1;
    double slope = dy/dt;

    return rate1 + slope*x;

}
```

We interpolate using the **floor** and **ceil** built-in math routines of the rate we want to interpolate. For instance, in the `FloatLeg` function `calcPayFloat`, we call

```cpp
floatVal = interpolate(floatLegRate_[floor(diff)],floatLegRate_[ceil(diff)],
  floor(diff),ceil(diff),diff);
```

It is important to note that this is a simple form of interpolation. In actual practice to get more accurate interpolated values, we would want to bootstrap the yield curve using liquid instruments like T-bill futures and Eurodollar futures or use a numerical technique like cubic splines.

The main function is

MAIN.cpp

```cpp
#include <strstrea.h>
#include <fstream.h>
```

```cpp
#include <stdlib.h>
#include <iostream.h>
#include <string.h>
#include <math.h>
#include <map>
#include "Swap.h"
#define SIZE_X 100

void main()
{
  cout.setf(ios::showpoint);
  cout.precision(8);

  cout << "Swap Pricing Pay Fixed  " << endl << endl;
  Date start = "3/29/2004";
  cout << "Start date = " << start << endl;
  Date maturity = "3/28/2013";
  cout << "Maturity = " << maturity << endl;
  Date valuation = "10/14/2005"; //today";
  cout << "Valuation = " << valuation << endl;
  Date effectiveDate = "today";
  double notional = 3300000;
  cout << "Notional = " << notional << endl;
  double swapRate = 0.03969;
  cout << "Swap Rate = " << swapRate << endl;

  std::vector<double> mat;
  std::map<double,double> libor;
  std::map<double,double> discRate;
  char buffer[SIZE_X];
  char dataBuffer[SIZE_X];
  char* str = NULL;
  double yr = 0.0;
  double rate = 0.0;
  int swapType = 1;  // receive fixed-pay float ; 1 = pay fixed-receive
                     // float


  const char* file = "c:\\swapData.txt";
  ifstream fin;              // input file stream
  fin.clear();
  fin.open(file);

  if (fin.good())
  {
      while (!fin.eof())
      {
          fin.getline(buffer,sizeof(buffer)/sizeof(buffer[0]));
          //cout << buffer << endl;
          istrstream str(buffer);
          // Get data
          str >> dataBuffer;
          yr = atof(dataBuffer);

          str >> dataBuffer;
          if (strcmp(dataBuffer,"MO") == 0)
              yr = (double) yr/12;
```

```
            else if (strcmp(dataBuffer,"WK") == 0)
                yr = (double) yr/52;
            else if (strcmp(dataBuffer,"DY") == 0)
                yr = (double) yr/365;
            mat.push_back(yr);

            str >> dataBuffer;
            rate = atof(dataBuffer);
            libor[yr] = rate;

            str >> dataBuffer;
            rate = atof(dataBuffer);
            discRate[yr] = rate;
        }
    }
    else
        cout << "File not good!" << "\n";

    fin.close();

    Swap s(notional,maturity,start,start+1,valuation,libor,discRate,
        swapRate,swapType);
}
```

We get the following results:

```
Fixed Accrued = 5821.2000
Float Accrued = -5867.3096
Accrued = -46.109589
Principal = -176178.34
Market Value = -176224.45
```

The risk measures are as follows:

```
fixed duration = 5.8713815
fixed DV01 = 1937.5559
float duration = 0.20821918
float DV01 = -68.712329
Swap DV01 = 1868.8436
```

1.13   BERMUDAN SWAPTION PRICING IN MATLAB

Interest rate swaps have the characteristics of futures contracts. As such, they are used to lock in future interest rate positions, usually for longer periods than can be obtained with exchange-traded futures. Financial managers, though, who want downside protection for their position with the potential for gains if conditions become favorable, can also take a position in *swaptions* or options on swaps. Swaptions give the holder the right, but not the obligation, to enter into a swap at maturity: for example, a fixed-rate payer's position (or a floating-rate payer's position), with the exercise price set by the fixed rate on the swap. Bermudan swaptions, however, give the holder the right to enter on discrete prespecified

dates throughout the life of the swaption. The following Matlab implementation[23] values a
Bermudan swaption:

bermudan_swaption.m

```
function []=bermudan_swaption()

%This program can work for arbitrary no. of factors. You have to specify no.
%of factors as well as volatility structure for each factor. The volatility
%structure can be obtained from principal component analysis of correlation
%matrix and adjusting to calibrated volatilities as done in excellent paper
%by Rebonato. See my web page for the references
%(http://www.geocities.com/anan2999). It does not take correlation
%structure as input. You can also specify CEV constant alpha for skew.
%Remember changing this constant changes effective volatility.

%randn('state',[1541045451;4027226640]) % add a good random number seed
%here if you wish.
%if you don't matlab will choose its own seed.

delta=.25; %Tenor spacing. usually .25 or .5

P=5000;   % No. of paths, do not try more than 5000 paths unless you are
          % very patient
T_e1=6.0;                  %maturity of underlying swap in years(must be an
                           %exact multiple of delta)
T_x1=5.75;                 %last exercise date of the swaption (must be an
                           %exact multiple of delta)
T_s1=3.0;                  %lockout date (must be an exact multiple of delta)


T_e=T_e1/delta+1;
T_x=T_x1/delta+1;
T_s=T_s1/delta+1;
N=T_e;

F=2;    % number of factors. If you change this line also change volatility
        % structure appropriately
alpha=1.0;%CEV constant alpha for skew.Remember changing this value changes
          %effective volatility
%It is 1.0 for lognormal model.
k=.1; % strike, fixed coupon
pr_flag=+1; %payer receiver flag; assumes value of +1 for a payer swaption
%and a value of -1 for a receiver swaption.


n_spot=2;
L=repmat(.10,[P,T_e+1]);
vol=repmat(0,[T_e,F]);
for n=1:N,
   for f=1:F,
      if(f==1)
         vol(n,f)=.15; %volatility of first factor
      end
      if(f==2)
         vol(n,f)= (.15-(.009*(n)*.25).^.5); %volatility of second factor
```

```
        end
    end
end
%You can add more volatility factors in the above line but please also
%change F accordingly
%drift=repmat(0,[P,F]);
money_market=repmat(1,[T_x,P]);
swap=repmat(0,[T_x,P]);
B=repmat(1,[P,T_e]);


money_market(2,:)=money_market(1,:).*(1+delta*L(:,1))';
increment=repmat(0,[P,1]);
drift=repmat(0,[P,F]);

for t= 2 : T_x,

    t


  normal_matrix=randn([P,F]);
  drift(:,:)=0;
   for n= t : T_e,
      increment(:,1)=0;

                  %       n
      for f=1:F,

          drift(:,f)=drift(:,f)+ delta*vol(n-n_spot+1,f).*
                      ((L(:,n).^alpha)./(1+delta.*L(:,n))); %

          increment(:,1)=increment(:,1)+vol(n-n_spot+1,f).*
                          (L(:,n).^alpha)./L(:,n)...
             .*(normal_matrix(:,f).*sqrt(delta)-.5.*vol(n-n_spot+1,f).*
               (L(:,n).^alpha)./L(:,n)...
             .*delta+drift(:,f).*delta);
      end

      L(:,n)=L(:,n).*exp(increment(:,1));
      L(L(:,n)<.00001,n)=.00001;
   end

  B(:,t)=1.0;
  for n=t+1:T_e,
     B(:,n)=B(:,n-1)./(1+delta.*L(:,n-1));
  end


  money_market(t+1,:)=money_market(t,:).*(1+delta*L(:,n_spot))';

  if((t>= T_s) & (t <=T_x))
     for n=t:(T_e-1), %//the swap leg is determined one date before
                       %//the end

                   swap(t,:)=swap(t,:)+  (B(:,n+1).*
                              (L(:,n)-k).*pr_flag*delta)' ;
```

```
         end
      end
      n_spot=n_spot+1;

end


value=repmat(0,[P,1]);
stop_rule=repmat(T_x,[P,1]);

value(swap(T_x,:)>0,1) = (swap(T_x,swap(T_x,:)>0))';
coeff=repmat(0,[T_x,6]);

for t=(T_x-1):-1:T_s,
   i=0;
   a=0;
   y=0;
   for p=1:P,
      if (swap(t,p)> 0.0)
         i=i+1;
         a(i,1)=1;
         a(i,2)=swap(t,p);
         a(i,3)=swap(t,p)*swap(t,p);
         a(i,4)=money_market(t,p);
         a(i,5)=money_market(t,p)*money_market(t,p);
         a(i,6)=money_market(t,p)*swap(t,p);

         y(i,1)= money_market(t,p)/money_market(stop_rule(p,1),p) *
                    value(p,1);

      end

   end


   temp=inv(a'*a)*(a'*y);
   coeff(t,:)=temp';

   expec_cont_value=repmat(0,[P,1]);
   exer_value=repmat(0,[P,1]);

   expec_cont_value(:,1)=(coeff(t,1)+coeff(t,2).*swap(t,:)+
                          coeff(t,3).*swap(t,:)...
      .*swap(t,:)+coeff(t,4).*money_market(t,:)+
        coeff(t,5).*money_market(t,:)...
      .*money_market(t,:)+coeff(t,6).*money_market(t,:).*swap(t,:))';

exer_value(swap(t,:)>0,1)=(swap(t,swap(t,:)>0))';


 value((exer_value(:,1)>expec_cont_value(:,1))&(swap(t,:)>0)',1)...
    =exer_value((exer_value(:,1)> expec_cont_value(:,1))&(swap(t,:)>0)',1);

 stop_rule((exer_value(:,1)>expec_cont_value(:,1))&(swap(t,:)>0)',1)=t;
```

```
end

   price=0;
   for p=1:P,
      price=price+ (value(p,1)/(money_market(stop_rule(p,1),p)))/P;

   end

   price
```

ENDNOTES

1. This is the case for a plain vanilla fixed-for-floating. A hedge on a bond portfolio with an amortization of the principal or a hedge on the total return on bond portfolio would require use of constant maturity swaps (or index amortization swaps) and total return swaps, which do not have swap futures equivalents (as of today).
2. A *Eurodollar* is a dollar deposited in a U.S. or foreign bank outside the United States. The Eurodollar interest rate is the rate of interest earned on Eurodollars deposited by one bank with another bank.
3. It can be shown that if an underlying asset of a long futures contract is strongly positively correlated with interest rates, futures prices will be higher than forward prices because futures are settled daily, and the gain can be invested at a higher-than-average rate of interest since the positive correlation will make it more likely rates will increase. Similarly, when the underlying asset is strongly negatively correlated with interest rates, the futures position will incur an immediate loss, and this loss will tend to be financed at a lower-than-average rate of interest. An investor with a long position in a forward contract rather than a futures contract is not affected in this way by rate movements.
4. Hull, J. (1997), *99*.
5. Id. 99.
6. Id. 100.
7. Id. 100.
8. Id. 100.
9. Hull, J. (1997), 97.
10. See *http://www.academ.xu.edu/johnson/*.
11. In actuality, the manager could purchase only five contracts because she can only purchase an integer multiple of contracts. Thus, she would be underhedged by 0.115 T-bill units, but if she bought six contracts, she would be overhedged by 0.985 T-bill units.
12. We can also compute the duration using a continuously compounded yield, y_i, $1 \leq i \leq n$, as

$$D = \sum_{i=1}^{n} t_i \left[\frac{c_i e^{-y_i t_i}}{B} \right]$$

where $B = \sum_{i=1}^{n} c_i e^{-y_i t_i}$.

13. The term "yield modified duration" refers to the traditional analytic formulation for modified duration using a flat discount rate.
14. To compute DV01, shift the yield curve up by one basis point, recompute the duration using yield + 1bp, and then subtract the initial duration before the one basis point shift.
15. Reproduced with permission from "Hedging a Fixed-Income Portfolio with Swap Futures," CBOT Interest Rate Swap Complex White Paper.
16. Audley, D., Chin, R, and Ramamuthy, S., "Term Structure Modeling" in *Interest Rate, Term Structure, and Valuation Modeling*, edited by Fabozzi, F., Wiley (2002)., pg. 95.
17. Id., pg. 95.
18. Typically, $n = 2$ as most bonds use semiannual compounding.
19. A cubic "spline" is a piecewise polynomial function, made up of individual polynomial sections or segments that are joined together at (user-selected) points known as *knot points*. A cubic spline is a function of order three, and a piecewise cubic polynomial that is twice differentiable at each knot point. At each knot point, the slope and curvature of the curve on either side must match. An exponential cubic function would fit an exponential curve through the discount points. Thus, cubic and exponential splines are used to fit a smooth curve to bond prices (yields) given the term discount factors.

    See James and Webber (2000), *Interest Rate Modeling*, Wiley, pp. 430-432; Waggoner, D. (1997); Pienaar, R. and Choudhry., M. article in Fabozzi (2002), "Fitting the Term Structure of Interest Rates Using the Cubic Spline Methodology," pg. 157-185; O. De la Grandville (2001), *Bond Pricing and Portfolio Analysis*, MIT Press, pp. 248-252; Vasicek, O. and Fong, H. (1982), "Term Structure Modeling Using Exponential Splines," *Journal of Finance* 37, 1982, pp. 339-361.
20. Developed by Stefano Galiani (2003).
21. See MATLAB Fixed-Income Toolkit User's Guide (2002), The MathWorks.
22. The *Date* class is an open source library written by James M. Curran (1994).
23. Written by Ahsan Amin. See *http://www.geocities.com/anan2999/*.

CHAPTER **2**

COPULA FUNCTIONS

SECTIONS

2.1 Definition and Basic Properties of Copula Functions
2.2 Classes of Copula Functions
2.3 Archimedean Copulae
2.4 Calibrating Copulae
2.5 Numerical Results for Calibrating Real-Market Data
2.6 Using Copulas in Excel
Endnotes

Copula functions are essential instrumentalities in the pricing of structured credit products given the ability of these functions to incorporate correlation dependencies of the underlying credits. They can be characterized in terms of density functions (for elliptical copulae) and generator functions (for Archimedean copulas). Copulae are instrumental in pricing credit products like credit default swaps, credit swap indices (CDXs), and collateralized debt obligations (CDOs) that require modeling dependency and correlation structures of the underlying reference entities. In §2.1, we provide the definition and basic properties of copula functions. In §2.2, we discuss classes of copula functions, including the multivariate Gaussian copula and multivariate Student's t copula. In §2.3, we review Archimedean copulae, a large and flexible class of copulae for modeling dependency structures. In §2.4, we discuss calibrating copulae. We review using the exact maximum likelihood method for the Gaussian and Student's t copula. We discuss the inference functions for margins methods (IFM), as well as the canonical maximum likelihood method for calibrating the copula parameters. We also discuss the Bouyè, Mashal, and Zeevi methods. In addition, we provide Matlab implementations for both of these calibration methods. In §2.5, we discuss and provide numerical results from calibrating copulae to real-market data. The work follows directly from Galiani (2003). In §2.6, some Excel copulae examples in Excel are given.

2.1 DEFINITION AND BASIC PROPERTIES OF COPULA FUNCTIONS

An n-dimensional copula is a function $C : [0, 1]^n \rightarrow [0, 1]$ that has the following properties:

1. $C(\mathbf{u})$ is increasing in each component $\mathbf{u}_k$ with $k \in \{1, 2, ..., n\}$.

2. For every vector $\mathbf{u} \in [0, 1]^n$, $C(\mathbf{u}) = 0$ if at least one coordinate of the vector $\mathbf{u}$ is 0, and $C(\mathbf{u}) = \mathbf{u}_k$ if all the coordinates of $\mathbf{u}$ are equal to 1 except the k-th one.

3. For every $\mathbf{a}, \mathbf{b} \in [0, 1]^n$ with $\mathbf{a} \leq \mathbf{b}$ given a hypercube $\mathbf{B} = [\mathbf{a}, \mathbf{b}] = [a_1, b_1] \times [a_2, b_2] \times \cdots \times [a_n, b_n]$ whose vertices lie in the domain of C, its volume[1] $V_C(\mathbf{B}) \geq 0$.

The definition shows that C is a multivariate distribution function with uniformly distributed marginals. The statistical interpretation of the preceding properties will become further meaningful once we adapt the definition of copula functions to a vector or random variables. But first, we will need an auxiliary theory, which constitutes one of the most relevant results in the copula methodology.

Theorem 1 (Sklar):   Let G be an n-dimensional distribution function with margins $F_1, F_2, \ldots, F_n$. Then there exists an n-dimensional copula C such that, for $x \in \Re^n$, we have

$$G(x_1, x_2, \ldots, x_n) = C(F_1(x_1), F_2(x_2), \ldots, F_n(x_n)). \tag{2.1}$$

Moreover, *if* $F_1, F_2, \ldots, F_n$ are continuous, then C is unique. Sklar's theorem expresses the basic idea of dependence modeling via copula functions, by stating that for any multivariate distribution function, the univariate marginals (the distribution functions in case of random variables) and the dependence structure can be separated, with the latter completely described by a copula function. As Scaillet (2000), Sklar's theorem has an important corollary:

Corollary 1:   Let G and C be, respectively, an n-dimensional distribution function (with continuous univariate marginals $(F_1, F_2, \ldots, F_n)$ and an n-dimensional copula function. Then for any $u \in [0, 1]^n$, we have

$$C(u_1, u_2, \ldots, u_n) = G(F_1^{-1}(u_1), F_2^{-1}(u_2), \ldots, F_n^{-1}(u_n)), \tag{2.2}$$

where $F_i^{-1}(u_i)$ denotes the inverse of the cumulative distribution function, namely, for $u_i \in [0, 1]$, $F_i^{-1}(u_i) = \inf\{x : F_i(x) \geq u_i\}$. The importance of equation (2.2) will be clear in the following sections after we present a general framework for simulation of random numbers generated by a specific copula. Let $(X_1, X_2, \ldots, X_n)'$ be an n-dimensional vector of random variables with distribution functions $(F_1, F_2, \ldots, F_n)$ and joint distribution function G. Then, by Sklar's theorem, if $(F_1, F_2, \ldots, F_n)$ are continuous functions, $(X_1, X_2, ..., X_n)'$ has a unique copula, as described by the following representation:

$$\begin{aligned} G(x_1, x_2, \ldots, x_n) &= P(X_1 \leq x_1, \ldots, X_n \leq x_n) \\ &= C(F_1(x_1), F_2(x_2), \ldots, F_n(x_n)) \end{aligned}$$

This representation of copula functions allows to further re-establish the last two properties of definition 1. In fact, property (2) follows from the fact that, by the so-called "probability-integral transform" (see Casella and Berger [2000]), if the random variables X and Y have continuous distribution function F_X and F_Y, then the random variables

$U = F_X(X)$ and $V = F_Y(Y)$ are uniformly distributed on $[0, 1]$ and, therefore, in the bivariate case,

$$C(u, 1) = P(U \leq u, V \leq 1) = P(U \leq u) = u$$

and

$$C(u, 0) = P(U \leq u, V \leq 0) = 0$$

Property (3) ensures that the copula function C respects the defining characteristic of a proper multivariate distribution function, assigning non-negative weights to all rectangular subsets in $[0, 1]^n$.

By applying Sklar's theorem and by exploiting the relation between the distribution and the density function,[2] we can easily derive the multivariate copula density $c(F_1(x_1), \ldots, F_n(x_n))$ associated with a copula $C(F_1(x_1), \ldots, F_n(x_n))$:

$$f(x_1, ..., x_n) = \frac{\partial^n [C(F_1(x_1), ..., F_n(x_n))]}{\partial F_1(x_1)...\partial F_n(x_n)} \cdot \prod_{i=1}^{n} f_i(x_i)$$

$$= c(F_1(x_1), ..., F_n(x_n)) \cdot \prod_{i=1}^{n} f_i(x_i),$$

where we define

$$c(F_1(x_1), \ldots, F_n(x_n)) = \frac{f(x_1, \ldots, x_n)}{\prod\limits_{i=1}^{n} f_i(x_i)}. \tag{2.3}$$

As we will see in §2.2, knowledge of the associated copulate density will be particularly useful in order to calibrate its parameters to real-market data.

2.2 CLASSES OF COPULA FUNCTIONS

There are different families of copula functions that can be classified. The most common are the Gaussian and t copulas belonging to the elliptical family.[3]

Multivariate Gaussian Copula

Definition 1: Let R be a symmetric, positive definite matrix with $diag(R) = \mathbf{1}$ and let $\mathbf{\Phi}_R$ be the standardized multivariate normal distribution correlation matrix R. Then the multivariate Gaussian copula is defined as

$$C(u_1, u_2, \ldots, u_n; R) = \mathbf{\Phi}_R(\Phi^{-1}(u_1), \Phi^{-1}(u_2), \ldots, \Phi^{-1}(u_n)), \tag{2.4}$$

where $\Phi^{-1}(u)$ denotes the inverse of the normal cumulative distribution function. The associated multinormal copula density is obtained by applying equation (2.3):

$$c(\Phi(x_1), \ldots, \Phi(x_n)) = \frac{f^{gaussian}(x_1, \ldots, x_n)}{\prod\limits_{i=1}^{n} f_i^{gaussian}(x_i)}$$

$$= \frac{\frac{1}{(2\pi)^{n/2}|R|^{1/2}} \exp\left(-\frac{1}{2}\boldsymbol{x}'R^{-1}\boldsymbol{x}\right)}{\prod\limits_{i=1}^{n} \frac{1}{\sqrt{2\pi}} \exp\left(-\frac{1}{2}x_i^2\right)}$$

Thus, fixing $u_i = \Phi(x_i)$, and denoting $\varsigma = (\Phi^{-1}(u_1), \ldots, \Phi^{-1}(u_n))'$ the vector of the Gaussian univariate inverse distribution functions, we have the following:

$$c(u_1, u_2, \ldots, u_n; R) = \frac{1}{|R|^{1/2}} \exp\left[-\frac{1}{2}\varsigma'(R^{-1} - I)\varsigma\right] \qquad (2.5)$$

Figure 2.1 shows the surface of the Gaussian copula density as depicted in (2.5) for the bivariate case with correlation r.

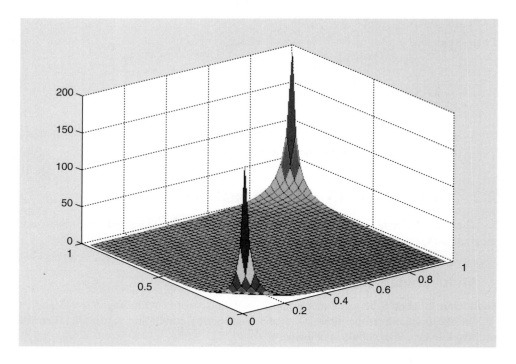

Figure 2.1 Gaussian copula density for bivariate case. *Source: Galiani, S. (2003).*

The following Matlab code computes the Gaussian copula density surface.

gaussian_copula_density.m

```
% This script plot the density of a bivariate gaussian copula function
% Pairwise correlation is set at 50%

R=ones(2,2);
r=.5;

R(1,2)=r;
R(2,1)=r;
X=zeros(2,1);
U=zeros(2,1);
gc=zeros(39,39);
h=0;

for i=0.025:.025:.975
    h=h+1;
    k=0;
    for j=0.025:.025:.975
        X=[i;j];
        k=k+1;
        U=norminv(X);
        block1=1/(det(R)^0.5);
        block2=-0.5*U'*(inv(R)-ones(2,2))*U;
        gauss_grid(h,k)=block1*exp(block2);
    end
end
surf(gauss_grid)
```

Multivariate Student's *T* Copula

Definition 2:   Let R be a symmetric, positive definite matrix with $diag(R) = \mathbf{1}$ and let $T_{R,v}$ be the standardized multivariate Student's t distribution with correlation matrix R and v degrees of freedom.[4] Then the multivariate Student's t copula function is defined as

$$C(u_1, u_2, \ldots, u_n; R, v) = T_{R,v}(t_v^{-1}(u_1), t_v^{-1}(u_2), \ldots, t_v^{-1}(u_n)) \qquad (2.6)$$

where $t_v^{-1}(u)$ denotes the inverse of the Student's t cumulative distribution function. The associated Student's t copula density is obtained by applying equation (2.3):

$$c(u_1, u_2, ..., u_n; R, v) = \frac{f^{Student}(x_1, \ldots, x_n)}{\prod\limits_{i=1}^{n} f_i^{Student}(x_i)} \qquad (2.7)$$

$$= |R|^{-1/2} \frac{\Gamma\left(\frac{v+n}{2}\right)}{\Gamma\left(\frac{v+1}{2}\right)} \left[\frac{\Gamma\left(\frac{v}{2}\right)}{\Gamma\left(\frac{v+1}{2}\right)}\right]^n \frac{\left(1 + \frac{\varsigma' R^{-1} \varsigma}{v}\right)^{-\frac{v+n}{2}}}{\prod\limits_{i=1}^{n} \left(1 + \frac{\varsigma_i^2}{v}\right)^{-\frac{v+1}{2}}}$$

where $\varsigma = (t_v^{-1}(u_1), t_v^{-1}(u_2), \ldots, t_v^{-1}(u_n))'$.

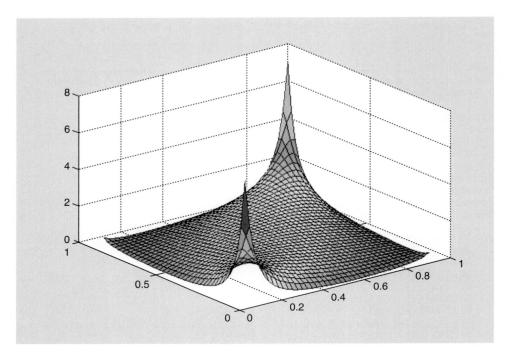

Figure 2.2 Student's t copula density for bivariate case.   *Source: Galiani, S. (2003).*

Figure 2.2 shows the surface of the Student's t copula density as given in (2.7) for a bivariate case with correlation r.

The following Matlab code computes a t copula density surface:

t_copula_density1.m

```
% This script plots che bivariate Student's t copula with 50% correlation
% and 3 degrees of freedom

R=ones(2,2);
r= .5;

R(1,2)=r;
R(2,1)=r;
X=zeros(2,1);
U=zeros(2,1);
gc2=zeros(39,39);
h=0;
DoF=3; % degrees of freedom
d=2; %dimension
Block_1=0;
Block_2=0;
for i=0.025:.025:.975
    h=h+1;
```

```
   k=0;
   for j=0.025:.025:.975
       X=[i;j];
       k=k+1;
       y=(tinv(X,DoF));
       A=gamma((DoF+d)/2)*((gamma(DoF/2))^(d-1));
       B=((gamma((DoF+1)/2))^d)*((det(R))^0.5);
       Block_1=A/B;
       A=0;
       B=0;

       Block_2=1;
       for l=1:d
           C=(1+((y(l)^2)/DoF))^(-(DoF+1)/2);
           Block_2=Block_2*C;
           C=0;
       end
       D=y'*inv(R)*y/DoF;
       Block_3=(1+D)^(-(DoF+d)/2);
       D=0;
       t_grid(h,k)=(Block_1/Block_2)*Block_3;
   end
end

surf(t_grid)
```

2.3 ARCHIMEDEAN COPULAE

Archimedean copulae constitute an important class of copula functions not only because of their analytical tractability (many of the most common Archimedean copulae have closed form expression), but also because they provided a large spectrum of different dependence structures.

Following the analysis of Nelson (1999), consider a function $\varphi : [0,1] \to [0,\infty)$ such that:

- φ is continuous.

- $\varphi'(u) < 0$ for all $u \in [0,1]$.

- $\varphi(1) = 0$.

Define the pseudo-inverse of φ as the function $\varphi^{[-1]} : [0,\infty) \to [0,1]$ such that:

$$\varphi^{[-1]}(t) = \begin{cases} \varphi^{-1}(t) & \text{for } 0 \leq t \leq \varphi(0) \\ 0 & \text{for } \varphi(0) \leq t \leq \infty \end{cases}$$

Now, if φ is convex, then the function $C : [0,1]^2 \to [0,1]$, defined as

$$C(u,v) = \varphi^{[-1]}\left[\varphi(u) + \varphi(v)\right] \tag{2.8}$$

is an Archimedean copula and φ is called the generator of the copula. Furthermore, if $\varphi(0) = \infty$, the pseudo-inverse describes an ordinary inverse function (that is, $\varphi^{[-1]} = \varphi^{-1}$) and we call φ and C, respectively, a strict generator and a strict Archimedean copula.

Gumbel Copula: Let $\varphi(t) = (-\ln t)^\theta$ with $\theta \geq 1$. Then, using equation (2.8), we have

$$C_\theta^{Gumbel}(u, v) = \varphi^{-1}[\varphi(u) + \varphi(v)] = \exp\left\{-\left[(-\ln u)^\theta + (-\ln v)^\theta\right]^{1/\theta}\right\}.$$

Clayton Copula: Let $\varphi(t) = (t^{-\theta} - 1)/\theta$ with $\theta \in [-1, \infty) \setminus \{0\}$. Then, using (2.8), we have

$$C_\theta^{Clayton}(u, v) = \max[(u^{-\theta} + v^{-\theta} - 1)^{1/\theta}, 0].$$

Note that if $\theta > 0$, then $\varphi(0) = \infty$, and we can simplify the preceding equation as

$$C_\theta^{Clayton}(u, v) = (u^{-\theta} + v^{-\theta} - 1)^{1/\theta}. \tag{2.9}$$

Frank Copula: Let $\varphi(t) = -\ln \frac{e^{-\theta t} - 1}{e^{-\theta} - 1}$ with $\theta \in \Re \setminus \{0\}$. Then, using equation (2.8), we have

$$C_\theta^{Frank}(u, v) = -\frac{1}{\theta} \ln \left[1 + \frac{(e^{-\theta u} - 1)(e^{-\theta v} - 1)}{e^{-\theta} - 1}\right]. \tag{2.10}$$

We can generalize the Archimedean copulae framework to the multivariate case. Following the analysis of Embrechts, Lindskog, and McNeil (2001), we have the following theorem:

Theorem 2(Kimberling):   Let $\varphi : [0, 1] \to [0, \infty)$ be a continuous, strictly decreasing function such that $\varphi(0) = \infty$ and $\varphi(1) = 0$, and let φ^{-1} be the inverse of φ. Then, for all $n \geq 2$, the function $C : [0, 1]^n \to [0, 1]$ defined as

$$C(u_1, u_2, \ldots, u_n) = \varphi^{-1}[\varphi(u_1) + \varphi(u_2) + \ldots + \varphi(u_n)]$$

is an n-dimensional Archimedean copula if and only if φ^{-1} is completely monotone[5] on $[0, \infty)$.

2.4   CALIBRATING COPULAE

Calibrating copula parameters to real-market data is an important step in pricing structured credit products to ensure accuracy and robustness in pricing. In the following analysis, we consider a random sample represented by the time series $\boldsymbol{X} = (X_{1t}, X_{2t}, ..., X_{Nt})_{t=1}^T$ where N stands for the number of underlying assets—e.g., loans—and T represents the number of observations (on a daily monthly, quarterly, or yearly basis) available.

Exact Maximum Likelihood Method (EML)

Let Θ be the parameter space and θ be the k-dimensional vector of parameters to be estimated. Let $L_t(\theta)$ and $l_t(\theta)$ be, respectively, the likelihood and the log-likelihood function for the observation at time t. Define the log-likelihood function $l(\theta)$ as the following:

$$l(\theta) = \sum_{t=1}^T l_t(\theta) \tag{2.11}$$

Consider the canonical expression for density function as expressed by equation (2.3). We can expand (2.11) as follows:

$$l(\theta) = \sum_{t=1}^{T} \ln c(F_1(x_1^t), ..., F_N(x_N^t)) + \sum_{t=1}^{T}\sum_{n=1}^{N} \ln f_n(x_n^t). \tag{2.12}$$

Define the maximum likelihood estimator, as the vector $\widehat{\theta}$ such that

$$\widehat{\theta} = (\widehat{\theta}_1, \widehat{\theta}_2, \dots, \widehat{\theta}_k) \in \arg\max\{l(\theta) : \theta \in \Theta\}.$$

Gaussian Copula: Let $\Theta = \{R : R \in \Re^{N x N}\}$ denote the parameter space with R being a symmetric and positive definite matrix. Applying equation (2.12) to the case of the gaussian copula density given in equation (2.5) yields

$$l^{gaussian}(\theta) = -\frac{T}{2}\ln|R| - \frac{1}{2}\sum_{t=1}^{T} \varsigma_t'(R^{-1} - I)\varsigma_t. \tag{2.13}$$

Assuming that the log-likelihood function in (2.13) is differentiable in θ and that the solution of the equation $\frac{\partial}{\partial\theta}\ell(\theta) = 0$ defines a global maximum, we can easily recover the maximum likelihood estimator $\widehat{\theta} = \widehat{R}$ for the gaussian copula whose log-likelihood is given in equation (2.13):

$$\frac{\partial}{\partial R^{-1}}\ell^{gaussian}(\theta) = \frac{T}{2}R - \frac{1}{2}\sum_{t=1}^{T}\varsigma_t'\varsigma_t$$

and therefore

$$\widehat{R} = \frac{1}{T}\sum_{t=1}^{T}\varsigma_t'\varsigma_t. \tag{2.14}$$

Student's t Copula: Let $\theta = \{(v, R) : v \in [2, \infty), R \in \Re^{N x N}\}$, with R being a symmetric and positive definite matrix, denote the parameter space. We can apply (2.14) to the case of the Student's t copula density given in (2.7). In this case, the calculation is more involved, leading to the following:

$$\ell^{Student}(\theta) = T \ln \frac{\Gamma\left(\frac{v+N}{2}\right)}{\Gamma\left(\frac{v}{2}\right)} - NT \ln \frac{\Gamma\left(\frac{v+1}{2}\right)}{\Gamma\left(\frac{v}{2}\right)} - \frac{T}{2}\ln|R| -$$
$$\frac{v+N}{2}\sum_{t=1}^{T}\ln\left(1 + \frac{\varsigma_t'R^{-1}\varsigma_t}{v}\right) + \tag{2.15}$$
$$\frac{v+1}{2}\sum_{t=1}^{T}\sum_{n=1}^{N}\ln\left(1 + \frac{\varsigma_{nt}^2}{v}\right).$$

Unlike the case of Gaussian copula, the calibration of the Student's t copula via the EML method is more complicated because it requires a simultaneous estimation (see, for example, Johnson and Kotz (1972)) of the parameters of the marginals and the parameters related to the dependence structure. But this procedure, as indicated by Mashal and Naldi (2002), requires a large amount of data and is computationally intensive. For that reason, the alternative methodologies of the inference functions for margins method (IFM) and canonical maximum likelihood method (CML) are employed.

The Inference Functions for Margins Method (IFM)

The IFM, based on the work of Joe and Xu (1996), exploiting the fundamental idea of copula theory (that is, the separation between the univariate margins and the dependence structure), expresses equation (2.12) as

$$\ell(\theta) = \sum_{t=1}^{T} \ln c(F_1(x_1^t; \theta_1), \dots, F_N(x_N^t; \theta_N); \boldsymbol{\alpha}) + \sum_{t=1}^{T} \sum_{n=1}^{N} \ln f_n(x_n^t; \theta_n). \quad (2.16)$$

The peculiarity of (2.16) relies in the separation between the vector of the parameters for the univariate marginals $\boldsymbol{\theta} = (\theta_1, \dots, \theta_N)$ and the vector of the copula parameters $\boldsymbol{\alpha}$. In other words, the calibration of the copula parameters to market data is performed via a two-stage procedure:

1. Estimation of the vector of the parameters for the marginal univariates $\boldsymbol{\theta} = (\theta_1, ..., \theta_N)$ via the EML method. For instance, considering the time series of the ith underlying asset, we have[6]

$$\widehat{\theta}_i = \arg\max_{\theta_t} \sum_{t=1}^{T} \ln f_i(x_i^t; \theta_i).$$

2. Estimation of the vector of copula parameters $\boldsymbol{\alpha}$, using the previous estimators $\widehat{\boldsymbol{\theta}} = (\widehat{\theta}_1 \dots, \widehat{\theta}_N)$:

$$\widehat{\alpha}_{IFM} = \arg\max_{\alpha} \sum_{t=1}^{T} \ln c\left(F_1(x_1^t; \widehat{\theta}_1), \dots, F_N(x_n^t; \widehat{\theta}_N); \boldsymbol{\alpha}\right).$$

The IFM estimator is then defined as the vector $\boldsymbol{\theta}^{IFM} = (\widehat{\boldsymbol{\theta}}, \widehat{\alpha}_{IFM})$.

The Canonical Maximum Likelihood Method (CML)

Both the EML and IFM methods are based on an exogenous specification, and thus imposition, of the parametric form of the univariate marginals.[7] An alternative method, which does not imply any *a priori* assumption on the distributional form of the marginals, is the CML method and relies on the concept of the *empirical marginal transformation*. The transformation tends to approximate the unknown parametric marginals $\widehat{F}_n(\cdot)$, for $n = 1, \dots, N$, with the empirical distribution functions $\widehat{F}_n(\cdot)$, defined as follows

$$\widehat{F}_n(\cdot) = \frac{1}{T} \sum_{t=1}^{T} 1_{\{X_{nt} \leq \cdot\}} \text{ for } n = 1, \dots, N, \quad (2.17)$$

where $1_{\{X_{nt} \leq \cdot\}}$ represents the indicator function. The CML is then implemented via a two-stage procedure:

1. Transformation of the initial data set $X = (X_{1t}, X_{2t}, \ldots, X_{Nt})_{t=1}^{T}$ into uniform variates, using the empiricial marginal distribution—that is, for $t = 1, \ldots, T$, let
$$\widehat{u}_t = (\widehat{u}_1^t, \widehat{u}_2^t, \ldots, \widehat{u}_N^t) = \left[\widehat{F}_1(X_{1t}), \widehat{F}_2(X_{2t}), \ldots, \widehat{F}_N(X_{Nt}) \right].$$

2. Estimation of the vector of the copula parameters $\boldsymbol{\alpha}$, via the following relation:
$$\widehat{\boldsymbol{\alpha}}_{CML} = \arg \max_{\boldsymbol{\alpha}} \sum_{t=1}^{T} \ln c\left(\widehat{u}_1^t, \widehat{u}_2^t, \ldots, \widehat{u}_N^t; \boldsymbol{\alpha} \right).$$

The CML estimator is then defined as the vector $\boldsymbol{\theta}^{CML} = \widehat{\boldsymbol{\alpha}}_{CML}$.

2.5   NUMERICAL RESULTS FOR CALIBRATING REAL-MARKET DATA

In this section, we will present an application, as shown by Galiani (2003), of the CML method for calibrating the parameter of the Student's t copula to real-market data. We consider a portfolio of four stocks (Fiat, Merrill Lynch, Ericsson, and British Airways) with 990 daily observations spanning from August 14, 1999 to July 15, 2003. There are two approaches provided: the first developed by Bouyè *et al.*, based on a recursive optimization procedure for the correlation matrix; the second, proposed by Mashal and Zeevi, based on the rank correlation estimator given by the Kendall's tau.

Bouyè, Durrelman, Nikeghbali, Riboulet, and Roncalli Method

This procedure is composed of a series of subsequent steps and is summarized and implemented as follows:

1. Starting from the random sample X of stock returns, transform the initial data set into the set of uniform variates $\widehat{U}$ using the empirical marginal transformation and using the canonical maximum likelihood method (CML) given in §2.4.3.

2. For each value of the degrees of freedom v on a specified range, assess the correlation matrix R_v^{CML} using the following routine:

   i. For each fixing date t, let $\xi_t = (t_v^{-1}(\widehat{u}_{1t}), t_v^{-1}(u_{2t}), \ldots, t_v^{-1}(\widehat{u}_{2t}))'$ for $t = 1, \ldots, T$.

   ii. Estimate the exact maximum likelihood (EML) estimator $\widehat{R}$ of the correlation matrix for the Gaussian copula, using equation (2.14). Then set $R_0 = \widehat{R}$.

   iii. Obtain $R_{v,k+1}$ via the following recursive scheme:[8]
$$R_{v,k+1} = \frac{v+N}{Tv} \sum_{t=1}^{T} \frac{\xi_t' \xi_t}{\left(1 + \frac{\xi_t' R_{v,k}^{-1} \xi_t}{v}\right)}$$

iv. Rescale matrix entries in order to have unit diagonal elements:

$$(R_{v,k+1})_{i,j} = \frac{(R_{v,k+1})_{i,j}}{\sqrt{(R_{v,k+1})_{i,i}(R_{v,k+1})_{j,j}}}$$

v. Repeat procedure iii–iv until $R_{v,k+1} = R_{v,k}$ and set $R_v^{CML} = R_{v,k}$.

3. Find the CML estimator v^{CML} of the degrees of freedom by maximizing the log-likelihood function of the Student's t copula density:

$$v^{CML} = \arg\max_{v \in \Theta} \sum_{t=1}^{T} \log c^{Student}(\widehat{u}_1^t, \widehat{u}_2^t, \ldots, \widehat{u}_N^t; R_v^{CML}, v)$$

Figure 2.3 plots the log-likelihood function of the t copula density as a function of the degrees of freedom, by which we can see that the estimated number of degrees of freedom is 10.

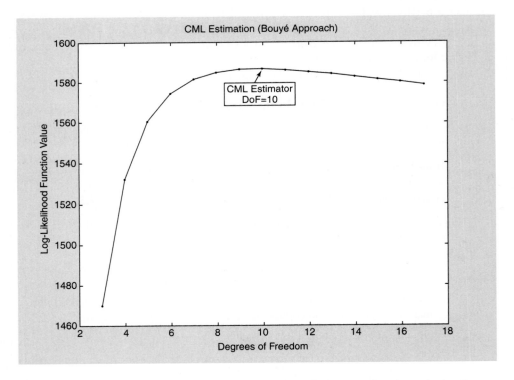

Figure 2.3 Log-likelihood function of the t copula density using Bouyè method. *Source: Galiani, S. (2003).*

IMF_t_CORR.m

```
function [U_sample,CORR]=IFM_t_CORR(R,DoF,M)

% This function, starting from a random sample M, estimate the correlation
% matrix for the Student's t copula via the Bouye(2000), p.42 algorithm.
% Moreover it returns the uniform variate sample via the
% probability-integral transformation with Student's t margins.
% R:    correlation matrix for the gaussian copula
% DoF:  degrees of freedom for the multivariate t copula density
% M:    random sample of equity returns

N=size(R,2);
T=size(M,1);
U_emp=zeros(size(M));
U_st=zeros(size(M));
t_CORR=zeros(N);
CORR=zeros(N);

for n=1:N
    U_emp(:,n)=emp_dis(M(:,n));
end

for i=1:T
    U_st(i,:)=tinv(U_emp(i,:),DoF);
end

for k=1:100
    dummy_CORR=zeros(N);

        if k==1
            for i=1:T
                term=(U_st(i,:)'*U_st(i,:))/(1+(U_st(i,:)*
                    inv(R)*U_st(i,:)'/DoF));
                dummy_CORR=dummy_CORR+term;
            end
            t_CORR=dummy_CORR*(DoF+N)/(T*DoF);
            for xx=1:N
                for yy=1:xx
                    CORR(xx,yy)=t_CORR(xx,yy)/(sqrt(t_CORR(xx,xx))*
                            sqrt(t_CORR(yy,yy)));
                    CORR(yy,xx)=CORR(xx,yy);
                end
            end
        else
            for i=1:T
                term=(U_st(i,:)'*U_st(i,:))/(1+(U_st(i,:)*inv(CORR)*
                    U_st(i,:)'/DoF));
                dummy_CORR=dummy_CORR+term;
            end
            t_CORR=dummy_CORR*(DoF+N)/(T*DoF);
            for xx=1:N
                for yy=1:xx
                    CORR(xx,yy)=t_CORR(xx,yy)/(sqrt(t_CORR(xx,xx))*
                            sqrt(t_CORR(yy,yy)));
                    CORR(yy,xx)=CORR(xx,yy);
                end
            end
        end
```

```
        end
end

U_sample=U_st;
```

emp_dis1.m

```
function X=emp_dis(Y)
% Compute the empirical marginal transformation, for the asset return
% samples, as described in Mashal(2002), "Beyond Correlation", pag.15
% As input we provide the i-th row of our d-columns sample
% i: #observation        d: #asset in the basket

X=zeros(length(Y),1);                    % create a vector of d dimension
count=0;
for k=1:length(Y)
    for s=1:length(Y)
        if Y(s)<=Y(k)
            count=count+1;
        end
    end
    X(k)=count/length(Y);                % compute the empirical
                                         % distribution function

    if X(k)==1
        X(k)=.999999;                    % otherwise, if 1, then we have
                                         % problem in using the t inverse

    end
    count=0;
end
```

t_copula_density2.m

```
function c=t_copula_density(U,DoF,Corr)

% gives the t-copula density for fixed input of "U" ( t-th row of the
% uniform sample with N elements), degrees of freedom "DoF", and
% correlation matrix "Corr"
%
N=length(U);
A=0;
B=0;
C=0;
D=0;
Block_1=0;
Block_2=1;
Block_3=0;

% Now, we split formula 4, pag. 12 of Mashal(2002) "Beyond Correlation" in
% 3 blocks

A=gamma((DoF+N)/2)*((gamma(DoF/2))^(N-1));
B=((gamma((DoF+1)/2))^N)*((det(Corr))^0.5);
Block_1=A/B;
```

```
for n=1:N
    C=(1+((U(n)^2)/DoF))^(-(DoF+1)/2);
    Block_2=Block_2*C;
end

D=U'*inv(Corr)*U/DoF;
Block_3=(1+D)^(-(DoF+N)/2);

c=(Block_1/Block_2)*Block_3;
```

pseudo_sample_IFM.m

```
% Starting from a random sample M, this script, generates a matrix (T*N) of
% uniform variates through the probability-integral transformation with
% gaussian margins.

% T:    # of observation in the time series for each asset
% N:    # of assets

M = xlsread('C:\copula\DataSet_new.xls'); % equity return database
N=size(M,2);
T=size(M,1);
ML_CORR=zeros(N);
Average=zeros(N,1);
Deviation=zeros(N,1);
U_nor1=zeros(size(M));
U_nor2=zeros(size(M));

for i=1:N
    Average(i)=mean(M(:,i));
    Deviation(i)=std(M(:,i),1);
    U_nor1(:,i)=normcdf((M(:,i)-Average(i))/Deviation(i));

end

for i=1:T
    U_nor2(i,:)=norminv(U_nor1(i,:));
    ML_CORR=ML_CORR+U_nor2(i,:)'*U_nor2(i,:);
end

ML_CORR=ML_CORR/T;
```

t_copula_CML

```
function MLE=t_copula_CML(DoF)
% calculate the target function to be maximized as described in Step 3
% pag. 43 of Mashal's (2002) paper
pseudo_sample
T=size(U,1);                      % number of observation for each stock
Log_L=zeros(T,1);
Sum_Log_L=0;
% For each observation compute the t-copula density and sum over
for t=1:T
    Log_L(t)=log(t_copula_density(U(t,:),DoF,CORR_EST));
```

```
    Sum_Log_L=Sum_Log_L+Log_L(t);
end

MLE=Sum_Log_L;
```

Mashal and Zeevi Method

The Bouyè procedure can be computationally heavy when dealing with several under-lying assets and large data sets, and, as pointed out by Mashal and Zeevi (2002), affected by numerical instability due to the inversion of close to singular matrices. Consequently, Mashal and Zeevi propose to estimate the correlation matrix for the Student's t copula via a rank correlation estimator, namely the Kendall's tau, exploiting the result included in the following theorem:

Theorem 3:   Let $X \sim E_N(\mu, \Sigma, \varphi)$, where for $i, j \in \{1, 2, \ldots, N\}$, X_i and X_J are continuous. Then,

$$\tau(X_i, X_j) = \frac{2}{\pi} \arcsin R_{i,j} \tag{2.18}$$

where $E_N(\mu, \Sigma, \varphi)$, denotes the N-dimensional elliptical distribution with parameters (μ, Σ, φ), and $\tau(X_i, X_j)$ and $R_{i,j}$ indicate, respectively, the Kendall's tau[9] and the Pearson's linear correlation coefficient for the random variables (X_i, X_j).

Proof: See Lindkog, McNeil, and Schmock (2001).

1. Starting from the random sample X of stock prices, transform the initial data set into the set of uniform variate $\widehat{U}$ using the empirical marginal transformations described in §2.4.3.

2. From equation (2.18), estimate the correlation matrix R^{CML}.

3. Find the CML estimator v^{CML} of the degrees of freedom by maximizing the log-likelihood function of the Student's t copula density:

$$v^{CML} = \arg\max_{v \in \Theta} \sum_{t=1}^{T} \log c^{Student}(\widehat{u}_1^t, \widehat{u}_2^t, \ldots, \widehat{u}_N^t; R^{CML}, v)$$

Figure 2.4 plots the log-likelihood function of the t copula density as a function of the degrees of freedom, by which we can see that the estimated number of degrees of freedom is 9.

The corresponding calibrated correlation matrix R_9^{CML} is shown in Table 2.1.

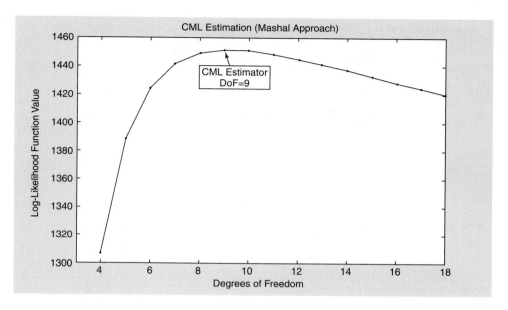

Figure 2.4   Log-likelihood function of the t copula density using Mashal and Zeevi method. *Source: Galiani, S. (2003).*

Table 2.1   Correlation Matrix

1	0.34771	0.81475	0.77631
0.34771	1	0.62666	0.65706
0.81475	0.62666	1	0.77288
0.77631	0.65706	0.77288	1

The following is the Matlab implementation of the Mashal and Zeevi method:

t_copula_density3.m

```
function c=t_copula_density(U,DoF,Corr)

% gives the t-copula density for fixed input of "U" ( i-th row of the
% pseudo sample with d elements), degrees of freedom "DoF", and
% correlation matrix "Corr"
%
d=length(U);
y=zeros(d,1);          % create the vector of univariate t r.v.s.
z=zeros(d,1);
z=DoF;
y=(tinv(U,z))';        % vector the inverse of the t cdf

% Now, we split formula 4, pag. 12 of Mashal(2002) "Beyond Correlation"
% in 3 blocks

A=gamma((DoF+d)/2)*((gamma(DoF/2))^(d-1));
```

```
B=((gamma((DoF+1)/2))^d)*((det(Corr))^0.5);
Block_1=A/B;
A=0;
B=0;

Block_2=1;
for k=1:d
    C=(1+((y(k)^2)/DoF))^(-(DoF+1)/2);
    Block_2=Block_2*C;
    C=0;
end

D=y'*inv(Corr)*y/DoF;
Block_3=(1+D)^(-(DoF+d)/2);
D=0;

c=(Block_1/Block_2)*Block_3;
```

emp_dis2.m

```
function X=emp_dis(Y)
% Compute the empirical marginal transformation, for the asset return
% samples, as described in Mashal(2002), "Beyond Correlation", pag.15
% As input we provide the i-th row of our d-columns sample
% i: #observation        d: #asset in the basket

X=zeros(length(Y),1);                     % create a vector of d dimension
count=0;
for k=1:length(Y)
    for s=1:length(Y)
        if Y(s)<=Y(k)
            count=count+1;
        end
    end
    X(k)=count/length(Y);                 % compute the empirical
                                          % distribution function

    if X(k)==1
        X(k)=.999999;                     % otherwise, if 1, then we have
                                          % problem in using the t inverse

    end
    count=0;
end
```

kendall.m

```
function TAU=KENDALL(A,B);

% This function computes the Kendall's tau for a bivariate vector of
% observations

A=A(:);
B=B(:);
N=length(A);
N1=0;N2=0;S=0;
```

```
for J=1:N
    A1=A(J+1:N)-A(J);
    A2=B(J+1:N)-B(J);
    AA=A1.*A2;
    i=find(AA>=0);
    lni=length(i);
    k=find(~AA(i));                    % find the zero products.
    dis=length(AA)-lni;               % discordant pairs.
    con=lni-length(k);                % concordant pairs
    l=length(find(~(~A1(i(k)))));     % add up the extra zeros
    m=length(find(~(~A2(i(k)))));
    N1=N1+con+dis+l;
    N2=N2+con+dis+m;
    S=S+con-dis;
end
TAU=S/sqrt(N1*N2);
```

pseudo_sample.m

```
% Starting from a random sample M, this script creates a pseudo sample and
% compute the estimated correlation matrix using Kendall's Tau as described
% in Mashal(2001), "Beyond Correlation", p.41.

% T:    # of observation in the time series for each asset
% N:    # of assets

M = xlsread('C:\copula\DataSet_new.xls'); % equity price database
N=size(M,2);
T=size(M,1);
U=zeros(size(M));
corr_matrix=zeros(N);

% for each underlying asset we calculate the empirical distribution
for n=1:N
    U(:,n)=emp_dis(M(:,n));
end

% create the correlation matrix (via Kendall's tau), using the procedure
% described in page 42-42 of Mashal(2001) "Beyond Correlation"

for i=1:N
    for j=i:N
        if i==j
            corr_matrix(i,j)=1;
        else
        corr_matrix(i,j)=sin(pi*0.5*KENDALL(U(:,i),U(:,j)));
            corr_matrix(j,i)=corr_matrix(i,j);
        end
    end
end


CORR_EST=corr_matrix;
CORR_LIN=corrcoef(U);
```

The corresponding calibrated correlation matrix R^{CML} is shown in Table 2.2.

Table 2.2 Calibrated Correlation Matrix

1	0.44818	0.90208	0.83975
0.44818	1	0.67615	0.68552
0.90208	0.67615	1	0.84178
0.83975	0.68552	0.84178	1

2.6   USING COPULAS IN EXCEL

Figure 2.5 shows random Monte Carlo simulations to value a portfolio using bivariate Frank copula. Figure 2.6 shows a simulation for the Clayton copula.

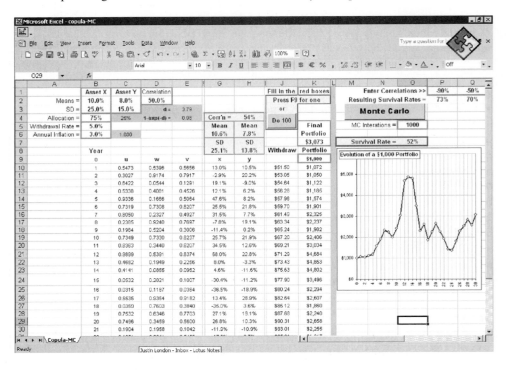

Figure 2.5 Random Monte Carlo simulations.

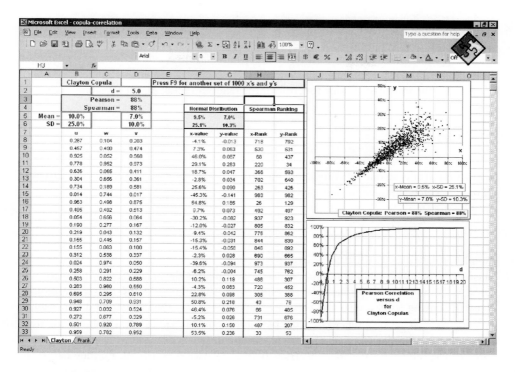

Figure 2.6 Clayton copula simulation.

ENDNOTES

1. The volume $V_C(\mathbf{B})$ of a n-box $\mathbf{B} = [\mathbf{a}, \mathbf{b}]$ is defined as follows:

$$V_C(\mathbf{B}) = \sum_d \operatorname{sgn}(\mathbf{d})C(\mathbf{d})$$

$$= \sum_{i_1=1}^{2} \sum_{i_2=1}^{2} \cdots \sum_{i_n=1}^{2} (-1)^{i_1+i_2+\ldots+i_n} C(d_{1i_1}, d_{2i_2}, \ldots, d_{ni_n}) \geq 0$$

where $d_{j1} = a_j$ and $d_{j2} = b_j$ for all $j \in \{1, 2, \ldots, n\}$.

2. In the univariate case, the density function $f(x)$ of a random variable X can be obtained by the cumulative distribution function via the following relation:

$$f(x) = \frac{\partial F(x)}{\partial x}.$$

3. Based on the definition of Fang, Kotz, and Ng (1987), if $\mathbf{X}$ is an n-dimensional vector of random variables and for some $\boldsymbol{\mu} \in \Re^n$, and some $n x n$ nonnegative definite, symmetric matrix $\boldsymbol{\Sigma}$, the characteristic function $\varphi_{X-\mu}(\mathbf{t})$ of $\mathbf{X} - \boldsymbol{\mu}$ is a function of the quadratic form $t'\Sigma t$, then $\mathbf{X}$ has an elliptical distribution with parameters $(\boldsymbol{\mu}, \boldsymbol{\Sigma}, \varphi)$ and we write $\mathbf{X} \sim \mathbf{E}^n(\boldsymbol{\mu}, \boldsymbol{\Sigma}, \varphi)$.

4. Following Johnson and Kotz (1972), p. 134, given a random vector $\mathbf{X} = (X_1, \ldots, X_n)'$ with a joint standardized multinormal distribution with correlation matrix R and a χ_v^2-distributed random variable S, independent from $\mathbf{X}$, we define the standardized multivariate Student's t joint density function with correlation matrix R and v degrees of freedom, as the joint distribution function of the random vector $\mathbf{Y} = (\frac{X_1}{S/\sqrt{v}}, \ldots, \frac{X_n}{S/\sqrt{v}})'$:

$$f(\mathbf{y}) = \frac{\Gamma\left(\frac{v+n}{2}\right)}{\Gamma\left(\frac{v}{2}\right)} \frac{1}{(\pi v)^{n/2} |R|^{1/2}} \left(1 + \frac{\mathbf{y}'R^{-1}\mathbf{y}}{v}\right)^{-\frac{(v+n)}{2}}$$

5. A function $f(t)$ is said to be completely monotone on the interval D if it has derivatives of all orders which alternate in sign, that is

$$(-1)^k \frac{d^k}{dt^k} f(t) \geq 0$$

for all t in the interior of D and $k = 0, 1, 2, 3 \ldots$.

6. Mashal and Naldi (2002) suggest procedures for estimating the parameters of the marginals based on a numerical optimization routine for the likelihood of the univariate returns. Namely, starting from a univariate return sample, $\{X_t\}_{t=1}^T$, they construct a new sample $\{\widehat{X}_t\}_{t=1}^T = \{\frac{X_t - m}{H}\}_{t=1}^T$ where m is the location parameter and H is the scale factor, to be distributed as a Student's t random variable with v degrees of freedom. Therefore, given a parameter space $\Theta = \{\theta : m \in \Re, H > 0, v > 2\}$ with $\theta = (m, H, v)$, they define the maximum likelihood estimator $\widehat{\theta} = \left(\widehat{m}, \widehat{H}, \widehat{v}\right)$ as $\widehat{\theta} = \arg\max_{\theta \in \Theta} \prod_{t=1}^T f_v^{student}\left(\widehat{X}_t\right)$.

7. Note that for equation (2.15), we have fixed $\varsigma = (t_v^{-1}(u_1), t_v^{-1}(u_2), \ldots, t_v^{-1}(u_N))'$. Similarly, with regard to equation (2.13), we have $\varsigma = (\Phi^{-1}(u_1), \ldots, \Phi^{-1}(u_N))'$.

8. This equation is derived by the maximum output of the log-likelihood function for the t copula density given in equation (2.15):

$$\frac{\partial \ell^{Student}(\theta)}{\partial R^{-1}} = \frac{T}{2} R - \frac{v + N}{2} \sum_{t=1}^T \frac{\frac{\xi_t' \xi_t}{v}}{\left(1 + \frac{\xi_t' R^{-1} \xi_t}{v}\right)}$$

from where we note that the ML estimator of R must satisfy the following equation:

$$R_{ML} = \frac{v + N}{Tv} \sum_{t=1}^T \frac{\xi_t' \xi_t}{\left(1 + \frac{\xi_t' R_{ML}^{-1} \xi_t}{v}\right)}$$

9. Using the definition given by Embrechts, Lindskog, and McNeil (2001), let (x, y) and $(\widetilde{x}, \widetilde{y})$ be two observations from a vector (X, Y) of continuous random variables. Then (x, y) and $(\widetilde{x}, \widetilde{y})$ are said to be concordant if

$$(x - \bar{x}) - (y - \bar{y}) > 0$$

and discordant otherwise. The Kendall's tau is then defined as the probability of concordance minus the probability of discordance; namely, given two pairs (X, Y) and $\left(\widetilde{X}, \widetilde{Y}\right)$ of independent random variables with the same distribution $F(.,.)$, we have:

$$\tau = P\left[(X - \bar{X})(Y - \bar{Y}) > 0\right] - P\left[(X - \bar{X})(Y - \bar{Y}) < 0\right]$$

As suggested by Meneguzzo and Vecchiato (2002), given two series X_t and Y_t with $t = 1, \ldots, T$, the consistent estimator of the Kendall's tau is then computed as

$$\tau = \frac{2}{T(T-1)} \sum_{i<j} \operatorname{sgn}\left[(X_i - X_j)(Y_i - Y_j)\right],$$

where

$$\operatorname{sgn}(x) = \left\{ \begin{array}{rl} 1 & \text{if } x \geq 0 \\ -1 & \text{if } x < 0 \end{array} \right.$$

C H A P T E R **3**

MORTGAGE-BACKED SECURITIES

SECTIONS

Mortgage-backed securities (MBSs) and mortgage pass-throughs (PT) are claims on a portfolio of mortgages. MBSs are created when a federal agency, mortgage banker, bank, or investment company buys up mortgages of a certain type—i.e., FHA (Federal Home Administration) or VA (Veterans' Administration) insured—and then sells claims on the cash flows from the portfolio as MBSs, with the proceeds of the MBS sale being used to finance the purchase of the mortgages. There are two types of MBS: agency and conventional (private-label).[1]

Agency MBSs, such as a GNMA pass-through, are securities with claims on a portfolio of mortgages insured against default risk by FHM, VA, or FmHA (Farmers Mortgage Home Administration). A mortgage banker, bank, or investment company presents a pool of FHA, VA, or FmHA mortgages of a certain type (30-year fixed, 15-year variable rate, etc.) to GNMA (Ginnie Mae). If the mortgage pool is in order, GNMA will issue a separate guarantee that allows the MBSs on the mortgage pool to be issued as a GNMA PT. Other agency MBSs include the Federal Home Loan Mortgage Corporation (FHLMC) MBSs, which are claims on a portfolio of conventional mortgages. The FHLMC issues agency MBSs, whereby the FHLMC buys mortgages from the mortgage originator, and then creates an MBS referred to as a *participation certificate*, which it issues through a network of dealers. FHLMC has a swap program whereby FHLMC swaps MBSs for a savings and loan's or commercial bank's portfolio of mortgages of a certain type. Other government agencies such as FNMA (Fannie Mae) issue several types of MBS: participation certificates, swaps, and PTs. With these certificates, homeowners' mortgage payments pass from the originating bank through the issuing agency to the holds of the certificates.

Conventional types, also known as private-label types, are issued by commercial banks (via their holding companies), S&Ls, mortgage bankers, and investment companies. Conventional issued MBSs include those issued by Prudential Home, Chase Mortgage, Citi-Corp Housing, Ryland/Saxon, GE Capital, and Countrywide. Conventional PTs must be registered with the SEC. These PTs are often insured with external insurance in the form of a letter of credit (LOC) of the private-label issuer, as well as internal insurance through the creation of senior and junior classes of the PT structured by the private-label issuer.

There is both a primary and a secondary market for MBS. In the primary market, investors buy MBSs issued by agencies or private-label investment companies either directly or through dealers. Many of the investors are institutional investors. Thus, the creation of MBS has provided a tool for having real estate financed more by institutions. In the primary market, MBS issue denominations are typically between $25,000 to $250,000 (with some as high as $1M) and some have callable features. In the secondary market, MBSs are traded over-the-counter (OTC). OTC dealers are members of the Mortgage-Backed Securities Dealer Association (MSDA).

MBSs are some of the most complex securities to model and value due to their sensitivity to prepayment and interest rates, which affects the timing, frequency, and size of cash flows to investors. Cash flows (CFs) from MBSs are the monthly CFs from the portfolio of mortgages (referred to as the *collateral*). Cash flows include interest on principal, scheduled principal, and prepaid principal. Cash flow analysis is essential in the valuation of any MBS given their impact by the underlying features of the MBS, including *weighted average maturity* (WAM), *weighted average coupon rate* (WAC), *pass-through rate* (PT rate), and *prepayment rate* or *speed*. The WAM is effectively the duration, or weighted length of time, of all the payment of MBS cash flows to be paid out to investors. The WAC is the rate on a portfolio of mortgages (collateral) that is applied to determine scheduled principal. The PT rate is the interest on principal and is lower than the WAC, with the difference going to the MBS issuer. The prepayment rate or speed is the assumed prepayment rate made by homeowners of mortgages in the pool.

In this chapter, we discuss MBS pricing and modeling in detail. In §3.1, we discuss prepayment and PSA models for MBS pricing. In §3.2, we give numerical examples using Excel of how the prepayment models work. In §3.3, we discuss MBS pricing, quoting, and the value and return to investors based on different prepayment and interest rate assumptions. In §3.4, we discuss prepayment risk and the average life of MBS. In §3.5, we review in detail a numerical implementation in C++ and Excel for valuation and cash flow analysis of MBS using Monte Carlo simulation. In §3.6, we give numerical examples using the Fixed-Income Toolbox in Matlab. In §3.7, we discuss MBS derivatives, including collateralized mortgage obligations (CMOs) and sequential-pay tranche structures. We give examples using Excel. In §3.8, we give an implementation of a CMO in C++. In §3.9, we discuss planned amortization classes (PAC) and their structures. In §3.10, we review stripped MBSs, including interest-only (IO) and principal-only (PO) securities. In §3.11, we discuss interest rate risk of MBSs. Finally, in §3.12, we discuss hedging MBSs and using MBSs for balance sheet asset-liability management.

3.1 PREPAYMENT MODELS

MBS valuation models typically assume a prepayment rate or speed. Investors and issuers apply different prepayment models in analyzing MBS. Most models, though, are compared to a benchmark model or rate. The benchmark model is the one provided by the Public Securities Association (PSA). PSA measures speed by the Conditional Prepayment Rate (CPR). CPR is the proportion of the remaining mortgage balance that is prepaid each month and is quoted on an annual basis. The monthly rate is referred to as the Single-Monthly Mortality rate (SMM) and is given by:

$$SMM = 1 - (1 - CPR)^{1/12} \tag{3.1}$$

The estimated monthly prepayment is:

$$\textit{Monthly prepayment} = SMM \ \cdot$$
$$[\textit{Beginning of month balance} - \textit{Sched. prin. for month}]$$

For example, if CPR $= 6\%$, beginning-of-the-month balance $=$ \$100M, and scheduled principal for month $=$ \$3M, then the estimated prepaid principal for the month would be \$0.499M:

$$SMM = 1 - [1 - .06]^{1/12} = .005143$$
$$\textit{Monthly prepaid principal} = .005143[\$100M - \$3M] = \$0.499M$$

In the PSA model, CPR depends on the maturity of the mortgages. PSA's standard model assumes that for a 30-year mortgage (360 months), the CPR is equal to .2% the first month, grows at that rate for 30 months to equal 6%, and stays at 6% for the rest of the mortgage's life. This model is referred to as the 100% PSA model. Figure 3.1 shows the prepayment rate as a function of time in months.

The estimation of CPR for month t is:

$$CPR = \begin{cases} 0.06 \left(\frac{t}{30}\right), & \text{if } t \le 30 \\ 0.06, & \text{if } t > 30 \end{cases} \tag{3.2}$$

As an example, the CPR for month five is:

$$CPR = .06 \left(\frac{5}{30}\right) = .01$$
$$SMM = 1 - [1 - .01]^{1/12} = .000837$$

PSA's model can be defined in terms of different speeds by expressing the standard model (100% PSA) in terms of a higher or lower percentage, such as 150% or 50%. In a period of lower rates, the PSA model could be 150%, and in a period of higher rates, it

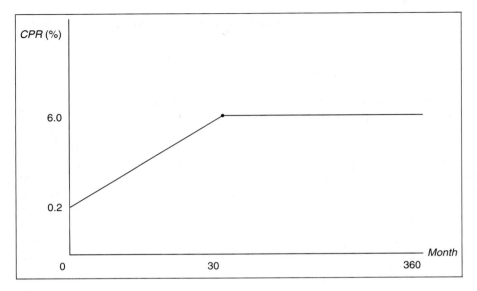

Figure 3.1 100% PSA Model.

could be 50%. For the 100% PSA model, the average time a 30-year mortgage is held is 17 years; for a 225% PSA model, it is 8 years. Figure 3.2 shows the different prepayment rates as a function of time in months.

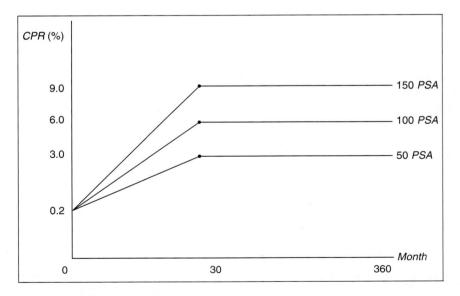

Figure 3.2 PSA Models.

Suppose we want to compute the CPR and SMM for month five with 165 PSA speed. Then we compute the following based on (3.1) and (3.2):

$$CPR = .06 \left(\frac{5}{30} \right) = .01$$

$$165CPR = 1.65(.01) = .0165$$

$$SMM = 1 - [1 - .0165]^{1/12} = .0001386$$

3.2   NUMERICAL EXAMPLE OF PREPAYMENT MODEL

Let p = monthly scheduled mortgage payment, F_0 = the face value of the underlying mortgage pool of the MBS, $M = WAM$ = weighted average of the number of months remaining until maturity, I = interest rate payment, SP = scheduled principal payment, PP = prepaid principal, R_A = annual interest rate (WAC), $B_i, i = 1, \ldots, 360$, the remaining mortgage balance in month i, and $CF_i, i = 1, \ldots, 360$, the cash flow in the ith month. Note that the balance in month 1 is the initial face value of the MBS pool, $B_1 = F_0$. The following formula gives p:

$$p = \frac{F_0}{\left(\frac{1-1/(1+(R_A/12))^M}{R_A/12} \right)} \tag{3.3}$$

Consider a mortgage portfolio with an underlying face value of $100M, a WAC = 9%, a WAM = 360 months, and a prepayment speed = 100% PSA. We need to compute the various cash flows for the first month. The first monthly principal payment is as follows:

$$p = \frac{\$100M}{\left(\frac{1-1/(1+(.09/12))^{360}}{.09/12} \right)} = \$804,600$$

The interest payment is:

$$I = \left(\frac{.09}{12} \right) \$100M = \$750,000$$

The scheduled principal payment is:

$$SP = \$804,600 - \$750,000 = \$54,600$$

The estimated prepaid principal in the first month is:

$$CPR = \left(\frac{1}{30} \right) .06 = .002$$

$$SMM = 1 - [1 - .002]^{1/12} = .0001668$$

$$PP = .0001668[\$100M - \$54,620] = \$16,667$$

The first-year cash flow is computed as:

$$CF_1 = p + PP + I$$
$$= \$804,600 + \$750,000 + \$16,667 = \$821,295$$

The beginning balance for the second month is:

$$B_2 = B_1 - SP - PP$$
$$= \$100M - \$54,600 - \$16,667M = \$99.929M$$

The second-month cash flows are computed as follows. The second monthly payment is:

$$p = \frac{\$99.9287M}{\left[\frac{1-1/(1+(.09/12))^{359}}{.09/12}\right]} = \$804,488$$

The interest payment is:

$$I = \left(\frac{.09}{12}\right)\$99.9287M = \$749,465$$

and the scheduled principal payment is:

$$SP = \$804,488 - \$749,465 = \$55,023$$

The estimated prepaid principal is:

$$CPR = \left(\frac{2}{30}\right).06 = .004$$
$$SMM = 1 - [1 - .004]^{1/12} = .0003339$$
$$PP = .0003330[\$99.9287M - \$55,023] = \$33,352$$

Thus, the second-month cash flows are computed as:

$$CF_2 = \$749,400 + \$55,023 + \$33,352 = \$837,840$$

The remaining month cash flows are computed similarly.

Consider now a mortgage portfolio with a face value of \$100M, a WAC = 8.125%, a WAM = 357 months, a PT rate = 7.5%, and a prepayment = 165% PSA. Note that because the WAM is not 360 months, but rather 357 months, the pool age is "seasoned" so that the first month of payments actually starts in month four, and not month one. Moreover, interest payments are calculated using the PT rate. However, scheduled principal and mortgage payments are computed using the WAC rate.

In this example, the schedule monthly mortgage payment is:

$$p = \frac{\$100M}{\left[\frac{1-1/(1+(.08125/12))^{357}}{.08125/12}\right]} = \$743,970$$

The interest payment (which uses the PT rate) is

$$I = \left(\frac{.075}{12}\right) \$100M = \$625,000$$

and the scheduled principal payment (which uses the WAC rate) is

$$SP = \$743,970 - (.08125/12)(\$100M) = \$66,880.$$

The estimated prepaid principal using the 165% PSA model is:

$$CPR = 1.65 \left(\frac{4}{30}\right) .06 = .0132$$

$$SMM = 1 - [1 - .0132]^{1/12} = .0011067$$

$$PP = .0011067[\$100M - \$66,880] = \$110,600$$

The first-month cash flow (starting in month four) is:

$$CF_1 = \$625,000 + \$66,880 + \$110,600 = \$802,480$$

The beginning mortgage balance for month two is:

$$\$100M - \$66,880 - \$110,600 = \$99.822M$$

The scheduled monthly mortgage payment in the second month is:

$$p = \frac{\$99.822M}{\left[\frac{1-1/(1+(.08125/12))^{356}}{.08125/12}\right]} = \$743,140$$

The second-month interest payment is:

$$I = \left(\frac{.075}{12}\right) \$99.822M = \$623,890$$

The scheduled principal payment in month two is:

$$SP = \$743,140 - (.08125/12)(\$99.822M) = \$67,260$$

The estimated prepaid principal is:

$$CPR = 1.65 \left(\frac{5}{30}\right) .06 = .0165$$

$$SMM = 1 - [1 - .0165]^{1/12} = .00139$$

$$PP = .00189[\$99.822M - \$67,260] = \$138,210$$

Thus, the second-month cash flow is computed as:

$$CF_2 = \$623,890 + \$67,260 + \$138,210 = \$829,360$$

Table 3.1 shows the cash flows for the first few months.

The Excel spreadsheet MBS1.xls shows the complete computations for every month. Parameters can be changed (for different assumptions) to generate different cash flows.

Table 3.1

Month	Balance	Sch. Payment	Interest	Sch.Pr.	CPR	SMM	Prepayment	CF	Ending Bal.
1	100,000,000.00	743,967.06	625,000.00	66,883.73	0.0132	0.0011067	110,597.15	802,480.87	99,822,519.13
2	99,822,519.13	742,153.62	623,890.74	66,271.98	0.0165	0.0013855	138,213.22	828,375.94	99,618,033.93
3	99,618,033.93	740,145.25	622,612.71	65,648.15	0.0198	0.0016652	165,771.24	854,032.10	99,386,614.54
4	99,386,614.54	737,942.81	621,166.34	65,012.61	0.0231	0.0019457	193,248.74	879,427.69	99,128,353.20
5	99,128,353.20	735,547.31	619,552.21	64,365.76	0.0264	0.0022271	220,623.21	904,541.17	98,843,364.23
6	98,843,364.23	732,959.93	617,771.03	63,707.98	0.0297	0.0025093	247,872.18	929,351.19	98,531,784.07
7	98,531,784.07	730,181.99	615,823.65	63,039.70	0.0330	0.0027925	274,973.22	953,836.56	98,193,771.16
8	98,193,771.16	727,214.96	613,711.07	62,361.30	0.0363	0.0030765	301,903.97	977,976.35	97,829,505.88

Source: Johnson, S. (2004)

3.3   MBS PRICING AND QUOTING

The prices of an MBS are quoted as a percentage of the underlying mortgage balance. The mortgage balance at time t, F_t, is quoted as a proportion of the original balance. This is called the pool factor pf_t:

$$pf_t = \frac{F_t}{F_0} \tag{3.4}$$

Suppose, for example, an MBS backed by a collateral mortgage pool originally worth $100M, a current pf of .92, and quoted at $95 - 16$ (note: 16 is 16/32) would have a market value of $87.86M, as calculated:

$$F_t = (pf_t)F_0$$
$$= (.92)(\$100M) = \$92M$$

so that

$$\text{Market Value} = (.9550)(\$92M) = \$87.86M$$

The market value is the clean price; it does not take into account accrued interest, denoted AI. For an MBS, accrued interest is based on the time period from the settlement date (two days after the trade) to the first day of the next month. For example, if the time period is 20 days, the month is 30 days, and the WAC = 9%, then AI is $.46M:

$$AI = \left(\frac{20}{30}\right)\left(\frac{.09}{12}\right)\$92M = \$460,000$$

The full market value would be $88.32M:

$$\text{FullMktValue} = \$87.86M + \$460,000 = \$88.32M$$

The market price per share is the full market value divided by the number of shares. If the number of shares is 400, then the price of the MBS based on a $95 - 16$ quote would be $220,080:

$$\text{MBS price} = \frac{\$88.32M}{400} = \$220,800$$

The value of an MBS is equal to the present value (PV) of security's cash flows (CFs); thus, the value is a function of the MBS's expected CFs and the interest rate. In addition, for MBSs, the CFs are also dependent on rates R: A change in rates will change the prepayment of principal and either increase or decrease early CFs:

$$V_{MBS} = f(CFs, R)$$

where

$$CF = f(R).$$

Since cash flows, CFs, are a function of rates, the value of MBS is more sensitive to interest rate changes than a similar corporate bond. This sensitivity is known as *extension risk*. Note the following relationships:

$$\textit{if } R \downarrow \Rightarrow \text{ lower discount rate} \Rightarrow V_M \uparrow \text{ (just like any other bond)}$$

and

$$\textit{if } R \downarrow \Rightarrow \text{ Increases prepayment} :\Rightarrow V_M \uparrow$$
$$\Rightarrow \text{ Earlier CFs} \uparrow$$

On the other hand,

$$\textit{if } R \uparrow \Rightarrow \text{ higher discount rate} \Rightarrow V_M \downarrow$$

and

$$\textit{if } R \uparrow \Rightarrow \text{ Decreases prepayment} :\Rightarrow V_M \downarrow$$
$$\Rightarrow \text{ Earlier CFs} \downarrow$$

so that an increase in rates will reduce the market value of the MBS, leading to extension risk.

There are various exogenous and endogenous factors that influence prepayment other than refinancing rates. One is housing turnover—the long-term rate at which borrowers in a pool prepay their mortgages because they sell their homes. Another is the seasoning period, the number of months over which base voluntary prepayments (housing turnover, cash-out refinancing, and credit upgrades, but not rate refinancing or defaults) are assumed to increase to long-term levels. Other factors include credit curing—the long-term rate at which borrowers prepay their mortgages because improved credit and/or increased home pool prices enable them to get better rates and/or larger loans. As the pool burns out, the rate of curing declines.[2] Default, expressed as a percentage of the PSA Standard Default Assumption (SDA), affects prepayment, as well as the maximum rate-related CPR for burnout— CPR is lower for a pool that has experienced no prior rate-related refinancing. The lower the ratio, the faster the pool burns out.[3]

Many Wall Street firms use proprietary reduced-form prepayment models that use past prepayment rates and endogenous variables to explain prepayment. These models are calibrated to fit observed payment data, unrestricted by theoretical considerations.[4]

3.4 PREPAYMENT RISK AND AVERAGE LIFE OF MBS

Average life is the weighted average of the MBS's or MBS collateral's time periods, with the weights being the periodic cash flow payments divided by the total principal. For example, the original average life of the 30-year, $100M, 9%, 100 PSA mortgage (the first example in §3.2) portfolio is 12.077 years, computed as follows:

$$Ave.\ life = \frac{1}{12}\frac{(1(\$71,295) + 2(\$88,376) + \ldots + 360(\$135,281))}{\$100,000,000} = 12.077$$

In general, the average life of the MBS can be computed by the following formula:

$$Ave.\ life = \frac{1}{12}\frac{\sum_{i=1}^{360} i * CF_i}{F_0} \tag{3.5}$$

Prepayment risk can be measured in terms of how responsive (sensitive) an MBS's or MBS collateral's average life is to changes in prepayment speed (change in PSA) or equivalently to changes in rates (because rate changes are the major factor affecting speed):

$$prepayment\ risk = \frac{\Delta Ave.\ life}{\Delta PSA} \cong \frac{\Delta Ave.\ life}{\Delta R} \tag{3.6}$$

An MBS or its collateral would have zero prepayment risk if

$$prepayment\ risk = \frac{\Delta Ave.\ life}{\Delta PSA} = 0.$$

One of the more significant innovations in finance occurred in the 1980s with the development of derivative MBSs, such as Planned Amortization Classes (PACs), which had different prepayment risk features, including some derivatives with zero prepayment risk.

Assumptions of prepayment rates can be made based on the probability of refinancing rates changing. For example, if there is a high probability that the Federal Open Markets Committee (the Fed) will lower rates (based, for example, on media reports that they intend to do so in the near future), refinancing rates can be expected to fall as well so that more homeowners will refinance their mortgages at lower rates. This in turn will increase the speed of prepayment and thus of the cash flows to investors. PSA rates should then be adjusted upward. Conversely, if the Fed is expected to raise rates as a response to, say, inflation, refinancing rates can be expected to rise, decreasing prepayment risk and lengthening the average life of the MBS. PSA rates should then be adjusted downward.

The best way to model refinancing rate scenarios is through Monte Carlo simulation. One first constructs an interest rate tree—i.e., a binomial tree[5]—with both the spot rates and refinancing rates at each node. One runs many simulation paths sampling from possible interest rate paths that rates could possibly take in the tree. For each simulation path, one estimates the cash flows based on the refinancing rates at each step along the path. (Each time step along the path corresponds to a time step made in the short-rate tree.) Specifically, Monte Carlo simulation can be used to determine the MBS's theoretical value or rate of return through the following steps:

1. Simulate interest rates. Use a binomial interest-rate tree to generate different paths for spot rates and refinancing rates.

2. Specify a prepayment model based on the spot rates.

3. Generate CF paths for a mortgage portfolio, MBS, or tranche.

4. Determine the PV of each path, the distribution of the path, the average (theoretical value), and standard deviation. Alternatively, given the market value, determine each path's rate of return, distribution, average, and standard deviation.

Step 1

In step 1, to simulate interest rates, we generate interest rate paths from a binomial interest-rate tree.[6] For example, assume a three-period binomial tree of one-year spot rates, R_t^S, and refinancing rates, R_t^{ref}, where $R_0^S = 6\%$, $R_0^{ref} = 8\%$, $u = 1.1$, and $d = .9091 = 1/1.1$. With three periods, there are four possible rates after three periods (years), and there are eight possible paths in the binomial tree shown in Figure 3.3. Table 3.2 shows eight short-rate paths simulated from the preceding binomial tree (the eight possible paths rates can take in the tree).

Suppose we have a mortgage portfolio with a par value of $1M, a WAM = 10 years, a WAC = 8%, PT rate = 8%, annual cash flow payments, the mortgages are insured against default risk, and has a balloon payment at the end of year 4 equal to the balance at the

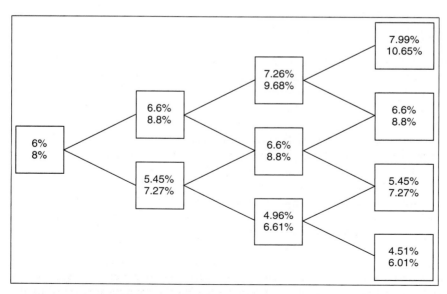

Figure 3.3 Binomial tree for spot and refinancing rates.

Table 3.2

	Year 1	Year 2	Year 3	Year 4
Path 1	8.0000%	7.2728%	6.6117%	6.0107%
Path 2	8.0000%	7.2728%	6.6117%	7.2728%
Path 3	8.0000%	7.2728%	8.0000%	7.2728%
Path 4	8.0000%	8.8000%	8.0000%	7.2728%
Path 5	8.0000%	7.2728%	8.0000%	8.0000%
Path 6	8.0000%	8.8000%	8.0000%	8.0000%
Path 7	8.0000%	8.8000%	9.6800%	8.8000%
Path 8	8.0000%	8.8000%	9.6800%	10.6480%

beginning of year 4 (e.g. the scheduled principal in year 4). We compute the scheduled monthly mortgage payment:

$$p = \frac{\$1,000,000}{\frac{1-(1/1.08)^{10}}{.08}} = \$149,029$$

If we initially assume no prepayment risk, then we obtain the cash flows shown in Table 3.3. The balloon payment at the end of year 4 is:

$$Balloon = Balance(yr4) - Sch.prin(yr4)$$
$$= \$775,149 - \$86,957 = \$688,946$$

The cash flow in year 4 can be computed as

$$CF_4 = Balloon + p$$
$$= \$688,946 + \$149,029 = \$837,973$$

or equivalently, as

$$CF_4 = Balance(yr4) + Interest$$
$$= \$775,903 + \$62,513 = \$837,973$$

Table 3.3

Year	Balance	P	Interest	Scheduled Principal	CF
1	$1,000,000	$149,029	$80,000	$69,029	$149,029
2	$930,970	$149,029	$74,478	$74,551	$149,029
3	$856,419	$149,029	$68,513	$80,516	$149,029
4	$775,903	$149,029	$62,072	$86,957	$837,975

Step 2

The second step of the Monte Carlo process is to specify a prepayment model. Suppose we specify the prepayment schedule shown in Table 3.4. The CPR is determined by the value of the spread $X = WAC - R^{ref}$.

Table 3.4

		Range		CPR
	X	$\leq$	0	5%
0	$<$	X	$\leq$	0.5%	10%
0.5%	$<$	X	$\leq$	1.00%	20%
1.00%	$<$	X	$\leq$	1.25%	30%
1.25%	$<$	X	$\leq$	2.0%	40%
2.0%	$<$	X	$\leq$	2.5%	50%
2.5%	$<$	X	$\leq$	3.0%	60%
	X	$>$	3.0%	70%

Step 3

The third step of the valuation process is the estimation of cash flows for each path based on the simulated path of refinancing rates, the spread X, and thus the CPR (see Table 3.5).

The calculation of the cash flows for the first path are shown as follows. In year 1, the scheduled mortgage payment is:

$$p = \frac{\$1,000,000}{\frac{1-(1/1.08)^{10}}{.08}} = \$149,029$$

The interest payment is:

$$I = 0.08(\$1,000,000) = \$80,000$$

The scheduled principal is:

$$SP = \$149,029 - \$80,000 = \$69,029$$

Table 3.5 (continued next page)

Path 1 Year	1 Ref	2 Balance	WAC	3 Interest	4 Sch. Prin.	5 CPR	6 Prepaid	7 CF
1	0.072728	1000000	0.08	80000	69029.49	0.2	186194.1	335223.6
2	0.066117	744776.4	0.08	59582.11	59641.48	0.4	274054	393277.6
3	0.060107	411081	0.08	32886.48	38647.68	0.4	148973.3	220507.5
4		223460	0.08	17876.8				241336.8

Path 2 Year	1 Ref	2 Balance	WAC	3 Interest	4 Sch. Prin.	5 CPR	6 Prepaid	7 CF
1	0.072728	1000000	0.08	80000	69029.49	0.2	186194.1	335223.6
2	0.066117	744776.4	0.08	59582.11	59641.48	0.4	274054	393277.6
3	0.072728	411081	0.08	32886.48	38647.68	0.2	74486.66	146020.8
4		297946.6	0.08	23835.73				321782.4

Source: Johnson, S. (2004)

Table 3.5 (continued)

Path 3	1	2		3	4	5	6	7
Year	Ref	Balance	WAC	Interest	Sch. Prin.	CPR	Prepaid	CF
1	0.072728	1000000	0.08	80000	69029.49	0.2	186194.1	335223.6
2	0.08	744776.4	0.08	59582.11	59641.48	0.05	34256.75	153480.3
3	0.072728	650878.2	0.08	52070.25	61192.16	0.2	117937.2	231199.6
4		471748.8	0.08	37739.91				509488.7

Path 4	1	2		3	4	5	6	7
Year	Ref	Balance	WAC	Interest	Sch. Prin.	CPR	Prepaid	CF
1	0.088	1000000	0.08	80000	69029.49	0.05	46548.53	195578
2	0.08	884422	0.08	70753.76	70824.26	0.05	40679.89	182257.9
3	0.072728	772917.8	0.08	61833.43	72665.69	0.2	140050.4	274549.5
4		560201.7	0.08	44816.14				605017.9

Path 5	1	2		3	4	5	6	7
Year	Ref	Balance	WAC	Interest	Sch. Prin.	CPR	Prepaid	CF
1	0.072728	1000000	0.08	80000	69029.49	0.2	186194.1	335223.6
2	0.08	744776.4	0.08	59582.11	59641.48	0.05	34256.75	153480.3
3	0.088	650878.2	0.08	52070.25	61192.16	0.05	29484.3	142746.7
4		560201.7	0.08	44816.14				605017.9

Path 6	1	2		3	4	5	6	7
Year	Ref	Balance	WAC	Interest	Sch. Prin.	CPR	Prepaid	CF
1	0.088	1000000	0.08	80000	69029.49	0.05	46548.53	195578
2	0.08	884422	0.08	70753.76	70824.26	0.05	40679.89	182257.9
3	0.088	772917.8	0.08	61833.43	72665.69	0.05	35012.61	169511.7
4		665239.5	0.08	53219.16				718458.7

Path 7	1	2		3	4	5	6	7
Year	Ref	Balance	WAC	Interest	Sch. Prin.	CPR	Prepaid	CF
1	0.088	1000000	0.08	80000	69029.49	0.05	46548.53	195578
2	0.096	884422	0.08	70753.76	70824.26	0.05	40679.89	182257.9
3	0.088	772917.8	0.08	61833.43	72665.69	0.05	35012.61	169511.7
4		665239.5	0.08	53219.16				718458.7

Path 8	1	2		3	4	5	6	7
Year	Ref	Balance	WAC	Interest	Sch. Prin.	CPR	Prepaid	CF
1	0.088	1000000	0.08	80000	69029.49	0.05	46548.53	195578
2	0.096	884422	0.08	70753.76	70824.26	0.05	40679.89	182257.9
3	0.10648	772917.8	0.08	61833.43	72665.69	0.05	35012.61	169511.7
4		665239.5	0.08	53219.16				718458.7

Source: Johnson, S. (2004)

The prepaid principal is:

$$PP = 0.20(\$1,000,000 - \$69,029) = \$186,194$$

The cash flow in year 1 is:

$$CF_1 = \$80,000 + \$69,029 + \$186,194 = \$335,223$$

For year 2, along path 1, we have a balance of:

$$B_2 = \$1,000,000 - \$69,029 - \$186,194 = \$744,776$$

The scheduled monthly mortgage payment is:

$$p = \frac{\$744,446}{\frac{1-(1/1.08)^9}{.08}} = \$119,223$$

The interest payment is:

$$I = 0.08(\$744,776) = \$59,582$$

The scheduled principal payment is:

$$SP = \$119,223 - \$59,582 = \$59,641$$

The prepaid principal in the second year is:

$$PP = 0.4(\$755,776 - \$59,641) = \$274,054$$

The cash flow is:

$$CF_2 = \$59,582 + \$59,641 + \$274,052 = \$393,277$$

In year 3, on path 1, the balance is:

$$B_3 = \$744,776 - \$59,641 - \$274,054 = \$411,081$$

The scheduled monthly mortgage payment is:

$$p = \frac{\$411,081}{\frac{1-(1/1.08)^8}{.08}} = \$71,543$$

The interest payment is:

$$I = 0.08(\$411,081) = \$32,886$$

The scheduled principal payment is:

$$SP = \$71,543 - \$32,886 = \$38,648$$

The prepaid principal in the third year is:

$$PP = 0.4(\$411,081 - \$38,648) = \$148,973$$

The cash flow is:

$$CF_3 = \$32,886 + \$38,648 + \$148,973 = \$220,507$$

Finally, in year 4, the balance is:

$$B_4 = \$411,081 - \$38,648 - \$148,943 = \$223,460$$

The interest payment is:

$$I = 0.08(\$223,460) = \$17,877$$

The cash flow is:

$$CF_4 = B_4 + I$$
$$= \$223,460 + \$17,877 = \$241,337$$

The cash flows for all the other paths are computed similarly.

Step 4

The fourth step of the valuation process is the valuation of the cash flows along each of the paths. The PV of each path's cash flows are determined by specifying the appropriate discount rates. Because the mortgages are insured against default risk, the only risk investors are exposed to is prepayment risk. The risk premium for such risk is known as the *option adjusted spread* (OAS). The OAS is a measure of the spread over the government Treasury bonds rates provided by the MBS when all embedded options have been into account.[7] One can view the OAS as the market price for unmodeled risks (risks that the model cannot capture), such as the forecast error associated with prepayments. The OAS is the spread, such that when added to all the spot rates on all interest rate paths, make the average present value of the paths equal to the observed market price (plus accrued interest). Thus, it equates the observed market *price* of a security to its theoretical *value*. Mathematically, it is equivalent to the solution of K in

$$
\begin{aligned}
P^{Market} &= \frac{1}{N} \left[PV(path\ 1) + PV(path\ 2) + \ldots + PV(path\ N) \right] \\
&= \frac{1}{N} \left[\sum_{i=1}^{T} \frac{CF_i^{path\ 1}}{(1 + Z_i^1 + K)^i} + \sum_{i=1}^{T} \frac{CF_i^{path\ 2}}{(1 + Z_i^2 + K)^i} + \ldots + \right. \\
&\qquad \left. \sum_{i=1}^{T} \frac{CF_i^{path\ N}}{(1 + Z_i^N + K)^i} \right]
\end{aligned}
\qquad (3.7)
$$

where Z_i^j is the zero rate at time i—i.e, month $i = 1, \ldots, T$ on path $j = 1, ..., N$. Typically, $T = 360$ and $N = 1,024$.

The cash flow "yield" that is a standard measure in evaluating any MBS is the *static spread*. This is the yield spread in "a static scenario (i.e., no volatility interest rates) of the bond over the theoretical Treasury spot rate curve, not a single point on the Treasury yield curve."[8] The magnitude of this spread depends on the steepness of the yields curve: the steeper the curve, the greater the difference between the bond and Treasury yields.[9] There are two ways to compute the static spread. The first approach is to use today's yield curve to discount future cash flows and keep the mortgage refinancing rate fixed at today's mortgage rate.[10]

Because the mortgage refinancing rate is fixed, the investor can usually specify a reasonable prepayment rate, which can be used to estimate the bond's future cash flows until the maturity of the bond. The second approach, known as the *zero volatility OAS*, computes the static spread by allowing the mortgage rates to go up the curve as implied by forward interest rates.[11] In this case, a prepayment model is needed to determine the vector of future prepayment rates (a prepayment schedule) implied by the vector of future refinancing rates. After a static spread and OAS is computed, the implied cost of the prepayment option embedded in any MBS can be computed by calculating the different between the OAS (at the assumed volatility of interest rates) and the static spread. That is

$$Option\ cost = Static\ spread - OAS \qquad (3.8)$$

Consequently, because, in general, a tranche's option cost is more stable than its OAS in the face of uncertainty of interest rate movements, then, for small market moves, the OAS of a tranche may be approximated by recalculating the static spread and subtracting its option cost. This is quite useful because the OAS is computationally expensive to evaluate while the static spread is cheap and easy to compute.[12]

It is important to point out that investors in MBSs hold the equivalent of long positions in noncallable bonds and short positions in call (prepayment) options.[13] The noncallable bond is a collection of zero-coupon bonds—i.e., Treasury strips—and the call option gives the borrower the right to prepay the mortgage at any time prior to maturity of the loan.[14] Thus, the value of MBSs is the difference between the value of the noncallable bond and the value of the call (prepayment) option. The OAS is the spread differential between the bond component and the option value component of the MBS. The two main inputs into the computation of an OAS are the cash flows generated as a function of the principal (scheduled and unscheduled) and coupon payments, as well as the interest rate paths generated under an assumed term structure of the zero-coupon curve for discounting the cash flows.[15] At each cash flow date, the spot rate (observed from the interest rate path taken at the corresponding time step of the term structure) determines the discount factor for each cash flow.[16]

Denote z_t to be the appropriate zero discount rate for maturity t (i.e., t years or months), seen today (time 0) (and similarly, f_{tj}, the forward discount rate of maturity t seen at time j), and K, the option adjusted spread. In our simple four-step binomial example, the one-year forward (zero) rate at time 0 is $f_{10} = 8.0\%$; the one-year forward rates at time step 1 are $f_{11} = \{8.6\%, 7.45\%\}$; the one-year forward rates at time step 2 are $f_{12} = \{9.26\%, 8\%, 6.96\%\}$; and the one-year forward rates at time step 3 are $f_{13} = \{9.986\%, 8.6\%, 7.45\%, 6.51\%\}$.

The value of each path is obtained by discounting each cash flow by its risk-adjusted zero-spot rate, z. In our example of four time steps, the value of the MBS on path i is

$$V_i = \frac{CF_1}{1 + z_1} + \frac{CF_2}{(1 + z_2)^2} + \frac{CF_3}{(1 + z_3)^3} + \frac{CF_4}{(1 + z_4)^4}$$

where, because we can express zero rates in terms of forward rates, we have

$$z_1 = f_{10},$$
$$z_2 = ((1 + f_{10})(1 + f_{11}))^{1/2} - 1$$
$$z_3 = ((1 + f_{10})(1 + f_{11})(1 + f_{12}))^{1/3} - 1$$
$$z_4 = ((1 + f_{10})(1 + f_{11})(1 + f_{12})(1 + f_{13}))^{1/4} - 1$$

In general, on path $i = 1, \ldots, N$,

$$z_T = \{(1 + f_{10})(1 + f_{11})(1 + f_{12})...(1 + f_{12T})\}^{1/T} - 1$$

Note that in our example, we have assumed one-year forward rates, but in a more complex and realistic implementation, we would be simulating future one-month rates over a period of 360 months. Thus, for each path, we would be simulating 360 one-month future interest rates, mortgage refinancing rates, and cash flows instead of just four, and we would be simulating many more paths—i.e., 1024, instead of eight.

The zero-rate calculations for path one are

$$z_1 = 0.08$$
$$z_2 = ((1.08)(1.074546))^{1/2} - 1 = 0.077269$$
$$z_3 = ((1.08)(1.074546)(1.069588))^{1/3} - 1 = 0.074703$$
$$z_4 = ((1.08)(1.074546)(1.069588)(1.06508))^{1/4} - 1 = 0.072289$$

so that the MBS value for path one is

$$V_1 = \frac{\$335,224}{1.08} + \frac{\$393,278}{(1.077269)^2} + \frac{\$220,507}{(1.04703)^3} + \frac{\$241,337}{(1.072289)^4} = \$1,009,470.$$

Table 3.6 shows the MBS computed for each of the eight paths.

The final step is to compute the theoretical value of the MBS by averaging over all values taken on each path. In this example, the theoretical value of the mortgage portfolio is the average of the MBS values computed on each of the eight paths:

$$\bar{V} = \frac{1}{N}\sum_{i=1}^{N} V_i \qquad (3.9)$$

Evaluating (3.8), the theoretical value is $997,235 or 99.7235% of par. Note, in addition to the theoretical value, we also can determine the variance of the distribution:

$$Var(V) = \frac{1}{N}\sum_{i=1}^{N}[V_i - \bar{V}]^2 \qquad (3.10)$$

Equivalently, we can also compute the theoretical value by taking the weighted average of each MBS value computed on each path, where the weight is the probability of obtaining that value on the path (each up and down move is assumed to be 0.5), shown in Table 3.7.

Table 3.6 (continued next page)

Path 1 Year	7 CF	8 Z1,t-1	9 Zt0	10 Value	11 Prob.
1	335223.6	0.08	0.08	310392.2	0.5
2	393277.6	0.074546	0.07727	338883.5	0.5
3	220507.5	0.069588	0.074703	177647.1	0.5
4	241336.8	0.06508	0.072289	182547.5	
			Value =	1009470	0.125
Path 2 Year	7 CF	8 Z1,t-1	9 Zt0	10 Value	11 Prob.
1	335223.6	0.08	0.08	310392.2	0.5
2	393277.6	0.074546	0.07727	338883.5	0.5
3	146020.8	0.069588	0.074703	117638.5	0.5
4	321782.4	0.074546	0.074664	241252.6	
			Value =	1008167	0.125

Source: Johnson, S. (2004)

Table 3.6 (continued)

Path 3 Year	7 CF	8 Z1,t-1	9 Zt0	10 Value	11 Prob.
1	335223.6	0.08	0.08	310392.2	0.5
2	153480.3	0.074546	0.07727	132252.5	0.5
3	231199.6	0.08	0.078179	184465.3	0.5
4	509488.7	0.074546	0.07727	378300.6	
			Value =	1005411	0.125

Path 4 Year	7 CF	8 Z1,t-1	9 Zt0	10 Value	11 Prob.
1	195578	0.08	0.08	181090.8	0.5
2	182257.9	0.086	0.082996	155393.5	0.5
3	274549.5	0.08	0.081996	216742.2	0.5
4	605017.9	0.074546	0.080129	444493.9	
			Value =	997720.3	0.125

Path 5 Year	7 CF	8 Z1,t-1	9 Zt0	10 Value	11 Prob.
1	335223.6	0.08	0.08	310392.2	0.5
2	153480.3	0.074546	0.07727	132252.5	0.5
3	142746.7	0.08	0.078179	113892.1	0.5
4	605017.9	0.086	0.080129	444493.9	
			Value =	1001031	0.125

Path 6 Year	7 CF	8 Z1,t-1	9 Zt0	10 Value	11 Prob.
1	195578	0.08	0.08	181090.8	0.5
2	182257.9	0.086	0.082996	155393.5	0.5
3	169511.7	0.08	0.081996	133820.4	0.5
4	718458.7	0.086	0.082996	522269.5	
			Value =	992574 1	0.125

Path 7 Year	7 CF	8 Z1,t-1	9 Zt0	10 Value	11 Prob.
1	195578	0.08	0.08	181090.8	0.5
2	182257.9	0.086	0.082996	155393.5	0.5
3	169511.7	0.0926	0.086188	132277.2	0.5
4	718458.7	0.086	0.086141	516246.6	
			Value =	985008	0.125

Path 8 Year	7 CF	8 Z1,t-1	9 Zt0	10 Value	11 Prob.
1	195578	0.08	0.08	181090.8	0.5
2	182257.9	0.086	0.082996	155393.5	0.5
3	169511.7	0.0926	0.086188	132277.2	0.5
4	718458.7	0.09986	0.08959	509741.1	
			Value =	978502.5	0.125

Source: Johnson, S. (2004)

Table 3.7

Value	Prob.
1009470	0.125
1008167	0.125
1005411	0.125
997720.3	0.125
1001031	0.125
992574.1	0.125
985008	0.125
978502.5	0.125
Wt. Value	**$997,235**

3.5   MBS PRICING USING MONTE CARLO IN C++

To price MBSs in C++, we create and define an MBS class that contains methods for MBS pricing via Monte Carlo simulations of spot rate paths in a binomial tree.

```
#ifndef _MBS_H__
#define _MBS_H__

#include <vector>
#include "math.h"
#include "time.h"
#include "Utility.h"
#include "TNT.h"
#define SIZE_X 100
#define SIZE_Y 100

using namespace std;
```

We define two global double array variables that will be used to store the spot rates and discount rates in the binomial tree.

```
static TNT::Array2D<double> spotRate(SIZE_X,SIZE_Y);
static TNT::Array2D<double> discountRate(SIZE_X,SIZE_Y);
```

The *MBS* class contains an overloaded constructor that accepts the notional principal, coupon, weighted average WAC, weighted average maturity (WAM), and option adjusted spread (OAS). The class contains a method `calcPrice` that first builds a binomial tree and then simulates the interest rate paths on the tree using Monte Carlo. The `calcPrice` method accepts the initial spot rate, mortgage refinance rate, the number of steps in the binomial tree, and the number of simulations. The *MBS* class also contains a method to compute the conditional prepayment rate (CPR) `calcCPR`, which accepts the current refinance rate and a method `computeZeroRates` that computes the current discount factor by accepting as input the current time step in the binomial tree and the stored history of discount rates on the current path. The MBS class contains a `calcPayment` function that computes the current mortgage payment by receiving the remaining principal and time to maturity as input. Finally, the MBS class contains a `getPrice` that returns the calculated MBS price, a `getStdDev` method that returns the standard deviation of the computed MBS price, and a `getStdError` method that returns the standard error of the computed MBS price.

MBS.h

```
// MBS.h: interface for the MBS class.
//
//////////////////////////////////////////////////////////////////////

#ifndef _MBS_H__
#define _MBS_H__

#if _MSC_VER > 1000
#pragma once
#endif // _MSC_VER > 1000
#include <vector>
#include "math.h"
#include "time.h"
#include "Utility.h"
#include "TNT\TNT.h"
#define SIZE_X 100
#define SIZE_Y 100

using namespace std;
static TNT::Array2D<double> spotRate(SIZE_X,SIZE_Y);
static TNT::Array2D<double> discountRate(SIZE_X,SIZE_Y);

class MBS
{
  public:
        MBS();
        MBS(double principal, double coupon, double WAC, double WAM,
          double OAS) :
                faceValue(principal), coupon(coupon), WAC(WAC), WAM(WAM),
                OAS(OAS), T(WAM) { }
        virtual ~MBS() { }
        double calcPayment(double principal, double T);   // compute
                                                          // payment
                                                          // amount
        void calcPrice(double initRate, double financeRate, int N,
          long int M);
        double calcCPR(double rate);
        void buildTree(double initRate, double financeRate, int N);
        double computeZeroRates(int cnt, vector<double> rate);
        double calcSMM(double x);
        double getPrice();
        double getStdDev();
        double getStdErr();
        double getMaturity();
        double getWAM();
        double getWAC();
        double getOAS();
  private:
        double OAS;                  // option adjusted spread
        double faceValue;            // principal amount
```

```
        double coupon;              // coupon rate
        double WAM;                 // weighted average maturity
        double WAC;                 // weighted average coupon
        vector<double> zeroRates;   // store discount zero coupon rates
        double T;                   // maturity of MBS
        double mbsPrice;            // price
        double stdDev;              // standard deviation
        double stdErr;              // standard error
};

#endif _MBS_H__
```

The method definitions are

MBS.cpp

```
// MBS.cpp: implementation of the MBS class.
//
////////////////////////////////////////////////////////////////////

#include "MBS.h"

////////////////////////////////////////////////////////////////////
// Construction/Destruction
////////////////////////////////////////////////////////////////////

void MBS::buildTree(double initRate, double financeRate, int N)
{

        Utility util;
        double u = 1.1;
        double d = 1/u;
        double p = (exp(initRate*T) - d)/(u - d);
        double deviate = 0.0;
        long seed = 0;
        double refRate = financeRate;
        long* idum = 0;
        double pay = faceValue;
        double faceAmount = 0.0;
        double interest = 0.0;
        double schedulePrincipal = 0.0;
        double prepaidPrincipal = 0.0;
        double CPR = 0.0;
        double balance = faceValue;
        double sum = 0.0;
        double totalsum = 0.0;
        double SMM = 0.0;
        TNT::Array1D<double> CF(SIZE_X);    // cash_flow
        vector<double> disc(0.0);

        srand(unsigned(time(0)));
        seed = (long) rand() % 100;
        idum = &seed;
        // build binomial tree for rates
        for (int i = 0; i <= N; i++)
        {
```

```
                      for (int j = 0; j <= i; j++)
                      {
                              spotRate[i][j] = initRate*pow(u,j)*pow(d,i-j);
                              discountRate[i][j] = spotRate[i][j] + OAS;
                      }
              }


        faceAmount = faceValue;
        int k = 0;
        long int M = 10000;
        int cnt = 0;
        double r = 0.0;
        int j = 0;

        for (k = 0; k < M; k++)
        {
                sum = 0.0;
                balance = faceValue;
                refRate = financeRate;
                j = 0;
                disc.clear();
                disc.empty();
                disc.push_back(discountRate[0][0]);

                for (i = 0; i < N; i++)
                {
                        balance = balance - (schedulePrincipal +
                                        prepaidPrincipal);
                        deviate = util.gasdev(idum);

                        if (deviate > 0)
                        {
                                j++;
                                refRate = refRate*u;
                        }
                        else
                        {
                                j--;
                                if (j < 0)
                                        j = 0;
                                refRate = refRate*d;
                        }
                        disc.push_back(discountRate[i+1][j]);
                        interest = coupon*balance;
                        pay = calcPayment(balance,WAM-i);
                        schedulePrincipal = pay - interest;

                        if (balance >= schedulePrincipal)
                        {
                                CPR = calcCPR(refRate);
                                SMM = calcSMM(CPR);
                                prepaidPrincipal = SMM*(balance -
                                  schedulePrincipal);

                                if (i != N-1)
                                        CF[i] = interest +
```

```
                                                      schedulePrincipal +
                                                      prepaidPrincipal;
                                    else
                                            CF[i] = interest + balance;

                                    r = computeZeroRates(i,disc);
                                    sum = sum + CF[i]/(pow(1+r,i+1));

                        }
                        else
                                goto x;

                }
                x:
                totalsum = totalsum + sum;
        }
        double ave = (totalsum/M);
        std::cout << "MBS price = " << ave << endl;
}

double MBS::calcCPR(double rate)
{
        double CPR = 0.0;
        double value = WAC - rate;

        /*
        if (value <= 0)
                CPR = 0.05;
        else if ((value <= 0.005) && (value > 0))
                CPR = 0.10;
        else if ((value <= 0.01) && (value > 0.005))
                CPR = 0.20;
        else if ((value <= 0.0125) && (value > 0.01))
                CPR = 0.30;
        else if ((value <= 0.02) && (value > 0.0125))
                CPR = 0.40;
        else if ((value <= 0.025) && (value > 0.02))
                CPR = 0.50;
        else if ((value <= 0.03) && (value > 0.025))
                CPR = 0.60;
        else
                CPR = 0.70;
        */

        CPR = 100*(1-pow((1-(value/100)),12));

        return CPR;

}

double MBS::calcPayment(double fv, double T) {
        return (fv*coupon)/(1-pow(1/(1+coupon),T));
}

void MBS::calcPrice(double initRate, double financeRate, int N,
  long int M){
```

```
Utility util;       // utility class for generating
                    // random deviates
double u = 1.1;     // up move in binomial tree
double d = 1/u;     // down move in binomial tree
double p = (exp(initRate*T) - d)/(u - d);  // up probablity
double deviate = 0.0;                       // random deviate
long seed = 0;                              // seed
double refRate = financeRate;   // refinance rate
long* idum = NULL;              // pointer to seed value for RNG
double pay = faceValue;         // face value of MBS
double faceAmount = 0.0;        // face amount
double interest = 0.0;          // interest payment
double schedulePrincipal = 0.0; // scheduled principal payments
double prepaidPrincipal = 0.0;  // prepaid principal payments
double CPR = 0.0;               // conditional prepayments
double SMM = 0.0;               // monthly mortality
double balance = faceValue;     // balance remaining
double sum = 0.0;               // sum of discounted cash flows
                                // along a path
double totalsum = 0.0;  // total sum of all discounted cash flows
double totalsum2 = 0.0;
TNT::Array1D<double> CF(SIZE_X); // cash_flow
vector<double> disc(0.0);        // stores discount rates

// build binomial tree for rates
for (int i = 0; i <= N; i++)
{
        for (int j = 0; j <= i; j++)
        {
                spotRate[i][j] = initRate*pow(u,j)*pow(d,i-j);
                discountRate[i][j] = spotRate[i][j] + OAS;
        }
}

srand(unsigned(time(0)));
seed = (long) rand() % 100;
idum = &seed;
faceAmount = faceValue;
int k = 0;
int cnt = 0;
double r = 0.0;
int j = 0;

for (k = 0; k < M; k++)
{
        sum = 0.0;
        balance = faceValue;
        refRate = financeRate;
        j = 0;
        disc.clear();
        disc.push_back(discountRate[0][0]);

        for (i = 0; i < N; i++)
        {
                balance = balance - (schedulePrincipal +
                        prepaidPrincipal);
                deviate = util.gasdev(idum);
```

```
                              if (deviate > 0)
                              {
                                      j++;
                                      refRate = refRate*u;
                              }
                              else
                              {
                                      j--;
                                      if (j < 0)
                                       j = 0;
                                      refRate = refRate*d;
                              }
                              disc.push_back(discountRate[i+1][j]);
                              interest = coupon*balance;
                              pay = calcPayment(balance,WAM-i);
                              schedulePrincipal = pay - interest;

                              if (balance >= schedulePrincipal)
                              {
                                 CPR = calcCPR(refRate);
                                 SMM = calcSMM(CPR);
                                   prepaidPrincipal = SMM*(balance -
                                                      schedulePrincipal);

                                   if (i != N-1)
                                      CF[i] = interest + schedulePrincipal +
                                                 prepaidPrincipal;
                                   else
                                       CF[i] = interest + balance;

                                 r = computeZeroRates(i,disc);
                                 sum = sum + CF[i]/(pow(1+r,i+1));

                              }
                              else    // break out of loop
                                 goto x;

                      }
                      x:
                         totalsum = totalsum + sum;
                         totalsum2 = totalsum2 + sum*sum;
              }
              double ave = (totalsum/M);

              mbsPrice = ave;
              stdDev = sqrt(totalsum2 - (double)(totalsum*totalsum)/M)*(exp(-
              2*initRate*T)/(M-1));
              stdErr = (double) stdDev/sqrt(M);
}


double MBS::calcSMM(double CPR) {
        return (1 - pow((1 - CPR),(double)1/12));
}

double MBS::computeZeroRates(int cnt, vector<double> rate) {
```

```
            double value = WAC+1;
            for (int j = 1; j <= cnt; j++)
                value = value*(1 + rate[j]);

            if (cnt == 0)
                value = WAC;
            else
                value = pow(value,(double)1/(cnt+1)) - 1;

            return value;
}

double MBS::getPrice() {
      return mbsPrice;
}

double MBS::getStdDev() {
      return stdDev;
}

double MBS::getStdErr() {
      return stdErr;
}

double MBS::getMaturity() {
        return T;
}

double MBS::getWAM() {
        return WAM;
}

double MBS::getWAC() {
        return WAC;
}

double MBS::getOAS() {
        return OAS;
}
```

Consider pricing an MBS with the parameters used previously:

Main.cpp
```
#include <fstream.h>
#include <stdlib.h>
#include <iostream.h>
#include <string.h>
#include <math.h>
#include <map>

#define SIZE_X 100
#include "CMO.h"

void main()
```

```
{
            std::cout.precision(7);
            double principal = 1000000;       //  underlying principal
                                              //  (notional) of MBS
            double coupon = 0.08;             //  coupon rate
            double WAC = 0.08;                //  weighted average
                                              //  coupon rate
            double WAM = 10;                  //  weighted average maturity
            double OAS = 0.02;                //  option adjusted spread
            double initSpotRate = 0.06;       //  spot rate
            double initRefinanceRate = 0.08;  //  refinance rate
            int N = 10;                       //  number of time steps in tree
            long int M = 100000;              //  number of simulation paths
            MBS mbs(principal,coupon,WAC,WAM,OAS);

            std::cout << "Running Monte Carlo to price MBS..." << endl << endl;
            mbs.calcPrice(initSpotRate,initRefinanceRate,N,M);
            std::cout << "MBS Price = " << mbs.getPrice() << endl;
            std::cout << "Std Deviation = " << mbs.getStdDev() << endl;
            std::cout << "Std Error = " << mbs.getStdErr() << endl << endl;

            std::cout << "Pricing MBS with Simulations of Binomial
               Tree Paths..." << endl;
            MBS mbs1(principal,coupon,WAC,N,OAS);
            mbs1.buildTree(initSpotRate,coupon,N);

            vector<Tranche> tranche;
            Tranche trA('A',500000,0.06);
            tranche.push_back(trA);
            Tranche trB('B',300000,0.065);
            tranche.push_back(trB);
            Tranche trC('C',200000,0.07);
            tranche.push_back(trC);
            Tranche trZ('Z',100000, 0.075);
            tranche.push_back(trZ);

            std::cout << endl;
            std::cout << "Pricing CMO Tranches..." << endl << endl;
            CMO cmo(mbs,tranche);
            cmo.calcCashFlows(initSpotRate,initRefinanceRate,N,M);
}
```

The results are as follows:

```
MBS Price = 964386.69
Std Deviation = 110.07
Std Error = 1.10
```

We can improve the accuracy by increasing the number of simulations. For instance, if $M = 100,000$, then:

```
MBS Price = 964469.78
Std Deviation = 34.86
Std Error = 0.11
```

Thus, the price of the MBS is priced at roughly 96.5% of par. The more time steps, however, improves the accuracy of the computed price.

Continuous Time Model

The binomial model is a simple discrete model and does not capture the movement of interest rates in practice because at each step, rates can only go up or down—they cannot stay the same or move in between time steps. To capture a realistic evolution of interest rate movements, an arbitrage-free model of the term structure of interest rates is typically used. The short rate is assumed to follow a diffusion (a continuous time stochastic) process. The general form of these models is described in terms of changes in the short rate, as follows:

$$dr_t = \kappa(\theta - r)dt + \sigma r^\alpha dz_t, \quad r(0) = r_0$$

where dr_t represents an infinitesimal change in r_t over an infinitesimal time period, dt, and dz_t is a standard Wiener process. κ is the speed of mean-reversion, θ is the long-run mean of the interest rate process, α is the proportion conditional volatility exponent, and σ is the instantaneous standard deviation of changes in r_t. The various short-rate models differ by the parameter α. The Vasicek model assumes it is 0, the Cox-Ingersoll-Ross (CIR) model assumes it to be 0.5, and the Courtadon model assumes it to be 1.

In order to simulate the process, we discretize it as follows (assume Courtadon):

$$\Delta r_t = \kappa(\theta - r_t)\Delta t + \sigma r_t \sqrt{\Delta t} z_t, \quad r(0) = r_0$$

Many interest rate models have some form of mean reversion, reverting the generated interest rate paths to some "long-run" level. Without reversion, interest rates could obtain unreasonably high and low levels. Volatility, over time, would theoretically approach infinity. Similarly, a large percentage volatility assumption would result in greater fluctuations in yield, which in turn results in a greater probability of the opportunity to refinance. The increased probability in refinancing is a greater value attributed to the implied call option, and a higher resulting option cost.[17]

In addition to a more realistic term structure, we need to expand our prepayment model to reflect the effects of multiple factors that impact prepayment. We can utilize the Richard and Roll (1989) prepayment model, which is based on empirical estimation of the mortgagor's financing condition. The model tries to explain prepayments by observing actual prepayments and relating them to the measurable factors suggested by their economic theory of prepayments. The prepayment model makes a few assumptions. The maximum CPR is 50% and the minimum CPR is 0%. The midpoint CPR at 25% occurs at a WAC-refinance rate differential at 200 basis points. At midpoint, the maximum slope is 6% CPR for a 10 basis point rate shift.

The Richard and Roll (1989) model identifies four factors that should be included in any prepayment model:[18]

1. Refinancing incentive: borrower's incentive to refinance

$$RI(t) = a + b(\arctan(c + d(WAC - r_t)))$$

where[19]

$$a = (\max CPR + \min CPR)/2$$
$$b = 100(\max CPR - a)/(\pi/2)$$
$$d = \max slope/b$$
$$c = -d \; x \; midpoint \text{ diff.}$$

2. Seasoning (age of the mortgage):

$$Age(t) = \min(\frac{t}{30}, 1)$$

3. Seasonality (monthly multiplier): yearly trends in housing turnover[20]

$$MM(t) = (0.94, 0.76, 0.74, 0.95, 0.98, 0.92, 0.98, 1.10, 1.18, 1.22, 1.23, 0.98)$$

where t is the tth month, $t = 1...12$.

4. Burnout multiplier: A spike in refinancing due to incentives is followed by a burnout

$$BM(t) = 0.3 + 0.7\frac{B(t)}{B(0)}$$

where $B(t)$ is the mortgage balance at time t and $B(0)$ is the initial mortgage pool balance.

The annualized prepayment rate, $CPR(t)$, is equal to

$$CPR(t) = RI(t)xAge(t)xMM(t)xBM(t).$$

The cash flows for the MBS under this expanded prepayment model are as follows:

- $MP(t)$ is the scheduled mortgage payment for period (month) t:

$$MP(t) = B(t) \left(\frac{WAC/12}{1 - (1 + WAC/12)^{-WAM+t}} \right)$$

- $IP(t)$ is the interest payment for period t:

$$IP(t) = B(t) \left(\frac{WAC}{12} \right)$$

- $PP(t)$ is the principal prepayment for period t

$$PP(t) = SMM(t)(B(t) - SP(t))$$

where

$$SMM(t) = 1 - \sqrt[12]{1 - CPR(t)} \text{ and } SP(t) = MP(t) - IP(t).$$

- $SP(t)$ is the scheduled principal payment for period t, and $SMM(t)$ is the single monthly mortality-rate at time t.

The reduction in the mortgage balance for each month is given by

$$B(t+1) = B(t) - TPP(t)$$

where $TPP(t)$ is the total principal payment for period t. As before, we computed the expected cash flows at time t, $CF(t)$, of the MBS, and thus the MBS price P, using these formulas and Monte Carlo:

$$P = E^Q \left[\sum_{t=0}^{M} PV(t) \right] = E^Q \left[\sum_{t=0}^{M} df(t)CF(t) \right]$$

where

PV = Present value for cash flow at time t.

$$df(t) = \prod_{k=1}^{t} \frac{1}{(1 + r_k)} = \text{Discounting factor for time } t.$$

$$CF(t) = MP(t) + PP(t) = TTP(t) + IP(t)$$
$$MP(t) = SP(t) + IP(t)$$
$$TPP(t) = SP(t) + PP(t).$$

Monte Carlo simulation can be used to help people like portfolio managers identify whether current MBS market prices are rich or cheap compared to their theoretical values and variances, and make potentially profitable trades to capture "mispricings" in the market compared to their "true" theoretical values. One can use the information from the simulation to estimate the average life of each path and the mean and variance from all the paths. From this, one can estimate prepayment risk.

There are two types of cash flow analysis approaches. The first, static cash flow analysis, assumes a constant PSA, while the second, vector (or dynamic) cash flow analysis assumes that the PSA changes over time. The static cash flow methodology estimates CFs based on different PSA speeds, and then calculates the yields on the CFs for prices and for different PSA speeds, assuming a constant interest rate volatility assumption. Static CF analysis is useful in determining what is a good price given the estimated yields based on PSA speeds, duration, average life, and other features of the mortgage or MBS. Table 3.8 shows static analysis for different par value, price, and PSA speeds assumptions.

Based on CF analysis, an investor would be willing to pay 90.75% of par or less for the MBS, if they required a yield of 9.76% for an MBS investment with a PSA of 165 (or equivalently for an investment with an average life of 2.93, and duration of 2.57).

Vector analysis is a more dynamic approach. Vector analysis can be used like static CF analysis to determine prices given required yields. The example at the bottom of Table 3.8 shows vector analysis in which different PSA speeds are assumed for three subperiods.

In general, a decrease in PSA will benefit longer-maturity tranches more than shorter maturity tranches. Slowing down prepayment increases the OAS for all tranches, more for

Table 3.8

Par Value	PSA Yield			Mean	Std Dev.
(Price as % of Par)	50%	100%	165%		
$44.127M	8.37%	9.01%	9.76%	9.047%	.5681
(90.75)					
$45.100M	7.82%	8.31%	8.88%	8.3367%	.4330
(92.75)					
$46.072M	7.29%	7.63%	8.03%	7.6500%	.5234
(94.75)					
$47.045M	6.78%	6.97%	7.20%	6.9800%	.1717
(96.75)					
$48.017M	6.28%	6.34%	6.40%	6.3400%	.0490
(98.75)					
Average Life (Years)	5.10	3.80	2.93		
Maturity	9.40	7.15	5.40		
Duration	4.12	3.22	2.57		
Vector Analysis:					
Month:	PSA				
1–36	50	100	165		
37–138	200	200	400		
139–357	300	300	400		
At $48.127M:					
Yield	6.02%	6.01%	6.00%	6.0100%	.00816
Average Life	3.51	2.71	2.63		
Duration	2.97	2.40	2.34		

Source: Johnson, S. (2004)

those tranches trading above par, as well as increases their price. However, changes in price are not as great for shorter duration tranches, as their prices do not move as much from a change in OAS as a longer duration tranche. Conversely, an increase in PSA will reduce the OAS and price of all tranches, especially if they are trading above par. Interest-only (IO) tranches and IO types of tranches will be adversely affected by an increase as well. A reduction in interest rate volatility increases the OAS and price of all tranches, though most of the increase is realized by the longer maturity tranches. The OAS gain for each of the tranches follows more or less the OAS durations of those tranches.[21] An increase in interest rate volatility will distribute the collateral's loss such that the longer the tranche duration, the greater the loss.

As part of the valuation model, option-adjusted duration and option-adjusted convexity are important measures. In general, duration measures the price sensitivity of a bond to a small change in interest rates. Duration can be interpreted as the approximate percentage change in price for 100-basis point parallel shift in the yield curve.[22]

For example, if a bond's duration is 3.4, this suggests that a 100-basis point increase in rates will result in a price decrease of approximately 3.4%. A 50-basis point increase in yields will decrease the price by roughly 1.7%. The smaller the basis point change, the better the approximated change will be.

The effective duration of an MBS (or any fixed-income security) can be approximated as follows:

$$Effective\ Duration = \frac{V_- - V_+}{2V_0 \Delta r} \qquad (3.11)$$

where

V_- = Price if yield is decreased (per \$100 of par value) by Δr.

V_+ = Price if yield is increased (per \$100 of par value) by Δr.

V_0 = Initial price (per \$100 of par value).

Δr = Number of basis points change in rates used in calculate V_- and V_+.

Effective duration—in contrast to modified duration, which is the standard measure of duration—assumes that prices in the formula (3.11) are computed assuming cash flow changes when interest rates change. Modified duration, on the other hand, assumes that if interest rates change, the cash flow does not change so that modified duration is an appropriate measure for option-free securities like Treasury bonds, but not for securities with embedded options like MBSs, where cash flows are affected by rate changes. Consequently, MBSs use effective duration, also known as OAS duration, which can be computed using an OAS model as follows. First, the bond's OAS is found using the current term structure of interest rates. Next, the bond is reprised holding OAS constant, but shifting the term structure twice—one shift increases yields and one shift decreases yields generating two prices, V_- and V_+, respectively.[23]

Subsequently, effective duration can be used with a binomial tree or with CF analysis to measure the duration of a bond with option risk or an MBS. The following steps are utilized for using a binomial tree to value a bond with an embedded option. First, take a yield curve estimated with bootstrapping and value the bond, V_0, using the calibration approach. Then, let the estimated yield curve with bootstrapping decrease by a small amount and then estimate the price of the bond using the calibration approach: V_-. Let the estimated yield curve with bootstrapping decrease by a small amount, and then estimate the price of the bond using the calibration approach: V_+. Finally, calculate the effective duration in (3.11). Similarly, using static cash flow analysis, you can calculate effective duration as follows. For a given PSA, determine the prices associated with small yield changes (you can also use a model in which you assume PSA changes as rates change), and then use the formula (3.11). It is important to note that effective duration assumes only parallel shifts in the term structure and will not correctly predict the bond price change if shifts are not parallel.

Convexity is a measure of a security that is the approximate change in price that is not explained by duration. It can be viewed as the second-order term of the Taylor expansion of the bond price as a function of yield. Bonds with positive convexity will have a greater percentage increase in price than the percentage price decrease if the yield changes by a given number of basis points. Conversely, bonds with negative convexity will have a greater percentage price decrease than percentage price increase if yields change a given number of basis points. Although positive convexity is a desirable feature of a bond, a pass-through security can exhibit either positive or negative convexity, depending on the current mortgage refinancing rate relative to the rate on the underlying mortgage loans. Convexity can be computed as:

$$\frac{V_+ + V_- - 2(V_0)}{2V_0(\Delta r)^2} \tag{3.12}$$

If cash flows do not change when yields change, then the resulting convexity from (3.12) is a good approximation to the standard convexity of an option-free bond. However, if prices in (3.12) are derived by changing the cash flows change (by changing prepayment rates) when yields change, the resulting convexity is called *effective convexity*.[24] If prices are obtained by simulating the OAS via Monte Carlo simulation or by an OAS model, the resulting value is known as OAS convexity.

As an example of computing duration and convexity, consider a PSA 165 MBS with the following prices and yields shown in Table 3.9.

Table 3.9

Price	Yield
102.1875	6.75%
100.2813	7.00%
98.4063	7.25%

From (3.12), we find the duration is

$$\frac{102.1875 - 98.4063}{2(100.2813)(.0025)} = 7.54$$

and the convexity is

$$\frac{102.1875 + 98.4063 - 2(100.2813)}{2(100.2813)(.0025)^2} = 24$$

Thus, for a 25% change in the yield, the bond price will change by 7.54%, with a positive convexity of 24%—meaning 24% of the price change is not captured by the duration.

Figure 3.4 shows the simulated cash flows for a 30-year MBS with a 8.5% coupon on a $1,000,000 pool.

For MBS-pricing models where the underlying factor follows a diffusion process, see Kariya and Kobayashi (2000) for a one-factor (interest rate) valuation model and Kariya, Ushiyama, and Pliska (2002) for a three-factor (interest rate, mortgage rate, and housing price) valuation model.[25]

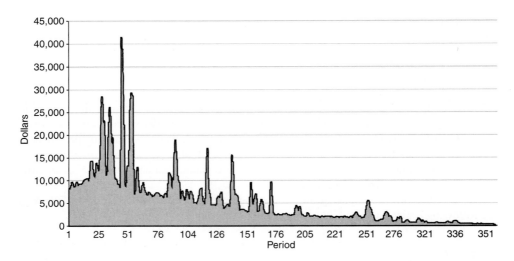

Figure 3.4 Simulated cash flows for a 30-year MBS.   *Source: Bandic, I. (2002), pg. 23.*

3.6 MATLAB FIXED-INCOME TOOLKIT FOR MBS VALUATION

The Matlab Fixed-Income Toolkit can be used for MBS valuation and for computing many MBS measures, such as effective duration, convexity, and OAS. The following variables are inputs in MBS valuation in Matlab:

- **Price:** Clean price for every $100 of face value.

- **Yield:** Mortgage yield, compounded monthly (in decimal).

- **Settle:** Settlement date. A serial date or date string. Settle must be earlier than or equal to Maturity.

- **OriginalBalance:** Original balance value in dollars (balance at the beginning of each TermRemaining).

- **TermRemaining:** (Optional) Number of full months between settlement and maturity.

- **Maturity:** Maturity date. A serial date number of date string.

- **IssueDate:** Issue date. A serial date number or date string.

- **GrossRate:** Gross coupon rate (including fees), in decimal. Equal to WAC.

- **CouponRate:** Net coupon rate, in decimal. Default = GrossRate. Equal to PT rate.

- **Delay:** (Optional) Delay (in days) between payment from homeowner and receipt by bondholder. Default = 0 (no delay between payment and receipt).

- **NMBS:** Number of mortgage-backed securities.

- **PrepaySpeed:** (Optional) Relation of the conditional prepayment rate (CPR) to the benchmark model. Default = 0. Set PrepaySpeed to [] if you input a customized prepayment matrix.

- **PrepayMatrix:** (Optional) Used only when PrepayModel and PrepaySpeed are unspecified. Customized prepayment vector: A NaN-padded matrix of size max(TermRemaining)-by-NMBS. Each column corresponds to each MBS, each row corresponds to each month after settlement.

- **ZeroMatrix:** A matrix of three columns. Column 1: serial date numbers. Column 2: spot rates with maturities corresponding to the dates in Column 1. Column 3: Compounding of rates in Column 1. Values are 1 (annual), 2 (semiannual), 3 (three times per year), 4 (quarterly), 6 (bimonthly), 12 (monthly), and −1 (continuous).

- **Interpolation:** Interpolation method. Computes the corresponding spot rates for the bond's cash flow. Available methods are (0) nearest, (1) linear, and (2) cubic spline. Default = 1.

All inputs (except PrepayMatrix and ZeroMatrix) are NMBS x 1 vectors. The following variables are inputs for pricing bonds, which can in turn be used to find the implied yield curve for pricing mortgage-backed securities:

- **Face:** (Optional) Face value of each bond in the portfolio. Default = 100.

- **Yield:** Scalar or vector containing yield to maturity of instruments.

- **Settle:** Settlement date. A scalar or vector of serial date numbers. Settle must be earlier than or equal to Maturity.

- **Maturity:** Maturity date. A scalar or vector of serial date numbers of date strings.

- **ConvDates:** Conversion dates for the bonds. A matrix of serial date numbers.

- **CouponRates**: Matrix containing coupon rates for each bond in the portfolio in decimal form. The first column of this matrix contains rates applicable between Settle and dates in the first column of ConvDates.

- **Period:** (Optional) Number of coupons per year of the bond. A vector of integers. Allowed values are 0, 1, 2, 3, 4, 6, and 12. Default = 2 (semiannual).

- **Basis:** (Optional) Day count basis of the instrument. A vector of integers. 0 = actual/actual (default), 1 = 30/360, 2 = actual/360, 3 = actual/365, 4 = 30/360 (PSA compliant), 5 = 30/360 (ISDA compliant), 6 = 30/360 (European), and 7 = actual/365 (Japanese).

- **EndMonthRule:** (Optional) End-of-month rule. A vector. This rule applies only when Maturity is an end-of-month date for a month having 30 or fewer days. 0 = ignore rule, meaning that a bond's coupon payment date is always the same numerical day of the month. 1 = set rule on (default), meaning that a bond's coupon payment date is always the last actual day of the month.

2

Suppose we want to compute the cash flows and balances of an FHLMC mortgage pool with an initial balance of $10,000,000, PSA of 150, WAC = 8.125%, term of 360 months, and a remaining term of 357 months (the pool has been "seasoned" for three months). We use the following Matlab code:

```
OriginalBalance = 1000000;
GrossRate = 0.08125;
OriginalTerm = 360;
TermRemaining = 357;
PrepaySpeed = 125;
[Balance, Payment, Principal, Interest, Prepayment] =
  mbspassthrough(OriginalBalance,...
 GrossRate, OriginalTerm, TermRemaining, PrepaySpeed)
```

This code produces the output shown in Table 3.10 (Balance, Payment, Principal, Interest, and Prepayment).

Table 3.10

Month	Balance	Payment	Principal	Interest	Prepayment
1	998,490.00	7439.7	668.8373	6770.8	836.6
2	996,780.00	7433.4	672.8021	6760.6	1045.4
3	994,850.00	7425.7	676.6479	6749	1253.8
4	992,700.00	7416.3	680.3719	6735.9	1461.6
5	990,350.00	7405.4	683.9716	6721.4	1668.7
6	987,790.00	7392.9	687.4443	6705.5	1875
7	985,020.00	7378.9	690.7876	6688.2	2080.4
8	982,040.00	7363.4	693.9991	6669.4	2284.7
9	978,850.00	7346.3	697.0763	6649.2	2487.7
10	975,460.00	7327.7	700.017	6627.7	2689.5
350	5,640.00	832.5	788.7487	43.8	36.7
351	4,820.00	827.1	788.9469	38.2	31.4
352	4,000.00	821.8	789.1451	32.6	26.1
353	3,190.00	816.4	789.3434	27.1	20.8
355	1,590.00	805.9	789.7401	16.2	10.3
356	790.00	800.7	789.9385	10.7	5.2
357	0.00	795.5	790.137	5.3	0

Source: Johnson, S. (2004)

These values are computed in the same way as in §3.2. Given a portfolio of mortgage-backed securities, we could compute the clean prices and accrued interest using the Matlab `mbsprice` function. Suppose the yield on the portfolio is 7.25%, the WAC (gross coupon) is 8.5%, the maturity is January 10, 2034, the issue date is January 10, 2004, and we want the price on five settlement dates: March 10, 2004; May 17, 2004; May 17, 2005; January 10, 2006; and June 10, 2006 with PT (coupon) rates of 7.5%, 7.875%, 7.75%, 7.95%, and 8.125%, on each of the MBS securities, respectively. Assume the delay in the start of payments is 20 days:

```
% MBS.m  : compute MBS prices and accrued interest
Yield = 0.0725;
Settle = datenum(['10-Mar-2004';'17-May-2004';'17-May-2005';'10-Jan-
2006';'10-Jun-2006']);
Maturity = datenum('10-Jan-2034');
IssueDate = datenum('10-Jan-2004');
GrossCoupon = 0.085;
CouponRate = [0.075; 0.07875; 0.0775; 0.0795; 0.08125];
Delay = 20;
Speed = 150;
[Price, Accrt] = mbsprice(Yield, Settle, Maturity, IssueDate, ...
        GrossRate, CouponRate, Delay, Speed)
```

Table 3.11 shows the prices and accrued interest at each of the settlement dates.

Table 3.11

Settlement Date	Price	Accrued Interest
March 10, 2004	101.0937	0.0000
May 17, 2004	103.2801	0.1531
May 17, 2005	102.3677	0.1507
Jan 10, 2006	103.3897	0.0000
June 10, 2006	104.3008	0.0000

Suppose that we want to compute the OAS of the mortgage pool at the March 10, 2004 settlement date with a roughly a 28-year WAM remaining, given assumptions of a 100, 150, and 200 PSA speeds using the computed price and coupon on March 10, 2004 for the preceding mortgage pool. In Matlab, we first need to create a zero matrix constructed (implied) by bond prices (assume all bonds pay semiannual coupons) and yields:

```
Bonds = [datenum('11/21/2004')   0.045    100   2   3   1;
         datenum('02/20/2005')   0.0475   100   2   3   1;
         datenum('07/31/2007')   0.0500   100   2   3   1;
         datenum('08/15/2010')   0.0550   100   2   3   1;
         datenum('03/15/2012')   0.0575   100   2   3   1;
         datenum('02/15/2015')   0.0600   100   2   3   1;
         datenum('03/31/2020')   0.0650   100   2   3   1;
         datenum('08/15/2025')   0.0720   100   2   3   1;
         datenum('07/20/2034')   0.0850   100   2   3   1];

Yields = [0.0421; 0.0452;  0.0482; 0.0510;  0.0532;  0.0559;
0.0620; 0.0682; 0.0785];
% Since the above is Treasury data and not "selected" agency data, an
% ad-hoc method of altering the yield has been chosen for demonstration
% purposes
Yields = Yields + 0.025*(1./[1:9]');

% Get parameters from Bonds matrix
Settle = datenum('10-Mar-2004');
Maturity    = Bonds(:,1);
CouponRate  = Bonds(:,2);
Face        = Bonds(:,3);
```

```
Period        = Bonds(:,4);
Basis         = Bonds(:,5);
EndMonthRule = Bonds(:,6);

% compute bond prices
[Prices, AccruedInterest] = bndprice(Yields, CouponRate, ...
  Settle, Maturity, Period, Basis, EndMonthRule, [], [], [], [], ...
  Face);

% uses the bootstrap method to return a zero curve given a portfolio of
% coupon bonds and their prices
[ZeroRatesP, CurveDatesP] = zbtprice(Bonds, Prices, Settle);
SpotCompounding = 2*ones(size(ZeroRatesP));
ZeroMatrix = [CurveDatesP, ZeroRatesP, SpotCompounding];
Maturity = datenum('10-Jan-2034');
IssueDate = datenum('10-Jan-2004');
GrossRate = 0.085;
Delay = 20;
Interpolation = 1;
PrepaySpeed = [100 150 200];
Price = 101.0937;
CouponRate = 0.075;
Settle = datenum('10-Mar-2004');

OAS = mbsprice2oas(ZeroMatrix, Price, Settle, Maturity, ...
        IssueDate, GrossRate, CouponRate, Delay, Interpolation, ...
        PrepaySpeed)
```

The OAS results are shown in Table 3.12

Table 3.12

PSA	OAS
100	82.6670
150	101.8518
200	114.6088

We can compute the effective duration and convexity of the mortgage pool using the functions mbsdurp (duration given price), mbsdury (duration given yield), mbsconvp (convexity given price), and mbsconvy (convexity given yield). For instance, continuing with the example, we can compute the yearly duration, modified duration, and convexity of the pool on March 10, 2004 for the 100, 150, and 200 PSA speed assumptions by making the function calls following the code:

```
% compute regular duration and modified duration
[YearDuration, ModDuration] = mbsdurp(Price, Settle, Maturity,
  IssueDate, GrossRate,   CouponRate, Delay, PrepaySpeed)

% compute convexity
Convexity = mbsconvp(Price, Settle, Maturity, IssueDate, GrossRate,
  CouponRate, Delay,PrepaySpeed)
```

Table 3.13 shows duration, modified duration, and convexity for 100, 150, and 200 PSAs.

Table 3.13

PSA	Year Duration	Mod. Duration	Convexity
100	7.0669	6.8148	82.3230
150	6.1048	5.8881	62.2476
200	5.3712	5.1814	48.3368

3.7 COLLATERALIZED MORTGAGE OBLIGATIONS (CMOS)

CMOs are securities backed by a pool of mortgages, MBSs, stripped MBSs, or CMOs. They are structured so that there are several classes of bonds; these classes are called tranches. Each tranche has a different priority claim on the principal. There are two general types of CMOs: sequential-pay tranches and planned and amortization class (PAC). In a sequential-pay tranche, each bond class is prioritized in terms of the order of the principal payment. Principal for each tranche is paid sequentially by priority: The first priority tranche's principal is paid entirely (retired) before the next class, which has its principal paid before the next class, and so on. This process continues until all the tranches in the structure are paid off. In general, the YTM of the first tranche is the lowest because it has the shortest average life and the least prepayment risk. Each successive tranche has a longer average life and a higher YTM.

The last tranche in many plain vanilla structures does not receive interest until all the tranches with shorter maturities are paid off. These classes are known as accrual bonds or "Z bonds" due to their similarity to zero-coupon bonds. The interest that would be paid to the Z bond is used to pay the principal in the shorter maturity tranches, which shortens their average lives.

Figure 3.5 shows a hypothetical distribution of principal and interest cash flows between the sequential pay bonds and the Z bond.

Suppose we form sequential-pay tranches from the mortgage portfolio described in Table 3.14: $100M mortgage portfolio, WAM = 357 months, WAC = 8.125%, PT rate = 7.5%, and prepayment speed = 165.

The distribution of cash flows is made as follows. Principal payments are first made to A, then to B, then to C, and so on down to the residual tranches. Principal payment includes both scheduled principal payment and prepaid principal. The coupon payment is based on the remaining balance in the tranche. Table 3.15 shows the structured tranche payments.

To attract certain types of investors, floating-rate and inverse floating-rate tranches are created. These two tranches can be created from an existing one such as the C tranche. For example, a floating rate class (FR) and inverse floating rate class (IFR) in C can be constructed such that the floating rate is, for example, LIBOR + 50 basis points, and the

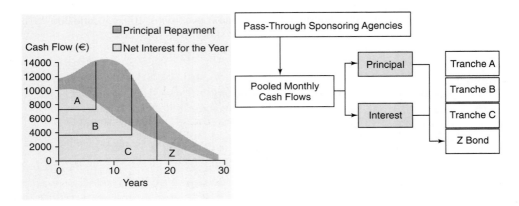

Figure 3.5 Sequential Pay Bonds and Z Bonds.

Table 3.14

Tranche	Par	PT Rate
A	$48.625M	7.5%
B	$9M	7.5%
C	$42.375M	7.5%

inverse floating rate is $28.5 - 3$ (LIBOR). The FR class is 75% of tranche C, and the IFR class is 25%. Thus, the tranches can be constructed as shown in Table 3.16.

Note that in the inverse floating rate equations, 28.5 is referred to as the cap rate (K) and 3 is called the leverage rate (L). Because the floating and inverse floating classes were created from class C, which paid a rate of 7.5%, the K and L were found such that:

$$.75[LIBOR + .5\%] + .25[K - L(PLIBOR) = 7.5\%$$

If LIBOR is 6%, then:

$$FR = 6\% + .5\% = 6.5\%$$
$$IFR = 28.5 - 3(6\%) = 10.5$$
$$.75(6.5\%) + .25(10.5\%) = 7.5\%$$

CMOs often have tranches with different rates. Such CMOs often include a special type of tranche known as a notional interest-only class, which receives only the residual interest. Notional IO classes are often described as paying a certain base interest on a notional principal. Consider the following CMO with an NIO shown in Table 3.17.

The notional principal of the NIO class is $13.75M. The interest-only (IO) class receives the excess interest of 7.5% over the rate paid on each class. For example, from class A, the IO class would receive 1.5% ($7.5\% - 6\%$) on $48.625M, which is $0.729375M. Capitalizing $.729375M at 7.5% yields a notional principal of $9.725M for the IO class on class A. The sum of the notional principals for each class yields the IO's notional principal of $13.75M, as shown in Table 3.18.

Table 3.15

Month	Balance 100,000,000.00	Interest	Principal	Tranch A Begin. Bal. 48,625,000.00	48,625,000.00 Interest	Principal
1	100,000,000.00	625,000.00	177,480.87	48,625,000.00	303,906.25	177,480.87
2	99,822,519.13	623,890.74	205,473.91	48,447,519.13	302,796.99	205,473.91
3	99,617,045.22	622,606.53	233,389.97	48,242,045.22	301,512.78	233,389.97
4	99,383,655.25	621,147.85	261,205.39	48,008,655.25	300,054.10	261,205.39
5	99,122,449.86	619,515.31	288,896.53	47,747,449.86	298,421.56	288,896.53
6	98,833,553.33	617,709.71	316,439.78	47,458,553.33	296,615.96	316,439.78
80	51,965,586.84	324,784.92	512,605.38	590,586.84	3,691.17	512,605.38
81	51,452,981.45	321,581.13	508,049.13	77,981.45	487.38	77,981.45
82	50,944,932.32	318,405.83	503,532.52	0.00	0.00	0.00
83	50,441,399.80	315,258.75	499,055.22	0.00	0.00	0.00
84	49,942,344.58	312,139.65	494,616.89	0.00	0.00	0.00
85	49,447,727.69	309,048.30	490,217.17	0.00	0.00	0.00
99	42,968,082.27	268,550.51	432,494.82	0.00	0.00	0.00
100	42,535,587.45	265,847.42	428,635.94	0.00	0.00	0.00
101	42,106,951.51	263,168.45	424,810.66	0.00	0.00	0.00
102	41,682,140.85	260,513.38	421,018.70	0.00	0.00	0.00
103	41,261,122.15	257,882.01	417,259.77	0.00	0.00	0.00
104	40,843,862.38	255,274.14	413,533.58	0.00	0.00	0.00
105	40,430,328.80	252,689.56	409,839.84	0.00	0.00	0.00
106	40,020,488.96	250,128.06	406,178.29	0.00	0.00	0.00
356	74,797.79	467.49	37,597.30	0.00	0.00	0.00
357	37,200.49	232.50	37,200.49	0.00	0.00	0.00

Tranche B Beginning Bal. 9000000	9000000 Principal	Interest	Tranche C Month	C: Beg. Bal Cum Int 42375000	Principal 0	Interest
9000000	0	56250	1	42375000	0	0
9000000	0	56250	2	42639843.8	0	0
9000000	0	56250	3	42904687.5	0	0
9000000	0	56250	4	43169531.3	0	0
9000000	0	56250	5	43434375	0	0
9000000	0	56250	54	56411718.8	0	0
9000000	196997.83	56250	55	56676562.5	0	0
8803002.17	899641.259	55018.764	56	56941406.3	0	0
7903360.91	894022.233	49396.006	57	57206250	0	0
904465.071	850793.615	5652.9067	65	59325000	0	0
53671.45651	53671.4565	335.4466	66	59589843.8	527084	372436.52
0	0	0	67	59062759.6	575606	369142.25
0	0	0	68	58487153.2	570502	365544.71
0	0	0	69	57916651	565442	361979.07
0	0	0	356	74797.7939	37597.3	467.48621
0	0	0	357	37200.4934	37200.5	232.50308

Source: Johnson, S. (2004)

Table 3.16

Tranche	Par	PT Rate
A	$48.625M	7.5%
B	$9M	7.5%
FR	$31.782M	LIBOR + 50 bps
IFR	$10.549M	28.5 − 3 (LIBOR)

Table 3.17

Tranche	Par	PT Rate
A	$48.625M	6.0%
B	$9M	6.5%
Z	$42.375M	7.0%
NIO	$13.750M	7.5%

Table 3.18

Tranche	Par	PT Rate	(.075−PT Rate) Par	Notional Principal
A	$48.625M	6.0%	$729,375	$9.725M
B	$9M	6.5%	$90,000	$1.2M
Z	$42.375M	7.0%	$211,875	$2.825M
			Total	$13.75M

Suppose we have a $30,000,000 FHLMC mortgage pool with three tranches, A, B, and C, each with a size of $10,000,000. Assume the first tranche pool "balloons out" in 60 months, the second pool "balloons out" in 90 months, and the third is regularly amortized to maturity. The prepayment speeds are assumed to be 100, 165, and 200 for each tranche, respectively. Suppose that the delay before the first pass-through payment made after issue is 30 days, the WAC (*GrossRate* in Matlab) is 8.125%, the PT rate (*CouponRate* in Matlab) is 7.5%, the issue date is March 1, 2004, the settlement date is March 1, 2004, and the maturity is March 1, 2034. The following Matlab code computes cash flows between settle and maturity dates, the corresponding time factors in months from settle, and the mortgage pool factor (the fraction of loan principal outstanding) for each tranche:

```
% mbsfamounts
% [output] CFlowAmounts: vector of cash flows starting from Settle
% through end of the last month (Maturity)
%                CflowDates: indicates when cash flows occur, including
% at Settle.  A negative number at Settle indicates
% accrued interest is due.
%                TFactors: vector of times in months from Settle,
% corresponding to each cash flow.
%                Factors: vector of mortgage factors (the fraction of
% the balance still outstanding at the end of each month).
Settle = [datenum('1-Mar-2004');
          datenum('1-Mar-2004');
          datenum('1-Mar-2004')];
```

```
Maturity = [datenum('1-Mar-2034')];
IssueDate = datenum('1-Mar-2004');
GrossRate = 0.08125;
CouponRate = 0.075;
Delay = 30;
PSASpeed = [100; 165; 200];
[CPR, SMM] = psaspeed2rate(PSASpeed);
PrepayMatrix = ones(360,3);
PrepayMatrix(1:60,1) = SMM(1:60,1);
PrepayMatrix(1:90,2) = SMM(1:90,2);
PrepayMatrix(:,3)=SMM(:,3)
 [CFlowAmounts, TFactors, Factors] = mbscfamounts(Settle, Maturity,
     IssueDate, ...
   GrossRate, CouponRate, Delay, [], PrepayMatrix)
```

The cash flows for the difference sequential tranches are shown in Table 3.19.

We can compute the price and accrued interest of each of the mortgage pools by using the following code:

```
[Price, AccrInt] = mbsprice(Yield, Settle, Maturity, IssueDate,
GrossRate, CouponRate, Delay, PrepaySpeed, PrepayMatrix)
```

Table 3.19

Month	Tranche A CF	Tranche B CF	Tranche C CF
1	0	0	0
2	70,708.00	71,794.00	72,379.00
3	72,368.00	74,534.00	75,702.00
4	74,015.00	77,256.00	79,004.00
5	75,649.00	79,957.00	82,283.00
59	95,117.00	105,150.00	108,680.00
60	94,592.00	104,190.00	107,470.00
61	94,070.00	103,240.00	106,270.00
62	7,580,500.00	102,290.00	105,080.00
63	0.00	101,350.00	103,910.00
64	0.00	100,420.00	102,750.00
88	0.00	80,383.00	78,340.00
89	0.00	79,637.00	77,455.00
90	0.00	78,897.00	76,579.00
91	0.00	78,163.00	75,713.00
92	0.00	4,811,500.00	74,857.00
93	0.00	0.00	74,009.00
358	0.00	0.00	2,017.40
359	0.00	0.00	1,976.90
360	0.00	0.00	1,936.80
361	0.00	0.00	1,897.30

The price and accrued interest is shown in Table 3.20. No tranche pool has any accrued interest because the settlement date is the same as the issue date.

Table 3.20

	Price	Accrued Interest
Tranche A	101.1477	0
Tranche B	100.8520	0
Tranche C	100.7311	0

We can compute the effective duration and convexity of the mortgage pool using the mbsdurp (duration given price), mbsdury (duration given yield), mbsconvp (convexity given price), and mbsconvy (convexity given yield). For instance, continuing with the example, we can compute the yearly duration, modified duration, and convexity of the pool on March 10, 2004 for the 100, 150, and 200 PSA speed assumptions by making the function calls following the code:

```
% compute regular duration and modified duration
[YearDuration, ModDuration] = mbsdurp(Price, Settle, Maturity,
IssueDate, GrossRate,
   CouponRate, Delay, PrepaySpeed)

% compute convexity
Convexity = mbsconvp(Price, Settle, Maturity, IssueDate, GrossRate,
CouponRate, Delay,
    PrepaySpeed)
```

The duration, modified duration, and convexity results returned from the Matlab functions above for 100, 150, and 200 PSAs are shown in Table 3.21. Figure 3.6 shows simulated cash flows for a sequential-pay CMO.

Table 3.21

PSA	Year Duration	Mod. Duration	Convexity
100	7.0669	6.8148	82.3230
150	6.1048	5.8881	62.2476
200	5.3712	5.1814	48.3368

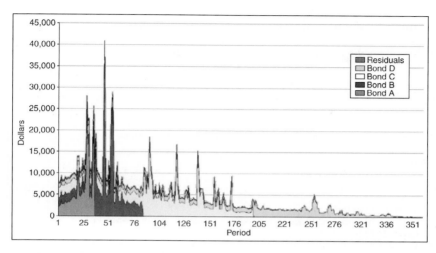

Figure 3.6   Simulated CMO Cash Flows.   *Source: Bandic (2002), 28.*

3.8   CMO IMPLEMENTATION IN C++

CMO.h

```cpp
#ifndef _CMO__
#define _CMO__

#include <vector>
#include <algorithm>
#include <numeric>
#include "Constants.h"
#include "MBS.h"

using namespace std;

class Tranche
{
  public:
        Tranche() {}
        Tranche(char clas, double balance, double coupon)
          : initBalance_(balance), balance_(balance), coupon_(coupon),
            clas_(clas) {}
        virtual ~Tranche() {}
        double initBalance_;
        double balance_;
        double coupon_;
        vector<double> cashFlows_;
        vector<double> sumCF_;
        vector<double> inter_;
        vector<double> principal_;
        vector<double> discount_;
        vector<double> T_;
        double price_;
```

```
        double interest_;
        double princip_;
        double averageLife_;
        char clas_;
};

class CMO
{
  public:
        CMO(MBS m, vector<Tranche> tr) : mbs(m), tranche(tr)
        {
          for (int i = 0; i < tranche.size(); i++)
                collateral_.push_back(tranche[i].balance_);
        }
        virtual ~CMO() { }
        void calcTrancheCF();
        inline double calcCPR(double SMM) { return 100*(1-pow((1-
           (SMM/100)),12)); }
        inline double calcSMM(double scheduleBal, double actualBal) {
          return 100*((double)(scheduleBal - actualBal)/scheduleBal);
        }
        inline double calcPSA(double age, double CPR) {

          return 100*((double)(CPR/(0.2*min(age,30))));
        }
      }
      inline double calcRefinance(double r) {

          double WAC = mbs.getWAC();
          double a = (double) 0.5/2;
          double b = (double) 100*((0.5 - a)/(PI/2));
          double d = (double) 0.06/b;
          double c = (double) -d*0.02;
          return (double) (a + b*(atan(c + d*(WAC - r))));
        }
        inline double calcBurnout(int t, Tranche tr, double balance) {

          return (double) (0.3 + 0.7*((double)balance/1000000));
        }
        inline double calcMP(int t, Tranche tr, double balance)  {

          double WAC = mbs.getWAC();
          double WAM = mbs.getWAM();

          return balance*(((double)WAC/12)/(1-pow((1+(double)WAC/12),
             -WAM+t)));
        }
        inline double calcIP(int t, Tranche tr, double r,
           double balance) {

          double WAC = mbs.getWAC();

          return (balance)*((double)(tr.coupon_/12));
        }
        inline double calcPP(int t, Tranche tr, double r,
           double balance) {

          double SMM = calcSMM1(t,tr,r,balance);
```

```
            double SP = calcSP(t,tr,r,balance);

            return SMM*(balance - SP);

        }
        inline double calcMM(int t) {

            double MM[12] = { 0.94, 0.76, 0.74, 0.95, 0.98, 0.92, 0.98,
                             1.10, 1.18, 1.22, 1.23, 0.98};
            int rem =  t % 12;

            if (t == 1)
                    rem = 1;

            return MM[rem-1];

        }
        inline double calcCPR1(int t, Tranche tr, double r,
            double balance) {

            double RI = calcRefinance(r);
            double age = calcAge(t);
            double MM = calcMM(t);
            double BM = calcBurnout(t,tr,balance);

            return RI*age*MM*BM;

        }
        inline double calcAge(int t) {
            return min((double)t/30,1);
        }
        inline double calcSMM1(int t,Tranche tr, double r,
            double balance) {

            double CPR = calcCPR1(t,tr,r,balance);

            return (1 - pow((1 - CPR),(double)1/12));
        }
        inline double calcSP(int t, Tranche tr, double r,
            double balance) {

            double MP = calcMP(t,tr,balance);
            double IP = calcIP(t,tr,r,balance);

            return MP - IP;
        }
        void calcCashFlows(double initRate, double financeRate, int N,
            int M);
    private:
        MBS mbs;
        vector<Tranche> tranche;
        vector<double> collateral_;
};

#endif
```

Here are the method definitions:

CMO.cpp

```
#include "CMO.h"
#include "Utility.h"

void CMO::calcCashFlows(double initRate, double financeRate, int N, int M)
{
    Utility util;
    int i, t = 0;
    double r = 0.0715;
    const double kappa = 0.29368;
    const double vol = 0.11;
    const double theta = 0.08;
    double deviate = 0;
    long seed = 0;
    long* idum = 0;
    double balance = 0;
    double sum = 0;
    double S[4] = {0};
    double sum1 = 0;
    double sum2 = 0;
    double sum3 = 0;
    double sumA = 0;
    double sumB = 0;
    double sumC = 0;
    double sumD = 0;
    double CPR = 0;
    double interest = 0.0;
    double mbsPrice = 0;
    double stdErr = 0;
    double stdDev = 0;
    double totalsum = 0;
    double totalsumA = 0;
    double totalsumB = 0;
    double totalsumC = 0;
    double totalsumD = 0;
    double totalsum2 = 0;
    double schedulePrincipal = 0;
    double prepaidPrincipal = 0;
    double discount = 0;
    double principal = 0;
    double pay = 0.0;
    double r1 = 0.0;
    double rr = 0.0;
    int cnt = 0;
    double trancheBal = 0.0;
    double T = mbs.getMaturity();
    double WAM = mbs.getWAM();
    double OAS = mbs.getOAS();
    double dt = (double) T/N;
    double interest1 = 0;
    vector<double> disc(0.0);
    vector<double> time1;
    TNT::Array1D<double> CF(SIZE_X);    // cash_flow
```

```
vector<double> p;

srand(unsigned(time(0)));
seed = (long) rand() % 100;
idum = &seed;

for (t = 1; t <= N; t++)
  time1.push_back((double)(t-1)/12);

for (i = 0; i < M; i++)
{
  r = initRate;
  sum = 0;
  sumA = 0;
  sumB = 0;
  sumC = 0;
  sumD = 0;
  schedulePrincipal = 0;
  prepaidPrincipal = 0;
  balance = 1000000;
  cnt = 1;
  disc.clear();
  disc.empty();
  disc.push_back(r);
  p.clear();
  p.push_back(0);

  for (int j = 0; j < tranche.size(); j++)
  {
    tranche[j].balance_ = collateral_[j];
    tranche[j].inter_.clear();
    tranche[j].principal_.clear();
    trancheBal = calcPP(0,tranche[j],r,tranche[j].balance_) +
       calcMP(0,tranche[j],tranche[j].balance_);
    tranche[j].principal_.push_back(trancheBal);
    tranche[j].interest_ = calcIP(0,tranche[j],r,tranche[j].balance_);
    tranche[j].inter_.push_back(tranche[j].interest_);
    S[j] = 0;
  }

  for (t = 1; t <= N; t++)
  {
    balance = balance - (schedulePrincipal + prepaidPrincipal);
    deviate = util.gasdev(idum);
    r = r + kappa*(theta - r)*dt + vol*r*sqrt(dt)*deviate;
    disc.push_back(r);
    interest = calcIP(t,tranche[cnt-1],r,balance);
    schedulePrincipal = calcMP(t,tranche[cnt-1],balance);
    prepaidPrincipal = calcPP(t,tranche[cnt-1],r,balance);
    tranche[cnt-1].balance_ = tranche[cnt-1].balance_ -
       schedulePrincipal - prepaidPrincipal;
    principal = schedulePrincipal + prepaidPrincipal;
    tranche[cnt-1].principal_.push_back(principal);
    tranche[cnt-1].princip_ = principal;
    p.push_back(principal);

    if (tranche[cnt-1].balance_ > 0)
```

```
      interest1 = calcIP(t,tranche[cnt-1],r,tranche[cnt-1].balance_);
else
  interest1 = 0;

tranche[cnt-1].inter_.push_back(interest1);
tranche[cnt-1].interest_ = interest1;

for (int k = 1; k <= tranche.size(); k++)
{
  if (k != cnt)
  {
      interest1 = calcIP(t,tranche[k-1],r,tranche[k-1].balance_);

      if (tranche[k-1].balance_ != 0 )
      {
        tranche[k-1].inter_.push_back(interest1);
        tranche[k-1].interest_ = interest1;
      }
      else
      {
        tranche[k-1].inter_.push_back(0.0);
        tranche[k-1].interest_ = 0.0;
      }

      tranche[k-1].principal_.push_back(0.0);
      tranche[k-1].princip_ = 0.0;
  }

  rr = mbs.computeZeroRates(t-1,disc);
  S[k-1] = (tranche[k-1].interest_ + tranche[k-1].princip_)/
     (pow(1+rr+OAS,(double)(t-1)/12));

  if (k == 1)
    sumA = sumA + S[k-1];
  else if (k == 2)
    sumB = sumB + S[k-1];
  else if (k == 3)
    sumC = sumC + S[k-1];
  else
    sumD = sumD + S[k-1];
}

if (tranche[cnt-1].balance_ > 0)
{
  if (balance >= schedulePrincipal)
  {
    if (t != N)
        CF[t-1] = schedulePrincipal + interest + prepaidPrincipal;
    else
        CF[t-1] = interest + balance;

    rr = mbs.computeZeroRates(t-1,disc);
    sum = sum + CF[t-1]/(pow(1+rr+OAS,(double)(t-1)/12));
  }
  else
    goto x;
}
```

```
              else
              {
                tranche[cnt-1].balance_ = 0;
                cnt++;
              }
        }
      x:
              totalsum = totalsum + sum;
              totalsumA = totalsumA + sumA;
              totalsumB = totalsumB + sumB;
              totalsumC = totalsumC + sumC;
              totalsumD = totalsumD + sumD;
              totalsum2 = totalsum2 + sum*sum;
    }

    calcTrancheCF();
    for (int j = 0; j < tranche.size(); j++)
    {
            sum1 = 0;
            sum2 = 0;
            for (i = 0; i < tranche[j].principal_.size(); i++)
            {
              sum1 = sum1 + (time1[i])*(tranche[j].principal_[i]);
              sum2 = sum2 + tranche[j].principal_[i];
            }
            tranche[j].averageLife_ = sum1/sum2;
    }
    sum1 = 0;
    sum = accumulate(p.begin(),p.end(),0);
    for (j = 0; j < p.size(); j++)
            sum1 = sum1 + time1[j]*p[j];

    std::cout << endl;
    std::cout << "collateral price = " << totalsum/M <<  " " << "Ave.Life = "
        << sum1/sum << endl;
    std::cout << "Tranche A price =  " << totalsumA/M << " " << "Ave.Life = "
        << tranche[0].averageLife_ << endl;
    std::cout << "Tranche B price =  " << totalsumB/M << " " << "Ave.Life = "
        << tranche[1].averageLife_ << endl;
    std::cout << "Tranche C price =  " << totalsumC/M << " " << "Ave.Life = "
        << tranche[2].averageLife_ << endl;
    std::cout << "Tranche Z price =  " << totalsumD/M << " " << "Ave.Life = "
        << tranche[3].averageLife_ << endl;

    T = mbs.getMaturity();
    stdDev = sqrt(totalsum2 - (double)(totalsum*totalsum)/M)*
        (exp(-2*initRate*T)/(M-1));
    stdErr = (double) stdDev/sqrt(M);
}

void CMO::calcTrancheCF()
{
  vector<Tranche>::iterator iter;
  vector<double>::iterator iter1;
  vector<double>::iterator iter2;
  int cnt = 1;
```

```
for (iter = tranche.begin(); iter != tranche.end(); iter++)
{
   iter2 = iter->inter_.begin();
      cnt = 1;
      for (iter1 = iter->principal_.begin(); iter1 !=
         iter->principal_.end(); iter1++)
      {
         std::cout << "Mo." << cnt << "  Class: " << iter->clas_
            << " " << "Principal= " << *iter1
            << " " << "Coupon= " << *iter2 << endl;
         iter2++;
         cnt++;
      }
   }
}
```

The main method is as follows:

Main.cpp
```
void main()
{

   std::cout.precision(7);
   double principal = 1000000;       // underlying principal notional)
                                     // of MBS

   double coupon = 0.08;             // coupon rate
   double WAC = 0.08;                // weighted average coupon rate
   double WAM = 10;                  // weighted average maturity
   double OAS = 0.02;                // option adjusted spread
   double initSpotRate = 0.06;       // spot rate
   double initRefinanceRate = 0.08;  // refinance rate
   int N = 10;                       // number of time steps in tree
   long int M = 100000;              // number of simulation paths

   MBS mbs(principal,coupon,WAC,WAM,OAS);

   vector<Tranche> tranche;
   Tranche trA('A',500000,0.06);
   tranche.push_back(trA);
   Tranche trB('B',300000,0.065);
   tranche.push_back(trB);
   Tranche trC('C',200000,0.07);
   tranche.push_back(trC);
   Tranche trZ('Z',100000, 0.075);
   tranche.push_back(trZ);

   std::cout << endl;
   std::cout << "Pricing CMO Tranches..." << endl << endl;
   CMO cmo(mbs,tranche);
   cmo.calcCashFlows(initSpotRate,initRefinanceRate,N,M);

}
```

The output is as follows:

```
Pricing CMO Tranches...

Mo.1    Class: A Principal= 51851.6  Coupon= 2500
Mo.2    Class: A Principal= 115430   Coupon= 1922.85
Mo.3    Class: A Principal= 114668.5 Coupon= 1349.507
Mo.4    Class: A Principal= 113798.2 Coupon= 780.5165
Mo.5    Class: A Principal= 113024   Coupon= 215.3967
Mo.6    Class: A Principal= 111815.5 Coupon= 0
Mo.7    Class: A Principal= 0        Coupon= 0
Mo.8    Class: A Principal= 0        Coupon= 0
Mo.9    Class: A Principal= 0        Coupon= 0
Mo.10   Class: A Principal= 0        Coupon= 0
Mo.1    Class: B Principal= 31110.96 Coupon= 1625
Mo.2    Class: B Principal= 0        Coupon= 1625
Mo.3    Class: B Principal= 0        Coupon= 1625
Mo.4    Class: B Principal= 0        Coupon= 1625
Mo.5    Class: B Principal= 0        Coupon= 1625
Mo.6    Class: B Principal= 0        Coupon= 1625
Mo.7    Class: B Principal= 110373.5 Coupon= 1027.143
Mo.8    Class: B Principal= 108932.9 Coupon= 437.0903
Mo.9    Class: B Principal= 107334.2 Coupon= 0
Mo.10   Class: B Principal= 0        Coupon= 0
Mo.1    Class: C Principal= 20740.64 Coupon= 1166.667
Mo.2    Class: C Principal= 0        Coupon= 1166.667
Mo.3    Class: C Principal= 0        Coupon= 1166.667
Mo.4    Class: C Principal= 0        Coupon= 1166.667
Mo.5    Class: C Principal= 0        Coupon= 1166.667
Mo.6    Class: C Principal= 0        Coupon= 1166.667
Mo.7    Class: C Principal= 0        Coupon= 1166.667
Mo.8    Class: C Principal= 0        Coupon= 1166.667
Mo.9    Class: C Principal= 0        Coupon= 1166.667
Mo.10   Class: C Principal= 105320.6 Coupon= 552.2968
Mo.1    Class: Z Principal= 10370.32 Coupon= 625
Mo.2    Class: Z Principal= 0        Coupon= 625
Mo.3    Class: Z Principal= 0        Coupon= 625
Mo.4    Class: Z Principal= 0        Coupon= 625
Mo.5    Class: Z Principal= 0        Coupon= 625
Mo.6    Class: Z Principal= 0        Coupon= 625
Mo.7    Class: Z Principal= 0        Coupon= 625
Mo.8    Class: Z Principal= 0        Coupon= 625
Mo.9    Class: Z Principal= 0        Coupon= 625
Mo.10   Class: Z Principal= 0        Coupon= 625

collateral price = 682754.6 Ave.Life = 0.4104376
Tranche A price =  564751.1 Ave.Life = 0.2279203
Tranche B price =  321741.6 Ave.Life = 0.5318972
Tranche C price =  108757.8 Ave.Life = 0.6266037
Tranche Z price =  5460.491 Ave.Life = 0
```

3.9   PLANNED AMORTIZATION CLASSES (PACS)

Planned amortization classes (PACs) (also called planned redemption obligations) are tranches set up such that they have zero (or at least minimum) prepayment risk. PACs are set up by applying low and high PSA speeds to the collateral. The PAC bond then receives a promise of the minimum CF each month, with a support bond created that receives the rest. These support classes, sometimes referred to as companions, absorb principal payments and pay off sooner if the PSA exceeds the PAC range. If the PSA is below the range, the companion classes have a longer life and amortization schedule. In either case, the PAC classes experience less volatility than they would in a sequential-pay structure because of the stability provided by the companions.

PACs are much less sensitive to prepayment risk than standard pass-throughs as long as the PSA speed falls between the low and high PSA thresholds used. Suppose one applied 90 and 300 PSA models to the collateral of a $100M mortgage pool with a WAC = 8.125%, WAM = 357 months, and PT rate = 7.5%. This would yield two different monthly principals over the 357-month period. We also need to factor in a seasoning factor, a factor that accounts for the prepayment based on the season, which we assume to be 3. Table 3.22 shows the cash flows for a PAC with the above features.

To show how these calculations were made, we know that in the first month (period 1), the PAC balance is $100,000,000. The computed interest for this first month is:

$$I_1 = (0.075/12) * (100,000,000) = \$625,000$$

The computed PAC principal payment is:

$$p = \frac{(0.08125/12)(100,000,000)}{1 - (1/(1 + 0.08125/12))^{357}} = \$743,967.06$$

The PAC scheduled principal payment is:

$$743,967.06 - (0.085/12)(100,000,000) = 66,883.73$$

The low PAC PSA speed is assumed to be 90. We compute the PAC adjuster seasoning factor, which we take to be:

$$Min\left(\frac{month + seasoning\, factor}{number\, of\, months\, until\, fixed\, CPR}, 1\right)$$

Thus, in the first month, this value is:

$$Min\left(\frac{1+3}{30}, 1\right) = 0.13333$$

The PAC adjuster seasoning factor is then applied to the PAC CPR:

$$\left(\frac{PSA}{100}\right)(Fixed\, CPR)(adjuster\, seasoning\, factor) = \left(\frac{90}{100}\right)(0.06)(0.1333)$$
$$= 0.0072$$

Table 3.22

Pac Period	Pac Low PSA Pr	Pac high PSA Pr	Pac Min. Principal	Pac Int 0.08	collateral Balance 100,000,000.00	collateral Interest 625,000.00	collateral Prncipal
1	127,042.38	268,982.80	127,042.38	381,088.87	100,000,000.00	625,000.00	177,480.87
2	142,460.86	319,853.03	142,460.86	380,294.85	99,822,519.13	623,890.74	205,473.91
3	157,844.28	370,548.61	157,844.28	379,404.47	99,617,045.22	622,606.53	233,389.97
4	173,185.47	420,991.54	173,185.47	378,417.95	99,383,655.25	621,147.85	261,205.39
5	188,477.28	471,103.66	188,477.28	377,335.54	99,122,449.86	619,515.31	288,896.53
6	203,712.56	520,806.83	203,712.56	376,157.55	98,833,553.33	617,709.71	316,439.78
7	218,884.17	570,023.17	218,884.17	374,884.35	98,517,113.54	615,731.96	343,811.60
102	363,181.39	371,031.65	363,181.39	129,910.54	41,682,140.85	260,513.38	421,018.70
103	361,690.25	364,654.51	361,690.25	127,640.65	41,261,122.15	257,882.01	417,259.77
104	360,206.39	358,384.81	358,384.81	125,380.09	40,843,862.38	255,274.14	413,533.58
105	358,729.77	352,220.75	352,220.75	123,140.18	40,430,328.80	252,689.56	409,839.84
106	357,260.36	346,160.58	346,160.58	120,938.80	40,020,488.96	250,128.06	406,178.29
107	355,798.12	340,202.57	340,202.57	118,775.30	39,614,310.67	247,589.44	402,548.63
356	150,750.84	2,573.92	2,573.92	31.76	74,797.79	467.49	37,597.30
357	150,372.35	2,507.45	2,507.45	15.67	37,200.49	232.50	37,200.49

Source: Johnson, S. (2004)

The SMM is:

$$SMM = (1 - (1 - PAC\ CPR)^{1/357} = (1 - (1 - 0.0072)^{1/357} = 0.00060199$$

The PAC prepaid principal is:

$$SMM(balance - scheduled\ principal) \cdot$$
$$0.00060199(100,000,000 - 66,883.73) = \$60,158.65$$

The PAC cash flow is:

$$PAC\ Interest + PAC\ Scheduled\ Principal +$$
$$PAC\ Prepaid\ Principal = 625,000 + 66,883.73 + 60,148.65$$
$$= \$752,042.38$$

We can now compute the PAC low PSA total prepayment amount:

$$PAC\ Scheduled\ Principal + PAC\ Prepaid\ Principal = 66,883.72 + 60,158.65$$
$$= \$127,042.38$$

The same computations are then made for the high PSA level of 300. The main difference is that the PAC CPR in this case is:

$$\left(\frac{PSA}{100}\right)(Fixed\ CPR)(adjuster\ seasoning\ factor) = \left(\frac{300}{100}\right)(0.06)(0.1333)$$
$$= 0.024$$

The PAC bond has an average life of 7.26 years. Moreover, between PSA speeds of 90 and 300, the PAC bond's average life is 7.26 years, implying no prepayment risk. Table 3.23 shows average life for the PAC and support bond for various PSA assumptions.

Table 3.23

PSA Speed	PAC	Support	Collateral
0	10.36	23.84	20.36
50	8.04	21.69	15.36
90	7.26	20.06	12.26
100	7.26	18.56	11.67
150	7.26	12.56	9.33
200	7.26	8.36	7.69
250	7.26	5.35	6.52
300	7.26	3.11	5.64
350	6.61	2.91	4.98
400	6.06	2.74	4.45

The PAC bond can be broken into other PAC tranches. The most common is a sequential-pay PAC. For example, one can form six sequential-pay PACs using the previous collateral. The average life for the PAC classes will be stable within the 90–300 PSA range; 90–300 is referred to as the *collar*. Some PACs will move outside that range. This is referred to as the *effective collar*. The more classes you have, the more narrow you make the windows, making the PAC resemble a bullet bond. Such PACs could be sold to liability-management funds to meet liabilities with certain liabilities or durations—cash flow matching. In the 1980s, one could find CMOs (especially PACs) with as many as 70 tranches; in the early 1990s, the average number of tranches was 24. Like the PACs, the support bond also can be divided into different classes: sequential-pay, floaters, accrual bonds, and so on.

Targeted amortization classes (TACs) also offer prepayment protection within a defined PSA range, but not below the PSA used to price the CMO. This could result in a lengthening of average life if prepayments slow down, and for this reason, TACs offer higher yields in relation to comparable PACs.

Figure 3.7 shows the cash flows paid to a hypothetical GNMA PAC 100/300.

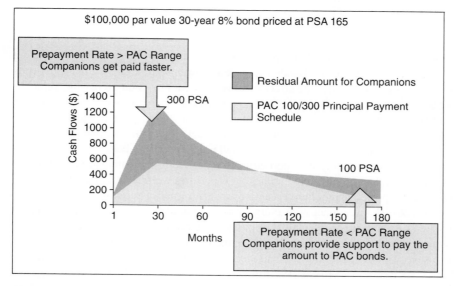

Figure 3.7 GNMA PAC 100/300 Cash Flows.

3.10 PRINCIPAL- AND INTEREST-ONLY STRIPS

Stripped MBSs were introduced by FNMA in 1986. Any MBS can be "stripped" and sold separately by directing a collateral's cash flows into principal-only (PO) or interest-only (IO) securities. IO classes receive just the interest on the mortgages. PO classes receive just the principal payments. The yield on PO bonds depends on the speed of prepayment. The faster the prepayment, the greater the yield. For instance, PO investors who paid $75 million for a mortgage portfolio with a principal of $100 million would receive a higher yield if the $100 million were paid early (e.g., first years) than if it were spread out. POs have an inverse price-interest rate sensitivity relationship: If interest rates decrease, then prepayments increase so that the PO (yield) return increases and its price (value) increases. Analogously, if interest rates increase, then prepayments decrease so that the PO (yield) return decreases and its price (value) decreases.

Because IO investors receive interest on the outstanding principal, they want prepayments to be slow. For example, IO investors holding an IO claim on a $400 million 7.5% pool would receive $30 million (= $400 * 0.075) if the principal were paid immediately. By contrast, if the principal were paid off by equal increments over four years, the return would be $75 million (see Table 3.24).

Table 3.24

Year 1	$(\$400M)(0.75) = \$30.0M$
Year 2	$(\$300M)(0.75) = \$22.5M$
Year 3	$(\$200M)(0.75) = \$15.0M$
Year 4	$(\$100M)(0.75) = \$7.5M$
Total	$\$75M$

Because a rate decrease augments speed, it lowers the return on an IO bond, causing its value to decrease. Whether IO bonds decrease in response to a rate decrease depends on whether this effect dominates the effect of lower discount rates on increasing value. In other words, when interest rates decrease, the prepayments increase, which decreases the return, and the value of the IO must be balanced against the increase in value from the effect of lower discount rates. The two effects may offset one another so that it is possible that there is a direct relationship between value and return for an IO bond.

Like CMOS, stripped MBSs are a derivative product. Both strips are extremely volatile and, as stated, dependent on prepayment rates. POs perform well in high prepayment environments when the principal purchased at a discount is returned at par, faster than expected, making them a bullish investment with a large, positive duration. IOs perform better if prepayments are slow because the principal remains outstanding for a longer period and interest payments continue, making them an investment with a negative duration—i.e., their price increases as interest rates increase and vice versa. IOs are often used to hedge interest rate risks in MBS or CMO portfolios. Portfolio losses that are caused by an increase in rates are partially or fully offset by a corresponding appreciation in the IO position, depending on the structure of the hedge.

Consider a stripped MBS with a collateral pool of $100 million, WAM = 357 months, WAC = 0.08125, PT rate = 0.075, and a PSA = 165. The cash flows are given as shown in Table 3.25.

Table 3.25

Period	Balance 100000000	Interest	Sch. Prin.	Prepaid Prin.	Principal	Stripped MBS PO	IO
1	100000000	625000	65216.47156	110598.9911	175815.4627	175815.4627	625000
2	99824184.54	623901.153	65592.16276	138216.4665	203808.6293	203808.6293	623901.2
3	99620375.91	622627.349	65951.60553	165774.6371	231726.2426	231726.2426	622627.3
4	99388649.67	621179.06	66294.44744	193250.204	259544.6515	259544.6515	621179.1
5	99129105.01	619556.906	66620.34673	220619.862	287240.2088	287240.2088	619556.9
6	98841864.81	617761.655	66928.97288	247860.3319	314789.3047	314789.3047	617761.7
7	98527075.5	615794.222	67220.00709	274948.3929	342168.4	342168.4	615794.2
104	40930020.29	255812.627	59884.94969	353521.5406	413406.4903	413406.4903	255812.6
105	40516613.8	253228.836	59775.10019	349946.5766	409721.6768	409721.6768	253228.8
106	40106892.12	250668.076	59665.45219	346403.4839	406068.9361	406068.9361	250668.1
107	39700823.19	248130.145	59556.00532	342891.9853	402447.9906	402447.9906	248130.1
108	39298375.2	245614.845	59446.75922	339411.8057	398858.5649	398858.5649	245614.8
109	38899516.63	243121.979	59337.71351	335962.6724	395300.3859	395300.3859	243122
110	38504216.25	240651.352	59228.86783	332544.3152	391773.183	391773.183	240651.4
111	38112443.06	238202.769	59120.22181	329156.4661	388276.6879	388276.6879	238202.8
112	37724166.38	235776.04	59011.77508	325798.8595	384810.6346	384810.6346	235776
113	37339355.74	233370.973	58903.52728	322471.2322	381374.7594	381374.7594	233371
356	75665.72172	472.910761	37703.25592	328.3705641	38031.62648	38031.62648	472.9108
357	37634.09524	235.213095	37634.09524	-3.02093E-12	37634.09524	37634.09524	235.2131

3.11 INTEREST RATE RISK

The MBS interest rate risk is similar to that of other fixed-income securities: When interest rates fall, price goes up and vice versa. However, the prepayment optionality "embedded" in MBS impacts the degree of price movement based on the relationship between the security's coupon rate and current mortgage rates. When a pass-through coupon is either at or above current mortgage rates, homeowners are more likely to exercise the prepayment option. As the likelihood of prepayment increases, the price of the MBS pass-through does not go up as much as that of an otherwise identical security with no optionality due to the increased prepayment risk. This is known as *negative convexity*.

When a pass-through coupon is below current mortgage rates, or "out of the money," homeowners are unlikely to exercise the prepayment option. Although the prepayment option is less likely to be exercised, the price of the pass-through still exhibits negative convexity because investors maintain their principal investment at lower levels than the current market rate for longer periods of time. This is known as *extension risk*. Figure 3.8 shows the inverse relationship between the price of a regular fixed-income security and interest rates. Figure 3.9 shows the negative convexity of an MBS.

3.12 DYNAMIC HEDGING OF MBS

Institutions hold significant positions in mortgage-backed securities (MBSs) for a variety of reasons. Hedging interest rate risk of MBSs is an important concern whether the positions reflect trades on relative value or inventory holdings due to main businesses. MBSs hedging is complicated by the fact that the timing of the cash flows is dependent on the prepayment behavior of the pool. In particular, mortgagors are more likely to prepay given the incentive to refinance when interest rates fall. Thus, fixed-rate investors are implicitly writing a call option on the corresponding fixed-rate bond.[26] Though other factors influence

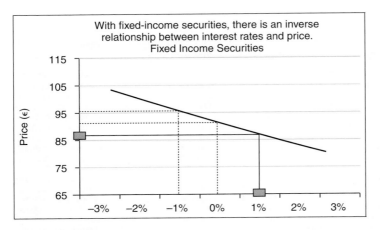

Figure 3.8 Inverse relationship between the price of a regular fixed income security and interest rates.

prepayments—e.g., seasonality and burnout—interest rates are the predominant factor in valuing MBSs. Because of this predominance, U.S. Treasury securities, or more specifically, Treasury note (T-note) futures, are often used to hedge MBSs. There are two reasons: (1) T-note futures are very liquid instruments; and (2) the prices of those instruments are determined by the underlying term structure of interest rates and thus relate directly to the value of MBSs.[27] We follow the work of Boudoukh, Richardson, Stanton, and Whitelaw (1995) in the following discussion.

There are two common approaches to hedging MBSs using T-note futures. The first is purely empirical and involves the regression of past returns on MBSs against past returns on T-note futures. The estimated regression coefficient from the resulting relation can then be used to hedge the interest rate risk of MBSs using the risk in T-notes. The advantage of

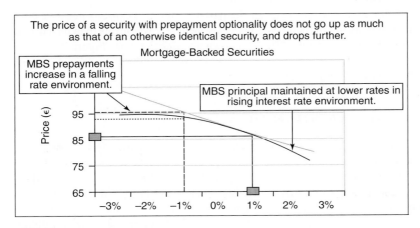

Figure 3.9 Negative convexity of a MBS.

this method is that it does not involve strong assumptions regarding the underlying model for the evolution of interest rates or prepayments.[28] The disadvantage is that the method is static in nature. It does not explicitly adjust the hedge ratio for changes in interest rates and mortgage prepayments, which can potentially be detrimental from mishedging a large portfolio exposure.[29] Consequently, the observations used in the regression represent an average of the relation between MBSs and T-note futures only over the sample period, which may or may not be representative of the current period.

As an alternative, a second approach is model-based. It involves specification of the interest rate process and a prepayment model. The assumptions then help map an MBS pricing functional to interest rates and possibly other factors.[30] The approach represents a dynamic method for determining co-movements between MBS prices and T-note futures prices. These co-movements are completely specified by conditioning on current values of the relevant economic variables and on particular parameter values. The basic idea is to estimate a conditional hedge ratio between returns on an MBS and returns on a T-note futures. This is important for MBSs because, as interest rates change, expected future prepayments change, and thus the timing of the future prepayments change, and thus timing of the future cash flows also changes.

To estimate the conditional hedge ratio, a structural model is usually required (as with model-based MBS valuation approaches). There are two drawbacks: First, there is no consensus regarding what is a reasonable specification of how the term structure moves through time, and how these movements relate to prepayment behavior. The model price is going to be closely related to these possibly ad-hoc assumptions, which may be reasonable or unreasonable.[31] Second, and more subtle, is the recognition that the parameter values themselves may often be "chosen" or estimated from a static viewpoint.[32] For instance, empirical prepayment models often reflect ad hoc prepayment rates on data sets housing and interest rate factors. But any of the well-documented MBS-hedging fiascoes would imply that the resulting regression coefficients, which present an average of the relation of the past, do not have the same link to the variable factors describing the current period. In other words, static in-sample regression estimated coefficients are not accurate estimators of future out-of-sample coefficients.

One method that has worked well in reducing the error between in-sample and out-of-sample estimators is the probability density estimation method.

The Multivariable Density Estimation Method

Multivariate density estimation (MDE) is a method for estimating the joint density of a set of variables. Given the joint and marginal densities of these variables, the corresponding distributions and conditional moments, such as the mean, can be calculated. The estimation relates the expected return on an MBS to the return on a T-note futures, conditional on relevant information available at any point in time. We have T observations, $\mathbf{z}_1, \mathbf{z}_2, \ldots, \mathbf{z}_T$, where each $\mathbf{z}_t$ is an m-dimensional vector that might include the MBS and T-note futures returns, as well as several variables describing the state of the economy. One popular consistent measure of the joint density is the Parzen (fixed window width) density estimator:

$$\widehat{f}(\mathbf{z}^*) = \frac{1}{Th^m} \sum_{t=1}^{T} K\left(\frac{z^* - z_t}{h}\right)$$

where $K(\cdot)$ is called the kernel function (with the property that it integrates to unity) and is often chosen to be a density function, h is window or smoothing parameter (which helps determine how tight the kernel function is), and $\widehat{f}(z^*)$ is the estimate of the probability density at $\mathbf{z}^*$. The density at any point $\mathbf{z}^*$ is estimated as the average of densities centered at the actual data points $\mathbf{z}_t$. The further a data point is away from the estimation point, the less it contributes to the estimated density. Consequently, the estimate is highest near high concentrations of data points and lowest when observations are sparse.[33] A commonly used kernel is the multivariate normal density:

$$K(\mathbf{z}) = \frac{1}{(2\pi)^{m/2}} e^{-\frac{1}{2}\mathbf{z}'\mathbf{z}}$$

Let $\mathbf{z}_t = (R_{t+1}^{mbs}, R_{t+1}^{TN}, \mathbf{x}_t)$, where R_{t+1}^{mbs} and R_{t+1}^{TN} are the one-period returns on the MBS and T-note futures from t and $t+1$, respectively, and $\mathbf{x}_t$ is an $(m-2)$-dimensional vector of factors known at time t. We can then obtain the conditional mean, $E\left[R_{t+1}^{mbs}|R_{t+1}^{TN}, \mathbf{x}_t\right]$—i.e., the expected MBS return given movements in the T-note return—conditional on the current economic state as described by $\mathbf{x}_t$. Specifically,

$$
\begin{aligned}
E\left[R_{t+1}^{mbs}|R_{t+1}^{TN}, \mathbf{x}_t\right] &= \int R_{t+1}^{mbs} \frac{f(R_{t+1}^{mbs}, R_{t+1}^{TN}, \mathbf{x}_t)}{f_1(R_{t+1}^{TN}, \mathbf{x}_t)} dR^{mbs} \\
&= \frac{\sum_{i=1}^{t} R_{t+1-i}^{mbs} K_1^{t-i}(\cdot, \cdot)}{\sum_{i=1}^{t} K_i^{t-i}(\cdot, \cdot)}
\end{aligned}
\tag{3.13}
$$

where $K_1^{t-i}(\cdot, \cdot) = K_1((R_{t+1-i}^{TN} - R_{t+1}^{TN})/h^{TN}), (\mathbf{x}_{t-i} - \mathbf{x}_t)/h))$.

$K_1(\cdot, \cdot)$ is the marginal density, $\int K(z)dR^{mbs}$, which is also a multivariate normal density. The expected return in equation (3.13) is simply a weighted average of past returns where the weights depend on the levels of the conditioning variables relative to their levels in the past.

Given $E\left[R_{t+1}^{mbs}|R_{t+1}^{TN}, \mathbf{x}_t\right]$, a hedge ratio can be formed by estimating how much the return on the MBS changes as a function of changes in the T-note futures return, conditional on currently available information $\mathbf{x}_t$. That is

$$\frac{\partial E\left[R_{t+1}^{mbs}\,|\,R_{t+1}^{TN},\mathbf{x}_t\right]}{\partial R_{t+1}^{TN}} = \frac{\sum\limits_{i=1}^{t} R_{t+1-i}^{mbs}\,\frac{\partial K_1^{t-i}(\cdot,\cdot)}{\partial R_{t+1}^{TN}}}{\sum\limits_{i=1}^{t} K_1^{t-1}(\cdot,\cdot)} -$$

$$\frac{\sum\limits_{i=1}^{t} R_{t+1-i}^{mbs} K_1^{t-i}(\cdot,\cdot) \sum\limits_{i=1}^{t} \frac{\partial K_1^{t-1}(\cdot,\cdot)}{\partial R_{t+1}^{TN}}}{\left[\sum\limits_{i=1}^{t} K_1^{t-i}(\cdot,\cdot)\right]^2}$$

$$(3.14)$$

where

$$\frac{\partial K_1^{t-i}(\cdot,\cdot)}{\partial R_{t+1}^{TN}} = -\left[\frac{(R_{t+1-i}^{TN} - R_{t+1}^{TN})}{(h^{TN})^2}\right] K_1^{t-i}(\cdot,\cdot).$$

A couple of points can be made. First, equation (3.14) provides a formula for the hedge ratio between an investor's MBS position and T-note futures. For example, if $\frac{\partial E\left[R_{t+1}^{mbs}\,|\,R_{t+1}^{TN},\mathbf{x}_t\right]}{\partial R_{t+1}^{TN}}$ equals 0.5, then for every \$1 of an MBS held, the investor should short \$0.50 worth of T-note futures. Second, the hedge ratio will change dynamically, depending on the current economic state described by $\mathbf{x}_t$. For example, suppose $\mathbf{x}_t$ is an $m-2$ vector of term structure variables. As these variables change, whether they are the level, slope, or curvature of the term structure, the hedge ratio may change in response. Thus, the appropriate position in T-note futures will vary over time. Third, the hedge ratio is a function of the unknown return on the T-note futures. If the conditional relation between MBS returns and T-note futures returns is always linear, then the same hedge ratio will be appropriate, regardless of how T-note futures move. If the relation is not linear, then the investor must decide what type of T-note moves to hedge. For example, the investor might want to form the MBS hedge in the neighborhood of the conditional mean of the T-note futures return because many of the potential T-note futures will lie in that region. On the other hand, it may be the case that the investor is concerned about the tails of the distribution T-note futures returns, and thus adjusts the hedge ratio to take account of potential extreme moves in interest rates and T-note futures. Fourth, the hedge ratio is horizon specific. In contrast to the instantaneous hedge ratio, the method's implied hedge ratio directly reflects the distribution of MBS returns over the relevant horizon. Thus, different hedge ratios may be appropriate for daily, weekly, or monthly horizons.

The static OLS regression coefficient, or hedge ratio, is given by

$$\beta = \frac{\sum\limits_{i=1}^{t} R_{t+1-i}^{mbs} R_{t+1-i}^{TN} - T\mu_{mbs}\mu_{TN}}{\sum\limits_{i=1}^{t} (R_{t+1-i}^{TN} - \mu_{TN})^2}$$

$$(3.15)$$

where $\mu_{mbs} = \frac{1}{T}\sum\limits_{i=1}^{t} R_{t+1-i}^{mbs}$ and $\mu_{TN} = \frac{1}{T}\sum\limits_{i=1}^{t} R_{t+1-i}^{TN}.$

In contrast, the dynamic hedging method explicitly takes into account the current economic state. Equation (3.14) can be rewritten as

$$
\frac{\partial E\left[R_{t+1}^{mbs}\,|\,R_{t+1}^{TN},\mathbf{x}_t\right]}{\partial R_{t+1}^{TN}} = \sum_{i=1}^{t} R_{t+1-i}^{mbs}\left[\frac{(R_{t+1-i}^{TN}-R_{t+1}^{TN})}{(h^{TN})^2}\right]w_i(t) -
$$

$$
\left[\sum_{i=1}^{t} R_{t+1-i}^{mbs}w_i(t)\right]\cdot \tag{3.16}
$$

$$
\left[\sum_{i=1}^{t}\left(\frac{(R_{t+1-i}^{TN}-R_{t+1}^{TN})}{(h^{TN})^2}\right)w_i(t)\right]
$$

where $w_i(t) = \dfrac{K_1^{t-i}(\cdot,\cdot)}{\sum\limits_{i=1}^{t} K_1^{t-i}(\cdot,\cdot)}$.

The hedge ratio in (3.16) is constructed by taking past pairs of MBS and T-note futures returns, and then differentially weighting these pairs' co-movements by determining how "close" $(R_{t+1-i}^{TN}, \mathbf{x}_{t-i})$ pairs are to a chosen value of R_{t+1}^{TN} and current information $\mathbf{x}_t$. The dynamic hedge ratio is similar in spirit to a regression hedge, except that the weights are no longer constant, but instead depend on current information. $w_i(t)$ puts little weight on the observation pair $(R_{t+1-i}^{mbs}, R_{t+1-i}^{TN})$ if the current information $\mathbf{x}_t$ is not close to $\mathbf{x}_{t-i}$ in a distributional sense. The hedge ratio adjusts to current economic conditions. For example, if interest rates are currently high, but the term structure is inverted, then more weight will be given to past co-movements between MBS and T-note futures in that type of interest rate environment.

Boudoukh, Richardson, Stanton, and Whitelaw (1995) apply the method to weekly 30-year fixed-rate GNMA MBS (with 8%, 9%, and 10% coupons) and T-note futures data over the period January 1987 to May 1994. The GNMA prices represent dealer-quoted prices on $X\%$ coupon-bearing GNMAs traded for forward delivery on a *to be announced* (TBA) basis.[34] Performing an out-of-sample analysis, their research shows that the dynamic hedging method performs considerably better than the static regression method. For instance, in hedging weekly returns on 10% GNMA, the dynamic method reduces the volatility of the GNMA return from 41 to 24 basis points, whereas a static method manages only 29 basis points of residual volatility. Furthermore, only 1 basis point of the volatility of the dynamically hedged return can be attributed to risk associated with U.S. Treasuries in contrast to 14 basis points of interest rate risk in the statically hedged return.

The results of Boudoukh, Richardson, Stanton, and Whitelaw (1995) shown in Table 3.26 compares the mean, volatility, and autocorrelation of unhedged returns on GNMA TBAs and hedged returns using two different approaches. The approaches involve hedging GNMAs with T-note futures, resulting in the hedged return, $R_{t+1}^{mbs} - \beta_{t+}R_{t+1}^{TN}$, where R_{t+1}^{mbs} and R_{t+1}^{TN} are the out-of-sample returns on GNMAs and T-note futures respectively, and the hedge ratio, is estimated using the prior 150 weeks of data in one of two ways: (1) a linear hedge based on a regression of past R_{t+1}^{mbs} on R_{t+1}^{TN}, and (2) a MDE hedge using the distribution of R_{t+1}^{mbs} and R_{t+1}^{TN}, conditional on the 10-year yield at time t. The estimation is performed on a rolling basis and covers the out-of-sample period, December 1989 to May 1994. Results are reported for both weekly and overlapping monthly returns.

Table 3.26

	GNMA 8		GNMA 9		GNMA 10	
	1 wk.	4 wks.	1 wk.	4 wks.	1 wk.	4 wks.
Unhedged						
Mean (%)	.078	.326	.077	.316	.069	.286
Vol. (%)	.685	1.364	.531	.999	.414	.746
Autocorr.	.011	.138	-.019	.109	-.045	.082
Linear Hedge						
Mean (%)	.007	.041	.017	.086	.024	.126
Vol. (%)	.318	.599	.309	.573	.286	.524
Autocorr.	.015	-.107	.012	.021	.060	.039
MDE Hedge						
Mean (%)	.006	.123	.020	.178	.027	.189
Vol. (%)	.285	.583	.245	.472	.242	.440
Autocorr.	.011	-.096	.016	-.083	.036	-.085

Source: Boudoukh, Richardson, Stanton, and Whitelaw (1995)

Figure 3.10 shows hedge ratios for hedging weekly 10% (top) and 8% (bottom) GNMA returns using the 10-year T-note futures. Hedge ratios are estimated on a 150-week rolling basis using both a linear regression and MDE. The MDE hedge ratios condition on the level of the 10-year T-note yield.

Figure 3.11 shows the expected weekly return on a 10% (top) and an 8% (bottom) GNMA as a function of the contemporaneous 10-year T-note futures return, conditional on three different levels of the 10-year T-note yield. The relation is estimated using MDE over the period January 1987 to May 1994. Returns are in percent per week.

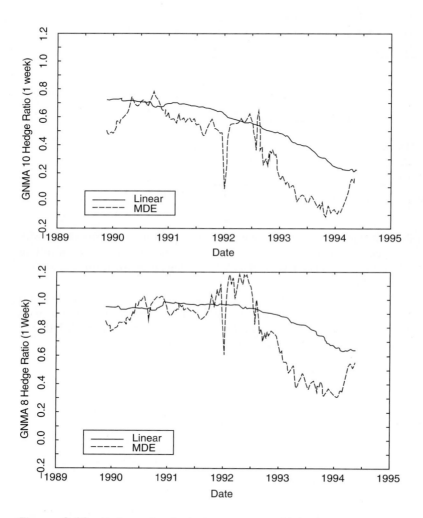

Figure 3.10 Hedge ratios for hedging weekly 10% (top) and 8% (bottom) GNMA returns using the 10-year T-note futures. *Source: Boudoukh, Richardson, Stanton, and Whitelaw (1995).*

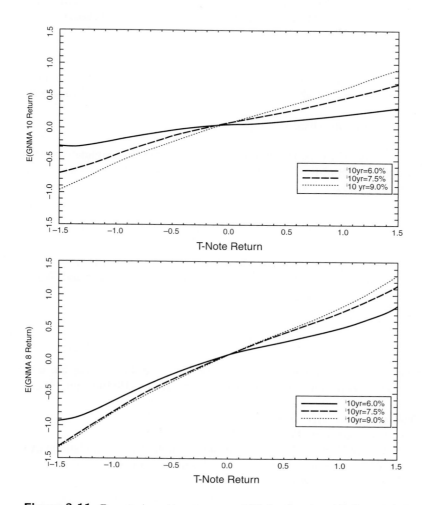

Figure 3.11 Expected weekly return on a 10% (top) and an 8% (bottom) GNMA as a function of the contemporaneous 10-year T-note futures return, conditional on three different levels of the 10-year T-note yield.   *Source: Boudoukh, Richardson, Stanton, and Whitelaw (1995).*

ENDNOTES

1. Throughout this chapter, we follow the direct work of Dr. Stafford Johnson, Professor of Finance at Xavier University, at *http://www.academ.xu.edu/johnson/*.
2. Obazee, P. (2002), pp. 338–339. See "Understanding the Building Blocks for OAS Models" in *Interest Rate, Term Structure, and Valuation Modeling.* Edited by Frank J. Fabozzi, Wiley & Sons.
3. Id., pp. 338–339.
4. Id., pp. 338–339.
5. In practice, one would use a more sophisticated term structure model than the binomial model such as the Hull-White, Black-Derman-Toy, Black-Karasinski, or Cox-Ingersoll-Ross interest rate models.
6. We give the C++ code later in the chapter.
7. Hull, J. (1996), pg. 391.
8. Fabozzi, F., Richard, S., and Horwitz, D. (2002), pp. 445. "Monte Carlo Simulation/OAS Approach to Valuing Residential Real Estate-Backed Securities" in *Interest Rate, Term Structure, and Valuation Modeling*, Wiley & Sons.
9. Id., pp. 445–446.
10. Id., pp. 445–446.
11. Id., pg. 446.
12. Id., pg. 453.
13. Obazee, P. (2002), pp. 315–344. See "Understanding the Building Blocks for OAS Models" in *Interest Rate, Term Structure, and Valuation Modeling.* Edited by Frank J. Fabozzi, Wiley & Sons.
14. Id., pg. 317.
15. Id., pg. 318.
16. Id., pg. 319.
17. Bandic, I., pg. 11.
18. The refinancing incentive and seasoning factor were previously discussed, but are now given analytical formula specifications based on Richard and Roll's (1989) empirical observations.
19. Formulas from Davidson/Herskovitz (1996).
20. Monthly parameters were taken from Figure 3 in Richard Roll (1989).
21. Fabozzi, F., Richard, S., and Horwitz, D. (2002), pg. 459. "Monte Carlo Simulation/OAS Approach to Valuing Residential Real Estate-Backed Securities" in *Interest Rate, Term Structure, and Valuation Modeling*, Wiley & Sons.
22. Id., pg. 454.
23. Fabozzi, F., Richard, S., and Horwitz, D. (2002), pg. 454.
24. Id., pg. 455.
25. The one-factor model has the capacity to describe the burnout effect of prepayment by embedding heterogeneity of prepayment behavior into the MBS valuation as a function of mortgage rates. In contrast, the three-factor model is based on discrete-time, no-arbitrage pricing theory, making an association between prepayment behavior and cash flow patterns where prepayment behavior is due to refinancing(caused by changes in interest rates) and

rising housing prices by incentive response functions. (See Kariya and Kabayashi, 2000, and Kariya, Ushiyama, and Pliska, 2002.)

26. Boudoukh, Richardson, Stanton, and Whitelaw (1995), pg. 1.
27. Id., pg. 1.
28. Id., pg. 1.
29. For a discussion of some of the problems associated with static hedges, see, for example, Breeden (1991) and Breeden and Giarla (1992). With respect to linear regression hedges in particular, Batlin (1987) discusses the effect of the prepayment option on the hedge ratio between MBSs and T-note futures.
30. Davidson and Herkowitz (1992) provide an analysis of the various theoretical methodologies for valuing MBSs in practice. The advantages and disadvantages of each approach are discussed in detail. With respect to the particular issue of hedging MBSs, Roberts (1987) gives an analysis, focusing primarily on model-based approaches to MBS valuation.
31. Id.
32. Id., pg. 2.
33. Id., pg. 3.
34. The TBA market is most commonly employed by mortgage originators who have a given set of mortgages that have not yet been pooled. However, trades can also involve existing pools, on an unspecified basis. This means that, at the time of the agreed-upon transaction, the characteristics of the mortgage pool to be delivered (e.g., the age of the pool, its prepayment history, and so on) are at the discretion of the dealer. Nonetheless, as long as new mortgages with the required coupon are being originated, these pools are likely to be delivered because seasoned pools are more valuable in the interest rate environment that characterizes a sample period. Thus, GNMA TBAs are best viewed as forward contracts on generic, newly issued, securities.

CHAPTER 4

COLLATERALIZED DEBT OBLIGATIONS

SECTIONS

In this chapter, we discuss the structured financial products of collateralized debt obligations (CDOs). In §4.1, we discuss the structure of CDOs. In §4.2, we discuss synthetic CDOs. In §4.3, we review the importance of balance sheet risk management with CDOs. In §4.4, we discuss the distribution of default losses on a portfolio. In §4.5, we look at the CDO equity tranche. In §4.6, we discuss CDO tranche pricing. In §4.7, we look at a pricing equation of a CDO tranche. In §4.8, we provide a simulation algorithm for CDO pricing. In §4.9, we provide a CDO pricing implementation in Matlab. In §4.10, we provide a CDO pricing implementation in C++ and give an example. In §4.11, we discuss CDO^2 (CDO of CDOs) pricing. In §4.12, we discuss fast loss calculation for CDO and CDO^2 using conditional normal approximations and provide a fast algorithm for computing CDO tranche loss in Matlab.

4.1 STRUCTURE OF CDOS

A collateralized debt obligation (CDO) is a diversified portfolio of illiquid and credit-risky assets such as high-yield bonds—e.g., collateralized bond obligations (CBOs)—and bank leverage loans—e.g., collateralized loan obligations (CLOs). A CDO might also include structured fixed income securities, distressed debt, emerging market debts, and commercial real estate-linked debt. The CDO is managed by a special purpose vehicle (SPV) company. CDOs are structured and packaged into tranches that have different risk and return characteristics based on their prioritization. The CDO tranche structure allocates interest income and principal prepayment from the pool of different debt instruments based on the tranche prioritization. Figure 4.1 shows a typical CDO structure.

Senior notes are paid before mezzanine and lower-rated notes. Thus, on every payment date, scheduled interest and principal debt payments are made first to the senior tranches, then to the mezzanine tranches, and then the lower-rated tranches. The equity tranche receives any remaining cash proceeds. The equity tranche is called the "first-loss" position in the collateral portfolio because it is exposed to the risk of the first dollar loss in the portfolio. The CDO receives a credit rating based on its ability to service debt with the cash flows generated by the underlying assets. The debt service "depends on the collateral diversification and quality guidelines, subordination, and structural production (credit enhancement and liquidity protection)."[1] As one moves down the CDO's capital structure, the level of risk increases. The equity holders incur the highest risk but have the option to call the transaction after the end of the non-call period, which in most cases lasts three to five years.

The typical CDO consists of a ramp-up period, during which the collateral portfolio is formed, a reinvestment period, during which the collateral portfolio is actively managed, and an unwind period, during which the liabilities are repaid in order of seniority using collateral principal proceeds. During the reinvestment phase, the "equity class distributions consist of excess interest on the full portfolio, minus collateral interest income remaining after the payment of debt interest and other fees." In the repayment period, excess interest payments gradually decrease as the collateral principal proceeds are used to repay the debt in order of seniority. After all the debt classes have been redeemed, and if the equity class has not elected to call the transaction, the remaining principal payments pass to the equity.[2]

A CDO collateralized by bonds is called a *collateralized bond obligation* (CBO), and a CDO collateralized by bank loans in called a *collateralized loan obligation* (CLO). In CBOs and CLOs, a note is issued by a trust or SPV as a claim against an underlying portfolio of bonds and bank loans, respectively. Often these notes are issued in multiple

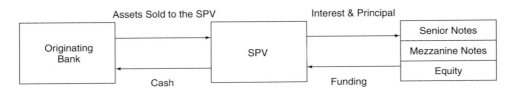

Figure 4.1 CDO structure. *Source: Picone, D. (2001), 15.*

tranches, based on different credit risk characteristics, varying from AAA to unrated equity, to investors with different investment objectives.

The risk of loss on the reference portfolio is divided into tranches based on seniority. Losses first affect the equity or "first-loss" tranche, then the "mezzanine" tranche, and then the "senior" and "super-senior" tranches. The mezzanine tranche is highly sensitive to business cycles and is typically investment-grade, while the super-senior tranches are senior to an AAA tranche.[3] CDO investors take on exposure to a particular tranche based on their risk appetite, effectively selling credit protection to the CDO issuer. The CDO issuer, in turn, hedges its risk by selling credit protection on the reference portfolio in the form of single-name credit default swaps. Parties on the other side of these hedging transactions are the ultimate sellers of credit risk to the CDO investor, with the CDO issuer acting as an intermediary.[4]

Figure 4.2 shows an example capital structure, where high-yield bonds collateralize CDO liabilities.

Most CDOs can be placed into either of two main groups: arbitrage and balance sheet transactions.[5] Arbitrage CDOs can be broken down into cash flow and market value CDOs, while balance sheet CDOs can be broken down into balance sheet cash flow CDOs. Throughout this chapter, we follow the direct work of Picone (2001), who explains the various types of CDOs (see also Lehnert, Altrock, Rachev, Trück, and Wilch [2005]).

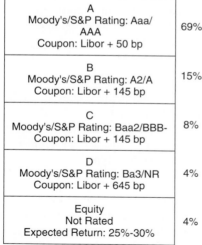

Figure 4.2 CDO collateral structure.   *Source: Picone, D. (2001).*

Cash Flow CDOs

A cash flow CDO is one where the collateral portfolio is not subjected to active trading and management by the CDO manager. The uncertainty concerning the interest and principal repayments is determined by the number and timing of the collateral assets that default. The payoffs of the note tranches are directly linked to the cash flows resulting from the underlying collateral portfolio. Losses due to defaults are the main source of risk as payoffs.

Market Value CDOs

A market CDO is one where the performance of the CDO tranches is primarily a mark-to-market performance—i.e., all securities in the collateral are marked to market with high frequency. Market value CDOs leverage the performance of the asset manager in the underlying collateral asset class. As part of normal due diligence, a potential CDO investor needs evaluate the ability of the manager, the institutional structure around him, and the suitability of the management style to a leveraged investment vehicle.

Balance Sheet Cash Flows CDOs

Balance sheet CDOs are structures for the purpose of capital relief, where the asset securitized is a lower yielding debt instrument. The capital relief reduces funding costs or increases return on equity, by removing from the balance sheet the assets that take too much regulatory capital. These transactions rely on the quality of the collateral that is represented by guaranteed bank loans with a very high recovery rate. The relative low coupon attached to these assets results in a smaller spread cushion than the corresponding arbitrary structure. However, given their relative superior quality, they require less subordination when used in a CDO deal. In the majority of the cases, the sold assets are loan-secured portfolios. The size of a typical balance sheet CDO is in general very large, as the transaction must have an impact on the ROE of the institution looking for capital relief.

Arbitrage CDOs

The goal of arbitrage CDOs is to capture the arbitrage opportunity that exists in the credit-spread differential, between high-yield collateral and high-rated notes. The idea is to create a collateral with a funding cost loan lower than the returns expected from the notes issued. Most arbitrage deals are private ones, where the size is not large and the number of assets included in the deal are very limited compared to the cash flow type.

Arbitrage Market Value CDOs

Arbitrage market value CDOs, unlike balance sheet CDOs where there is no active trading of loans in the portfolio, go through a very extensive trading by the collateral manager, necessary to exploit perceived price appreciations. The type of CDO relies on the market value of the pool securitized, which is monitored on a daily basis. Every security traded in capital markets, with an estimated price volatility, can be included in this type of CDO. In fact, the primary consideration is the price volatility of the underlying collateral. The important aspect is the collateral manager's capacity to generate high total rate of return. The CDO manager has a great deal of flexibility in terms of the asset included in the deal. During the revolver period, the collateral manager can increase or decrease the funding amount that changes the leverage of the structure.

Arbitrage Cash Flow CDOs

Collateral assets are typically purchased at market price and are negotiable instruments. Most of these assets are bonds. However, syndicated loans, usually tradable, have been included in past transactions. As arbitrage deals, the collateral assets can be refinanced more economically by retranching the credit risk and funding cost in a more diversified portfolio. Unlike arbitrage market value CDOs, collateral assets are not traded frequently.

Credit Enhancement in Cash Flow Transactions

Senior notes in cash flow transactions are protected by subordination, over-collateralization, and excess spread. The senior notes have a priority claim on all cash flows generated by the collateral; therefore, non-senior notes' performance is subordinated to the good performance of senior notes. Over-collateralization provides a further protection to senior notes by imposing a minimum collateral value with two coverage tests: par value and interest coverage tests. Par value tests require that the senior notes (and subsequently other notes) are a certain percentage of the underlying collateral (e.g., 110%). The par value test is applicable to lower-rated notes such as mezzanines. In this case, the trigger percentage, below which fails the test, is selected at a lower rate (e.g., 105%). An interest coverage test is applied to ensure that interest income is sufficient to cover losses and still make interest payment to the senior notes. This credit support is also known as excess spread.

Credit Enhancement in Market Value Transactions: Advance Rates and the Over-Collateralization Test

Advance rates are the primary form of credit enhancement in market value transactions. The advance rate is the maximum percentage of the market rate that can be used to issue debt. Rating agencies assign different advance rates to different types of collateral. They depend on the volatility of the asset return, and on the liquidity of the asset in the market. Assets with a higher return volatility and lower liquidity are given lower advance rates. Table 4.1 shows a sample table that Fitch would apply to different asset classes. For instance, it is possible to issue AA debt with 95% of the market value of CD or CP as collateral assets. To issue BB debt, one would have to use 100% of the market value of the same instrument.

For market value transactions, there are usually multiple over-collateralization tests. To illustrate how the test works, consider the collateral and liability structure of Table 4.2.

After applying the AA advance rates, Table 4.3 shows that the senior advance amounts exceeds the total AA debt, defined as borrowing amount surplus, by £28 million. This is the market value loss that the AA structure can sustain before breaching the over-collateralized (OC) test.

Tables 4.4 and 4.5 show the borrowing amount surpluses of the AA+BBB debt and the AA+BBB+B debt, respectively. As for Table 4.3, the borrowing surpluses of £23 and £25 million are the market value losses that the AA+BBB and AA+BBB+B structure can sustain before violating their OC tests, respectively.

Table 4.1 Fitch's Advance Rates

Asset Category	AA	A	BBB	BB	B
Cash and Equivalents	100%	100%	100%	100%	100%
CD and CP	95%	95%	95%	100%	100%
Senior Secured Bank Loans	85%	90%	91%	93%	96%
BB-High-Yield Debt	71%	80%	87%	90%	92%
< BB-High-Yield Debt	69%	75%	85%	87%	89%
Convertible Bonds	64%	70%	81%	85%	97%
Convertible Preferred Stock	59%	65%	77%	83%	86%
Mezzanine Debt, Distressed, Emerging Market	55%	60%	73%	80%	85%
Equity, Illiquid Debt	40%	50%	73%	80%	85%

Source: Fitch.

Table 4.2 CDO Market Value Transaction

Collateral			Notes			
Assets	Market Value Million Euro	%	Tranche	Rating	Face Value Million Euro	%
CD and CP	£230	46	Senior Facility	AA	£175	35
BB-High-Yield Debt	£225	45	Senior Notes	AA	£200	40
Convertible Bonds	£10	2	Mezzanine Notes	BBB	£50	10
Mezzanine Debt	£25	5	Subordinate Notes	B	£25	5
Equity	£10	2	Equity	NR	£50	10
Total	**£500**	**100%**	**Total**		**£500**	**100%**

Source: Picone, D., 5.

Table 4.3 AA Debt OC Test

Collateral				
Assets	Market Value (Million Euro)	Percent	AA Advance Rates	Senior Advance Amounts (Million Euro)
CD and CP	£230	46%	95%	£219
BB-High-Yield Debt	£225	45%	71%	£160
Convertible Bonds	£10	2%	64%	£6
Mezzanine Debt	£25	5%	55%	£14
Equity	£10	2%	40%	£4
Total	**£500**	**100%**		**£403**

Total AA Senior Debt Face Value (Senior Facility + Senior Notes): £375

Borrowing Amount Surplus: £28

Source: Picone, D., 6.

Table 4.4 AA+BBB Debt OC Test

Collateral

Assets	Market Value (Million Euro)	Percent	BBB Advance Rates	Senior Advance Amounts (Million Euro)
CD and CP	£230	46%	95%	£219
BB-High-Yield Debt	£225	45%	87%	£196
Convertible Bonds	£10	2%	81%	£8
Mezzanine Debt	£25	5%	73%	£18
Equity	£10	2%	73%	£7
Total	£500	100%		£448

Total AA+BBB Debt Face Value: £425

Borrowing Amount Surplus: £23

Source: Picone, D., 6.

Table 4.5 AA+BBB+B Debt OC Test

Collateral

Assets	Market Value (Million Euro)	Percent	B Advance Rates	Senior Advance Amounts (Million Euro)
CD and CP	£230	46%	100%	£230
BB-High-Yield Debt	£225	45%	92%	£207
Convertible Bonds	£10	2%	87%	£9
Mezzanine Debt	£25	5%	85%	£21
Equity	£10	2%	85%	£9
Total	£500	100%		£475

Total AA+BBB+B Debt Face Value: £450

Borrowing Amount Surplus: £25

Source: Picone, D., 6.

A collateral manager must ensure that the market value tests are not breached due to fluctuations in the underlying prices. A breach of the OC test is quite serious, and when it happens, the collateral manager must remedy it within a cure period that is usually between two to ten days. There are usually two options:

1. To sell securities with a lower advance rate and buy one/more with a higher advance rate.

2. To sell securities with a lower advance rate and repay the debt starting with more senior notes.

The first action is preferred when the OC test is slightly out of compliance. The second is a drastic cure. If the collateral manager cannot comply with the OC test, the debt holders have the power to take control of the fund and liquidate the portfolio in the event of default.

Minimum Net Worth Test

The minimum net worth test is also designated to offer credit protection to the senior noteholders, by creating an equity cushion. This is achieved by imposing that the excess market asset value (MAV), minus the debt notes, is equal to or greater than the equity face value, times a percentage:

$$MAV - Debt \geq \%^* Equity$$

In cases where the test fails, the manager has a cure period to bring the CDO into compliance, by either (1) redeeming part or all of the senior notes or (2) by generating enough capital gains by selling some assets. The latter is preferable because the manager would not de-leverage the deal. If the collateral manager cannot comply with the minimum net worth test, and an event of default occurs, the debt holders have the power to call the deal.

Figure 4.3 shows an actual CBO structure and termsheet for Iccrea Banca Spa that was transacted on March 22, 2004. The CBO was securitized by the Italian Co-operative Bank floating rate bonds. Table 4.6 shows the note structure.

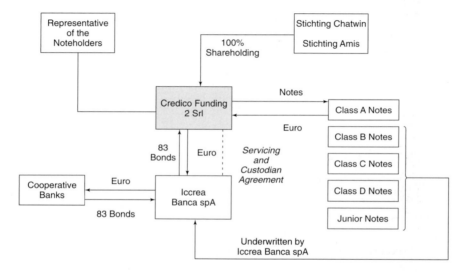

Figure 4.3 *Source: Iccrea Banca Spa CBO.*

Table 4.6 Note Structure

Class	Initial Principal Balance	Class Size	Rating	Spread Over 3m Euribor	Average Life	Expected Maturity Date	Legal Maturity Date
A	EUR [1.131] mn	[87.0]%	AAA	+25 bp	6.0 yrs	[Mar 2010]	[Mar 2012]
B	EUR [39] mn	[3.0]%	AA	+40 bp	6.0 yrs	[Mar 2010]	[Mar 2012]
C	EUR [65] mn	[5.0]%	A	+80 bp	6.0 yrs	[Mar 2010]	[Mar 2012]
D	EUR [26] mn	[2.0]%	BBB	+120 bp	6.0 yrs	[Mar 2010]	[Mar 2012]
E	EUR [39] mn	[3.0]%	NR	+300 bp	N/A	N/A	N/A

Transaction Characteristics

Credico Funding 2 Srl ("Credico 2") is the second securitization of Italian Co-operative Bank (BCC) assets. The first was launched in March 2002.

Credico is backed by a pool of 83 senior unrated, unsecured, and unlisted floating rate bonds ("the Bond Portfolio") issued on March 29, 2003 by 83 of the 462 Italian Co-operative Banks (BCCs). These were transferred to Credico Funding 2 Srl on April 15, 2004 for an aggregate purchase price of approximately € 1,200 million. Final maturity of each Bond in the Bond Portfolio is March 2010.

Credico 2 will issue six classes of notes, rated AAA, AA, A, and BBB. The mezzanine and junior notes will be underwritten by Iccrea.

All the tranches will carry a 20% risk weighting in Italy, according to Bank of Italy final confirmation.

Only Class A will carry a 20% risk weighting in the major European jurisdictions (i.e., Germany, UK, Ireland, Benelux, France, Spain, and Netherlands). Table 4.7 lists the parties involved in the transaction.

Table 4.8 provides the CDO transaction details.

4.2 SYNTHETIC CDOs

A synthetic CDO is constructed using credit default swaps rather than bonds or loans in the underlying portfolio. This gives the structure a much larger degree of flexibility because the credit risk is synthetically transferred out of the originators' balance sheet and into the SPV through a credit default swap while the underlying credit ownership of the underlying pool remains on the originator's book. In contrast to cash CDOs, where the tranche holder has made an initial investment, synthetic CDOs have no initial investment, and the value of the tranche can be positive or negative.[6] Moreover, in contrast to CBOs and CLOs, not all tranches of a synthetic CDO must be sold off in the form of notes. Assuming constant interest rates, a cash CDO tranche is equal to a synthetic CDO tranche, plus a cash amount equal to the remaining principal of the tranche.[7] Protection can also be purchased in the form of pure derivative transactions. The structure can be set up without the legally complicated transfer of loans as in most conventional cash flow CDOs; assets are actually transferred into the SPV. The structure is also not affected by peculiarities of the specification of the underlying loans or bonds. Within the class of corporate credit risk, synthetic CDOs tend to focus on either the investment-grade sector or the high-yield sector, though recently the range of collateral used in synthetic CDO transactions has included residential MBSs, commercial MBSs, CDO tranches (CDOs of CDOs), and other structured finance securities.[8]

The first synthetic CDO deals were done by banks in 1997.[9] These bank balance sheet deals were "motivated by either a desire to hedge credit risk, a desire to reduce regulatory capital, or both."[10] Following these early deals, the same synthetic CDO technology has been used to create CDO tranches with risk-return profiles that investors found attractive. These later deals, driven by the needs of credit investors rather than banks, are termed *arbitrage deals*.[11] In the early days of the synthetic CDO market (1997–1999), nearly all synthetic CDOs were motivated by balance sheet considerations. However, arbitrage deals have been growing rapidly and now account for a significant majority of market activity. Also, in the early days of the synthetic CDO market, deals included a complete set of tranches (equity, mezzanine, senior) whose notional amounts summed to the notional amount of the reference portfolio. Now, most synthetic CDO activity consists of "so-called single-tranche CDOs, where only one tranche of the CDO's capital structure is sold."[12]

Figure 4.4 shows the notional amount of synthetic CDO tranches issued from January 2002 to February 2004, broken down by collateral type. Over this time period, total issuance volume has grown rapidly and has averaged $37 billion per month.[13] Investment grade corporate debt is the most common collateral type. Structured finance is the second-largest collateral type and has been growing in importance as declining corporate credit spreads have reduced the attractiveness of corporate credit risk to investors. The relatively small amount of high-yield synthetic CDOs reflects "the lack of liquidity in the high-yield segment of the single-name credit default swap market."[14]

Table 4.7 The Parties to the Transaction

Issuer	Credico Funding 2 Srl, a special purpose vehicle established under the Italian Securitization Law 130/99
Seller	ICCREA Banca S.p.A. ("ICCREA")
Representative of the Noteholders	Bankers Trustee Company Limited
Servicer/Custodian/ Financing Bank	ICCREA Banca S.p.A.
Stichtingen	Stichting Chatwin and Stichting Amis are Dutch foundations (stichtingen) established under the laws of the Netherlands
Computation and Principal Paying Agent/Agent Bank	Deutsche Bank, AG, London
Italian Paying Agent/Account Bank	Deutsche Bank S.p.A.
Listing and Luxembourg Paying Agent	Deutsche Bank Luxembourg SA
Management Services Provider	SPV Management Limited
Corporate Services Provider	Deloitte Touche Tohmatsu Tax Services S.r.l.
Settlement	Monte Titoli/Euroclear/Clearstream
Listing	Luxembourg Stock Exchange
Arranger	ICCREA Banca S.p.A.
Advisor	Société Générale
Rating Agencies	Fitch Ratings, Moody's, and S&P
Joint Underwriters	Bank of America/CAI/Société Générale
Expected Launch Date	[April 19, 2004]
Expected Closing Date	[April 26, 2004]

Table 4.8 Transaction Structure (continued next page)

Collateral	Pool of [76] senior unrated and [7] senior rated by S&P, unsecured and unlisted floating rate bonds ("the Bond Portfolio") issued on [29 March 2004] by [83] of the 462 BCCs. These will be transferred to Credico 2 on [15th April 2004] for an aggregate purchase price of around €[1.200] million. Final maturity of each bond in the Bond Portfolio is March 2010.
Interest Rate	Class A Notes Interest is three-month EURIBOR plus [0.25] % p.a. Class B Notes Interest is three-month EURIBOR plus [0.40] % p.a. Class C Notes Interest is three-month EURIBOR plus [0.80] % p.a. Class D Notes Interest is three-month EURIBOR plus [1.20] % p.a. Class E Notes Interest is three-month EURIBOR plus [3] % p.a.
Interest Payment Date	The underlying bonds pay quarterly interest in arrears from [·] at a rate of 3M Euribor + [·] bp. The Notes will follow the same interest payment profile and will therefore be naturally hedged. The first Note interest payment date will be [·] (short first coupon), with subsequent dates being [·],[·],[·] every year.
Expected Redemption Date	The earlier of (i) the Interest Payment Date falling in [·] and (ii) the later of the Interest Payment Date immediately following the occurrence of the Cumulative Loss Event and the Interest Payment Date falling in [·].
Legal Maturity Date	[2013]
Redemption	Sequential bullet.
Credit Enhancement/ Liquidity	Subordination of B, C, D, and E tranches, and a liquidity reserve of up to [0.22]% of the initial Bond Portfolio amount (built up from excess spread in the first 15 months of the transaction, and replenished if used over the life of the transaction). In addition, over the life of the transaction, on any Interest Payment Date, a coupon of three-month EURIBOR plus [·] % p.a will be trapped and credited on an Additional Reserve Account in order to cover any shortfall of the Bond Portfolio.
Denomination:	EUR [100,000]
Governing Law of the Notes	[Italian]
Cumulative Loss Event	A Cumulative Loss Event occurs when the aggregate of the Principal Deficiencies recorded in previous collection periods exceeds [6%] of the initial principal amount of the Bond Portfolio.
Principal Deficiency	The difference between (i) the outstanding principal amount of a Defaulted Bond and (ii) its relative Recovery derived from the sale of this Defaulted Bond.
Reserve Amount	[0.22%] of the initial Bond Portfolio amount (built up from excess spread in the first 15 months of the transaction).

Table 4.8 Transaction Structure (continued next page)

Additional Reserve Amount	During the life of the transaction, the coupon due on the junior class will be trapped and credited on an Additional Reserve Account and released at the maturity date.
Eligible Investments	Any such euro-denominated senior debt securities or other debt instruments providing a fixed principal amount at maturity and issued/guaranteed by an institution whose debt obligations are rated not below the minimum ratings required by the Rating Agencies for this purpose.
Issuer Available Funds:	**Revenue Available Funds**

	i	Any indemnity received under the transaction documents;
	ii	Any collections in respect of interest on the Bond Portfolio;
	iii	Any balance standing to the credit of the Interest Account;
	iv	Any interest accrued on and credited to any of the Accounts; and
	v	Any amount resulting from the liquidation of Eligible Investments minus the Principal Funds Investments Amount and Reserve Funds Investments Amount (the "Revenue Eligible Investments Amount").

Principal Available Funds

	i	Any collections in respect of principal on the Bond Portfolio;
	ii	Any recovery derived from the sale of any Defaulted Bond (up until but excluding the Expected Redemption Date); the Principal Funds Investments Amount; and
	iii	Any balance standing to the credit of the Principal Account.

Pre-Enforcement Priority of Payments	**Revenue Available Funds** will be applied on each Interest Payment Date in making the following payments:

	i	All amounts due and payable to the Representative of the Noteholders;
	ii	a) All amounts due and payable to the other transaction parties, b) any other amounts to be paid in order to preserve the corporate existence of the Issuer, and c) any amount necessary to replenish the Expenses Reserve Account up to the Retention Amount (€[10,000]);
	iii	All amounts of interest due on the Class A Notes;
	iv	(Up until but excluding the Expected Redemption Date) to credit to the Principal Account an amount equal to the Class A Notes Principal Deficiency;
	v	Any amount due to the Financing Bank under the Letter of Undertaking;
	vi	All amounts of interest due on the Class B Notes;
	vii	(Up until but excluding the Expected Redemption Date) to credit to the Principal Account an amount equal to the Class B Notes Principal Deficiency;
	viii	All amounts of interest due on the Class C Notes;

Table 4.8 Transaction Structure (continued next page)

	ix	(Up until but excluding the Expected Redemption Date) to credit to the Principal Account an amount equal to the Class C Notes Principal Deficiency;
	x	All amounts of interest due on the Class D Notes;
	xi	(Up until but excluding the Expected Redemption Date) to credit to the Principal Account an amount equal to the Class D Notes Principal Deficiency;
	xii	(Up until but excluding the Expected Redemption Date) to credit to the Principal Account an amount equal to the Class E Junior Notes Principal Deficiency;
	xiii	To credit to the Reserve Fund Account amounts up until the balance equals the Reserve Amount or, as applicable, to replenish it to the Reserve Amount;
	xiv	To pay any monies due to Iccrea as seller of the Bonds pursuant to the terms of the Transfer Agreement;
	xv	To credit to the Additional Reserve Fund Account all amounts of interest due on the Class E Notes until the Maturity Date;
	xvi	At the Maturity Date, all amounts of interest due on the Class E Junior Notes credited on the Additional Reserve Fund Account;
	xvii	To credit any residual amount to the Principal Account.
		If on any Interest Payment Date, there are not sufficient Revenue Available Funds to make all payments due under (i) to (iv) above, until redemption in full of the Class A Notes, the Issuer shall on that Interest Payment Date, apply the amounts standing to the credit of the Reserve Fund Account and the Additional Reserve Fund Account toward such shortfalls.
Principal Available Funds		Prior to the Expected Redemption Date, the Principal Available Funds (except for Eligible Investments) will not be applied to make any payment on the Notes and will be invested in Eligible Investments.
Mandatory Redemption		On the Expected Redemption Date, and thereafter, on each Interest Payment Date, the Principal Available Funds will be applied by or on behalf of the Issuer in making the following payments (in each case, only if and to the extent that payments of a higher priority have been made in full):
	i	Principal on the Class A Notes until redemption in full of the Class A Notes;
	ii	Principal on the Class B Notes until redemption in full of the Class B Notes;
	iii	Principal on the Class C Notes until redemption in full of the Class C Notes;
	iv	Principal on the Class D Notes until redemption in full of the Class D Notes;

Table 4.8 Transaction Structure (continued)

	v	Principal on the Class E Junior Notes until redemption in full of the Class E Junior Notes;
	vi	The items (i) to (xvii) with the exclusions of items (iv), (vii), (ix), (xi), (xiii), and (xiv) of the Pre-Enforcement Priority of Payments—Revenue Available Funds, to the extent that there were not sufficient Revenue Available Funds; and
	vii	Retain any residual amount in the Principal Account.
Principal Deficiency		Principal Deficiency will arise only after the relative Recovery is collected and will be calculated immediately following the Collection Period when the recovery was collected.
		Such Principal Deficiency shall be allocated:
	i	To the Junior Notes up to the Principal Amount Outstanding of the Junior Notes;
	ii	To the Class D Notes if the Principal Deficiency is higher than the Principal Amount Outstanding of the Junior Notes and the Class E Notes, up to the Principal Amount Outstanding of the Class D Notes;
	iii	To the Class C Notes if the Principal Deficiency is higher than the Principal Amount Outstanding of the Junior Notes, the Class E Notes, and the Class D Notes, up to the Principal Amount Outstanding of the Class C Notes;
	iv	To the Class B Notes if the Principal Deficiency is higher than the Principal Amount Outstanding of the Junior Notes, the Class E Notes, the Class D Notes, and the Class C Notes, up to the Principal Amount Outstanding of the Class B Notes; and
	v	To the Class A Notes if the Principal Deficiency is higher than the Principal Amount Outstanding of the Junior Notes, the Class E Notes, the Class D Notes, the Class C Notes, and the Class B Notes, up to the Principal Amount Outstanding of the Class A Notes.
Optional Redemption		If the Issuer at any time satisfies the Representative of the Noteholders that (i) the Issuer would be required to deduct or withhold from the Principal or Interest owed to the Senior Notes any tax, duty, or charges (other than the above); or (ii) as a result of a change in law, it is or will become unlawful for the Issuer to perform or comply with any of its obligations in respect of the Notes or the Transaction Documents to which it is party, then the Issuer may redeem the Notes on any subsequent Interest Payment Date falling, at its option, after the first 18 months of the Transaction.

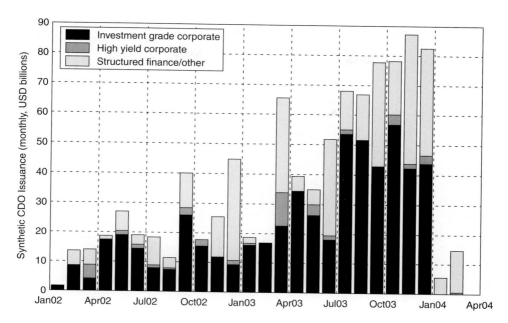

Figure 4.4   There are two types of synthetic CDOs: funded and unfunded.   *Source: Gibson, M. (2004), 2.*

Fully Funded Synthetic CDOs

In a fully funded synthetic CDO, the SPV issues notes for approximately 100% of the reference portfolio. The proceeds of these notes are generally invested in high-quality securities used as collateral that have a 0% risk weight. In order to hedge its risk exposure in its loan portfolio, the originating bank enters into a CDS with either the same SPV or with an OECD bank. With the CDS, the loan originator buys credit protection in return for a premium based on the credit quality of the obligor. The premium received is then added to the interest received by the note investors. Typically, in a funded CDO tranche, the CDO investor pays the notional amount of the tranche at the beginning of the deal, and any defaults cause a writedown (reduction) of the principal (of the tranche) until it is depleted. Throughout the deal, the investor receives LIBOR plus a spread that reflects the riskiness of the tranche. The investor's funds are put into a collateral account and invested in low-risk securities (government or AAA-rated debt).[15]

A schematic representation is shown in Figure 4.5 and Figure 4.6.

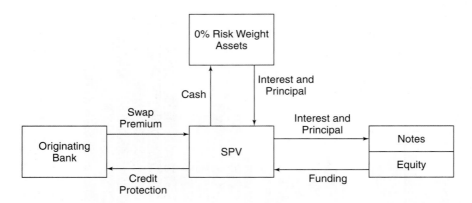

Figure 4.5 Fully funded synthetic CDO with CDS with an SPV.   *Source: Picone, D. (2001).*

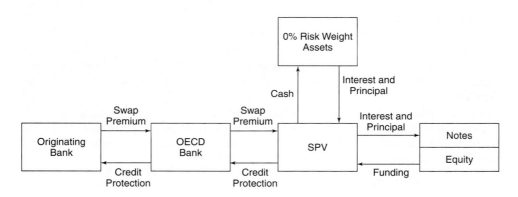

Figure 4.6 Fully funded synthetic CDO with CDS with an OECD bank.   *Source: Picone, D. (2001).*

The equity retained by the originator brings a 100% risk weight. Therefore, as with the structure in Figure 4.4, the originating bank would achieve a regulatory capital release of 6%. Additional regulatory capital required would depend on the presence of an OECD bank in the structure. If the CDS is transacted directly with the SPV (as in Figure 4.5), and if the note proceeds are invested in 0% risk weighted assets, no more regulatory capital is added to the transaction. If the CDS is directly with an OECD bank (as in Figure 4.6), the regulatory capital on the CDS is 1.6% (e.g., 20% * 8%) of the notional amount of the swap. If the CDS has a notional amount equal to reference portfolio, then the total regulatory capital charge of this transaction would be 3.6%.

Partially and Unfunded Funded Synthetic CDOs

In fully funded CDOs, the bank originator does not achieve efficient capital use given the regulatory capital requirements. A fully funded CDO-CLO can sometimes be a relatively expensive facility. However, it is also true that as *term funding* debt, a CDO-CLO structure remains less exposed to the risk that credit spreads may widen. A more efficient allocation of capital can be achieved with a partially funded CDO. The structure behind a partially funded CDO transaction is quite similar to that of a fully funded structure. The originator bank buys credit protection directly from an SPV (as in Figure 4.4) or from an OECD bank (as in Figure 4.5). The difference is that the SPV issues a lower amount of notes because it guarantees a lower amount of collateral. The unfunded portion, the super senior, characterizes this structure. The super senior is very high-quality commercial paper, with essentially no probability of loss exposure. The originating bank enters in a CDS (super senior CDS) with an OECD bank for the amount of the super senior portion. There is also a Junior CDS portion that can be transacted with either the SPV or an OECD bank.

Unfunded tranches are similar to swaps.[16] No money changes hands at the beginning of the deal. The investor receives "a spread and pays when defaults in the reference portfolio affect the investor's tranche (after any subordinate tranches have been eaten away by previous defaults)."[17] Because unfunded tranches rely on the investor's future ability and willingness to pay into CDOs, they create counterparty credit risk that must be managed.

Figures 4.7 and 4.8 illustrate the mechanics of the partially funded CDO.

The treatment of regulatory capital for European banks is currently different from jurisdiction to jurisdiction. In contrast, in the United States, the Federal Reserve Bank has issued several provisions that apply only to U.S. banks. Some conditions are necessary to receive better treatment of regulatory capital. If the conditions are met, and if the credit risk is transferred to another OECD bank with a CDS, the super senior tranche receives a risk weight of 20% with a capital charge of 8%.

The regulatory capital rules on the equity piece and on the junior CDS are the same as those applied on fully funded CDOs. Thus, the last step is to add the regulatory capital required on the funded and unfunded parts of the structure. If one applies those percentages to the portion of the super senior part (87%), the total regulatory capital is 3.4% (4% for the super senior CDS and 2% for the equity part).

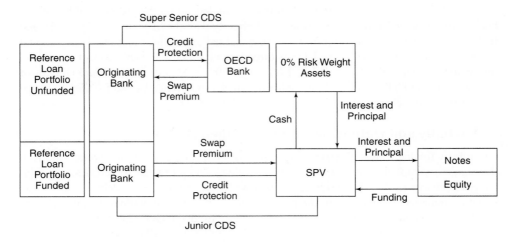

Figure 4.7 Partially funded synthetic CDO with CDS with an SPV. *Source: Investing in Collateralized Debt Obligations, Frank J. Fabozzi, Laurie S. Goodman.*

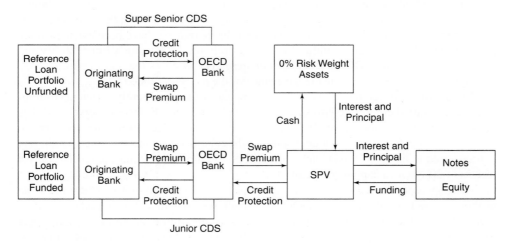

Figure 4.8 Partially funded synthetic CDO with CDS with an OECD bank. *Source: Investing in Collateralized Debt Obligations, Frank J. Fabozzi, Laurie S. Goodman.*

4.3 BALANCE SHEET MANAGEMENT WITH CDS

Banks seek the least expensive funding cost. Thus, many banks have a preference toward partially funded structures. Figure 4.9 makes a funding cost comparison between fully and partially funded CDO structures.

With the partially funded structure, a bank can achieve a reduction in the funding cost. In Figure 4.9, the bank has an overall transaction cost drop of 9 bps (34 bps–25 bps). Moreover, for one unit of equity used in the partially funded structure, the originator would pay 7.26 bps versus 17 bps for the fully funded structure.

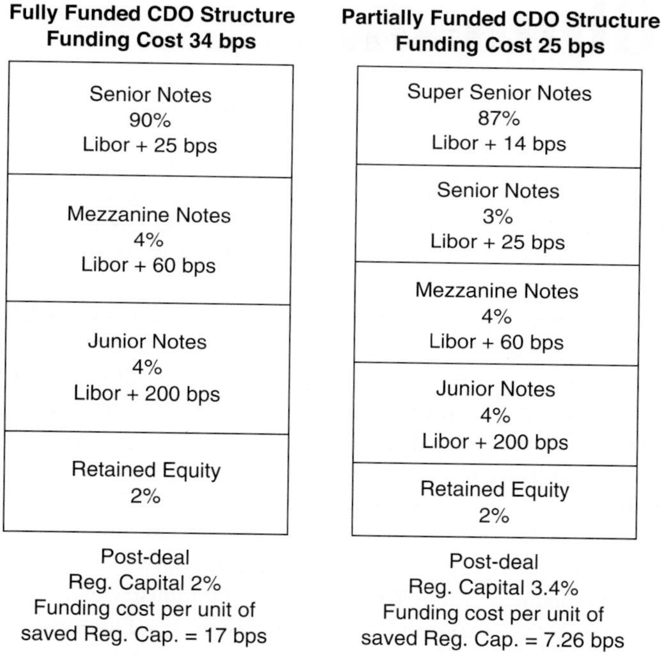

Fully Funded CDO Structure Funding Cost 34 bps	Partially Funded CDO Structure Funding Cost 25 bps
Senior Notes 90% Libor + 25 bps	Super Senior Notes 87% Libor + 14 bps
Mezzanine Notes 4% Libor + 60 bps	Senior Notes 3% Libor + 25 bps
Junior Notes 4% Libor + 200 bps	Mezzanine Notes 4% Libor + 60 bps
Retained Equity 2%	Junior Notes 4% Libor + 200 bps
	Retained Equity 2%
Post-deal Reg. Capital 2% Funding cost per unit of saved Reg. Cap. = 17 bps	Post-deal Reg. Capital 3.4% Funding cost per unit of saved Reg. Cap. = 7.26 bps

Figure 4.9 Funding costs with a fully and partially funded synthetic CDO.   *Source: Picone, D. (2001).*

4.4 THE DISTRIBUTION OF DEFAULT LOSSES ON A PORTFOLIO

Assume that all the loans in Figure 4.10 are Baa1 loans, with a maturity of six years, a cumulative default probability of 37%,[18] and a recovery rate of 65%. The expected loss on the portfolio is then (1-0.65)*0.37 = 0.0048 = 0.48%. Consequently, the expected losses have to rise by a factor of four before hitting the junior notes. Figure 4.10 shows the statistical distribution of losses that might occur in this transaction.

The CDO structure is free of any interest rate mismatch—i.e., it pays Libor and receives Libor. The average spread of 100 bps compensates the originating bank for taking the credit

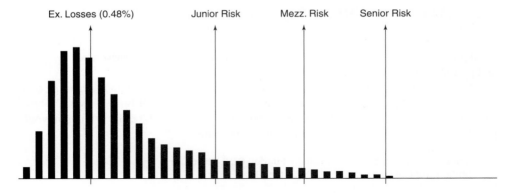

Figure 4.10 Distribution of Expected Losses. *Source: Picone, D. (2001).*

risk of expected losses on the underlying loan portfolio. The credit spreads, ranging from 25 to 200 bps, compensate note investors for taking different risks based on the risk exposure of the note tranche. Thus, we can remove the Libor and leave the spreads, as shown in Table 4.9.

In general, a CDS is designed to mimic the credit behavior of a floating rate note, such as the loans in Table 4.6. The loan spread, which is constant until the loan matures, is equivalent to the fixed leg of a CDS. In fact, the CDS seller, who seeks credit exposure, receives a spread of X basis point per year until the credit reference matures or defaults. Because the fixed leg of a CDS is a constant spread, we can remove the loans and add the CDS on the asset side, as shown in Table 4.10.

With the CDO in Table 4.10, the bank is now exposed to the credit risk of 50 synthetic assets. To hedge its position, the bank borrows via four different credit risk notes—e.g., super senior, senior, mezzanine, and junior tranches. Retaining the equity gives it the right to a possible dividend. Some of the loans in Table 4.10 may be in the industry and same country. Thus, it is safe to assume that they may be affected by the same risk factors. As a consequence, we may treat them as one loan with a notional equal to the sum of the notional of each loan. In other words, we can treat the CDO as a basket CDS with a reference pool of each loan as a credit exposure.

Table 4.9 CDO Structure with Hedged Interest Rate Risk

CDO Structure						
Assets	**%**	**Spreads**	**Liabilities**	**%**	**Spreads**
Loan 1	2%	100 bps	Super Senior Notes	87%	15 bps
Loan 2	2%	100 bps	Senior Notes	3%	25 bps
Loan 3	2%	100 bps	Mezzanine Notes	4%	80 bps
....	...	100 bps	Junior Notes	4%	200 bps
Loan 50	2%	100 bps	Retained Equity	2%	Dividend

Source: Picone, D. (2001), pg. 15.

Table 4.10 CDO Structure with Hedged Interest Rate Risk and with CDS in Place of Loans

Assets	%	Spreads	Liabilities	%	Spreads
		CDO Structure			
CDS 1	2%	100 bps	Super Senior Notes	87%	15 bps
CDS 2	2%	100 bps	Senior Notes	3%	25 bps
CDS 3	2%	100 bps	Mezzanine Notes	4%	80 bps
....	...	100 bps	Junior Notes	4%	200 bps
CDS 50	2%	100 bps	Retained Equity	2%	Dividend

Source: Picone, D. (2001), pg. 15.

Table 4.11 shows, on the asset side, a basket side with equal notional and a diversity score of 30, on a reference pool with an average rating of Baa1. The diversity score in Table 4.11 indicates that the 50 loans behave almost as 30 uncorrelated loans. Viewed from this perspective, a CDO is a hedged portfolio. The assets are a portfolio of synthetic loans, and the liabilities are tranches with different ratings. By hedging its balance sheet from credit risk (and from interest rate risk), the bank is trying to achieve a higher return than investing in risk-less treasury bonds. By partially funding the CDO structure, the bank has also achieved a leverage position, with potentially huge returns. However, the hedge is not perfect because the expected losses may erode equities up to the senior note tranche.

We follow Gibson (2004) in the following discussion of how to compute the distribution of default losses on a CDO portfolio (see also Vasicek (1987); Galiani (2003); and Gupton et al. (1997) for loss distribution computations). These approaches each utilize the general loss distribution computation of the CreditMetrics framework established by JP Morgan, which is based on the Merton model of pricing corporate debt.[19] To price or measure the risk of a synthetic CDO tranche, the probability distribution of default losses on the reference portfolio is a key input. The computation of the loss distribution can be done in an analytically tractable way. Assume that the correlation of defaults within the reference portfolio is driven by a common factor. One computes the loss distribution conditional on the factor, and then integrates out the factor to get the unconditional loss distribution. The approach described by Gibson (2004) synthesizes various research that tackle this problem

Table 4.11 CDO Structure with a Basket CDS

Assets	%	Spreads	Liabilities	%	Spreads
		CDO Structure			
pool of N		100 bps	Super Senior Notes	87%	15 bps
equal notional CDS		100 bps	Senior Notes	3%	25 bps
diversity score: 30		100 bps	Mezzanine Notes	4%	80 bps
average rating: Baa1		100 bps	Junior Notes	4%	200 bps
		100 bps	Retained Equity	2%	Dividend

Source: Picone, D. (2001), pg. 16.

in a similar way.[20] Each credit in the reference portfolio of $i = 1, ..., N$ credits is described by the following parameters:

A_1 Notational amount of credit i

$q_i(t)$ Risk-neutral probability that credit i defaults before t

R_i Recovery rate of credit i

Notional amounts are known quantities, risk-neutral default probabilities can be estimated using each credit's single-name credit default swap (CDS) spreads, and recovery rates are assumed known and constant. This analysis uses risk-neutral default probabilities and recovery rates derived from market spreads (in contrast to historical default probabilities or rating transition matrices). Creditworthiness is assumed to depend on a reference credit's normalized asset value x_i. Default occurs when x_i falls below a threshold $\bar{x}$. The asset value x_i is assumed to depend on a single common factor M:

$$x_i = a_i M + \sqrt{1 - a_i^2} Z_i \tag{4.1}$$

where x_i, M, and Z_i are mean-zero, unit-variance random variables with distribution functions F_i, G, and H_i. The random variables $M, Z_1, ..., Z_n$, are assumed to be independently distributed—i.e., Z_i $\Phi(0, 1)$. M denotes the normalized return of the systematic risk factor.

The factor loading a_i is constrained to lie between zero and one. One can view a_i as the correlation obligor i with the market factor. Denote the correlation of asset value between credits i and j is equal to $a_i a_j$. The default threshold $\bar{x}$ is equal to $F_i^{-1}(p_i(t))$. The conditional default probability $p_i(t|M)$, which in this setup can also be written as Prob$x_i < \bar{x}$ is equal to

$$p_i(t|M) = H_i\left(\frac{\bar{x}_i - a_i M}{\sqrt{1 - a_i^2}}\right) \tag{4.2}$$

using (4.1) or (4.2)

$$p_i(t|M) = H_i\left(\frac{F_i^{-1}(p_i(t)) - a_i M}{\sqrt{1 - a_i^2}}\right)$$

The distribution of losses on the reference portfolio takes on a discrete number of values. Each credit either takes no loss or a loss of $A_i(1 - R_i)$. If A_i and R_i are equal across credits, the number of discrete values will be equal to $N + 1$, corresponding to no defaults, one default, two defaults, and so on, up to N defaults. We assume that A_i and R_i are equal across credits and drop the i subscript for ease of notation. With this assumption, the distribution of losses and the distribution of the number of defaults become interchangeable; simply multiply the number of defaults by $A(1 - R)$ to get losses. If A_i and R_i are not equal across credits, the method described can still be used. However, the computational burden increases with the number of discrete values the portfolio's losses are distributed over. If the number of discrete values grows too large, it may be necessary to coarsen the loss distribution, as described by Andersen, Sidenius, and Basu (2003) to keep the number of discrete values down to a manageable size.

The distribution of the number of defaults conditional on the common factor M can be computed with the following recursion. Let $p^K(l, t|M)$ denote the probability that exactly l defaults occur by t, conditional on the common factor M, in a reference portfolio of size K. Assume we know the default distribution for a set of K credits:

$$p^K(l, t|M) \qquad l = 0, ..., K$$

Add one credit, with a conditional default probability $q_{K+1}(t|M)$. The default distribution for the new reference portfolio of $K + 1$ credits is:

$$
\begin{aligned}
&p^{K+1}(l, t|M) && (4.3)\\
&p^{K+1}(0, t|M) = p^K(0, t|M)(1 - q_{K+1}(t|M)) + p^K(l - 1, t|M)q_{K+1}(t|M)\\
&\quad l = 1, ..., K.\\
&p^{K+1}(K + 1, t|M) = p^K(K, t|M)q_{K+1}(t|M)
\end{aligned}
$$

Starting with the degenerate default distribution for $K = 0$, $p^0(0, t|M) = 1$, we can use the recursion (4.3) to solve for the default distribution for the reference portfolio of N credits:

$$p^N(l, t|M) \qquad l = 0, ..., N. \tag{4.4}$$

When we have the conditional default distribution, the unconditional default distribution $p(l, t)$ can be solved as

$$p(l, t) = \int_{-\infty}^{\infty} p^N(l, t|M)g(M)dM \tag{4.5}$$

where g is the probability density of M. The integral is calculated with numerical integration—e.g., Simpson's rule.

Because the functions $p(l, t|M)$ and $g(M)$ are typically smooth and well-behaved, numerical integration is straightforward and quite fast. For each t of interest, $N + 1$ numerical integrations are required, each requiring many evaluations of the recursion (4) for different values of M.[21] The calculation of the default distribution must be repeated for each date t on which a payment may occur (e.g., 20 payment dates for a five-year CDO with quarterly payments). At this point, it may be useful to give a numerical example of what a default probability distribution looks like. For the numerical example, let $N = 100$, the factor loading $a_i = \sqrt{0.3}$, the risk-neutral default probabilities equal $1 - e^{-0.01t}$ (default hazard of 1 percent per year), $t = 1$ year, and the common and idiosyncratic factors (M and Z_i) be normally distributed.

Under these assumptions, Table 4.12 shows numerical examples of conditional and unconditional default probability distributions. As the common factor M increases, moving to the right across the table, the weight of the distribution shifts toward fewer defaults. The unconditional distribution, which is computed by integrating out the common factor as in (4.5), can be interpreted as a weighted average of the conditional distributions, weighted by the relative probability of the different values of the common factor.

Table 4.12 Conditional and Unconditional Default Probability Distributions

Number of defaults	Conditional default distribution $p(l,t|M)$					Unconditional default distribution $p(l,t)$
	M = −2	M = −1	M = 0	M = 1	M = 2	
0	0.001	0.186	0.763	0.971	0.998	0.644
1	0.005	0.316	0.206	0.029	0.002	0.166
2	0.019	0.265	0.028	*	*	0.072
3	0.048	0.147	0.002	*	*	0.039
4	0.087	0.060	*	*	*	0.023
5	0.127	0.020	*	*	*	0.015
6	0.152	0.005	*	*	*	0.010
7	0.154	0.001	*	*	*	0.007
8	0.136	*	*	*	*	0.005
9	0.105	*	*	*	*	0.004
10	0.072	*	*	*	*	0.003
11	0.045	*	*	*	*	0.002
12	0.025	*	*	*	*	0.002
13	0.013	*	*	*	*	0.001
14	0.006	*	*	*	*	0.001
15	0.003	*	*	*	*	0.001
16	0.001	*	*	*	*	0.001
17	*	*	*	*	*	0.001
18	*	*	*	*	*	*
⋮	⋮	⋮	⋮	⋮	⋮	⋮
100	*	*	*	*	*	*

* = less than 0.001

Source: Gibson, M. (2004), pg. 7.

4.5 CDO EQUITY TRANCHE

The CDO equity tranche can be viewed as a hybrid security. It exhibits the features of a coupon bond, corporate equity, and a call option on the collateral and a managed fund. As a coupon bond, CDO equity is issued at or near par and has a final maturity date. As with convertible bonds, payments are not contractually specified, although the range of expected distributions is established at the time of issuance. In a similar way to a call option, the value of CDO equity increases with the price and volatility of the underlying assets. As with any actively managed investment, the contribution of the manager is a crucial determinant of CDO equity performance.

CDO Equity Tranche Performance

The equity of a CDO represents a leveraged investment in the underlying asset class and in the asset management skills of the CDO manager. The leverage is achieved by issuing investment and subinvestment grade debt as term asset-backed securities. Credit losses are the obvious drivers of the CDO equity tranche performance and can affect investors in two ways. First, as collateral shrinks because of defaults (in cash flow CDOs) or realized price deterioration (in market value CDOs), the amount of underlying assets reduces and with it the size of received interest payments. Second, if the par size of the collateral falls below a trigger point (OC and Interest Cover tests) specified by the rating agencies, the excess interest that normally passes to the equity holders is redirected to pay down the senior liabilities, thereby de-leveraging the CDO. Equity payments resume only after the ratio of collateral par to liabilities is restored above the trigger level. Redirection of equity distributions can also be triggered by a drop in the interest income relative to the interest cost of the transaction. In performing CDO transactions, the remaining interest that needs allocating to equities is equivalent to excess spread often in the range of 2.5% to 3%, implying a 25% to 30% running return on the equity.

The CDO Embedded Option

Depending on the collateral asset type and the timing of the transaction, the call option embedded in CDO equity may be quite valuable. Figure 4.11 shows the historical spread over Libor on the Goldman Sachs Single B Bond Index and the estimated cost of funding CDO liabilities—the wider the gap between the income from the assets and the cost of the liabilities, the greater the investment incentive for CDO equity. The upside from calling the transaction hugely depends on the type of collateral, making the distinction between CBO and CLO imperative.

Those CDOs where the collateral is represented by bonds purchased at low prices (when interest rates were high) and where the structure is financed through cheap term notes (current low interest rates) offer most benefit of a possibility of significant capital appreciation. Floating-rate collaterals such as leveraged loans can easily be refinanced. The underlying

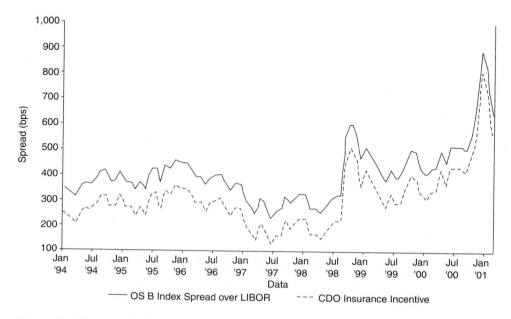

Figure 4.11 GS Single B Bond Index over Libor and bond-backed CDO issuance incentive. *Source: Picone, D. (2001), 22.*

borrowers can prepay outstanding loans and refinance at a lower spread. For this reason, a manager of a loan-backed CDO will be in a very difficult position to generate outsized capital appreciation. In other words, they do not offer as much potential for significant appreciation. As the remaining expected returns fall, the equity holders are likely to exercise their option during the repayment period, either to take advantage of potential appreciation in CBOs, or to minimize the impact of a difficult credit environment with CLOs.

The Price of Equity

The price of CDO equity is expected to have a natural downward path as soon as the principal begins to be redeemed. Figure 4.12 shows the cash flow profile of equity distributions over time for a CBO transaction. The distributions are per quarter. The same CBO is fully analyzed in the next article. We have created the example equity distributions under the assumption that the underlying collateral portfolio experiences a constant annual default rate of 3%. The equity distributions only receive interest until quarter 17. The remaining principal is received in the last four quarters. In generating this payment time path, we have assumed that the equity holders do not call the transaction. In reality, equity investors are likely to call a well-performing transaction when leverage falls, usually between six and eight years.

We expect the price of CDO equity to change over time. Other effects, such as changes in the value of the collateral portfolio, the value of the call option, and changes in the floating rates attached to the notes will also affect the price path of equity over time. Because the CDO equity is a call option on the collateral, we expect the CDO equity price to go down as final maturity approaches. The change in the floating rates affect the yield spread between the income from the collateral and the funding cost of the issued notes. An in-

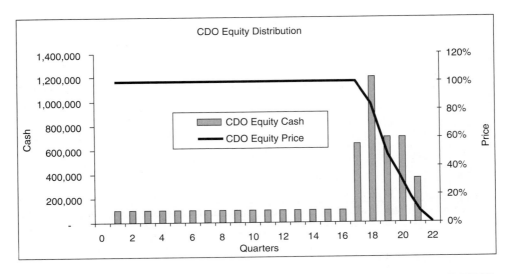

Figure 4.12 Price and Cash Distribution of a CDO equity tranche. *Source: Picone, D. (2001), 25.*

crease in the floating rates compresses the interest margin in the transaction that can be used to cover losses. Also, we can expect the leverage to affect the return profile of the equity piece. More highly leveraged deals have steeper return profiles. Figure 4.13 shows the returns of two CDO equity pieces with various loss rates: The more highly levered equity piece yields more until 6% losses but loses more after that. Besides, the deal with greater leverage would also have tighter OC levels, which would trigger sooner and deliver the structure. To generate the returns, we have used the same CDO structure as before.

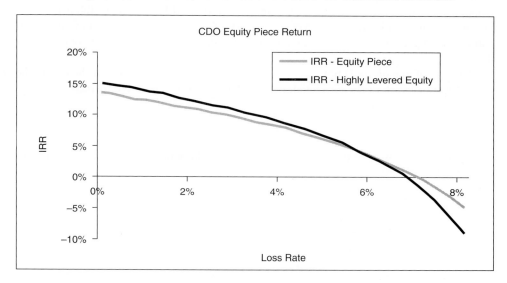

Figure 4.13 CDO equity investor return with different loss rate scenarios.   *Source: Picone, D. (2001), 25.*

Using Moody's Binomial Expansion Technique to Structure Synthetic CDOs

Moody's uses the Binomial Expansion Technique (BET) to determine the amount of credit risk present in the collateral. The BET reduces the actual pool of collateral assets with correlated default probabilities to a homogenous pool of assets with uncorrelated default probabilities via the diversity score. The diversity score D provides the number of uncorrelated bonds or loans that mimic the behavior of the original pool. For example, at maturity, one of the D bonds may or may not have defaulted—i.e., there are only two outcomes: default or nondefault. Furthermore, the probability that one particular bond defaults is independent on the probability that any other bond defaults. The consequence of such an assumption is the probability that N of the D bonds default can be calculated with the binomial distribution $P \sim Binomial(D, N, p)$:

$$P_N = \left(\begin{array}{c} D \\ N \end{array} \right) p^N (1-p)^{D-N} \tag{4.6}$$

where p is the average probability of default of the pool, stressed by the appropriate factor.

Once the collateral risk is calculated, it is compared to the credit protection offered by the structure to arrive at the correct rating of all CDO tranches. At default, the losses first hit the junior notes, then the mezzanine, and finally the senior notes. The calculation is performed via simulating the number of defaults that the transaction can experience through its life. Starting with the initial state of no default, each *homogeneous* bond is taken to its maturity through binomial branches of default with probability p and no default with probability $1 - p$. The expected loss that hits the CDO structure is calculated and mapped against the Moody's Idealized Cumulative Expected Losses in the Table 4.13. For example, from a collateral with average maturity of five years, the maximum amount of cumulative expected loss for an *Aaa* senior note with the same maturity must not be greater than 0.002%.

The loss of one of the D homogeneous assets defaulting is calculated as the loss in the present value of cash flows associated with the defaulted bond, adjusted by recovery.

The probability of this event is:

$$EL_1 = P_1 * L_1 \tag{4.7}$$

The expected losses of the pool are calculated by taking the sum of all losses under all the scenarios, $N = 0, 1, 2, \ldots, D$

$$EL = \sum_{N=0}^{D} P_N * L_N \tag{4.8}$$

and the unexpected losses are

$$UL = \sum_{N=0}^{D} P_N * (L_N - EL)^2 . \tag{4.9}$$

Thus, to use the BET, we need to calculate the following collateral variables: the default probability, the losses, and the diversity score.

Occasionally, the collateral pool may be made of two (or more) highly uncorrelated assets, having different average properties. Moody's models this case with a variation of the BET called Double BET. With the Double BET, ones approaches the two pools as two independent pools. In this case, the probability that a assets in pool A, and b assets in pool B default, are two independent events distributed as $P \sim Binomial(D_A, D_B, N_A, N_B, p_A, p_B)$:

$$P_{a+b} = \left(\begin{array}{c} D_a \\ a \end{array} \right) p_A^a (1 - p_A)^{D_a - a} \left(\begin{array}{c} D_b \\ b \end{array} \right) p_B^b (1 - p_B)^{D_b - b} \tag{4.10}$$

The loss of having $a + b$ defaults can be calculated as the present value of the cash flows associated to those $a + b$ defaulted bonds, over the present value of all cash flows.

The expected losses of the combined pool is calculated by taking the sum of all the expected losses under all the scenarios, $a + b = 0, 1, 2, ..., N_A + N_B$.

$$EL = \sum_{i=0}^{D_a} \sum_{j=0}^{D_b} P_{ij} L_{ij} \tag{4.11}$$

Table 4.13 Moody's Idealized Cumulative Expected Losses

	Year									
	1	2	3	4	5	6	7	8	9	10
Aaa	0.000%	0.000%	0.000%	0.001%	0.002%	0.002%	0.003%	0.004%	0.005%	0.006%
Aa1	0.000%	0.002%	0.006%	0.012%	0.017%	0.023%	0.030%	0.037%	0.045%	0.055%
Aa2	0.001%	0.004%	0.014%	0.026%	0.037%	0.049%	0.061%	0.074%	0.090%	0.110%
Aa3	0.002%	0.010%	0.032%	0.056%	0.078%	0.101%	0.125%	0.150%	0.180%	0.220%
A1	0.003%	0.020%	0.064%	0.104%	0.144%	0.182%	0.223%	0.264%	0.315%	0.385%
A2	0.006%	0.039%	0.122%	0.190%	0.257%	0.321%	0.391%	0.456%	0.540%	0.660%
A3	0.021%	0.083%	0.198%	0.297%	0.402%	0.501%	0.611%	0.715%	0.836%	0.990%
Baa1	0.050%	0.154%	0.308%	0.457%	0.605%	0.754%	0.919%	1.085%	1.249%	1.430%
Baa2	0.094%	0.259%	0.457%	0.660%	0.869%	1.084%	1.326%	1.568%	1.782%	1.980%
Baa3	0.231%	0.578%	0.941%	1.309%	1.678%	2.035%	2.382%	2.734%	3.064%	3.355%
Ba1	0.488%	1.111%	1.722%	2.310%	2.904%	3.438%	3.883%	4.340%	4.780%	5.170%
Ba2	0.858%	1.909%	2.849%	3.740%	4.626%	5.374%	5.885%	6.413%	6.958%	7.425%
Ba3	1.546%	3.030%	4.329%	5.385%	6.523%	7.419%	8.041%	8.641%	9.191%	9.713%
B1	2.574%	4.609%	6.369%	7.618%	8.866%	9.840%	10.522%	11.127%	11.682%	12.210%
B2	3.938%	6.419%	8.553%	9.972%	11.391%	12.458%	13.206%	13.833%	14.421%	14.960%
B3	6.391%	9.136%	11.567%	13.222%	14.878%	16.060%	17.050%	17.909%	18.579%	19.195%
Caa	14.300%	17.875%	21.450%	24.134%	26.813%	28.600%	30.388%	32.174%	33.963%	35.750%

and the unexpected losses

$$UL = \sum_{i=0}^{D_A} \sum_{j=0}^{D_B} P_{ij} \left(L_{ij} - EL \right)^2 \qquad (4.12)$$

Default Probability

The default probabilities are calculated using the ratings of the collateral assets. When public ratings are not available, Moody's determines *shadow* ratings. The default probabilities are then adjusted by taking into account the underlying asset maturities to give the cumulative default probabilities. The collateral cumulative default probability is calculated as the weighted average of the assets cumulative default probabilities where the weights are the assets par values:

$$CDP = \frac{\sum\limits_{N=0}^{M} CP_N \cdot A_N}{\sum\limits_{N=0}^{M} A_N} \qquad (4.13)$$

where

CP_N is the cumulative default probability of bond N.

A_N is the par value of bond N.

M_N is the total number of assets.

Loss Severity

Loss severity depends on the assumed recovery value and time of recovery. Moody's assumes that the recoveries are not affected by the asset rating, but they depend on the seniority and security of the obligation. Moody's also assumes that the base case recovery rate is a minimum of 30% of the market value or 25% of par value. For emerging markets, the recovery rates drop to a minimum of 20% of the market value or 15% of par value. Historical recovery rates for various loan tranches are given in Table 4.14.

Table 4.14 Recovery Rates Used by Moody's for Different Seniority

Loan/Bond	Recovery Rates
Senior Secure Loans	70%
Senior Unsecured Loans	-
Senior Secured Bonds	52%
Senior Unsecured Bonds	49%
Subordinated Bonds	33%

Source: Picone (2001)

Diversity Score

Moody's has solved the problem of estimating default correlation through the diversity score. This measures the number of uncorrelated assets in the pool that would experience the level of default in the original pool. Because default correlation is higher in poorly diversified portfolios, a low diversity score value is a sign of a riskier portfolio. To calculate the diversity score, the industry classifications are used. The industry concentrations are calculated using bond par values as weights. After the concentration is measured, the diversity score is calculated by using the values of Table 4.15 in the "Diversity Score" column.

Moody's also distinguishes diversity scores for bonds originated in emerging markets from all other regions. From Table 4.12, a pool of four EM bonds have a diversity score of two, whereas with the same number of U.S. high-yield bonds, the diversity score is three. To arrive at the Latin America Diversity Score, the following adjustment is used: $LADS = 1 + (DS - 1) * 0.5$.

Table 4.15 Diversity Score

Number of Bond Issuers per Industry/Region	Diversity Score	Diversity Score for Latin America
1.00	1.00	1.00
1.50	1.20	1.10
2.00	1.50	1.25
2.50	1.80	1.40
3.00	2.00	1.50
3.50	2.20	1.60
4.00	2.30	1.65
4.50	2.50	1.75
5.00	2.70	1.85
5.50	2.80	1.90
6.00	3.00	2.00

Source: Picone (2001).

Correlation Risk of CDO Tranches

As Gibson states, the pricing of CDO tranches "reflects investors' expectation of the correlation of defaults in the reference portfolio throughout the life of the CDO.[22]" Market quotes of CDO tranches constitute a market view on correlation at different points in the portfolio capital structure and thus on the shape of the portfolio loss distribution. Because this correlation is unobservable, CDO tranches are exposed to correlation risk. Figure 4.14 shows how the mark-to-market value of the three hypothetical stylized CDO tranches varies with the correlation among the credits in the reference portfolio of $N = 100$ credits (assuming asset correlation across credits of 0.3 and using the par spreads in Table 4.16, revaluating each tranche as the asset correlation across credits various between 0 and 0.9).

Table 4.16

Tranche	Attachment points (percent)	Notional amount ($ millions)	Par spread (basis points)
Equity	0–3	30	1507
Mezzanine	3–10	70	315
Senior	10-100	900	7
Entire portfolio	0–100	1,000	60

Source: Gibson, M. (2004), pg. 11.

A higher correlation of defaults implies a greater likelihood that losses will wipe out the equity and mezzanine tranches and inflict losses on the senior tranche.[23] Thus, the value of the senior tranche falls as correlation rises. Conversely, higher correlation also makes the extreme case of very few defaults more likely. Thus, the value of the equity tranche rises as correlation rises. Equity tranche investors gain more in a scenario with very few defaults than they lose from a scenario with many defaults. (They are only exposed to the first few defaults.)[24] Mezzanine tranches are subject to both effects, which can broadly cancel each other out and make mezzanine tranches less sensitive to correlation, as shown in Figure 4.14. Correlation effects are particularly strong for some of the most recent innovations in credit markets, including single-tranche CDOs and first-to-default basket swaps (discussed in Chapter 5, "Credit Derivatives").

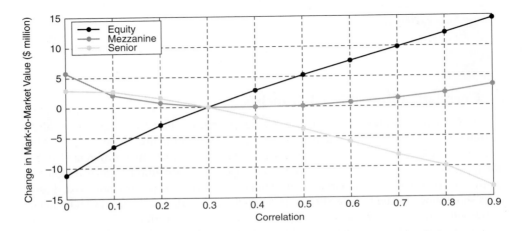

Figure 4.14 *Source: Gibson, M. (2004), 19.*

In order to obtain the default correlation between two obligors i, j, we can use the general correlation formula for two random variables:

$$
\begin{aligned}
Corr(x_i, x_j) &= \frac{Cov(x_i, x_j)}{\sqrt{\mathrm{var}(x_i)\,\mathrm{var}(x_j)}} \\
&= \frac{E(x_i x_j) - E(x_i)E(x_j)}{\sqrt{p_i(1 - p_i)}\sqrt{p_j(1 - p_j)}} \\
&= \frac{p_{ij} - p_i p_j}{\sqrt{p_i(1 - p_i)}\sqrt{p_j(1 - p_j)}}
\end{aligned}
$$

where x_i is a Bernoulli random variable with mean p_i and standard deviation $\sqrt{p_i(1 - p_i)}$. The joint probability of default of the two obligors, p_{ij}, can be derived from the joint distribution of asset returns. The value of p_i can be derived from equation (4.2).

There are two measures of implied correlation: compound and base correlations. In the compound correlation approach, each tranche is considered separately. A pricing model is chosen, and each tranche is priced using a single (flat) correlation number as input to the pricing model.[25] By an iteration process, the compound correlation can be determined as the input correlation number, which produces a spread that is equal to the market quote.[26] One drawback of the compound correlation method is that it does not "produce unique solutions, since the compound correlation is a function of both the upper and lower attachment point of the tranche."[27]

The base correlation approach, proposed by JP Morgan, in contrast to compound correlations, considers the value of several tranches simultaneously by applying a bootstrapping process.[28] Consider a tranched credit product with upper attachment points $K_j, j = 1, ..., n$. Let ρ_{K_j} denote the base correlation of a tranche with upper attachment point K_j. The expected loss of the first equity tranche $EL_{\rho_{K_1}}(0, K_1)$ is already traded in the market, as well as the expected losses of the nonequity tranches $EL(K_1, K_2)$, $EL(K_2, K_3)$, ... The expected losses of the other equity tranches are calculated by bootstrapping

$$
EL_{\rho_{K_2}}(0, K_2) = EL_{\rho_{K_1}}(0, K_1) + EL(K_1, K_2)
$$
$$
EL_{\rho_{K_2}}(0, K_3) = EL_{\rho_{K_1}}(0, K_2) + EL(K_2, K_3)
$$

and so on. According to McGinty and Ahluwalia (2004), base correlation is defined as "the correlation inputs required for a series of equity tranches that give the tranche values consistent with quoted spreads, using the standardized large pool model."[29] For a discussion of base correlation, see Willemann (2004).

For an examination of correlation modeling and implied correlation calibration of the CreditRisk+ (CR+) model (of Credit Suisse First Boston [1997]) to reproduce iTraxx Europe tranche quotes, see Lehnert, Altrock, Rachev, Trück, and Wilch (2005). Lehnert, Altrock, Rachev, Trück, and Wilch find that using initial parameters, CR+ produces much less heavy tails compared to the losses of the senior tranches traded in the market.

Consequently, they conclude that in order to reproduce such quotes, parameters of CR+ have to be adjusted such that a loss distribution with fatter tails is produced.

4.6   CDO TRANCHE PRICING

CDOs can be used to price using the copula framework given the dependence structure (e.g., Gaussian and Student's t copulae) affects pricing results. We follow Galiani (2003) in the following discussion (see also Gibson (2004) and Gregory and Laurent (2002) for CDO pricing discussions).

We define the notion used in the pricing:

- n is the number of reference entities included in the collateral pool.

- N_i is the notional amount of the i-th reference obligation.

- R_i is the deterministic recovery rate of the i-th reference obligation.

- $T = t_n$ is the legal maturity of the contract, measured in years, from the current time $t_0 = 0$.

- τ_i is the default stopping time for the i-th obligor, which is the time of the first jump of a Cox process n with intensity $\lambda_i(t)$.

- $D(0, t)$ is the risk-free discount rate (assumed to be deterministic).

- s is the fair price of the CDO tranche, expressed in basis points per annum, as a fraction of the outstanding tranche notional.

We denote $L_i = (1 - R_i)N_i$ and $Q_i(t) = 1_{\tau_i < t}$ as the loss given default and the default indicator, respectively, at time t of the i-th obligor. The default indicator is equal to one if $\tau_i < t$ and zero otherwise. We define the accumulated loss $L(t)$ on the collateral portfolio as:

$$L(t) = \sum_{i=1}^{n} L_i Q_i(t) = \sum_{i=1}^{n} L_i 1_{\{\tau_i < t\}} \tag{4.14}$$

The distribution of losses between noteholders will vary according to the seniority of the tranches. Let A and B be the lower and upper triggers, respectively, such that the default leg of a tranche will be given by the contingent stream of payments, due to the losses incurred in the collateral pool, above the threshold A and below B. A and B are called the *attachment point and de-attachment points* of the tranche, respectively—the points at which losses can be incurred by the tranche between A and B. For instance, in a three-tranche CDO, if the tranche defined between A and B is the mezzanine tranche, then losses below A belong to the equity tranche and those above B belong to the senior tranche. Thus, the seniority of the tranche is defined by the relative location of the two attachment points, A and B. If A = 0, then it is called the *equity* tranche; if $A > 0$ and $B < \sum_{i=1}^{n} N_i$, it is called the *mezzanine* tranche; and if $B = \sum_{i=1}^{n} N_i$, it is called the *senior* tranche.

Therefore, the cumulative loss $L^{A,B}(t)$ on a given tranche, will be zero if $L(t) < A$, equal to $L(t) - A$ if $A \le L(t) < B$, and $B - A$ if $L(t) \ge B$. More formally, we have:

$$L^{A,B}(t) = (L(t) - A)1_{\{A,B\}}L(t) + (B - A)1_{\left\{B, \sum_{i=1}^{n} N_i\right\}}L(t) \tag{4.15}$$

4.7   PRICING EQUATION

Like the analysis for pricing basket default swaps, the fair price of a CDO tranche is defined by the equivalence of the default (DL) and premium (PL) legs.

Using the representation given by Laurent and Gregory (2002), we can express the default leg as the expected value of the default payments stream discount from the time of default:

$$DL = E^* \left[\int_0^T D(0,t) dL^{A,B}(t) \right] \tag{4.16}$$

The premium leg can be written as the expectation of present value of the premium payments, weighted by the outstanding capital (original amount minus accumulated losses) at each payment date, to be paid $1/\alpha$ times[30] per year:

$$PL = E^* \left[\alpha \sum_{i=1}^n s_{A,B} D(0,t_i) \min \left\{ \max \left[B - L(t_i), 0 \right], B - A \right\} \right] \tag{4.17}$$

In equation (4.17), we note that, in case of no defaults in the collateral pool (or, up to a number of defaults such that the accumulated losses are less than A), the discounted premium is weighted to the total notional amount of the tranche; in case of losses between A and B, the reference nominal amount is accordingly reduced, until being equal to 0, when the cumulative losses exceed the upper attachment point B.

The fair price of the CDO tranche is then defined to be spread $s_{A,B}^*$ such that

$$s_{A,B}^* = PL(s_{A,B}^*) - DL(s_{A,B}^*) = 0$$

and thus

$$s_{A,B}^* = \frac{E^* \left[\int_0^T D(0,t) dL^{A,B}(t) \right]}{E^* \left[\alpha \sum_{i=1}^n D(0,t_i) \min \left\{ \max \left[B - L(t_i), 0 \right], B - A \right\} \right]}. \tag{4.18}$$

Despite the compactness of the preceding formula, the computational effort needed to determine the distribution of the accumulated losses and, therefore, the spread s^*, is quite involved, as the next section explains.

4.8   SIMULATION ALGORITHM

Monte Carlo simulation can be used to estimate the loss distribution of the collateral pool of a CDO and its reflection in computing the fair spread $s_{A,B}^*$ of a tranche with lower and upper loss attachment and de-attachment points given by A and B, respectively. The first part of the pricing procedure is similar to price default basket swaps. Furthermore, given the high-dimensionality of the problem (collateral pools with at least 50 reference entities), a variance reduction technique is highly recommended in order to lower the number of simulations required for convergence. The procedure can be summarized as follows:

1. For each reference entity, calibrate the parameters of the default time distribution function by computing the implied default intensities $\lambda_n(t)$ for $t = T_1, T_2, ..., T_M$ being the set of expiry dates of credit default swaps available in the market.

2. Calibrate the parameters of the copula function chosen for modeling the dependence among the obligors in the pool (see Chapter 2, "Copula Functions," §2.4).

3. For each simulation k, repeat the following routine:

    (a) Generate an n-dimensional vector of correlated uniform random variables using the algorithms presented in Chapter 5, §5.9.2.

    (b) For each obligor, translate the corresponding uniform variate into a default time using the procedure presented in Chapter 5, §5.9.3.

    (c) Sort the n-dimensional vector of default times, τ^k, in ascending order, and select the vector of default times $\Gamma^k = \{\tau_1^k, \tau_2^k, ..., \tau_n^k\}$ such that $\tau_j^k \leq T \,\forall\, j \in \{1, 2, ..., n\}$.

    (d) Calculate the stream of contingent default payments according to the following routine:

        i. Based on the specific realization of the vector Γ^k, compute the accumulated loss in the collateral pool by calculating $L^k(t)$, as described in equation (4.1).

        ii. If $L^k(T) < A$, the default payments are set equal to 0.

        iii. If $A \leq L^k(t) < B$, select the default trigger time $\tau_a^k = \inf\{t > 0 | L(t) \geq A\}$, and for each defaulter $\ell \in \{1, 2, ..., L\}$ whose default time is greater than or equal to τ_a^k, compute the obligor's discounted default payment DP_w^k, namely, given the collection of default times $\Gamma_{A,B}^k = \{\tau_a^k, \tau_{a+1}^k, ..., \tau_L^k\}$, compute $DP_w^k = D(0, \tau_w^k)L_w = D(0, \tau_w^k)(1 - R_w)N_w$ for $w \in \{a, a+1, ..., L\}$ and, finally, sum over all the specified defaulters—that is,

        $$DP^k = \sum_{w=a}^{L} DP_w^k.$$

        If $L^k(T) \geq B$, select τ_a^k as described previously, and calculate the upper default trigger time $\tau_b^k = \inf\{t > 0 | L(t) \geq B\}$. Then, for each defaulter $\ell = \{1, 2, \ldots, L\}$ whose default time is greater than or equal to τ_a^k and less than τ_w^k, compute the discounted default payment DP_w^k, namely, given the collection of default times $\Gamma_{A,B}^k = \{\tau_a^k, \tau_{a+1}^k, \ldots, \tau_b^k\}$, compute $DP_w^k = D(0, \tau_w^k)L_w = D(0, \tau_w^k)(1 - R_w)N_w$ for $w \in \{a, a+1, ..., b\}$ and, finally, sum over all the specified defaulters—that is, $DP^k =$

        $$\sum_{w=a}^{b} DP_w^k.$$

    (e) Calculate the premium leg according to the following routine:

        i. Based on the specific realization of the vector Γ^k, for each one of the premium dates $\{t_1, t_2, \ldots, t_n\}$, compute the accumulated loss $L^k(t_i)$ for $i \in \{1, 2, \ldots, n\}$ and then calculate the premium leg

$$PL^k = \alpha \sum_{i=1}^{n} D(0, t_i) \min \left\{ \max \left[B - L^k(t_i), 0 \right], B - A \right\}.$$

4. Calculate the arithmetic average of DP^k and PL^k and apply equation (4.5) to determine the fair spread $s^*_{A,B}$.

4.9 CDO PRICING IN MATLAB[31]

The following Matlab functions are used for pricing CDO tranches. CDO_tranche.m prices the tranche and generates the default times by calls to gaussian_time.m and generates discounted cash flows in cash_flow.m.

CDO_tranche.m

```
function [price_eq,price_mezz,price_sen]=CDO_tranche(ref_ent,T,k)

% this function computes the fair price of a synthetic CDO tranched in three
% portions, 0-3%, 3-14% and 14%-100%. Spread for each reference entity is
% fixed @ 150 bps. We let recoveries and pairwise correlation changing in
% order to produce a chart of CDO breakeven spread vs. correlation &
% recovery.

% Inputs:

% ref_ent:   # of reference entities in the pool
% T:         # maturity of the deal
% k:         # of simulation


tic
%inizialize a vector of zeros for each of the three tranches
CDO_P1=zeros(5,5);
CDO_P2=zeros(5,5);
CDO_P3=zeros(5,5);
%inizialize a vector of zeros for different recoveries
Recovery =zeros(ref_ent,5);
hazard=zeros(5,1);
% set the obligors' spread to 150bps p.a.
spread =150/10000;

% since the CDS term structure is flat, the relationship hazard
% rate=spread/(1-recovery) holds. Therefore, for each recovery we calculate
% the corresponding hazard rate.
for rec_cycle=1:5
    Recovery(:,rec_cycle)=(.2*rec_cycle)-.2; % recovery ranges from
                                             % 0% to 80%
    hazard(rec_cycle)=spread/(1-Recovery(1,rec_cycle));
end

ZC=0.05; % constant interest rate

Amount=zeros(ref_ent,1); %vector of notional amount for each credit
```

```
Amount(:)=100; % each credit has a notional amount of 100 units
C=zeros(3,1); % we fix three attachment points: 0%,3%,14%
D=zeros(3,1); % we fix three detachment points: 3%,14%,100%
C(1)=(0/100)*sum(Amount);
D(1)=(3/100)*sum(Amount);
C(2)=(3/100)*sum(Amount);
D(2)=(14/100)*sum(Amount);
C(3)=(14/100)*sum(Amount);
D(3)=(100/100)*sum(Amount);

time=zeros(ref_ent,1);
index=zeros(ref_ent,1);

R=[0:.2:0.8]; %constant pairwise correlation ranges from 0% to 80%
% start the correlation loop
for R_cycle=1:5
    for xx=1:ref_ent
        for yy=1:xx
            if xx==yy
                corr(xx,yy)=1;
            else
                corr(xx,yy)=R(R_cycle); %populate the correlation matrix
                corr(yy,xx)=R(R_cycle);
            end
        end
    end
    def_t=gaussian_time(corr,k,ref_ent); % generate pseudodefault times
                                         % with gaussian copula and
                                         % constant hazard rate


    S_fees=zeros(5,3);     % dummy variable for memorizing the simulated
                           % payment leg
    S_default=zeros(5,3);  % dummy variable for memorizing the simulated
                           % default leg
    M_fees=zeros(5,3);     % variable which memorize the payment leg for
                           % each loop of recovery&corr
    M_default=zeros(5,3);  % variable which memorize the payment leg for
                           % each loop of recovery&corr

    for n=1:k % start the simulation loop
        for rec_cycle=1:5 %start the recovery loop
            [time,index]=sort(def_t(n,:)); % sort the pseudo vector of
                                           % default times
            tau=[time./hazard(rec_cycle);index]; % generate the vector
                                                 % of default time by
                                                 % dividing by the
                                                 % corresponding hazard
                                                 % rate
            for u=1:3 % start the loop for each of the three tranches
                recovery=0;
                fees=0;
                % calculate the premium and default leg
                [default,fees]=cash_flow(T,tau,Recovery(1,rec_cycle),ZC,
                  Amount(1),C(u),D(u));
                S_fees(rec_cycle,u)=S_fees(rec_cycle,u)+fees;
                S_default(rec_cycle,u)=S_default(rec_cycle,u)+default;
```

```
            end
        end

    end
    for u=1:3
        for rec_cycle=1:5
            M_fees(rec_cycle,u)=S_fees(rec_cycle,u)/k; % average DV01
            M_default(rec_cycle,u)=S_default(rec_cycle,u)/k; % average
                                                    % default leg
        end
    end

    for rec_cycle=1:5
        CDO_P1(R_cycle,rec_cycle)=(M_default(rec_cycle,1)/
          (M_fees(rec_cycle,1)))*10000; % B\E spread for the 0-3% tranche
        CDO_P2(R_cycle,rec_cycle)=(M_default(rec_cycle,2)/
          (M_fees(rec_cycle,2)))*10000; % B\E spread for the 3-14% tranche
        CDO_P3(R_cycle,rec_cycle)=(M_default(rec_cycle,3)/
          (M_fees(rec_cycle,3)))*10000; % B\E spread for the 14-100% tranche
    end
end

price_eq=CDO_P1;
price_mezz=CDO_P2;
price_sen=CDO_P3;


figure(1)
surf((0:.2:.8),R,price_eq);
title('Equity Tranche (0%-3%)')
xlabel('Recovery');
ylabel('Correlation');
zlabel('Tranche spread (bps per annum)');


figure(2)
surf((0:.2:.8),R,price_mezz);
title('Mezzanine Tranche (3%-14%)')
xlabel('Recovery');
ylabel('Correlation');
zlabel('Tranche spread (bps per annum)');


figure(3)
surf((0:.2:.8),R,price_sen);
title('Senior Tranche (14%-100%)')
xlabel('Recovery');
ylabel('Correlation');
zlabel('Tranche spread (bps per annum)');

toc
```

cash_flow.m

```
function [PV_def, PV_premium]=cash_flow(expiry,def_time,rec,zc_rate,
  capital,C,D)
% This function computes the value of the premium (DV01, spread still to be
% determined) and default legs of a CDO. Inputs are:

% expiry: CDO maturity
% def_time: simulated default time
% rec: recovery
% zc_rate: constant ZC rate
% capital: nominal amount of each reference entity
% C: attachment point
% D: detachment point

PV_def=0;
PV_premium=0;
num=size(def_time,2);
loss=zeros(num,1); % loss give default for each credit
tot_loss=0; % cumulative portfolio loss
periodic_loss=zeros(expiry,1); % stores the accumulated loss at each
                               % payment date
out_capital=zeros(expiry,1); % outstanding tranche capital at each
                             % payment date
fee=zeros(expiry,1);
total_fee=0;
indicator=0;
c=0;
% calculate the total loss in the k-th simulation
for i=1:num
    if def_time(1,i)<expiry % if the simulated default time for the generic
                            % credit is < than the CDO maturity, there is
                            % a loss
        loss(i)=(1-rec)*capital;
        tot_loss=tot_loss+loss(i); % sum the individual losses
    end
end

%% DEFAULT LEG SIMULATION %%

% if the loss is below the lower treshold C there's no default payment
if tot_loss<C
    PV_def=0;
% if the loss is above C and below D there's a default payment
elseif tot_loss>C & tot_loss<D
    for i=1:num
        if def_time(1,i)<expiry
            indicator=indicator+loss(i); % we memorize the cumulative
                                         % losses
            if indicator>C % tranche begins to absorbe losses in excess
                           % of C
                if c==0
                    disc_fact_def=0;
                    r=zc_rate;
                    disc_fact_def=(1+r)^(-def_time(1,i)); % discount factor
                                                          % at default
                    PV_def=PV_def+(indicator-C)*disc_fact_def; % only the
                      % loss exceeding C is absorbed (look at the footnote
```

```
                                % 32 in the simulation algorithm p. 51 of my paper)
                        c=1;
                else
                        disc_fact_def=0;
                        r=zc_rate;
                        disc_fact_def=(1+r)^(-def_time(1,i));
                        PV_def=PV_def+loss(i)*disc_fact_def;
                end
            end
        end
    end
% if portfolio losses are exceeding D, the C-D% tranche only absorb losses
% up to D%.
elseif tot_loss>D
    for i=1:num
        if def_time(1,i)<expiry
            indicator=indicator+loss(i);
            if indicator>C & indicator<D % check if losses are in the
                                         % C-D% range
                if c==0
                    disc_fact_def=0;
                    r=zc_rate;
                    disc_fact_def=(1+r)^(-def_time(1,i));
                    PV_def=PV_def+(indicator-C)*disc_fact_def;
                    c=1;
                else
                    disc_fact_def=0;
                    r=zc_rate;
                    disc_fact_def=(1+r)^(-def_time(1,i));
                    PV_def=PV_def+loss(i)*disc_fact_def;
                end
            elseif indicator>D % look at footnote 33 p. 52 of my paper
                if c==1
                    disc_fact_def=0;
                    r=zc_rate;
                    disc_fact_def=(1+r)^(-def_time(1,i));
                    absorbed_loss=D-(indicator-loss(i)); % look at footnote
                                                         % 33 p. 52 of my
                                                         % paper
                    PV_def=PV_def+(absorbed_loss*disc_fact_def);
                    c=2;
                end
            end
        end
    end
end


%% PREMIUM LEG SIMULATION %%

for i=1:expiry
    periodic_loss(i)=0;
    for j=1:num
        if def_time(1,j)<i
            % calculated the accumulated portfolio losses
            periodic_loss(i)= periodic_loss(i)+(1-rec)*capital;
        end
```

```
        end
        out_capital(i)=min(max(D-periodic_loss(i),0),D-C); % oustanding capital
                                                           % at each payment
                                                           % date

        fee(i)=((1+zc_rate)^(-i))*out_capital(i);
        PV_premium=PV_premium+fee(i); % DV01


end
```

gaussian_time.m

```
function def_times1=gaussian_time(R,num,n)

% This function generates pseudo default stopping times (generated by a
% multinomial gaussian copula with correlation matrix "R") for the "n"
% obligors included in the basket. "num" stands for the    of simulations.
% We call the output of the function "pseudo" cause we still have to
% divide the result of the function by the specific hazard rate. But given
% the relationship h=S/(1-Rec), the hazard rate will vary at each recovery
% loop, so we will perform the ratio in the CDO_tranche.m function.

% Now we use the simulation algorithm for generating normal variates from
% gaussian copula suggested by ELM(01), pag. 26

x1=zeros(num,n);
y=zeros(num,n);

A=chol(R);
clear R;
z=randn(num,n);
for i=1:num
y(i,:)=z(i,:)*A;
end
clear A;
clear z;

Gauss_U1=normcdf(y);              % 0-1 variates normally distribuited
clear y;
x1=-log(Gauss_U1);
clear Gauss_U1;

def_times1=x1; % we do not divide by the hazard rate cause it depends on
               % the recovery rate at each loop
```

Consider a flat zero curve at 5% p.a. and 5-year maturity CDO with the following characteristics:

Tranche	Attachment Points
Equity Tranche	0%–3%
Mezzanine Tranche	9%–14%
Senior Tranche	14%–100%

The following are the graphical outputs. Figure 4.15 is the equity tranche, and Figure 4.16 is the mezzanine tranche. Figure 4.17 displays the numerical computations of the tranche pricing of a CDO structure with a homogenous collateral pool ($n = 100$ reference entities with the same notional amount, $N_i = 100$), with a constant single name default swap curve set as $s = 150$ basis points p.a. and constant pairwise correlation $r_{i,j} = r$.

Galiani (2002) notes that there are different relationships between prices and correlation for CDO tranches: Senior tranches show a positive relation between prices and correlation, while the opposite is true for the equity tranche. Mezzanine tranches seem to behave similarly to the equity piece as far as correlation sensitivity is concerned, especially for recovery values under 60%; the dependence on recovery values is nevertheless straightforward because, for higher correlation values, the sign of the relation resembles the behavior of the junior tranche.

With regard to the recovery dependence, although senior tranche spreads appear to be monotonically decreasing, the opposite is true for equity tranches. The behavior, first described in Boscher and Ward (2002), even if counterintuitive at first glance, can be reasonably explained by analyzing the shape of loss distribution of the collateral pool for different assumptions of the recovery rate. To this end, starting from (4.14), we can compute the first two moments of the loss distribution, obtaining:

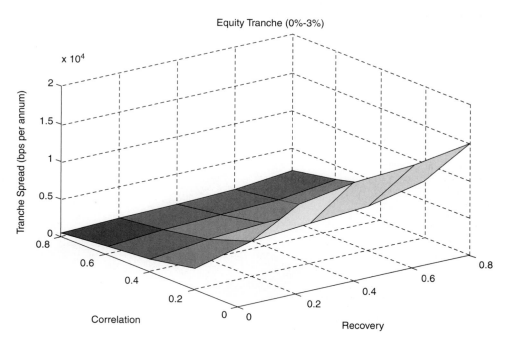

Figure 4.15 Equity tranche. *Source: Galiani, S. (2003), 54.*

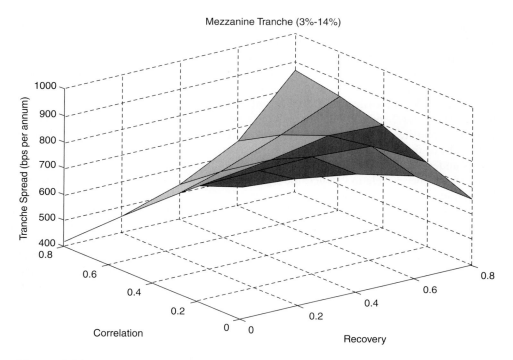

Figure 4.16 Mezzanine tranche.   *Source: Galiani, S. (2003), 54.*

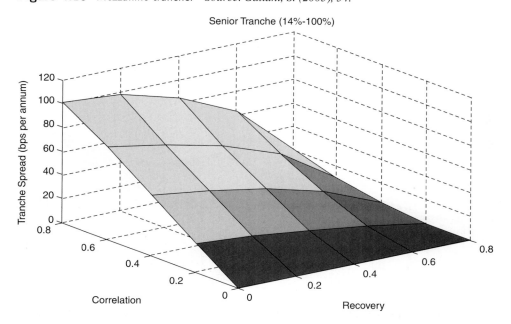

Figure 4.17 Senior tranche.   *Source: Galiani, S. (2003), 54.*

$$E\left[L(t)\right] = E\left[\sum_{i=1}^{n} L_i Q_i(t)\right]$$

$$= \sum_{i=1}^{n} L_i E\left[1_{\tau_i < t}\right]$$

$$= \sum_{i=1}^{n} (1 - R_i) N_i F_i(t) \tag{4.19}$$

$$V\left[L(t)\right] = \sum_{i=1}^{n} V[L_i(t)] + \sum_{i=1}^{n} \sum_{\substack{j=1 \\ i \neq j}}^{n} r_{ij} \sqrt{V[L_i(t)]V[L_j(t)]} \tag{4.20}$$

where

$$V[L_i(t)] = (1 - R_i)^2 N_i^2 F_i(t)(1 - F_i(t)).$$

In the case of a homogenous collateral pool (same notional n for each reference entity and same recovery rate R), with constant pairwise correlation $r_{ij} = r$ and flat credit default curve,[32] we have $V[L_i(t)] = V[L_j(t)]$ for all $i, j \in \{1, 2, ..., n\}$; this implies that (4.20) can be rewritten as follows

$$V[L_i(t)] = nV[L_i(t)] + n(n-1)rV[L_i(t)].$$

We then define the unexpected loss UL as the square root of the portfolio loss variance:

$$UL(t) = \sqrt{nV[L_i(t)] + n(n-1)rV[L_i(t)]}$$
$$= \sqrt{n + n(n-1)r}(1-R)N\sqrt{F(t)(1-F(t))} \tag{4.21}$$

It is clear that the dispersion of the loss distribution, denoted by UL, is an increasing function with respect to the correlation r. Regarding the effect of the recovery rates, setting $Q = \sqrt{n + n(n-1)r}N = Q$ and differentiating (4.12) with respect to the recovery rate R yields

$$\frac{\partial UL(t)}{\partial R} = Q\left[\frac{\partial(1-R)}{\partial R}\sqrt{F(t)(1-F(t))} + (1-R)\frac{\partial\sqrt{F(t)(1-F(t))}}{\partial R}\right]$$

$$= Q\left[-\sqrt{F(t)(1-F(t))} + \frac{st(1-R)^{-1}(1-F(t))(1-2F(t))}{2\sqrt{F(t)(1-F(t)}}\right].$$

Let $W = \frac{st}{(1-R)}$. After some simple algebraic manipulations, we get

$$\frac{\partial UL(t)}{\partial R} = Q\sqrt{1-F(t)}\left[-\sqrt{F(t)} + W\frac{1-2F(t)}{2\sqrt{F(t)}}\right].$$

For $R < 1$ and $s > 0$, the term in brackets is negative, thus showing that the unexpected loss (the standard deviation) of the collateral pool is a monotonically decreasing function of the recovery rate.

Figure 4.18 plots the loss distribution of the CDO collateral pool ($n = 100$) as a function of the recovery rate.

As expected, recovery rate acts as a scale-location parameter of the loss distribution, shifting the center of the distribution to the left tail[33] and reducing the standard deviation of the loss distribution (in the case of increasing recovery rates). This clearly affects CDO prices, increasing the required spread for junior tranches and lowering it for senior tranches.

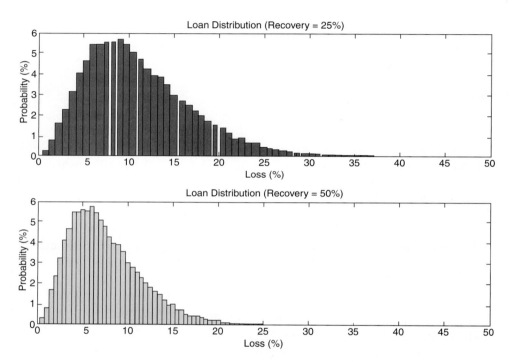

Figure 4.18   Collateral pool simulates losses ($r = 0.1$ and constant intensity $h = k = 3\%$) with Gaussian copula.   *Source: Galiani, S. (2003), 57.*

4.10   CDO PRICING IN C++

CDO.h

```
#ifndef _CDO__
#define _CDO__


#include "datecl.h"
#include <vector>
#include <map>
#include <iostream>
#include "MatrixUtil.h"
```

```
#define N 1
#define NUM_TRANCHES 3
#define NUM_REF 100
#define numSim 10000
#define MATURITY 5
#define ZC 0.05
#define ENTITY_NOTIONAL 10000
#define SPREAD 150

class Tranche
{
 public:
        Tranche(double C, double D, string desc) :
           lowerAttachment(C*ENTITY_NOTIONAL*NUM_REF),
          upperAttachment(D*ENTITY_NOTIONAL*NUM_REF), desc_(desc) {}
        vector<double> cash_Flow(int expiry, vector<double> defTime,
           double rec, double capital,double C, double D, int numReference)
        {
                vector<double> results;
                double PV_def=0;
                double PV_premium=0;
                // loss given default for each credit
                double* loss = new double[numReference];
                double tot_loss = 0;          // cumulative portfolio loss
                // stores the accumulated loss at each payment date
                double* periodic_loss = new double[numReference];
                // outstanding tranche capital at each payment date
                double* out_capital = new double[numReference];
                double* fee = new double[numReference];
                double total_fee = 0;
                double indicator = 0;
                double disc_fact_def = 0;
                double absorbed_loss = 0;
                double r = 0.0;
                int c = 0;
                int j = 0;
                int num = N;

                // calculate the total loss in the k-th simulation
                for (int i = 0; i < numReference; i++)
                {
                // if the simulated default time for the generic credit
                // is < than the CDO maturity, there is a loss
                   if (defTime[i] < expiry)
                   {
                        loss[i] = (1- rec)*capital;
                        // sum the individual losses
                        tot_loss = tot_loss + loss[i];
                   }
                }
                // DEFAULT LEG SIMULATION %%
                // if the loss is below the lower treshold C there's no
                // default payment
                if (tot_loss < C)
                        PV_def=0;  // if the loss is above C and below D
                                   // there's a default payment
```

```
        else if ((tot_loss >= C) && (tot_loss < D))
        {
            for (i= 0; i < numReference; i++)
            {
                if (defTime[i] < expiry)
                    {
                        // we memorize the cumulative losses
                    indicator=indicator+loss[i];
                        // tranche begins to absorbe losses in
                        // excess of C
                    if (indicator > C)
                    {
                        if (c == 0)
                        {
                            disc_fact_def=0;
                            r = ZC;
                            // discount factor at default
                            disc_fact_def= exp(-defTime[i]*r);
                                // only the loss exceeding C is
                                // absorbed (look at the footnote
                                // 32 in the simulation algorithm
                                // p.51 of my paper)
                                PV_def=PV_def+(indicator-C)*
                                   disc_fact_def;
                                c = 1;
                        }
                        else
                        {
                            disc_fact_def=0;
                            r= ZC;
                            disc_fact_def= exp(-defTime[i]*r);
                            PV_def=PV_def+loss[i]*disc_fact_def;
                        }
                    }
                }
            }
        }
        // if portfolio losses are exceeding D, the C-D% tranche
        // only absorb losses up to D
        else if (tot_loss > D)
        {
            for (i = 0; i < numReference; i++)
            {
                if (defTime[i] < expiry)
                {
                    indicator= indicator + loss[i];
                        // check if losses are in the C-D% range
                    if ((indicator > C) && (indicator < D))
                        {
                        if (c == 0)
                            {
                                r= ZC;
            disc_fact_def = exp(-defTime[i]*r);
            PV_def=PV_def+(indicator-C)*disc_fact_def;
            c=1;
                            }
                else
```

```
                                          {
                                              r= ZC;
                                              disc_fact_def= exp(-defTime[i]*r);
                                          PV_def=PV_def+loss[i]*disc_fact_def;
                                          }
                                      }
                                          // look at footnote 33 p. 52 of my paper
                                      else if (indicator > D)
                                      {
                                          if (c == 1)
                                          {
                                              r= ZC;
                                              disc_fact_def= exp(-defTime[i]*r);
                                                 // look at footnote 33 p. 52
                                                 // of my paper
                                              absorbed_loss = D -
                                                 (indicator-loss[i]);
                                              PV_def=PV_def+(absorbed_loss*
                                                 disc_fact_def);
                                              c=2;
                                          }
                                      }
                                  }
                              }
                      }
                  results.push_back(PV_def);


        // PREMIUM LEG SIMULATION

        for (i= 0; i < expiry; i++)
        {
                periodic_loss[i]=0;
                for (j= 0; j < numReference; j++)
                {
                if (defTime[j] < i)
                        // calculated the accumulated portfolio losses
                        periodic_loss[i] = periodic_loss[i]+
                           (1-rec)*capital;
                }
                // oustanding capital at each payment date
                out_capital[i] = min(max(D-periodic_loss[i],0),D-C);
                fee[i]= exp(-ZC*i)*out_capital[i];
                PV_premium=PV_premium+fee[i]; // DV01
        }

        results.push_back(PV_premium);
        results.push_back(indicator/(ENTITY_NOTIONAL*NUM_REF));

        return results;
        }
        void setExpectedLoss(double loss) { expectedLoss_ = loss; }
        double getExpectedLoss() const { return expectedLoss_; }
        double getUpperAttachment() { return upperAttachment; }
        double getLowerAttachment() { return lowerAttachment; }
        void setSpread(double spread) { spread_ = spread; }
        double getSpread() const { return spread_; }
```

```
        void setDesc(string desc) { desc_ = desc; }
        string getDesc() const { return desc_; }
private:
        double expectedLoss_;
        double upperAttachment;
        double lowerAttachment;
        double recovery;
        double spread_;
        string desc_;
        double totalLoss;      // cumulative portfolio loss
        double out_capital;    // outstanding tranche capital at each
                               // payment date
        double periodic_loss;  // stores the accumulated loss at each
                               // payment date
};

class CDO
{
 public:
        CDO() : T(MATURITY), numReference_(NUM_REF) { }
        double priceTranche(int numReference)
        {
                MatrixUtil mu;
                double C = 0.0;
                double D = 0.0;
                double spread = (double) SPREAD/10000;
                Array2D<double> R1(numReference,numReference);
                int size = R1.dim1();
                std::cout << "pool size = " << size << endl;
                vector<double> defaultTime;
                vector<double> normaldev;
                vector<double>::iterator iter;
                vector<double> val;
                map<double,int> expMap;

                double y = 0;
                double tau = 0.0;
                double fees = 0.0;
                double loss = 0.0;
                double PV_default = 0.0;
                double* dev = new double[numReference];
                int rec_cycle = 0;

                Array1D<double> hazard(N);
                Array1D<double> R(N);
                Array1D<double> expectLoss(N);
                Array1D<double> recovery(N);
                Array2D<double> corr(numReference,numReference);
                Array2D<double> S_fees(N,NUM_TRANCHES);
                Array2D<double> S_default(N,NUM_TRANCHES);
                Array2D<double> M_fees(N,NUM_TRANCHES);
                Array2D<double> M_default(N,NUM_TRANCHES);
                Array2D<double> totLoss(N,NUM_TRANCHES);
                Array2D<double> expLoss(N,NUM_TRANCHES);
                //std::cout.precision(5);

                for (int j = 0; j < N; j++)
```

```
        {
        // start the loop for each of the three tranches
                for (int u = 0; u < NUM_TRANCHES; u++)
                {
                    S_fees[j][u] = 0;
                    S_default[j][u] = 0;
                    M_fees[j][u] = 0;
                    M_default[j][u] = 0;
                    totLoss[j][u] = 0;
                }
                hazard[j] = 0.03;    // hazard rate
                recovery[j] = 0.40; // recovery rate
        }

        for (int R_cycle = 0; R_cycle < N; R_cycle++)
        {
                for (int xx = 0; xx < numReference; xx++)
                {
                    for (int yy = 0; yy < numReference; yy++)
                    {
                        if (xx == yy)
                            corr[xx][yy] = 1.0;
                        else
                        {
                            corr[xx][yy] = 0.2*(R_cycle+1);
                                // populate the correlation
                                // matrix
                            corr[yy][xx] = 0.2*(R_cycle+1);
                        }
                        R1[xx][yy] = corr[xx][yy];
                    }

                }

                for (int i = 0; i < numSim; i++)
                {
                    defaultTime.clear();
                    defaultTime.empty();
                    defaultTime = mu.genCholesky4(R1);

                    for (int j = 0; j < N; j++)
                    {
                        int l = 0;
                        for (iter = defaultTime.begin();
                          iter != defaultTime.end(); iter++)
                        {

                                defaultTime[l] = (double)
                                  *iter/hazard[j];
                                l++;
                        }
                        // tau = *iter/hazard[expMap[*iter]];
                        // std::cout << "tau = " << tau << endl;
                        // generate the vector of default time by
                        // dividing by the corresponding
                        // hazard rate
```

```
                       sort(defaultTime.begin(),
                         defaultTime.end());
                       // start the loop for each of the three
                       // tranches
                       for (int u= 0; u < NUM_TRANCHES; u++)
                       {
                       // calculate the premium and default leg
                       C = tranche[u].getLowerAttachment();
                       D = tranche[u].getUpperAttachment();
                       val= tranche[u].cash_Flow(MATURITY,
                         defaultTime,recovery[j],ENTITY_NOTIONAL,
                         C,D,numReference);
                       iter = val.begin();
                       PV_default = *iter;
                       iter++;
                       fees = *iter;
                       iter++;
                       loss = *iter;
                       totLoss[j][u] = totLoss[j][u] + loss;
                       S_fees[j][u] = S_fees[j][u]+fees;
                       S_default[j][u] = S_default[j][u]+
                         PV_default;

                       }
                   }
                defaultTime.empty();
                defaultTime.clear();
          }

       for (int rec_cycle = 0; rec_cycle < N; rec_cycle++)
       {
            for (int u = 0; u < NUM_TRANCHES; u++)
            {
              // average DV01
              M_fees[rec_cycle][u]=
                S_fees[rec_cycle][u]/numSim;
              // average default leg
              M_default[rec_cycle][u]=S_default[rec_cycle]
                [u]/numSim;
              expLoss[rec_cycle][u] = totLoss[rec_cycle]
                [u]/numSim;
            }
       }

       for (rec_cycle = 0; rec_cycle < N; rec_cycle++)
       {
   for (int u = 0; u < NUM_TRANCHES; u++)
        {
     spread= ((M_default[rec_cycle][u])/(M_fees
       [rec_cycle][u]))*10000;
         // B\E spread for the 0-3% tranche
         loss = expLoss[rec_cycle][u];
         tranche[u].setSpread(spread);
         tranche[u].setExpectedLoss(loss);
             std::cout << tranche[u].getDesc() << " " <<
       tranche[u].getSpread() << " " <<
             tranche[u].getExpectedLoss() << endl;
```

```
                                        }
                                }
                        }
                        delete [] dev;

                        return 0.0;

                }
                void addTranche(Tranche t) { tranche.push_back(t); }
                int getNumTranches() { return numTranches_; }
                int getNumReferences() { return numReference_; }
                virtual ~CDO() { }
        private:
                //Date maturity;
                vector<Tranche> tranche;
                int T;
                int numReference_;
                int numTranches_;
};

#endif
```

The main function is:

```
Main.cpp
#include <strstream>
#include <iostream>
#include <fstream>
#include "Basket.h"
#define SIZE_X 1000
using namespace std;

void main()
{
        CDO cdo;

        std::cout << "Pricing CDO..." << endl;
        Tranche tranche1(0,0.03,"equity");
        Tranche tranche2(0.03,0.14,"mezzanine");
        Tranche tranche3(0.14,1.00,"senior");


        cdo.addTranche(tranche1);
        cdo.addTranche(tranche2);
        cdo.addTranche(tranche3);
        cdo.priceTranche(100);
}
```

Example 1

Suppose we want to price the senior, mezzanine, and equity tranches of a CD with the attachment points shown in the following table.

	Lower Attachment	Upper Attachment
Senior Tranche	14%	100%
Mezzanine Tranche	3%	14%
Equity Tranche	0%	3%

For simplicity, we assume a homogenous pool with 100 obligors and each with a hazard rate of 3%. Using Monte Carlo with 10,000 simulations yields what is displayed in the following table.

	Price (bps)	Standard Deviation
Senior Tranche	52.76	0.0642
Mezzanine Tranche	1372.9	0.1115
Equity Tranche	4672.1	0.1137

4.11   CDO² PRICING

Li and Liang (2005) provide a pricing formula for a CDO^2 tranche with m baby or underlying CDOs, and with a total of N underlying credits. For each baby CDO, we have the loss up to time t as

$$L_B^N(t) = \sum_{k=1}^{N} N_i^k (1 - R_i) 1_{\{\tau_i < t\}} \tag{4.22}$$

where N_i^k is the notional amount of the ith credit in the kth baby CDO, and τ_i is the default time of the ith credit. The tranche loss, $\bar{L}_B^k$ for the kth baby CDO with the attachment point A_L^B and detachment point A_U^B is:

$$\bar{L}_B^k = \max\left(L_B^k(t) - A_L^B, 0\right) - \max\left(L_B^k(t) - A_U^B, 0\right) \tag{4.23}$$

The tranche loss for the CDO^2 or "mother CDO" with the attachment point A_L^M and detachment point A_U^M is:

$$\bar{L} = \max\left(\sum_{k=1}^{n} \bar{L}_B^k(t) - A_L^M, 0\right) - \max\left(\sum_{k=1}^{n} \bar{L}_B^k(t) - A_U^M, 0\right) \tag{4.24}$$

As the preceding payoff shows, the payoff function that the pricing of CDO^2 depends on is the joint loss distribution from all underlying baby CDO portfolios.

4.12   FAST LOSS CALCULATION FOR CDOS AND CDO²S

Let $q_i(t|Y_M) = \Pr[\tau_i \le t|Y_M]$ be the conditional marginal default probability for credit i before time t where Y_M is the conditional common state variable. The total loss distribution as a sum of independent variables can then be calculated using a few methods, such as Fourier transformation, recursive method. or conditional normal approximation.[34] The conditional mean and variance of the total loss variable, $L|Y_M$:

$$M_v = \sum_{i=1}^{n} N_i(1 - R_i) \cdot q_i(t|Y_M)$$

$$\sigma_v^2 = \sum_{i=1}^{n} N_i^2(1 - R_i)^2 \cdot q_i(t|Y_M)(1 - q_i(t|Y_M))$$

Li and Liang (2005) assume a conditional normal approximation approach. Such an approach uses a normal distribution to approximate the preceding conditional total loss distribution by assuming that the normal distribution has the same mean and variance as computed previously.[35] The normal distribution is chosen due to the central limit theorem, which states that the sum of independent distributions (but not identical distribution) approaches to a normal distribution as the number of the independent distributions increases.

Li and Liang (2005), using the conditional normal approach, give the conditional expected loss for the tranche that can be easily computed in closed form, as follows:

$$E[L^T(t)|v] = \left(M_v - A_L^T\right) \Phi \left(\frac{M_v - A_L^T}{\sigma_v}\right) + \sigma_v \cdot \phi \left(\frac{M_v - A_L^T}{\sigma_v}\right)$$
$$- \left(M_v - A_U^T\right) \Phi \left(\frac{M_v - A_U^T}{\sigma_v}\right) + \sigma_v \cdot \phi \left(\frac{M_v - A_U^T}{\sigma_v}\right)$$

where ϕ is a one-dimensional normal density function. With the calculated conditional expected loss, the unconditional expected loss is obtained simply by integrating over the common factor Y_m:

$$E[L^T(t)] = \int_{-\infty}^{\infty} E[L^T(t)|y] \cdot \phi(y)dy$$

For an equity tranche, one can use the following method to preserve the expected loss of the whole portfolio, and to achieve a better approximation. We allow negative loss introduced in the conditional normal approximation in the equity tranche payoff function. An equity tranche with detachment point, A_U^T in this case, can be expressed as follows:

$$L_{equity}^T(t) = L(t) - \max(L(t) - A_U^T, 0)$$

The conditional expected loss for the equity tranche is:

$$E[L_{equity}^T(t)|v] = M_v - \left(M_v - A_U^T\right) \Phi \left(\frac{M_v - A_U^T}{\sigma_v}\right) - \sigma_v \cdot \phi \left(\frac{M_v - A_U^T}{\sigma_v}\right)$$

This has been proven to work well for index equity tranches of sizes more than 3%.[36] Alternatively, we can also use the inverse Gaussian distribution to approximate for the equity tranche because inverse Gaussian distribution takes only positive value.

Similarly, synthetic CDO^2 pricing depends on the joint loss distribution from all underlying baby CDO portfolios. Conditioning on the normal variable Y_M, we can compute the mean and covariance of loss variables, $L_k|Y_M, k = 1, ..., n$:

$$\mu_k^v = \sum_{i=1}^N N_i^k (1 - R_i) \cdot q_i(t|Y_M)$$

$$\Sigma_{k,k'}^v = \sum_{i=1}^n N_i^k N_i^{k'} (1 - R_i)^2 \cdot q_i(t|Y_M)(1 - q_i(t|Y_M))$$

It can be seen from this expression that the conditional covariance of two loss distributions of sub-portfolios would depend on the overlapping of the two portfolios.[37] Even though each credit default is independent to each other conditional on common factor, the overlapping of names in the two portfolios would result in a high correlation between the losses of the two portfolios. The conditional normal approximation approach uses multi-normal distributions to approximate the conditional loss distributions. The multi-normal distributions have the same means and covariance matrix as computed previously. As the CDO^2 loss is a function of underlying CDO loss variables, and with the conditional normal specification, the conditional expected loss can be calculated with a multi-dimensional integration:

$$E\left[\bar{L}_t | v\right] = \int \ldots \int \bar{L}(L_b^1, \ldots, L_b^n) dL_b^1 dL_b^2 \ldots dL_b^n$$

The dimension of this integration equals to the number of underlying CDOs. A Monte Carlo simulation is used to compute this multi-dimensional integration. With the calculated conditional expected loss, the unconditional expected loss is obtained simply by integrating crossing the common factor Y_M:

$$E[\bar{L}_t] = \int_{-\infty}^{\infty} E[\bar{L}_t | y] \cdot n(y) dy$$

where $n(y) = \frac{1}{\sqrt{2\pi}} e^{-y^2}$ is the standard normal density function.

For the pricing of a CDO or CDO^2, it is sufficient to know the portfolio loss distributions over different time horizons. Starting with an equity tranche with a strike A, the tranche loss up to time t, $L_T(t)$, is:

$$L_T(t) = \max(L(t), 0) - \max(L(t) - A, 0) = L(t) - \max(L(t) - A, 0)$$

Fast Algorithm for Computing CDO Tranche Loss in Matlab

Pavel Okenuv (2005) provides a Matlab implementation to compute the expected loan portfolio CDO tranche loss in the Gaussian factor model using numerically fast integration.

gs_loss.m

```
% This implements one factor Gaussian model.
% [loss]=gsloss(L,w,p,a,d,N)
% L = exposures,as fraction of total
% portfolio, taking into account the recovery rate
% Example: loan 1 is 0.01 fraction of the total portfolio, recovery
```

```
% rate is 40% then L(1)=0.01*(1-0.4)
% w = loading factors
% p = default probabilities
% a = attachement point
% d = detachment point
% N = number of names in the portfolio
% loss = expected tranche loss as percentage of the portfolio nominal
% expressed in basis points

function [loss]= gsloss(L,w,p,a,d,N)

Pi=3.14159265;
% This integration routine serves as an example only. We highly
% recommend that the user should replace it with his/her favorite high
% order routine.
% Set integration parameters
IP=200; % number of points used by integration routine
BD=10;   % integration interval [-BD,BD]
z=linspace(-BD,BD,IP+1); % creates equally spaced grid for integration
% Loss computation
loss=0;

for i=1:IP

  m=0; % m conditional mean
v=0; % v conditional variance

for k=1:N
   pm=normcdf((norminv(p(k))-w(k)*z(i))/sqrt(1-w(k)*w(k)));
m=m+L(k)*pm;
v=v+L(k)*L(k)*pm*(1-pm);
  end

  s=sqrt(v); % s conditional standard deviation
  temp=m*(normcdf((d-m)/s)-normcdf((a-m)/s));
  temp=temp+s*1/sqrt(2*Pi)*(exp(-(a-m)^2/(2*s^2))-exp(-(d-m)^2/(2*s^2)));
  temp=temp+(d-a)*normcdf((1-m)/s)-d*normcdf((d-m)/s)+a*normcdf((a-m)/s);
  loss=loss+temp*1/sqrt(2*Pi)*exp(-z(i)^2/2)*2*BD/IP;
end

loss=loss*10000; % express as basis points
```

ENDNOTES

1. Picone, D., pg. 2.
2. Id., pg. 2.
3. Gibson, M. (2004), pg. 1.
4. Id., pg. 1.
5. Id.
6. Hull, J. and White, A. (2004), pg. 17.
7. Id., pg. 17.
8. Gibson, M., pg. 1.
9. According to Goodman (2002), the first synthetic CDOs in 1997 were conducted by Swiss Bank Corporation ("Glacier Finance Ltd.") and JP Morgan ("BISTRO").
10. Gibson, M. (2004), pg. 2.
11. Id., pg. 2.
12. Id., pg. 3.
13. Id., pg. 2.
14. Id., pg. 2.
15. Id., pg. 3.
16. Gibson, M. (2004), pg. 3.
17. Id.
18. 37% corresponds to the six-year cumulative probability of default as calculated by Moody's.
19. According to Merton (1974), a firm defaults if its asset value falls below a certain threshold. Thus, the firm value is the underlying process that derives credit events. In contrast to other credit risk models, CreditMetrics can also handle migrations in the credit quality of an obligor, by employing a threshold for each possible migration from one credit rating to another. A key characteristic of the CreditMetrics model is that the full loss distribution cannot be calculated analytically but relies on Monte Carlo simulation. In order to perform the simulation, the following variables must be determined:

    - For each obligor, its possible values at the end of the horizon are specified. In the case of no default, it equals the sum of its discounted cash flows. In the case of default, it equals its recovery rate.

    - Using the assumption of standard normally distributed asset returns, we can translate a historically estimated probability of default into a threshold of default for each obligor.

    - The correlation between two obligors.

20. See Li (2000); Boscher and Ward (2002); Andersen, Sidenius, and Basu (2003); and Hull and White (2003).
21. On an AMD Athlon 2.2 GHz PC with 1GB of RAM, Gibson (2004) computes the unconditional default distribution for $N = 100$, which takes 10 seconds using the Scilab software package (*http://www.scilab.org*).
22. Gibson, M. (2004), pg. 18.
23. Gibson, M. (2004), pg. 18.
24. Id., pg. 18.

25. Lehnert, N., Altrock, R., Rachev, S., Trück, S., and Wilch, A. (2005), pg. 10.
26. Id., pg. 10.
27. Id., pg. 10.
28. Id., pg. 10.
29. McGinty and Ahuluwalia (2004).
30. Assuming a 30/360 day count convention, we have $\alpha = 1$ for payments with annual frequency, $\alpha = 1/2$ for payments with semiannual frequency, and $\alpha = 1/4$ for payments with quarterly frequency.
31. The Matlab code was written by Stefano Galiani.
32. The assumption of a flat spread curve implies an interesting relation between the contract spread, the hazard rate, and the recovery rate, namely

$$h = \frac{s}{1 - R}$$

For a formal proof, see Meneguzzo and Vecchiato (2002), pp. 54-44. Furthermore, based on this property, it is possible to express the default time distribution function as:

$$F(t) = 1 - \exp(-ht)$$
$$= 1 - \exp\left(-\frac{s}{1 - R}t\right)$$

33. Under the assumption specified here, this claim can be easily proved by differentiating ( ) with respect to the recovery rate R, leading to

$$\frac{\partial E[L(t)]}{\partial R} = -nN\left[1 - \left(1 + \frac{st}{1 - R}\right)\exp\left(-\frac{st}{1 - R}\right)\right]$$

which is nonpositive for $s > 0$ and $R < 1$.
34. Li and Liang (2005), pg. 13.
35. Li and Liang (2005), pg. 13.
36. Id., pg. 14.
37. Id., pg. 14.

CHAPTER 5

CREDIT DERIVATIVES

SECTIONS

In this chapter, we discuss credit derivatives—derivatives that enable the efficient transfer and repackaging of credit risk. Credit derivatives such as credit default swaps (CDS) enable financial institutions to protect their loan portfolio and balance sheets from underlying credit risks and credit-related events such as a widening, ratings downgrade, and default of individual obligors. For instance, credit derivatives enable banks to transfer the credit risk, and a large part of the regulatory capital off their books, while keeping the loan business.

The credit derivatives market has experienced tremendous growth over the past five years. From virtually nothing in 1995, total market notional now approaches $1 trillion. Much of this growth has been due to the increasing realization of the advantages credit derivatives possess over their cash counterparts. For instance, a standard CDS can be replicated by using a cash bond and the repo market. Precluding arbitrage opportunities, it is more efficient and cheaper to use a CDS, an unfunded product, to replicate credit risks than a standard funded cash bond instrument. With the introduction of unfunded products, credit derivatives have for the first time separated the issue of funding from credit risk.[1] This has made credit markets more accessible to those with high funding costs and cheaper to leverage credit risk.[2]

In their more exotic form, credit derivatives enable "the credit exposure of a particular asset or group of assets to be divided up and redistributed into a more concentrated or diluted form that appeals to the various risk appetites of investors."[3] For instance, collateralized debt obligations (CDOs) and tranched portfolio default swap enable yield-seeking investors to leverage their credit risk and return by buying first-loss products. More risk-averse investors can buy lower-risk, lower-return second-loss products.

In this chapter, we examine various credit products as well credit derivatives pricing models. In §5.1, the mechanics and structure of credit defaults swaps (CDSs) are discussed. In §5.2, CDS day counting conventions are reviewed. In §5.3, general valuation principles of CDSs are discussed. In §5.4, we review hazard rate functions, which are used to compute default probabilities. In §5.5, Poisson and Cox processes for modeling the default time and number of defaults over a timer horizon are discussed. In §5.6, we discuss valuation of CDSs using a deterministic intensity model. In §5.7, we review hazard rate calibration to real Bloomberg market data. In §5.8, we discuss credit curve construction and calibration to market data. In §5.9, we discuss multi-name credit derivatives with credit default basket swaps and indices. In §5.10, we provide a Matlab implementation for pricing CDSs based on a pricing algorithm given in §5.6. In §5.11, we provide a C++ implementation for pricing credit baskets and credit indices. In §5.12, we discuss credit linked notes.

5.1 CREDIT DEFAULT SWAPS

Credit default swaps (CDSs) are the standard unfunded credit derivative for hedgers and investors of credit risk. A CDS is a bilateral swap contract between a protection buyer and a protection seller. The protection buyer (short the credit) purchases credit protection from a protection seller (long the credit) against the risk of default of an asset such as a corporate bond issued by a specified *reference entity*. The protection buyer pays a fee, generally quarterly, determined by the specified CDS spread.

CDSs generally mature on the 20th day of either March, June, September, or December using a modified following day counting convention. The most liquid CDSs have five-year maturities and notional amounts of $10 million.

Following a defined credit event such as default, a credit downgrade, bankruptcy, failure to pay interest or principal, repudiation, or restructuring, the protection buyer receives a payment intended to compensate against the loss on a long position in the underlying credit. For instance, suppose Bank of America (BoA) made a three-year $10 million term loan to Ford Motor Company on February 5, 2004 that matures February 7, 2007. BoA is concerned about the deterioration in Ford's credit quality and a possible default on the loan. In order to protect itself, BoA can buy three-year protection (maturing March 20, 2007) on Ford (the reference obligor) from a protection seller using a Ford-issued bond—i.e., 6.75% '07 senior unsecured—as the reference asset.[4]

If the quoted CDS spread on Ford is 156 basis points at the time of the CDS contract, then every quarter, BoA pays $10,000,000 \times 0.25 \times 0.0157 = \$39,250$ to the protection seller. In actuality, the amount the protection buyer pays is $(A/360) \times 10,000,000 \times 0.0157 = (A/360) \times \$157,000$ where A is the actual number of days in a quarter between payment dates. In addition, if the credit event occurs between two default premium payment dates, then the protection buyer pays that part of the default swap premium that has accrued since the last payment date—the accrued interest.

The specification of the default payment settlement can either be cash or physical settlement. In a cash settlement, payment by the protection seller is fixed or is the difference between par and the recovery value of the reference asset following the credit event. Under physical delivery, the protection buyer delivers the defaulted reference securities to the protection seller and receives the difference between par and the market price of the asset after default. The price of the defaulted asset is generally determined by a dealer poll conducted within 14–30 days of the credit event to allow the recovery value to stabilize. In some cases, it may not be possible to price, in which case there may be provisions in the documentation to allow the price of another asset of the same credit quality and similar maturity to be substituted.

If Ford defaults on the issued reference bond before the CDS matures, a credit event is said to occur. To qualify as an actual event, the defaulted amount must exceed a materiality threshold, and the amount must remain unpaid after a grace period of some days.[5]

Assume there is a 40% recovery rate on the bonds. Under cash settlement, the protection seller would pay $6,000,000 to BoA, and BoA would pay the protection seller the accrued default payment up to the default date. Under physical settlement, BoA would deliver 10,000 (defaulted) Ford 6.75% '07 bonds, with a total notional of $10,000,000 (the notional of the CDS) to the protection seller and receive $10,000,000 in return.[6] Because liquidity in defaulted securities can be very low, the CDS contract usually contains more than one bond issue by the reference credit that can be delivered. Consequently, BoA will choose to deliver bonds with the lowest market value so that the CDS gives it a "cheapest-to-deliver" option.

Suppose the recovery rate on the reference asset is 40%; then, Figure 5.1 shows the cash flows if there is no default and if there is default.

A CDS is a par product and so does not totally hedge the loss on an asset that is currently trading away from par. A default swap over hedges the credit risk if the asset trades at a discount, and under hedges the credit risk if the asset trades at a premium. If the asset price falls significantly in price without a credit event, the investor can purchase protection in a smaller face value or can use amortizing default swap where the size of the hedge amortizes to the face value of the bond as maturity approaches.[7]

On a mark-to-market basis, the value of a CDS changes in line with changes in the credit quality of the issuer, as reflected in the issuer's changing default swap spread, because the mark-to-market of a default swap has to reflect the cost of entering into an offsetting transaction. For a protection buyer, the mark-to-market of the default swap position reflects the cost of entering into a short position with the same maturity date as the long protection position.

Denote $S(T)$ as the current default swap spread to the maturity date, $S(0)$ as the default swap spread at trade inception, and $PV01$ as the present value of a zero-recovery, one-basis-point annuity with the maturity of the default swap that terminates following a credit event. Then the mark-to-market value if given by

$$MTM = (S(T) - S(0)) \times PV01$$

Over time, the mark-to-market of the CDS declines with its shortening maturity. If the credit quality of the issuer deteriorates, the mark-to-market of a long protection position

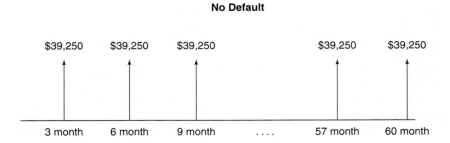

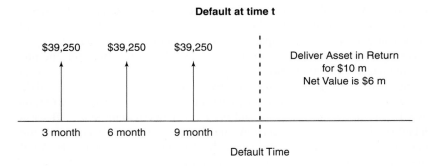

Figure 5.1 CDS cash flows.

(short the credit) will increase, whereas if the credit quality increases, the mark-to-market of the long position will decline.

5.2   CDS Day Counting Conventions

The day that a CDS is executed is the trade date t. The next day, known as $t + 1$, is the effective date, and $t + 3$ days is the settlement date. In general, CDS trade books use a *modified following* day counting convention. Under a modified following convention, if a settlement or payment date falls on a weekend day or a holiday, the next following business day is used for calculation purposes. The premium payments of the protection buyer are calculated on an actual/360 basis, while the protection seller's payments are computed on an actual/365 basis.

5.3   General Valuation of Credit Default Swaps

To value a credit default swap, the spread is chosen so that the net present value of the cash flows between the protection buyer and seller is set equal to zero. Default swaps can be valued within the well-known reduced-form framework of Duffie (1998), Lando (1998), and Duffie and Singleton (1999).[8] In the reduced-form model, in contrast to the structural models proposed by Merton (1973), default times are assumed to follow a jump process with an exogenous intensity. As long as the intensity is assumed to be a linear function of affine diffusion variables, it can be econometrically estimated from observed prices and credit spreads using the methodology of Duffie and Singleton.[9] Moreover, reduced-form models can be used to study default correlation. An important assumption of the model, which facilitates construction of the doubly stochastic Poisson process called a Cox process in Lando (1998), is that multiple defaults are independent conditional on the sample paths of the default intensities.[10] This implies that default correlation is synonymous with the correlation of the default intensities. However, as pointed out by Schonbucher and Schubert (2001), "the default correlations that can be reached with this approach are typically too low when compared with empirical default correlations."

Assume the default swap matures at time T. The payments on the "premium" leg occur at times $\widetilde{A} = \{T_1, ..., T_n\}$, n discrete payment dates; $\Delta_i = \Delta(T_{i-1}, T_i)$ is the day count fraction on the interval (T_{i-1}, T_i), $T_0 = 0$, fixed in advance at time 0 up to the default time τ if it occurs before maturity T, or until maturity T if no default occurs. We assume $T_n \leq T$ (typically $T_n = T$). Denote $R \in (0, 1)$ as the recovery rate of the defaulted reference asset. Denote $\mathbf{1}_{\{\tau<T\}}$ as the indicator function that is equal to 1 if $\tau < T$ and 0 otherwise. Let $D(t, T) = B(t)/B(T)$ be the bank account numeraire where $B(t) = B(0, t) = \exp\left(-\int_0^t r(u)\,du\right)$, and $r(t)$ is the instantaneous risk-free rate, where $t \in [T_{i-1}, T_i)$— i.e., T_i is the first payment date of $T_1, ..., T_n$ following t. Moreover, let the discount bond price $P(t, T) = E^Q\left(\frac{B(t)}{B(T)}|\Im_t\right)$, where $\Im_t$ is the filtration (information) at time t. To reduce notation, $E_t[.] = E[\cdot|\Im_t]$. Denote E^Q as the expectation under the risk-neutral probability measure.

Typically, three fundamental assumptions are postulated in the valuation:

1. The interest rate process and the default process are independent under the risk-neutral martingale measure Q.

2. Defaults can happen only at a set of finite, discrete dates.

3. Default payments are settled immediately upon default.

The total payments by the protection buyer (PB) are

$$CDS^{PB}(t, T; \tau)$$
$$= sN\sum_{i=1}^n D(t, T_i)\Delta_i \mathbf{1}_{\{\tau<T\}} + sND(t, \tau)\Delta_i \frac{(\tau - T_{i-1})}{(T_i - T_{i-1})}\mathbf{1}_{\{\tau<T_n\}} \qquad (5.1)$$

where the rightmost term is the accrued interest, $A(T_{\beta(t)-1}, \tau)$, from the previous payment date up until the time of default $\tau > t$, that the protection buyers pays to the seller at default. Thus, protection buyer payment can be broken into the premium leg (PL) plus the accrued premium[11] (AP) since the last payment date. If there is no default, the protection seller

(PS) pays nothing to the protection buyer, but if there is a default before maturity, then the protection seller pays the unrecovered portion of the loan, which has a value of:

$$CDS^{PS}(t, T; \tau) = (1 - R) D(t, \tau) N \mathbf{1}_{\{\tau < T\}} \qquad (5.2)$$

The value of the CDS at time $t > 0$ is the premium leg (payments made by the protection buyer) minus the default leg (payments made by the protection seller upon default):

$$CDS(t, T) = CDS^{PB} - CDS^{PS}$$

The initial value of the CDS is the value of the spread s that makes the payments of $CDS^{PB}(t, T; \tau)$ equal to $CDS^{PS}(t, T; \tau)$ at time 0 so that the value of the swap is zero to both parties. Setting equation (5.1) to (5.2) at time 0 yields

$$sN \sum_{i=\beta(t)}^{n} D(0, T_i) \Delta_i \mathbf{1}_{\{\tau > T\}} + sND(0, \tau) \Delta_i \frac{(\tau - T_{\beta(t)-1})}{(T_i - T_{i-1})} \mathbf{1}_{\{\tau < T_n\}}$$

$$= (1 - R) D(0, \tau) N \mathbf{1}_{\{\tau < T\}}$$

so that

$$s = \frac{(1 - R) D(0, \tau) \mathbf{1}_{\{\tau < T\}}}{\sum_{i=1}^{n} D(0, T_i) \Delta_i \mathbf{1}_{\{\tau > T_i\}} + D(0, \tau) \Delta_i \frac{(\tau - T_{\beta(t)-1})}{(T_i - T_{i-1})} \mathbf{1}_{\{\tau < T_n\}}} \qquad (5.3)$$

or

$$s = \frac{(1 - R) \exp\left(-\int_0^\tau r(u)\, du\right) \mathbf{1}_{\{\tau < T\}}}{\sum_{i=1}^{n} \exp\left(-\int_0^{T_i} r(u)\, du\right) \Delta_i \mathbf{1}_{\{\tau > T_i\}} + \exp\left(-\int_0^\tau r(u)\, du\right) \Delta_i \frac{(\tau - T_{i-1})}{(T_i - T_{i-1})}}.$$

$$(5.4)$$

Thus, the net present value of the CDS at time $0 < t < \tau$ is as follows:

$$CDS(t, T)$$

$$= \mathbf{1}_{\{\tau > t\}} N \left[s \sum_{i=1}^{n} D(t, T_i) \Delta_i \mathbf{1}_{\{\tau > T\}} \right.$$

$$\left. + sD(t, \tau) \Delta_i \frac{(\tau - T_{i-1})}{(T_i - T_{i-1})} \mathbf{1}_{\{\tau < T_n\}} - (1 - R) D(t, \tau) \mathbf{1}_{\{\tau < T\}} \right] \qquad (5.5)$$

5.4   HAZARD RATE FUNCTION

Given a filtered probability space $\left(\Omega, \Im, (\Im_t)_{t \geq 0}, P\right)$, let τ be the $(\Im_t)$ − stopping time at which default occurs, with a distribution function $F(t) = P(\tau \leq t)$ and probability density function $f(t)$. Denote $P(t < \tau < t + \Delta t | \tau > t)$ the probability that the default will occur in the interval $(t, t + \Delta t)$, given that the reference entity has survived up to time t, we define the hazard function $h = \lambda(t)$ as

$$\lambda(t) = \lim_{\Delta t \to 0} P(t < \tau \le t + \Delta t | \tau > t).$$

The relation between $\lambda(t)$, $f(t)$, and $F(t)$ can be established as follows:

$$\lambda(t) = \frac{P(t < \tau \le t + \Delta t | \tau > t)}{P(\tau > t)} = \lim_{\Delta t \to 0} \frac{\int_t^{t+\Delta t} f(u)\,du}{\int_t^{\infty} f(u)\,du}$$

$$= \frac{f(t)}{1 - F(t)} = \frac{\frac{\partial}{\partial t} F(t)}{1 - F(t)} = -\frac{\partial}{\partial t} \log(1 - F(t)).$$

Solving the differential equation, we get

$$F(t) = 1 - \exp\left(-\int_0^t \lambda(u)du\right) \tag{5.6}$$

and

$$f(t) = \lambda(t) \exp\left(-\int_0^t \lambda(u)du\right) \tag{5.7}$$

From (5.5), we define the survival probability $S(t) = 1 - F(t) = P(\tau > t)$ so that

$$S(t) = \exp\left(-\int_0^t \lambda(u)du\right). \tag{5.8}$$

It should be noted that the distribution function $F(t)$ and the survival function $S(t)$ provide two mathematically equivalent ways of specifying the distribution of the random variable of time-until-default.[12]

5.5   POISSON AND COX PROCESSES

To compute the value of (5.4), we need to model the default time τ (also known as a stopping time of a credit event). We model the default time τ as a Cox process. As Lando describes, a Cox process is a generalization of the Poisson process where the intensity is allowed to be random, such that if conditioned on a particular realization of the intensity $\lambda(\cdot, \omega)$, the jump process becomes an inhomogeneous Poisson process with intensity $\lambda(s, \omega)$.[13] Under such a process, τ is the first jump-time of a time-inhomogeneous (doubly stochastic Poisson) counting (integer-valued) process $N(t)$ defined by

$$N(t) := \begin{cases} \sum_{i \in N} \mathbf{1}_{\{\tau_i \le t\}} & \text{for } t > 0 \\ 0 & \text{for } t = 0 \end{cases}$$

where $\mathbf{1}_{\{\tau_i \leq t\}}$ is the indicator function of the $(\Im_t)$−stopping time τ_i. Furthermore, the process for $0 \leq t < T$ satisfies the following conditions:

1. The increment $N(T) - N(t)$ is independent of the σ−algebra $\Im_t$.

2. The increment $N(T) - N(t)$ is distributed according to a Poisson law with a strictly increasing, non-negative, and invertible parameter (known as a hazard function)

$$\Lambda(t) = \int_0^t \lambda(u) du$$

where $\lambda(t)$ is a non-negative, progressively measurable intensity process:[14]

$$P(N(T) - N(t) = n) = \frac{\left(\int_t^T \lambda(u) du \right)^n}{n!} \exp \left(-\int_t^T \lambda(u) du \right).$$

In particular, $N(0) = 0$, and

$$P(N(0) = 0) = \exp \left(-\int_0^t \lambda(u) du \right)$$

and N possesses stationary independent increments. $\Lambda(t)$ is known as the predictable compensator process and gives a lot of information about the probabilities of jumps over the next time step. $\Lambda(t)$ is increasing because $N(t)$ is also increasing. The model assumes that $N(t + \Delta t) - N(t)$ can only be 1 or 0 so that

$$\begin{aligned} E\left[\Lambda\left(t + \Delta t \right) - \Lambda\left(t \right) | \Im_t \right] \\ = 1 \cdot P\left[N\left(t + \Delta t \right) - N\left(t \right) = 1 | \Im_t \right] + 0 \cdot P\left[N\left(t + \Delta t \right) - N\left(t \right) = 0 | \Im_t \right] \\ = P\left[N\left(t + \Delta t \right) - N\left(t \right) = 1 | \Im_t \right] \end{aligned}$$

Thus, the compensated process $N(t) - \Lambda(t)$ is a local martingale. Because the compensator is predictable, its increments over the next time step are deterministic. Thus, the compensator gives "a running measure of the local jump probabilities of the counting process."[15]

The time-in homogenous process N can be written as a time-in homogenous process $N(t) = M(\Lambda^{-1}(t))$ with constant intensity equal to 1. M is a unit-jump increasing, right continuous process with stationary increments and $M(0) = 0$. If N jumps for the first time at τ, then M jumps for the first time at $\Lambda(\tau)$. Because M is Poisson with intensity one, its first jump at $\Lambda(\tau)$ is distributed as an exponential random variable with parameter 1, so that under a risk-neutral probability measure Q

$$Q\left(\Lambda(\tau) < s \right) = 1 - \exp(-s).$$

To simulate the first jump τ of N, let Y be a unit exponential random variable and define the default time as

$$\tau = \inf \left(t : \int_0^t \lambda(u)\, du \geq Y \right) \tag{5.9}$$

We could write the intensity process as a function of the current level of state variables. These state variables include time, stock prices, credit ratings, and other relevant variables for predicting likelihood of default. In this case, we would denote the intensity as $\lambda(X_t)$, where X is a $\Re^d$-valued stochastic process. However, for simplicity, we will assume that the hazard rate is only a function of time.

In the risk-neutral world under a risk-neutral probability measure Q, we need the following informational setup (denoting $\sigma(\cdot)$ as the sigma algebra):

$$G_t = \sigma \left(\mathbf{1}_{\{\tau \leq u\}} : 0 \leq u \leq t \right)$$
$$H_t = \sigma \left(X_s : 0 \leq s \leq t \right)$$
$$\Im_t = G_t \vee H_t$$

where we assume that we have a probability space $(\Omega, \Im, P)$ that supports a standard unit rate Poisson process N and is equipped with the filtration $\Im_t$, which corresponds to knowing the evolution of the state variables up to time t and whether default has occurred or not.[16] We will make use of the following fact:

$$E\left[\mathbf{1}_{\{\tau \geq T\}} \,\middle|\, \Im_t \right] = \mathbf{1}_{\{\tau > t\}} \exp \left(- \int_t^T \lambda(s)\, ds \right)$$

We make use of the fact that the conditional expectation is 0 on the set $\{\tau \leq t\}$ and that the set $\{\tau > t\}$ is an atom of G_t in the following proof:[17]

$$E\left[\mathbf{1}_{\{\tau \geq T\}} \,\middle|\, \Im_t \right] = \mathbf{1}_{\{\tau > t\}} E\left(\mathbf{1}_{\{\tau \geq T\}} \,\middle|\, \Im_t \right)$$
$$= \mathbf{1}_{\{\tau > t\}} \frac{P(\{\tau \geq T\} \cap \{\tau > t\} \,|\, \Im_t)}{P(\tau > t \,|\, \Im_t)}$$
$$= \mathbf{1}_{\{\tau > t\}} \frac{P(\tau \geq T \,|\, \Im_t)}{P(\tau > t \,|\, \Im_t)}$$
$$= \mathbf{1}_{\{\tau > t\}} \frac{\exp\left(-\int_0^T \lambda(s)\, ds \right)}{\exp\left(-\int_0^t \lambda(s)\, ds \right)}$$
$$= \mathbf{1}_{\{\tau > t\}} \exp\left(-\int_t^T \lambda(s)\, ds \right).$$

We can also assume the stochastic discount factor for rates, $D(t,T) = \exp\left(-\int_t^T r(u)\, du \right)$, and the default time τ are independent whenever intensities are deterministic.

5.6   VALUATION USING A DETERMINISTIC INTENSITY MODEL

We can value the CDS using a deterministic intensity model by taking the risk-neutral expectation of (5.4):

$$
= E^Q \left\{ \mathbf{1}_{\{\tau>t\}} N \left[s \sum_{i=1}^{n} D(t, T_i) \Delta_i \mathbf{1}_{\{\tau>T_i\}} \right. \right.
$$

$$
\left. \left. + s D(t, \tau) \Delta_i \frac{(\tau - T_{i-1})}{(T_i - T_{i-1})} \mathbf{1}_{\{\tau<T_n\}} - (1-R) D(t, \tau) \mathbf{1}_{\{\tau\leq T\}} \right] \middle| \Im_t \right\}
$$

$$
= \mathbf{1}_{\{\tau>t\}} N E^Q \left[s \sum_{i=1}^{n} E^Q [D(t, T_i) \mathbf{1}_{\{\tau>T\}}] \Delta_i \right.
$$

$$
+ s E^Q \left[D(t, \tau) \Delta_i \mathbf{1}_{\{\tau<T_n\}} \right] \frac{(\tau - T_{i-1})}{(T_i - T_{i-1})}
$$

$$
\left. - (1-R) E^Q \left[D(t, \tau) \mathbf{1}_{\{\tau<T\}} \right] \middle| \Im_t \right]
$$

$$
= \mathbf{1}_{\{\tau>t\}} N E^Q \left[s \sum_{i=1}^{n} P(t, T_i) \mathbf{1}_{\{\tau>T_i\}} \Delta_i \right. \tag{5.10}
$$

$$
\left. + s \Delta_i P(t, \tau) \mathbf{1}_{\{\tau<T_n\}} \frac{(\tau - T_{i-1})}{(T_i - T_{i-1})} - (1-R) P(t, \tau) \mathbf{1}_{\{\tau<T\}} \right] \middle| \Im_t \right]
$$

$$
= \mathbf{1}_{\{\tau>t\}} N \left[s \sum_{i=1}^{n} P(t, T_i) \Delta_i \exp \left(- \int_t^{T_i} \lambda(s) ds \right) \right.
$$

$$
+ s \Delta_i \int_t^{T_n} P(t, u) \frac{(u - T_{i-1})}{(T_i - T_{i-1})} dQ\{\tau \leq u | \Im_t\}
$$

$$
\left. - (1-R) \int_t^T P(t, u) \lambda(u) \exp \left(- \int_t^u \lambda(s) ds \right) du \right]
$$

so that

$$
CDS(t, \tau, T, s) = \mathbf{1}_{\{\tau>t\}} N \left[s \sum_{i=1}^{n} P(t, T_i) \Delta_i \exp \left(- \int_t^{T_i} \lambda(s) ds \right) \right.
$$

$$
+ s \Delta_i \int_t^{T_n} P(t, u) \left(\frac{(u - T_{i-1})}{(T_i - T_{i-1})} \right) \tag{5.11}
$$

$$\cdot \lambda(u) \exp\left(- \int_t^u \lambda(s)ds \right) du$$

$$- (1-R) \int_t^T P(t,u)\lambda(u) \exp\left(- \int_t^u \lambda(s)ds \right) du \Bigg]$$ (5.11)

If we set (5.11) to 0 and solve for the spread, we get at $t = 0$

$$s = \cfrac{(1-R) \int_0^{T_n} \lambda(u) P(0,u) \exp\left(- \int_0^u \lambda(s)ds \right) du}{\left(\sum_{i=1}^n \left\{ \Delta_i P(0,T_i) \exp\left(- \int_0^{T_i} \lambda(s)ds \right) + \int_{T_{i-1}}^{T_i} \Delta_i \lambda(u) \left(P(0,u) \exp\left(- \int_0^u \lambda(s)ds \right) \frac{(u-T_{i-1})}{(T_i-T_{i-1})} \right) du \right\} \right)}$$ (5.12)

We note that the denominator in (5.12) is the risky premium value of a one basis point move in the spread (RPV01), namely the risky PV01. O'Kane and Turnbull note that the integral in the protection leg recovery payment expression (the numerator in (5.12)) can be tedious to evaluate. Without any loss of accuracy, they simply assume that the credit event can occur only on a finite number M of discrete points per year.[18] For a T_n maturity default swap, we have $M \times T_n$ discrete times, which can be labeled as $m = 1, ..., M \times T_n$. We then have

$$PL = (1-R) \sum_{m=1}^{M \times T_n} P(0,T_m) \cdot$$

$$\left(\exp\left(- \int_0^{T_{m-1}} \lambda(s)ds \right) - \exp\left(- \int_0^{T_m} \lambda(s)ds \right) \right).$$ (5.13)

The lower the value of M, the fewer calculations required, but the accuracy is also reduced. O'Kane and Turnbull (2003) point out that the expression for the accrued premium

$$sN \sum_{i=1}^n \int_{T_{i-1}}^{T_i} \Delta_i \lambda(u) P(0,u) \left(\exp\left(- \int_0^u \lambda(s)ds \right) \frac{(u-T_{i-1})}{(T_i-T_{i-1})} \right) du$$

is a complicated expression to evaluate directly, but can be approximated as[19]

$$\frac{sN}{2} \sum_{i=1}^n \Delta_i \lambda(u) P(0,u) \left((Q(0,T_{n-1}) - Q(0,T_n)) \frac{(u-T_{i-1})}{(T_i-T_{i-1})} \right) du$$ (5.14)

by noting that if a default does occur between two premium dates, the average accrued premium is half the full premium due to be paid at the end of the premium period and assuming a piecewise constant hazard rate. The full value of premium leg is

$$s \times N \times RPV01$$

where

$$RPV01 = \sum_{i=1}^{n} \Delta_i P(0, T_i) \left[Q(0, T_i) + \frac{1_{AP}}{2} \left(Q(0, T_{i-1}) - Q(0, T_i) \right) \right]$$

where $1_{AP} = 1$ if the CDS contract specifies accrued premium and 0 otherwise,[20] and $Q(T_v, T_n)$ is the arbitrage-free survival probability of the reference entity from valuation time T_ν, $\nu = 0, \dots, n - 1$, to the premium payment time T_n. Assuming a piecewise constant hazard rate, we can define

$$Q(T_v, T_n) = \begin{cases} \exp\left(-\lambda_{0,1}\tau\right) & \text{if } 0 < \tau \le 1 \\ \exp\left(-\lambda_{0,1} - \lambda_{1,3}(\tau - 1)\right) & \text{if } 1 < \tau \le 3 \\ \exp\left(-\lambda_{0,1} - 2\lambda_{1,3} - \lambda_{3,5}(\tau - 3)\right) & \text{if } 3 < \tau \le 5 \\ \exp\left(-\lambda_{0,1} - 2\lambda_{1,3} - 2\lambda_{3,5} - \lambda_{5,7}(\tau - 5)\right) & \text{if } 5 < \tau \le 7 \\ \exp\left(-\lambda_{0,1} - 2\lambda_{1,3} - 2\lambda_{3,5} - 2\lambda_{5,7} - \lambda_{7,10}(\tau - 7)\right) & \text{if } \tau \ge 7 \end{cases}$$

where $\tau = T_n - T_\nu$ and assuming the hazard rate remains flat beyond the 10Y maturity.

Assuming the hazard rate function is piecewise constant, we can write (5.12) to value a 1Y default swap as

$$s = \frac{(1 - R) \int_0^{T_n} \lambda_{0,1} P(0, u) \exp\left(-\lambda_{0,1} u\right) du}{\sum_{i=1}^{n} \left\{ \Delta_i P(0, T_i) \exp\left(-\lambda_{0,1} T_i\right) + \int_{T_{i-1}}^{T_i} \lambda_{0,1} \Delta_i P(0, u) \left(\exp\left(-\lambda_{0,1} u\right) \frac{(u - T_{i-1})}{(T_i - T_{i-1})} \right) du \right\}}$$

or using O'Kane and Turnbull's approximation to simplify calculations

$$s = \frac{(1 - R) \sum_{m=1}^{12} P(0, T_m) \left(\exp\left(-\lambda_{0,1} T_{m-1}\right) - \exp\left(-\lambda_{0,1} T_m\right) \right)}{\frac{1}{2} \sum_{\substack{i=3 \\ Step3}}^{12} \Delta(T_{i-3}, T) P(0, T_i) \left(\exp\left(-\lambda_{0,1} T_{i-3}\right) - \exp\left(-\lambda_{0,1} T_i\right) \right)}$$

assuming quarterly payments, a monthly discretization ($M = 12$), and accrued premium.

Usually, the market sets the CDS spread s to a value $s^{mid}(t, T)$ (average of the bid and ask) that makes the CDS fair at time t, the value of s that makes $CDS(t, T; \tau, s^{mid}(t, T), N) = 0$. In the market, CDS quotes are made at time t through bid and ask value for the "fair" spread $s^{mid}(t, T)$ for a set of maturities $T = t + 1y$ up to $T = t + 10y$.

It can also be shown that a Nelson-Siegel curve approximation can be used to bootstrap the survival function and thereby generate the forward implied default probability curve. Starting with $S_0 = 1$, then

$$S_1 = \frac{\frac{1}{2}(1-R)(Z_0 + Z_1) - s_1\tau_1(Z_0 + 2Z_1)/6}{\left(\left(\frac{1}{2}(1-R)(Z_0 + Z_1) - s_1\tau_1(Z_0 + 2Z_1)/6\right) + s_1\tau_1 Z_1\right)}$$

and

$$S_n = \frac{(1-R)\left(\sum\limits_{i=1}^{n-1}(Z_{i-1} + Z_i)(S_{i-1} - S_i) + \frac{1}{2}(Z_{n-1} + Z_n)S_{n-1}\right) - s_n\left(\sum\limits_{i=1}^{n-1}\frac{1}{6}(Z_{i-1} + 2Z_i)\tau_i(S_{i-1} - S_i) + Z_i S_i \tau_i - \frac{1}{6}(Z_{n-1} + 2Z_n)\tau_n S_{n-1}\right)}{\left(\frac{1}{2}(Z_{n-1} + Z_n)(1-R) - s_n\tau_n(Z_{n-1} + 2Z_n)/3\right) + s_n\tau_n Z_n}$$

with the restriction that we force $0 \le S_n \le S_{n-1} \le 1$ and where

- s_n is the par spread for maturity n.

- Z_i is the risk-less discount factor from time 0 to T_i.

- S_i is the no-default probability from time 0 to T_i.

- τ_i is the accrual period from T_{i-1} to T_i.

- $(S_{i-1} - S_i)$ is the probability of a credit event occurring during the period T_{i-1} to T_i.

5.7   HAZARD RATE FUNCTION CALIBRATION

For simplicity, many practitioners assume the hazard rate is deterministic—i.e., constant, $\Lambda(T) = \lambda$, or piecewise-constant

$$\Lambda(T) = \begin{cases} \lambda_{0,1} & T_0 < t \le T_1 \\ \lambda_{1,2} & T_1 < t \le T_2 \\ \dots & \\ \lambda_{n-1,n} & T_{n-1} < t \le T_n \end{cases} \tag{5.15}$$

as shown in Figure 5.2.

We could assume that the curve is piecewise linear. However, this only makes a difference if (1) we do not have quoted spreads for many maturities, and (2) the curve is steeply sloped. This is generally not the case because most names only have liquidity at the five-year default swap, and the curve is therefore assumed to be flat.[21] The main exception is when we have an inverted spread curve, usually associated with distressed credit.[22]

Given 1Y, 3Y, 5Y, 7Y, and 10Y default swap spread values, we would assume that we have a hazard rate term structure with five sections: $\lambda_{0,1}$, $\lambda_{1,3}$, $\lambda_{3,5}$, $\lambda_{5,7}$, and $\lambda_{7,10}$.

We follow the common assumption in the calibration methodology that postulates that hazard rates are piecewise constant between the CDS maturity dates. If we denote with

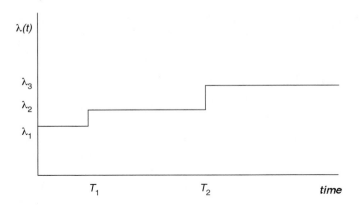

Figure 5.2 Piecewise-Linear Hazard function.

$[T_1, T_2, ..., T_n]$ the expiration (in years) of the CDS contracts traded and quoted in the market, this implies that the hazard function $\lambda(t)$ can be expressed as

$$\lambda(t) = \sum_{i=1}^{n} c_i \mathbf{1}_{T_{i-1}, T_i}(t),$$

for some positive constants c_i and $i = 1, ..., n$.

This assumption implies that the distribution function $F(t)$ in (5.4) can be written as:

$$F(t) = 1 - \exp\left[-\sum_{j=1}^{k} c_j(T_j - T_{j-1}) \right],$$

$$k = \begin{cases} 1 & \text{if } t \le t_1 \\ 2 & \text{if } t_1 < t \le t_2 \\ \cdots & \cdots \\ n & \text{if } t > t_{n-1} \end{cases}$$

(5.16)

By inserting (5.16) into the spread pricing equation (5.12) for the CDS with the shortest maturity T_1, and appropriately fixing the recovery rate for each reference entity, we can recover c_1. Knowing c_1, one can calibrate c_2 using the market spread relative to the CDS expiring at T_2, and in this fashion calibrate all the remaining c_j's up to time T_n. The process of iteratively solving for the hazard rates c_j is known as *bootstrapping*.

Example 1

Suppose a protection buyer buys three-year CDS protection on $10 million of notional of Ford Motor Credit on March 1, 2004 (the trade date). The effective date would be $t+1$ day, March 2, 2004; the settlement date would be $t+3$ days, or March 7, 2004; and the maturity date would be March 20, 2007 because the CDSs mature on the 20th day of March, June, September, and December. Typically, default swaps use a *modified following* day counting convention so that if the settlement or payment date falls on a weekend day or a holiday, the next following business day will be used for calculation purposes. For instance, the first two payment dates will be March 22, 2004 and June 21, 2004, respectively, because March 20, 2004 falls on a Saturday and June 20, 2004 falls on a Sunday. The three-year CDS quoted in Figure 5.1 is 156 basis points.

Table 5.1 shows the payment schedule.

For instance, the screen shown in Figure 5.3 is a set of CDS quotes for Ford taken from Bloomberg on March 5, 2004.

Notice that only the one-year, three-year, and five-year are actively quoted. Because different broker-dealers may offer different bid-ask quotes, a protection buyer should check with various broker-dealers to get the best quote. For instance, one can get an indicator quote from a broker-dealer Dresner Bank, as shown in Figure 5.4.

From equation (5.12), we can approximate the actual fair spread of Ford. In order to do so, we need to bootstrap the Treasury yield curve or interpolate the U.S. agency zero rate curve. Using Bloomberg, we find the Treasury and zero rates on March 5, 2004, as shown in Figure 5.5.

We can also find the discount factors from the U.S. Libor swap curve or U.S. discount note curves, as shown in Figure 5.6.[23]

We will bootstrap using the U.S. Government agency curve. The screen in Figure 5.7 shows a comparison between the U.S. Government agency zero and the U.S. Libor swap (Act/360). The curves are very close between one and seven years. In practice, most trading desks bootstrap using either the U.S. Libor swap curve or the Euribor swap curve.

We can back out the implied hazard rate in equation (5.12). We assume that the hazard rate is piecewise constant—i.e, $\lambda(s) = h$. Suppose we want to calculate the implied default probability for the three-year CDS for Ford Motor Credit. In this case, $T = 1$ and we assume $R = 0.40$. After we have bootstrapped the yield curve for all maturity payment dates (we can use linear interpolation), we can compute the value of all discount bonds.

Table 5.1

Num. Days	Tenor (Actual/360)	Payment Date	Payment
21	0.0583	Mon. March 22, 2004	$9,094.80
92	0.2556	Mon. June 21, 2004	$39,873.60
92	0.2556	Mon. Sept. 20, 2004	$39,873.60
92	0.2556	Mon. Dec. 20, 2004	$39,873.60
92	0.2556	Mon. March 21, 2005	$39,873.60
93	0.2583	Mon. June 21, 2005	$40,294.80
92	0.2556	Tue. Sept. 20, 2005	$39,873.60
92	0.2556	Tue. Dec. 20, 2005	$39,873.60
91	0.2528	Tue. March 20, 2006	$39,436.80
93	0.2583	Tue. June 20, 2006	$40,294.80
93	0.2583	Wed. Sept. 20, 2006	$40,294.80
91	0.2528	Wed. Dec. 20, 2006	$39,436.80
91	0.2528	Tues. Mar. 20, 2007	$39,436.80

Figure 5.3 CDS Spreads. *Source: Reproduced with permission from Bloomberg.*

Figure 5.4 CDS Auto Spreads. *Source: Reproduced with permission from Bloomberg.*

```
Page                                                              P089 Corp    FMCH
Hit <PAGE> for more info or <MENU> for list of curves.
                        FAIR MARKET YIELD CURVES – HISTORY

Curve                    90                      80

Title              USD Govt               USD Trsy
Date               Agncy Zeros            Composite
3MO                3/ 5/04                3/ 5/04
6MO                1.2853                 0.9202
1YR                1.3650                 0.9559
2YR                1.3984                 1.1034
3YR                1.9668                 1.5751
4YR                2.4743                 2.0784
5YR                2.9214                 2.5121
7YR                3.3146                 2.8465
8YR                3.8891                 3.3884
9YR                4.0665                 3.6600
10YR               4.3047                 3.7455
15YR               4.5120                 3.9580
20YR               5.0496                 4.4816
25YR               5.3044                 4.7609
30YR               5.3225                 4.8929
                   5.4648                 4.6968


Australia 61 2 9777 8600    Brazil 5511 3048 4500      Europe 44 20 7330 7500        Germany 49 69 920410
Hong Kong 852 2977 6000     Japan 81 3 3201 8900   Singapore 65 6212 1000  U.S. 1 212 318 2000   Copyright 2004 Bloomberg L.P.
                                                                                     H185-9-2 05-May-04 19:08:48
```

Figure 5.5 Fair Market Yield curves. *Source: Reproduced with permission from Bloomberg.*

```
<HELP> for explanation.                                           P165 M–Mkt   MMCV

Hit <PAGE> for graph or <MENU> for list of curves.                            Page 2/2

                             MULTIPLE CURVES
Date 3/ 5/2004
```

	LIBOR US	US DISCOUNT NOTES	
	Yield	Yield	Yield
1 DAY		0.92000	
7 DAY	1.07375	0.96000	
15 DAY		0.97000	
21 DAY		0.98000	
30 DAY	1.10000	0.97000	
45 DAY		0.98000	
60 DAY	1.11000	0.98000	
90 DAY	1.12000	0.99000	
4 MONTH	1.14000	1.00000	
5 MONTH	1.16000	1.01000	
6 MONTH	1.19000	1.03000	
7 MONTH	1.22000	1.05000	
8 MONTH	1.25000	1.06000	
9 MONTH	1.29000	1.09000	
1YEAR	1.42000	1.18000	

```
Australia 61 2 9777 8600    Brazil 5511 3048 4500      Europe 44 20 7330 7500        Germany 49 69 920410
Hong Kong 852 2977 6000     Japan 81 3 3201 8900   Singapore 65 6212 1000  U.S. 1 212 318 2000   Copyright 2004 Bloomberg L.P.
                                                                                     H185-9-2 05-May-04 19:08:48
```

Figure 5.6 U.S. Libor Swap curve. *Source: Reproduced with permission from Bloomberg.*

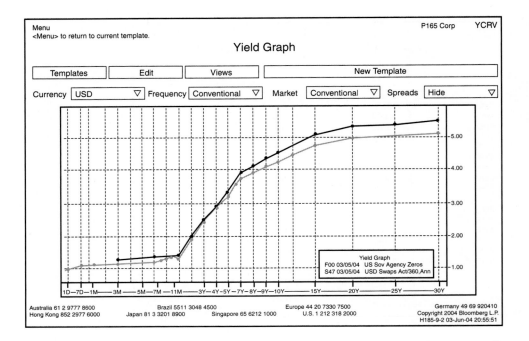

Figure 5.7 U.S. Libor and Discount note rates.   *Source: Reproduced with permission from Bloomberg.*

The one-year CDS average rate is 90 basis points, which is 0.009. We can rewrite (5.12) as follows:

$$s = \frac{(1-R)\int_0^1 hP(0,u)\exp\left(-\int_0^u hds\right)du}{\left(\sum_{i=1}^n \left\{\Delta_i P(0,T_i)\exp\left(-\int_0^{T_i} hds\right) + \int_{T_{i-1}}^{T_i}\Delta_i hP(0,u)\left(\exp\left(-\int_0^u hds\right)\frac{(u-T_{i-1})}{(T_i-T_{i-1})}\right)du\right\}\right)} \tag{5.17}$$

The integrals can be solved using a numerical integration method like Simpson's method. However, a more practical solution is made using the O'Kane and Turnbull approximation. The one-year maturity CDS (with the first five payment dates in Figure 5.4) using the O'Kane and Turnbull approximation assuming quarterly payment frequency, using a monthly discretization ($M = 12$), is

$$0.009 = \frac{0.6 \sum_{m=1}^{12} P(0, T_m) \left(\exp(-\lambda_{0,1}T_{m-1}) - \exp(-\lambda_{0,1}T_m)\right)}{(1/2) \sum_{i=1}^{5} \Delta_i P(0, T_i) \left(\exp\left(-\lambda_{0,1}T_{i-1}\right) + \exp\left(-\lambda_{0,1}T_i\right)\right)}$$

where $T_0 = 0.0, T_1 = 0.0833, T_2 = 0.167, T_3 = 0.25, ..., T_{12} = 1.00$. A numerical iterative procedure must be used to solve for $\lambda_{0,1}$ because it is a nonlinear equation in $\lambda_{0,1}$. Solving, the above equation[24] we find $\lambda_{0,1} = 0.016338 = 1.63\%$. To compute $\lambda_{1,3}$, we solve,

$$0.01495$$

$$= \frac{0.6 \sum_{m=1}^{36} P(0, T_m) \left(\exp\left(-\lambda_{0,1} - \lambda_{1,3}\left(T_{m-1} - 1\right)\right) - \exp\left(-\lambda_{0,1} - \lambda_{1,3}\left(T_m - 1\right)\right)\right)}{(1/2) \sum_{i=1}^{13} \Delta_i P(0, T_i) \left(\exp\left(-\lambda_{0,1} - \lambda_{1,3}\left(T_{i-1} - 1\right)\right) + \exp\left(-\lambda_{0,1} - \lambda_{1,3}\left(T_i - 1\right)\right)\right)}$$

and find $\lambda_{1,3} = 0.02739 = 2.74\%$.

To compute $\lambda_{3,5}$, we solve,

$$0.01885$$

$$= \frac{\left(0.6 \sum_{m=1}^{60} P(0, T_m) \left(\exp\left(-\lambda_{0,1} - \lambda_{1,3}\left(T_{m-1} - 1\right) - \lambda_{3,5}(T_{m-1} - 3)\right) - \exp\left(-\lambda_{0,1} - \lambda_{1,3}\left(T_m - 1\right) - \lambda_{3,5}(T_m - 3)\right)\right)\right)}{\left((1/2) \sum_{i=1}^{21} \Delta_i P(0, T_i) \left(\exp\left(-\lambda_{0,1} - \lambda_{1,3}\left(T_{i-1} - 1\right) - \lambda_{3,5}(T_{i-1} - 3)\right) + \exp\left(-\lambda_{0,1} - \lambda_{1,3}\left(T_i - 1\right) - \lambda_{3,5}(T_i - 3)\right)\right)\right)}$$

and we find $\lambda_{3,5} = 3.69\%$.

In order to calculate these hazard rates, we will use a *Hazard* class that contains methods for their computation:

HazardRate.h

```
#ifndef _HAZARD__
#define _HAZARD__

#include <map>
#include <vector>
#include <math.h>

#define R 0.6   // recovery rate
#define absolute(x) (x > 0) ? x : -x
#define MAX_ITER      25
```

```
#define THIRTY_SIX     36
#define TWELVE         12
#define SIXTY          60
#define EIGHTY_FOUR  84

class HazardRate
{
  public:
        HazardRate() {}
        HazardRate(std::vector<double> sp) : spread(sp) {}
        virtual ~HazardRate() {}
        void init();        // initialize and store tenors and
                            // discount rates
        void calcDiscountBonds();  // calculates discount bond
                                   // prices
        double calcHazard(int num);  // calculates hazard rates
        double calcDeriv(double h, int num);    // calculates first
                                                // derivatives in
        double calcFunc(double h, int num);
        double Q(int num, double h, double t);
  private:
        std::vector<double> P;   // stores discount coupon bond
                                 // prices
        std::map<int,double> T;   // stores zero coupon maturities
        std::vector<double> delta; // stores tenors between payment
                                   // dates
        std::vector<double> r;    // stores discount rates
        std::vector<double> haz;   // stores hazard rates
        std::vector<double> spread;  // stores spread quotes
};

#endif _HAZARD__
```

We must first read in or compute all the tenors and discount rates. The tenors can be computed from a credit payment schedule and the discount rates can be bootstrapped from the yield curve. The data could be read from a text file or read from a socket pipe to a data feed with proper API programming.[25] Suppose that the spread data is

```
1 YR    82.50    97.50
3 YR   143.00   156.00
5 YR   182.00   189.50
7 YR   195.00   200.50
```

We read the spread data in from a text file in the main routine:

Hazard_Main.cpp

```
#include <strstrea.h>
#include <fstream.h>
#include <stdlib.h>
#include <iostream.h>
#include <string.h>
#include "Hazard.h"

void main()
```

```cpp
{
  std::vector<double> mat;
  char buffer[SIZE_X];
  char dataBuffer[SIZE_X];
  std::vector<double> spread;
  char* str = NULL;
  double yr = 0.0;
  double bid = 0.0;
  double ask = 0.0;
  // path to file could be read in as an argument to main function
  const char* file = "c:\\spreads.txt";  // file name

  ifstream fin;  // input file stream
  fin.clear();
  fin.open(file);

  if (fin.good())
  {
      while (!fin.eof())
      {
          fin.getline(buffer,sizeof(buffer)/sizeof(buffer[0]));
          istrstream str(buffer);
          // Get data
          str >> dataBuffer;
          yr = atof(dataBuffer);

          str >> dataBuffer;
          if (strcmp(dataBuffer,"MO") == 0)
            yr = (double) yr/12;
          else if (strcmp(dataBuffer,"WK") == 0)
            yr = (double) yr/52;
          else if (strcmp(dataBuffer,"DY") == 0)
            yr = (double) yr/365;

          mat.push_back(yr);
          str >> dataBuffer;
          bid = atof(dataBuffer);

          str >> dataBuffer;
          ask = atof(dataBuffer);
          spread.push_back((double)((bid + ask)/2)/10000);
      }
  }
  else
    cout << "File not good!" << "\n";

  fin.close();

}
```

The C++ routines that computes these values are:

HazardRate.cpp

```cpp
#include "HazardRate.h"

void HazardRate::calcDiscountBonds()
{
        for (int i = 0; i <= EIGHTY_FOUR; i++)
                P.push_back(exp(-r[i]*T[i]));
}

double HazardRate::calcHazard(int num)
{
        double h = 0.01;
        double temp = h;
        double diff = 0.0;
        double f, f1 = 0.0;
        const double error = 0.000001;
        int cnt = 0;

        do
        {
                temp = h;
                f = calcFunc(h,num);
                f1 = calcDeriv(h,num);
                h = h - f/f1;
                diff = h - temp;
                cnt++;

        }
        while (absolute(diff) > error);
        haz.push_back(h);
        return h;
}

double HazardRate::calcFunc(double h,int num)
{

        double sum = 0;
        double sum1 = 0;
        double v = 0.0;

        if ((num > 0) && (num <= 1))
        {
                for (int i = 1; i <= 5; i++)
                        sum = sum + delta[i-1]*P[i-1]*(Q(num,h,T[i-1]) +
                          Q(num,h,T[i]));

                for (i = 1; i <= 12; i++)
                        sum1 = sum1 + P[i-1]*(Q(num,h,T[i-1]) -
                          Q(num,h,T[i]));

                v = R*sum1 - 0.5*spread[0]*sum;
        }
        else if ((num > 1) && (num <= 3))
```

```
        {
                for (int i = 1; i <= 13; i++)
                        sum = sum + delta[i-1]*P[i-1]*(Q(num,h,T[i-1]) +
                                Q(num,h,T[i]));

                for (i = 1; i <= 36; i++)
                        sum1 = sum1 + P[i-1]*(Q(num,h,T[i-1]) -
                                Q(num,h,T[i]));

                v = R*sum1 - 0.5*spread[1]*sum;

        }
        else if ((num > 3) && (num <= 5))
        {
                for (int i = 1; i <= 21; i++)
                        sum = sum + delta[i-1]*P[i-1]*(Q(num,h,T[i-1]) +
                                Q(num,h,T[i]));

                for (i = 1; i <= 60; i++)
                        sum1 = sum1 + P[i-1]*(Q(num,h,T[i-1]) -
                                Q(num,h,T[i]));

                v = R*sum1 - 0.5*spread[2]*sum;

        }
        else if ((num > 5) && (num <= 7))
        {
                for (int i = 1; i <= 29; i++)
                        sum = sum + delta[i-1]*P[i-1]*(Q(num,h,T[i-1]) +
                                Q(num,h,T[i]));

                for (i = 1; i <= 84; i++)
                        sum1 = sum1 + P[i-1]*(Q(num,h,T[i-1]) -
                                Q(num,h,T[i]));

                v = R*sum1 - 0.5*spread[3]*sum;

        }
        else if (num > 7)
        {
                for (int i = 1; i <= 41; i++)
                        sum = sum + delta[i-1]*P[i-1]*(Q(num,h,T[i-1]) +
                                Q(num,h,T[i]));

                for (i = 1; i <= 120; i++)
                        sum1 = sum1 + P[i-1]*(Q(num,h,T[i-1]) -
                                Q(num,h,T[i]));

                v = R*sum1 - 0.5*spread[4]*sum;
        }

        return v;
}

double HazardRate::calcDeriv(double h, int num)
{
        double sum = 0;
        double sum1 = 0;
```

```
double v = 0.0;
int i = 0;

if ((num > 0) && (num <= 1))
{
   for (i = 1; i <= 5; i++)
        sum = sum + delta[i-1]*P[i-1]*(T[i-1]*Q(num,h,T[i-1]) +
           T[i]*Q(num,h,T[i]));

   for (i = 1; i <= 12; i++)
        sum1 = sum1 + P[i-1]*(-T[i-1]*Q(num,h,T[i-1]) +
           T[i]*Q(num,h,T[i]));

   v = R*sum1 - 0.5*spread[0]*sum;


}
else if ((num > 1) && (num <= 3))
{
    for (i = 1; i <= 13; i++)
       sum = sum + delta[i-1]*P[i-1]*((T[i-1]-1)*Q(num,h,T[i-1]) +
                (T[i]-1)*Q(num,h,T[i]));

    for (i = 1; i <= 36; i++)
        sum1 = sum1 + P[i-1]*(-(T[i-1]-1)*Q(num,h,T[i-1]) +
           (T[i]-1)*Q(num,h,T[i]));

    v = R*sum1 - 0.5*spread[1]*sum;
}
else if ((num > 3) && (num <= 5))
{
    for (i = 1; i <= 21; i++)
        sum = sum + delta[i-1]*P[i-1]*((T[i-1]-1)*Q(num,h,T[i-1]) +
        (T[i]-1)*Q(num,h,T[i]));

    for (i = 1; i <= 60; i++)
        sum1 = sum1 + P[i-1]*(-(T[i-1]-3)*Q(num,h,T[i-1]) +
           (T[i]-1)*Q(num,h,T[i]));

    v = R*sum1 - 0.5*spread[2]*sum;


}
else if ((num > 5) && (num <= 7))
{
    for (i = 1; i <= 29; i++)
       sum = sum + delta[i-1]*P[i-1]*((T[i-1]-1)*Q(num,h,T[i-1]) +
       (T[i]-1)*Q(num,h,T[i]));

   for (i = 1; i <= 84; i++)
      sum1 = sum1 + P[i-1]*(-(T[i-1]-5)*Q(num,h,T[i-1]) +
         (T[i]-1)*Q(num,h,T[i]));

   v = R*sum1 - 0.5*spread[3]*sum;
}
else if (num > 7)
{
   for (int i = 1; i <= 41; i++)
        sum = sum + delta[i-1]*P[i-1]*(Q(num,h,T[i-1]) +
```

```
                         Q(num,h,T[i]));

            for (i = 1; i <= 120; i++)
                sum1 = sum1 + P[i-1]*(-(T[i-1]-7)*Q(num,h,T[i-1]) +
                (T[i]-1)*Q(num,h,T[i]));

            v = R*sum1 - 0.5*spread[4]*sum;
        }

        return v;

}

double HazardRate::Q(int num, double h, double T)
{

        double q = 0.0;

        if ((num > 0) && (num <= 1))
                q = exp(-h*T);
        else if ((num > 1) && (num <= 3))
                q = exp(-haz[0] - h*(T-1));
        else if ((num > 3) && (num <= 5))
                q = exp(-haz[0] - 2*haz[1] - h*(T-3));
        else if ((num > 5) && (num <= 7))
                q = exp(-haz[0] - 2*haz[1] - 2*haz[2] - h*(T-5));
        else // assume hazard rate remains constant beyond 10Y maturity
                q = exp(-haz[0] - 2*haz[1] - 2*haz[2] - 2*haz[3] - h*(T-7));

        return q;
}
```

The tenors and discount rates are entered or read in from a file in the initialization routine.

After bootstrapping the yield curve and calibrating the hazard rates to the Ford Motor Credit market quotes, we generate the following default time distribution function surface, shown in Figure 5.8, for different assumptions of recovery rates.

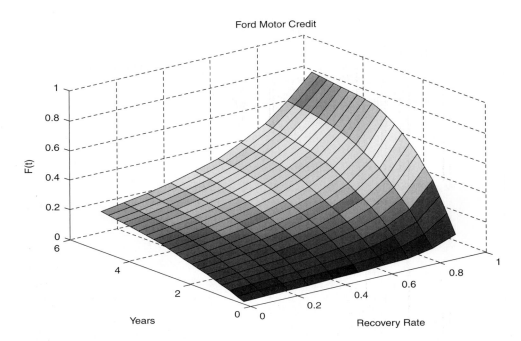

Figure 5.8 Default time distribution function surface.   *Source: Galiani, S. (2003), pg. 36.*

5.8   CREDIT CURVE CONSTRUCTION AND CALIBRATION

As discussed previously, in order to price credit derivatives, it is necessary to construct a credit curve from the prices of liquid instruments like bonds or from asset swap spreads. In the construction process, we can make use of a fundamental result of Duffie and Singleton (1997) for pricing a defaultable coupon-bearing bond using a reduced-form model. We can value a defaultable bond by discounting the promised cash flows by a credit risk-adjusted discounted factor. In general, the credit risk-adjusted factor (or total discount factor) is the product of the risk-free discount factor and the pure credit discount factor if the underlying factors affecting default and those affecting interest rates are independent.[26] Consequently, we value a bond as

$$V(0) = \sum_{i=1}^{n} C_i \exp\left(- \int_0^{t_i} (r(s) + (1 - R)h(s))\, ds \right)$$

where C_i is the promised cash flow at time t_i. We assume that the implied forward default hazard rate is piecewise constant, as is often assumed—i.e., $h(t) = h_i$—and that the implied recovery rate $R = R_i$, $t_{i-1} < t < t_i$

$$V(0) = \sum_{i=1}^{n} C_i \exp\left(- \int_0^{t_i} (r(s) + (1 - R_i)h_i)\, ds \right).$$

In sum, the following steps are used to construct the credit curve:

1. Bootstrap the forward rate curve using a stripping procedure of the Libor swap curve.

2. Find the expected recovery rate by calibration/estimation.

3. Calibration of the spread curve to determine the implied default hazard rates.

Sometimes, step 2 is bypassed by making assumptions about the recovery rate of each obligor based on historical default and recovery rates for obligors of similar credit ratings in the same industry. Furthermore, the calibration of the term structure of default hazard rates (step 3) is separate from the calibration of the expected recovery rates in step 2 because joint calibration typically yields unstable results.[27] In practice, real-world determinations of recovery rates are effected by time delays, dealer polls, and delivery options.

In step 3, the hazard rate calibration methods can assume a parametric form, in which case a functional form of $h(0, s)$ is assumed and some measure (e.g., mean-square) of deviation of the market prices from the calculated prices is minimized. Alternatively, a bootstrap procedure can be used. In such a case, the hazard rate is assumed piecewise constant and starting from the short maturity, the hazard rate is "bootstrapped" similarly to the bootstrapping procedure for the interest rate term structure.

5.9   CREDIT BASKET DEFAULT SWAPS PRICING

A loan or bond portfolio manager will usually find it cheaper to buy protection on a basket of credits (multinames) rather than buying single-name credit default swap protection for each obligor. A credit basket default swap-pricing methodology, such as the copula-based framework, can capture the dependency structure of the obligors in the basket, which in turn is reflected in the fair basket price. The higher the correlation of default probabilities among the credits in the basket, the lower the basket price because the credits behave like one another and thus are similar to a single individual credit. For instance, a basket with all auto sector names, such as Ford, General Motors, Toyota, and Daimler-Chrysler, will be cheaper than a basket with credits in different and diversified business sectors.

Auto credits in a basket are all exposed to the same systematic default risks of the auto sector in particular and economy in general, and so given the high default correlation and dependency structure, an increase in the default probability of one name is likely to be followed by an increase in the default probability of other names.[28] In other words, a default by one credit (and thus a default stopping time) is likely to be followed by default of other credits (and other default stopping times). Conversely, a basket with many diversified credits with low or uncorrelated default probabilities has a price that approximates the sum of credit default protection on each of the individual names in the basket, which is more expensive. A default by one name in the basket is not likely to be followed by a default by another name if the names have low default correlation.

Basket prices can be valued using generalized Monte Carlo simulation that incorporates the copula methodology. The simulation of default times of the various credits in the basket is an important step.

Generation of Correlated Default Stopping Times

The simulation of default times within a portfolio context is intricately related with the specific choice of the copula function used to capture the dependency structure among obligors and to the parametric form of the univariate marginals used to define survival functions for each entity. Based on this observation, Li proposed to decompose the simulation algorithm into a two-stage procedure:

1. Generation of correlated uniform random variables on $[0, 1]$ from an N-dimensional copula.

2. Translation of correlated uniform random variables into default times via the inverse of the marginal distribution function.

The first step is specific to the particular choice of copula function; the second is connected with the default time arrival setting discussed in §5.5.

Sampling from Elliptical Copulae

Multivariate Gaussian Copula

The procedure for generating random variables from the Gaussian copula $C_R^{Gaussian}$ with correlation matrix R proceeds as follows:

1. Find a suitable (e.g., Cholesky) decomposition A of R, such that $R = A \cdot A^T$.

2. Draw an N-dimensional vector $\mathbf{z} = (z_1, z_2, ..., z_N)'$ of uncorrelated standard normal variates.

3. Set $\mathbf{x} := \mathbf{z}'\mathbf{A}$.

4. Set $\mathbf{x}$ back to an N-dimensional vector $\mathbf{u}$ of uniform variables on $[0, 1]$ by computing $\mathbf{u} = \mathbf{\Phi}(\mathbf{x})$.

   Then, $\mathbf{u} \sim C_R^{Gaussian}$.

Multivariate Student's t Copula

The procedure for generating random variables from the Gaussian copula $C_{R,\nu}^{Student}$ with correlation matrix R and ν degrees of freedom proceeds as follows:

1. Find a suitable (e.g., Cholesky) decomposition A of R, such that $R = A \cdot A^T$.

2. Draw an N-dimensional vector $\mathbf{z} = (z_1, z_2, ..., z_n)'$ of uncorrelated standard normal variates.

3. Draw an independent χ_ν^2 random variable s.

4. Set $\mathbf{y} := \mathbf{z}'A$.

5. Set $\mathbf{x} := \mathbf{y}\sqrt{\frac{v}{s}}$.

6. Map **x** back to an N-dimensional vector **u** of uniform variates on $[0, 1]$ by computing $\mathbf{u} = t_v(\mathbf{x})$.

Then, $\mathbf{u} \sim C_{R,v}^{Student}$.

Figure 5.9 shows $3,000$ samples from the Gaussian and t copula. Note how samples from the t copula, compared with the Gaussian copula, accumulate in the upper-right and lower-left region, thus confirming the impact of the tail dependence in modeling the occurrence of extreme events.

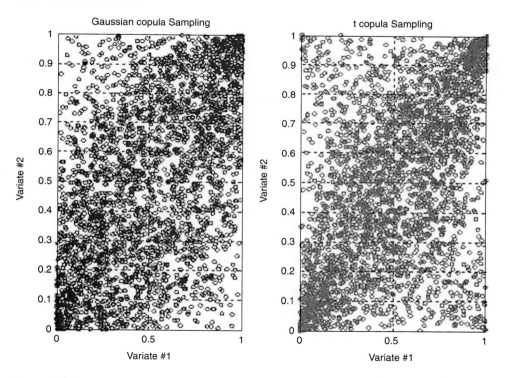

Figure 5.9   3,000 samples from the gaussian and t copula.   *Source: Galiani, S. (2003), pg. 36.*

The Matlab implementation is:

copula_sample.m

```
function M=copula_sample(n,r)

% this function plots random variables extracted by a bivariate gaussian
% and Student's t copula with correlation coefficient "r" and "n" degrees
% of freedom

corr=ones(2);
corr(1,2)=r;
corr(2,1)=r;
```

```
% Now we use the simulation algorith suggested by ELM(01), pag. 26

A=chol(corr);
z=randn(2,1);
s=chi2rnd(n);
y=(z'*A)';
Gauss_U=normcdf(y);
x=(sqrt(n)/sqrt(s))*y;
t_U=tcdf(x,n);
M=[Gauss_U',t_U'];
```

copula_comp.m
```
function sample=copula_comp(num,n,r)
% this function shows bivariate r.v.s. from a normal and t copula with
% "num" simulation runs, "n" degrees of freedom and correlation "r"

U=zeros(num,4);
for k=1:num
    U(k,:)=copula_sample(n,r);
end
subplot(1,2,1); plot(U(:,1),U(:,2),'ob','MarkerSize',2)
grid on;
title('Gaussian copula Sampling');
xlabel('Variate #1');
ylabel('Variate #2');
subplot(1,2,2); plot(U(:,3),U(:,4),'or','MarkerSize',2)
grid on;
title('t copula Sampling');
xlabel('Variate #1');
ylabel('Variate #2');
sample=U;
```

The Distribution of Default Arrival Times

Schonbucher notes that for every simulation run, the path of the default intensity is known and suggests the following simulation procedure in order to estimate the distribution of default for the N obligors:

1. Simulate an N-dimensional vector $\mathbf{u} = (u_1, u_2, ..., u_N)'$ of uniform variates from a copula C.

2. Calibrate the intensities $\lambda_n(t)$ of survival function in equation (5.10) using the methodology discussed in §5.7 for each reference entity $n \in 1, 2, ..., N$.

Basket CDS Pricing Algorithm

The following are the steps required to compute the value of a basket CDS. It can be used to price instruments like credit indices, such as the TracX, Iboxx, and Dow Jones Credit Index.

1. Input start date, maturity date, frequency of payments (e.g., quarterly), and notional amount of the CDS or basket.

2. Compute the number of days between each start date and end payment date by using Actual/360 day counting convention.[29]

3. Generate the schedule of payment dates.

4. Obtain the term structure—e.g., swap curve—from a data source such as U.S. swap curve—e.g., 1YC1 on Bloomberg (can use Bloomberg API to extract quotes or enter them into Excel).

5. Bootstrap swap curve to generate the discount factors corresponding to payment dates.

6. Calibrate the market-traded CDS spread curves for each reference entity in the basket. Thus, for each reference entity, calibrate the parameters of the default time distribution function by computing implied default intensities $\lambda_n(t)$ (hazard rates) for $t = [T_1, T_2, ..., T_M]$, the set of expiry dates of CDSs available in the market, such that the hazard rate for each of the names replicates market-traded CDS quotes.[30]

7. Compute survival and default probabilities from calibrated hazard rates in step 6.

8. Calibrate the parameters of the copula function chosen for modeling the dependence among the obligors in the basket.

9. Generate a correlation matrix R of the reference names and do a Cholesky decomposition to generate correlated deviates for simulated default times, e.g. find a lower triangular matrix A such that $C = AA'$.

10. For each simulation, repeat the following routine:

    (a) Generate an N-dimensional vector of correlated uniform random variables using the algorithms presented in "Sampling from Elliptical Copulae."

    (b) For each obligor, translate the corresponding uniform variate into default time using the procedure presented in "The Distribution of Default Arrival Times."

    (c) Sort the N-dimensional vector of default times τ in ascending order, and according to the seniority of the contract (k-th to default), select the k-th coordinate.

    (d) Based on the specific realization of the order statistic $\tau_{(k)}$, compute the discounted value of the premium payments, accrued interest, and default payments.

11. Compute the arithmetic averages of the previous quantities and apply equation (5.12) to determine the fair spread.

Steps 10 and 11 are given by the following pseudocode:

```
Step 10:

    // initialize variables
    inflows = 0
    outflows = 0
    M = number of simulations

    // initialize random number generator (RNG), e.g. Mersenne
    // Twister
    for i = 1 to M
    {

        for each reference name in the basket
        {

        // generate default times
        generate uniform random number U from RNG for each name in
        the basket and store in vector

        generate independent normal variate z corresponding to each
        U, e.g. z = Φ⁻¹(U).

        generate correlated normal deviates from Cholesky matrix R,
        R = AA', with independent normal deviates, e.g. z'A

        if (correlated deviate < default probability)
           identify and store identity of which name defaulted

        if CDS curve is flat
           default time = ln(1-correlated deviate)/hazard rate
        else      // in reality CDS term structure is not flat
           default time = solved numerically   // see Li paper( )

        Store default times
        }
        Sort the N-dimensional vector of default times τ in ascending
        order, and according to the seniority of the contract (k-th
        to default), select the k-th coordinate.
        if min default time > maturity of the CDS basket
        // no defaults occurred
        {
            inflow = 0                // buyer protection receives nothing
            total_protection_leg = sum of notional*(actual/360)*(spread)
            outflow = outflow + total_protection_leg
        }
        else
        {
          // use recovery rate of identified defaulted obligor
          inflow = inflow + notional*(1-recovery rate)*(discount rate
                        corresponding to default time)

          // must take into account interest accrued on default times
          // that do not fall exactly on a payment date. When you
          // default mid-period, the protection buyer is only liable
          // for the portion of protection payment on a pro-rata
```

```
                // basis

            sum_payments = sum of discounted protection payments up to
                           time of default
                  // =(value of 1 basis point)*(min
                  // default time of all times in the basket)
            outflow = outflow + sum_payments
         }
   }
}
```

Step 11:

```
   basket payoff = average inflow -- average outflow
   basket spread = (average inflow/average outflow)*(spread)
```

5.10   CREDIT BASKET PRICING IN MATLAB

interpolated_zero.m

```
function rate=interpolated_zero(t,zcr)
% This function computes the zero rate for a specific date with linear
% interpolation

for j=1:16                    % loop through all the zero rates date knots
    if zcr(j,1)>t & t>(1/12);
        rate=zcr(j-1,2)+((t-zcr(j-1,1))/(zcr(j,1)-zcr(j-1,1)))*
            ((zcr(j,2)-zcr(j-1,2)));
    elseif t<(1/12)
        rate=zcr(j,2);
        break
    end

end
```

premium_leg.m

```
function PV=premium_leg(expiry,def_time,disc_fact)

% This function calculate the present value of the premium leg of a basket
% default swap. We can have two scenarios: the default time is beyond the
% contract expiry date or is within. In the first case we just compute the
% PV of the cash flows for the whole maturity of the contract. This is
% carried in the main function. In the other case we compute the cash flows
% PV just until the default stopping time.

sum_disc=0;
for i=1:expiry
    if def_time>i                      % if there is no default at time
                                       % "i" we simply add the discount
                                       % factors
        sum_disc=sum_disc+disc_fact(i);
    else
```

```
        break                          % in case of default we stop adding.
                                       % The accrual factor is then
                                       % calculated in the other leg of the
                                       % contract
    end
end
PV=sum_disc;
```

default_leg.m

```
function [PV_def,accrued_premium]=default_leg(expiry,def_time,rec,zc_rate)

% This function calculate the present value of the default leg of a basket
% default swap. (The accrued premium is included).
disc_fact_def=0;
last_payment=0;
r=interpolated_zero(def_time,zc_rate);   % in case of a default we calculate
                                         % the corresponding zero rates by
                                         % linear interpolation
disc_fact_def=(1+r)^(-def_time);
PV_def=(1-rec)*disc_fact_def;
for n=1:expiry
    if def_time<n
        last_payment=n-1;
        break
    end
end
accrued_premium=(def_time-last_payment)*disc_fact_def;
```

basket_spread.m

```
function [a,b,c]=basket_spread(expiry,def_time,rec,zc_rate,discount)

% This function computes the fair spread for each realization of the
% simulated stopping time

% compute the expected premium leg

expected_fees=premium_leg(expiry,def_time,discount);

% compute the expected default leg (default payment + accrued premium)
[exp_rec,accrued]=default_leg(expiry,def_time,rec,zc_rate);

a=expected_fees;
b=exp_rec;
c=accrued;
```

gaussian_time_AV.m

```
function [def_times1 ,def_times2]=gaussian_time_AV(R,hazard,num)

% This function generates default stopping times (generated by a
% multinomial gaussian copula with correlation matrix "r") for the
% obligors included in the basket. Inputs are the correlation matrix
% and the hazard rates for each time and each obligor

% Now we use the simulation algorithm for generating normal variates
% from gaussian copula suggested by ELM(01), pag. 26

n=size(R,1);                   % number of obligors in the basket
k=size(hazard,1);              % number of hazard rates available
                               % (corresponding to the number of default
                               % swap premia in the market)
hazard_sum=zeros(k,n);
x1=zeros(num,n);
x2=zeros(num,n);
y=zeros(num,n);
dst1=zeros(num,n);
dst2=zeros(num,n);

A=chol(R); %choleski decomposition
z=randn(num,n); % draw a sample of normal r.v.s. uncorrelated
for i=1:num
y(i,:)=z(i,:)*A;
end
Gauss_U1=normcdf(y);           % 0-1 variates normally distributed
Gauss_U2=normcdf(-y);
% antithetic variate
x1=-log(Gauss_U1);
x2=-log(Gauss_U2);

for sim=1:num

hazard_sum=zeros(k,n);

o1=zeros(n,1);
o2=zeros(n,1);

for j=1:n                      % for each name in the basket compute the
                               % default times
    for i=1:k                  % we discretize the integral depicted in
                               % Schonbucher (2003), pag. 347
        if i==1
            hazard_sum(i,j)=hazard(i,j);
        else
            hazard_sum(i,j)=hazard_sum(i-1,j)+hazard(i,j);
        end
        if hazard_sum(i,j)>=x1(sim,j)
            if i==1
                dst1(sim,j)=x1(sim,j)/hazard(1,j);
                o1(j)=1;
            else
                dst1(sim,j)=((x1(sim,j)-hazard_sum(i-1,j))/hazard(i,j))+
                    (i-1);
                o1(j)=1;
```

```
                  end
                  break
              end
          end
      if hazard_sum(k,j)<=x1(sim,j) & o1(j)~=1
          dst1(sim,j)=((x1(sim,j)-hazard_sum(k-1,j))/hazard(k,j))+(k-1);
      end
  end

  for j=1:n                    % for each name in the basket compute the
                               % default times
      for i=1:k                % we discretize the integral depicted in
                               % Schonbucher (2003), pag. 347
          if i==1
              hazard_sum(i,j)=hazard(i,j);
          else
              hazard_sum(i,j)=hazard_sum(i-1,j)+hazard(i,j);
          end
          if hazard_sum(i,j)>=x2(sim,j)
              if i==1
                  dst2(sim,j)=x2(sim,j)/hazard(1,j);
                  o2(j)=1;
              else
                  dst2(sim,j)=((x2(sim,j)-hazard_sum(i-1,j))/hazard(i,j))+
                      (i-1);
                  o2(j)=1;
              end
              break
          end
      end
      if hazard_sum(k,j)<=x2(sim,j) & o2(j)~=1
          dst2(sim,j)=((x2(sim,j)-hazard_sum(k-1,j))/hazard(k,j))+(k-1);
      end
  end


  end
def_times1=dst1;
def_times2=dst2;
```

gaussian_basket_AV.m

```
function [dist,price]=gaussian_basket_AV(T,k,corr,order,hazard,ZC,Recovery)
% This function computes the fair value of a kth to default basket swap
% through simulation by mean of a gaussian copula. With Variance reduction
% scheme (antithetic variates).
% Inputs provided by the users are:
    % T:          basket maturity
    % k:          # simulations
    % R:          correlation matrix
    % order:      1 for 1st to default, 2 for 2nd to default....
    % hazard:     term structure of hazard rate
    % ZC:         zero coupon rates
    % Recovery:   recovery values for each name in the basket
```

```
tic

S_fees=0;
S_recovery=0;
S_acc=0;
time1=zeros(size(hazard,2));
index1=zeros(size(hazard,2));
time2=zeros(size(hazard,2));
index2=zeros(size(hazard,2));
t_dist=zeros(size(k,1));


DF=zeros(T,1);
for i=1:T                           % compute the discount factor
                                    % for each payment date
    for j=1:16                      % loop through all the zero
                                    % rates date knots
        if ZC(j,1)==i;
            DF(i)=(1+ZC(j,2))^(-i);
        end
    end
end
[def_t1, def_t2]=gaussian_time_AV(corr,hazard,k); %load the vector of
                                                  %default times from
                                                  %a normal copula

default=0;
for n=1:k
    if min(def_t1(n,:))<T % count how many defaults
        default=default+1;
    end
end
defaulter=zeros(default,1);

ttt=1;


for n=1:k                       % start k-th simulation path
    fees1=0;
    recovery1=0;
    acc1=0;
    fees2=0;
    recovery2=0;
    acc2=0;
    [time1,index1]=sort(def_t1(n,:)); %sort the vector
    [time2,index2]=sort(def_t2(n,:));
    tau1=time1(order); % minimum default time
    m1=index1(order); % defaulter
    tau2=time2(order);
    m2=index2(order);
    if tau1<T %default case
        [fees1,recovery1,acc1]=basket_spread(T,tau1,Recovery(m1),ZC,DF);
        defaulter(ttt)=m1;
        ttt=ttt+1;

    else %no default
        for l=1:T
```

```
                fees1=fees1+DF(i);
            end
        recovery1=0;
        acc1=0;
    end
    if tau2<T
        [fees2,recovery2,acc2]=basket_spread(T,tau2,Recovery(m2),ZC,DF);
    else
        for l=1:T
                fees2=fees2+DF(i);
        end
        recovery2=0;
        acc2=0;
    end
    fees=0.5*(fees1+fees2);
    recovery=.5*(recovery1+recovery2);
    acc=.5*(acc1+acc2);
    S_fees=S_fees+fees;
    S_recovery=S_recovery+recovery;
    S_acc=S_acc+acc;

end
M_fees=S_fees/k;
M_recovery=S_recovery/k;
M_acc=S_acc/k;
price=(M_recovery/(M_acc+M_fees))*10000;
count1=0;
count2=0;
count3=0;
count4=0;
for g=1:default %count the frequency of default for each obligors
    if defaulter(g)==1
        count1=count1+1;
    elseif defaulter(g)==2
        count2=count2+1;
    elseif defaulter(g)==3
        count3=count3+1;
    elseif defaulter(g)==4
        count4=count4+1;
    end
end

dist=([default^2 count1 count2 count3 count4]/default)';
toc
```

t_time_AV.m

```
function [def_times1 ,def_times2]=t_time_AV(R,hazard,num,DoF)

% This function generates default stopping times (generated by a
% multinomial t copula with correlation matrix "r" and "DoF" degrees
% of freedom) for the obligors included in the basket. Inputs are the
% correlation matrix and the hazard rates for each time and each obligor

% Now we use the simulation algorithm for generating variates from t
% copula suggested by ELM(01), pag. 26
```

```
n=size(R,1);                  % number of obligors in the basket
k=size(hazard,1);             % number of hazard rates available
                              % (corresponding to the number of
                              % default swap premia in the market)
hazard_sum=zeros(k,n);
x1=zeros(num,n);
x2=zeros(num,n);
x=zeros(num,n);
y=zeros(num,n);
dst1=zeros(num,n);
dst2=zeros(num,n);

A=chol(R);
z=randn(num,n);
s=chi2rnd(DoF,num,1);
for i=1:num
y(i,:)=z(i,:)*A;
x(i,:)=(sqrt((DoF/s(i))))*y(i,:);

end

t_U1=tcdf(x,DoF);             % 0-1 variates t-distribuited
t_U2=tcdf(-x,DoF);            % 0-1 variates t-distribuited

x1=-log(t_U1);
x2=-log(t_U2);
for sim=1:num

hazard_sum=zeros(k,n);

o1=zeros(n,1);
o2=zeros(n,1);

for j=1:n                     % for each name in the basket compute the
                              % default times
    for i=1:k                 % we discretize the integral depicted in
                              % Schonbucher (2003), pag. 347
        if i==1
            hazard_sum(i,j)=hazard(i,j);
        else
            hazard_sum(i,j)=hazard_sum(i-1,j)+hazard(i,j);
        end
        if hazard_sum(i,j)>=x1(sim,j)
            if i==1
                dst1(sim,j)=x1(sim,j)/hazard(1,j);
                o1(j)=1;
            else
                dst1(sim,j)=((x1(sim,j)-hazard_sum(i-1,j))/hazard(i,j))+
                (i-1);
                o1(j)=1;
            end
            break
        end
    end
    if hazard_sum(k,j)<=x1(sim,j) & o1(j)~=1
        dst1(sim,j)=((x1(sim,j)-hazard_sum(k-1,j))/hazard(k,j))+(k-1);
```

```
        end
end

for j=1:n               % for each name in the basket compute the
                        % default times
    for i=1:k           % we discretize the integral depicted in
                        % Schonbucher (2003), pag. 347
        if i==1
            hazard_sum(i,j)=hazard(i,j);
        else
            hazard_sum(i,j)=hazard_sum(i-1,j)+hazard(i,j);
        end
        if hazard_sum(i,j)>=x2(sim,j)
            if i==1
                dst2(sim,j)=x2(sim,j)/hazard(1,j);
                o2(j)=1;
            else
                dst2(sim,j)=((x2(sim,j)-hazard_sum(i-1,j))/hazard(i,j))+
                    (i-1);
                o2(j)=1;
            end
            break
        end
    end
    if hazard_sum(k,j)<=x2(sim,j) & o2(j)~=1
        dst2(sim,j)=((x2(sim,j)-hazard_sum(k-1,j))/hazard(k,j))+(k-1);
    end
end

end
def_times1=dst1;
def_times2=dst2;
```

t_basket_AV.m

```
function [dist,price]=t_basket_AV(T,k,corr,order,hazard,ZC,Recovery,DoF)
% This function computes the fair value of a first to default basket swap
% through simulation by mean of a Student's t copula. Inputs provided by
% the users are:
    % T:          basket maturity
    % k:          # simulations
    % R:          correlation matrix (full)
    % order:      1 for 1st to default, 2 for 2nd to default....
    % hazard:     term structure of hazard rate for each obligor
    % ZC:         zero coupon rates
    % Recovery:   recovery values for each name in the basket
    % DoF:        degrees of freedom of the t copula

tic

S_fees=0;
S_recovery=0;
S_acc=0;
time1=zeros(size(hazard,2));
index1=zeros(size(hazard,2));
```

```matlab
time2=zeros(size(hazard,2));
index2=zeros(size(hazard,2));
t_dist=zeros(size(k,1));

DF=zeros(T,1);
for i=1:T                    % compute the discount factor for each
                             % payment date
    for j=1:16               % loop through all the zero rates date knots
        if ZC(j,1)==i;
            DF(i)=(1+ZC(j,2))^(-i);
        end
    end
end
[def_t1, def_t2]=t_time_AV(corr,hazard,k,DoF);

default=0;
for n=1:k
    if min(def_t1(n,:))<T
        default=default+1;
    end
end
defaulter=zeros(default,1);

ttt=1;


for n=1:k                    % start k-th simulation path
    fees1=0;
    recovery1=0;
    acc1=0;
    fees2=0;
    recovery2=0;
    acc2=0;
    [time1,index1]=sort(def_t1(n,:));
    [time2,index2]=sort(def_t2(n,:));
    tau1=time1(order);
    m1=index1(order);
    tau2=time2(order);
    m2=index2(order);
    if tau1<T
        [fees1,recovery1,acc1]=basket_spread(T,tau1,Recovery(m1),ZC,DF);
        defaulter(ttt)=m1;
        ttt=ttt+1;
    else
        for l=1:T
            fees1=fees1+DF(i);
        end
        recovery1=0;
        acc1=0;
    end
    if tau2<T
        [fees2,recovery2,acc2]=basket_spread(T,tau2,Recovery(m2),ZC,DF);
    else
        for l=1:T
            fees2=fees2+DF(i);
        end
```

```
                    recovery2=0;
                    acc2=0;
            end
            fees=0.5*(fees1+fees2);
            recovery=.5*(recovery1+recovery2);
            acc=.5*(acc1+acc2);
            S_fees=S_fees+fees;
            S_recovery=S_recovery+recovery;
            S_acc=S_acc+acc;



end
M_fees=S_fees/k;
M_recovery=S_recovery/k;
M_acc=S_acc/k;
price=(M_recovery/(M_acc+M_fees))*10000;
count1=0;
count2=0;
count3=0;
count4=0;
for g=1:default
    if defaulter(g)==1
        count1=count1+1;
    elseif defaulter(g)==2
        count2=count2+1;
    elseif defaulter(g)==3
        count3=count3+1;
    elseif defaulter(g)==4
        count4=count4+1;
    end
end

dist=([default^2 count1 count2 count3 count4]/k)';
price=(M_recovery/(M_acc+M_fees))*10000;
toc
```

This m-script loads the array of the zero-coupon rates bootstrapped from Euribor and EuroSwap Rates, from an Excel spreadsheet

```
Book = xlsread('C:\ZC\_Rates\ZC.xls');
ZC=zeros(41,2);
ZC(:,1)=Book(:,4);
ZC(:,2)=Book(:,5)/100;
clear Book;
```

5.11 CREDIT BASKET PRICING IN C++

The following C++ code is the class definition for a credit Basket derivative.

BASKET.h
```
#ifndef _BASKET_H__
#define _BASKET_H__
```

```
#include "datecl.h"
#include <vector>
#include <string>
#include "time.h"
#include <algorithm>
#include <map>
#include <numeric>
#include "CDO.h"
#ifndef _DEVIATES
#include "MatrixUtil.h"
#endif

#define numSimulations 10000000
#define NOTIONAL 1000000
#define RECOVERY 0.4
#define NUM 4
#define FV 100
#define NUM_SIM 500000
#define step 0.25

static vector<double> hazard;
static vector<int> dayDiff;
static vector<int> matLength;
static vector<double> accrual;
static vector<double> discountRate;
static map<double,double> TR;
static map<double,double> rate;
static int counter = 0;


static void discount(double d) {
  discountRate.push_back(d);
}

static double interpolate(double rate1, double rate2, double t1,
   double t2, double x) {
  double dy = rate2 - rate1;
  double dt = t2 - t1;
  double slope = dy/dt;

  return rate1 + slope*x;
}


class Exposure
{
  public:
      int paySize;
      void setPaySize(double p) { paySize = p; }
      int getPaySize() { return paySize; }
      vector<int> getMatYears() {
          return T;
      }
      vector<double> getHazRate() {
          return hazRate;
      }
```

```
    Exposure(vector<int> matYears, vector<double> spreads,
      string name_, double recovery): T(matYears),
      recoveryRate(recovery), tradeDate("today"),
        notional(NOTIONAL), riskfreeRate(0.02), name(name_) {

        effectiveDate = tradeDate + 1;
        if (effectiveDate == Date::SATURDAY)
            effectiveDate = effectiveDate + 2;
        else if (effectiveDate == Date::SUNDAY)
            effectiveDate = effectiveDate + 1;

        for (int i = 0; i < matYears.size(); i++)
        {
            spreads[i] = (double) spreads[i]/10000;
            Date maturity = effectiveDate.AddYears(matYears[i]);
            maturityDate = computeDate(maturity);
            hazardRate = 0.4;
            spread = spreads[i];
            effectiveDate = tradeDate +  1;
            accrualBasis = computeAccrualBasis(effectiveDate,
                maturityDate);
            accrual.push_back(accrualBasis);
            accrualBasis = accrual[0];
            calcPaymentDates1();
            calibrateHazardRates(i+1);
        }
    }
    Exposure(Date matDate, double hazRate, double s) :
        recoveryRate(0.4), tradeDate("today"),
        notional(NOTIONAL), riskfreeRate(0.02) {

        effectiveDate = tradeDate + 1;
        if (effectiveDate == Date::SATURDAY)
            effectiveDate = effectiveDate + 2;
        else if (effectiveDate == Date::SUNDAY)
            effectiveDate = effectiveDate + 1;

        if (matDate.day != 20)
            matDate.day = 20;
        if (matDate.day_of_week == Date::SATURDAY)
            matDate.day = 21;
        if (matDate.day_of_week == Date::SUNDAY)
            matDate.day = 22;

        maturityDate = matDate;
        hazardRate = hazRate;
        spread = s;
        accrualBasis = computeAccrualBasis(effectiveDate,maturityDate);
        accrual.push_back(accrualBasis);
        calcPaymentDates();
    }
    ~Exposure() { };
    void computePaymentDates(Date start, Date end);
    double calcFixedLeg(double h) {

        hazardRate = h;
        int time = computeNumDays(effectiveDate,maturityDate);
```

```
        int time1 = time + 1;
        double survivalProb = (double) exp(-hazardRate*
           ((double)time/365));
        double discountFactor = (double) exp(-riskfreeRate*
           ((double)time1/365));

        return notional*spread*accrualBasis*discountFactor*survivalProb;
    }
    double calcFixedLegDeriv(double h) {

        hazardRate = h;
        int time = computeNumDays(effectiveDate,maturityDate);
        int time1 = time + 1;
        double survivalProb = exp(-hazardRate*((double)time/365));
        double discountFactor = exp(-riskfreeRate*((double)time1/365));

        return (-(double)time/365)*notional*spread*accrualBasis*
           discountFactor*survivalProb;
    }
    double calcNPVFixedTwo(double h) {

        hazardRate = h;
        double survivalProb = exp(-hazard[0]*
           ((double)(matLength[0])/365));
        double survivalProb1 = exp(-hazardRate*
           ((double)(dayDiff[1])/365));
        double discountFactor = exp(-riskfreeRate*
           ((double)(matLength[0] + 1)/365));
        double discountFactor1 = exp(-riskfreeRate*
           ((double)(matLength[1] + 1)/365));

        return notional*spread*accrualBasis*discountFactor*
           survivalProb + notional*spread*((double)dayDiff[1]/360)*
           discountFactor1*survivalProb*survivalProb1;
    }
    double calcNPVFixedTwoDeriv(double h) {

        hazardRate = h;
        double survivalProb = exp(-hazard[0]*
           ((double)(matLength[0])/365));
        double survivalProb1 = exp(-hazardRate*
           ((double)(dayDiff[1])/365));
        double discountFactor = exp(-riskfreeRate*
           ((double)(matLength[1] + 1)/365));

        return -((double)dayDiff[1]/365)*notional*spread*((double)
           dayDiff[1]/360)*discountFactor*survivalProb*survivalProb1;
    }
    double calcNPVFixedThree(double h) {

        hazardRate = h;
        double survivalProb = exp(-hazard[0]*
           ((double)(matLength[0])/365));
        double survivalProb1 = exp(-hazard[1]*((double)(dayDiff[1])/365));
        double survivalProb2 = exp(-hazardRate*
           ((double)(dayDiff[2])/365));
        double discountFactor = exp(-riskfreeRate*
```

```
      ((double)(matLength[0] + 1)/365));
    double discountFactor1 = exp(-riskfreeRate*
      ((double)(matLength[1] + 1)/365));
    double discountFactor2 = exp(-riskfreeRate*
      ((double)(matLength[2] + 1)/365));

    return notional*spread*((double)dayDiff[0]/360)*
      discountFactor*survivalProb
      + notional*spread*((double)dayDiff[1]/360)*
      discountFactor1*survivalProb*survivalProb1
      + notional*spread*((double)dayDiff[2]/360)
      *discountFactor2*survivalProb*survivalProb1*survivalProb2;

}
double calcNPVFixedFour(double h) {

    hazardRate = h;
    double survivalProb = exp(-hazard[0]*
      ((double)(matLength[0])/365));
    double survivalProb1 = exp(-hazard[1]*((double)(dayDiff[1])/365));
    double survivalProb2 = exp(-hazard[2]*((double)(dayDiff[2])/365));
    double survivalProb3 = exp(-hazardRate*
      ((double)(dayDiff[3])/365));
    double discountFactor = exp(-riskfreeRate*
      ((double)(matLength[0] + 1)/365));
    double discountFactor1 = exp(-riskfreeRate*
      ((double)(matLength[1] + 1)/365));
    double discountFactor2 = exp(-riskfreeRate*
      ((double)(matLength[2] + 1)/365));
    double discountFactor3 = exp(-riskfreeRate*
      ((double)(matLength[3] + 1)/365));

    return notional*spread*((double)dayDiff[0]/360)*
      discountFactor*survivalProb
      + notional*spread*((double)dayDiff[1]/360)*
      discountFactor1*survivalProb*survivalProb1
      + notional*spread*((double)dayDiff[2]/360)*
      discountFactor2*survivalProb*survivalProb1*survivalProb2
      + notional*spread*((double)dayDiff[3]/360)*discountFactor3*
      survivalProb*survivalProb1*survivalProb2*survivalProb3;

}
double calcNPVFixedFive(double h) {

    hazardRate = h;
    double survivalProb = exp(-hazard[0]*
      ((double)(matLength[0])/365));
    double survivalProb1 = exp(-hazard[1]*((double)(dayDiff[1])/365));
    double survivalProb2 = exp(-hazard[2]*((double)(dayDiff[2])/365));
    double survivalProb3 = exp(-hazard[3]*((double)(dayDiff[3])/365));
    double survivalProb4 = exp(-hazardRate*
      ((double)(dayDiff[4])/365));
    double discountFactor = exp(-riskfreeRate*
      ((double)(matLength[0] + 1)/365));
    double discountFactor1 = exp(-riskfreeRate*
      ((double)(matLength[1] + 1)/365));
    double discountFactor2 = exp(-riskfreeRate*
```

```
            ((double)(matLength[2] + 1)/365));
        double discountFactor3 = exp(-riskfreeRate*
          ((double)(matLength[3] + 1)/365));
        double discountFactor4 = exp(-riskfreeRate*
          ((double)(matLength[4] + 1)/365));

        return notional*spread*((double)dayDiff[0]/360)*
          discountFactor*survivalProb
          + notional*spread*((double)dayDiff[1]/360)*
          discountFactor1*survivalProb*survivalProb1
          + notional*spread*((double)dayDiff[2]/360)*
          discountFactor2*survivalProb*survivalProb1*survivalProb2
          + notional*spread*((double)dayDiff[3]/360)*discountFactor3*
          survivalProb*survivalProb1*survivalProb2*survivalProb3
          + notional*spread*((double)dayDiff[4]/360)*discountFactor4*
          survivalProb*survivalProb1*survivalProb2*survivalProb3*
          survivalProb4;
    }
    double calcNPVFixed(double h, int i)
    {
        hazardRate = h;
        double survivalProb = 1.0;
        double discountFactor = 0;
        double sum = 0.0;

        for (int j = 0; j < i; j++)
        {
            discountFactor = exp(-riskfreeRate*((double)(matLength[j] +
              1)/365));
            if (j != i-1)
                survivalProb *= exp(-hazard[j]*
                  ((double)(dayDiff[j])/365));
            else
                survivalProb *= exp(-hazardRate*
                  ((double)(dayDiff[j])/365));

            sum += notional*spread*((double)dayDiff[i-1]/360)*
              discountFactor*survivalProb;
        }

        return sum;
    }
    double calcNPVFixedThreeDeriv(double h) {

        hazardRate = h;
        double survivalProb = exp(-hazard[0]*
          ((double)(matLength[0])/365));
        double survivalProb1 = exp(-hazard[1]*((double)(dayDiff[1])/365));
        double survivalProb2 = exp(-hazardRate*
          ((double)(dayDiff[2])/365));
        double discountFactor2 = exp(-riskfreeRate*
          ((double)(matLength[2] + 1)/365));

        return-((double)dayDiff[2]/365)*notional*spread*
        ((double)dayDiff[2]/360)*discountFactor2*survivalProb*
        survivalProb1*survivalProb2;
    }
```

```
double calcNPVFixedFourDeriv(double h) {

    hazardRate = h;
    double survivalProb = exp(-hazard[0]*
      ((double)(matLength[0])/365));
    double survivalProb1 = exp(-hazard[1]*((double)(dayDiff[1])/365));
    double survivalProb2 = exp(-hazard[2]*((double)(dayDiff[2])/365));
    double survivalProb3 = exp(-hazardRate*
      ((double)(dayDiff[3])/365));
    double discountFactor3 = exp(-riskfreeRate*
      ((double)(matLength[3] + 1)/365));

    return -((double)dayDiff[3]/365)*notional*spread*((double)
      dayDiff[3]/360)*discountFactor3*survivalProb*survivalProb1*
      survivalProb2*survivalProb3;
}

double calcNPVFixedFiveDeriv(double h) {

    hazardRate = h;
    double survivalProb = exp(-hazard[0]*
      ((double)(matLength[0])/365));
    double survivalProb1 = exp(-hazard[1]*((double)(dayDiff[1])/365));
    double survivalProb2 = exp(-hazard[2]*((double)(dayDiff[2])/365));
    double survivalProb3 = exp(-hazard[3]*((double)(dayDiff[3])/365));
    double survivalProb4 = exp(-hazardRate*
      ((double)(dayDiff[4])/365));
    double discountFactor3 = exp(-riskfreeRate*
      ((double)(matLength[4] + 1)/365));

    return -((double)dayDiff[4]/365)*notional*spread*((double)
      dayDiff[4]/360)*discountFactor3*survivalProb*survivalProb1*
      survivalProb2*survivalProb3*survivalProb4;
}
double calcNPVFixedDeriv(double h, int i) {

    hazardRate = h;
    double survivalProb = 1.0;
    double discountFactor =  exp(-riskfreeRate*
      ((double)(matLength[i-1] + 1)/365));

    for (int j = 0; j < i; j++)
    {
        if (j != i-1)
            survivalProb *= exp(-hazard[j]*
              ((double)(dayDiff[j])/365));
        else
            survivalProb *= exp(-hazardRate*
              ((double)(dayDiff[j])/365));
    }
        return -((double)dayDiff[i-1]/365)*notional*spread*
          discountFactor*survivalProb;

}
double calcNPVFloatingTwo(double h) {

    hazardRate = h;
```

```
        double defaultProb = 1 - exp(-hazard[0]*
          ((double)matLength[0])/365);

        double defaultProb1 = 1 - exp(-hazardRate*
          ((double)dayDiff[1])/365);
        double survivalProb = exp(-hazard[0]*((double)dayDiff[0])/365);
        double discountFactor = exp(-riskfreeRate*
          (double)(matLength[0]+1)/365);
        double discountFactor1 = exp(-riskfreeRate*
          (double)(matLength[1] + 1)/365);
        double accruedInterest1 = 0.5*notional*spread*
          ((double)dayDiff[1]/360);
        double accruedInterest = 0.5*notional*spread*
          ((double)dayDiff[0]/360);
        payments.push_back(accruedInterest);
        payments.push_back(accruedInterest1);

        return (notional*(1 - recoveryRate) - accruedInterest)*
          discountFactor*defaultProb
          + (notional*(1 - recoveryRate) - accruedInterest1)*
          discountFactor1*survivalProb*defaultProb1;

    }
    double calcNPVFloatingThree(double h) {

        hazardRate = h;

        double defaultProb = 1 - exp(-hazard[0]*
          ((double)matLength[0])/365);
        double defaultProb1 = 1 - exp(-hazard[1]*
          ((double)dayDiff[1])/365);
        double defaultProb2 = 1 - exp(-hazardRate*
          ((double)dayDiff[2])/365);

        double survivalProb = exp(-hazard[0]*((double)dayDiff[0])/365);
        double survivalProb1 = exp(-hazard[1]*((double)dayDiff[1])/365);

        double discountFactor = exp(-riskfreeRate*
          (double)(matLength[0]+1)/365);
        double discountFactor1 = exp(-riskfreeRate*
          (double)(matLength[1]+ 1)/365);
        double discountFactor2 = exp(-riskfreeRate*
          (double)(matLength[2]+ 1)/365);

        double accruedInterest = 0.5*notional*spread*
          ((double)dayDiff[0]/360);
        double accruedInterest1 = 0.5*notional*spread*
          ((double)dayDiff[1]/360);
        double accruedInterest2 = 0.5*notional*spread*
          ((double)dayDiff[2]/360);

        payments.push_back(accruedInterest);
        payments.push_back(accruedInterest1);
        payments.push_back(accruedInterest2);

        return (notional*(1 - recoveryRate) - accruedInterest)*
```

```
         discountFactor*defaultProb
         + (notional*(1 - recoveryRate) - accruedInterest1)*
         discountFactor1*survivalProb*defaultProb1
         + (notional*(1 - recoveryRate) - accruedInterest2)*
         discountFactor2*survivalProb*survivalProb1*defaultProb2;
}
double calcNPVFloatingFour(double h)
{

    hazardRate = h;
    double defaultProb = 1 - exp(-hazard[0]*
      ((double)matLength[0])/365);
    double defaultProb1 = 1 - exp(-hazard[1]*
      ((double)dayDiff[1])/365);
    double defaultProb2 = 1 - exp(-hazard[2]*
      ((double)dayDiff[2])/365);
    double defaultProb3 = 1 - exp(-hazardRate*
      ((double)dayDiff[3])/365);

    double survivalProb = exp(-hazard[0]*((double)dayDiff[0])/365);
    double survivalProb1 = exp(-hazard[1]*((double)dayDiff[1])/365);
    double survivalProb2 = exp(-hazard[2]*((double)dayDiff[2])/365);

    double discountFactor = exp(-riskfreeRate*
      (double)(matLength[0]+1)/365);
    double discountFactor1 = exp(-riskfreeRate*
      (double)(matLength[1]+ 1)/365);
    double discountFactor2 = exp(-riskfreeRate*
      (double)(matLength[2]+ 1)/365);
    double discountFactor3 = exp(-riskfreeRate*
      (double)(matLength[3]+ 1)/365);


    double accruedInterest = 0.5*notional*spread*
      ((double)dayDiff[0]/360);
    double accruedInterest1 = 0.5*notional*spread*
      ((double)dayDiff[1]/360);
    double accruedInterest2 = 0.5*notional*spread*
      ((double)dayDiff[2]/360);
    double accruedInterest3 = 0.5*notional*spread*
      ((double)dayDiff[3]/360);

    payments.push_back(accruedInterest);
    payments.push_back(accruedInterest1);
    payments.push_back(accruedInterest2);
    payments.push_back(accruedInterest3);

    return (notional*(1 - recoveryRate) - accruedInterest)*
      discountFactor*defaultProb
      + (notional*(1 - recoveryRate) - accruedInterest1)*
      discountFactor1*survivalProb*defaultProb1
      + (notional*(1 - recoveryRate) - accruedInterest2)*
      discountFactor2*survivalProb*survivalProb1*defaultProb2
      + (notional*(1 - recoveryRate) - accruedInterest3)*
      discountFactor3*survivalProb*survivalProb1*survivalProb2*
      defaultProb3;
```

```
}
double calcNPVFloatingFive(double h)
{

    hazardRate = h;
    double defaultProb = 1 - exp(-hazard[0]*
      ((double)matLength[0])/365);
    double defaultProb1 = 1 - exp(-hazard[1]*
      ((double)dayDiff[1])/365);
    double defaultProb2 = 1 - exp(-hazard[2]*
      ((double)dayDiff[2])/365);
    double defaultProb3 = 1 - exp(-hazard[3]*
      ((double)dayDiff[3])/365);
    double defaultProb4 = 1 - exp(-hazardRate*
      ((double)dayDiff[4])/365);

    double survivalProb = exp(-hazard[0]*((double)dayDiff[0])/365);
    double survivalProb1 = exp(-hazard[1]*((double)dayDiff[1])/365);
    double survivalProb2 = exp(-hazard[2]*((double)dayDiff[2])/365);
    double survivalProb3 = exp(-hazard[3]*((double)dayDiff[3])/365);

    double discountFactor = exp(-riskfreeRate*
      (double)(matLength[0]+1)/365);
    double discountFactor1 = exp(-riskfreeRate*
      (double)(matLength[1]+ 1)/365);
    double discountFactor2 = exp(-riskfreeRate*
      (double)(matLength[2]+ 1)/365);
    double discountFactor3 = exp(-riskfreeRate*
      (double)(matLength[3]+ 1)/365);
    double discountFactor4 = exp(-riskfreeRate*
      (double)(matLength[4]+ 1)/365);

    double accruedInterest = 0.5*notional*spread*
      ((double)dayDiff[0]/360);
    double accruedInterest1 = 0.5*notional*spread*
      ((double)dayDiff[1]/360);
    double accruedInterest2 = 0.5*notional*spread*
      ((double)dayDiff[2]/360);
    double accruedInterest3 = 0.5*notional*spread*
      ((double)dayDiff[3]/360);
    double accruedInterest4 = 0.5*notional*spread*
      ((double)dayDiff[4]/360);

    payments.push_back(accruedInterest);
    payments.push_back(accruedInterest1);
    payments.push_back(accruedInterest2);
    payments.push_back(accruedInterest3);
    payments.push_back(accruedInterest4);

    return (notional*(1 - recoveryRate) - accruedInterest)*
      discountFactor*defaultProb
      + (notional*(1 - recoveryRate) - accruedInterest1)*
      discountFactor1*survivalProb*defaultProb1
      + (notional*(1 - recoveryRate) - accruedInterest2)*
      discountFactor2*survivalProb*survivalProb1*defaultProb2
      + (notional*(1 - recoveryRate) - accruedInterest3)*
      discountFactor3*survivalProb*survivalProb1*
```

```
                survivalProb2*defaultProb3
                + (notional*(1 - recoveryRate) - accruedInterest4)*
                discountFactor4*survivalProb*survivalProb1*survivalProb2*
                survivalProb3*defaultProb4;
        }
        double calcNPVFloating(double h, int i) {

            hazardRate = h;
            double defaultProb = 1.0;
            double discountFactor = 1.0;
            double survivalProb = 1.0;
            double accruedInterest = 0.0;
            double sum = 0.0;

            for (int j = 0; j < i; j++)
            {
                discountFactor *= exp(-riskfreeRate*
                  ((double)dayDiff[j]+1)/365);
                survivalProb *= exp(-riskfreeRate*((double)dayDiff[j]+1)/365);
                defaultProb *= 1 - exp(-hazardRate*((double)dayDiff[j])/365);
                accruedInterest = 0.5*notional*spread*
                  (((double)dayDiff[j]+1)/360);
                payments.push_back(accruedInterest);
                if (j == 0)
                    sum += (notional*(1-recoveryRate) - accruedInterest)*
                        discountFactor*defaultProb;
                else
                    sum += (notional*(1-recoveryRate) - accruedInterest)*
                        discountFactor*survivalProb*defaultProb;
            }

            return sum;

        }
        double calcNPVFloatingTwoDeriv(double h) {

            hazardRate = h;
            double defaultProb = 1 - exp(-hazard[0]*
              ((double)matLength[0])/365);
            double defaultProb1 = 1 - exp(-hazardRate*
              ((double)dayDiff[1])/365);

            double survivalProb = exp(-hazard[0]*((double)dayDiff[0])/365);
            double discountFactor1 = exp(-riskfreeRate*
              (double)(matLength[1] + 1)/365);
            double accruedInterest = 0.5*notional*spread*
              ((double)dayDiff[1]/360);

            double z = ((double)dayDiff[1]/365)*
                (notional*(1 - recoveryRate) - accruedInterest)*
                  discountFactor1*survivalProb*defaultProb1;

            return z;
        }
        double calcNPVFloatingThreeDeriv(double h) {

            hazardRate = h;
```

```
            double defaultProb2 = 1 - exp(-hazardRate*
              ((double)dayDiff[2])/365);

            double survivalProb  = exp(-hazard[0]*((double)dayDiff[0])/365);
            double survivalProb1 = exp(-hazard[1]*((double)dayDiff[1])/365);
            double discountFactor2 = exp(-riskfreeRate*
              (double)(matLength[2] + 1)/365);
            double accruedInterest2 = 0.5*notional*spread*
              ((double)dayDiff[2]/360);

            double z = ((double)dayDiff[2]/365)*
              (notional*(1 - recoveryRate) - accruedInterest2)*
                discountFactor2*survivalProb*survivalProb1*defaultProb2;

            return z;
        }
        double calcNPVFloatingFourDeriv(double h) {

            hazardRate = h;
            double defaultProb3 = 1 - exp(-hazardRate*
              ((double)dayDiff[3])/365);

            double survivalProb  = exp(-hazard[0]*((double)dayDiff[0])/365);
            double survivalProb1 = exp(-hazard[1]*((double)dayDiff[1])/365);
            double survivalProb2 = exp(-hazard[2]*((double)dayDiff[2])/365);

            double discountFactor3 = exp(-riskfreeRate*
              (double)(matLength[3] + 1)/365);
            double accruedInterest3 = 0.5*notional*spread*
              ((double)dayDiff[3]/360);

            return ((double)dayDiff[3]/365)*(notional*(1 - recoveryRate) -
              accruedInterest3)*discountFactor3*survivalProb*survivalProb1*
              survivalProb2*defaultProb3;
        }
        double calcNPVFloatingFiveDeriv(double h) {

            hazardRate = h;
            double defaultProb4 = 1 - exp(-hazardRate*
              ((double)dayDiff[4])/365);

            double survivalProb  = exp(-hazard[0]*((double)dayDiff[0])/365);
            double survivalProb1 = exp(-hazard[1]*((double)dayDiff[1])/365);
            double survivalProb2 = exp(-hazard[2]*((double)dayDiff[2])/365);
            double survivalProb3 = exp(-hazard[3]*((double)dayDiff[3])/365);

            double discountFactor4 = exp(-riskfreeRate*
              (double)(matLength[4] + 1)/365);
            double accruedInterest4 = 0.5*notional*spread*
              ((double)dayDiff[4]/360);

            return ((double)dayDiff[4]/365)*(notional*(1 - recoveryRate)  -
              accruedInterest4)*discountFactor4*survivalProb*survivalProb1*
              survivalProb2*survivalProb3*defaultProb4;

        }
```

```
    double calcFloatingLegDeriv(double h) {

        hazardRate = h;
        double accruedInterest = calcRebate(effectiveDate);
        int time = computeNumDays(effectiveDate,maturityDate);
        int time1 = time + 1;
        double defaultProb = 1 - exp(-hazardRate*((double)time/365));
        double discountFactor = exp(-riskfreeRate*((double)time1/365));

        return ((double)time/365)*(notional*(1 - recoveryRate) -
          accruedInterest)*discountFactor*defaultProb;

    }
    double calcNPVFloatingDeriv(double h, int i)
    {

        hazardRate = h;
        double defaultProb = 1 - exp(-hazardRate*
          ((double)dayDiff[i-1])/365);
        double discountFactor = exp(-riskfreeRate*
          ((double)matLength[i-1] + 1)/365);
        double accruedInterest = 0.5*notional*spread*
          ((double)dayDiff[i-1]/360);
        double survivalProb = 1;

        if (i != 1)
        {
            for (int j = 0; j < i; j++)
            {
                survivalProb *= exp(-hazard[j]*((double)dayDiff[j])/365);
            }
        }

        return ((double)dayDiff[i-1]/365)*(notional*(1 - recoveryRate) -
          accruedInterest)*discountFactor*survivalProb*defaultProb;
    }
    double calcFloatingLeg(double h) {

        hazardRate = h;
        double accruedInterest = calcRebate(effectiveDate);
        payments.push_back(accruedInterest);
        int time = computeNumDays(effectiveDate,maturityDate);
        int time1 = time + 1;
        double defaultProb = (double) 1 - exp(-hazardRate*
          ((double)time/365));
        double discountFactor = exp(-riskfreeRate*((double) time1/365));

        return (notional*(1 - recoveryRate) - accruedInterest)*
          discountFactor*defaultProb;
    }
    int computeNumDays(Date start, Date end1) {

        return end1 - start + 1;
    }
    void setNumDays(int numDay) {

        numDays = numDay;
```

```
    }
    double calcRebate(Date defaultDate) {

        int time1 = maturityDate - effectiveDate;
        return 0.5*notional*spread*((double)time1/360);


    }
    double calcRebate1() {

        int time1 = dayDiff[1];
        return 0.5*notional*spread*((double)time1/360);
    }
    void calcPaymentDates()
    {
        Date d, paymentDay;
        int cnt = 1;
        payments.empty();
        payments.clear();

        std::cout << "payment size = " << payments.size() << "cnt = " <<
          cnt << endl;
        Date firstDate = computeDate(effectiveDate);
        std::cout << "first Payment Date " << firstDate << endl;
        paymentDates.push_back(firstDate);
        int diff = firstDate - effectiveDate + 1;

        periodLength.push_back(diff);
        payments.push_back(notional*spread*((double)diff/365));
        survival.push_back(exp(-hazardRate*((double)diff/365)));

        do
        {
            if (cnt != 1)
                d = firstDate.AddMonths(3);
            else
                d = firstDate;
            paymentDay = computeDate(d);
            paymentDates.push_back(paymentDay);
            int length = paymentDates[cnt] - paymentDates[cnt-1];
            int duration = paymentDates[cnt] - tradeDate + 1;
            survival.push_back(exp(-hazardRate*((double)duration/365)));
            double val = (notional*spread*((double)length/365))*
              survival[cnt-1]*discountRate[cnt-1];
            std::cout << "val = " << val << endl;
            payments.push_back(val);
            periodLength.push_back(length);
            cnt++;
        }
        while (paymentDay != maturityDate);

        totalPay = accumulate(payments.begin(),payments.end(),
          (float)0.0);
        std::cout << "payment size = " << payments.size() <<
          "cnt = " << cnt << endl;
        setPaySize(payments.size());
        payments.empty();
        payments.clear();
```

```
    }
void calcPaymentDates1()
{
    Date d, paymentDay;
    int cnt = 1;
    payments.empty();
    payments.clear();

    Date firstDate = computeDate(effectiveDate);
    paymentDates.push_back(firstDate);
    int diff = firstDate - effectiveDate + 1;
    periodLength.push_back(diff);
    payments.push_back(notional*spread*((double)diff/365));
    survival.push_back(exp(-hazardRate*((double)diff/365)));

    do
    {
        if (cnt != 1)
            d = firstDate.AddMonths(3);
        else
            d = firstDate;
        paymentDay = computeDate(d);
        paymentDates.push_back(paymentDay);
        int length = paymentDates[cnt] - paymentDates[cnt-1];
        int duration = paymentDates[cnt] - tradeDate + 1;
        survival.push_back(exp(-hazardRate*((double)duration/365)));
        double val = (notional*spread*((double)length/365))*
          survival[cnt-1]*discountRate[cnt-1];
        payments.push_back(val);
        periodLength.push_back(length);
        cnt++;
    }
    while (paymentDay <= maturityDate);

    totalPay = accumulate(payments.begin(),payments.end(),(float)0.0);
    setPaySize(payments.size());
    payments.empty();
    payments.clear();
}
Date computeDate(Date maturity)
{
    if ((maturity.month == Date::JANUARY) || (maturity.month ==
      Date::FEBRUARY))
    {
        maturity.month = Date::MARCH;
        maturity.day = 20;
        if (maturity.day_of_week == Date::SATURDAY)
            maturity.day = 21;
        if (maturity.day_of_week == Date::SUNDAY)
            maturity.day = 22;
    }
    else if (maturity.month == Date::MARCH)
    {
        if (maturity.day < 20)
        {
            maturity.day = 20;
```

```
                    if (maturity.day_of_week == Date::SATURDAY)
                        maturity.day = 21;
                    if (maturity.day_of_week == Date::SUNDAY)
                        maturity.day = 22;
                }
                else if (maturity.day != 20)
                {
                    maturity.month = Date::JUNE;
                    maturity.day = 20;
                    if (maturity.day_of_week == Date::SATURDAY)
                        maturity.day = 21;
                    if (maturity.day_of_week == Date::SUNDAY)
                        maturity.day = 22;
                }
        }
        else if ((maturity.month == Date::APRIL) ||
          (maturity.month == Date::MAY))
        {
            maturity.month = Date::JUNE;
            maturity.day = 20;
            if (maturity.day_of_week == Date::SATURDAY)
                maturity.day = 21;
            if (maturity.day_of_week == Date::SUNDAY)
                maturity.day = 22;
        }
        else if (maturity.month == Date::JUNE)
        {
            if (maturity.day < 20)
            {
                maturity.day = 20;
                if (maturity.day_of_week == Date::SATURDAY)
                    maturity.day = 21;
                if (maturity.day_of_week == Date::SUNDAY)
                    maturity.day = 22;
                }
                else if (maturity.day != 20)
                {
                    maturity.month = Date::SEPTEMBER;
                    maturity.day = 20;
                    if (maturity.day_of_week == Date::SATURDAY)
                        maturity.day = 21;
                    if (maturity.day_of_week == Date::SUNDAY)
                        maturity.day = 22;
                }
        }
        else if ((maturity.month == Date::JULY) ||
          (maturity.month == Date::AUGUST))
        {
            maturity.month = Date::SEPTEMBER;
            maturity.day = 20;
            if (maturity.day_of_week == Date::SATURDAY)
                maturity.day = 21;
            if (maturity.day_of_week == Date::SUNDAY)
                maturity.day = 22;
        }
        else if (maturity.month == Date::SEPTEMBER)
        {
```

```
                    if (maturity.day < 20)
                    {
                        maturity.day = 20;
                        if (maturity.day_of_week == Date::SATURDAY)
                            maturity.day = 21;
                        if (maturity.day_of_week == Date::SUNDAY)
                            maturity.day = 22;
                    }
                    else if (maturity.day != 20)
                    {
                        maturity.month = Date::DECEMBER;
                        maturity.day = 20;
                        if (maturity.day_of_week == Date::SATURDAY)
                            maturity.day = 21;
                        if (maturity.day_of_week == Date::SUNDAY)
                            maturity.day = 22;
                    }
            }
            else if ((maturity == Date::OCTOBER) || (maturity ==
              Date::NOVEMBER))
            {
                maturity.month = Date::DECEMBER;
                maturity.day = 20;
                if (maturity.day_of_week == Date::SATURDAY)
                    maturity.day = 21;
                if (maturity.day_of_week == Date::SUNDAY)
                    maturity.day = 22;
            }
            else if (maturity.month == Date::DECEMBER)
            {
                if (maturity.day < 20)
                {
                    maturity.day = 20;
                    if (maturity.day_of_week == Date::SATURDAY)
                        maturity.day = 21;
                    if (maturity.day_of_week == Date::SUNDAY)
                        maturity.day = 22;
                }
                else if (maturity.day != 20)
                {
                    maturity.month = Date::MARCH;
                    maturity.day = 20;
                    if (maturity.day_of_week == Date::SATURDAY)
                        maturity.day = 21;
                    if (maturity.day_of_week == Date::SUNDAY)
                        maturity.day = 22;
                    maturity.year = maturity.year + 1;
                }
            }
            return maturity;
}
double computeAccrualBasis(Date start, Date end) {

    // compute accrual basis
    numDays = computeNumDays(effectiveDate,maturityDate);
    setNumDays(numDays);
    matLength.push_back(numDays);
```

```
            counter++;
            if (dayDiff.size() == 0)
                dayDiff.push_back(numDays);
            else
            {
                int diff1 = matLength[counter-1] - matLength[counter-2] + 1;
                dayDiff.push_back((int)diff1);
            }
            accrualBasis = (double) numDays/360;
            return accrualBasis;
    }
    void setMaturityDate(Date d1)
    {
        if ((d1 != Date::JUNE) && (d1 != Date::SEPTEMBER)
            && (d1 != Date::DECEMBER) && (d1 != Date::MARCH))
        {
            //cout << "Maturity month must be March, June, Sept., or
                Dec." << endl;
            maturityDate = "6/20/2009";   // default maturity
        }
        else
            maturityDate = d1;

    }
    void calibrateHazardRates(int num)
    {

        int j = 0;
        double h = hazardRate;
        double f, fd;
        double error = 0.0;
        double dfixedleg = 0.0;
        double dfloatingleg = 0.0;

        switch (num)
        {
        case 1:
            do
            {
                f = calcFloatingLeg(h) - calcFixedLeg(h);
                dfixedleg = calcFixedLegDeriv(h);
                dfloatingleg = calcFloatingLegDeriv(h);
                fd = dfloatingleg - dfixedleg;
                h = h - 0.01*(f/fd);
                error = -0.01*f/fd;
            }
            while (fabs(error) > 0.00001);
            break;
        case 2:
            do
            {
                f = calcNPVFloatingTwo(h) - calcNPVFixedTwo(h);
                dfixedleg = calcNPVFixedTwoDeriv(h);
                dfloatingleg = calcNPVFloatingTwoDeriv(h);
                fd = dfloatingleg - dfixedleg;
                h = h - 0.01*(f/fd);
                error = -0.01*f/fd;
```

```
                    }
                    while (fabs(error) > 0.00001);
                    break;
              case 3:
                    do
                    {
                         f = calcNPVFloatingThree(h) - calcNPVFixedThree(h);

                         dfixedleg = calcNPVFixedThreeDeriv(h);
                         dfloatingleg = calcNPVFloatingThreeDeriv(h);
                         fd = dfloatingleg - dfixedleg;
                         h = h - 0.01*(f/fd);
                         error = -0.01*f/fd;
                    }
                    while (fabs(error) > 0.00001);
                    break;
              case 4:
                    do
                    {
                         f = calcNPVFloatingFour(h) - calcNPVFixedFour(h);

                         dfixedleg = calcNPVFixedFourDeriv(h);
                         dfloatingleg = calcNPVFloatingFourDeriv(h);
                         fd = dfloatingleg - dfixedleg;
                         h = h - 0.01*(f/fd);
                         error = -0.01*f/fd;
                    }
                    while (fabs(error) > 0.00001);
                    break;
              case 5:
                    do
                    {
                         f = calcNPVFloatingFive(h) - calcNPVFixedFive(h);
                         dfixedleg = calcNPVFixedFiveDeriv(h);
                         dfloatingleg = calcNPVFloatingFiveDeriv(h);
                         fd = dfloatingleg - dfixedleg;
                         h = h - 0.01*(f/fd);
                         error = -0.01*f/fd;
                    }
                    while (fabs(error) > 0.00001);
                     break;
              }
              hazardRate = h;
              hazard.push_back(hazardRate);
              hazRate.push_back(hazardRate);
              std::cout << getName() << " " << T[num-1] <<
                 "year   hazardRate = " << hazardRate << endl;
        }
     void setName(string name_) { name = name_; }
          string getName() { return name; }
private:
   friend class Basket;
   double hazardRate;
   vector<double> hazRate;
   map<Date,double> matHaz;
   double accrualBasis;
   double totalPay;
```

```
        Date defaultTime;
        vector<int> periodLength;
        vector<Date> paymentDates;
        vector<double> payments;
        vector<double> survival;
        double survivalRate;
        double recoveryRate;
        double riskfreeRate;
        string name;
        Date maturityDate;
        double notional;
        int numDays;
        Date tradeDate;  // start date
        Date effectiveDate;
        double spread;
        double rebate;
        vector<int> T;
};

struct BondPrice
{
    double price;
    double coupon;
    int numPeriods;
};

class Basket
{
   public:
        Basket() { kthToDefault = 1; }
        ~Basket() {};
        void bootstrap(vector<double> price, vector<double> coupon,
          vector<double> period);
        void bootstrap(map<double,double> TR);
        double genCorrelatedDeviates();
        double priceBasket();
        double priceCDOBasket(int numReference, int expiry,
          vector<Tranche> tranche);
        void computePaymentDates(Date start, Date end);
        void setEffectiveDate(Date d1);
        void setTradeDate(Date d1);
        void setMaturityDate(Date d1);
        void setkthtoDefault(int kthDefault);
        void addExposure(Exposure& ex) {
            exposure.push_back(ex);
        }
        double calcSumDiscPayments(Date d, int j);
        double calcDefaultTime(double d, int j);
        int getNumExposures();
        void printHazard() {

            int num = exposure.size();
            vector<double>::iterator iter;
            vector<double> v;
            vector<int> year = exposure[0].getMatYears();

            std::cout << "                    ";
```

```
            for (int i = 0; i < num; i++)
                std::cout << exposure[i].getName() << "          ";
        std::cout << endl << endl;

            for (i = 0; i < num; i++) {
                std::cout << "Year " << year[i] << "       ";
                v = exposure[i].getHazRate();
                for (iter = v.begin(); iter != v.end(); iter++) {
                    std::cout << "    " << *iter;
                }
                std::cout << endl;
            }
        }
private:
    vector<Exposure> exposure;
    int frequency;          // frequency of payments
    Date tradeDate;         // start date
    Date effectiveDate;
    Date maturityDate;      // maturity of basket
    int numExposures;       // number of exposures in the basket
    vector<Date> paymentDates;
    vector<double> spotRates;
    vector<Date> numDays;
    vector<double> cdsSpreads;
    vector<double> termStructure;
    vector<double> coupons;
    vector<double> bondPrice;
    vector<double> period;
    int kthToDefault;
    vector<double> discountRate;
    vector<double> discountSum;
    double faceValue;
};

#endif
```

The method definitions are as follows:

BASKET.cpp
```
#include "Basket.h"
#include <map>
#define NUM 5
#define step 0.25

void Basket::bootstrap(vector<double> price, vector<double> coupon,
  vector<double> period)
{
        copy(price.begin(),bondPrice.begin(),bondPrice.end());
        copy(coupon.begin(),coupons.begin(),coupons.end());
        copy(period.begin(),period.begin(),period.end());

        spotRates[0] = (((coupons[0] + faceValue)/bondPrice[0])-1)*2;
        discountSum[0] = pow(1/(1 + spotRates[0]),period[0]);

        for (int i = 1; i <= bondPrice.size(); i++)
        {
```

```
                        spotRates[i] = 2*(pow((coupons[i] +
                          faceValue)/(bondPrice[i] - coupons[i]*discountSum[i-1]),
                          (1/period[i]))-1);
                        discountSum[i] = discountSum[i-1] +
                          pow(1/(1 + spotRates[i]),period[i]);
            }
}

void Basket::setkthtoDefault(int kthDef) {
        kthToDefault = kthDef;
}
void Basket::setTradeDate(Date d1) {
        tradeDate = d1;
}

void Basket::setEffectiveDate(Date d1) {
        effectiveDate = d1;
}

void Basket::setMaturityDate(Date d1) {
        maturityDate = d1;
}

double Basket::priceBasket()
{
        int i, j, k;
        MRNG mrng;   // Mersenne generator
        MatrixUtil mu;  // Matrix Utility
        double* z = new double[NUM];
        double aveInflow = 0.0;
        double aveOutflow = 0.0;
        vector<double> defaultTime;
        vector<double> normaldev;
        TNT::Array1D<double> dev(NUM);
        double minTime = 0.0;
        double basketPrice = 0.0;
        double sum, outflow = 0.0;
        double inflow = 0.0;        // cash inflows
        double y = 0.0;             // default time
        int m = exposure.size();  // number of exposure in the basket
        int def = 0;
        double total_protection_leg = 0.0;
        double total_fixed_leg = 0.0;
        Array2D<double> R(NUM,NUM);
        map<double,int> expMap;
        std::cout.precision();

        for (i = 0; i < NUM; i++)
        {
                for (j = 0; j < NUM; j++)
                {
                        if (i == j)
                                R[i][j] = 1;
                        else
                                // flat correlation
                                R[i][j] = R[j][i] = 0.62;
                }
```

```
                }
        }

        // sample correlation structure
        /*
        R[0][1] = R[1][0] = 0.44180;
        R[0][2] = R[2][0] = 0.90208;
        R[0][3] = R[3][0] = 0.83975;
        R[1][2] = R[2][1] = 0.67615;
        R[1][3] = R[3][1] = 0.68552;
        R[2][3] = R[3][2] = 0.84178;
        */

        for (i = 1; i <= NUM_SIM; i++)
        {
                sum = 0.0;
                normaldev.empty();
                defaultTime.empty();
                normaldev.clear();
                defaultTime.clear();

                // for each name in the basket
                for (j = 0; j < m; j++)
                {
                        dev = mu.genCholesky(R);
                        normaldev.push_back(mu.normalCalc(dev[j]));
                        y = calcDefaultTime(-log(normaldev[j]),j);
                        defaultTime.push_back(y);
                        expMap[defaultTime[j]] = j;
                }
                vector<double>::iterator iter;
                vector<double>::iterator defIter;

                sort(defaultTime.begin(),defaultTime.end());
                defIter = defaultTime.begin();
                minTime = *defIter;

                switch (kthToDefault)
                {
                        case 1:
                            {
                            k = expMap[minTime];
                            break;
                            }
                        case 2:
                            {
                            defIter++;
                            minTime = *defIter;
                            k = expMap[minTime];
                            break;
                            }
                        case 3:
                            {
                            defIter++;
                            defIter++;
                            minTime = *defIter;
                            k = expMap[minTime];
```

```
                                    break;
                                    }
                            default:
                              k = expMap[minTime];
                              break;
                    }

              Date effectiveDate = "today";

              int months = (int) (minTime - (minTime/100))*12;
              int years = (int) minTime / 100;
              Date defTime = effectiveDate.AddYears(years);
              defTime = effectiveDate.AddMonths(months);
              int diff = defTime - exposure[k].effectiveDate;

              if (defTime > exposure[k].maturityDate)
              {
              // inflow = inflow + 0;
              // receive nothing
              total_fixed_leg = exposure[k].totalPay;
              outflow = outflow + total_fixed_leg;
              // pay total discounted spread on notional
              // = sum of notional*(num days/360)*(spread)
              }
       else
       {
                    total_protection_leg = ((exposure[k].notional)*(1 -
                       exposure[k].recoveryRate))*exp(-
                       (exposure[k].riskfreeRate)*((double)diff/365));
                    inflow = inflow + total_protection_leg;
                    // sum of discounted protection payments up to
                    // time of default
                    // = (value of 1 basis pt)*(min default
                    // time of all names in basket)
                    outflow = outflow + calcSumDiscPayments(defTime,k);

                    }
       }
       std::cout << "inflow = " << inflow << endl;
       std::cout << "outflow = " << outflow << endl;
       aveInflow = (double) inflow/M;
       aveOutflow = (double) outflow/M;

       basketPrice = (aveInflow/aveOutflow)*(exposure[k].spread)*10000;
       std::cout << "basketPrice = " << basketPrice << endl;

       return 0;
}


double Basket::calcSumDiscPayments(Date defDate, int j)
{
       double sum = 0.0;
       double discPay = 0.0;

       for (int i = 0; i < exposure[j].getPaySize(); i++)
       {
```

```
                        if (exposure[j].paymentDates[i] < defDate)
                        {
                                int length = defDate - exposure[j].paymentDates[i];
                                discPay = exposure[j].payments[i]*
                                  exp(-(exposure[j].riskfreeRate)*
                                  ((double)length/365));
                                sum = sum + discPay;
                        }
            }
        return sum;
}

int Basket::getNumExposures() {
        return numExposures;
}

double Basket::calcDefaultTime(double dev, int j) {

        double tau = 0.0;
        double hazard_sum[10];
        double o[10] = {0.0};

        int k = exposure[0].hazRate.size()-1;
        int i = 0;
        double y = 0.0;

        for (i = 0; i <= k; i++)
        {
                if (i == 0)
                        hazard_sum[0] = exposure[j].hazRate[0];
                else
                        hazard_sum[i] = hazard_sum[i-1] +
                          exposure[j].hazRate[i];

                if (hazard_sum[i] >= dev)
                {
                        if (i == 0)
                        {
                                tau = dev/exposure[j].hazRate[0];
                                o[j] = 1.0;
                        }
                        else
                        {
                                tau = ((dev - hazard_sum[i-1])/
                                  (exposure[j].hazRate[i]))+i;
                                o[j] = 1.0;
                        }
                        break;
                }
        }
        if ((hazard_sum[k] <= dev) && (o[j] != 1))
                tau = ((dev - hazard_sum[k-1])/
                  (exposure[j].hazRate[k])) + k;

        return tau;
}
```

In order to compute the correlates deviates, we use a matrix utility class *MatrixUtil* that utilizes the Template Numerical Toolkit (TNT) matrix functions for computing Cholesky and matrix decompositions. The class also utilizes a Mersenne Twister random number generator from a *Random* class for generating random deviates.

Suppose we want to price a five-year basket with four reference entities with the following spreads:

	Maturity (yrs)				
	1	2	3	4	5
Apple	100	150	160	170	185
IBM	75	120	200	220	250
GM	400	450	500	530	580
Northwest	420	450	500	520	550

and correlation structure of:

1	0.44180	0.90208	0.83975
0.44180	1	0.67615	0.25903
0.90208	0.67615	1	0.84178
0.83975	0.25903	0.841878	1

The main function is:

BasketPricing_Main.cpp
```cpp
#include <strstream>
#include <iostream>
#include <fstream>
#include "Basket.h"
#define SIZE_X 1000
using namespace std;

void main()
{

  Basket basket;
  basket.setEffectiveDate("today");
  char buffer[SIZE_X];
  char dataBuffer[SIZE_X];
  char* str = NULL;
  double disc = 0.0;
  // make sure the path to the folder is correct
  const char* file = "c:\\BasketCDSPricing\\Discount.txt";

  ifstream fin;                 // input file stream
  fin.clear();
  fin.open(file);

  if (fin.good())
  {
      while (!fin.eof())
      {
        fin.getline(buffer,sizeof(buffer)/sizeof(buffer[0]));
        istrstream str(buffer);
```

```
        // Get data
        str >> dataBuffer;
        disc = atof(dataBuffer);
        discount(disc);
    }
}
else
            std::cout << "File not good!" << "\n";

fin.close();

vector<int> expDates1;
expDates1.push_back(1);
expDates1.push_back(2);
expDates1.push_back(3);
expDates1.push_back(4);
expDates1.push_back(5);

vector<double> s1, s2, s3, s4, s5;
s1.push_back(100);
s1.push_back(150);
s1.push_back(160);
s1.push_back(170);
s1.push_back(185);

s2.push_back(75);
s2.push_back(120);
s2.push_back(200);
s2.push_back(220);
s2.push_back(250);

s3.push_back(400);
s3.push_back(450);
s3.push_back(500);
s3.push_back(530);
s3.push_back(580);

s4.push_back(420);
s4.push_back(450);
s4.push_back(500);
s4.push_back(520);
s4.push_back(550);

std::cout << "Calibrating Hazard Rates..." << endl << endl;

Exposure exp1(expDates1,s1,"Apple",0.4);
Exposure exp2(expDates1,s2,"IBM",0.4);
Exposure exp3(expDates1,s3,"GM",0.4);
Exposure exp4(expDates1,s4,"Northwest",0.4);

basket.addExposure(exp1);
basket.addExposure(exp2);
basket.addExposure(exp3);
basket.addExposure(exp4);

std::cout << endl;
std::cout << "Pricing Basket..." << endl;
```

```
  //basket.setkthtoDefault(2);
  basket.priceBasket();
}
```

The output is as follows:

```
Calibrating Hazard Rates...

Apple 1year hazardRate = 0.0169168
Apple 2year hazardRate = 0.0345374
Apple 3year hazardRate = 0.0307447
Apple 4year hazardRate = 0.0344349
Apple 5year hazardRate = 0.0431177

IBM 1year hazardRate = 0.0126858
IBM 2year hazardRate = 0.0239344
IBM 3year hazardRate = 0.0525948
IBM 4year hazardRate = 0.0720684
IBM 5year hazardRate = 0.107577

GM 1year hazardRate = 0.0677314
GM 2year hazardRate = 0.14406
GM 3year hazardRate = 0.228336
GM 4year hazardRate = 0.334723
GM 5year hazardRate = 0.502378

Northwest 1year hazardRate = 0.0711293
Northwest 2year hazardRate = 0.14406
Northwest 3year hazardRate = 0.228336
Northwest 4year hazardRate = 0.325314
Northwest 5year hazardRate = 0.460316

basketPrice = 784.92
```

Note that the basket price is less than the price of buying five-year CDS protection on each of the reference entities separately due to the correlation structure. In practice, most trading desks price baskets using a flat correlation structure. For instance, if the correlation is assumed to be 0.446 among all the obligors, the basket price is 785.23 basis points.

5.12   CREDIT LINKED NOTES (CLNS)

A credit linked note (CLN) enables an investor to purchase and fund an asset with a return linked to the credit risk of the asset itself and an additional credit risk transferred by way of a credit default swap between the issuer and the bank. A CLN structure enables the "risks transferred using a credit default swap to be embedded into a security and issued to an investor."[31] The investor receives a coupon and par redemption unless there has been a credit event by the underlying reference credit, in which case redemption is equal to par

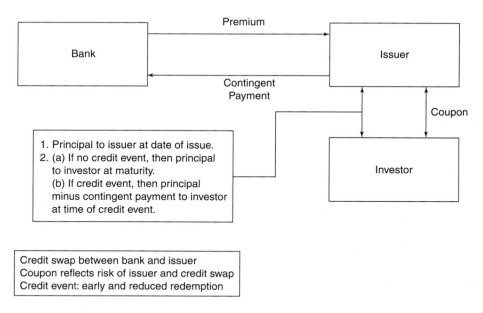

Figure 5.10 CLN transaction.

minus a contingent payment.[32] The transaction between the bank and the note issuer is a credit default swap, as shown in Figure 5.10.

The investor assumes two main risks. First, the investor is exposed to reference credit default risk (via the credit default swap between the issuer and bank), and second, that of the credit worthiness of the medium term note (MTN) issuer. If the reference credit defaults, this event would trigger an early and reduced redemption value of the notes. Should the issuer default, the investor is exposed to its recovery and to the mark-to-market of the credit swap at the time. This exposure to these two risks is reflected in the yield on the note, which is the sum of the return of the issuer and the premium of the credit swap. To reduce the risks to the investor, a paper-based, intangible company known as a special purpose vehicle (SPV), which typically has a AAA credit rating, insures against the reference credit risk by packaging a credit derivative inside a structured note. As such, a CLN can be viewed as a credit asset such as a loan or bond that is packaged by the SPV with a sold insurance option, frequently a credit default option or a total return swap. The SPV is established by a "parent" company specifically to obtain legal ownership of the underlying assets. The SPV then sells a credit default option to provide default protection on the selected reference asset, which is unrelated to the assets within the SPV. The issuer receives a premium for taking exposure to the reference credit. This premium forms part of the coupon that is paid to the investor. If there is a credit event by the reference credit, the note redeems early, a contingent payment is made to the bank, and the balance is paid to the investor. As there is no taxation at the SPV level, the premium from the sold option and the return on the credit asset flow straight through to the investor who purchases the CLN. This provides investors with access to credit risk that may otherwise be inaccessible due to a lack of infrastructure or liquidity. For example, an investor in the United States without any overseas banking relationships can gain exposure to bank loans in Japan if the loans are packaged in a CLN, as shown in Figure 5.11.

Because the performance of a CLN is dependent on two different assets, there are two scenarios in which the note could default: the highly-rated asset defaults, an unlikely but possible scenario, or the reference asset of the sold option defaults. If the reference asset defaults, the SPV typically sells the highly-rated assets it originally bought and uses some of the proceeds to pay the default loss due the protection buyer. The remaining proceeds go to the CLN investor, who receives only a percentage of the original investment. At this point, the CLN is terminated.

The price of a credit linked note, typically quoted as a spread over some benchmark, such as LIBOR or U.S. Treasuries, is equal to the sum of the cash flows coming into the SPV. For example, if an SPV owns the bonds within a trust earning UST + 20 bps and is short a credit default option with a premium of 295 bps, the price of the note linking the credit derivative to the bond is UST + 315 bps, as shown in Figure 5.12.

An organization can create a synthetic bond that is cheaper (or, put differently, that has a higher yield) than the equivalent market asset by selling a credit default option on the asset and combining it with a highly rated asset-backed security in an SPV. The default premium plus the return on the asset-backed security creates a credit linked note with a higher yield than the reference bond itself. For example, the 10-year bond of an auto manufacturer trades at LIBOR + 270 bps. The SPV sells a 10-year default swap on the bond for $1 million notional, receiving a premium of 330 bps per annum. At the same time, the SPV buys a $1 million AAA-rated asset-backed security that provides a return of LIBOR + 10 bps. The SPV packages the cash flows into a credit linked note with a return of LIBOR + 340 bps, creating a synthetic bond that yields 70 bps more than the bond issued by the auto manufacturer, as shown in Figure 5.13.

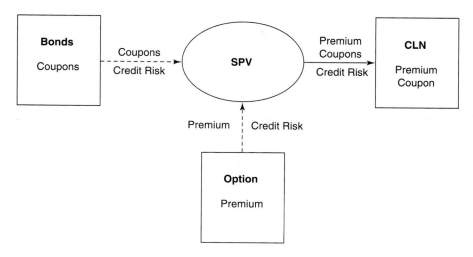

Figure 5.11 CLN structure.

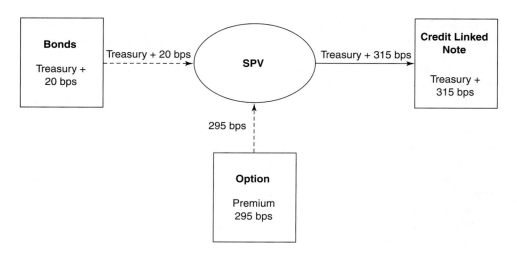

Figure 5.12 CLN payments.

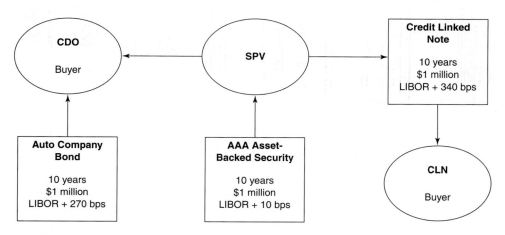

Figure 5.13 Creation of a synthetic bond with a CLN.

If the reference asset (auto company bond) defaults, the SPV sells the asset-backed-securities to make the loss payment. At expiration, CLN pays the remaining funds to the note holder. Suppose the recovery rate is 40%; then the SPV will sell the AAA asset-backed securities for $1 million and pay $600,000 to the CDO buyer as a recovery payment on their defaulted auto company bond, and will pay the remainder, $400,000, to the CLN holder, as shown in Figure 5.14.

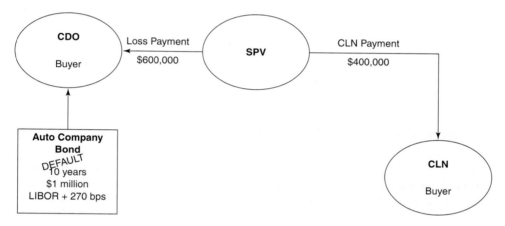

Figure 5.14 Default of reference asset.

CLNs with Collateralized Loan or Bond Obligations (CLOs or CBOs)

Aside from linking credit derivatives to assets such as loans or bonds, credit linked notes can be created by combining a default option with a collateralized loan obligation (CLO) or a collateralized bond obligation (CBO). CLOs and CBOs are formed by packaging non-investment-grade loans and bonds in an SPV. For example, an organization may package a portfolio of defaulted bank loans in an SPV to create a highly-rated CLO. The CLO, in turn, can be linked to a credit default swap through another SPV to create a credit linked note.

To attract a wider pool of investors, an SPV will often tranche the CLO/CBO as well as the CLN. Figure 5.15 shows an SPV with a senior, subordinate, and junior tranche. Each tranche is assigned a credit rating, indicating the likelihood that there will be default. Typically, only the highest-rated CLO/CBO is used to create a CLN. This helps to ensure that the performance of the CLN is mostly dependent on the reference asset in the sold default option position.

CDOs, which encompass CBO and CLOs, are discussed in detail in Chapter 4, "Collateralized Debt Obligations."

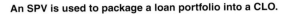

An SPV is used to package a loan portfolio into a CLO.

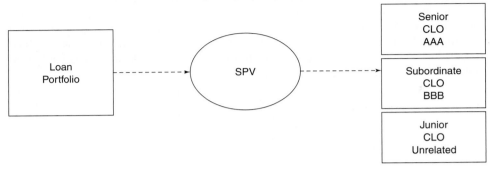

Figure 5.15 SPV with a senior, subordinate, and junior tranche.

Pricing Tranched Credit Linked Notes

The price of a CLN is equal to the sum of the cash flows coming into the SPV, regardless of its structure. With a tranched note, however, the cash flows must be divided between the tranches such that the sum of inputs equals the sum of outputs. For example, consider an SPV that earns LIBOR + 315 bps on $20 million face worth of assets. The SPV issues two tranches of credit linked notes: a $15 million face senior tranche earning LIBOR and a $5 million junior tranche receiving a return of LIBOR plus a spread. Because $15 million of the $20 million face simply receives LIBOR, the only unknown cash flow is the spread distributed to the junior tranche. Using the assumption that the sum of inputs equals the sum of outputs, the spread can be calculated as shown in Figure 5.16.

```
              The equation is solved for spread.

        Sum of Inputs = Sum of Outputs
20 x (LIBOR + 315 bps) = 15 x LIBOR + 5 x (LIBOR + spread)
       LIBOR + 315 bps = 15/20 x LIBOR + 5/20 x (LIBOR + spread)
       LIBOR + 315 bps = 15/20 x LIBOR + 5/20 x LIBOR + 5/20 x spread
       LIBOR + 315 bps = LIBOR + 5/20 x spread
               315 bps = 5/20 x spread
              1260 bps = spread
```

Figure 5.16 Spread calculation.

Regulatory Capital

Credit linked notes offer an ideal means for banks to reduce regulatory capital. Regulatory capital is the percentage of equity capital that a bank must maintain in relation to its assets (e.g., loans), typically 8%. Equity is relatively expensive to fund. For example, bank stockholders may require a 15% rate of return per annum in comparison to an interbank loan funded at LIBOR. One way to reduce costly equity capital requirements is to lower the risk of credit assets. By creating a CLN from its loan portfolio, a bank can transfer the credit risk from the bank to the CLN investors. As a result, only 20% of the recommended 8% holding is required. Take, for example, a bank with $5 billion in loans. The bank is required to have funded approximately 8%, or $400 million, of these loans with expensive equity capital. However, consider the same scenario when the bank forms an SPV that issues CLNs. This offering removes the underlying credit risk from the bank's balance sheet, which, in turn, reduces the regulatory capital to $80 million, an 80% decrease from the original requirement.

ENDNOTES

1. O'Kane, D. (2001), "Credit Derivatives Explained," Lehman Brothers Structured Credit Research, March, pg. 3.
2. Id., pg. 3.
3. Id., pg. 3.
4. According to the British Bankers' Association (2002), banks, security houses, and hedge funds dominate the protection-buyers market, with banks representing 50% of the demand. On the protection-sellers side, banks and insurance companies dominate.
5. Schonbucher, P., *Credit Derivatives Pricing Models*, Wiley & Sons, Inc. (2003).
6. The Ford bonds have a par face value of $1,000 and thus a total notional of $10,000 \times 1,000 = \$10,000,000$. However, if BoA doesn't own the bonds already to deliver or have an underlying position in the bonds it needs to unwind, then BoA will have to purchase them in the market; however, it will pay less than $10,000,000 for them because the defaulted bonds will be worth less than par—i.e., $400. This gives BoA an option to deliver the cheapest bonds with the lowest market value.
7. Id., pg. 28.
8. Duffie, D., and Singleton, K. (1999), "Modeling Term Structures of Defaultable Bonds," *Review of Financial Studies*, 12(4), pp. 687–720.
9. Yu, Fan. (2003), "Default Correlation in Reduced-Form Models," University of California, Irvine, working paper, September.
10. Id., pg. 1.
11. If T_i is the premium payment date prior to the default date τ, then the accrued premium AP to be paid by the protection buyer is computed as

$$AP = sN\Delta_{i+1}\frac{\tau - T_i}{T_{i+1} - T_i} = sN\frac{T_{i+1} - T_i}{360}\frac{\tau - T_i}{T_{i+1} - T_i} = sN\frac{\tau - T_i}{360}$$

where s is the fraction of the nominal or notional value N (expressed in basis points per annum).
12. Li, D. (1998), "Constructing a Credit Curve." Risk, Credit Risk Special Report. November, pg. 40.
13. Lando, D., "On Cox Processes and Credit Risky Securities," Department of Operations Research, University of Copenhagen (March 1998).
14. We assume that $\lambda : \Re_+ \to \Re$ and $\int_0^\infty \lambda(u)du = \infty$.

15. Schonbucher, P. *Credit Derivatives Pricing Models*, John Wiley & Sons, Inc. (2003), pg. 91.
16. Id., pg. 6.
17. Id., pg. 7.
18. O'Kane and Turnbull (2003), pg. 9.
19. We assume that the valuation date is at time 0, T_0, and so $T_i - T_0 = T_i$. However, the equation can be modified by using T_v as the valuation date and using $T_i - T_v$ instead where $v = 0, .., i - 1$.
20. O'Kane and Turnbull (2003), pg. 8.
21. O'Kane and Turnbull (2003), pg. 12.
22. Ibid.
23. Historical yield and spread data can be obtained from Bloomberg by going into the Yield Curve Analytics/Matrices menu in the Corporate Bond menu and using Fair Market Yld Curves-History.
24. We use the tenors in Table 5.1 for the Δ_i and the discount bond yields from the LIBOR U.S. rates.
25. In the program, we hard code the tenors and interest rate data and store them in vectors in the initialization *init* function.
26. Li, D. (1998), pg. 40.
27. Schonbucher, P., pg. 70.
28. On May 6, 2005, Standard & Poor's cut the credit rating of both GM and Ford to junk status. Both GM and General Motors Acceptance Corp., its finance arm, were downgraded to BB, two notches below investment grade, while Ford and Ford Motor Credit, its finance arm, were downgraded to BB+. Moody's cut Ford to its lowest investment grade.
29. The market convention for CDS is quarterly payments, Actual/360, modified following, effective one calendar day from the trade date and maturing on either March 20, June 20, September 20, or December 20.
30. The calibration of the hazard rates can be accomplished through a nonlinear recursive or gradient solver, such as the Newton-Raphson procedure.
31. Kasapi, A. (1999), pg. 67.
32. Id., pg. 67.

Chapter 6

Weather Derivatives

SECTIONS

The impact of weather on many commercial businesses and recreational activities is significant and varies both geographically and seasonally. Many businesses, including agriculture, insurance, energy, and tourism, are either favorably or adversely affected by weather. For this reason, the financial markets have created an innovative new class of instruments called *weather derivatives*, through which risk exposure to weather (and temperature) may be transferred or reduced. Weather derivatives are contingent claims written on weather indices, which in turn, are variables whose values are constructed from weather data. Commonly referenced weather indices include, but are not restricted to, Daily Average Temperature (DAT), Cumulative Annual Temperature (CAT), Heating Degree Days (HDDs), Cooling Degree Days (CDDs), precipitation, snowfall, and wind. In contrast to other contingent claims, weather derivatives pricing poses some difficulties because pricing based on the traditional risk-neutral no-arbitrage arguments do not work; underlying weather indices at present are not securitized by liquid traded instruments. There also exist some difficulties in implementing statistical, equilibrium-based pricing techniques, because the observed weather indices are non-stationary, and "characterized by long-term variations and trends, potentially with cycles much longer than what the data records reveal."[1] In contrast, an actuarial present value pricing approach is rather simple and intuitively appealing, although it cannot capture such cycles and trends in the weather like statistical models. In this chapter, we explore various pricing models for weather derivatives, including use of statistical and stochastic models.

In §6.1, we provide a background of the weather derivatives market and how it originated. In §6.2, we discuss weather contracts, including CME futures contracts and options contracts on weather indices. In §6.3, we cover modeling temperature based on the work of Alaton et al. (2000). In §6.4, we discuss general parameter estimation of the model in §6.3. In §6.5, we review mean-reversion estimation, while in §6.6, we discuss volatility estimation. In §6.7, we discuss pricing weather derivatives contracts, including European call and put options on HDDs. In §6.8, we cover historical burn analysis as a method for pricing. In §6.9, we discuss time-series weather forecasting based on the work of Campbell and Diebold (2005). In §6.10, we give a Monte Carlo implementation in C++ to price weather options.

6.1   WEATHER DERIVATIVES MARKET

The market for weather derivatives started in 1997 as a response from businesses effected by El Niño in order to hedge against seasonal weather risk, which can lead to significant earnings decline. The El Niño conditions were associated with warm winters in the eastern and midwestern U.S., resulting in significant energy cost savings for consumers and businesses. In addition, these conditions suppressed hurricane activities in the Atlantic and led to minimal economic losses due to hurricanes. However, the same weather pattern was also associated with extreme floods in California, resulting in both economic loss and loss of life.

After the El Niño episode, the market for weather derivatives expanded rapidly, and contracts started to be traded over-the-counter (OTC) as individually negotiated contracts. The weather derivatives market went from being essentially nonexistent in 1997 to a market in 1998 estimated at $500 million, but it was still illiquid, with large spreads and limited secondary market activity. The market grew to more than $5 billion in 2005, with better liquidity. This OTC market was primarily driven by companies in the energy sector. To increase the size of the market and to remove credit risk from the trading of the contracts, the Chicago Mercantile Exchange (CME) started an electronic marketplace for weather derivatives in September 1999. This was the first exchange where standard weather derivatives could be traded. Although weather risk has an enormous impact on many businesses, including energy producers and consumers, supermarket chains, the leisure industry, and the agricultural industries, it is primarily the energy sector that has driven the demand for weather derivatives and has caused the weather risk management industry to now evolve rapidly.[2]

The growth in the weather derivatives market in the mid-1990s can be attributed to the deregulation of the energy and utility industries in the U.S. Faced with growing competition and uncertainty in demand, energy and utility companies sought effective hedging tools to stabilize their earnings. In the deregulated environment, energy merchants quickly realized that weather conditions were the main source of revenue uncertainties. Weather affects both short-term demand and long-term supply of energy. For instance, as shown in Figure 6.1, the electricity load depends heavily on the temperature level.

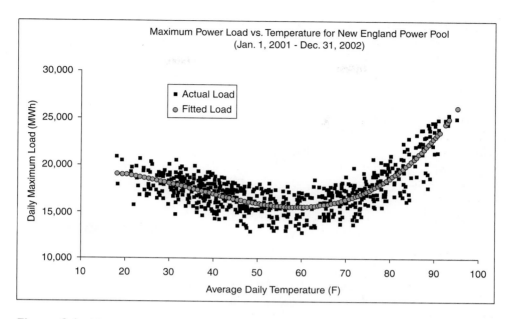

Figure 6.1 Maximum Power Load versus Temperature for New England.   *Source: Cao, Li, and Wei (2004).*

The maximum power load is at the lowest when the average daily temperature is around 65°F and becomes higher when the temperature increases or decreases. Similarly, natural gas consumption is highly dependent on temperature, as shown in Figure 6.2.

Thus, short-term demand of power and energy (discussed in Chapter 7, "Energy and Power Derivatives") is largely driven by weather conditions. On the other hand, a specific pattern of weather conditions (e.g., a strong global warming trend) can also affect "the long-term supply as energy producers re-adjust their production levels."[3]

Campbell and Diebold (2005) suggest a number of interesting considerations that make weather derivatives different from "standard" derivatives. First, the underlying asset (weather) is not traded in a spot market. Second, unlike financial derivatives, which are useful for price hedging but not for quantity hedging, weather derivatives are useful for quantity hedging but not necessarily for price hedging (although the two are obviously related). That is, weather derivative products provide protection against weather-related changes in quantities, complementing extensive commodity price risk management tools already available through futures. Third, although liquidity in weather derivative markets has improved, it will likely never be as good as in traditional commodity markets, because weather is by its nature a location-specific and nonstandardized commodity, unlike, say, a specific grade of crude oil. One cannot take delivery of the weather underlying the contract. Consequently, while standard derivatives are used to hedge prices, weather derivatives are used to hedge quantity changes. For instance, a weather derivatives option might have a payoff of $1,000 for each day that it rains over the next two months in return for a premium payment of $10,000 that reflects that risk.

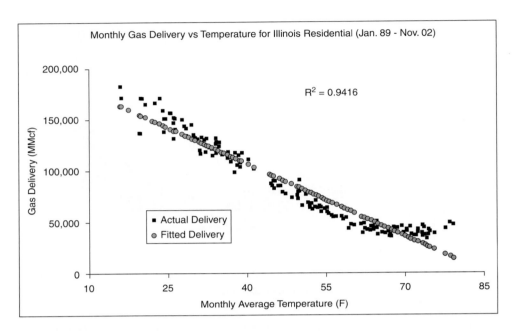

Figure 6.2 Monthly Gas Delivery versus Temperature for Illinois Residential. *Source: Cao, Li, and Wei (2004).*

The European market has not developed as quickly as the U.S. market, but there are a number of factors that suggest growth potential. One of them is the fact that Europe's energy industry is not yet fully deregulated, and as deregulation spreads throughout the industry, the volume in weather deals traded in Europe should increase. This will improve liquidity of the market and encourage new entrants into the market.

When entrants outside the energy sector become more interested in the weather derivatives market, there will also be an enormous growth potential. As mentioned earlier, there are companies in many different areas that are affected by the weather. When these companies start to look at the weather derivatives market for hedging purposes, increased liquidity as well as new products will probably follow.

Another key for the market to grow is the existence of standardized contracts. London International Financial Futures Exchange (LIFFE) is currently developing pan-European weather futures, which should increase the size of the overall weather derivatives market. There are also some barriers that must be removed if the market is to grow. For example, the quality and cost of weather data varies considerably across Europe. Companies that want to analyze their performance against historical weather data must often buy information from the national meteorological offices, and that could, in some countries, be quite expensive. It is also important that the quality of the weather data is good so that companies can rely on it when pricing derivatives.

6.2   WEATHER CONTRACTS

Weather derivatives are usually structured as swaps, futures, and call/put options based on different underlying weather indices. Some commonly used indices are Heating and Cooling Degree Days, rain (precipitation), wind, stream flow, and snowfall. Many weather derivatives are based on degree-days (temperature) indices, because they are most often used. We will focus on temperature weather derivatives.

We start with some basic definitions and terminology. We define the temperature T_i as follows: Given a specific weather station, let $T_i^{\max}$ and $T_i^{\min}$ denote the maximal and minimal temperatures (in degrees Celsius) measured on day i. We define the temperature for day i as:

$$T_i = \frac{T_i^{\max} + T_i^{\min}}{2} \tag{6.1}$$

Let T_i denote the temperature for day i. Define the Heating Degree Days, HDD_i, as

$$HDD_i = \max\{65°\text{F} - T_i, 0\} \tag{6.2}$$

and the Cooling Degree Days, CDD_i, generated on that day, as

$$CDD_i = \max\{T_i - 65°\text{F}, 0\}. \tag{6.3}$$

Note that the number of HDDs or CDDs for a specific day is just the number of degrees that the temperature deviates from a reference level. It has become industry standard in the U.S. to set this reference level at $65°$ Fahrenheit ($18°$C). The names Heating and Cooling Degree Days originate from the U.S. energy sector. The reason is that if the temperature is below $18°$C, people tend to use more energy to heat their homes, whereas if the temperature is above $18°$C, people start turning their air conditioners on, for cooling. Most temperature-based weather derivatives are based on the accumulation of HDDs or CDDs during a certain period, usually one calendar month or a winter/summer period. Typically, the HDD season includes winter months from November to March, and the CDD season is from May to September. April and October are often referred to as the "shoulder months."

CME Weather Futures

The CME offers standardized futures contracts on temperatures based on the CME Degree Day index, which is the cumulative sum of daily HDDs or CDDs during a calendar month, as well as options on these futures. The CME Degree Day index is currently specified for 11 U.S., five European, and two Japanese cities. The HDD/CDD index futures are agreements to buy or sell the value of the HDD/CDD index at a specific future date. The notional value of one contract is \$100 times the Degree Day index, and the contracts are quoted in HDD/CDD index points. The futures are cash-settled, which means that there is a daily marking-to-market based upon the index, with the gain or loss applied to the customer's account. A CME HDD or CDD call option is a contract that gives the owner the right, but not the obligation, to buy one HDD/CDD futures contract at a specific price, usually called the strike or exercise price. The HDD/CDD put option analogously gives the owner the right, but not the obligation, to sell one HDD/CDD futures contract. On the CME, the options on futures are European style, which means that they can only be exercised at the expiration date.

The CME futures have the number of HDDs (or CDDs) over one month or one season for 15 U.S. cities as the underlying temperature index. The HDD index over the time interval $[t_1, t_2]$ is defined in a continuous-time setting as $\int_{t_1}^{t_2} \max(65 - T_t, 0)dt$, whereas the CDD index is defined as $\int_{t_1}^{t_2} \max(T_t - 65, 0)dt$.[4]

For the five European cities, one can trade in futures written on the cumulative (average) temperature (CAT) index and the HDD index over a month or season. The CAT index over a timer interval $[t_1, t_2]$ is defined as $\int_{t_1}^{t_2} T_t dt$, where the temperature is measured in degrees of Celsius and not Fahrenheit. The contracts are denominated in GBP instead of USD. Moreover, the temperature level for the HDD-contracts is set at $18°C$.

For the two Japanese cities (Tokyo and Osaka), the futures are written on the so-called Pacific Rim index, which measures the average daily temperature over a month or a season. The Pacific Rim index over the period $[t_1, t_2]$ is defined as $\frac{1}{t_2-t_1} \int_{t_1}^{t_2} T_t dt$, and the contracts are denominated in Japanese yen.[5]

The CME also offers trading in plain vanilla European options on the different temperature index futures. There exists call and put options for different strike and maturities for all HDD, CDD, CAT, and Pacific Rim index futures. Among the major market makers for the CME are Aquila Energy, Koch Energy Trading, Southern Energy, Enron, and Castlebridge Weather Markets. All these firms are also active in the OTC market for weather derivatives.

Following Benth and Šalytè–Benth (2005), consider the price dynamics of futures written on the HDD index over a specified period $[t_1, t_2]$, $t_1 < t_2$ from December to March (e.g., the winter season). Assuming a constant continuously compounding rate r, the futures price at time $t < t_1$ written on the HDD index is defined as the $\Im_t$–adapted stochastic process $F_{HDD}(\tau, t_1, t_2)$ satisfying

$$e^{-r(t_2-t)}E^Q\left[\int_{t_1}^{t_2} \max(c - T_t, 0)dt - F_{HDD}(\tau, t_1, t_2)|\Im_t\right] = 0 \qquad (6.4)$$

where Q is the risk-neutral probability and c is equal to 65°F or 18°C, depending on whether the contract is for a U.S. or European city. Given the adaptedness of $F_{HDD}(t_1, t_2)$, we find the futures price to be

$$F_{HDD}(\tau, t_1, t_2) = E^Q\left[\int_{t_1}^{t_2} \max(c - T_t, 0)dt|\Im_t\right]. \qquad (6.5)$$

Analogously, the CDD-futures price is

$$F_{CDD}(\tau, t_1, t_2) = E^Q \left[\int_{t_1}^{t_2} \max(T_t - c, 0) dt | \Im_t \right]. \tag{6.6}$$

By the same reasoning, one can derive the price of a CAT futures and a Pacific Rim futures to be

$$F_{CAT}(\tau, t_1, t_2) = E^Q \left[\int_{t_1}^{t_2} T_t dt | \Im_t \right], \tag{6.7}$$

and

$$F_{PRIM}(\tau, t_1, t_2) = E^Q \left[\frac{1}{t_2 - t_1} \int_{t_1}^{t_2} T_t dt | \Im_t \right]. \tag{6.8}$$

Note that

$$F_{PRIM}(\tau, t_1, t_2) = \frac{1}{t_2 - t_1} F_{CAT}(\tau, t_1, t_2). \tag{6.9}$$

Moreover, because $\max(c - x, 0) = c - x + \max(x - c, 0)$, we have the following:

$$F_{HDD}(\tau, t_1, t_2) = c(t_2 - t_1) - F_{CAT}(\tau, t_1, t_2) + F_{CDD}(\tau, t_1, t_2)$$

Outside the CME, there are a number of different contracts traded in the OTC market. The buyer of a HDD call, for example, pays the seller a premium at the beginning of the contract. In return, if the number of HDDs for the contract period is greater than the predetermined strike level, the buyer will receive a payoff. The size of the payoff is determined by the strike and the tick size. The *tick size* is the amount of money that the holder of the call receives for each degree-day above the strike level for the period. Often the option has a cap on the maximum payout unlike, for example, traditional options on stocks. A standard weather option can be formulated by specifying the following parameters:

- The contract type (call or put)

- The contract period (e.g., month of January)

- The underlying index (HDD or CDD)

- An official weather station from which the temperature data are obtained

- The strike level

- The tick size

- The maximum payoff (if there is any)

To find a formula for the payout of an option, let K denote the strike level and the tick size. Let the contract period consist of n days. Then, the number of HDDs and CDDs for that period are

$$H_n = \sum_{i=1}^{n} HDD_i \text{ and } C_n = \sum_{i=1}^{n} CDD_i \qquad (6.10)$$

respectively. Now we can write the payoff of an uncapped HDD call as:

$$\alpha \max\{H_n - K, 0\} \qquad (6.11)$$

The payouts for similar contracts like HDD puts and CDD calls/puts are defined in the same way. Figure 6.3 shows an example of HDD- and CDD-based forward and option contracts.

Examples of HDD- and CDD-Based Forward and Option Contracts

	HDD Forward	CDD Put Option
Current time	December 1, 2001	January 1, 2002
Location	Phil, Int'l Airport, Philadelphia	Hartsfield Airport, Atlanta
Long Position	ABC Bank	Air Conditioning Ltd.
Short Position	Power Supply Ltd.	XYZ Bank
Accumulation Period	February, 2002	July, 2002
Tick Size	84,000 per HDD	$10,000 per CDD
Strike Level	855 HDDs	550 CDDs
Actual Level	650 HDDs	510 CDDs
Payoffs at Maturity (Long Position)	$(650 - 850) \times 4000 = -\$800,000$	$(550 - 510) \times 10000 = \$400,000$

Figure 6.3 *Source: Cao, Li, and Wei (2004).*

6.3 MODELING TEMPERATURE

To properly model weather derivatives, we must generate the stochastic process that temperature, the underlying variable, follows and understand its behavior and movements. There are strong seasonal variations and patterns in temperature. Thus, temperature cannot be modeled well with random walks. There are other observations to consider: Temperatures exhibit high autocorrelation, which means that short-term behavior will differ from the long-term behavior. Finally, there is no underlying asset because temperature (or precipitation) cannot be bought or sold. There is no way to construct a portfolio of financial assets that replicates the payoff of a weather derivative. Given these issues with temperature, the Black Scholes framework does not apply. Figure 6.4 shows a typical pattern of average daily temperatures in Stockholm, Sweden starting January 1, 1994 and ending January 1, 2005.

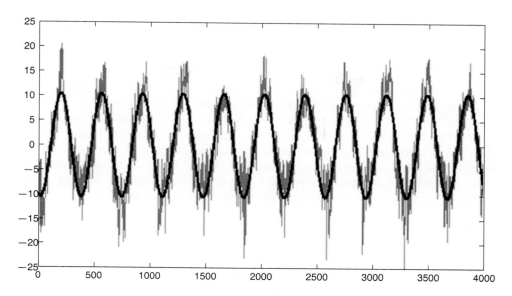

Figure 6.4   Average Temperature in Stockholm, Sweden (Jan. 2004- Jan. 2005).   *Source: Alaton, P., Djehiche, B. and Sillberger, D. (2000).*

Given the seasonal and cyclical nature of temperature, the model should incorporate mean reversion in the process. The mean temperature seems to vary between about 20°C during the summers and −10°C during the winters. After a quick glance at Figure 6.1, we guess that it should be possible to model the seasonal dependence with, for example, some sine-function. This function would have the form

$$\sin(\omega t + \theta)$$

where t denotes the time, measured in days. We let $t = 1, 2, \ldots$ denote January 1, January 2, and so on. Because we know that the period of the oscillations is one year (neglecting leap years), we have $\omega = \frac{2\pi}{365}$. Because the yearly minimum and maximum mean temperatures do not usually occur at January 1 and July 1, respectively, we have to introduce a phase angle θ. Moreover, a closer look at the data series reveals a positive trend in the data. It is weak, but it does exist. The mean temperature actually increases each year. There can be many reasons to this. One reason is the fact that we may have a global warming trend all over the world. Another is the so called urban heating effect, which means that temperatures tend to rise in areas nearby a big city, because the city is growing and warming its surroundings. To catch this weak trend from data, we will assume, as a first approximation, that the warming trend is linear. We could have assumed it to be polynomial, but due to its weak effect on the overall dynamics of the mean temperature, it is only the linear term of this polynomial that will dominate.

Summing up, a deterministic model for the mean temperature at time t, T_t^m would have the form

$$T_t^m = A + Bt + C \sin(\omega t + \theta) \tag{6.12}$$

where the parameters A, B, C, and θ have to be chosen so that the curve fits the data well.

Temperature movements are not deterministic—they are affected by global and seasonal weather changes. Thus, to obtain a more realistic model, we now have to add some sort of noise to the deterministic model (6.12). One choice is a standard Wiener process, $(W_t, t \geq 0)$. Indeed, this is reasonable not only with regard to the mathematical tractability of the model, but also because Figure 6.5 shows a good fit of the plotted daily temperature differences with the corresponding normal distribution, although the probability of getting small differences in the daily mean temperature will be slightly underestimated.

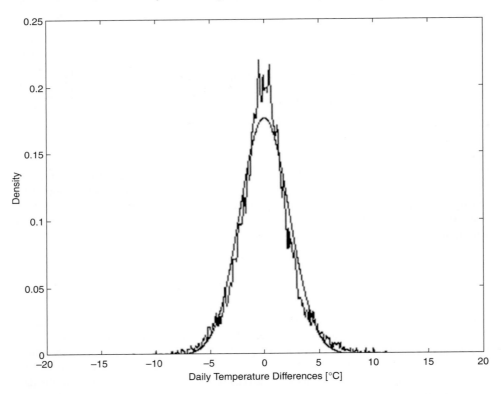

Figure 6.5 Daily Temperature Distribution. *Source: Alaton, P., Djehiche, B. and Sillberger, D. (2000), 9.*

Noise Process

A closer look at the data series reveals that the variation σ_t^2 of the temperature varies across the different months of the year, but nearly constant within each month. Especially during the winter, the quadratic variation is much higher than during the rest of the year. Therefore, we make the assumption that σ_t is a piecewise constant function, with a constant value during each month.[6] We specify σ_t as

$$\sigma_t = \begin{cases} \sigma_1 \text{ during January} \\ \sigma_2 \text{ during February} \\ \vdots \\ \sigma_n \text{ during December} \end{cases}$$

where $\sigma_i, i = 1, ..., 12$ are positive constants. Thus, the driving noise process of the temperature would be $(\sigma_t W_t, t \geq 0)$.

Mean-Reversion

We know that the temperature cannot, for example, rise day after day for a long time. This means that our model should not allow the temperature to deviate from its mean value for more than short periods of time. In other words, the stochastic process describing the temperature we are looking for should have a mean-reverting property. Putting all the assumptions together, we model temperature by a stochastic process solution of the following SDE[7]

$$dT_t = a(T_t^m - T_t)dt + \sigma_t dW_t \tag{6.13}$$

where $a \in \Re$ determines the speed of mean-reversion. The solution of such an equation is usually called an Ornstein-Uhlenbeck process. Alaton et al. (2000) suggests adding another term to the drift because equation (6.13) is not actually mean-reverting to T_t^m in the long run, as shown by Dornier and Queruel (2000):[8]

$$\frac{dT_t^m}{dt} = B + \omega C \cos(\omega t + \theta) \tag{6.14}$$

Given the mean temperature T_t^m is not constant, this term will adjust the drift so that the solution of the SDE has the long run mean T_t^m.

Starting at $T_s = x$, we now get the following model for the temperature

$$dT_t = \left(\frac{dT_t^m}{dt} + a(T_t^m - T_t) \right) dt + \sigma_t dW_t, \ t>s \tag{6.15}$$

whose solution is

$$T_t = (x - T_s^m)e^{-a(t-s)} + T_t^m + \int_s^t e^{-a(t-\tau)} \sigma_\tau dW_\tau \tag{6.16}$$

where

$$T_t^m = A + Bt + C \sin(\omega t + \theta). \tag{6.17}$$

6.4 PARAMETER ESTIMATION

To estimate the unknown parameters A, B, C, θ, a, and σ, one can use least squares regression techniques. To find the numerical values of the parameters in (6.17), we can estimate the parameters of

$$Y_t = a_1 + a_2 t + a_3 \sin(\omega t) + a_4 \cos(\omega t) \tag{6.18}$$

by fitting the function in (6.18) to the temperature data using the method of least squares. We must find the parameter vector $\xi = (a_1, a_2, a_3, a_4)$ that solves

$$\min_{\xi} ||\mathbf{Y} - \mathbf{X}||^2 \tag{6.19}$$

where $\mathbf{Y}$ is the vector with elements (6.18) and $\mathbf{X}$ is the (historical) data vector. The constant in the model (6.17) are then obtained by

$$A = a_1 \tag{6.20}$$

$$B = a_2 \tag{6.21}$$

$$C = \sqrt{a_3^2 + a_4^2} \tag{6.22}$$

$$\theta = \arctan\left(\frac{a_4}{a_3}\right) - \pi \tag{6.23}$$

As an example, Alaton et al. (2000) estimates the parameters in (6.18) using temperature data from the Bromma Airport in Stockholm, Sweden from the last 40 years. The following function for the mean temperature is given by:

$$T_t^m = 5.97 + 6.57 \cdot 10^{-5} t + 10.4 \sin\left(\frac{2\pi}{365} t - 2.01\right) \tag{6.24}$$

The amplitude of the sin-function is about $10°C$, which means that the difference in temperature between a typical winter day and a summer day is about $20°C$.[9]

6.5 VOLATILITY ESTIMATION

Alaton et al. (2000) provides to estimators for σ from the data (collected for each month). Given a specific month μ of N_i days, denote the outcomes of the observed temperatures during the month μ by $T_j, j = 1, \ldots, N_i$. The first estimator is based on the quadratic variation of T_t (see Basawa and Prasaka Rao [1980], 212–213).[10]

$$\widehat{\sigma}_i^2 = \frac{1}{N} \sum_{j=0}^{N_\mu - 1} (T_{j+1} - T_j)^2 \tag{6.25}$$

The second estimator is derived by discretizing (6.15) and viewing the discretized equation as a regression equation. During a given month μ, the discretized equation is

$$T_j = T_j^m - T_{j-1}^m + a T_{j-1}^m + (1-a) T_{j-1} + \sigma_\mu \varepsilon_{j-1}, \; j = 1, \ldots, N_\mu \tag{6.26}$$

where $\{\varepsilon_j\}_{j=1}^{N_m-1}$ are independent standard normally distributed random variables—e.g., $\varepsilon_j \sim N(0,1)$. Let $\widetilde{T}_j = T_j - (T_j^m - T_{j-1}^m)$. Then we can write (6.26) as

$$\widetilde{T}_j = aT_{j-1}^m + (1-a)T_{j-1} + \sigma_\mu \varepsilon_{j-1}, \tag{6.27}$$

which can be seen as a regression of today's temperature on yesterday's temperature. Thus, an efficient estimator of σ_i is (see Brockwell and Davis [1990]):[11]

$$\widehat{\sigma}_\mu^2 = \frac{1}{N_\mu - 2} \sum_{j=0}^{N_\mu} (\widetilde{T}_j - aT_{j-1}^m + (1-a)T_{j-1})^2 \tag{6.28}$$

To evaluate the estimator in (6.28), one needs to find an estimator of the mean-reversion parameter a, which is done in the next section.

6.6   MEAN-REVERSION PARAMETER ESTIMATION

The mean-reversion parameter can be estimated using the martingale estimation function methods given by Bibby and Sorensen (1995).[12] Let $b(T_t; a)$ denote the drift term of the temperature stochastic process in (6.15):

$$b(T_t; a) = \frac{dT_t^m}{dt} + a(T_t^m - T_t) \tag{6.29}$$

Following Alaton et al. (2000), based on observations collected during n days, an efficient estimator $\widehat{a}_n$ of a is obtained as *a* zero of equation:

$$G_n(\widehat{a}_n) = 0 \tag{6.30}$$

where

$$G_n(a) = \sum_{i=1}^{n} \frac{\dot{b}(T_{i-1}; a)}{\sigma_{i-1}^2} (T_i - E[T_i|T_{i-1}]) \tag{6.31}$$

and $\dot{b}(T_t; a)$ denotes the derivatives of the drift in (6.29) with respect to a. To solve (6.30), one only needs to determine each of the conditional expectation terms $E[T_i|T_{i-1}]$ in (6.31). By equation (6.16) for $t \geq s$,

$$T_t = (T_s - T_s^m)e^{-a(t-s)} + T_t^m + \int_s^t e^{-a(t-\tau)}\sigma_\tau dW_\tau \tag{6.32}$$

which yields

$$E[T_i|T_{i-1}] = (T_{i-1} - T_{i-1}^m)e^{-a} + T_i^m \tag{6.33}$$

where as before

$$T_t^m = A + Bt + C\sin(\omega t + \theta).$$

Therefore,

$$G_n(a) = \sum_{i=1}^{n} \frac{T_{i-1}^m - T_{i-1}}{\sigma_{i-1}^2} \left(T_i - (T_{i-1} - T_{i-1}^m)e^{-a} - T_i^m\right) \tag{6.34}$$

from which one finds the mean-reversion estimator

$$\widehat{a}_n = -\log\left(\frac{\sum_{i=1}^{n} Y_{i-1}(T_i - T_i^m)}{\sum_{i=1}^{n} Y_{i-1}(T_{i-1} - T_{i-1}^m)}\right) \tag{6.35}$$

is the unique zero of equation (6.30), where

$$Y_{i-1} = \frac{T_{i-1}^m - T_{i-1}}{\sigma_{i-1}^2} \ i = 1, 2, \dots, n. \tag{6.36}$$

6.7 PRICING WEATHER DERIVATIVES

Model Framework

We define the following parameters for the pricing model:

- T_t^m: modeled average temperature at time t

- T_t: current temperature at time t

- a: mean reversion parameter

- σ: volatility of the temperature

- W_t: Wiener process

The market for weather derivatives is a typical example of an incomplete market, because the underlying variable, the temperature, is not tradable. Therefore, we have to consider the market price of risk λ, in order to obtain unique prices for such contracts. Because there is not yet a real market from which we can obtain prices, we assume for simplicity that the market price of risk is constant. Furthermore, we assume that we are given a risk-free asset with constant interest rate r and a contract that for each degree Celsius pays one unit of currency. Thus, under a martingale measure Q, characterized by the market price of risk λ, the temperature process also denoted by T_t satisfies the following dynamics:

$$dT_t = \left(\frac{dT_t^m}{dt} + a(T_t^m - T_t) - \lambda\sigma_t\right) dt + \sigma_t dW_t \tag{6.37}$$

where $\{W_t, t \geq 0\}$ is a Q–Wiener process. Following Alaton et al. (2000), we start computing the expected value and the variance of T_t because the price of a derivative is expressed as a discounted expected value under the risk-neutral martingale measure Q. We will use Girsanov's theorem to change to the drift under the physical measure P. However, because

Girsanov's transformation only changes the drift, the variance of T_t is the same under both measures. Therefore,

$$\text{Var}[T_t|\Im_s] = \int_s^t \sigma_u^2 e^{-2a(t-u)} du. \tag{6.38}$$

Furthermore, it follows from (6.16) that

$$E^P[T_t|\Im_s] = (T_s - T_s^m)e^{-a(t-s)} + T_t^m. \tag{6.39}$$

Thus, in view of equation (6.37), we must have the following:

$$E^Q[T_t|\Im_s] = E^P[T_t|\Im_s] - \int_s^t \lambda \sigma_u e^{-a(t-u)} \tag{6.40}$$

Evaluating the integrals in one of the intervals where σ is constant, we get that

$$E^Q[T_t|\Im_s] = E^P[T_t|\Im_s] - \frac{\lambda \sigma_i}{a}(1 - e^{-a(t-s)}) \tag{6.41}$$

and the variance is

$$\text{Var}[T_t|\Im_s] = \frac{\sigma^2}{2a}\left(1 - e^{-2a(t-s)}\right). \tag{6.42}$$

The covariance of the temperature between two different days is for $0 \le s \le t \le u$:

$$\text{Cov}[T_t, T_u|\Im_s] = e^{-a(u-t)}\,\text{Var}[T_t|\Im_s] \tag{6.43}$$

As Alaton et al. (2000) shows, suppose now that t_1 and t_n denote the first and last day of a month and start the process at some time s from the month before $[t_1, t_n]$. To compute the expected value and variance of T_t in this case, we split the integrals in (6.40) and (6.38) into two integrals where σ is constant in each one. We then get

$$E^Q[T_t|\Im_s] = E^P[T_t|\Im_s] - \frac{\lambda}{a}(\sigma_i - \sigma_j)e^{-a(t-t_1)} + \frac{\lambda \sigma_i}{a}e^{-a(t-s)} - \frac{\lambda \sigma_j}{a} \tag{6.44}$$

and the variance is

$$\text{Var}[T_t|\Im_s] = \frac{1}{2a}\left(\sigma_i^2 - \sigma_j^2\right)e^{-2a(t-t_1)} - \frac{\sigma_i^2}{2a}e^{-2a(t-s)} + \frac{\sigma_j^2}{2a}. \tag{6.45}$$

The generalization to a larger time interval now becomes straightforward.

Pricing a Heating Degree Day Option

To price a standard HDD call option, we use the payoff given in (6.5)

$$\chi = \alpha \max(H_n - K, 0) \tag{6.46}$$

where

$$H_n = \sum_{i=1}^{n} \max(65° F - T_t, 0). \tag{6.47}$$

The payoff depends on the accumulation of HDDs during some time period (e.g., in the winter during the month of January).

For simplicity, we assume that the tick size is $\alpha = 1$. The contract in (6.46) is a type of arithmetic average Asian option. In the case of a log-normally distributed underlying process, no exact formula for the price of such an option is known, so we try to make some sort of approximation. We know that under the risk-neutral measure Q, and given information at time s,

$$T_t \sim N(\mu_t, \sigma_t^2)$$

where μ_t is given by (6.44) and σ_t^2 is given by (6.45). Suppose the probability that max $(65 - T_t, 0) = 0$ is extremely small on a winter day. Then, for such a contract, we can write

$$H_n = 65n - \sum_{i=1}^{n} T_{t_i}. \tag{6.48}$$

We now determine fair pricing under a (normal) distributional model. Following Alaton et al. (2000), we know that $T_t, i = 1, ..., n$ are all samples from an Ornstein-Uhlenbeck process, which is a Gaussian process. This means that the vector $(T_{t_1}, T_{t_2}, \ldots, T_{t_n})$ is Gaussian. Because the sum of (6.48) is a linear combination of the elements of the vector, H_n is also Gaussian.[13] We compute the first and second moments. We have, for $t < t_1$,

$$E^Q[H_n|\Im_s] = E^Q\left[65n - \sum_{i=1}^{n} T_{t_i}|\Im_s\right] = 65n - \sum_{i=1}^{n} E^Q[T_{t_i}|\Im_t] \tag{6.49}$$

and

$$\mathrm{Var}[H_n|\Im_s] = \sum_{i=1}^{n} \mathrm{Var}[T_{t_i}|\Im_s] + 2\sum_{j=1}^{n}\sum_{i<j} \mathrm{Cov}[T_{t_i}, T_{t_j}|\Im_t]. \tag{6.50}$$

Suppose we make the previous calculations and find that:

$$E^Q[H_n|\Im_t] = \mu_n \text{ and } \mathrm{Var}[H_n|\Im_t] = \sigma_n^2 \tag{6.51}$$

Then, $H_n \sim N(\mu_n, \sigma_n)$. Thus, the price at $t \le t_1$ of the claim (6.46) is given by

$$c_{HDD}(t) = e^{-r(t_n-t)} E^Q[\max(H_n - K, 0)|\Im_t]$$

$$= e^{-r(t_n-t)} \int_{K}^{\infty} (x - K) f_{H_n}(x) dk$$

$$= e^{-r(t_n-t)} \left((\mu_n - K)\Phi(-\alpha_n) + \frac{\sigma_n}{\sqrt{2\pi}} e^{-\frac{\alpha_n^2}{2}}\right) \tag{6.52}$$

where $\alpha_n = (K - \mu_n)/\sigma_n$ and Φ denotes the cumulative standard normal distribution function (see also Platen and West [2004], pg. 23[14]).

Similarly, we can derive the formula for the price of an HDD put option with the claim payoff of:

$$y = \max(K - H_n, 0) \tag{6.53}$$

The price is

$$
\begin{aligned}
p_{HDD}(t) &= e^{-r(t_n - t)} E^Q\left[\max(K - H_n, 0)|\Im_t\right] \\
&= e^{-r(t_n - t)} \int_0^K (K - x) f_{H_n}(x) dx \\
&= e^{-r(t_n - t)} \left\{ (K - \mu_n)\left(\Phi(\alpha_n) - \Phi\left(-\frac{\mu_n}{\sigma_n}\right)\right) + \right. \\
&\qquad \left. \frac{\sigma_n}{\sqrt{2\pi}}\left(e^{-\frac{\alpha_n^2}{2}} - e^{-\frac{1}{2}\left(\frac{\mu_n}{\sigma_n}\right)^2}\right)\right\}.
\end{aligned}
\tag{6.54}
$$

Formulas (6.52) and (6.54) for call and put, respectively, hold primarily for contracts during winter months, which typically is the period from November to March.[15] During the summer months, we cannot use these formulas without restrictions. If the mean temperatures are very close to, or even higher than, 65°F (18°C), we no longer have $\max(65 - T_{t_i}, 0) \neq 0$. For such contracts, we can use Monte Carlo simulation.

Zeng (2000) discusses a pure actuarial statistical approach (see also Platen and West [2004]), as well as a prediction-based pricing approach for weather derivatives. In the latter approach, a normal distribution is fit to the historical CDD data by assuming that the option CDD follows a normal distribution with the mean and standard deviation equal to the sample mean and standard deviation, respectively, of the historical data. The probability of "non-exceedance" is evenly divided into the highest, middle, and lowest thirds, as shown in Figure 6.6.

The fitted distribution is then sampled such that the number of samples corresponding to the highest, middle, and lowest thirds are proportional to the above, near, and below climate norms (denoted p_A, p_N, and p_B, respectively). For instance, unlike traditional Monte Carlo, which samples the fitted distribution evenly across the probabilistic distribution, the prediction-based approach only samples from the highest, middle, and lowest thirds, respectively, of the distribution so as to incorporate the probabilistic climate prediction into the sample CDD values (a biased sampling Monte Carlo approach). The payoffs are averaged over from this sampled distribution just like in traditional Monte Carlo. The method exploits the fact that the rank-order correlation of the historical data will be high given the seasonal nature of temperature (for instance, a high July temperature tends to be associated with a high June-July-August (JJA) temperature), and that the predicted anomaly probabilities for the temperature p_A, p_N, and p_B are assumed to approximate the probabilities that the CDD will be above, near, and below the climate norm, respectively.[16]

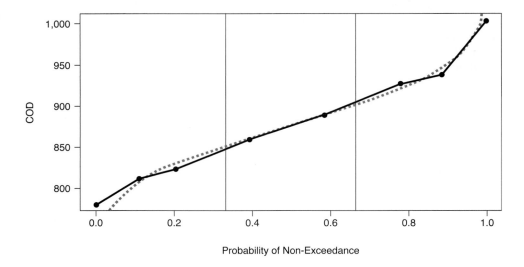

Figure 6.6 The probability of non-exceedance.   *Source: Zeng (2000).*

6.8 HISTORICAL BURN ANALYSIS

The method of historical burn analysis evaluates the contract against historical data and takes the average of realized payoffs as the fair value estimate. For instance, suppose a call option is written on a city's CDDs for the month of July, and suppose we have 20 years of daily temperatures. To apply the historical burn analysis method, for each July of the past 20 years, we calculate the option payoff using the realized CDDs. The average of the 20 payoffs is the estimate for the call option value. Thus, this method's key assumption is that the past always reflects the future on average. To be more precise, the method assumes that the distribution of the past payoffs accurately depicts the future payoff's distribution. This is a far-reaching requirement in most cases. For instance, we have only 20 payoff observations in the previous example, which can hardly capture the complete characteristics of the true distribution.

Cao, Li, and Wei (2004) apply this method to call options written on the three-month (January, February, and March) cumulative HDDs for Atlanta, Chicago, and New York. Table 6.1 shows the calculations. They first calculate the realized cumulative HDDs for each year, and then evaluate the option's payoff[17] accordingly. (The exercise prices are set at 1,500, 3,200, and 2,500 for Atlanta, Chicago, and New York, respectively.) When Cao, Li, and Wei (2004) use all 20 historical observations for Atlanta, for example, the average payoff is 92.15; when the most recent 19 observations are used, the average payoff is 82.37, and so on. When they use only the most recent 10 observations, the fair value estimate is 22.50. Going back 10 years versus 20 years would lead to a difference of more than 300% in value estimates! The estimates for the option on New York's HDDs have the smallest dispersion. But even there, the highest estimate is 70% higher than the lowest estimate.

We can argue that we should use as long a time series as possible to enhance accuracy. However, using more data will cover more temperature variations, but a derivative

Table 6.1

Year	HDDs for Jan. 1 - March 31			HDD Call Option Payoff			Years in Average	Estimate of Call Option Value		
	Atlanta	Chicago	New York	Atlanta	Chicago	New York		Atlanta	Chicago	New York
1979	1778	3851	2841	278	651	341				
1980	1672	3474	2702	172	274	202				
1981	1698	3183	2708	198	0	208				
1982	1587	3760	2791	87	560	291				
1983	1749	3002	2443	249	0	0				
1984	1660	3424	2724	160	224	224				
1985	1723	3591	2567	223	391	67				
1986	1416	3208	2533	0	8	33				
1987	1602	2813	2504	102	0	4				
1988	1649	3417	2593	149	217	93	10	22.50	63.70	69.60
1989	1242	3150	2417	0	0	0	11	34.00	77.64	71.73
1990	1009	2627	2078	0	0	0	12	39.67	71.17	66.08
1991	1354	3066	2217	0	0	0	13	36.62	66.31	63.54
1992	1325	2862	2439	0	0	0	14	49.93	89.50	63.79
1993	1514	3277	2667	14	77	167	15	57.27	98.47	74.47
1994	1410	3524	2921	0	324	421	16	69.25	92.31	69.81
1995	1295	3096	2370	0	0	0	17	70.29	119.82	82.82
1996	1666	3410	2608	166	210	108	18	77.39	113.17	89.78
1997	1102	3226	2377	0	26	0	19	82.37	121.63	95.68
1998	1545	2637	2060	45	0	0	20	92.15	148.10	107.95
							Highest	92.15	148.10	107.95
							Lowest	22.50	63.70	63.54
							Highest/Lowest	4.10	2.32	1.70

Source: Cao, Li, and Wei (2004)

security's payoff depends on the future temperature behavior, which may be quite different from past history. This is especially true if the maturity of the derivative security is short. Ultimately, the decision boils down to a trade-off between statistical power and representativeness.[18] The commonly accepted sample length in the industry appears to be between 20 to 30 years. Furthermore, we could combine the burn analysis with temperature forecasts to arrive at a more representative price estimate.

Like an insurance or actuarial method, the method of historical burn analysis is incapable of accounting for the market price of risk associated with the temperature variable.[19] These methods are only useful from the perspective of a single dealer.[20] To establish a unique market price that incorporates a risk premium, we need a dynamic, forward-looking model such as

$$dY(t) = \beta[\theta(t) - Y(t)]dt + \sigma(t)Y_t^r dW(t) \tag{6.55}$$

where $Y(t)$ is the current temperature, $\theta(t)$ is the deterministic long-run level of the temperature, β is the speed at which the instantaneous temperature reverts to the long-run level $\theta(t)$, $\sigma(t)$ is the volatility (which is season-dependent), $r = 0, 0.5$, or 1, and $W(t)$ is a Wiener process that models the temperature's random innovations. The process in (6.55) needs to be discretized as

$$Y_t - Y_{t-1} = \beta[\theta(t) - Y_t]\Delta t + \sigma(t)Y_t^r \Delta W_t$$

in order to estimate β and the parameters imbedded in $\theta(t)$ and $\sigma(t)$, where the functional forms for $\theta(t)$ and $\sigma(t)$ can be specified based on careful statistical analyses. Once the process in (6.55) is estimated using a method like ordinary least squares, we can then value any contingent claim by taking expectation of the discounted future payoff; i.e.,

$$X = e^{-r(T-t)} E\left[g(Y_t, Y_{t+1}, ..., Y_T)\right] \tag{6.56}$$

where X is the current value of the contingent claim, r is the risk-free interest rate, T is the maturity of the claim, and $g(Y_t, Y_{t+1}, ..., Y_T)$ is the payoff at time T, which usually is a function of the realized temperatures, $Y_t, Y_{t+1}, ..., Y_T$ (e.g., a contract on cumulative HDDs or CDDs).

Given the complex form of $\theta(t)$ and $\sigma(t)$ and the path-dependent nature of most payoffs, the formula in (6.55) usually does not have closed-form solutions. Monte Carlo simulations must be used. There are two additional drawbacks of this continuous setup. First, it does not allow a place for the market price of risk. Instead, a risk-neutral valuation is imposed without any theoretical justification. Second, the process in (6.55) cannot reflect the persistent serial correlations typically present in daily temperatures.[21] As a result of these drawbacks, time-series discrete processes and models that can incorporate serial correlation have been proposed for forecasting the temperature, as discussed in the next section (see Campbell and Diebold [2002]; Cao and Wei [2003]).

6.9   TIME-SERIES WEATHER FORECASTING

As Figure 6.4 shows, the daily average temperature moves in a given city repeatedly and regularly through periods of high temperature (summer) and low temperature (winter). However, seasonal fluctuations differ noticeably across cities both in terms of amplitude and detail of pattern.[22] But most cities' unconditional temperature distributions are bimodal, with peaks characterized by cool and warm temperatures.[23] Temperature time-series across cities suggests that a seasonal component will be an important factor in any time-series model fit to daily average temperature, as "average temperature displays pronounced seasonal variation, with both the amplitude and precise seasonal patterns differing noticeably across cities."[24] Campbell and Diebold (2000) use a low-ordered Fourier series as opposed to daily dummies to model seasonality for two reasons. First, use of a low-ordered Fourier series produces a smooth seasonal pattern, which accords with the basic intuition that "the progression through different seasons is gradual rather than discontinuous."[25] Second, the Fourier approximation "produces a huge reduction in the number of parameters to be estimated, which significantly reduces computing time and enhances numerical stability."[26]

Campbell and Diebold (2000) also incorporate nonseasonal factors that may be operative in the dynamics of daily average temperature, though dominated by seasonality; in particular, a deterministic linear trend and cycle—persistent (but covariance stationary) dynamics apart from trend and seasonality.[27] These cyclical dynamics are captured using autoregressive lags, which facilitates numerically stable parameter estimates. Thus, an autoregressive model to forecast or estimate future average temperature is suggested:

$$T_t = Trend_t + Seasonal_t + \sum_{l=1}^{L} \rho_{t-1} T_{t-l} + \sigma \varepsilon_t \qquad (6.57)$$

where

$$Trend_t = \beta_0 + \beta_1 t$$

and

$$Seasonal_t = \sum_{p=1}^{P} \left(\delta_{c,p} \cos \left(2\pi p \frac{d(t)}{365} \right) + \delta_{s,p} \sin \left(2\pi p \frac{d(t)}{365} \right) \right) \qquad (6.58)$$

$$\varepsilon_t \overset{iid}{\sim} N(0,1)$$

and where $d(t)$ is a repeating step function that cycles through $1, \ldots, 365$ (i.e., each day of the year assumes one value between 1 and 365). The model is estimated using ordinary least squares, regressing average temperature on constant, trend, Fourier, and lagged average temperature terms, using $L = 25$ autoregressive lags (in order to capture long-memory dynamics) and three Fourier sine and cosine terms ($P = 3$).

Campbell and Diebold (2002) find that the model in (6.57), based on the correlograms of the *squared* residuals, has conditional heteroskedasticity in the model and has drastic misspecification related to nonlinear dependence despite residual autocorrelations that are negligible and consistent with white noise. As a result, Campbell and Diebold (2002) re-specify the model as

$$T_t = Trend_t + Seasonal_t + \sum_{l=1}^{L} \rho_{t-1} T_{t-l} + \sigma_t \varepsilon_t \qquad (6.59)$$

where

$$Trend_t = \beta_0 + \beta_1 t$$

and

$$Seasonal_t = \sum_{p=1}^{P} \left(\delta_{c,p} \cos \left(2\pi p \frac{d(t)}{365} \right) + \delta_{s,p} \sin \left(2\pi p \frac{d(t)}{365} \right) \right) \qquad (6.60)$$

$$\sigma_t^2 = \sum_{q=1}^{Q} \left(\gamma_{c,q} \cos \left(2\pi q \frac{d(t)}{365} \right) + \gamma_{s,q} \sin \left(2\pi q \frac{d(t)}{365} \right) \right) + \sum_{r=1}^{R} \alpha_r \varepsilon_{t-r}^2 \qquad (6.61)$$

$$\varepsilon_t \overset{iid}{\sim} N(0,1)$$

where, as before, $d(t)$ is a repeating step function that cycles through $1, \ldots ,365$ (i.e., each day of the year assumes one value between 1 and 365), and one sets $L = 25$, $P = 3$, $Q = 2$, and $R = 1$.

Model (6.57) is identical to model (6.59) with the addition of the conditional variance equation (6.61), which allows for two types of volatility dynamics. First, it captures seasonality volatility by approximating seasonality in the conditional variance in the same way as equation (6.60) approximates seasonality in the conditional mean, via a Fourier series.[28] Second, the variance equation captures "autoregressive effects in the conditional variance movements, which often arise naturally in time-series contexts, in which shocks to the conditional variance may have effects that persist for several periods, precisely as in the seminal work of Engle (1982)."[29] The model is estimated using Engle's (1982) asymptotically efficient two-step approach. First, equation (6.59) is estimated by ordinary least squares, regressing average temperature on constant, trend, Fourier, and lagged average temperature terms. Second, the variance equation (6.61) is estimated by regressing squared residuals from equation (6.59) on constant, Fourier, and lagged squared residual terms. Square roots of the inverse of fitted values $\hat{\sigma}_t^{-1}$ are used as weights in a weighted least squares re-estimation of (6.59).[30]

Campbell and Diebold (2002) show that the estimated model for conditional heteroskedasticity reduces (but does not eliminate) residual excess kurtosis. Figures 6.7 and 6.8 show the correlograms and correlograms of squared residuals, respectively, for the daily average temperature in various U.S. cities.

Each panel displays autocorrelations of the squared residuals from our daily average temperature model

$$\left(T_t - Trend_t + Seasonal_t + T_t - Trend_t + Seasonal_t + \sum_{l=1}^{L} \rho_{t-1} T_{t-l} \right)^2$$

together with approximate 95% confidence intervals under the null hypothesis of white noise.[31] The correlograms shows that there was no evidence of serial correlation in the standardized residuals. The correlograms of the squared standardized residuals from model (6.59) are substantial improvement over those from model (6.55), suggesting that there is no significant deviation from white noise behavior and that the fitted model (6.59) is adequate.[32]

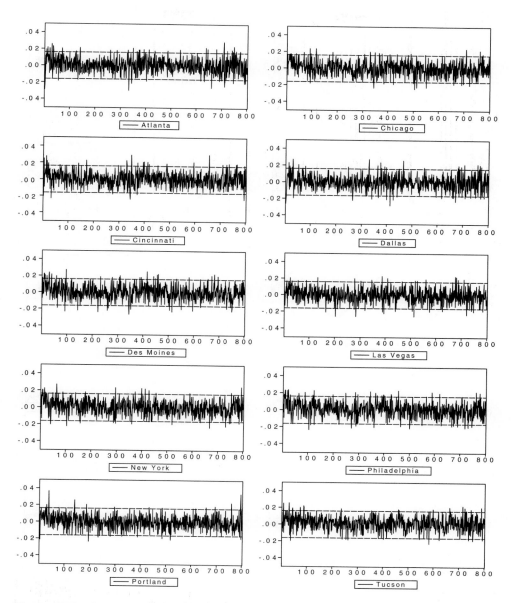

Figure 6.7 Correlograms.   *Source: Campbell and Diebold (2002).*

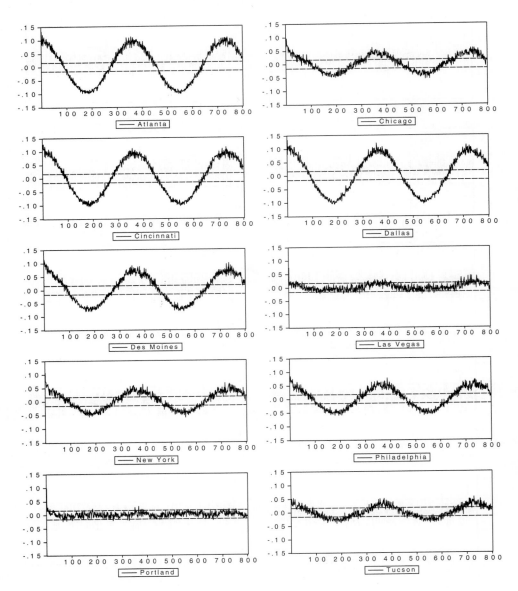

Figure 6.8 Correlograms of squared residuals.   *Source: Campbell and Diebold (2002).*

Figure 6.9 shows the actual values, fitted values, and residuals of the daily average temperature in various cities in the U.S.

Each panel displays actual values, fitted values, and residuals from an unobserved-components model

$$T_t = Trend_t + Seasonal_t + \sum_{l=1}^{L} \rho_{t-1} T_{t-l} + \sigma_t \varepsilon_t.$$

Figure 6.10 shows the estimated conditional standard deviations of the daily average temperature in various U.S. cities.

Each panel displays a time series of estimated conditional standard deviations of daily average temperature obtained from the model:

$$\widehat{\sigma}_t = \sum_{q=1}^{2} \left(\widehat{\gamma}_{c,q} \cos \left(2\pi q \frac{d(t)}{365} \right) + \widehat{\gamma}_{s,q} \sin \left(2\pi q \frac{d(t)}{365} \right) \right) + \widehat{\alpha} \varepsilon_{t-1}^2$$

Figure 6.11 shows the estimated seasonal patterns of daily average temperature (Fourier series versus daily dummies).

The panels shows smooth seasonal patterns estimated from Fourier models,

$$Seasonal_t = \sum_{p=1}^{3} \left(\delta_{c,p} \cos \left(2\pi p \frac{d(t)}{365} \right) + \delta_{s,p} \sin \left(2\pi p \frac{d(t)}{365} \right) \right),$$

and rough seasonal patterns estimated from dummy variable models,

$$Seasonal_t = \sum_{t=1}^{365} \delta_i D_{it}.$$

Figure 6.12 shows histograms of the estimated unconditional distributions of daily average temperature in various U.S. cities from 1996–2001.

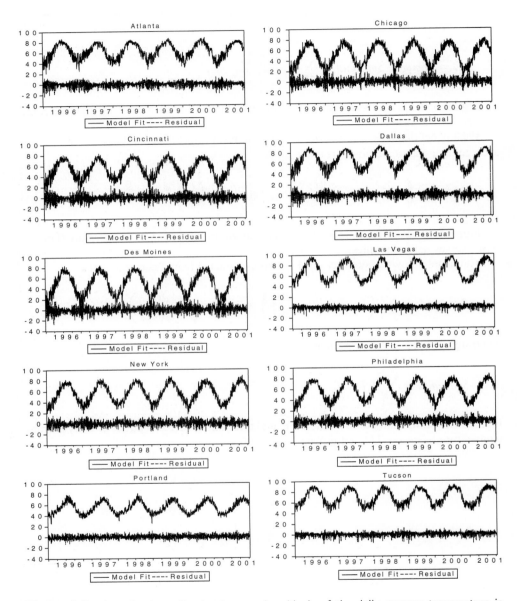

Figure 6.9 Actual values, fitted values, and residuals of the daily average temperature in various cities in the U.S.   *Source: Campbell and Diebold (2002).*

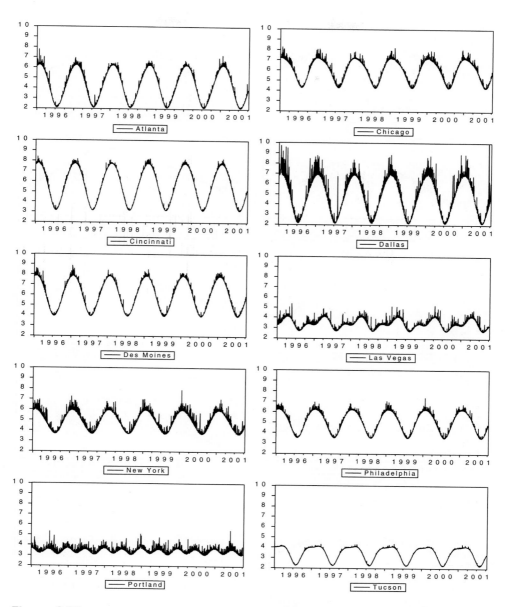

Figure 6.10 Estimated conditional standard deviations of the daily average temperature in various U.S. cities. *Source: Campbell and Diebold (2002).*

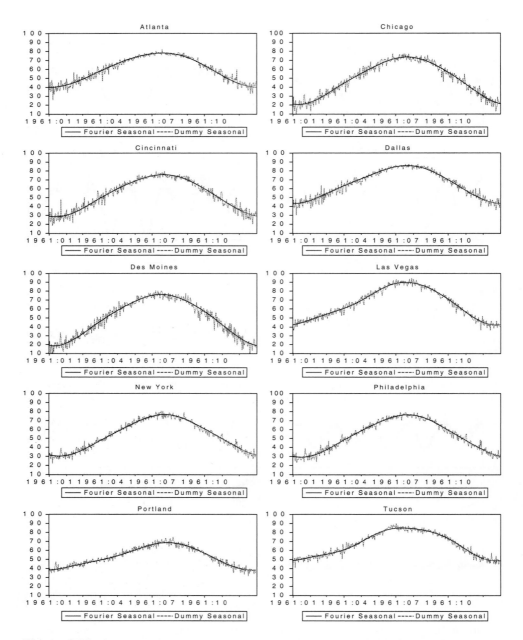

Figure 6.11 Estimated seasonal patterns of daily average temperature (Fourier series versus daily dummies). *Source: Campbell and Diebold (2002).*

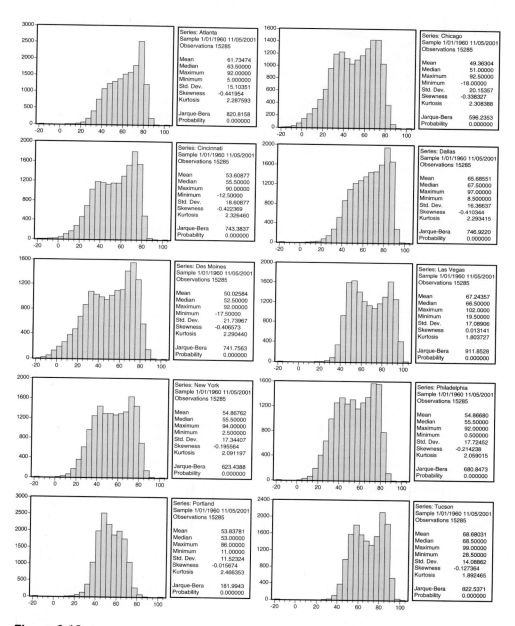

Figure 6.12 Histograms of the estimated unconditional distributions of daily average temperature in various U.S. cities from 1996-2001. *Source: Campbell and Diebold (2002).*

6.10   PRICING WEATHER OPTIONS IN C++

A weather option such as HDD or CDD can be thought of as an Asian option because the payoff depends on the average temperature over the period. We can price these options using Monte Carlo. We can adapt the code of an arithmetic Asian option to price a weather option—e.g., an HDD—by using the average formula in (6.1) and taking the individual payoff in (6.2) and the associated summed payoffs in (6.46). For each day in the period (of M days), we need to simulate the temperature N times (the number of times we sample the temperature during the day) and compute the high and low and take the average. This procedure is simulated K times, and the average payoff is taken over all paths and discounted to generate the expected value. We simulate the weather process using an Ornstein-Uhlenbeck process.

MCPricer_calcMCAsianPriceWeather.cpp

```
vector<double> MCPricer::calcMCAAsianPriceWeather(double price,
  double strike, double DDstrike, double vol, double rate,
    double div, double T, char type, long K, long M, long N)
{
        // initialize variables
        double A = 0.0;                 // arithmetic average
        double mu = 0.0;                // drift
        int i, j, k;                    // counters
        double deviate;                 // normal deviate
        double stddev = 0.0;            // standard deviation
        double stderror = 0.0;          // standard error
        double W = 0.0;                 // weather option price
        double sum = 0.0;               // sum payoffs
        double sum1 = 0.0;
        double sum2 = 0.0;              // sum squared payoffs
        double payoff = 0.0;            // payoff
        double val = 0.0;               // option value
        double dt = (double) T/N;       // compute step size
        double a = 0.10;                // mean reversion
        double Wbar = 65;               // long-run temperature
        double minW, maxW = 0;          // min and max temperature
        double tick_size = 100;         // tick size
        vector<double> value;           // store price, std dev., etc.
        vector<double> Wvec;            // store temperatures
    mrng.sgenrand(unsigned(time(0)));   // initializer RNG

        // number of simulations
        for (k = 0; k < K; k++)
        {
                payoff = 0;
                // for each day
                for (i = 0; i < M; i++)
                {
                W = Wbar;
                        Wvec.clear();
                        Wvec.empty();
                        // number of time steps (hours) in each day
                for (j = 0; j < N; j++)
                {
```

```
                                deviate = mrng.genrand();
                                   mu = -a*(W - Wbar);
                                W  = W + mu*dt + vol*sqrt(dt)*deviate;
                            // Ornstein-Uhlenbeck process
                                   Wvec.push_back(W);
                    }
                            // sort temperatures
                            sort(Wvec.begin(),Wvec.end());
                            minW = Wvec[0];
                            maxW = Wvec[Wvec.size()-1];
                    A = 0.5*(maxW + minW);
                    if (type == 'C')  // cooling days
                            payoff += tick_size*max(A - strike, 0);
                    else
                            payoff += tick_size*max(strike - A,0);
                    }
                    sum += payoff;
                    sum2 += payoff*payoff;
            }
            sum = (double) sum/(K*M);  // average over all pays and days
            sum2 = sum*sum;
            val = exp(-rate*T)*(sum);
            value.push_back(val);

            stddev = sqrt((sum2 - sum*sum/M)*exp(-2*rate*T)/(K-1));
            value.push_back(stddev);

            stderror = stddev/sqrt(K);
            value.push_back(stderror);

            value.push_back(payoff);

            if (type == 'C')
                    value.push_back(tick_size*(DDstrike - payoff));
            else
                    value.push_back(tick_size*(payoff - DDstrike));

    return value;
}
```

The main method is

MCPricer_weather_main.cpp

```cpp
#include "MCPricer.h"

void main()
{
    MCPricer mcp;
    long N = 5;
    long M = 100000;

    // weather options
    double W = 50;
    double strikeW = 65;
    double volW = 0.2;
```

```
    long numDays = 30;
    long K = 10000;
    long numSteps = 100;
    double HDDstrike = numDays*strikeW;
    double mat = (double) numDays/360;
    vector<double> val;
    cout.precision(8);

    val = mcp.calcMCAAsianPriceWeather(W,strikeW,HDDstrike,volW,rate,div,
        mat,'C',K,numDays,numSteps);
    std::cout << "Weather option price = " << val[0] << endl;
    std::cout << "Std deviation    = " << val[1] << endl;
    std::cout << "Std Error =        " << val[2] << endl;
    std::cout << "Actual HDD Price = "<< val[3] << endl;
    std::cout << "HDD Payoff at Maturity = " << val[4] << endl << endl;
}
```

The is the price of an HDD with a mean reversion of 0.1, a volatility of 0.2, a long-run mean of 65°F, with $K = 10000$ simulations, $M = 30$ days, and $N = 100$ time steps.

```
Weather option price = 14.462588
Std deviation = 0.14220213
Std Error = 0.0014220213
Actual HDD Price = 433.15165
HDD Payoff at Maturity = 151684.83
```

ENDNOTES

1. Platen and West (2004), 2.
2. Alaton, P., Djehiche, B., and Sillberger, D. (2000), 1.
3. Cao, Li, and Wei (2004), 1.
4. Benth, F. and Salyte-Benth, J. (2005), 9.
5. Id., 9.
6. Alaton, P., Djehiche, B., and Sillberger, D. (2000), 9.
7. Id., 9.
8. Dornier and Queruel (2002).
9. Alaton, P., Djehiche, B., and Sillberger, D. (2000), 10.
10. Basawa and Prasaka Rao (1980), 212–213.
11. Brockwell and Davis (1990).
12. Bibby and Sorenson (1995).
13. Alaton, P., Djehiche, B., and Sillberger, D. (2000), 16.
14. Platen and West (2004), 23.
15. Alaton, P., Djehiche, B., and Sillberger, D (2000), 17.
16. Zeng, L. (2000), 77.
17. These are reported in the six columns next to the first column. The last three columns show the option value estimates under different sample lengths.
18. Cao, Li, and Wei (2004), 14.
19. Id., 14.
20. Id., 14.

21. Cao, Li, and Wei (2004), 15.
22. Campbell, S. and Diebold, X. (2000), 5.
23. Id., 5.
24. Campbell, S. and Diebold, F. (2000), 6.
25. Id., 6.
26. Id., 6.
27. Id., 6.
28. Campbell, S. and Diebold, F. (2002), 9.
29. Engle (1982).
30. Campbell, S. and Diebold, F. (2002), 9.
31. Id.
32. Id., 10.

CHAPTER **7**

ENERGY AND POWER
DERIVATIVES

SECTIONS

The pricing of energy and power derivatives are reviewed in detail in this chapter. In §7.1, we discuss electricity markets. In §7.2, we review electricity pricing models including both one-factor and two-factor models, jump diffusion models, and stochastic volatility models. Estimation of model parameters is also discussed. In §7.3, we discuss electricity swing options. In §7.4, we review the Longstaff-Schwartz algorithm of least-squares Monte Carlo (LSM) for pricing American and Bermudan options. In §7.5, we then extend the application of LSM to pricing swing options based on the work of Doerr (2003) and

Meyer (2004). In §7.6, we incorporate upswings, downswings, and penalty functions, general features of swing options, into the LSM pricing algorithm. In §7.7, a swing option pricing implementation in Matlab of Doerr is provided. In §7.8, LSM simulation results are provided from the work of Doerr (2003). In §7.9, we discuss the pricing of energy commodity derivatives including cross-commodity spread options, as well as crack and spark spread options. In §7.10, we discuss jump diffusion models for pricing electricity derivatives, while in §7.11, we discuss stochastic volatility electricity pricing models. In §7.12, we discuss parameter estimation of the pricing models in §7.10 and §7.11 based on the work of Xiong (2004). Estimation methods like maximum likelihood (ML), generalized method of moments (GMM), ML of the conditional characteristic function (CCF), and spectral generalized method of moments (SGMM) are discussed. In §7.13, the parameter estimation methodology of Xiong (2004) is provided in Matlab. In §7.14, we review general energy commodity pricing models. We discuss natural gas derivatives, giving an overview of the market, in §7.15 and discuss pricing models based on the work of Xu (2004) in §7.16. In §7.17, a natural gas pricing implementation in Matlab of Xu is given. Finally, in §7.18, we discuss natural gas and electricity swaps.

7.1 ELECTRICITY MARKETS

Electricity, like weather, is characterized by its non-storability, in addition to its very limited transportability, making electricity delivered at different times and on different dates to be perceived by consumers as distinct commodities. On-peak and off-peak demand for electricity at different time periods (i.e., seasons) has a significant impact on electricity prices and is important in power markets as they determine, for instance, derivative contractual terms. Electricity prices are strongly dependent on the electricity needs (demand) of consumers and their determinants, including business activity and temporal weather conditions.

The non-storability and limited transportability of electricity affects the ability of "carrying" electricity across time and space and is essential in explaining the behavior of electricity spot and forward derivative prices as compared to other commodities. In other words, "arbitrage across time and space, which is based on storability and transportation, is seriously limited, if not completely eliminated, in electricity markets."[1] One would expect spot prices to be highly dependent on temporal and local supply and demand conditions if the links across time and space provided by arbitrage break down.[2]

Thus, the limits of arbitrage would be expected to affect decisively the relationship between spot and forward prices. Non-storability implies that arbitrage arguments cannot be used in defining a pricing model when electricity, like weather, is the underlying asset of a derivative contract. As a result, cost-of-carry models do not work (see Geman and Roncoroni [2001]) because they cannot capture the physical and temporal constraints of electricity as a non-storable commodity.

Transportation constraints on electricity are imposed by capacity limits of transmission lines and transportation loads, which can make transmission of electricity to certain regions impossible or uneconomical. The supply of electricity is also based on the availability of transportation line connections, which can be damaged by rare and extreme events such as power plant failures—e.g., the occurrence in August 2003 that led to severe power outages in the Midwest and Northeast. Such power failures can lead to dramatic price spikes. In the summer of 1998, the spot price of electricity in Eastern and Midwestern U.S. skyrocketed from $50/MWh to $70/MWh because of unexpected unavailability of some power generation plants and congestion on key transmission lines. As an example, consider Figure 7.1, which shows the historical on-peak electricity spot prices in Texas (ERCOT) and at the California and Oregon border (COB). The jumpy behavior in electricity spot prices is mainly attributed to the fact that "a typical regional aggregate supply function of electricity almost always has a kink at certain capacity levels and the supply curve has a steep upward slope beyond that capacity level."[3]

Figure 7.2 shows a comparison of wholesale electricity prices from 1999 to 2002 in the Midwest (ECAR) and Pennsylvania-Maryland-New Jersey (PJM) regions, the California-Oregon border, and at Palo Verde, a major hub for importing electricity into California, which show a large number of "spikes" in summer months.

These limitations make electricity contracts and prices "highly local; i.e., strongly dependent on the local determinants of supply and demand (such as characteristics of local generation plants, and local climate and weather conditions together with their derived uses of electricity)."[4] Given the non-storability and transportation limitations of electricity, derivative pricing is usually done in an incomplete market framework.

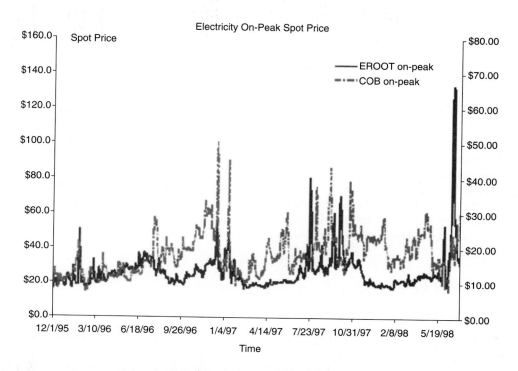

Figure 7.1 ERCOT and COB on-peak electricity spot prices.

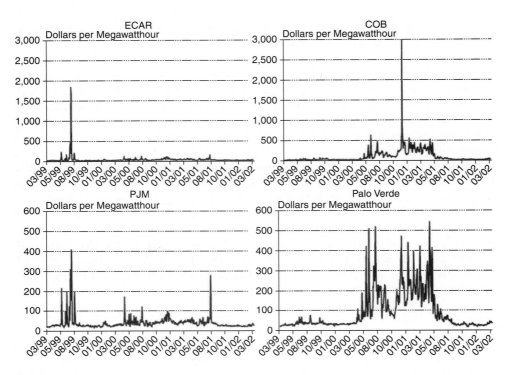

Figure 7.2 *Source: Commodity Futures Trading Commission (see Energy Information Administration, EIAGIS-NG Geographic Information System).*

The deregulation of the energy market has led to competitive wholesale electricity markets and has been accompanied by power derivative contracts, both OTC and exchange-traded, providing a variety of contract provisions to meet the needs of electricity market participants. In the U.S., electricity futures and options contracts have been listed in recent years by the Chicago Board of Trade (CBOT), the New York Mercantile Exchange (NYMEX), and the Minneapolis Grain Exchange.[5] The demand for these contracts has increased based on the increased forecasted demand for energy and investment in power generators. The Energy Information Administration (EIA) forecasts that meeting U.S. demand for electricity over the next decade will require about 198 gigawatts of new generating capacity.[6]

7.2 ELECTRICITY PRICING MODELS

Modeling the Price Process

Energy prices are mostly driven by supply and demand. Together with some characteristic properties of electricity, such as its heterogeneous nature with respect to time and location of its generation, its non-storability, and the incomplete market for electricity given arbitrage technical constraints, electricity spot prices exhibit pronounced short-term volatility. In addition, electricity prices exhibit the following properties that result from the peculiarities of supply and demand: mean-reversion, cyclical variations, and occasional prices spikes.

With mean-reversion, volatility decreases with increasing time horizon. There is a long-term equilibrium ("fair price") that is much less volatile than the spot price. The mean-reversion speed is determined by how quickly supply can react to sudden demand change (see Pilipovic (1998)).[7] Cyclical variations occur on different time-scales (time of day, day of week, seasons) and are driven by cyclical demand changes. This aspect of the price process can be considered deterministic and therefore can be easily separated from the stochastic time dependence.[8] Price spikes (surges) occasionally occur in addition to the large short-term volatility, but last only for a short time. Positive spikes can be caused by outages in the generation or transmission process (see Eydeland and Geman [1999]), while negative spikes occur when it is difficult to reduce generation capacity in periods of low demand.

Given these observations, simple geometric Brownian motion is not well suited to modeling electricity price processes because they do not capture spikes. Therefore, jump diffusion processes are frequently used. For instance, a discrete jump diffusion component can be added to a log-normal model. One-factor and two-factor lognormal mean-reverting processes with jumps have been proposed. We will examine the one-factor model.

One-Factor Model

Denote the spot price for electricity S_t. The stochastic process can be represented as the sum of two components—a deterministic function of time, $f(t)$, and a diffusion stochastic process, X_t, of a state variable (e.g., power load). That is,

$$S_t = f(t) + X_t. \tag{7.1}$$

We assume that X_t follows a stationary mean-reverting Ornstein-Uhlenbeck process:

$$dX_t = -\kappa X_t dt + \sigma dW_t \tag{7.2}$$

where $\kappa > 0$ is the speed of mean-reversion, $X(0) = x_0$, and dW_t represents an increment to a standard Brownian motion. Because $X_t = S_t - f(t)$, and assuming that the function $f(t)$ satisfies the appropriate regularity conditions, we can write (7.1) and (7.2) as

$$d(S_t - f(t)) = \kappa(f(t) - S_t)dt + \sigma dW \tag{7.3}$$

which shows that when S_t deviates from the deterministic term $f(t)$, it is pulled back at a rate proportional to its deviation. In this model, the only source of uncertainty comes from the stochastic behavior of X_t as described by (7.2).

Following Lucia and Schwartz (2001), the process followed by S_t can be expressed as the solution of the stochastic differential equation (provided that the function $f(t)$ satisfies the appropriate regularity conditions, such as $\int_{-\infty}^{\infty} f(t)^2 dt < \infty$ —i.e., the function is bounded), as follows:

$$dS_t = \kappa(\alpha(t) - S_t)dt + \sigma dW \tag{7.4}$$

where $\alpha(t)$ is the deterministic function of t defined by:

$$\alpha(t) = \frac{1}{\kappa}\frac{df(t)}{dt} + f(t) \tag{7.5}$$

which can be viewed as a particular case of the extended Vasicek model.

The assumed simple one-factor model is analytically tractable. An explicit solution for (7.2), in conjunction with (7.1), yields:

$$S_t = f(t) + X_0 e^{-\kappa t} + \sigma \int_0^t e^{\kappa(s-t)} dW(s) \tag{7.6}$$

We find that the conditional distribution of E_t is normal with conditional mean and variance given by (using $X_0 = E_0 - f(0)$):

$$\mathrm{E}[S_t] = \mathrm{E}[S_t|X_t] = f(t) + (S_0 - f(0))e^{-\kappa t} \tag{7.7}$$
$$\mathrm{Var}[S_t] = \mathrm{Var}[S_t|X_0] = \frac{\sigma^2}{2\kappa}\left(1 - e^{-2\kappa t}\right),\ \kappa > 0$$

where $\mathrm{E}[\cdot]$ is the expectation operator.

The price process of S_t tends to a mean value of $f(t)$ in the long run, given its initial value of S_0. The higher the value of κ (assuming $\kappa > 0$), the faster the convergence. The variance, in turn, decreases with the time horizon and has a finite limit of $\sigma^2/2\kappa$ as the horizon tends to infinity.

To price electricity derivatives, we need the risk-neutral process under a martingale measure for the state variable X_t, instead of the real process under the physical measure in (7.2). Taking into account the non-tradable nature of X_t, standard arbitrage arguments with two derivative assets allow us to obtain the risk-neutral process for X_t. Under the change of measure using Girsonov's transformation, we change the drift by setting $dW^* = dW - \lambda dt$, so that

$$dX_t = \kappa\left(\alpha^* - X_t\right)dt + \sigma dW^* \tag{7.8}$$

where

$$\alpha^* = -\frac{\lambda\sigma}{\kappa} \tag{7.9}$$

and dW^* is an increment to W_t^*, a standard Brownian motion under the risk-neutral probability measure, and λ denotes the market price of risk linked to the state variable X_t. While we assume λ is constant, it could be a function of t and the state variable X_t.

The explicit solution for the SDE in (7.8) yields:

$$S_t = f(t) + X_0 e^{-\kappa t} + \alpha^*(1 - e^{-\kappa t}) + \sigma \int_0^t e^{\kappa(s-t)} dW^*(s) \tag{7.10}$$

with α^* as defined in (7.9). We find from this that S_t is conditionally normally distributed under the risk-neutral measure, with the following conditional mean:

$$\text{E}^*[S_t] = f(t) + X_0 e^{-\kappa t} + \alpha^*(1 - e^{-\kappa t}) \tag{7.11}$$

We know that the value of any derivative security is its expected value of its payoff, under the risk-neutral measure, discounted back to the valuation date at the risk-free rate, which we assume to be constant. The value at time zero of a forward contract on the spot price of electricity maturing at time T must be:

$$V_0(X_t, T) = e^{-rT}\text{E}_0^*[S_T - F_0(S_0, T)] \tag{7.12}$$

where $F_0(X_0, T)$ is the forward price set at time zero for a contract maturing at time T, and r is the riskless continuously compounded interest rate. Because the value of a forward contract must be zero when initially entered into, we finally derive the following closed-form solution for the forward (futures) price of electricity[9] using (7.11) and (7.1) for $t = 0$:

$$F_0(S_0, T) = \text{E}_0^*[S_T] = f(T) + (S_0 - f(0))e^{-\kappa T} + \alpha^*(1 - e^{-\kappa T}) \tag{7.13}$$

with $\alpha^* = -\lambda\sigma/\kappa$.

Suppose the model in (7.1) is modified to incorporate the natural logarithm of the spot price instead of the spot price itself written as:

$$\ln S_t = f(t) + Y_t \tag{7.14}$$

so that

$$S_t = f(t)e^{Y_t}$$

where $f(t)$ is a known deterministic function of time, and Y_t is a stochastic process whose dynamics are given by:

$$dY_t = -\kappa Y_t dt + \sigma dW \tag{7.15}$$

with $\kappa > 0$ and $Y(0) = y_0$. The log-price follows a zero mean-reverting process, which implies the following price process under suitable conditions for $f(t)$:

$$dS_t = \kappa\left(b(t) - \ln S_t\right)S_t dt + \sigma S_t dW(t) \tag{7.16}$$

where

$$b(t) = \frac{1}{\kappa}\left(\frac{\sigma^2}{2} + \frac{d\log f(t)}{dt}\right) + \log f(t)$$

From (7.16), $\ln S_t$ has a conditional normal distribution with conditional mean and variance:

$$\text{E}_0[S_t] = \exp\left(\text{E}_0[\ln S_t] + \frac{1}{2}\text{Var}_0[\ln S_t]\right)$$

$$= \exp\left((f(t) + (\ln S_0 - f(0))e^{-\kappa t} + \frac{\sigma^2}{4\kappa}(1 - e^{-2\kappa t})\right)$$

and

$$\mathrm{Var}_0(S_t) = \exp\left(2\mathrm{E}_0[\ln S_t] + \mathrm{Var}_0[\ln S_t]\right)\left(\exp\left(\mathrm{Var}_0[\ln S_t]\right) - 1\right)$$
$$= \mathrm{E}_0[S_t]^2\left[\exp\left(\frac{\sigma^2}{2\kappa}(1 - e^{-2\kappa t})\right) - 1\right]$$

After changing the log price process to the risk-neutral measure under Girsonov's theorem, similar to (7.8), it can be shown that the forward (future) of the log electricity price is:[10]

$$F_0(S_0, T)$$
$$= \mathrm{E}_0^*[S_T] \tag{7.17}$$
$$= \exp\left[f(T) + (\ln S_0 - f(0))e^{-\kappa T} + \alpha^*(1 - e^{-\kappa T}) + \frac{\sigma^2}{4\kappa}\left(1 - e^{-2\kappa T}\right)\right]$$

where $\alpha^* = -\lambda\sigma/\kappa$. Note that the deterministic component of the behavior of the spot price (log-price) appears directly in the price of the forward (futures) contracts (see (7.13) and (7.17)), that term "being an important determinant of the shape of the forward (futures) curve."[11] In both the one-factor and log-factor models, all forward (futures) prices are perfectly correlated.[12]

Estimating the Deterministic Component

In order to implement the models in (7.1) and (7.14), it is necessary to specify the deterministic time function $f(t)$. This function tries to capture any relevant predictable components of the electricity prices behavior arising from genuine regularities along time. Although there are various choices available, the chosen function should have a deterministic general trend and capture seasonal and cyclical behavior. For instance, as suggested by Pilipovic (1998), a sinusoidal function like the cosine function could be used to reflect the general seasonal pattern of the price time series.

Lucia and Schwartz (2001) suggest the following function:

$$f(t) = \alpha + \beta D_t + \gamma \cos\left((t + \tau)\frac{2\pi}{365}\right) \tag{7.18}$$

where

$$D_t = \begin{cases} 1 & \text{if date } t \text{ is weekend or holiday} \\ 0 & \text{otherwise} \end{cases}$$

and cos is the cosine function measured in radians, and α, β, γ, and τ are all constant parameters. Here, the coefficient β tries to capture the changes in the level of the variable for weekends and holidays where electricity usage typically increases. The cosine function is expected to reflect the seasonal pattern in the evolution of the relevant variable throughout the year and so has annual periodicity.

Estimation of the Stochastic Process for the One-Factor Models

To estimate the stochastic process for the one-factor model from the spot price data, we discretize (7.1):

$$X_t = (1 - \kappa)X_{t-1} + \xi_t \tag{7.19}$$

for $t = 0, 1, 2, ..., N$, and where the innovations ξ_t are i.i.d normal random variables with mean 0 and variance σ^2. The same discretization can be used for the process Y_t in equation (7.15).

Given the discretization, we can estimate by the one-factor price and log-price models:

One-Factor Model

$$S_t = \alpha + \beta D_t + \gamma \cos\left((t + \tau)\frac{2\pi}{365}\right) + X_t \tag{7.20}$$

$$X_t = \phi X_{t-1} + u_t$$

One-Factor Log Price Model

$$\ln S_t = \alpha + \beta D_t + \gamma \cos\left((t + \tau)\frac{2\pi}{365}\right) + Y_t \tag{7.21}$$

$$Y_t = \phi Y_{t-1} + u_t$$

with the dummy variable defined in (7.18) and $\phi = 1 - \kappa$. For both models, the parameters are estimated simultaneously using nonlinear least squares. To be formal, one can write any of these models in the general form:

$$y_t = f(\mathbf{\Phi}, \mathbf{x_t}) + \xi_t \tag{7.22}$$

$$\xi_t = \phi\xi_{t-1} + u_t$$

The first equation expresses the dependent variable y_t (i.e., the price or the log-price variable) as a function of a vector of parameters, $\mathbf{\Phi}$, and the vector of explanatory variables $\mathbf{x_t}$. The second equation is the first order autoregressive equation of the disturbance term ξ_t in the first equation. Substituting ξ_t in the second equation, and rearranging terms, we get:

$$y_t = \phi y_{t-1} + f(\mathbf{\Phi}, \mathbf{x_t}) - \phi f(\mathbf{\Phi}, \mathbf{x_{t-1}}) + u_t \tag{7.23}$$

whose parameters ϕ and $\mathbf{\Phi}$ are estimated simultaneously using a nonlinear least squares procedure.[13] Finally, we take $\widehat{\kappa} = 1 - \widehat{\phi}$ as the estimate of the mean-reversion parameter κ, and the standard error of the regression as the estimate of σ. Lucia and Schwartz (2005) estimate the coefficients of these models (as well as for two-factor models) using this procedure based on daily electricity prices at the Nordic Power Exchange[14] from January 1, 1993 to December 31, 1999, as provided in Table 7.1.

Table 7.1

Parameter	Models based on the Price				Models based on the Log-price			
	Model 1		Model 2		Model 3		Model 4	
	Estimate	t-statistic	Estimate	t-statistic	Estimate	t-statistic	Estimate	t-statistic
α	153.051	8.146	145.732	8.670	4.938	38.711	4.867	46.192
β	-9.514	-28.085	-9.542	-28.277	-0.090	-28.339	-0.090	-28.523
γ			29.735	2.336			0.306	2.986
τ			6.691	0.269			0.836	0.043
β_2	-2.527	-0.754			-0.027	-0.878		
β_3	-4.511	-0.998			-0.041	-0.977		
β_4	-3.484	-0.664			-0.041	-0.849		
β_5	-13.248	-2.317			-0.185	-3.480		
β_6	-12.656	-2.114			-0.097	-1.744		
β_7	-7.038	-1.157			-0.062	-1.093		
β_8	-8.109	-1.347			-0.101	-1.807		
β_9	-10.061	-1.740			-0.094	-1.749		
β_{10}	-9.597	-1.795			-0.067	-1.352		
β_{11}	-7.304	-1.566			-0.052	-1.190		
β_{12}	-6.019	-1.674			-0.057	-1.703		
ϕ	0.990	355.4	0.989	340.4	0.986	299.0	0.984	277.5
κ	0.010		0.011		0.014		0.016	
S.E. of Regression	9.001		9.222		0.086		0.086	
Adjusted R^2	0.981		0.981		0.974		0.973	
Log likelihood	-9294.2		-9299.0		2652.9		2640.2	
Errors:								
M.A.E.	5.847		5.855		0.053		0.053	
M.A.P.E.	4.980		5.000		1.176		1.179	

Source: Lucia, J. and Schwartz, E. (2001), 32.

Model 1 and model 3 only contain the dummy variable and exclude the cosine cyclical component for the price and log-price, respectively.[15] In the four models, the independent coefficient α is significantly different from zero. The estimates of the coefficients β, ϕ, and σ are virtually indistinguishable between models 1 and 2, and between models 3 and 4. The null hypothesis of $\phi = 1$ is rejected by the usual t-test for every model. This means that the estimate for the reversion coefficient κ, though very small, turns out to be significant in all cases. The coefficient β corresponding to the dummy variable D_t is negative, as expected, and different from zero in the four models, but not all the coefficients of the monthly dummy variables are significant.[16]

Figures 7.3 and 7.4 plot the actual daily system prices against the fitted model estimates, as well as the associated residual errors of equation (7.23), also called the one period-ahead prediction errors.

Two-Factor Model

The one-factor model can be extended to two factors. According to Hillard and Reis (1998), we can model electricity prices based on the two-factor model:

$$dS_t = (r - \delta_t)S_t dt + \sigma_S S_t dW_t^S$$
$$d\delta_t = \alpha(\kappa_\delta - \delta_t)dt + \sigma_\delta dW_t^\delta \tag{7.24}$$

where r is the interest rate, σ_S is the variance of the geometric Brownian motion followed by S, and δ_t is a stochastic convenience yield that follows a mean-reverting process. The variance of the convenience yield represented by σ_δ, α_δ is the speed of adjustment, and

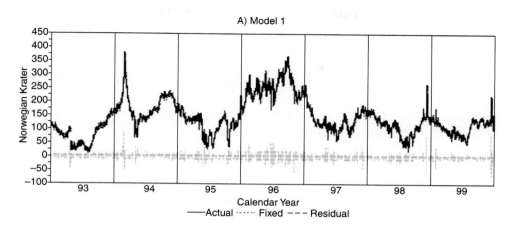

Figure 7.3 *Source: Lucia, J. and Schwartz, E. (2002). Reproduced with permission from Review of Dervatives Research.*

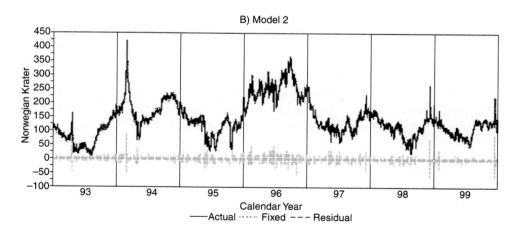

Figure 7.4 *Source: Lucia, J. and Schwartz, E. (2002). Reproduced with permission from Review of Dervatives Research.*

κ_δ is the long-run mean yield. The two Wiener processes W_t^S and W_t^δ are correlated with correlation coefficient ρ. As Doerr (2003) notes, since "the concept of convenience yield is usually only applied to storable commodities, this model is more appropriate for gas or oil prices than electricity."[17] However, it is relevant for swing options, as discussed in the next section. Moreover, the net convenience yield can be "interpreted as a theoretical construction to incorporate the special effects of supply, demand, and other particularities of the power market into one variable."[18] Those effects are "usually stochastic, implying a model for the stochastic behavior of convenience yield. As a key assumption of the model, electricity is therefore modeled as an asset with stochastic (positive or negative) dividend yield δ_t, which itself follows a mean-reverting Ornstein-Uhlenbeck process."[19] We assume that the market price of convenience yield risk is zero.

7.3   SWING OPTIONS

In order to hedge market risk arising from sudden changes in the commodity prices, consumers may use forwards or options on the commodity price. However, for some market participants, this reduction of risk is not sufficient because they do not know their exact future need of the commodity. In particular, this is a serious problem with commodities that cannot be stored (e.g., energy and electricity), or for which storage is very expensive. As a result of this problem, so-called swing options have been developed in order to give the holder a certain flexibility with respect to the amount purchased in the future.[20] Because energy is non-storable or expensive to store and exhibits extreme price fluctuations, swing contracts are typically used in the energy markets. This refers specifically to electricity, but swing contracts appear also in coal and gas markets.[21]

We will focus on swing options on electricity. However, the main characteristic properties of swing options—namely, the multiple early exercise features—are the same for all underlying commodities. Typical swing contracts contain a so-called base load agreement (see Jaillet, Ronn, and Tompaidis [2001]). The base load agreement is a set of forward contracts with different expiry dates, t_j, $j = 1, ..., N$. Each forward contract f_j is based on a fixed amount of electricity (or, in general, any commodity), q_j. At each expiry date, the holder has the option to purchase an excess amount or decrease the base load volume.[22] This means that the amount of electricity purchased at a predetermined price (i.e., the strike price) by the holder of the swing option can "swing" within a certain range $(q_j + \Delta_j)$. If Δ_j is positive (negative), the option exercised by the holder at an opportunity time t_j is called upswing (downswing). Thus, an upswing is a buy and a downswing is a sell. For a typical contract, there usually are further restrictions: The total number of upswings, U, and downswings, D, are limited—i.e., $U \le N$, $D \le N$, or $U + D \le N$, for some boundary $N > 0$.

The swing contract might include penalties if the overall volume bought during the term of the contract lies outside the predefined boundaries. These additional constraints lower the price of the swing option on one side. On the other side, they lead to a non-trivial exercise strategy of the option. The reason for this is that the decision to exercise a single swing right does not depend only on the electricity price at that time. Because the number of swing rights are limited, the exercise of one swing right reduces the number of rights available for later exercises. In addition, the exercise (or non-exercise) may result in penalties. Thus, to exercise a swing right, the payoff from exercise has to exceed the value of the remaining option. As a result, the optimal exercise strategy depends not only on the electricity price, but also on its history and its future distribution.

The combination of swing options with forward contracts is called a swing contract. Swing contracts allow one to add flexibility to the volume of the contract. A typical example for a swing contract is a supply contract. Here, the receiver has the right to receive an arbitrary volume of electricity up to some maximum load. Penalties are introduced in the form of "take-or-pay" clauses, which say that regardless of the volume received, a certain minimum amount of electricity has to be paid in any event. Such a contract can be decomposed into a swing option and a forward contract. The supplier of electricity is selling an implicit swing option.

We will follow the direct work of Doerr (2003) and Meyer (2004) in the discussion that follows on the pricing of swing options.

7.4   THE LONGSTAFF-SCHWARTZ ALGORITHM FOR AMERICAN AND BERMUDAN OPTIONS

The basic idea of the Longstaff-Schwartz algorithm, described in detail in Longstaff and Schwartz (2001) (and similar approaches like those reported in Clement and Protter (2002)), is to use least squares regression on a finite set of functions as a proxy for conditional expectation estimates. In a first step, the time axis has to be discretized—i.e., if the American option is alive within the time horizon $[0, T]$, early exercise is only allowed at discrete times $0 < t_1 < t_2 < ... < t_J = T$. The American option is thus approximated by a Bermudan option. For a particular exercise date t_k, early exercise is performed if the payoff from immediate exercise exceeds the continuation value—i.e., the value of the (remaining) option if it is not exercised at t_k. This continuation value can be expressed as conditional expectation of the option payoff with respect to the risk-neutral pricing measure Q. The expectation is taken conditional on the information set $\Im_{t_k}$, which is available at t_k. Representing the continuation value for a particular sample path ω by $F(\omega, t_k)$, we can write

$$F(\omega, t_k) = E^Q \left[\sum_{j=k+1}^{K} D(t_k, t_j) C(\omega, t_j, t_k, T) | \Im_{t_k} \right] \tag{7.25}$$

where $D(t_k, t_j)$ is the discount factor from t_k to t_j, and $C(\omega, t_j, t_k, T)$ denotes the path of cashflows generated by the option, conditional on the option not being exercised at or prior to time t_k and the holder following the optimal exercise strategy for all remaining opportunities t_j between t_k and T. Note that for every path ω, there is at most one exercise date j where $C(\omega, t_j, t_k, T) > 0$, because Bermudan options have only one exercise right. The decision of exercising at t_{J-1} is made by comparing the continuation value $F(\omega, t_{J-1})$ with the immediate payoff $P(S_{J-1})$, where S_{J-1} is the value of the underlying at time t_{J-1}. While $P(S_{J-1})$ is known, the continuation value has to be estimated.

To find an estimator, the continuation value is represented in a set of basis functions B_j:

$$F(\omega, t_{J-1}) = \sum_{i=0}^{\infty} a_i B_i(S_{J-1})$$

which is approximated by

$$\widehat{F}(\omega, t_{J-1}) = \sum_{i=0}^{M} a_i B_i(S_{J-1}). \tag{7.26}$$

The coefficient a_i is found by regressing the discounted values of $C(\omega, t_J, t_{J-1}, T)$ onto the basis functions. These cashflows are the cashflows that occur at time t_J. The regression is done over all paths that have a continuation value,—i.e., an option is in the money at time t_J. $\widehat{F}(\omega, t_{J-1})$ is an unbiased estimator of the continuation value.

The exercise decision can now be made by comparing the estimator $\widehat{F}(\omega, t_{j-1})$ with the immediate exercise payoff $P(S_{J-1})$ for each path. With the higher of both taken as new cashflow $C(\omega, t_{J-2}, t_{J-1}, T)$ at time t_{J-1}, the iteration is stepped further backward in time.

At the end, the resulting value of the option is calculated by averaging over the cashflows from each path ω:

$$V_{LSM}^{N} = \frac{1}{N} \sum_{i=1}^{N} C(\omega_i) \tag{7.27}$$

Here, $C(\omega_i)$ denotes the discounted cashflow of path ω_i.

The LSM Algorithm

Assume that all interest rates are zero and, therefore, discounting can be omitted. Before starting the actual algorithm, the paths that form the underlying spot prices have to be sampled. For N paths and J exercise opportunities (timesteps), this yields an N x J matrix S, where the matrix $S_{i,j}$ is the spot price in the ith path at time t_j. Next, the set of basis functions $(B_j)_{j=0}^{M}$ for the regression has to be chosen from a great variety of possibilities, including Hermite, Legendre, Chebyshev, Gegenbauer, or Jacobi polynomials.[23] However, Longstaff and Schwartz emphasize that their numerical tests indicate that Fourier or trigonometric series and even simple powers of the state variables also give accurate results. A basis function of order $M = 2$—i.e., quadratic polynomials—works well in the LSM algorithm and is used by Dorr.

$$B_0 = 1$$
$$B_1 = X$$
$$B_2 = X^2$$

The initial step of the actual algorithm is to determine the cashflow vector C^J at the last timestep t_J. These cashflows are easy to get because the continuation values are then zero—i.e.,

$$C_i^J = P(S_{i,J}) \tag{7.28}$$

where P is the payoff function. In the following, we focus on the payoff of a vanilla call option

$$P(S_{i,j}) = \max(S_{i,j} - X_j, 0) \tag{7.29}$$

where the strike prices X_j can vary from timestep to timestep.

Second, we consider the spot prices at timestep t_{J-1} and select those for which $P(S_{i,J-1}) > 0$. This yields the L_{J-1} x $1-$vector $\widehat{S}^{J-1}$ where L_{J-1} is the number of in-the-money paths at timestep t_{J-1}. The least squares regression of C^J onto the basis functions B_J is now performed by minimizing the expression

$$\left\| B^{J-1} a^{J-1} - C^J \right\| \tag{7.30}$$

where a^{J-1} is the $(M+1)$ x 1-vector of regression coefficients for timestep t_{J-1} and the matrix B^{J-1} is given by:

$$B^{J-1} = \begin{pmatrix} B_0(\widehat{S}_{1,J-1}) & \cdots & B_M(\widehat{S}_{1,J-1}) \\ \vdots & \cdots & \vdots \\ B_0(\widehat{S}_{L_{J-1},J-1}) & \cdots & B_M(\widehat{S}_{L_{J-1},J-1}) \end{pmatrix} \tag{7.31}$$

The solution of the minimization is given by:

$$a^{J-1} = ((B^{J-1})^T B^{J-1})^{-1} (B^{J-1})^T C^{J-1} \tag{7.32}$$

With that, we obtain the vector of continuation values Cont^{J-1} by:

$$\mathrm{Cont}_i^{J-1} = \sum_{k=0}^{M} a_k^{J-1} B_{i,k}^{J-1} \tag{7.33}$$

Once we have the continuation of values, we perform early exercise whenever

$$P(\widehat{S}_{i,J-1}) > \mathrm{Cont}_i^{J-1}. \tag{7.34}$$

The elements C_i^{J-1} of the cashflow vector C^{J-1} are then given by:

- $P(\widehat{S}_{i,J-1})$, if the early exercise condition (7.34) is true

- 0 otherwise

Subsequently, the elements of the cashflow vector C^J have to be set to zero for those paths where (7.34) is true.

We then step backward through time until we reach the first timestep.[24] At each timestep, early exercise is performed as described previously. Note that whenever a cashflow at timestep t_k is generated by early exercise in path i, all cashflows that occur in this path later than t_k (this is, at most, one) have to be removed.[25]

At the end, we can build the cashflow matrix C from the cashflow vectors C^k by concatenating the cashflow vectors C^k, $k = 1, ..., J$, and the option value is given by the arithmetic average of the row sums.[26]

7.5 EXTENSION OF LONGSTAFF-SCHWARTZ TO SWING OPTIONS

Following the presentation by Doerr,[27] we show how least-squares Monte Carlo can be adopted for the valuation of swing options. Because we now have more than one exercise right, however, we have to deal with an additional "dimension"—i.e., the number of exercises left. Consider a swing option with exercise opportunities at times t_1, t_2, t_3, t_4, and t_5, with five exercise opportunities and three exercise rights (upswings) with a strike price at each opportunity X. Sampling N paths yields N x 5-spot price matrix S. The main difficulties arising from the presence of more than one exercise rights are the following:

- The benefit from immediate exercise is not only the payoff, but the payoff plus the value of the remaining swing option (which has one upswing fewer than the original one).

- When early exercise is performed at time t_k, rearranging the cashflows at later opportunities requires the cashflow matrix of the swing option with one upswing less than the original one.

The generalized cashflow matrix of our algorithm must, therefore, have three dimensions:

- First dimension: number of paths

- Second dimension: number of timesteps (exercise opportunity)

- Third dimension: number of exercise rights (upswings) left

We denote the cashflow matrix for j upswings left as C^j. In our example, there are thus three N x 5 matrices C^1, C^2, and C^3. After the initial step, the cashflow matrices look as follows:

$$C^3 = \begin{pmatrix} \% & \% & P(S_{1,3}) & P(S_{1,4}) & P(S_{1,5}) \\ \% & \% & P(S_{2,3}) & P(S_{2,4}) & P(S_{2,5}) \\ \vdots & \vdots & \vdots & \vdots & \vdots \\ \% & \% & P(S_{N,3}) & P(S_{N,4}) & P(S_{N,5}) \end{pmatrix} \tag{7.35}$$

$$C^2 = \begin{pmatrix} \% & \% & \% & P(S_{1,4}) & P(S_{1,5}) \\ \% & \% & \% & P(S_{2,4}) & P(S_{2,5}) \\ \vdots & \vdots & \vdots & \vdots & \vdots \\ \% & \% & \% & P(S_{N,4}) & P(S_{N,5}) \end{pmatrix} \tag{7.36}$$

$$C^1 = \begin{pmatrix} \% & \% & \% & \% & P(S_{1,5}) \\ \% & \% & \% & \% & P(S_{2,5}) \\ \vdots & \vdots & \vdots & \vdots & \vdots \\ \% & \% & \% & \% & P(S_{N,5}) \end{pmatrix} \tag{7.37}$$

where

$$P(S) = \max(S - X, 0) \tag{7.38}$$

is the payoff of the upswing. The %-signs mean that these cashflows are undefined at this stage. For C^3, we can combine the last three timesteps in the initial step of the algorithm because it is obvious that early exercise takes place at t_3 whenever the payoff at this timestep is positive. Notice that this is the third timestep from the last.

Similarly, when two upswings are left, immediate early exercise is performed at t_4 and thus we can combine the last two timesteps for C^2. The matrix C^1 corresponds to the cashflow matrix in the Longstaff-Schwartz algorithm for Bermudan options. As an example, if we have only six paths, after the initial step, the matrices might look as follows:

$$C^3 = \begin{pmatrix} \% & \% & P_{1,3} & 0 & P_{1,5} \\ \% & \% & P_{2,3} & P_{2,4} & 0 \\ \% & \% & P_{3,3} & 0 & 0 \\ \% & \% & P_{4,3} & P_{4,4} & P_{4,5} \\ \% & \% & P_{5,3} & 0 & P_{5,5} \\ \% & \% & P_{6,3} & P_{6,4} & P_{6,5} \end{pmatrix} \tag{7.39}$$

$$C^2 = \begin{pmatrix} \% & \% & \% & 0 & P_{1,5} \\ \% & \% & \% & P_{2,4} & 0 \\ \% & \% & \% & 0 & 0 \\ \% & \% & \% & P_{4,4} & P_{4,5} \\ \% & \% & \% & 0 & P_{5,5} \\ \% & \% & \% & P_{6,4} & P_{6,5} \end{pmatrix} \tag{7.40}$$

$$C^1 = \begin{pmatrix} \% & \% & \% & \% & P_{1,5} \\ \% & \% & \% & \% & 0 \\ \% & \% & \% & \% & 0 \\ \% & \% & \% & \% & P_{4,5} \\ \% & \% & \% & \% & P_{5,5} \\ \% & \% & \% & \% & P_{6,5} \end{pmatrix} \tag{7.41}$$

Here, all $P_{i,j} = P(S_{i,j})$ are non-zero.

We now start stepping backwards in time. For t_4, we calculate the continuation values for one upswing left by least squares regression of the cashflow vector $\widehat{C}_5^1$ onto the basis functions.[28] In $\widehat{C}_5^1$, only the paths where the payoff at t_4 is positive are considered. We denote the vector of continuation values at timestep four with one upswing left at Cont_4^1.

With the continuation values, we can perform early exercise, and C^1 may look like:

$$
C^1 = \begin{pmatrix}
\% & \% & \% & 0 & P_{1,5} \\
\% & \% & \% & P_{2,4} & 0 \\
\% & \% & \% & 0 & 0 \\
\% & \% & \% & P_{4,4} & 0 \\
\% & \% & \% & 0 & P_{5,5} \\
\% & \% & \% & P_{6,4} & 0
\end{pmatrix}
$$

In our example, early exercise at t_4 was carried out for all possible paths—i.e., paths 2, 4, and 6. Note that for paths 4 and 6, the cashflows at t_5 have been removed. The cashflow matrices C^2 and C^3 remain unchanged in this step.

Now we move on to t_3. In order to get Cont_3^2, we first have to add the cashflow vectors C_4^2 and C_5^2. Denoting the sum vector as C_{4+5}^2, we obtain the relevant sum vector $\widehat{C}_{4+5}^2$ by omitting all paths where $P(S_{i,3})$ is zero. The continuation vector Cont_3^2 is then obtained by linear regression of $\widehat{C}_{4+5}^2$ on the basis functions.

The early exercise condition now reads:

$$
P(S_{i,3}) + \text{Cont}_3^1(i) > \text{Cont}_3^2(i) \tag{7.42}
$$

That means we have to calculate Cont_3^1 before we can perform early exercise in C^2. This calculation is easily done according to the usual Longstaff-Schwartz algorithm. For those paths where condition (7.42) is fulfilled, early exercise is performed. This means that for each corresponding path, i, $C_3^2(i)$ is set equal to the payoff $P(S_{i,3})$ and the cashflows $C_4^2(i)$ and $C_5^2(i)$ are replaced by $C_4^1(i)$ and $C_5^1(i)$, respectively. After this, early exercise for t_3 is performed in C^1. Although C^3 still remains unchanged in this step, the other cashflow matrices in our example might like the following:

$$
C^2 = \begin{pmatrix}
\% & \% & P_{1,3} & 0 & P_{1,5} \\
\% & \% & P_{2,3} & P_{2,4} & 0 \\
\% & \% & P_{3,3} & 0 & 0 \\
\% & \% & 0 & P_{4,4} & P_{4,5} \\
\% & \% & 0 & 0 & P_{5,5} \\
\% & \% & P_{6,3} & P_{6,4} & 0
\end{pmatrix} \tag{7.43}
$$

$$
C^1 = \begin{pmatrix}
\% & \% & 0 & 0 & P_{1,5} \\
\% & \% & P_{2,3} & 0 & 0 \\
\% & \% & 0 & 0 & 0 \\
\% & \% & 0 & P_{4,4} & 0 \\
\% & \% & 0 & 0 & P_{5,5} \\
\% & \% & P_{6,3} & 0 & 0
\end{pmatrix} \tag{7.44}
$$

For C^2, early exercise was performed in paths 1, 2, 3, and 6. Note that in path 6, the cashflows after t_3 had to be modified according to C^1 at the iteration step before—i.e., t_4. For C^1, early exercise occurs only in paths 2 and 6.

Moving on to t_2, early exercise must be performed for all three cashflow matrices. First, the continuation vectors are calculated by regressing $\widehat{C}_{3+4+5}^j, j = 1, 2, 3$ onto the basis functions as described previously. Then, early exercise is carried out starting with C^3 by evaluating the condition

$$P(S_{i,2}) + \text{Cont}_2^2(i) > \text{Cont}_2^3(i). \tag{7.45}$$

The condition for C^2 reads

$$P(S_{i,2}) + \text{Cont}_2^1(i) > \text{Cont}_2^2(i). \tag{7.46}$$

For C^1, we obtain

$$P(S_{i,2}) > \text{Cont}_2^1(i). \tag{7.47}$$

Because early exercise includes rearranging the cashflows after t_2 according to the cashflow matrix (with one upswing fewer) at the preceding iteration step, it is important that the procedure is first done with C^3, then with C^2, and finally with C^1. Repeating the same procedure for t_1, we end up with the final cashflow matrices C^1, C^2, and C^3. From these matrices, we obtain the value of the corresponding swing options by taking the average of the row sums.[29]

7.6   GENERAL CASE: UPSWINGS, DOWNSWINGS, AND PENALTY FUNCTIONS

Application of the LSM algorithm to price swing options must incorporate not only call (upswings), but also put features (downswings). In addition, the algorithm must incorporate penalty functions that depend on the total number of exercises (upswings and downswings).[30] These features have two important implications for the LSM algorithm. First, in the initial step, only the last timestep can be treated because continuation values might be negative because of penalty, and thus it could be sensible to let one or more exercise rights expire worthless. Second, we have an additional dimension—i.e., the number of downswings left.

We introduce some notation:

- u and d are the numbers of upswings and downswings exercised, respectively (in a particular iteration step).

- $u_{\max}$ and $d_{\max}$ are the total numbers of upswings and downswings, respectively.

- J is the number of timesteps (exercise opportunities).

The generalized cashflow tensor has now four dimensions (path, timestep, upswings exercised, and downswings exercised) and consists of $[(u_{\max}+1) \cdot (d_{\max}+1) - 1]$ cashflow matrices $C^{u,d}$. Each of these matrices has dimension N x J.

In the initial step, we have to evaluate the cashflows at the last exercise opportunities. With $\phi(u, d)$ denoting the penalty function for u upswings and d downswings exercised, we obtain the following cashflows in path i at the final timestep t_J : for $0 \le u < u_{\max}$, $0 \le d < d_{\max}$:

$$C_J^{u,d}(i) = \max[P_u(S_{i,J}) - \phi(u+1, d), P_d(S_{i,J}) - \phi(u, d+1), 0] \tag{7.48}$$

for $0 \le d < d_{\max}$:

$$C_J^{u_{\max},d}(i) = \max[P_d(S_{i,J}) - \phi(u_{\max}, d+1), 0] \qquad (7.49)$$

for $0 \le u < u_{\max}$:

$$C_J^{u,d_{\max}}(i) = \max[P_u(S_{i,J}) - \phi(u+1, d_{\max}), 0] \qquad (7.50)$$

where $P_{u,d}$ is the payoff of the upswing and downswing.

Now starting for a given path, to work backwards from t_J in time, we have to do the following at each step:

- Calculate the continuation values by least squares regression.

- Perform early exercise.

When performing early exercise, we have to step forward from $(u, d) = (0, 0)$ to $(u, d) = (u_{\max}, d_{\max})$. It does not matter whether we start with u or d, however. At timestep j (and thus iteration step $J + 1 - j$), the early exercise conditions for the up-swings are for $0 \le u < u_{\max}, 0 \le d < d_{\max}, u + d < j$:

$$P_u(S_{i,j}) + \text{Cont}_j^{u+1,d}(i) > \text{Cont}_j^{u,d}(i) \qquad (7.51)$$

For the downswings, we obtain for $0 \le u < u_{\max}, 0 \le d < d_{\max}, u + d < j$:

$$P_d(S_{i,j}) + \text{Cont}_j^{u,d+1}(i) > \text{Cont}_j^{u,d}(i) \qquad (7.52)$$

Eventually, the value of the swing option is obtained by calculating the average of the row sums of $C^{0,0}$ after the final iteration step. Note that in each row, there are at most $u_{\max} + d_{\max}$ non-zero cashflows.

7.7 SWING OPTION PRICING IN MATLAB

Refer to Appendix B, "Chapter 7 Code Files," to see the full listing of Matlab code written by Doerr (2004). The code provides the implementation of the LSM algorithm for pricing swing options using upswings, downswings, and penalty functions.

7.8 LSM SIMULATION RESULTS

Doerr (2003) computes the value of swing options using a one-factor and two-factor mean-reversion model. The follow parameters given in Table 7.2 are used for the one-factor model—see (7.2).

Figure 7.5 shows the swing option value as a function of the spot price for two different values of the mean-reversion speed. The swing consists of 6 upswings and 10 opportunities.

Figure 7.5 shows swing option value as a function of the spot price for two different values of the mean-reversion speed without (left) and with penalty (right). The swing consists of six upswings and four downswings at 10 opportunities. As a consequence of the downswings, the option value exhibits a minimum. Introducing a penalty

Table 7.2

spot value S	20
timesteps	10
time between two timesteps δt	1
exercise rights (upswings)	6
strike at each timestep K	20
mean reversion speed α	0.5
mean reversion level F	20.7387
volatility σ	0.392

Source: Doerr (2004).

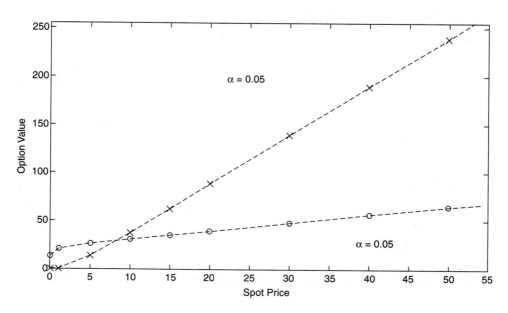

Figure 7.5   *Source: Doerr (2003). Reproduced with permission.*

$$\phi(v) = \begin{cases} 50 & \text{for } v \leq -1 \\ 30(v-2) & \text{for } v > 2 \\ 0 & \text{otherwise} \end{cases}$$

where $v = u - d$ and u and d are the total number of upswings and downswings, respectively, exercised, leads to an overall decrease of the option value, as shown in the left part of Figure 7.6.

The introduction of four downswings in addition to the six upswings (and keeping all other parameters constant[31]) must lead to an overall increase in the swing options value because the new option has more exercise rights while keeping all rights of the old option,[32] as shown in Figure 7.6. Because the downswings are in the money for low spot prices, the option's value as a function of the spot price now exhibits a minimum for both values of α.

Figure 7.7 shows the relative difference between the swing option values obtained by least squares Monte Carlo and finite differences. The calculations have been performed for a swing option with 10 opportunities and mean-reversion speeds of 0.05 (left, no downswings) and 0.5 (right, four downswings). The other parameters are those given in Table 7.2.

The relative deviations are significantly smaller than 1% and thus lie within numerical accuracy. For the Monte Carlo, the accuracy is about 0.3%.

Upper and Lower Boundaries

Because the numerical valuation of Swing options is—in general—quite costly, one tries to find approximation methods that are as simple as possible. In this context, it is important to find upper and lower bounds that can be considered as a first approximation step.

From simple considerations, we can deduce the following boundaries for a swing option with m exercise rights and N opportunities:

- Upper boundary: m Bermudan options (each of them with N opportunities according to the opportunities of the Swing option)

- Lower boundary: Callstrip—i.e., the sum of the m most valuable in the set of the N vanilla call options, which expire at the N opportunities of the Swing option

These boundaries are frequently discussed in the literature about this topic (see Jaillet, Ronn, and Tompaidis [2003], for example) and can be explained in the following way:

- Upper boundary: A holder of m Bermudan options can exercise in the same way a swing option's holder can. Furthermore, he has the right of exercising more than one option at the same opportunity. This means that he has more possibilities than the holder of the swing option, and thus a set of m Bermudan options is an upper boundary for the swing option.

- Lower boundary: The holder of a swing option can exercise at each opportunity, while the holder of the callstrip is restricted to m exercise dates, which are fixed at the beginning. The swing option's holder can exercise at these m dates, but he doesn't

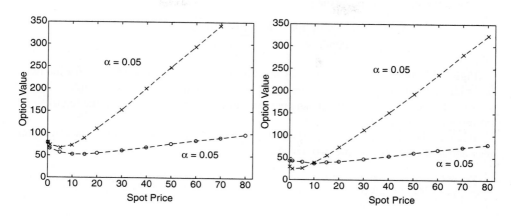

Figure 7.6   *Source: Doerr (2003). Reproduced with permission.*

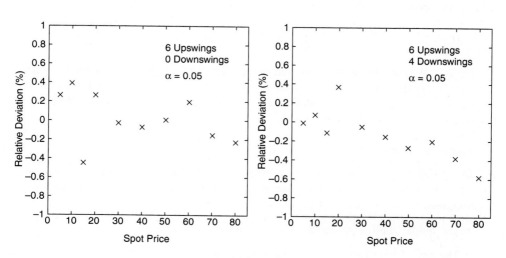

Figure 7.7   *Source: Doerr (2003), 36. Reproduced with permission.*

have to. Thus, the callstrip must be a lower boundary. In the next step, we want to investigate where the swing options value is situated between the two boundaries. We, therefore, introduce the position p:

$$p = \frac{\text{value of Swing option} - \text{lower boundary}}{\text{upper boundary} - \text{lower boundary}}$$

Figure 7.8 shows the empirical error as a function of the number of paths for the two-factor mean-reverting process given in (7.24) with the parameters shown in Table 7.3.

As with the one-factor process, an approximate straight line is given in the logarithmic representation in Figure 7.8.

It is obvious that p lies between 0 and 1. For fixed N, we now consider p as a function of m and immediately find the two trivial cases:

$$p(1) = 1 \tag{7.53}$$
$$p(N) = 0 \tag{7.54}$$

because for $m = 1(N)$, the swing option is the same as the Bermudan option (callstrip). As a computer experiment, $p(m)$ has been determined for both processes and various sets of process parameters.

The line u between the two limiting cases of (7.53) and (7.54) is given by

$$u(m) = \frac{N - m}{N - 1}$$

and the position $u(m)$ corresponds to a swing option value $V_u(m)$ of

$$V_u(m) = \frac{N - m}{N - 1} m \cdot Bermudan + \frac{m - 1}{N - 1} \cdot Callstrip.$$

Figure 7.9 shows the swing option value as a function of the spot price for the two-factor process. As for the one-factor process, adding downswings leads to an overall increase and the occurrence of a minimum (middle), and subsequent introduction of a penalty leads to an overall decrease of the option value (right).

Exercise Strategies

Doerr (2003) discusses various exercise strategies that impact the valuation of swing options. The valuation of the swing option has been (implicitly) based on the following assumptions:

- The holder applies the optimal exercise strategy.

- The payoff from early exercise can be realized immediately.

However, as Dörr points out, in reality these assumptions are not necessarily fulfilled. First, applying the optimal strategy requires knowledge at each opportunity as to whether it is better to exercise or not. Second, if physical delivery is settled, the holder may not be able to benefit from early exercise because he has to sell the electricity delivered. In this section,

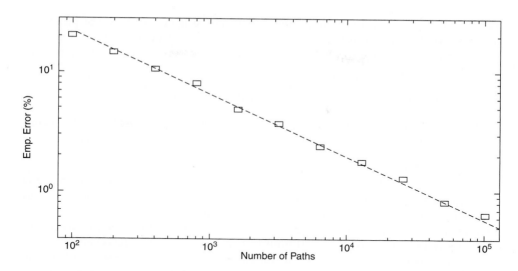

Figure 7.8   *Source: Doerr (2003), pg. 38. Reproduced with permission.*

Table 7.3

spot value S	20
timesteps	6
time between two timesteps δt	1
exercise rights (upswings)	4
strike at each timestep K	20
α	0.5
δ_0	0.05
κ	0.03
σ_S	0.4
σ_δ	0.05
ρ	0.5
r	0.04

Source: Doerr (2003), 36. Reproduced with permission.

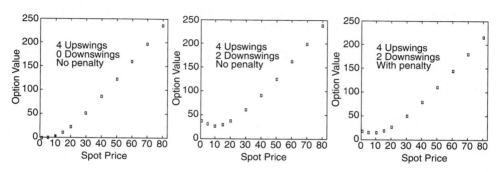

Figure 7.9   *Source: Doerr (2003), pg. 39. Reproduced with permission.*

we focus on the valuation of swing options in terms of different exercise strategies—i.e., we determine the expected payoff under the condition that a particular exercise strategy is applied. In particular, we try to find an approach to the value of a swing option for a holder who

- Does not know the optimal exercise strategy explicitly, or

- Cannot decide by himself when to exercise because he is exposed to external constraints

In the first case, the aim is to find a simple strategy that yields an option value close to the optimal exercise value. This strategy is to be found by simple considerations about the process parameters. An example for the second case could be the following. The holder has bought the swing option in order to protect himself from extremely high spot prices, but he does not know in advance when his need for electricity will occur. When there is no need for electricity, he cannot realize the payoff from an early exercise because he is not able to sell the electricity delivered. Under these circumstances, this holder is interested in knowing the difference between his expected payoff and the market price of the option, which is assumed to be based on optimal exercise. We restrict ourselves to the one-factor (logarithm) process discussed in §7.14. In this way, we keep the number of process parameters small. In particular, this allows us to investigate the interplay of mean-reversion and volatility systematically. Furthermore, some aspects of the early exercise problem can be treated analytically.

The Threshold of Early Exercise

At time t_0, the holder has to decide whether to exercise or not. If the holder decides not to exercise, the option turns into a vanilla call option. Therefore, early exercise is optimal if the payoff from realization is greater than the value of the call option—i.e.,

$$C(S, t_0, t) > S - K$$

where S and K denote the spot and strike prices, respectively. In the following, we keep the strike price K, the mean-reversion level F, and the time to maturity $t - t_0$ constant and consider the value of the vanilla call option as a function of the spot price S, the mean-reversion speed α, and the volatility σ. Omitting the time arguments

$$C(S, \alpha, \sigma) = A(t, t_0)e^{v(t,t_0)/2}N^0_{v(t,t_0)}(d_1) - KN^0_{v(t,t_0)}(d_2) \tag{7.55}$$

where A and v are given by

$$A(t, t_0) = S(t_0)^{e^{-\alpha(t-t_0)}} F^{1-e^{-\alpha(t-t_0)}} \tag{7.56}$$

and

$$v(t, t_0) = \frac{\sigma^2}{2\alpha}(1 - e^{-2\alpha(t-t_0)}). \tag{7.57}$$

With these parameters, d_1 and d_2 can be written as

$$d_1 = \log \frac{A}{K} + v = d_2 + v$$

and $N_b^a(\cdot)$ is the cumulative standard normal distribution defined by

$$N_b^a(\cdot) = \int\limits_{-\infty}^{y} \frac{1}{\sqrt{2\pi b}} e^{-\frac{(x-a)^2}{2b}} dx$$

Differing (7.55) with respect to S yields the delta of the call option:

$$\frac{\partial C}{\partial S} = e^{v/2} \frac{\partial A}{\partial S} \left(N_v^0(d_1) + \frac{1}{\sqrt{2\pi v}} e^{-\frac{d_1^2}{2v}} \right) - \frac{K}{A} \frac{\partial A}{\partial S} \frac{1}{\sqrt{2\pi v}} e^{-\frac{d_2^2}{2v}}$$

where

$$\frac{\partial A}{\partial S} = x S^{x-1} F^{1-x}$$

$$x = e^{-\alpha(t-t_0)}$$

Because $0 < x < 1$, we obtain the following limits as $S \to \infty$:

$$A \to \infty$$
$$\frac{\partial A}{\partial S} \to 0$$
$$d_1 \to \infty$$
$$d_2 \to \infty$$

From that, it follows directly that

$$\lim_{S \to \infty} \frac{\partial C}{\partial S} = 0.$$

Figure 7.10 shows a typical plot of a call option against spot price, together with the payoff from immediate exercise. Because both the call and the delta of the call are always greater than zero and delta approaches zero for $S \to \infty$, the equation

$$C(X, t_0, t) = \max(X - K, 0)$$

always has a solution for X—i.e., there is a (unique) threshold for early exercise.

We can show that this threshold is always greater than the mean-reversion level F. This is intuitively clear—why should we exercise early if we know that the spot price is "drawn up" toward F?

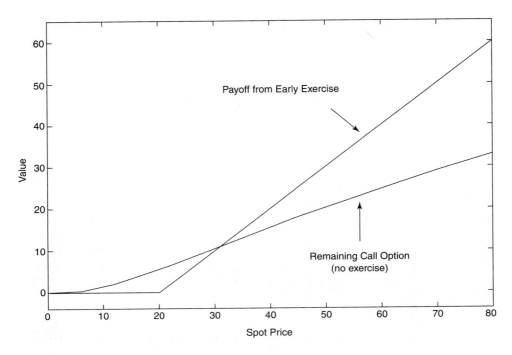

Figure 7.10   *Source: Doerr (2003), 48. Reproduced with permission.*

Doerr (2003) finds that the threshold for early exercise:

- Always exists if $\alpha > 0$

- Is always greater than the mean-reversion level

- Decreases with increasing α and approaches f in the limit $\alpha \to \infty$

- Increases with increasing σ

These results are illustrated in Figure 7.11. Intuitively, it is not surprising that the threshold (which lies always above the mean-reversion level) decreases with increasing mean-reversion speed. If α is large, we should immediately make use of early exercise, because the spot price is expected to be pulled down toward the mean-reversion level. However, if α is large, there is still some hope that the spot price will rise again toward values significantly above the mean-reversion level. Therefore, the need for early exercise is relaxed.

Interplay Between Early Exercise and Option Value

For Bermudan options, the holder can maximize his expected payoff by early exercise. The optimal exercise strategy is very simple: If the spot price at time t_0 exceeds the threshold X, he decides to exercise. However, applying the optimal strategy requires exact knowledge of X. In a simple case, it is quite easy to determine X numerically, but for more

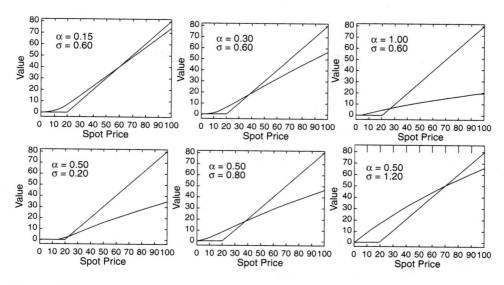

Figure 7.11   *Source: Doerr (2003), 51. Reproduced with permission.*

realistic situations (e.g., more than one opportunity), this may not be the case. Therefore, it is important to investigate the benefit from early exercise in more detail. This means that we should get a feeling for the sensitivity of the expected option payoff to the actual strategy. This shall now be achieved in an intuitive way. As can be seen in Figure 7.11, the cutting angle between the payoff from early exercise and the continuation function increases with increasing α. In Figure 7.12, this is illustrated in an even more drastic manner. For $\alpha = 0.05$, the curves are so close to each other that a suboptimal early exercise decision is expected to have virtually no impact on the expected option payoff. However, the opposite

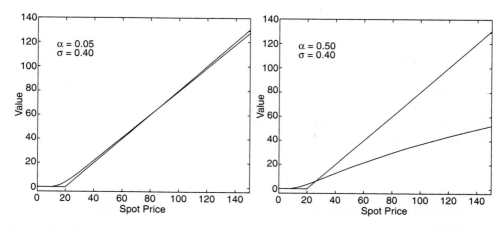

Figure 7.12   *Source: Doerr (2003), 52. Reproduced with permission.*

is right for $\alpha = 0.5$. In this case, the sensitivity of the expected payoff with respect to the actual strategy must be significant.

The cutting angle ϕ is given by:

$$\phi(\alpha, \sigma) = \frac{\pi}{4} - \arctan\left(\frac{\partial C}{\partial S}|_{S=X}\right)$$

We can use ϕ as an indicator for the sensitivity of the expected option payoff on the strategy. For the simple case described previously, it is obvious that the sensitivity increases with increasing ϕ. Because an analytic treatment of ϕ is very difficult (if possible), this has been done numerically. It has turned out that ϕ increases with increasing α, while it decreases with increasing volatility. However, the dependence on α seems to be much stronger than the dependence on σ. See Doerr (2003) for details.

7.9   PRICING OF ENERGY COMMODITY DERIVATIVES

Cross-Commodity Spread Options

In the petroleum industry, refinery managers are more concerned about the difference between their input and output prices than about the level of prices. Refiners' profits are tied directly to the spread, or difference, between the price of crude oil and the prices of refined products. Because refiners can reliably predict their costs other than crude oil, the spread is their major uncertainty. Crack spread options in crude oil markets, as well as the spark spread and locational spread options in electricity markets, are good examples of cross-commodity derivatives, which play a crucial role in risk management. Spark spread options are derivatives on electricity and the fossil fuels used to generate electricity. Such options are essential in asset valuation for fossil fuel electricity generation plants.[33] A European spark spread call (SSC) option pays a positive part of the difference between the electricity spot price and the generating fuel cost at the time of maturity. Its payoff function is

$$SSC(S_T^e, S_T^g, H, T) = \max\left(S_T^e - H \cdot S_T^g, 0\right) \tag{7.58}$$

where S_T^e and S_T^g are the prices of electricity and the generating fuel, respectively; the constant H is the strike heat price, which represents the number of units of generating fuel contracted to generate one unit of electricity.

A locational spread option pays off the positive part of the price difference between the prices of the underlying commodity at two different delivery points. In the context of electricity markets, locational spread options serve the purposes of hedging the transmission risk and can also be used to value transmission expansion projects[34] (see Deng, Johnson, and Songomonia [1998]). The payoff of a European locational spread call option (LSC) is

$$LSC(S_T^A, S_T^B, L, T) = \max\left(S_T^B - L \cdot S_T^A, 0\right) \tag{7.59}$$

where S_T^a and S_T^b are the commodity prices at locations A and B. The constant L is "a loss factor reflecting the transportation/transmission losses or costs associated with shipping one unit of the commodity from location A to B."[35]

A general cross-commodity spread call option (CSC) is an option with the following payoff at maturity time T:

$$CSC(S_T^1, S_T^2, K, T) = \max\left(S_T^1 - K \cdot S_T^2, 0\right) \tag{7.60}$$

where S_T^i is the spot price of commodity i $(i = 1, 2)$ and K is a scaling constant associated with the spot price of the second commodity. The interpretation of K is different depending on the type of cross-commodity option. For instance, K represents the strike heat rate H in a spark spread option, and it represents the loss factor L in a locational spread option.

The prices of European-type contingent claims on the underlying energy commodity, under various proposed models (discussed later), can be obtained through the inversion of the characteristic transform functions. Suppose $\mathbf{X}_t$ is a state vector in $\Re^n$ and $u \in C^n$. The generalized characteristic transform function is defined as:

$$\varphi(u, \mathbf{X}_t, t, T) = E^Q\left[e^{-r(T-t)} \exp(u \cdot \mathbf{X}_T)|\Im_t\right]$$
$$= \exp[A(t, u) + B(t, u)\mathbf{X}_t]$$

Let $G(v, \mathbf{X}_t, t, T; \mathbf{a}, \mathbf{b})$ denote the time t price of a contingent claim with payoff $\exp(\mathbf{a} \cdot \mathbf{X}_T)$ when $\mathbf{b} \cdot \mathbf{X}_T \leq v$ is true at time T, where $\mathbf{a}, \mathbf{b}$ are vectors in $\Re^n$ and $v \in \Re^1$. Then we have:

$$G(v, \mathbf{X}_t, t, T; \mathbf{a}, \mathbf{b}) = E^Q\lfloor e^{-r(T-t)} \exp\left(\mathbf{a} \cdot \mathbf{X}_t\right) \mathbf{1}_{\mathbf{b} \cdot \mathbf{X}_T \leq v}|\Im_t\rfloor$$

$$= \frac{\varphi(\mathbf{a}, \mathbf{X}_t, t, T)}{2} - \frac{1}{\pi} \int_0^\infty \frac{\text{Im}\left\{\varphi(\mathbf{a} + iw\mathbf{b}, \mathbf{X}_t, t, T)e^{-iwv}\right\}}{w} dw$$

For properly chosen v, $\mathbf{a}$, and $\mathbf{b}$, $G(v, \mathbf{X}_t, t, T; \mathbf{a}, \mathbf{b})$ serves as building blocks in pricing contingent claims such as forwards/futures, call/put options, and cross-commodity spread options.

The value of a European cross-commodity spread call option on two commodities can be found by taking the Fourier transform of (7.58). It can be shown that the price is given by

$$CSC(S_t^1, S_t^2, K, t) = E^Q\lfloor e^{-r(T-t)} \max(S_T^1 - K \cdot S_T^2, 0)|\Im_t\rfloor$$
$$= E^Q\lfloor e^{-r(T-t)} \exp(X_T^1)\mathbf{1}_{S_T^1 - K \cdot S_T^2 \geq 0}|\Im_t\rfloor -$$
$$K \cdot E^Q\lfloor e^{-r(T-t)} \exp(X_T^2)\mathbf{1}_{S_T^1 - K \cdot S_T^2 \geq 0}|\Im_t\rfloor$$
$$= G_1 - K \cdot G_2$$

where

$$G_1 = G(0, \ln S_t^1, \ln(K \cdot S_t^2), t, T; [1, 0, \cdots, 0]'; [-1, 1, 0, \cdots, 0]') \tag{7.61}$$
$$G_2 = G(0, \ln S_t^1, \ln(K \cdot S_t^2), t, T; [0, 1, \cdots, 0]'; [-1, 1, 0, \cdots, 0]')$$

and

$$G(v, \mathbf{X}_t, t, T; \mathbf{a}, \mathbf{b}) = \frac{\varphi(\mathbf{a}, \mathbf{X}_t, t, T)}{2} - \frac{1}{\pi} \int_0^\infty \frac{\text{Im}\left\{\varphi(\mathbf{a} + iw\mathbf{b}, \mathbf{X}_t, t, T)e^{-iwv}\right\}}{w} dw$$

is the price of the contingent claim at time t and

$$\varphi(u, X_t, Y_t, t, T) = E^Q \lfloor e^{-r(T-t)} \exp(u_1 X_T + u_2 Y_T) | \Im_t \rfloor$$

is the generalized transform function where **a** and **b** are vectors in R^n and $v \in R^1$ (see Duffie, Pan, and Singleton [1998] for derivation).

To price energy traded commodity derivatives, Deng (1999) considers three general models: regime-switching, deterministic volatility jump-diffusion, and stochastic volatility jump-diffusion. In each model, the parameters are assumed to be constant, and the jumps appear in the primary commodity price and the volatility processes (Model 3) only. Moreover, the jump sizes are distributed as independent exponential random variables in $\Re^n$, thus having the following transform function:

$$\phi_J^j(\mathbf{c}, t) = \prod_{k=1}^{n} \frac{1}{1 - \mu_j^k c_k} \tag{7.62}$$

where **c** is a vector of complex numbers.

Model 1

The jumps are in the logarithm of the primary commodity spot price, X_t. The sizes of type-j jumps ($j = 1, 2$) are exponentially distributed with mean μ_J^j. The transform function of the jump size distribution is $\phi_J^j(c_1, c_2, t) = \frac{1}{1 - \mu_J^j c_1}$ for $j = 1, 2$.

$$d \begin{pmatrix} X_t \\ Y_t \end{pmatrix}$$
$$= \begin{pmatrix} \kappa_1(\theta_1 - X_t) \\ \kappa_2(\theta_2 - Y_t) \end{pmatrix} dt + \begin{pmatrix} \sigma_1 & 0 \\ \rho_1 \sigma_2 & \sqrt{1 - \rho_1^2} \sigma_2 \end{pmatrix} dW_t + \sum_{i=1}^{2} \Delta Z_t^i \tag{7.63}$$

The closed-form solution of the transform function can be written out explicitly for this model as:

$$\varphi_1(u, X_t, Y_t, t, T) = \exp(\alpha(\tau) + \beta_1(\tau) X_t + \beta_2(\tau) Y_t)$$

where $\tau = T - t$. It can be shown that[36]

$$\beta_1(\tau, u_1) = u_1 e^{-\kappa_1 \tau}$$
$$\beta_2(\tau, u_1) = u_2 e^{-\kappa_2 \tau}$$
$$\alpha(\tau, u) = -r\tau - \sum_{j=1}^{2} \frac{\lambda_J^j}{\kappa_1} \ln \frac{u_1 u_J^j - 1}{u_1 u_J^j e^{-\kappa_1 \tau} - 1} + \frac{a_1 \sigma_1^2 u_1^2}{4\kappa_1} + \frac{a_2 \sigma_2^2 u_2^2}{4\kappa_2}$$
$$+ u_1 \theta_1 (1 - e^{-\kappa_1 \tau}) + u_2 \theta_2 (1 - e^{-\kappa_2 \tau})$$
$$+ \frac{u_1 u_2 \rho_1 \sigma_1 \sigma_2 (1 - e^{-(\kappa_1 + \kappa_2)\tau})}{\kappa_1 + \kappa_2}$$

with $a_1 = 1 - e^{-2\kappa_1 \tau}$ and $a_2 = 1 - e^{-2\kappa_2 \tau}$.

Model 2

Model 2 is a regime-switching model with the regime-jumps appearing only in the primary commodity price process. In the electricity markets, this is suitable for modeling the occasional price spikes in the electricity spot prices caused by forced outages of the major power generation plants or line contingency in transmission networks. The model can be used as a joint specification of electricity and the generating fuel price processes under the risk-neutral measure Q. For simplicity, Deng (1999) assumes that there are no jumps within each regime:

$$d\begin{pmatrix} X_t \\ Y_t \end{pmatrix}$$
$$= \begin{pmatrix} \kappa_1(\theta_1 - X_t) \\ \kappa_2(\theta_2 - Y_t) \end{pmatrix} dt + \qquad\qquad (7.64)$$
$$\begin{pmatrix} \sigma_1 & 0 \\ \rho_1\sigma_2 & \sqrt{1-\rho_1^2}\sigma_2 \end{pmatrix} dW_t + v(U_{t-})dM_t$$

U_t is the regime state process defined as a continuous-time two-state Markov process:

$$dU_t = 1_{U_{t=0}} \cdot \delta(U_t)dN_t^0 + 1_{U_{t=1}} \cdot \delta(U_t)dN_t^1 \qquad\qquad (7.65)$$

where N_t^i is a Poisson process with arrival intensity λ^i, $i = 0, 1$, and $\delta(0) = -\delta(1) = 1$. M_t is defined as a continuous-time Markov chain:

$$dM_t = -\lambda(U_t)\delta(U_t)dt + dU_t \qquad\qquad (7.66)$$

and W_t is a standard Brownian motion. $\{v(i) = (v_1(i), v_2(i))', i = 0, 1\}$ denotes the sizes of the random jumps in state variables when regime-switching occurs.

$\phi_{v(i)}(c_1, c_2, t) = \int_{\Re^2} \exp(c \cdot z)dv_{v(i)}(z)$ is the transform function of the regime-jump size distribution $v(i)$, $i = 1, 2$. Z^j, ΔZ^j, and ϕ_J^j are similarly defined as those in Model 1.

The transform function for the model cannot be solved completely in closed-form. We have

$$\varphi_2^0(x, y, t) = \exp\left(\alpha_0(t) + \beta_1(t)x + \beta_2(t)y\right)$$
$$\varphi_2^1(x, y, t) = \exp\left(\alpha_0(t) + \beta_1(t)x + \beta_2(t)y\right)$$

where $\beta(t) = \beta(t, u) = (\beta_1(t, u), \beta_2(t, u))'$ has the closed-form solution of

$$\beta_1(\tau, u_1) = u_1 \exp(-\kappa_1\tau)$$
$$\beta_2(\tau, u_1) = u_1 \exp(-\kappa_2\tau).$$

$\alpha(t) = \alpha(t, u) = (\alpha_0(t, u), \alpha_1(t, u))'$ needs to be numerically computed from

$$\frac{d}{dt}\begin{pmatrix} \alpha_0(t) \\ \alpha_1(t) \end{pmatrix} = -\begin{pmatrix} A_1(\beta(t), t) + \lambda^0\left[\frac{e^{(\alpha_1(t)-\alpha_0(t))}}{1-\mu_0\beta_1(t,u_1)} - 1\right] \\ A_1(\beta(t), t) + \lambda^1\left[\frac{e^{(\alpha_1(t)-\alpha_1(t))}}{1-\mu_1\beta_1(t,u_1)} - 1\right] \end{pmatrix}$$

$$\begin{pmatrix} \alpha_0(0, u) \\ \alpha_1(0, u) \end{pmatrix} = \begin{pmatrix} 0 \\ 0 \end{pmatrix}$$

with

$$A_1(\beta(t), t) = -r + \sum_{i=1}^{2} \left[\kappa_i \theta_i \beta_i + \frac{1}{2} \sigma_i^2 \beta_i^2 \right] - \rho_1 \sigma_1 \sigma_2 \beta_1 \beta_2.$$

Model 3

Model 3 is a stochastic volatility model in which the type-1 jumps are simultaneous jumps in the commodity spot price and volatility processes, and the type-2 jumps are in the commodity spot price only. All parameters are constants.

$$d \begin{pmatrix} X_t \\ V_t \\ Y_t \end{pmatrix} = \begin{pmatrix} \kappa_1(\theta_1 - X_t) \\ \kappa_V(\theta_V - V_t) \\ \kappa_2(\theta_2 - Y_t) \end{pmatrix} dt + \begin{pmatrix} \sqrt{V_t} & 0 & 0 \\ \rho_1 \sigma_2 \sqrt{V_t} & \sqrt{(1-\rho_1^2)V_t \sigma^2} & 0 \\ \rho_2 \sigma_3 \sqrt{V_t} & 0 & \sigma_3 \end{pmatrix} dW_t + \sum_{i=1}^{2} \Delta Z_t^i \tag{7.67}$$

where W_t is a standard Brownian motion in $\Re^3$. Z^i, $i = 1, 2$, is a compound Poisson process in $\Re^3$. The Poisson arrival intensity functions are $\lambda^1(X_t, V_t, Y_t, t) = \lambda_1$ and $\lambda^2(X_t, V_t, Y_t, t) = \lambda_2 V_t$. The transform functions of the jump-size distributions are

$$\phi_J^1(c_1, c_2, c_3, t) = \frac{1}{(1 - \mu_1^1 c_1)(1 - \mu_1^2 c_2)}$$

where μ_J^k is the mean size of the type-J $(J = 1, 2)$ jump in factor k, $k = 1, 2$. It can be shown that the transform function is of the form (see Deng [1999]):

$$\varphi_3(u, X_t, V_t, Y_t, t, T) = \exp\left(\alpha(t, u) + \beta_1(t, u) X_T + \beta_2(t, u) V_T + \beta_3(t, u) Y_T\right)$$

Deng uses these models to price a spark spread call option with a strike heat rate of $H = 9.5$ MMBtu/Mwh for the previous three models, as well as the geometric Brownian motion (GBM) model. The spark spread call option value converges to the current spot price under the GBM price model. However, under the mean-reversion jump-diffusion price models, it converges to a long-term value, as shown in Figure 7.13, which is most likely to be depending on fundamental characteristics of supply and demand.

Deng uses the model parameter estimates shown in Table 7.4. To estimate the parameters, Deng (1999) derives the moment conditions from the transform function of the unconditional distribution of the underlying price return. Deng assumes that the risk premium associated with the factor X is proportional to X—i.e., the risk premium is of the form $\xi_X \cdot X$. For simplicity, Deng assumes the risk premia associated with the jumps are zero. Deng then uses the electricity and natural gas spot and futures price series to get the estimates for the model parameters under the true measure and the risk premia by matching moment conditions as well as the futures prices.[37]

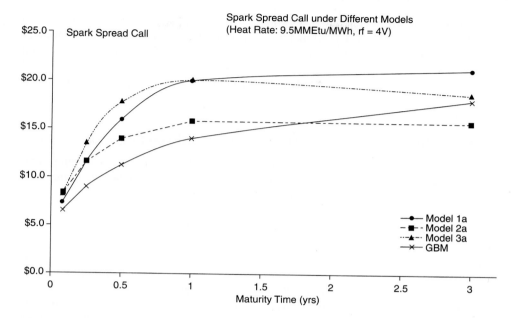

Figure 7.13   *Source: Deng (1999).*

Table 7.4

	Model 1a	Model 2a	Model 3a
κ_1	1.70	1.37	2.17
κ_2	1.80	1.80	3.50
κ_3	N/A	N/A	1.80
θ_1	3.40	3.30	3.20
θ_2	.087	0.87	0.85
θ_3	N/A	N/A	0.87
σ_1	0.74	0.80	N/A
σ_2	0.34	0.34	0.80
σ_3	N/A	N/A	0.54
ρ_1	0.20	0.20	0.25
ρ_2	N/A	N/A	0.20
λ_1	6.08	6.42	6.43
μ_{11}	6.19	0.26	0.23
μ_{12}	N/A	N/A	0.22
λ_2	7.00	8.20	5.00
μ_{21}	-0.11	-0.20	-0.14

Source: Deng (1999).

7.10   JUMP DIFFUSION PRICING MODELS

Various stochastic models have been proposed to capture the mean-reversion and spikes present in electricity prices. The affine jump-diffusion process is a popular choice because they are "flexible enough to capture certain properties such as multiple jumps, time-varying long-term mean, and stochastic volatility in various forms, which occur in many financial time series without sacrificing computational tractability."[38] Following the work of Xiong (2004), we have the models in the next sections.

Model 1a: Affine Mean-Reverting Jump-Diffusion Process

The diffusion part is represented by an Ornstein-Uhlenbeck process, and the jump component has exponentially distributed absolute value of jump size, with the sign of the jump determined by a Bernoulli variable. This is formulated as

$$dX_t = \kappa(\alpha - X_t)dt + \sigma dW_t + J_t dP_t \tag{7.68}$$

where the tuple $\theta = [\kappa, \alpha, \sigma^2, \omega, \psi, \lambda]$ are the unknown parameters. In particular, κ is the mean-reversion rate, α is the long-term mean, W_t is a standard Brownian motion with $dW_t \ N(0, dt)$ for an infinitesimal time interval dt, and P_t is a discontinuous, one-dimensional standard Poisson process with arrival rate ω. During dt, $dP_t = 1$ if there is a jump, and $dP_t = 0$ otherwise. The jump amplitude J_t is exponentially distributed with mean λ, and the sign of the jump J_t is distributed as a Bernoulli random variable with parameter ψ. It is assumed that the Brownian motion, Poisson process, and random jump amplitude are all Markov and pairwise independent.

The conditional characteristic function (CCF) of X_T, given X_t, $\phi(s, \theta, X_T)|X_t)$, takes the form

$$\varphi(s, \theta, X_T|X_t) = E[\exp(isX_T)|X_t]$$
$$= \exp(A(s, t, T, \theta) + B(s, t, T, \theta)X_t) \tag{7.69}$$

where $A(\cdot)$ and $B(\cdot)$ satisfy the following system of complex-valued ordinary differential equations (ODEs)

$$\frac{\partial A(s, t, T, \theta)}{\partial t} = -\kappa\alpha B(s, t, T, \theta)$$
$$- \frac{1}{2}\sigma^2(s, t, T, \theta) - \omega(\varphi(B(s, t, T, \theta)) - 1), \tag{7.70}$$
$$\frac{\partial B(s, t, T, \theta)}{\partial t} = \kappa B(s, t, T, \theta)$$

with boundary conditions

$$A(s, T, T, \theta) = 0, \quad B(s, T, T, \theta) = is. \tag{7.71}$$

Here, the "jump transform" $\varphi(B(s, t, T, \theta)$ is given by:

$$\varphi(B(s, t, T, \theta)) = \psi \int_0^\infty \exp\left(B(s, t, T, \theta)z\right) \frac{1}{\gamma} \exp\left(-\frac{z}{\gamma}\right) dz$$

$$+ (1 - \psi) \int_0^\infty \exp\left(-B(s, t, T, \theta)z\right) \frac{1}{\gamma} \exp\left(-\frac{z}{\gamma}\right) dz$$

$$= \frac{\psi}{1 - B(s, t, T, \theta)\gamma} + \frac{1 - \psi}{1 + B(s, t, T, \theta)\gamma} \tag{7.72}$$

Solving (7.69) for $A(\cdot)$ and $B(\cdot)$ and applying the corresponding boundary conditions yields the following:

$$A(s, t, T, \theta) = i\alpha s(1 - e^{-\kappa(T-t)}) - \frac{\sigma^2 s^2}{4\kappa}\left(1 - e^{-2\kappa(T-t)}\right)$$

$$+ \frac{i\omega(1 - 2\psi)}{\kappa}\left(\arctan(\gamma s e^{-\kappa(T-t)}) - \arctan(\gamma s)\right) \tag{7.73}$$

$$+ \frac{\varpi}{2\kappa} \ln\left(\frac{1 + \gamma^2 s^2 e^{-2\kappa(T-t)}}{1 + \gamma^2 s^2}\right)$$

$$B(s, t, T, \theta) = i s e^{-\kappa(T-t)}$$

Model 1b

This model allows for asymmetric upward and downward jumps (see Deng [1999], discussed previously), each with exponentially distributed jump magnitudes. The logarithm of the spot price X_t satisfies the SDE

$$dX_t = \kappa(\alpha - X_t)dt + \sigma dW_t + J_t^u dP_t^u(\omega) + J_t^d dP_t^d(\omega) \tag{7.74}$$

where κ is the mean-reversion rate, α is the long-term mean, and W_t is a standard Brownian motion with $dW_t \ N(0, dt)$. The jump behavior of X_t is governed by two types of jumps: upward jumps and downward jumps. The upward jumps J_t^u are exponentially distributed with positive mean γ_u and jump arrival rate ω_u. The downward jumps J_t^d are also exponentially distributed with negative mean γ_d and jump arrival rate ω_d. Again, P_t^u and P_t^d are two independent discontinuous, one-dimensional standard Poisson processes with arrival rate ω_u and ω_d, respectively.

The transform CCF can be written out as

$$\varphi(s, \theta, X_T | X_t) = E[\exp(isX_T)|X_t]$$

$$= \exp(A(s, t, T, \theta) + B(s, t, T, \theta)X_t),$$

where $A(\cdot)$ and $B(\cdot)$ satisfy the complex-valued system of ODEs:

$$\frac{\partial A(s,t,T,\theta)}{\partial t} = -\kappa\alpha B(s,t,T,\theta) - \frac{1}{2}\sigma^2(s,t,T,\theta) - \omega_u(\varphi_u(B(s,t,T,\theta))-1)$$
$$- \omega_d(\varphi_d(B(s,t,T,\theta))-1) \tag{7.75}$$
$$\frac{\partial B(s,t,T,\theta)}{\partial t} = \kappa B(s,t,T,\theta),$$

with boundary conditions:

$$A(s,T,T,\theta) = 0, \quad B(s,T,T,\theta) = is.$$

Here, the "jump transform" for the upward jump is given by:

$$\varphi_u(B(s,t,T,\theta)) = \int_0^\infty \exp\left(B(s,t,T,\theta)z\right)\left[\frac{1}{\gamma_u}\exp\left(-\frac{z}{\gamma_u}\right)\right]dz$$
$$= \frac{1}{1 - B(s,t,T,\theta)\gamma_u}$$

Similarly, the "jump transform" for the downward jump is given by:

$$\varphi_d(B(s,t,T,\theta)) = \frac{1}{1 - B(s,t,T,\theta)\gamma_d}$$

After some computations, one can solve for $A(\cdot)$ and $B(\cdot)$, applying the boundary conditions:

$$A(s,t,T,\theta) = i\alpha s(1 - e^{-\kappa(T-t)}) - \frac{\sigma^2 s^2}{4\kappa}\left(1 - e^{-2\kappa(T-t)}\right)$$
$$+ \frac{\omega_u}{\kappa}\ln\left(\frac{1 - is\gamma_u e^{-\kappa(T-t)}}{1 - is\gamma_u}\right)$$
$$+ \frac{\omega_d}{\kappa}\ln\left(\frac{1 - is\gamma_u e^{-\kappa(T-t)}}{1 - is\gamma_d}\right) \tag{7.76}$$
$$B(s,t,T,\theta) = ise^{-\kappa(T-t)}.$$

Model 2a: Time-Varying Drift Component

Model 1 (7.68) is extended by adding a time-varying component in the drift by replacing the long-term mean α with a deterministic function $\alpha(t)$. The logarithm of the electricity spot price is defined by:

$$dX_t = \kappa(\alpha(t) - X_t)dt + \sigma dW_t + J_t dP_t(\omega) \tag{7.77}$$

The model incorporates on-peak and off-peak effects into the price process by considering the following form for $\alpha(t)$:

$$\alpha(t) = \alpha_1\text{peak}_t + \alpha_2\text{offpeak}_t \tag{7.78}$$

where

$$
\text{peak}_t = \begin{cases} 1 & \text{if in on-peak periods} \\ 0 & \text{otherwise} \end{cases} \tag{7.79}
$$

$$
\text{offpeak}_t = \begin{cases} 1 & \text{if in off-peak periods} \\ 0 & \text{otherwise} \end{cases}
$$

This is also an affine process. By the same methods, the transform CFF is given by

$$
\begin{aligned}
\varphi(s, \theta, X_T | X_t) &= E[\exp(isX_T)|X_t] \\
&= \exp(A(s, t, T, \theta) + B(s, t, T, \theta)X_t),
\end{aligned}
$$

where $A(\cdot)$ and $B(\cdot)$ satisfy the following system of complex-valued ordinary differential equations (ODEs):

$$
\frac{\partial A(s, t, T, \theta)}{\partial t} = -\kappa\alpha B(s, t, T, \theta) - \frac{1}{2}\sigma^2(s, t, T, \theta) - \omega(\varphi(B(s, t, T, \theta)) - 1),
\tag{7.80}
$$

$$
\frac{\partial B(s, t, T, \theta)}{\partial t} = \kappa B(s, t, T, \theta),
$$

without boundary conditions:

$$
A(s, T, T, \theta) = 0, \quad B(s, T, T, \theta) = is.
$$

Solving (7.80) for $A(\cdot)$ and $B(\cdot)$ and applying the corresponding boundary conditions yields:

$$
\begin{aligned}
A(s, t, T, \theta) &= i\alpha s(1 - e^{-\kappa(T-t)}) - \frac{\sigma^2 s^2}{4\kappa}\left(1 - e^{-2\kappa(T-t)}\right) \\
&\quad + \frac{i\omega(1 - 2\psi)}{\kappa}\left(\arctan(\gamma s e^{-\kappa(T-t)}) - \arctan(\gamma s)\right) \\
&\quad + \frac{\varpi}{2\kappa}\ln\left(\frac{1 + \gamma^2 s^2 e^{-2\kappa(T-t)}}{1 + \gamma^2 s^2}\right)
\end{aligned}
\tag{7.81}
$$

$$
B(s, t, T, \theta) = ise^{-\kappa(T-t)}
$$

Here, let $t = t_0 < t_1 < \cdots < t_N = T$; then we have

$$
\begin{aligned}
L(s, t, T, \theta) &= \int_t^T \kappa\alpha(t)ise^{-\kappa(T-t)}\,dt \\
&= is\sum_{j=1}^N \alpha e^{-\kappa(T-t_j)}(1 - e^{-\kappa(t_j - t_{j-1})}),
\end{aligned}
\tag{7.82}
$$

where

$$
\alpha = \begin{cases} \alpha_1 & \alpha_1 \text{ if } [t_{j-1}, t_j] \text{ is in on-peak periods} \\ \alpha_2 & \text{otherwise} \end{cases}
\tag{7.83}
$$

Model 2b: Time-Varying Version of Model 1b

Consider the time-varying extension to Model 1b (7.77), where

$$dX_t = \kappa(\alpha(t) - X_t)dt + \sigma dW_t + J_t^u dP_t^u(\omega) + J_t^d dP_t^d(\omega) \tag{7.84}$$

where $\alpha(t)$ is defined in (7.78).

Similar to the previous models, the transform CCF is of the form

$$\varphi(s, \theta, X_T | X_t) = E[\exp(isX_T) | X_t]$$
$$= \exp(A(s, t, T, \theta) + B(s, t, T, \theta)X_t),$$

where

$$A(s, t, T, \theta) = i\alpha s(1 - e^{-\kappa(T-t)}) - \frac{\sigma^2 s^2}{4\kappa}\left(1 - e^{-2\kappa(T-t)}\right)$$
$$+ \frac{\omega_u}{\kappa}\ln\left(\frac{1 - is\gamma_u e^{-\kappa(T-t)}}{1 - is\gamma_u}\right)$$
$$+ \frac{\omega_d}{\kappa}\ln\left(\frac{1 - is\gamma_u e^{-\kappa(T-t)}}{1 - is\gamma_d}\right) \tag{7.85}$$
$$B(s, t, T, \theta) = ise^{-\kappa(T-t)}.$$

with $L(s, t, T, \theta)$ defined in equation (7.82).

7.11 STOCHASTIC VOLATILITY PRICING MODELS

Jumps alone are inadequate to replicate the level of skewness present in electricity prices. Kaminski (1997) and Deng (1999) emphasize the need to incorporate stochastic volatility in the modeling of electricity spot prices. Volatility in electric prices varies over time and is likely mean-reverting itself (see Goto and Karolyi [2003]). To capture stochastic volatility, various two-factor stochastic volatility models have been proposed by Deng (1999), Xiong (2004), and Villaplana (2002). We consider the two-factor affine process to model electricity spot prices.

Model 3a: Two-Factor Jump-Diffusion Affine Process with Stochastic Volatility

Let X_t be the logarithm of the spot price of electricity and V_t be the volatility of the price process, which evolves stochastically over time.

$$d\begin{bmatrix} X_t \\ V_t \end{bmatrix} = \begin{bmatrix} \kappa(\alpha - X_t) \\ \kappa_v(\alpha_v - V_t) \end{bmatrix} dt$$
$$+ \begin{bmatrix} \sqrt{(1-\rho^2)V_t} & \rho\sqrt{V_t} \\ 0 & \sigma_v\sqrt{V_t} \end{bmatrix}\begin{bmatrix} dW_t \\ dW_v \end{bmatrix} + \begin{bmatrix} J_t dP_t(\omega) \\ 0 \end{bmatrix} \tag{7.86}$$

where κ is the mean-reversion rate, α is the long-term mean of the log prices, P_t is a discontinuous, one-dimensional standard Poisson process with arrival rate ω, the amplitude of

J_t is exponentially distributed with mean γ, and the sign of J_t is distributed as a Bernoulli random variable with parameter ψ. The two random variables W_t and W_v are two standard Brownian motions with correlation ρ. Also, κ_v is the mean-reversion rate of the volatility V_t, α_v is the long-term mean of V_t, and σ_v is the volatility of V_t.

Suppose that the jump component in the logarithm of the spot price is defined as in Model 1a and Model 2a. Then, the "jump transform" is given by:

$$\varphi\left(\left[\begin{array}{c} A(\cdot) \\ B(\cdot) \end{array}\right]\right) = \int_0^\infty (\psi \exp(A(\cdot)z) + (1-\psi)\exp(-A(\cdot)z)\frac{1}{\gamma}\exp\left(-\frac{z}{\gamma}\right)dz$$

$$= \frac{\psi}{1-A(\cdot)\gamma} + \frac{1-\psi}{1+A(\cdot)\gamma} \tag{7.87}$$

The CCF is of the form

$$\varphi(s_x, s_v, \theta, X_T, V_T | X_t, V_t)$$
$$= E^\theta[\exp(is_x X_T + is_v V_T)|X_t, V_t]$$
$$= \exp(A(s_x, s_v, t, T, \theta)X_t + B(s_x, s_v, t, T, \theta)V_t + C(s_x, s_v, t, T, \theta)),$$

where $A(\cdot)$, $B(\cdot)$, and $C(\cdot)$ satisfy the following complex-valued Riccati equations:

$$\left\{\begin{array}{l} \frac{\partial A(\cdot)}{\partial t} = \kappa A(\cdot), \\ \frac{\partial B(\cdot)}{\partial t} = \kappa_v B(\cdot) \\ \qquad - \frac{1}{2}A(\cdot)(A(\cdot)+\rho\sigma_v B(\cdot)) - \frac{1}{2}B(\cdot)(A(\cdot)\rho\sigma_v + B(\cdot)\sigma_v^2) \\ \frac{\partial C(\cdot)}{\partial t} = -\kappa\alpha A(\cdot) - \kappa_v \alpha_v B(\cdot) - \omega(\varphi\left(\left[\begin{array}{c} A(\cdot) \\ B(\cdot) \end{array}\right] - 1\right) \end{array}\right. \tag{7.88}$$

with boundary conditions:

$$A(s_x, s_v, T, T, \theta) = is_x, \quad B(s_x, s_v, T, T, \theta) = is_v \quad C(s_x, s_v, T, T, \theta) = 0.$$

We can solve the first equation for $A(\cdot)$ and apply the initial conditions to obtain:

$$A(\cdot) = is_x e^{-\kappa(T-t)}$$

However, because there are not closed-form solutions for $B(\cdot)$ and $C(\cdot)$, we need to solve them numerically.

7.12   MODEL PARAMETER ESTIMATION

Following the work of Xiong (2004),[39] we discuss how to estimate the parameters of the models. Affine processes are flexible enough to allow us to capture the special characteristics of electricity prices, such as mean-reversion, seasonality, and "spikes." Moreover, under suitable regularity conditions, one can explore the information from the CCF of discretely sampled observations to develop computationally tractable and asymptotically efficient estimators of the parameters of affine processes. Moreover, the CCF is unique and contains the same information as the conditional density function through the Fourier transform. We can use it to recover the conditional density function via the Fourier transform and implement a usual maximum likelihood (ML) estimation. This is the approach of ML-CCF estimation. If the N-dimensional state variables are all observable, ML-CCF estimation can be implemented, and so obtained ML-CCF estimators are asymptotically efficient (see Singleton [2001]).

The estimation, however, can be costly in higher dimensions ($N \geq 2$) because we need to compute the multivariate Fourier inversions repeatedly and accurately in order to maximize the likelihood function. According to Singleton (2001), considerable computational saving can be achieved by using limited-information ML-CCF (LML-CFF) estimation (see Singleton [2001]). Suppose $\{\mathbf{X}_t, t = 1, 2, ...\}$ is a set of discretely sampled observations of an N-dimensional state variable with a joint CCF $\phi(s, \theta, \mathbf{X}_{t+1}|\mathbf{X}_t)$. Let η_j denote an N-dimensional selection vector where the jth entry is 1 and zeros elsewhere. Define $X_{t+1}^j = \eta_j \cdot \mathbf{X}_{t+1}$; then the conditional density of X_{t+1}^j conditioned on $\mathbf{X}_t$ is the inverse Fourier transform of $\phi(\xi\eta_j, \theta, \mathbf{X}_{t+1}|\mathbf{X}_t)$ with some scalar ξ:

$$f_j(X_{t+1}^j, \theta|\mathbf{X}_t) = \frac{1}{2\pi} \int\limits_{\Re} \phi(\xi\eta_j, \theta, \mathbf{X}_{t+1}|\mathbf{X}_t)e^{-i\xi\eta_j'\mathbf{X}_{t+1}}ds \qquad (7.89)$$

The basic idea behind this is to exploit the information in $f_j(X_{t+1}^j, \theta|\mathbf{X}_t)$ instead of information in the joint conditional density function:

$$f(X_{t+1}, \theta|X_t) = \frac{1}{(2\pi)^N} \int\limits_{\Re^N} \phi(s, \theta, X_{t+1}|X_t)e^{-is'X_{t+1}}ds \qquad (7.90)$$

Thus, the estimation involves at most N one-dimensional integrations instead of doing a N-dimensional integration. The estimators obtained are called LML-CCF estimators. Although the LML-CCF estimators do not exploit any information about the joint conditional density function, they are typically more efficient than the quasi-maximum likelihood (QML) estimators for affine diffusions (see Singleton [2001]).

But for those multi-factor models with unobservable (latent) state variables such as stochastic volatility models, the ML-CCF or LML-CCF estimators cannot be obtained. However, several papers discuss the methodologies related to CCF-based estimators of stochastic volatility models. Singleton (1999) proposed a Simulated Method of Moments (SMM-CCF) estimator; Jiang and Knight (1999) explored the Moment of System of Moments (MSM) estimators; Chacko and Viceira (2001) considered the so-called Spectral Generalized Method of Moments (SGMM). SGMM is more computationally tractable than the others (see Singleton [2001]). To deal with stochastic volatility models, Chacko and Viceira (2001) derive stationary (unconditional) characteristic function[40] from the CCF of the volatility, and utilized this CCF to obtain a so-called marginal CCF. An ML type estimation based on the so-called marginal CCF (ML-MCCF) to estimate stochastic volatility models is applied. Furthermore, SGMM estimators based on the so-called marginal CCF to estimate stochastic volatility models are introduced.

ML-CCF Estimators

ML estimation is the most common method of estimating the parameters of stochastic processes if the probability density has an analytical form. It provides a consistent approach to parameter estimation problems, and ML estimators become minimum variance unbiased estimators as the sample size increases. Suppose that $\mathbf{X}$ is an N-dimensional continuous random variable with probability density function $f(\mathbf{X}, \theta)$ where $\theta = \{\theta_1, ..., \theta_k\}$ are k unknown constant parameters that need to be estimated. Given a sequence of observations $\{\mathbf{X}_t\}$ sampled at $t = 1, 2, ..., n$, the log likelihood function at the sample is given by:

$$L(\mathbf{X}_1, ..., \mathbf{X}_n, \theta) = \sum_{t=1}^{n} \ln f(\mathbf{X}_t, \theta) \tag{7.91}$$

The maximum likelihood based estimators of θ are obtained by maximizing $L(\cdot)$

$$\widehat{\theta}_{ml} = \arg\max_{\theta} L(\mathbf{X}_1, \ldots, \mathbf{X}_n, \theta) = \arg\max_{\theta} \sum_{t=1}^{n} \ln(f(\mathbf{X}_t, \theta)). \tag{7.92}$$

For models we adopt, the CCF, $\phi(s, \theta, \mathbf{X}_{t+1}|\mathbf{X}_t)$, of the sample is known, often in closed-form, as an exponential of an affine function of $\mathbf{X}_t$. Thus, the conditional density function of $\mathbf{X}_{t+1}$ given $\mathbf{X}_t$ can be obtained by the Fourier transform of the CCF:

$$f(X_{t+1}, \theta|X_t) = \frac{1}{(2\pi)^N} \int_{\Re^N} \phi(s, \theta, X_{t+1}|X_t) e^{-is'X_{t+1}} ds \tag{7.93}$$

We can use the standard ML estimation based on this conditional density function to obtain ML-CCF estimators of the sample as:

$$\widehat{\theta}_{CCF} = \arg\max_{\theta} \sum_{t=1}^{n} \ln(f(\mathbf{X}_{t+1}, \theta|\mathbf{X}_t)) \tag{7.94}$$

Take Model 1a (7.65) as an example. The conditional density function of $\mathbf{X}_{t+1}$ given $\mathbf{X}_t$ of the sample is of the form:

$$f(X_{t+1}, \theta|X_t) = \frac{1}{2\pi} \int_{-\infty}^{\infty} \phi(s, \theta, X_{t+1}|X_t) e^{-isX_{t+1}} ds \tag{7.95}$$

$$= \frac{1}{2\pi} \int_{-\infty}^{\infty} e^{-isY_t} h(\theta, s) ds,$$

where

$$Y_t = (X_{t+1} - \alpha) - e^{-\kappa}(X_t - \alpha), \tag{7.96}$$

and

$$
h(\theta, s) = \exp\left(-\frac{\sigma^2 s^2}{4\kappa}(1 - e^{-2\kappa}) + \frac{i\omega(1 - 2\psi)}{\kappa}(\arctan(\gamma s e^{-\kappa}) - \arctan(\lambda s))\right.
$$
$$
\left. + \frac{\omega}{2\kappa}\ln\left(\frac{1 + \gamma^2 s^2 e^{-2\kappa}}{1 + \gamma^2 s^2}\right) \right) \tag{7.97}
$$

To assist in computing this integral (7.95), we define:

$$
F(Y_t, \theta) = f(X_{t+1}, \theta | X_t) = \frac{1}{2\pi}\lim_{R\to\infty}\int_{-R}^{R} e^{-isY_t}h(\theta, s)ds. \tag{7.98}
$$

Notice that $|h(\theta, s)|$ is continuous in s and $|h(\theta, s)| \le -\frac{\sigma^2 s^2}{4\kappa}(1 - e^{-2\kappa})$. Thus, we can truncate the integral to finite interval $[-R, R]$ outside of which the function $h(\theta, s)$ to be integrated is negligibly small. Then, for this choice of R,

$$
F(Y_t, \theta) \approx \frac{1}{2\pi}\int_{-R}^{R} e^{-isY_t}h(\theta, s)ds. \tag{7.99}
$$

Also, we can discretize Y_t into M subintervals such that[41]

$$
Y_n = n\Delta Y_t = n\left(\frac{Y_t}{M}\right),
$$
$$
s_k = k\Delta s = k\left(\frac{R}{M}\right),
$$
$$
F(Y_t, \theta) \approx \frac{1}{2\pi}\frac{R}{M}\sum_{n=-M}^{M-1\prime}(e^{-ink\frac{RY_t}{M}}h(\theta, \frac{nR}{M})). \tag{7.100}
$$

If we arrange $\frac{RY_t}{M} = 2\pi$, then we have

$$
F(Y_t, \theta) \approx \frac{1}{2\pi}\frac{R}{M}\sum_{n=-M}^{M-1\prime}(e^{-ink\frac{2\pi}{M}}h(\theta, \frac{nR}{M})). \tag{7.101}
$$

We can approximate $F(Y_t, \theta)$ by the discrete Fourier transform (DFT) of $h(\theta, \frac{nR}{M})$, and the integral in equation (7.95) can be estimated on a suitable grid of s values by a Fast Fourier transform (FFT) algorithm.

ML-MCCF Estimators

ML-CCF estimators are asymptotically efficient if all of the state variables are observable. But for those multi-factor models with unobservable state variables such as Model 3a and Model 3b, ML-CCF estimators cannot be obtained directly. If option prices are available, implied volatilities can be calculated from option prices observed in the market.

Various numerical methods have been proposed for estimating implied volatility functions from option prices (see Dupire [1994], Coleman, Li, and Verma [1999], and Hamida and Cont [2004]). Then one can use those values as the data of volatilities and implement ML-CCF estimation.

But in our case, option prices are not available. Following Chacko and Viceira (2001), we can integrate the unobservable variable (volatility) from the joint CCF of the log price and the volatility, and set $s_v = 0$, but also need to utilize the volatility information (not workable in our case). Singleton's SMM method integrates out the unobservable variables in the CCF by simulation. This requires a huge number of simulated paths of the volatility and can be quite time-consuming. Furthermore, this induces an estimation bias due to the discretization used in the simulation (see Chacko and Viceira [2001]). Meanwhile, compared to the SGMM method that will be introduced, ML-MCCF estimation avoids the so-called *ad-hoc* moment conditions selection problem and is easier to implement ease of stochastic volatility models.

Take Model 3a as an example. Recall that the volatility follows a square-root process such as

$$dV_t = \kappa_v(\alpha_v - V_t)dt + \sigma_v\sqrt{V_t}dW_v. \tag{7.102}$$

The infinitesimal generator of the square-root process is

$$Lf(v) = \frac{\sigma_v^2 v}{2}\frac{\partial^2 f}{\partial v^2} + \kappa_v(\alpha_v - v)\frac{\partial f}{\partial v}. \tag{7.103}$$

Let μ_t be the distribution function of and then it solves the forward Kolmogorov equation (7.103):

$$\mu_t(Lf) = \frac{d}{dt}\mu_t(f) \tag{7.104}$$

with $\mu_t(f) = \int f(v)d\mu_t$.

In particular, let μ be the stationary characteristic function of the volatility. In this case, with $f(v) = e^{iuv}$ and $\widehat{\mu}(u) = \mu(e^{iuv})$ we have

$$Le^{iuv} = -\frac{\sigma_v^2 v}{2}u^2 e^{iuv} + i\kappa_v(\alpha_v - v)ue^{iuv} \tag{7.105}$$

$$= (iv(\frac{i\sigma_v^2 u^2}{2} - \kappa_v u) + i\kappa_v\alpha_v u)e^{iuv}$$

and

$$\mu(Le^{iuv}) = (\frac{i\sigma_v^2 u^2}{2} - \kappa_v u)\int ive^{ivu}du + i\kappa_v\alpha_v u\int e^{iuv}du \tag{7.106}$$

$$= \left(\frac{i\sigma_v^2 u^2}{2} - \kappa_v u\right)\frac{d\widehat{\mu}(u)}{du} + i\kappa_v\alpha_v u\widehat{\mu}(u)$$

Because $\frac{d\mu(\cdot)}{dt} = 0$, we have

$$\left(\frac{i\sigma_v^2 u^2}{2} - \kappa_v u\right)\frac{d\widehat{\mu}(u)}{du} + i\kappa_v\alpha_v\widehat{\mu}(u) = 0 \tag{7.107}$$

with $\widehat{\mu}(0) = 1$. Then the solution for (7.107) has the form

$$\widehat{\mu} = \left(1 - \frac{iu\sigma_v^2}{s\kappa_v}\right)^{-2\kappa_v\alpha_v/\sigma_v^2}. \tag{7.108}$$

Recall that the joint CCF of the log price and volatility in this model is defined as

$$\phi(s_x, s_v, \theta, X_T, V_T | X_t, V_t)$$
$$= \exp\left(A(s_x, s_v, t, T, \theta)X_t + B(s_x, s_v, t, T, \theta)V_t + C(s_x, s_v, t, T, \theta)\right)$$

where $A(\cdot)$, $B(\cdot)$, and $C(\cdot)$ are the solutions of system (equation (7.88)). As the stochastic volatility V_t is unobservable, we cannot estimate the parameters of stochastic models directly from the joint CCF of the log price and volatility. Let's define the marginal CCF as

$$\phi(s_x, \theta, X_T | X_t)$$
$$= \int_0^\infty \phi(s_x, 0, \theta, X_T, V_T | X_t, V_t)d\mu \tag{7.109}$$

$$= e^{A(s_x,0,t,T,\theta)X_t+C(s_x,0,t,T,\theta)} \int_0^\infty e^{B(s_x,0,t,T,\theta)V_t}d\mu$$

$$= e^{A(s_x,0,t,T,\theta)X_t+C(s_x,0,t,T,\theta)}\widehat{\mu}(-iB(s_x,0,t,T,\theta))$$

Applying equation (7.108), we obtain the marginal CCF of the form

$$\phi(s_x, \theta, X_T | X_t) = e^{A(s_x,0,t,T,\theta)X_t+C(s_x,0,t,T,\theta)} \cdot$$
$$(1 - \frac{B(s_x,0,t,T,\theta)\sigma_v^2}{2\kappa_v})^{-2\kappa_v\alpha_v/\sigma_v^2}. \tag{7.110}$$

Through the Fourier transform, the marginal conditional density function is given by

$$f(X_{t+1}, \theta | X_t) = \frac{1}{2\pi} \int_\Re \phi(s_x, \theta, X_{t+1} | X_t)e^{-is_x X_{t+1}}ds. \tag{7.111}$$

Then, given a sample $\{X_t, t = 1, ..., n\}$, one can implement the maximum likelihood estimation based on this marginal distribution of the observed variables (electricity prices), and obtain ML-MCCF estimators as

$$\theta_{MCCF} = \arg\max_\theta \sum_{t=1}^{n-1} \ln f(X_{t+1}, \theta | X_t). \tag{7.112}$$

Note that because we only rely on the level of the electricity prices in the previous period, we lose efficiency. And the point estimates (including the SGMM estimators to be discussed), as pointed out by Chacko and Viceira (2001), are biased and inconsistent. In addition, the theoretical value for the bias is hard to calculate as we don't have closed forms for $B(\cdot)$ and $C(\cdot)$. Following Chacko and Viceira (2001), we try to correct the bias by a bootstrap method. In particular, we simulate 500 paths with a given parameter θ_0. For each path, there are 19,704 hourly observations (same length as the actual data). The estimates $\widehat{\theta}$, $i = 1, ..., n$, obtained from the simulated paths, result in a distribution for each parameter. We will regard the difference between the mean of those estimates and the given parameter as the bias—i.e.,

$$bias = \theta_0 - \frac{1}{n} \sum_{i=1}^{n} \widehat{\theta}_i, \tag{7.113}$$

with $n = 500$ in our setting.[42]

Spectral GMM Estimators

We describe the SGMM estimators constructed by Chacko and Viceira (2001). This method is essentially GMM in a complex variable setting. GMM estimation is one of the most fundamental estimation methods in statistics and econometrics (see Hansen [1982]). Unlike ML estimation, which requires the complete specification of the model and its probability distribution, full knowledge of the specification and strong distributional assumptions are not required for GMM estimation. GMM estimators are best suited to study models that are only partially specified, and they are attractive alternatives to likelihood-type estimators.

Definition 1:   Suppose that we have a set of random variables $\{x_t, t = 1, 2, ...\}$. Let $\boldsymbol{\theta} = \theta_1, ..., \theta_k$ be an unknown tuple with true value $\boldsymbol{\theta}_0$ to be estimated; θ_0, θ in some parameter space Θ. Then, the q-dimensional vector of functions $\mathbf{m}(x_t, \boldsymbol{\theta})$ is called an (unconditional) moment function if the following moment conditions hold:

$$E[\mathbf{m}(x_t, \boldsymbol{\theta}_0)] = \mathbf{0}. \tag{7.114}$$

Notice that θ is a k-tuple vector and $E[\mathbf{m}(x_t, \boldsymbol{\theta}_0)] = \mathbf{0}$ consists of q equations. If we have as many moment conditions as parameters to be estimated $(q = k)$, we can simply solve the k equations in k unknowns to obtain the estimates. If we have fewer moment conditions than unknowns $(q < k)$, then we cannot identify $\boldsymbol{\theta}$. In this case, we can "create" more moment conditions by the so-called weighting functions (often termed "instruments" in the GMM literature; see Matyas [1999]). If we have more functions than unknowns $(q > k)$, then this is an over-identified problem. Such cases of over-identification can easily arise, and the moment estimator is not well-defined. Different choices of moment conditions may lead to different estimates. GMM is a method to solve this kind of over-identification problem.

Consider the standard linear regression model as an example:

$$y = \mathbf{x}'\boldsymbol{\theta}_0 + \varepsilon. \tag{7.115}$$

Here y is the response variable, $\mathbf{x} = [x_1, x_2, \cdots, x_k]'$ is a k-dimensional vector of regressors, $\mathbf{x}'$ is its transpose, and $\boldsymbol{\theta} = [\theta_1, ..., \theta_k]'$ is the unknown vector of parameters with true value $\boldsymbol{\theta}_0$. We assume that ε has zero expectation and is uncorrelated with $\mathbf{x}$. Using the law of iterated expectations, we find that

$$E[\mathbf{x}\varepsilon] = E[E[\mathbf{x}\varepsilon|\mathbf{x}]] = E[\mathbf{x}E[\varepsilon|\mathbf{x}]] = \mathbf{0}. \tag{7.116}$$

Therefore, we can have the moment functions $\mathbf{m}((\mathbf{x},y),\boldsymbol{\theta}) = \mathbf{x}(y - \mathbf{x}'\theta)$. These moment functions are well defined, because, by the assumptions

$$E[\mathbf{m}((\mathbf{x},y),\boldsymbol{\theta}_0)] = E[\mathbf{x}(y - \mathbf{x}'\boldsymbol{\theta}_0)] = E[\mathbf{x}\varepsilon] = 0. \tag{7.117}$$

Suppose $n > k$ observations on the response variable are available—say $y_1, y_2, ..., y_n$. Along with each observed response y_t, we have a k-dimensional observation vector of regressors $\mathbf{x}_t$. We have exactly as many moment conditions as parameters to be estimated, because $\mathbf{x}_t$ is a k-dimensional vector. If we assume that the strong law of large numbers hold, then we have

$$\frac{1}{n}\sum_{t=1}^{n} \mathbf{m}((\mathbf{x},y),\widehat{\boldsymbol{\theta}}_0) \to E[\mathbf{m}((\mathbf{x},y),\boldsymbol{\theta}_0] = 0, \text{ almost surely.}$$

So the method of moments (MM) estimator for this model is just the solution of

$$\frac{1}{n}\sum_{t=1}^{n}\mathbf{x}_t(y_t - \mathbf{x}_t'\widehat{\boldsymbol{\theta}}_n) = \mathbf{0} \tag{7.118}$$

which gives

$$\widehat{\boldsymbol{\theta}}_n = \left(\sum_{t=1}^{n}\mathbf{x}_t\mathbf{x}_t'\right)^{-1}\sum_{t=1}^{n}\mathbf{x}_t y = (\mathbf{X}'\mathbf{X})^{-1}\mathbf{X}'\mathbf{y} \tag{7.119}$$

with $\mathbf{X} = [\mathbf{x}_1,...,\mathbf{x}_n]$ and $\mathbf{y} = [y_1,...,y_n]'$. Thus, the ordinary least squares (OLS) estimator is a MM estimator.

Notice that we specified relatively little information about the error term ε. For ML estimation, we would be required to give the distribution of the error term ε, as well as the autocorrelation and heteroskedasticity, which are also not required in formulating the moments conditions.

Now instead of assuming that the error term has zero expectation on certain observed variables, we can specify the moment conditions directly by requiring the error term to be uncorrelated with certain observed "instruments." Let's consider the previous model again. This time, we do not assume the error term has zero expectation, but that it is still uncorrelated to the regressors. Suppose we have a q-dimensional observed instrument $\mathbf{z}$, $(q > k)$ and $E[\mathbf{z}\varepsilon] = \mathbf{0}$. Thus, we have the moment conditions

$$E[\mathbf{z}\varepsilon] = E[\mathbf{z}(y - \mathbf{x}'\boldsymbol{\theta}_0)] = \mathbf{0}, \tag{7.120}$$

and the moment functions

$$\mathbf{m}((\mathbf{x},y,\mathbf{z}),\theta) = \mathbf{z}(y - \mathbf{x}'\boldsymbol{\theta}). \tag{7.121}$$

If $q = k$, then this is also a well-defined problem. Let $\mathbf{z_t}$ denote the corresponding k-dimensional observation vector of instrument to y_t. We assume that the strong law of large numbers holds, so that we have

$$\frac{1}{n} \sum_{t=1}^{n} \mathbf{m}((\mathbf{x}_t, y, \mathbf{z}_t), \widehat{\boldsymbol{\theta}_0}) \to E[\mathbf{m}((\mathbf{x}, y, \mathbf{z})\boldsymbol{\theta}_0] = \mathbf{0}, \text{ almost surely.} \tag{7.122}$$

Therefore, we solve

$$\frac{1}{n} \sum_{t=1}^{n} \mathbf{z}(y - \mathbf{x}'\widehat{\boldsymbol{\theta}_t}) = \mathbf{0} \tag{7.123}$$

which gives

$$\widehat{\boldsymbol{\theta}_n} = \left(\sum_{t=1}^{n} \mathbf{z_t}\mathbf{x_t}' \right)^{-1} \sum_{t=1}^{n} \mathbf{z_t} y = (\mathbf{Z}'\mathbf{X})^{-1}\mathbf{Z}'\mathbf{y} \tag{7.124}$$

with $\mathbf{Z} = [\mathbf{z_1}, ..., \mathbf{z_n}]$.

The definition of the CCF of sample implied that

$$E[\exp(is \cdot \mathbf{X}_T) - \phi(s, \theta, \mathbf{X}_T|\mathbf{X}_t)] = \mathbf{0}, \qquad \mathbf{s} \in \Re^n. \tag{7.125}$$

By taking real and imaginary parts of this function, we get the following pair of moment conditions:

$$\begin{aligned} E[\text{Re}(\exp(is \cdot \mathbf{X}_T) - \phi(s, \theta, \mathbf{X}_T|\mathbf{X}_t))] &= \mathbf{0}, \\ E[\text{Im}(\exp(is \cdot \mathbf{X}_T) - \phi(s, \theta, \mathbf{X}_T|\mathbf{X}_t))] &= \mathbf{0}. \end{aligned} \tag{7.126}$$

Thus, we can define a set of moment functions

$$\mathbf{m}(s, \theta, \mathbf{X}_T, \mathbf{X}_t) = \varepsilon_t(s, \theta, \mathbf{X}_T, \mathbf{X}_t) = \begin{bmatrix} \varepsilon_t^{\text{Re}}(s, \theta, \mathbf{X}_T, \mathbf{X}_t) \\ \varepsilon_t^{\text{Im}}(s, \theta, \mathbf{X}_T, \mathbf{X}_t) \end{bmatrix},$$

$$\varepsilon_t^{\text{Re}}(s, \boldsymbol{\theta}, \mathbf{X}_T, \mathbf{X}_t) = \text{Re}(\varepsilon_t(s, \boldsymbol{\theta}, \mathbf{X}_T, \mathbf{X}_t)) = \text{Re}(\exp(is \cdot \mathbf{X}_T) - \phi(s, \boldsymbol{\theta}, \mathbf{X}_T|\mathbf{X}_t)),$$

$$\varepsilon_t^{\text{Im}}(s, \boldsymbol{\theta}, \mathbf{X}_T, \mathbf{X}_t) = \text{Im}(\varepsilon_t(s, \boldsymbol{\theta}, \mathbf{X}_T, \mathbf{X}_t)) = \text{Im}(\exp(is \cdot \mathbf{X}_T) - \phi(s, \boldsymbol{\theta}, \mathbf{X}_T|\mathbf{X}_t)).$$

More generally, we can add a set of "instruments" or "weighting functions" to obtain more restrictions. So we can define the moment function based on the CCF as[43]

$$\mathbf{m}(s, \theta, \mathbf{X}_T, \mathbf{X}_t) = \boldsymbol{\varepsilon}_t(s, \theta, \mathbf{X}_T, \mathbf{X}_t) \otimes \mathbf{p}(\mathbf{X}_t),$$

where $\mathbf{p}(\mathbf{X}_t)$ are "instruments" independent of $\boldsymbol{\varepsilon}_t(s, \theta, \mathbf{X}_T, \mathbf{X}_t)$ and $\otimes$ is the Kronecker product. The SGMM estimator is of the form:

$$\widehat{\boldsymbol{\theta}}_{\text{SGMM}} = \arg\min_{\boldsymbol{\theta}} \left[\frac{1}{n} \sum_{t=1}^{n} \mathbf{m}(s, \boldsymbol{\theta}, \mathbf{X}_T, \mathbf{X}_t) \right]' \mathbf{W_n} \left[\frac{1}{n} \sum_{t=1}^{n} \mathbf{m}(s, \boldsymbol{\theta}, \mathbf{X}_T, \mathbf{X}_t) \right],$$

$$\theta \in \Theta.$$

Just as for other GMM estimators, the asymptotic variance of the SGMM estimator is minimized with the optimal weighting matrix $W_n = S^{-1}$, where S is the covariance matrix of the moment functions (see Chacko and Viceira [2001]). Under the usual regularity conditions, according to Chacko and Viceira (2001), the SGMM estimator, $\widehat{\theta}_{\text{SGMM}}$, inherits the optimality properties of GMM estimators such as consistency and asymptotic normality (see Hansen [1982]).

We can now apply SGMM to estimate stochastic volatility models like Model 3a and Model 3b. Recall that the marginal CCF of the sample is given by

$$\phi(s_x, \theta, X_{t+1}|X_t)$$
$$= e^{A(s_x,0,t,\theta)X_t+C(s_x,0,t,\theta)}\left(1 - \frac{B(s_x,0,t,\theta)\sigma_v^2}{2\kappa_v}\right)^{-2\kappa_v\alpha_v/\sigma_v^2} \qquad (7.127)$$

where $A(\cdot)$, $B(\cdot)$, and $C(\cdot)$ are the solutions of system (7.88) for Model 3a and Model 3b, respectively. Given a sample $\{X_t, t = 1, ..., T\}$, we have moment functions as follows:

$$\mathbf{m}(s_x, X_t, \theta) = \varepsilon_t(s_x, X_t, \theta) = \begin{bmatrix} \varepsilon_t^{\text{Re}}(s_x, X_t, \theta) \\ \varepsilon_t^{\text{Im}}(s_x, X_t, \theta) \end{bmatrix}, \qquad (7.128)$$
$$\varepsilon_t^{\text{Re}}(s_x, X_t, \theta) = (\cos(s_x X_{t+1}) - \text{Re}(\phi(s_x, 0, X_{t+1}|X_t))) \otimes \mathbf{p}(X_t),$$
$$\varepsilon_t^{\text{Im}}(s_x, X_t, \theta) = (\sin(s_x X_{t+1}) - \text{Im}(\phi(s_x, 0, X_{t+1}|X_t))) \otimes \mathbf{p}(X_t).$$

with $\phi(s_x, 0, X_{t+1}|X_t)$ defined as equation (7.127). Following Chacko and Viceira (2001), we can compute the n-th conditional moment by simple substitution $s_x = n$ into equation (7.128).

In order to construct the moment functions, Xiong (2004) uses the first six spectral moments by setting $s_x = 1, 2, ..., 6$ and $\mathbf{p}(X_t)$ as a T-dimensional vector of 1s. The estimates are biased and inconsistent (see Matyas [1999]). Using this methodology, Xiong finds the parameter estimates for Model 3a, shown in Table 7.5.

Table 7.5

	Estimate	Std.	T-ratio
κ	0.1152	0.0023	50.0870
α	-0.5086	0.0413	-12.3148
ω	1.0814	0.0170	63.6118
ψ	0.5781	0.0090	64.2333
γ	0.3522	0.0065	54.1846
ρ	-0.9710	0.0014	-693.5714
κ_ϖ	0.5483	0.0315	17.4063
α_ϖ	0.0261	0.0020	13.0500
σ_ϖ	0.1529	0.0171	8.9415
Log-likelihood	-11345.8013		

Source: Xiong (2004).

Simulation

Figure 7.14 shows the peak electricity prices (EP) superimposed by simulation paths for Model 1b. The plot also includes a sample plot of peak electricity prices, one typical simulated path, the 95% quantile, and 5% quantile of the simulation.

Figure 7.15 shows the offpeak EP superimposed by simulation paths for Model 1b. The plot also includes a sample plot of peak electricity prices, one typical simulated path, the 95% quantile, and 5% quantile of the simulation.

Figures 7.16 and 7.17 show a comparison of simulated price processes with Peak EP (Model 1b) and offpeak EP (Model 1b), respectively Note that the histogram in Figure 7.16 is of the change of the deseasonalized peak EP, and the histogram in Figure 7.17 is of the change of the deseasonalized offpeak EP. The overlaid black line is the corresponding distribution of the log returns of one typical simulated path. Note that this model underestimates the number of small changes and overestimates the medium-sized changes.

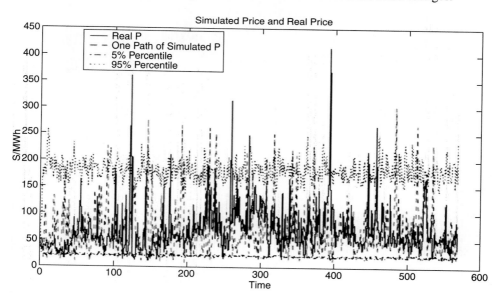

Figure 7.14   *Source: Xiong (2004). Reproduced with permission.*

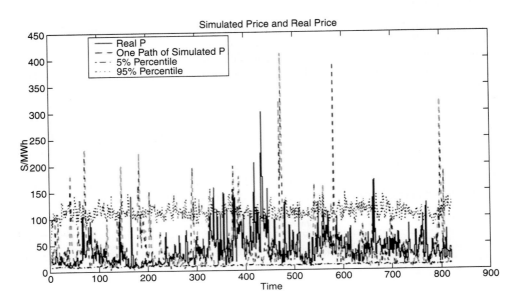

Figure 7.15 *Source: Xiong (2004). Reproduced with permission.*

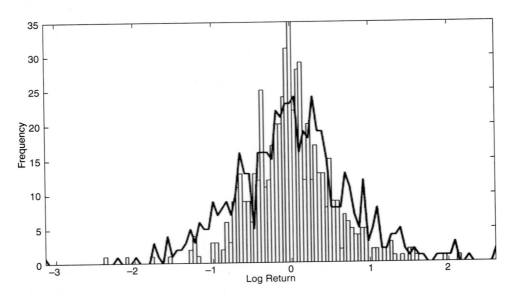

Figure 7.16 *Source: Xiong (2004). Reproduced with permission.*

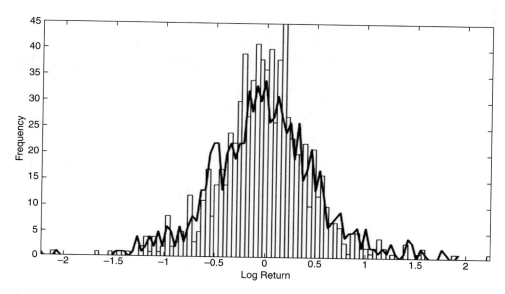

Figure 7.17 *Source: Xiong (2004). Reproduced with permission.*

7.13 PARAMETER ESTIMATION IN MATLAB

Refer to Appendix B to see the full listing of the Matlab code, written by Lei Xiong and Anthony Ware, that estimates the model parameters using the maximum likelihood methodology from Xiong (2004) given in the previous section. The market data Xiong and Ware used to calibrate and estimate the model parameters (stored in the array and used in the functions) is from the Alberta Nordic Pool (but not provided).

7.14 ENERGY COMMODITY MODELS

A common mean-reverting model used to model energy commodity prices for instruments like the crack spread contract[44] is the Schwartz-Ross model:

$$dS_t = \alpha(L - \ln S_t)S_t dt + \sigma S_t dW_t \tag{7.129}$$

where W_t is a standard Brownian motion, and α, L, and σ are all positive constant numbers. In this model, S_t mean reverts to the long-term mean $\widehat{L} = e^L$. Applying Ito's lemma for $X_t = \ln S_t$, we have

$$dX_t = \alpha(L - \frac{\sigma^2}{2\alpha} - X_t)dt + \sigma dW_t \tag{7.130}$$

which is an Ornstein-Uhlenbeck process. Rather than reversion to the long-term mean of the logarithm of the price, reversion to the price level itself can be modeled by the Dixit-Pinkyck model:

$$dS_t = \alpha(L - S_t)S_t dt + \sigma S_t dW_t \tag{7.131}$$

where W_t is a standard Brownian motion, and α, L, and σ are all positive constant numbers. Each of these parameters could be made time-varying and stochastic.

In contrast to other types of commodity prices like sugar and gold, energy commodity prices show no discernable trends. As shown in Figure 7.18, spot prices for crude oil (West Texas Intermediate at Cushing, Oklahoma), heating oil (New York Harbor), unleaded gasoline (New York Harbor), and natural gas (Henry Hub, LA) appear to fluctuate randomly.

Heating oil and gasoline prices tend to move with the crude oil prices, while spot markets of natural gas (discussed in the next section) peak periodically with no obvious warning. In general, energy commodities also have higher volatility than other types of commodities. Electricity commodities have the highest volatility, while financial commodities have the lowest, as shown in Figure 7.19, which displays the average annual historical spot market price volatility for various commodities from 1992 to 2001.

We can use these volatility estimates for σ in models (7.129) to (7.131).

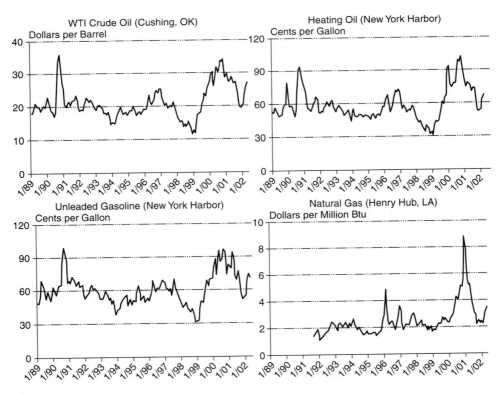

Figure 7.18   *Source: Commodity Futures Trading Commission (see Energy Information Administration/Derivatives and Risk Management in Energy Industries, U.S. Dept. of Energy, (2002), pg. 10).*

Commodity	Average Annual Volatility (Percent)	Market	Period
Electricity			
California-Oregon Border	309.9	Spot-Peak	1996-2001
Cinergy	435.7	Spot-Peak	1996-2001
Palo Verde	304.5	Spot-Peak	1996-2001
PJM	389.1	Spot-Peak	1996-2001
Natural Gas and Petroleum			
Light Sweet Crude Oil, LLS	38.3	Spot	1989-2001
Motor Gasoline, NYH	39.1	Spot	1989-2001
Heating Oil, NYH	38.5	Spot	1989-2001
Natural Gas	78.0	Spot	1992-2001
Financial			
Federal Funds Rate	85.7	Spot	1989-2001
Stock Index, S&P 500	15.1	Spot	1989-2001
Treasury Bonds, 30 Year	12.6	Spot	1989-2001
Metals			
Copper, LME Grade A	32.3	Spot	January 1989-August 2001
Gold Bar, Handy & Harman, NY	12.0	Spot	1989-2001
Silver Bar, Handy & Harman, NY	20.2	Spot	January 1989-August 2001
Platinum, Producers	22.6	Spot	January 1989-August 2001
Agriculture			
Coffee, BH OM Arabic	37.3	Spot	January 1989-August 2001
Sugar, World Spot	99.0	Spot	January 1989-August 2001
Corn, N. Illinois River	37.7	Spot	1994-2001
Soybeans, N. Illinois River	23.8	Spot	1994-2001
Cotton, East TX & OK	76.2	Spot	January 1989-August 2001
FCOJ, Florida Citrus Mutual	20.3	Spot	September 1998-December 2001
Meat			
Cattle, Amarillo	13.3	Spot	January 1989-August 2001
Pork Bellies	71.8	Spot	January 1989-August 2001

Figure 7.19 *Source: Energy Information Administration/Derivatives and Risk Management in the Energy Industries, U.S. Dept. of Energy (2002).*

7.15   NATURAL GAS

Natural Gas Markets

Natural gas is an important energy resource that consumers often demand and use as a cheaper alternative to other energy resources like electricity. The main use of natural gas[45] is in heating, power generation, as a household fuel, and as a chemical feedstock. Natural gas accounts for about a quarter of total energy consumption in North America. The deregulation of the natural gas industry in North America with the enactment of the American Natural Gas Policy Act of 1978 has led to a dynamic, highly competitive market with fluctuating prices. Before price deregulation, the market for domestic oil and gas derivatives was limited. Under price regulation, the U.S. Department of Energy (DOE), the Federal Energy Regulatory Commission (FERC), and the State public utility commissions (PUCs) directly or indirectly controlled the prices of domestic crude oil, petroleum products, wellhead natural gas, pipeline transmission, and retail gas service.

As a result of this deregulated environment, market participants like natural gas producers found themselves exposed to volatile price movements and to counterparty performance risk, which led to a substantial increase in the need for risk management. This in turn, led to the development of spot and forward markets in natural gas. As a result, the New York Mercantile Exchange (NYMEX) launched the world's first natural gas futures contract in April 1990. Since then, gas futures contracts have been widely used to hedge against price fluctuations in this volatile market. The standardization of contract terms, relatively small contract size, fungibility, lack of requirement of physical delivery, and rigorous performance requirements attracted many market participants like natural gas producers, marketers, processors, utilities, and end users, as well as speculators. Volume and open interest have grown rapidly establishing the gas contract as the fastest-growing instrument in NYMEX history. In 2002, the daily average volume of NYMEX market exceeded 97,000 contracts, which involves several times the average daily consumption of gas in North America. Figure 7.20 shows the major pricing points (hubs) for natural gas in the U.S. The Henry Hub in Louisiana is one the major hubs.

World trade in natural gas is divided among major regional markets dominated by pipeline infrastructures that provide the means of transporting the gas from producers to consumers and a single worldwide market for liquefied natural gas (LNG). The United States is the largest pipeline gas market. In 2000, the United States produced 19.3 trillion cubic feet of natural gas and consumed 23 trillion cubic feet. The supply gap was covered

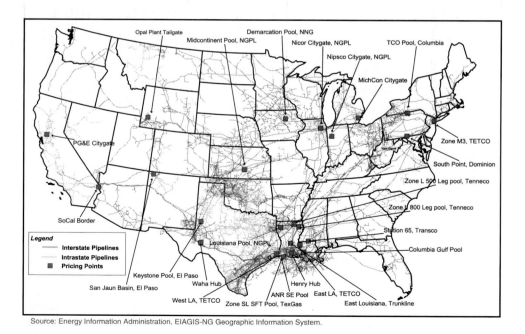

Source: Energy Information Administration, EIAGIS-NG Geographic Information System.

Figure 7.20 *Source: Energy Information Administration/ Derivatives and Risk Management in Energy Industries, U.S. Department of Energy (2002), pg. 19.*

by 3.2 trillion cubic feet of imports from Canada and 0.5 trillion cubic feet of LNG from the world market. The European countries produced 10.5 trillion cubic feet and consumed 16.2 trillion cubic feet, with the supply gap covered by Russian imports and small amounts of imported LNG. Russia was the world's largest producer of natural gas in 2000 at 20.3 trillion cubic feet, followed by the United States and Canada. Major exporters of LNG are Indonesia, Malaysia, Australia, Qatar, Oman, Nigeria, and Trinidad. Japan is the largest importer of LNG.

Natural gas, like electricity, is a network industry in the sense that all suppliers and users are linked by the physical distribution system for the commodity. Pipelines have no effective competition for moving gas within the United States. Figure 7.20 shows the general locations served by major pipelines and several of the spot markets (pricing points) that have emerged at major trans-shipment points (hubs).

Location arbitrage does not work as well for natural gas and electricity as it does for crude oil. Because gas pipelines and power lines have essentially no competitors, frustrated customers cannot buy supplies "off system." In addition, it is difficult to achieve competitive transmission pricing. Consequently, transmission charges are set in noncompetitive markets, with the result that arbitrary price differences between and across markets, not based on marginal costs, can persist in more or less independent, local markets.

Natural Gas Spot Prices

There are a number of fundamental factors that drive complex gas price behavior, including extraction, storage, transport, weather, policies, technological advances, and so on. Figure 7.21 illustrates the plot of daily gas spot prices, which are measured in dollars per million British thermal units (MMBTU), at the Henry Hub in Louisiana, one of the largest hubs in the U.S., from January 2, 1992 to December 30, 1999.

There are several important properties associated with the behavior of gas spot prices. Like electricity prices, gas prices exhibit mean-reversion. In addition, while prices move up and down frequently, they actually oscillate around an equilibrium level from the point of long-term view, which is the effect of mean-reversion.[46] The mean-reversion in natural gas appears to be correlated with the reaction of the market to events such as floods, summer heat waves, and other news-making events, which can create new and unexpected supply-and-demand imbalances in the market. A correction to either the supply side, to match the demand side, or the actual dissipation of the event, such as the temperatures reverting to their average seasonal levels, tends to cause the natural gas prices to come back to their average levels.[47] The speed of mean-reversion depends on how quickly it takes for supply and demand to return to a balanced state or for the events to dissipate. The long-term mean around which the prices oscillate is determined by the cost of production and the normal level of demand.[48]

Seasonality is also an important property of gas prices. Seasonality results primarily from regular demand fluctuations, which are driven by recurring weather-related factors. As we know, natural gas is a primary residential and commercial space heating fuel and is used increasingly as a fuel for electricity generation. The cold winter weather results in above-average consumption of natural gas, while in some hot summers, demand increases for power generation to run air conditioning and other cooling devices.[49] On the other hand,

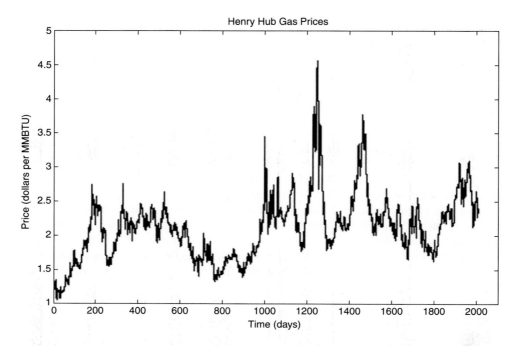

Figure 7.21 *Source: Xu (2004). Reproduced with permission.*

"the difficulty of storage and the limitation of transmission capacity make the supply side not elastic enough to match the suddenly increased demand side very quickly."[50]

7.16   GAS PRICING MODELS

We can model gas prices similar to electricity prices. Consider gas spot prices as the sum of a seasonal term $f(t)$ and an unseasonalized state term X_t, where X_t follows a one-factor mean reverting process with constant long-term mean and time-dependent volatility.

One-Factor Model

Following Xu (2004), let

$$S_t = f(t) + X_t \tag{7.132}$$

where

$$f(t) = bt + \sum_{i=1}^{N} \beta_i \cos\left(\frac{2\pi it}{365}\right) + \nu_i \sin\left(\frac{2\pi it}{365}\right) \tag{7.133}$$

and

$$dX_t = \alpha(L - X_t)dt + \sigma(t)X_t^r dW_t \tag{7.134}$$

where

$$\sigma(t) = \exp\left(c + \sum_{j=1}^{K} \lambda_j \cos\left(\frac{2\pi it}{365}\right) + \omega_j \sin\left(\frac{2\pi jt}{365}\right)\right)$$

where W_t is a Brownian motion, $r = 0, \frac{1}{2}$, or 1, and $b, \beta_i's, v_i's, \alpha, L, c, \lambda_j's$, and $\omega_i's$ are all constant. The volatility term $\sigma(t)$ is of an exponential form in order to ensure that it is positive. The linear term bt in $f(t)$ contributes to capture the tendency of the prices. The sine and cosine function in $f(t)$ and $\sigma(t)$ make them move up and down periodically as seasons change. Furthermore, the trigonometric functions corresponding to $N = 1$ and $K = 1$ capture the annual seasonality, because the period of these functions is 365, the number of days in the year; the trigonometric functions corresponding to $N = 2$ and $K = 2$ capture the semiannual seasonality, because the period of these functions is half a year.

Using Henry Hub prices from January 2, 1992 to December 30, 1999, Xu (2004) estimates the parameters of the one-factor model without seasonality using maximum likelihood estimation, as shown in Table 7.6.

Table 7.6

	Model 1 $r = 0$	Model 2 $r = 1/2$
α	0.0181	0.0139
L	2.1441	2.1526
σ	0.0870	0.0549

Source: Xu (2004).

Two-Factor Model

Consider a system of SDEs describing these models:

$$\begin{cases} dS_t = \alpha(L_t - S_t)dt + \sigma S_t^r dW_t^1 \\ dL_t = \mu(\gamma - L_t)dt + \tau L_t^r dW_t^2 \end{cases} \tag{7.135}$$

where $\alpha, \sigma, \mu, \gamma$, and τ are constant and $r = 0, \frac{1}{2}$, or 1. We assume that the Wiener processes dW_t^1 and dW_t^2 are uncorrelated. In this two-factor model, the natural gas spot price long-term mean is a random variable that follows its own mean-reverting process rather than geometric Brownian motion. Seasonality can be incorporated into this model. The gas spot price can be viewed as the sum of a seasonal term $f(t)$ and an unseasonalized state term X_t, which follows a two-factor mean-reverting process.

Mathematically, let

$$S_t = f(t) + X_t$$

where

$$f(t) = bt + \sum_{i=1}^{N} \beta_i \cos\left(\frac{2\pi it}{365}\right) + \eta_i \sin\left(\frac{2\pi it}{365}\right)$$

and X_t follows a mean-reverting process described by

$$\begin{cases} dS_t = \alpha(L_t - S_t)dt + \sigma(t)S_t^r\, dW_t^1 \\ dL_t = \mu(\gamma - L_t)dt + \tau L_t^r\, dW_t^2 \end{cases}$$

where

$$\sigma(t) = \exp\left(c + \sum_{j=1}^{K} \lambda_j \cos\left(\frac{2\pi i t}{365}\right) + \omega_j \sin\left(\frac{2\pi j t}{365}\right)\right).$$

In the preceding equations, W_t^i's are Wiener processes, $r = 0, \frac{1}{2}$, or 1, and b, β_i's, η_i's, α, μ, γ, τ, c, λ_j's, and ω_j's are all constant, while N and K are positive integers.

To price futures contracts on natural gas, we take the expectation of (7.135) under the risk-neutral measure:

$$\begin{cases} dS_t = \widetilde{\alpha}(L_t - S_t)dt + \sigma\sqrt{S_t}dW_t^1 \\ dL_t = \widetilde{\mu}(\gamma - L_t)dt + \tau\sqrt{L_t}dW_t^2 \end{cases}$$

where $\widetilde{\alpha}$, $\widetilde{\mu}$, and $\widetilde{\gamma}$ are the risk-neutral parameters, and we assume a square root process ($r = 1/2$). We then find that

$$\begin{cases} d\bar{S}_t = \widetilde{\alpha}(\bar{L}_t - \bar{S}_t)dt \\ d\bar{L}_t = \widetilde{\mu}(\widetilde{\gamma} - \bar{L}_t)dt \end{cases} \tag{7.136}$$

where $\bar{S}_t$ and $\bar{L}_t$ are the expectation values of S_t and L_t at time t respectively. Solving the second ODE for $\bar{L}_t$ with boundary condition that at $t = t_0$, $\bar{L}_t = L_{t_0}$, we obtain:

$$\bar{L}_t = (L_{t_0} - \widetilde{\gamma})e^{\widetilde{\mu}(t_0-t)} + \widetilde{\gamma} \tag{7.137}$$

Plugging in (7.136) into the first ODE in (7.135) for $\bar{S}$, with the boundary condition that at $t = t_0$, $\bar{S}_t = S_{t_0}$, we obtain that

$$\bar{S}_t = S_{t_0}e^{\widetilde{\alpha}(t_0-t)} + \frac{\widetilde{\alpha}}{\widetilde{\alpha} - \widetilde{\mu}}(L_{t_0} - \widetilde{\gamma})(e^{\widetilde{\mu}(t_0-t)} - e^{\widetilde{\alpha}(t_0-t)}) - \widetilde{\gamma}(1 - e^{\widetilde{\alpha}(t_0-t)})$$

$$= e^{\widetilde{\alpha}(t-T)}S_{t_0} + \frac{\widetilde{\alpha}}{\widetilde{\alpha} - \widetilde{\mu}}(e^{\widetilde{\mu}(t_0-t)} - e^{\widetilde{\alpha}(t_0-t)})L_{t_0} + \frac{\widetilde{\mu}\widetilde{\gamma}}{\widetilde{\alpha} - \widetilde{\mu}}(e^{\widetilde{\mu}(t_0-t)} - 1) -$$

$$\frac{\widetilde{\mu}\widetilde{\gamma}}{\widetilde{\alpha} - \widetilde{\mu}}(e^{\widetilde{\mu}(t_0-t)} - 1).$$

Because $F^{\widetilde{\theta}}(t, T, S_t) = \bar{S}_t$, and at initial time $t_0 = t$, $\bar{S}_{t_0} = S_t$, and $\bar{L}_{t_0} = L_{t_0}$, the gas futures price under the risk-neutral measure is

$$F^{\widetilde{\theta}}(t, T, S_t)$$

$$e^{\widetilde{\alpha}(t-T)}S_t + \frac{\widetilde{\alpha}}{\widetilde{\alpha} - \widetilde{\mu}}(e^{\widetilde{\mu}(t-T)} - e\widetilde{\alpha}(t - T)L_t +$$

$$\frac{\widetilde{\mu}\widetilde{\gamma}}{\widetilde{\alpha} - \widetilde{\mu}}(e^{\widetilde{\mu}(t-T)} - 1) - \frac{\widetilde{\mu}\widetilde{\gamma}}{\widetilde{\alpha} - \widetilde{\mu}}(e^{\widetilde{\mu}(t-T)} - 1). \tag{7.138}$$

If seasonality is included, then the futures price is

$$F^{\widetilde{\theta}}(t, T, S_t) = f(T) + e^{\widetilde{\alpha}(t-T)}(S_t - f(t)) +$$
$$\frac{\widetilde{\alpha}}{\widetilde{\alpha} - \widetilde{\mu}}(e^{\widetilde{\mu}(t-T)} - e\widetilde{\alpha}(t - T)L_t +$$
$$\frac{\widetilde{\mu}\widetilde{\gamma}}{\widetilde{\alpha} - \widetilde{\mu}}(e^{\widetilde{\mu}(t-T)} - 1) - \frac{\widetilde{\mu}\widetilde{\gamma}}{\widetilde{\alpha} - \widetilde{\mu}}(e^{\widetilde{\mu}(t-T)} - 1). \qquad (7.139)$$

Calibration

To calibrate and estimate the parameters of the model, maximum likelihood estimation can be used. *Calibration* is essentially a process of matching the information observed from the market so that the better the information matched, the more accurate the calibration. Seasonality can be inferred from the natural gas spot prices and futures prices. To reveal the seasonal term $f(t)$, a natural idea is to exploit the information in both spot and futures prices.

One-Factor Model Calibration

Denote the historical spot prices by $\{S_t\}_{t=1}^n$, and the futures prices by $\{F_{t,T_{ii}}|t = 1, 2, ..., n; i = 1, 2, ..., m\}$, where T_{ti} is the ith delivery after t, and m is the number of futures prices that we can observe at time t. These are the data we can obtain from the real market. On the other hand, under the assumption that the spot price follows the process described by equations (7.132)–(7.134), we have the theoretical futures price function $F^{\widetilde{\theta}}(t, T, S_t)$ for a one-factor model with seasonality given by

$$F^{\widetilde{\theta}}(t, T, S_t) = e^{\widetilde{\alpha}(t-T)}(S_t - \widetilde{L} - f(t)) + \widetilde{L} + f(T) \qquad (7.140)$$

where t is the observing time, T is the delivery time, and $\widetilde{\theta}$ is the set of active parameters— i.e., $[b, \beta_1, \beta_2, ..., \beta_N, \eta_1, \eta_2, ..., \eta_N, \widetilde{\alpha}, \widetilde{L}]$.

To match the real market data to the model, we need to find some appropriate parameters to make the theoretical futures prices and the actual futures prices as close as possible. If the distance between two vectors is defined in Euclidean space, then the estimation of $\widetilde{\theta}$ can be obtained by minimizing the sum of the squares of the differences between $F^{\widetilde{Q}}(t, T_{ti}, S_t)$ and $F_{t,T_{ii}}$, for $t = 1, 2, ..., n; i = 1, 2, ..., m$. In particular, we need to solve:

$$\widetilde{\theta} = \arg \min_{\widetilde{\theta}} \sum_{t=1}^n \sum_{i=1}^n (F^{\widetilde{\theta}}(t, T_{ti}, S_t) - F_{t,T_{ti}})^2 \qquad (7.141)$$

Xu (2004) estimates the risk-neutral parameters for the one-factor mean-reverting model with seasonality ($r = 0$) by minimizing (7.141) using artificial and real data (Henry Hub prices from January 2, 1992 to December 30, 1999), shown in Table 7.7.

The estimated seasonality parameters for model (7.133) (for $r = 0$, $1/2$, and 1) are given in Table 7.8[51] where 0 is used to denote values for some value less than $1e - 10$.

Table 7.7

	For artificial data			For real data
	Given	Mean of Est.	Std. of Est.	Est.
$\tilde{\alpha}$	0.0070	0.0070	1.4569e-13	0.0073
$\tilde{L}$	1.7000	1.7000	1.8859e-11	1.6663

Source: Xu (2004).

Table 7.8

	For artificial data			For real data
	Given	Mean of Est.	Std. of Est.	Est.
b	0.0003	0.0003	0	0.0003
β_1	0.1500	0.1500	0	0.1639
β_2	0.0500	0.0500	0	0.0558
η_1	-0.0500	-0.0500	0	-0.0468
η_2	-0.0300	-0.0300	0	-0.0295

Source: Xu (2004).

Two-Factor Model Calibration

Calibration in a two-factor model is an extension of calibration for a one-factor model. First, we "excavate" the hidden things, including the seasonal term $f(t)$ and the long-term mean-reversion factor L_t by matching the actual futures prices with the theoretical futures prices.[52] In this process, we can obtain X_t, parameters for $f(t)$ and some risk-neutralized parameters. Second, with the known X_t and L_t's values, we get parameters in these two stochastic processes by the maximum likelihood (ML) method.[53]

To find the hidden factor L_t and seasonal term $f(t)$ from futures prices, let

$$A_i = f(T_{ii}) + e^{\tilde{\alpha}(t-T_{ii})}(S_t - f(t)) + \frac{\tilde{\mu}\tilde{\gamma}}{\tilde{\alpha} - \tilde{\mu}}(e^{\tilde{\mu}(t-T_{ii})} - 1)$$

and

$$B_i = \frac{\tilde{\alpha}}{\tilde{\alpha} - \tilde{\mu}}(e^{\tilde{\mu}(t-T_{ii})} - e^{\tilde{\alpha}(t-T_{ii})}).$$

Then by equation (7.138), we have the futures price function $F^{\tilde{\theta}}(t, T_{ii}, S_t) = A_i + B_i L_t$. Notice that the futures price function involves not only $[\tilde{\alpha}, \tilde{\mu}, \tilde{\gamma}]$ and L_t, but also $f(t)$; hence, we can get all of them by matching futures prices.

Here, we let $\tilde{\theta} = [\tilde{\alpha}, \tilde{\mu}, \tilde{\gamma}, b, \beta_1, \ldots, \beta_N, \eta_1, \ldots, \eta_N]$ In the same way as before, L_t can be defined as a function of $\tilde{\theta}$:

$$L_t(\tilde{\theta}) = \frac{\sum_{i=1}^{m}(B_i F_{t,T_{ii}} - A_i B_i)}{\sum_{i=1}^{m} B_i^2} \tag{7.142}$$

Then we free $\widetilde{\theta}$ to obtain the optimal one by

$$\widetilde{\theta} = \arg \min_{\theta \in \Re^{n_0}} \sum_{t=1}^{n} \sum_{i=1}^{m} (F^{\widetilde{\theta}}(t, T_{ti}, S_t, L_t(\widetilde{\theta})) - F_{t,T_{ti}})^2 \qquad (7.143)$$

where n_0 is the vector length of $\widetilde{\theta}$. With the obtained $\widetilde{\theta}$, $\{L_t\}_{t=1}^{n}$, $\{f(t)\}_{t=1}^{n}$, and hence $\{X_t\}_{t=1}^{n}$ are all easily computed.

Table 7.9 shows the estimation of risk-neutral parameters of (7.138) for artificial and real data of Henry Hub prices.

Figure 7.22 shows the real and estimated seasonal term based on minimizing the sum of squares of the differences of the two-factor model is (7.143) for Henry Hub actual price data.

Figure 7.23 shows the estimated spot price X_t and long-term mean-reversion parameter L_t of the model using real data.

Xu (2004) estimates the parameters of the model in (7.134) for both artificial and real data using Henry Hub prices from January 2, 1992 to December 30, 1999. When $r = 0$ in equation (7.134), the parameters are given in Table 7.10.

When $r = 1/2$, the parameters are given in Table 7.11.

The parameters of the seasonal factor for all three models (e.g., $r = 0$, $1/2$, and 1) are shown in Table 7.12.

Figure 7.24 shows the fit of gas futures matching (by optimizing (7.143) between actual and estimated futures prices using a two-factor model with seasonality.

In the middle plot, the bold curve is the real futures curve. The thinner curve is the graph of the futures function given by (7.138). In the lower plot, the bold curve is the real futures curve. The thinner curve is the values of 250 paths of S_t simulated by equation (7.134), where the risk-neutral parameters shown in Table 7.5 are plugged in, and $r = 1$. For comparison, the upper plot shows the seasonal term $f(t)$ (solid curve), and the seasonal volatility function $\sigma(t)$ (dashed curve).

For analysis of the long-run behavior and forecasting of natural gas prices (as well as oil and coal) using stochastic dynamics of the price evolution, see Pindyk (1998). Pinkyk (1998) estimates various models using Kalman filter methods. Pindyk shows that under a theory of depletable resource production and pricing using the actual behavior of real prices over the past century, nonstructural models should incorporate mean-reversion to a stochastically fluctuating trend line that reflects long-run (total) marginal cost, which is unobservable.[54]

Table 7.9

	For artificial data			For real data
	Given	Mean of Est.	Std. of Est.	Est.
$\widetilde{\alpha}$	0.0110	0.0110	0	0.0111
$\widetilde{\mu}$	0.0020	0.0020	0	0.0018
$\widetilde{\gamma}$	2.0000	2.0000	0	2.0028

Source: Xu (2004). Reproduced with permission.

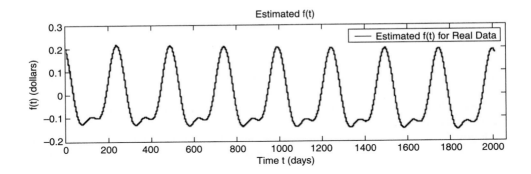

Figure 7.22   *Source: Xu (2004). Reproduced with permission.*

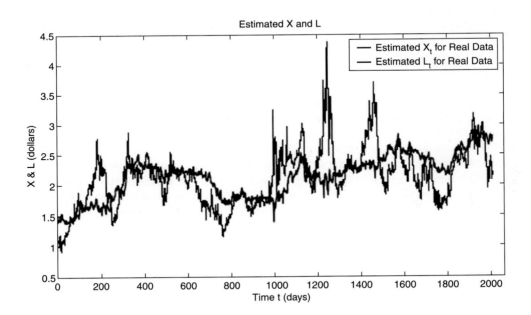

Figure 7.23   *Source: Xu (2004). Reproduced with permission.*

Table 7.10

	For artificial data			For real data
	Given	Mean of Est.	Std. of Est.	Est.
α	0.0240	0.0252	0.0045	0.0244
c	-2.6000	-2.6025	0.0180	-2.5616
λ_1	0.4000	0.4021	0.0203	0.4105
λ_2	0.0800	0.0777	0.0267	0.0790
ω_1	-0.2000	-0.7983	0.0202	-0.4982
ω_2	-0.0700	-0.0683	0.0231	-0.0660
μ	0.0050	0.0068	0.0030	0.0048
τ	0.0300	0.0299	0.0004	0.0329
γ	2.3000	2.2833	0.1297	2.2860

Source: Xu (2004).

Table 7.11

	For artificial data			For real data
	Given	Mean of Est.	Std. of Est.	Est.
α	0.0220	0.0230	0.0048	0.0221
c	-3.0000	-3.0030	0.0169	-2.9894
λ_1	0.3800	0.3787	0.0212	0.3791
λ_2	0.0750	0.0743	0.0198	0.0748
ω_1	-0.1800	-0.1828	0.0229	-0.1826
ω_2	-0.0300	-0.0333	0.0224	-0.0317
μ	0.0050	0.0075	0.0037	0.0050
τ	0.0230	0.0228	0.0004	0.0230
γ	2.3000	2.2866	0.1419	2.2793

Source: Xu (2004).

Table 7.12

	For artificial data			For real data
	Given	Mean of Est.	Std. of Est.	Est.
b	-0.0001	-0.0001	0	-1.4476e-5
β_1	0.1500	0.1500	0	0.1483
β_2	0.0600	0.0600	0	0.0574
η_1	-0.0500	-0.0500	0	-0.0527
η_2	-0.0300	-0.0300	0	-0.0292

Source: Xu (2004).

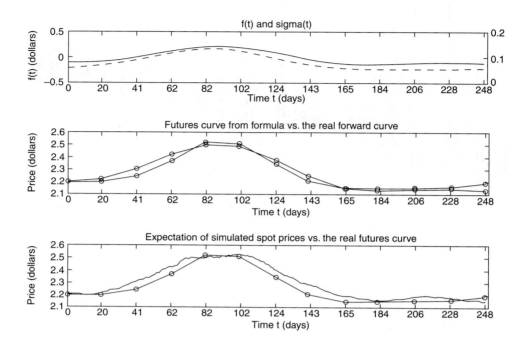

Figure 7.24   *Source: Xu (2004). Reproduced with permission.*

7.17   NATURAL GAS PRICING IN MATLAB

Refer to Appendix B to see the full listing of the key Matlab code, written by James Xu (2004), for pricing of natural gas futures using real-time gas data.

7.18   NATURAL GAS AND ELECTRICITY SWAPS

When one or both parties in a market face a spot market price that differs from the price in a reference market, basis risk may emerge. To manage this risk, forwards and futures contracts cannot be used because they work only for price certainty in a unified market. Instead, other derivative contract instruments like a basis contract may be needed to manage the resulting basis risk. Basis swaps, which are common in natural gas markets, are used to manage this risk. A basis swap allows an individual to lock in a fixed price at a location other than the delivery point of the futures contract. This can be done either as a physical or a financial deal. The most widely used natural gas futures market calls for delivery at the Henry Hub price in Louisiana. Basis contracts are available in the OTC markets to hedge locational, product, and even temporal differences between exchange-traded standard contracts and the particular circumstances of contract users. For example, suppose a local distribution company (LDC) in Tennessee can enter into a swap contract with a natural gas producer, using the Henry Hub prices as the reference price; however, the LDC would lose price certainty if the local spot market price differed from the Henry Hub price, as shown in Figure 7.25.

In this example, when the Henry Hub price is higher than the Tennessee price by more than it was at the initiation of the swap contract, the LDC gains, because its payment from the producer will exceed the amount it pays to buy gas in its local market.[55] Effectively, the LDC will pay less per thousand cubic feet than the fixed amount the LDC pays the producer. Conversely, if the Tennessee price is lower, the producer's payment will not cover the LDC's gas bill in its local market. In a natural gas basis swap, the OTC trader would pay the LDC the difference between the Tennessee price and the Henry Hub price (for the nominal amount of gas) in exchange for a fixed payment. The variety of contractual provisions is unlimited. For example, the flexible payment could be defined as a "daily or monthly average (weighted or unaveraged) price difference; it could be capped; or it could required the LDC to share the costs when the contract's ceiling price is exceeded."[56] What this OTC contract does is to close the gap between the Henry Hub price and the price on the LDC's local spot market, allowing the LDC to achieve price certainty.

The traders supplying basis contracts can survive only "if the basis difference they pay—averaged over time and adjusted for both financing charges and the time value of money—is less than the fixed payment from the LDC."[57] Competition among OTC traders can only reduce the premium for supplying basis protection. Reducing the underlying cause of volatile price differences would "require more pipeline capacity, more storage capacity, cost-based transmission pricing, and other physical and economic changes to the delivery system itself."[58]

Similarly, in the electricity futures markets, most firms have price exposure at delivery points such as COB, Palo Verde, as well as the PJM Interconnect and other locations. Thus, a firm that uses the NYMEX futures contract to manage price risk at other locations is exposed to basis risk—price differences at different locations. Traders and firms can use basis swaps and contracts to hedge their risk. Basis markets have evolved, allowing firms to hedge risks at most major trading points in the United States and Canada. These

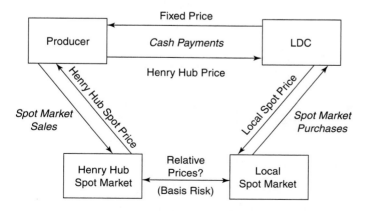

Figure 7.25   *Source: Energy Information Administration/ Derivatives and Risk Management in Energy Industries, U.S. Department of Energy (2002).*

basis markets are quite liquid, with narrow bid offer spreads (typically less than $0.02, but can be wider during volatile periods) and the ability to trade substantial volumes. Basis markets have also begun to develop in the electricity markets in the Western U.S. (e.g., COB, Palo Verde, and Mid-Columbia). Basis markets need not be physically connected by transmission wire or pipeline. For example, there is a Sumas natural gas basis market, even though it would be extremely hard to move gas from this point to the Henry Hub. Following Stoft, Belden, Goldman, and Pickle (1998), we illustrate financial transactions for different users to show the mechanics of these basis swaps.

Generator

To lock in an electricity price in Denver, a generator could sell a futures contract (or a price swap) and a basis swap (see Figure 7.26). Assume that the generator sells a futures contract for $18/MWh for delivery in six months and sells a basis swap agreeing to pay the Denver spot price in exchange for the COB price plus a premium. In six months, the generator sells electricity in Denver and receives the Denver spot price (B), pays the Denver spot price (B) to the basis counterparty, receives the COB spot price (A) plus a fixed premium from the counterparty, and buys a futures contract for the COB spot price (A). All of these transactions cancel out, and the generator should expect to receive the fixed price for the original futures contract, $18/MWh, in addition to the premium received from the basis counterparty. The preceding example represents a financial transaction. Physical transactions are also possible, where the generator provides power to the basis swap counterparty in return for the COB spot price plus a premium.

One risk associated with these transactions is that the generator may be unable to buy a futures contract at COB for the futures price used in the basis swap transaction. One way to avoid this risk is to use price swaps rather than futures contracts. The generator then pays

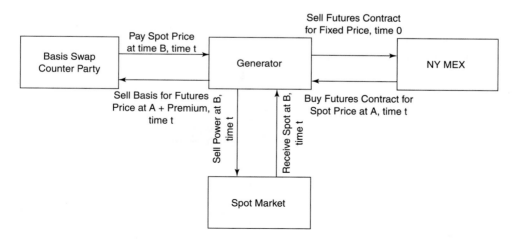

Figure 7.26 *Source: Stoft, S., Belden, T., Goldman, C., and Pickle, S. (1998), 35.*

the price swap counterparty the average of the Dow Jones COB Index, which would cancel out the average of the Dow Jones COB Index from the basis counterparty.[59]

End User

To lock in a fixed price for electricity in Denver, an end user would buy a futures contract (or price swap) and a basis swap (see Figure 7.27). Assume that the end user buys a futures contract for $18/MWh and agrees to pay the COB spot price plus a premium in return for the variable spot market price in Denver. The end user can execute this agreement physically or financially. In either case, the end user locks in an electricity price of $18/MWh plus the premium. The end user can also buy a price swap, rather than a futures contract, to lock in the price in Denver or other locations.

In a price swap, the buyer of the swap agrees to pay a fixed price, which is negotiated at the time of the transaction, and receive a price equal to the simple average of a given month's nonfirm, on-peak, COB index price published in the *Wall Street Journal*.[60] Although swaps can trade in any size, they are typically traded in increments of 25 MW on-peak. Because peak hours in the western United States include 16 hours per day (6 AM to 10 PM), six days a week (Monday through Saturday), the total notional volume equals the number of MWs multiplied by the number of days in the month (excluding Sundays and holidays), multiplied by 16. Just like the buyer of a future, the buyer of a swap profits when prices increase and loses when prices decrease relative to the fixed payment level. When the average of the on-peak Dow Jones COB prices exceeds the fixed price, the buyer of the swap (the fixed price payor) receives a positive cash flow from the transaction. When the average of the on-peak Dow Jones COB prices is below the fixed price, the seller of the swap receives a positive cash flow from the transaction. Swaps can be used to hedge or to speculate.

For example, to lock in an electricity price for July 1998, an end user would buy a price swap (see Figure 7.28). Assume that the end user agrees to pay $25/MWh and to

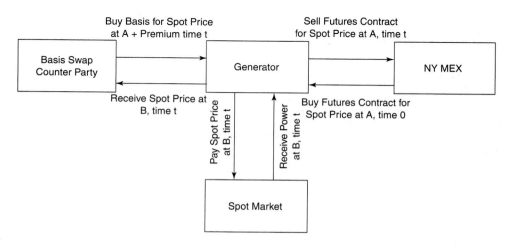

Figure 7.27   *Source: Stoft, S., Belden, T., Goldman, C., and Pickle, S. (1998), 35.*

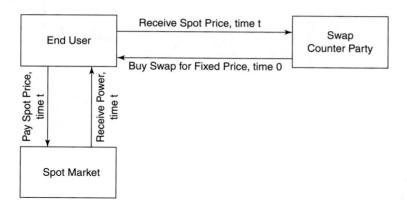

Figure 7.28 *Source: Stoft, S., Belden, T., Goldman, C., and Pickle, S. (1998), pg. 35.*

receive the average Dow Jones COB price. If the spot price at COB in July 2006 averaged $20/MWh, the end user would buy electricity in the spot market for $20/MWh, would receive $20/MWh from the swap counterparty, and would pay the swap counterparty $25/MWh. Using the price swap, the end user has a guaranteed electricity price of $25/MWh, but would be unable to take advantage of the lower-priced electricity if the price were to fall below $25/MWh.

Marketers can also execute these transactions on behalf of generators and end users in order to guarantee them a fixed price at a location other than the COB or Palo Verde. Marketers can also act as basis counterparties for generators and end users in these types of transactions. Generators and end users might work through marketers if they are uncomfortable using the financial tools associated with executing these transactions properly.

For a discussion of hedging and speculating in electricity and commodities using swaps and futures, see Stoft, Belden, Goldman, and Pickle (1998) and Schwartz (1997).

ENDNOTES

1. Lucia, J. and Schwartz, E. (2001), pg. 2.
2. Id., pg. 2.
3. Deng, S. (1999), pg. 4.
4. Id., pg. 2. In addition, regulatory issues such as market rules and market structure may also have an impact on the behavior in competitive electricity markets and, consequently, on their differences across countries.
5. Lucia, J. and Schwartz, E. (2001), pg. 2.
6. See EIA Report, Annual Energy Outlook (2002).
7. Dorr, U. (2003), pg. 3.
8. Id., pg. 3.
9. Lucia, J. and Schwartz, E. (2001), pg. 13.
10. Lucia, J. and Schwartz, E. (2001), pg. 15.
11. Id., pg. 15.

12. Id., pg. 15.
13. Lucia, J. and Schwartz, E. (2001), pg. 20.
14. Established in January 1993, and first covering the Norwegian market, the Nord pool is currently a non-mandatory common multinational market that also includes Sweden since January 1996, Finland since June 15, 1998, and the western part of Denmark since July 1, 1999. Nord Pool organizes two markets, a "physical market" (*Elspot*) and a "financial market" (*Eltermin* and *Eloption*) and also provides clearing services. Elspot is a "spot" market where day-ahead electric power contracts are traded for physical delivery for each one of the 24 hours during the following day.

Every contract in Elspot refers to a load, in megawatt-hours (WHw, 1MWh equals 1000 kWh), during a given hour, and a price per MWh. A price called the system price is fixed separately for each hour for the next day, based on the balance between supply and demand for all participants in the whole market area (the so-called Nordic Power Exchange Area), without considering capacity limits ("bottlenecks") in the grid among countries. A system price can thus be defined as the market clearing price at which market participants trade electricity for the entire exchange area when no transmission constrains apply. It is also used as a reference price in settlements at the Nord Pool's financial market.

15. $S_t = \alpha + \beta D_t + \sum_{t=2}^{12} \beta_t M_{tt} + X_t$ and $\ln S_t = \alpha + \beta D_t + \sum_{t=2}^{12} \beta_t M_{tt} + Y_t$

16. Lucia, J. and Schwartz, E. (2005), pg. 20.
17. Doerr, U. (2003), pg. 14.
18. Id.
19. Id., pg. 14.
20. Id., pg. 1.
21. Id., pg. 1.
22. Id., pg. 1.
23. Doerr, U. (2003), pg. 21.
24. See London (2004) for an implementation in C++ of the LSM applied to American equity options.
25. Doerr, U. (2003), pg. 22.
26. These sums have at most one non-zero addend.
27. See Doerr, U. (2003). Reproduced with permission.
28. Doerr, U. (2003), pg. 25.
29. Doerr, U. (2003), pg. 26.
30. Doerr, U. (2003), pg. 27.
31. The strikes of the downswings were set equal to the strikes of the upswings.
32. Doerr, U. (2004), pg. 34.
33. Deng, S. (1999), pg. 24.
34. Id., pg. 25.
35. Id., pg. 25.
36. See Deng (1999).
37. Deng, S. (1999).
38. Xiong, L. (2004), pg. 26.
39. Reproduced with permission.

40. As $t \rightarrow \infty$, there exists a limiting distribution for X_t. The limiting distribution is called the stationary distribution and its Fourier transform is called the stationary characteristic function (see Grimmett, G. and Stirzaker, D. (1982)).

41. Here we use the compound trapezoidal rule to approximate the integral, and $\sum_i{}'(A_i)$ denotes the sums of the A_i with the first and last term halved.

42. Xiong, L. (2004).

43. Let $\mathbf{A}$, $\mathbf{B}$ be $K \, x \, L$, $M \, x \, N$ matrices with elements indexed as

$$A[k, l], k = 0, 1, ..., K - 1, \qquad\qquad l = 0, 1, ..., L - 1$$
$$B[m, n], m = 0, 1, ..., M - 1, \qquad\qquad l = 0, 1, ..., N - 1$$

We define the Kronecker product $\mathbf{A} \otimes \mathbf{B}$ to be a $KM \, x \, LN$ matrix

$$\mathbf{A} \otimes \mathbf{B} = \begin{bmatrix} A[0, 0]\mathbf{B} & A[0, 1]\mathbf{B} & \cdots & A[0, L-1]\mathbf{B} \\ A[1, 0]\mathbf{B} & A[1, 1]\mathbf{B} & \cdots & A[1, L-1]\mathbf{B} \\ \vdots & \vdots & & \vdots \\ A[K-1, 0]\mathbf{B} & A[K-1, 1]\mathbf{B} & \cdots & A[K-1, L-1]\mathbf{B} \end{bmatrix}$$

with elements

$$(A \otimes B)[m + kM, n + lN] = A[k, l]B[m, n].$$

44. In 1994, NYMEX launched the crack spread contracts. NYMEX treats the crack spread purchases or sales of multiple futures as a single trade for the purposes of establishing margin requirements. The crack spread contract helps refiners to lock in a crude oil price and heating oil and unleaded gasoline prices simultaneously in order to establish a fixed refining margin. One type of crack spread contract bundles the purchase of three crude oil futures (30,000 barrels) with a sale a month later of two unleaded gasoline futures (20,000 barrels) and one heating oil future (10,000 barrels). The 3-2-1 ratio approximates the real-world ratio of refinery output—two barrels of unleaded gasoline and one barrel of heating oil from three barrels of crude oil. Buyers and sellers concern themselves only with the margin requirements for the crack spread contract. They do not deal with individual margins for the underlying trades. (See Energy Information Administration (2002), pg. 22.)

45. Natural gas is a combustible, gaseous mixture of simple hydrocarbon compounds, usually found in deep underground reservoirs formed by porous rock. Natural gas is fossil fuel composed almost entirely of methane, but does contain small amounts of other gases, including ethane, propane, butane, and pentane.

46. Xu, Z. (2004), pg. 7.

47. Xu, Z. (2004), pg. 8.

48. Id.

49. Id., pg. 8.

50. Id., pg. 8.

51. The seasonality estimates are the same for all three models ($r = 0, \frac{1}{2}$, and 1) because all three share the same futures price function given by equation (7.139).

52. Xu, Z. (2004), pg. 80.

53. Id., pg. 40.
54. Pindyk, R. (1998), pg. 33.
55. Energy Information Administration (2002), pg. 21.
56. Id., pg. 21.
57. Id., pg. 21.
58. Id., pg. 21.
59. Stoft, S., Belden, T., Goldman, C., and Pickle, S. (1998), pg. 40.
60. Stoft, S., Belden, T., Goldman, C., and Pickle, S. (1998), pg. 35.

PRICING POWER DERIVATIVES: THEORY AND MATLAB IMPLEMENTATION

Craig Pirrong
Professor of Finance, Bauer College of Business,
University of Houston

SECTIONS

8.1 INTRODUCTION

Energy derivatives have been around for awhile. Exchange futures derivatives on propane and heating oil were introduced in the 1970s. Futures on crude oil began trading in the 1980s, and natural gas futures were launched in the 1990s. The OTC market for energy derivatives has also developed, with crude oil and natural gas products leading the way. Common OTC structures are similar to those traded in interest rate or equity markets, and include fixed-for-floating swaps, forwards, and options. Some exotic products are also traded, and energy price contingencies are increasingly being incorporated into debt structures.

Linear products such as oil swaps are easy to value using standard arbitrage arguments, but energy presents considerable modeling challenges when valuing options. The problems are akin to those found in equity, fixed income, and currency markets, only more severe. In particular, normal distributions are a poor characterization of energy returns. Not only do such returns exhibit substantial excess kurtosis, but they are often skewed as well. Stochastic volatility and jumps are endemic. Energy also exhibits some complexities that are largely absent in financial markets. Most notably, seasonality is an important consideration for some energy products—natural gas being a prime example.

Despite these complications, those modeling derivatives for storable energy products can utilize various tricks-of-the-trade developed in equity, currency, and fixed income markets. Due primarily to the non-storability of power, however, things are not quite so easy in the newest frontier of energy trading—electricity derivatives. Electricity price dynamics are so far removed from the Brownian motion dynamics that underlay most standard valuation techniques that using them is akin to playing Russian Roulette with an automatic—things will go horribly wrong with probability one. Moreover, whereas quantity risks are typically limited or totally absent in financial markets and many energy markets, they are central in power markets. Furthermore, traditional models cannot incorporate quantity risk (an important consideration in many electricity valuation problems) in a natural way.

Thus, the modeler is confronted with a stark choice: use more complicated price processes (perhaps grafted onto some quantity process to create a Frankenstein-like hybrid), or utilize a fundamentals-based valuation approach in which quantity is an integral part of the model. The latter is feasible because the fundamentals in power markets are largely transparent. Weather, load, fuel prices, and outages are the major drivers of power prices, and all of these factors are observable. The main modeling challenge arises from the fact that electrical systems are extremely complex and of high dimension. The modeler perforce must judiciously abstract from this extreme complexity to create a tractable, low-dimension model. No tractable model can capture all of the features of real-world markets, but the one-eyed man is king in the land of the blind: a cleverly simplified fundamentals-based model can be much more effective than a pricing theory based on an exogenously specified characterization of price dynamics based on jump diffusions.

Electricity derivative valuation must confront another issue as well. Electricity markets are inherently incomplete. Even when we employ a standard valuation approach based on an exogenously specified price process, it must be recognized that electricity is not properly an asset. Not being storable, it is not possible to implement dynamic trading strategies that require holding positions in an unstorable. Therefore, we cannot employ standard hedging arguments—arguments that would break down in any event if we were to choose a discontinuous electricity price process. Similarly, many price drivers in a fundamental model—such as weather, load, and generation outages—are not traded assets either, and hence these risks cannot be hedged directly.

Market incompleteness implies that it is necessary to estimate market prices of the relevant risks. Thus, model calibration is an essential component of any valuation approach.

The remainder of this chapter examines these issues in detail. §8.2 provides a brief overview of electricity markets. This motivates an analysis of possible price processes in §8.3. This analysis suggests that price process-based approaches are problematic in power. I then turn attention to fundamentals-based models in §8.4. There I argue that very complicated fundamentals-based models, such as the "hybrid" models of Eydeland-Wolyniec (2002) are excessively complicated, and propose a simpler, lower-dimensional approach that can capture salient features of electricity price dynamic, readily permits the valuation and hedging of volume sensitive claims, and which can be calibrated to observable market data. The remainder of the chapter explores this simpler approach. §8.5 discusses in detail the Pirrong-Jermakyan fundamentals-based model, and §8.6 describes how to calibrate this model in a rigorous way to observed market data. §8.7 and §8.8 extend the analysis to options, and present Matlab code for valuing power options in this framework. §8.9 discusses the implications of the PJ model for the behavior of power options prices. §8.10 provides a brief summary of the chapter.

8.2 POWER MARKETS

In the U.S. and most other developed economies, electricity was traditionally supplied by vertically integrated utilities subject to price or rate-of-return regulation, or by state monopolies. These entities generated power, transmitted it over distances via high voltage lines, and distributed it to customers in monopoly geographic service territories. Starting in the 1980s, and progressing rapidly in the 1990s, electricity production, transmission, and distribution have been restructured. Although the details of this restructuring vary by country, and among regions in the United States, several salient features are found in most restructing regimes. First, vertical integration has been scaled back sharply, and in some instances vertically integrated firms have been replaced by separate generating, transmission, and distribution firms. Service territory monopolies have been eroded. Second, and relatedly, whereas wholesale and retail markets were unnecessary in vertically integrated electricity sectors, they are essential in restructured settings. Thus, most restructured electricity sectors have wholesale markets in which independent generators of electricity compete to supply load-serving entities and industrial and large commercial consumers of power. Moreover, some jurisdictions (such as Texas in the United States) have implemented competition at the retail level. In these cases, retail consumers have some choice over their household electricity supplier.

There are many variations in the designs of competitive wholesale power markets. Some markets are largely bilateral, over-the-counter ("OTC") markets. In these markets, owners of generation independently decide how to operate their assets, and enter into bilateral contracts with electricity users. Others markets are more formal and centralized. For instance, the PJM market in the United States operates centralized day-ahead and real-time markets for electricity. Owners of generation submit offers specifying the prices at which they are willing to generate various quantities of electricity, and load servers similarly specify bids at which they are willing to buy varying quantities. The market operator assembles the offers into supply curves and the bids into demand curves; determines the intersection of these curves to establish the market clearing price; and uses the generators' offers to dispatch the generation so as to minimize cost.

Restructuring has never been a smooth process anywhere—with California being the poster child for what can go wrong. These difficulties are attributable to the nature of electricity as a commodity. For practical purposes, electricity is not storable in large quantities.[1] Moreover, lack of electricity supply in real time leads to blackouts, which can cause massive economic losses. Because supplies of electricity cannot be stored for use when demand surges or generating units go offline, markets must be designed to ensure adequate generation supply at every instant of time. Electricity is also a highly localized commodity; constraints in transmission mean that power prices in proximate locations can differ substantially, and that these price differences can change dramatically over short periods of time.

Non-storability also means that inventories cannot be utilized to soften the impact of supply and demand shocks, as is the case for other commodities—including other energy commodities such as oil and natural gas. Because power demand can fluctuate substantially with variations in weather, and because power supply can also fluctuate due to mechanical failures at generating or transmission assets, the inability to use inventories as a shock absorber means that power prices can fluctuate wildly in response to random supply and demand changes.

The extreme movements in power prices (illustrated and discussed in more detail in the next section) create substantial risks for market participants. Moreover, many market players—including generators and load-serving entities—are subject to quantity risks. These risks create a need for hedging tools, and such tools have evolved in the wake of restructuring. Hedging tools include standard forward contracts and a variety of options. Some forward contracts are for very short delivery periods and are entered into very shortly before the delivery period—for instance, there are many day-ahead and even hour-ahead contracts in power markets. Other forward contracts are for blocks of power delivered over longer periods of time and entered into well in advance of the delivery period. For example, contracts calling for delivery of power rateably over the peak hours of an entire month are quite common. There are also a variety of options contracts in power markets, which are discussed in §8.7. Most power derivatives are traded OTC, although there are some exchange traded instruments available.

Although the derivative contracts traded in power are superficially quite similar to those traded in other energy derivatives markets, power's distinctive characteristics and price behaviors mean that valuation methods that work well for other commodities are problematic in the extreme for electricity. The next section explores electricity price behavior in more detail, and discusses the challenges inherent in applying traditional valuation approaches to pricing power forwards and options.

8.3 TRADITIONAL VALUATION APPROACHES ARE PROBLEMATIC FOR POWER

The traditional approach in derivatives pricing is to write down a stochastic process for the price of the asset or commodity underlying the contingent claim. This approach poses difficulties in the power market because of the extreme non-linearities and seasonalities in the price of power. These features make it impractical to write down a "reduced form" power price process that is tractable and that captures the salient features of power price dynamics.

Figure 8.1 depicts hourly power prices for the PJM market for 2001-2003. An examination of this figure illustrates the characteristics that any power price dynamics model must solve. Linear diffusion models of the type underlying the Black-Scholes model clearly cannot capture the behavior depicted in Figure 8.1; there is no tendency of prices to wander as a traditional random walk model implies. Prices tend to vibrate around a particular level (approximately $20 per megawatt hour) but sometimes jump upwards, at times reaching levels of $1000/MWh.

To address the inherent non-linearities in power prices illustrated in Figure 8.1, some researchers have proposed models that include a jump component in power prices. This presents other difficulties. For example, a simple jump model like that proposed by Merton (1973) is inadequate because in that model, the effect of a jump is permanent, whereas Figure 8.1 shows that jumps in electricity prices reverse themselves rapidly.

Moreover, the traditional jump model implies that prices can either jump up or down, whereas in electricity markets, prices jump up and then decline soon after. Barz and Johnson (1999) incorporate mean reversion and exponentially distributed (and hence positive) jumps to address these difficulties. However, this model presumes that big shocks to power prices damp out at the same rate as small price moves. This is implausible in some power markets. Geman and Roncoroni (2006) present a model that eases this constraint, but in which, conditional on the price spiking upward beyond a threshold level, (a) the magnitude of the succeeding down jump is independent of the magnitude of the preceding up jump,

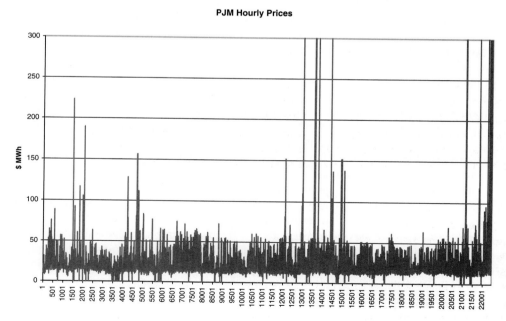

Figure 8.1 PJM hourly prices.

and (b) the next jump is necessarily a down jump (i.e., successive up jumps are precluded once the price breaches the threshold). Moreover, in this model, the intensity of the jump process does not depend on whether a jump has recently occurred. These are all problematic features.

Barone-Adesi and Gigli (2002) attempt to capture power spot price behavior using a regime shifting model. However, this model does not permit successive up jumps, and constraining down jumps to follow up jumps makes the model non-Markovian. Villaplana (2004) eases the constraint by specifying a price process that is the sum of two processes— one continuous, and the other with jumps—that exhibit different speeds of mean reversion. The resulting price process is non-Markovian, which makes it difficult to use for contingent claim valuation.

Estimation of jump-type models also poses difficulties. In particular, a reasonable jump model should allow for seasonality in prices and a jump intensity and magnitude that are also seasonal with large jumps more likely when demand is high than when demand is low. Given the nature of demand in the U.S., for instance, this implies that large jumps are most likely to occur during the summer months. Estimating such a model on the limited time series data available presents extreme challenges. Geman and Roncoroni (2006) allow such a feature, but most other models do not; furthermore, due to the computational intensity of the problem, even Geman-Roncoroni must specify the parameters of the non-homogeneous jump intensity function based on *a priori* considerations instead of estimating it from the data. Fitting regime-shifting models is also problematic, especially if they are non-Markovian as is necessary to make them a realistic characterization of power prices (Geman, 2005). Moreover, changes in capacity and demand growth will affect the jump intensity and magnitude. None of the extant models take this into account.

Even if jump models can accurately characterize the behavior of electricity prices under the "true measure," they pose acute difficulties as the basis for the valuation of power contingent claims. Jump risk is not hedgeable, and hence the power market is incomplete.[2] A realistic jump model that allows for multiple jump magnitudes (and preferably a continuum of jump sizes) requires multiple market risk prices for valuation purposes; a continuum of jump sizes necessitates a continuum of risk price functions to determine the equivalent measure that is relevant for valuation purposes. Moreover, these functions may be time varying. The high dimensionality of the resulting valuation problem vastly complicates the pricing of power contingent claims. Indeed, the more sophisticated the spot price model (with Geman-Roncoroni being the richest), the more complicated the task of determining the market price of risk functions.

The traditional valuation approach is also very difficult to apply to some important power valuation problems, notably those where quantity as well as price affect the payoff. Although most financial power contracts do not possess this feature, many physical contracts (such as load-serving transactions) do. Pricing volume-sensitive claims in the traditional framework requires grafting a quantity process to an already complicated price process. Moreover, the dependence between prices and quantities may be highly non-linear because power prices are a non-linear function of loads (quantities).

Given these difficulties, it is desirable to take an alternative approach to valuing power derivatives. Fortunately, such an alternative exists. This approach exploits the fact that the fundamentals that drive power prices are very transparent—a situation that contrasts starkly with that which prevails in currency, equity, or fixed income markets. The next section describes fundamentals-based models in detail.

8.4   FUNDAMENTALS-BASED MODELS

If traditional approaches are impractical for power, is all lost? Fortunately, no. Although a door has been closed, a window remains open. In other markets—think of currencies, for example—the fundamental price drivers are many and murky, and certainly not observable in real time. In contrast, in power markets, fundamentals are largely transparent. Exploiting this transparency, it is possible to construct fundamentals-based models to price power contingent claims. This is not to say that doing so is easy. Fundamental modeling must confront many challenges, most notably the complexity and incompleteness of power markets, but it is doable.

There are two basic, and related, fundamentals-based modeling schemes in the literature: Eydeland and Wolyniec ("EW") and Pirrong-Jermkyan ("PJ"). They share some similarities, but differ on key dimensions. Both capture the non-linearity of power prices by using non-linear functions to transform the linear processes for the fundamental price drivers. EW is a simulation-based approach that attempts to capture all of the fundamental drivers, whereas PJ is a PDE-based approach that relies on a few key drivers. More important, PJ relies on a theoretically rigorous approach for calibrating the model to observed market prices, whereas the calibration method in EW is more *ad hoc*.

EW (2002) present a detailed, fundamentals-based modeling approach. They propose modeling power prices using a very high dimension model of an electricity market that attempts to capture many of the complex features of power markets. At its heart, the EW approach recognizes that there are three major drivers to power prices: the cost of fuel used to generate electricity, demand (driven by weather, or measured directly as load), and the availability of generation resources (i.e., outages). EW recognize that in any power market, generation assets utilize a variety of fuels. For instance, in the U.S. most markets have some units fueled by coal, others by natural gas, others by nuclear fuel, and still others by fuel oil. As a result, EW specify forward price processes for all fuels used in a particular market. This, in turn, requires a specification of the correlation between all the fuels.

EW also recognize that the heterogeneity of generating assets in a market implies that different units will exhibit different probabilities of experiencing forced outages, different outage duration, and different scheduled outage patterns. They incorporate this into their model using unit-specific outage probabilities.

Conditional on information about the physical characteristics of plants—most notably their heat rates, which measure the amount of fuel required to produce one megawatt of power—fuel prices, and plant availability, EW can calculate the marginal cost of generating a given amount of power in a particular market. The curve specifying the relation between the quantity generated and marginal cost is commonly called the *generating stack*. EW recognize that the prices at which owners of generation are willing to sell power may diverge from marginal costs, however. Because these generator "bids," rather than marginal costs, will determine spot prices, EW posit that the supply curve in the market—the "bid stack"—differs from the generating stack, but that there is a stable relation between the former and the latter curves that is summarized by three parameters, the α parameters of the EW model.

These three parameters also play a key role in the calibration process. EW eschew reliance on historical data wherever possible, and instead advocate the calibration of the model to observable forward and option prices. The α parameters do all the heavy lifting in the EW framework. This calibration process kills two birds with one stone. Interpreted literally, it bridges the gap between the bid stack that actually drives prices and the generation stack that can be calculated from observable data. Moreover, although EW do not emphasize this point, it also addresses market incompleteness. In any market, forward prices can differ from expected spot prices due to the market price of risk. Choosing the α coefficients so that model prices estimated as expectations through simulations match market prices effectively adjusts the probability measure used to calculate the expectations.

Due to its high dimensionality, the EW approach must be implemented using Monte Carlo methods. Given specifications of the dynamics for all the driving variables—the various fuel prices, temperature, and outages—these variables can be simulated. One plugs the simulated values into the calibrated bid stack to get spot power prices. It is then possible to determine the payoff on a claim contingent on these prices. Averaging payoffs across simulations (and discounting appropriately) produces an estimate of the value of the claim.

Although the high dimensionality of the EW approach is attractive because it allows the modeler to capture some of the more complicated features of power markets, it comes at a cost. For example, it is necessary to estimate numerous correlations, but the data necessary to do so is often lacking. Moreover, it makes it computationally costly to calibrate the model. One must first choose the α, simulate the payoffs to all the claims, determine the sensitivity of each claim price to changes in the parameters, use these sensitivities to adjust the parameters for another simulation run, and continue until convergence is achieved. Iterating over Monte Carlo simulations is never a welcome task if it can be avoided.

More fundamentally, the calibration scheme lacks theoretical foundation. Several of the factors in the EW model—notably weather and outages—are not traded assets. Hence, under the equivalent measure that is appropriate for valuation, it is necessary to adjust the drift for the weather process and the outage probabilities. In fact, EW do not use market price data to calibrate these parameters. Instead, the entire burden of matching model and market prices falls on the parameters of the function relating the bid stack to the generating stack. Thus, EW effectively assume that all the difference between observed forward prices and marginal costs is due to the possibility that spot prices differ from marginal costs, and that none of this difference is due to non-zero market prices of risk for the non-traded factors.[3] This is a strong assumption that could have a substantial impact on the valuation of instruments not used to calibrate the model. For instance, this assumption could lead to substantial mis-valuations of weather or load-sensitive claims because it does not estimate the costs the market charges for these risks.

PJ propose a related, but different approach. Like EW, the PJ model is based on supply-demand fundamentals rather than a specification of an exogenous power price process. However, PJ advocate greater reliance on available historical data on loads and market bids than EW; this data is becoming more widely available, and communicates valuable information that should not be casually ignored. That is, rather than extract inferences on the relation of the bid and generating stacks through calibration to forward curves, PJ utilize historical data on these curves to identify this relation. This allows the calibration to forward prices to focus on the determination of the market risk prices. Given the limited number of power derivatives typically available, it is unwise to burden them with the multiple tasks of calibrating both the bid curves and the market risk prices.

Furthermore, PJ explicitly allow for a non-zero market price of risk for the key non-traded fundamental variable, load (or temperature), and calibrate the model to market prices to estimate this market price of risk function. This is a theoretically sound approach that generates information on market risk prices that can be employed to value other claims not utilized in the calibration process. Moreover, the PJ calibration approach is firmly grounded in the literature on the regularization of ill-posed problems.

Like all things in life, the PJ approach involves trade-offs. Most important, the calibration approach requires the use of finite difference methods. Due to the curse of dimensionality, these methods inherently limit the number of driving factors that can be included in the analysis. The original PJ approach relies on only two drivers—a fuel price and load (or temperature). These factors are clearly important. For instance, variations in load and fuel prices explain around 65 percent of the variations in PJM peak spot prices. Nonetheless, focusing on two factors does abstract from some real-world considerations. Because only one fuel price can be readily handled, it is not possible to take into account the full richness of fuel price dynamics and the generating stack. However, because in the U.S. natural gas is increasingly the marginal fuel, especially for peak hours in many markets, this assumption is not too objectionable. Moreover, PJ recognize that other factors—notably generation outages—can also influence power prices and have described modifications to the basic framework that incorporate these factors; see Pirrong-Jermakyan (2006) and Pirrong (2006a, 2006b) for details. To simplify the analysis, however, the remainder of this chapter focuses on the basic PJ model.

8.5   THE PJ MODEL—OVERVIEW

Load is the key driver in power prices in the PJM model. This model treats load as a controlled process. Defining load as Q_t, note that $Q_t \leq X$, where X is physical capacity of the generating and transmission system.[4] If load exceeds this system capacity, the system may fail, imposing substantial costs on power users. The operators of electric power systems (such as the independent system operator in the PJM region) monitor load and intervene to reduce power usage when load approaches levels that threaten the physical reliability of the system. Under certain technical conditions (which are assumed to hold herein), the arguments of Harrison and Taksar (1983) imply that under these circumstances, the controlled load process will be a reflected Brownian motion.[5] It is convenient to work in the natural logarithm of load, which we define as q_t. Formally, the log load will solve the following SDE:

$$dq_t = \alpha_q(q_t, t)dt + \sigma_q dW_{qt} - dL_t^u \qquad (8.1)$$

where L_t^u is the local time of the load on the capacity boundary.[6] The process L_t^u is increasing (i.e., $dL_t^u > 0$) if and only if $q_t = \ln(X)$, and with $dL_t = 0$, otherwise. That is, q_t is reflected at $\ln(X)$.

The dependence of the drift term $\alpha_q(q_t, t)$ on calendar time t reflects the fact that output drift varies systematically both seasonally and within the day. Moreover, the dependence of the drift on q_t allows for mean reversion. One specification that captures these features is:

$$\alpha_q(q_t, t) = \mu(t) + k[\theta_q(t) - q_t] - .5\sigma_q^2 \tag{8.2}$$

where the σ_q^2 term arises due to the log transformation. In this expression, q_t reverts to a time-varying mean $\theta_q(t)$. $\theta_q(t)$ can be specified as a sum of sine terms to reflect seasonal, predictable variations in electricity output. Alternatively, it can be represented as a function of calendar time fitted using non-parametric econometric techniques. The parameter $k \geq 0$ measures the speed of mean reversion; the larger k, the more rapid the reversal of load shocks. The function $\mu(t)$ represents the portion of load drift that depends only on time (particularly time of day). For instance, given $\theta_q(t) - q_t$, load tends to rise from around 3AM to 5PM and then fall from 5PM to 3AM on summer days.[7]

The load volatility σ_q in (8.1) is represented as a constant, but it can depend on q_t and t. There is some empirical evidence of slight seasonality in the variance of σ_q.

The second state variable is a fuel price. The process for the forward price of the marginal fuel is:

$$\frac{df_{t,T}}{f_{t,T}} = \alpha_f(f_{t,T}, t) + \sigma_f(f_{t,T}, t)dW_{ft} \tag{8.3}$$

where $f_{t,T}$ is the price of fuel for delivery on date T as of t and dW is a standard Brownian motion. Note that $f_{T,T}$ is the spot price of fuel on date T.

The processes $\{q_t, f_{t,T}, t \geq 0\}$ solve (8.1) and (8.3) under the "true" probability measure $\mathcal{P}$. To price power contingent claims, we need to find an equivalent measure $\mathcal{Q}$ under which deflated prices for claims with payoffs that depend on q_t and $f_{t,T}$ are martingales. Because $\mathcal{P}$ and $\mathcal{Q}$ must share sets of measure 0, q_t must reflect at X under $\mathcal{Q}$ as it does under $\mathcal{P}$. Therefore, under $\mathcal{Q}$, q_t solves the SDE:

$$dq_t = [\alpha_q(q_t, t) - \sigma_q\lambda(q_t, t)]tdt + \sigma_q dW_{qt}^* - dL_t^u$$

In this expression, $\lambda(q_t, t)$ is the market price of risk function and dW_{qt}^* is a $\mathcal{Q}$ martingale. Because fuel is a traded asset, under the equivalent measure $df_{t,T}/f_{t,T} = \sigma_f dW_{ft}^*$, where dW_{ft}^* is a $\mathcal{Q}$ martingale. The change in the drift functions is due to the change in measure.

Define the discount factor $Y_t = \exp(-\int_0^t r_s ds)$ where r_s is the (assumed deterministic) interest rate at time s. (Later we assume that the interest rate is a constant r.) Under $\mathcal{Q}$, the evolution of a deflated power price contingent claim C is:

$$Y_tC_t = Y_0C_0 + \int_0^t C_s dY_s + \int_0^t Y_s dC_s$$

In this expression, C_s indicates the value of the derivative at time s, and Y_s denotes the value of one dollar received at time s as of time 0. Using Ito's lemma, this can be rewritten as:

$$Y_tC_t = C_0 + \int_0^t Y_s(\mathcal{A}C + \frac{\partial C}{\partial s} - r_sC_s)ds$$
$$+ \int_0^t [\frac{\partial C}{\partial q}dW_{qs}^* + \frac{\partial C}{\partial f}dW_{fs}^*] - \int_0^t Y_s\frac{\partial C}{\partial q}dL_s^u$$

where $\mathcal{A}$ is an operator such that:

$$\mathcal{A}C = \frac{\partial C}{\partial q_t}[\alpha_q(q_t, t) - \sigma_q \lambda(q_t, t)]$$

$$+ .5\frac{\partial^2 C}{\partial q_t^2}\sigma_q^2 + .5\frac{\partial^2 C}{\partial f_{t,T}^2}\sigma_f^2 f_{t,T}^2 + \frac{\partial^2 C}{\partial q_t \partial f_{t,T}}\sigma_f \sigma_q \rho_{qf} f_{t,T}. \qquad (8.4)$$

For the deflated price of the power contingent claim to be a $\mathcal{Q}$ martingale, it must be the case that:

$$E[\int_0^t Y_s(\mathcal{A}C + \frac{\partial C}{\partial s} - r_s C_s)ds] = 0$$

and

$$E[\int_0^t Y_s \frac{\partial C}{\partial q}dL_s^u] = 0$$

for all t. Since (8.1) $Y_t > 0$, and (2) $dL_t^u > 0$ only when $q_t = X$, with a constant interest rate r, we can rewrite these conditions as:

$$\mathcal{A}C + \frac{\partial C}{\partial t} - rC = 0 \qquad (8.5)$$

and

$$\frac{\partial C}{\partial q} = 0 \text{ when } q_t = X \qquad (8.6)$$

It is obvious that (8.5) and (8.6) are sufficient to ensure that C is a martingale under $\mathcal{Q}$; it is possible to show that these conditions are necessary as well.

Expression (8.6) is a boundary condition of the Neumann type. This boundary condition is due to the reflecting barrier that is inherent in the physical capacity constraints in the power market.[8] The condition has an intuitive interpretation. If load is at the upper boundary, it will fall almost certainly. If the derivative of the contingent claim with respect to load is non-zero at the boundary, arbitrage is possible. For instance, if the partial derivative is negative, selling the contingent claim cannot generate a loss and almost certainly generates a profit.

Expression (8.5) can be rewritten as the fundamental valuation PDE:

$$rC = \frac{\partial C}{\partial t} + \frac{\partial C}{\partial q_t}[\alpha_q(q_t, t) - \sigma_q \lambda(q_t, t)]$$

$$+ .5\frac{\partial^2 C}{\partial q_t^2}\sigma_q^2 + .5\frac{\partial^2 C}{\partial f_{t,T}^2}\sigma_f^2 f_{t,T}^2 + \frac{\partial^2 C}{\partial q_t \partial f_{t,T}}\sigma_f \sigma_q \rho_{qf} f_{t,T} \qquad (8.7)$$

For a forward contract, after changing the time variable to $\tau = T - t$, the relevant PDE is:

$$
\frac{\partial F_{t,T}}{\partial \tau} = \frac{\partial F_{t,T}}{\partial q_t}[\alpha_q(q_t, t) - \sigma_q \lambda(q_t, t)]
$$
$$
+ .5\frac{\partial^2_{t,T}}{\partial q_t^2}\sigma_q^2 + .5\frac{\partial^2_{t,T}}{\partial f_{t,T}^2}\sigma_f^2 f_{t,T}^2 + \frac{\partial^2_{t,T}}{\partial q_t \partial f_{t,T}}f_{t,T}\sigma_f\sigma_q\rho_{qf} \qquad (8.8)
$$

where $F_{t,T}$ is the price at t for delivery of one unit of power at $T > t$.

This is a two-dimensional PDE, which presents some challenges that can be alleviated substantially in the case of forward contracts (but not options, alas) by exploiting the economics of power generation. Specifically, it is common to express the market price of power as the product of the price of the marginal fuel and a heat rate. The *heat rate* is the amount of fuel needed to produce one unit of power. The heat rate is a function of the efficiency of the generating unit at the margin, and because it is efficient to use progressively higher heat rate units to satisfy progressively higher loads, this function is increasing in load q. Formally, this relation is:

$$
P_t = f_{t,t}\phi(q_t)
$$

where P_t is the spot price of power at t, $\phi(q_t)$ is the heat rate function, with $\phi'(q_t) > 0$, and (typically) $\phi''(q_t) > 0$. This relation can be generalized as follows:

$$
P_t = f_{t,t}^\gamma \phi(q_t)
$$

Because the payoff to a forward contract expiring at t is tied to the spot price of power at that time, this function determines the payoff to a forward as a function of the state variables f and q. Moreover, it allows rewriting the forward price PDE as follows.

Posit that the forward price function is of the form

$$
F(q_t, f_{t,T}, \tau) = f_{t,T}^\gamma V(q_t, \tau).
$$

Then, making the appropriate substitutions into (8.8) produces the new one-dimensional PDE:

$$
\frac{\partial V}{\partial \tau} = .5\sigma_q^2\frac{\partial^2 V}{\partial q^2} + [\gamma\rho\sigma_f + a]\frac{\partial V}{\partial q} + .5\sigma_f^2\gamma(\gamma - 1)V \qquad (8.9)
$$

where $a = (\alpha_q(\tau, q) - \sigma_q\lambda(\tau, q))$, and where the equation must be solved subject to the von Neuman boundary condition $\partial V(X, \tau)/\partial q = 0$ and the initial condition $V(q_T, 0) = \phi(q_T)$. Once this function is solved for, the power forward price is obtained by multiplying $V(.)$ by $f_{t,T}^\gamma$. We can interpret $V(q_t, t, T)$ as the forward market heat rate observed as of t for delivery of power at T. The reduction in dimensionality is especially welcome when solving the computationally intense inverse problem for $\lambda(q, t)$.

Implementation of this approach requires knowledge of the heat rate function $\phi(.)$, which determines payoffs. For claims with payoffs that depend on a spot price (with a forward contract being an example), the methodologies set out in PJ (2006) can be used to relate the spot price to the state variables.[9] Similarly, for a claim with a payoff that depends on forward prices, the PJ model can be used to solve for these forward prices as a function of load and fuel price. These forward prices, in turn, can be used to establish the relation between option payoff and the state variables.

In either case, before valuing electricity options, it is first necessary to implement the PJ inverse problem solution to determine the market price of risk function $\lambda(q_t)$. The solution to the PDE (8.9) depends on this market price of risk, which is not directly observable. Instead, it can be implied from the observed forward prices in the marketplace. The next section describes the calibration methodology.

8.6   MODEL CALIBRATION

At first blush, it might appear that there is no need to estimate a market price of load risk. If we believe that only systematic risks should be priced in equilibrium and that idiosyncratic risks should not, because electricity prices are virtually uncorrelated with any measure of overall market performance, we might think that λ should be zero. We would be wrong. There is extensive evidence, summarized in PJ (2006), that the market price of risk is significant in power markets. Research by Bessembinder and Lemon (2002) suggests that this reflects the incomplete integration of power markets into the broader financial system.

Because the market price of risk is potentially large, it is imperative to take it into account when valuing derivatives. Unfortunately, the market price of risk is not observable directly. However, it can be inferred from prices of traded instruments. In particular, given a set of quoted forward prices, inverse problem methods can be applied to (8.9) to generate an implied market price of risk. In essence, these methods find a λ function that calibrates the forward prices produced by the model to the prices quoted in the marketplace. This is analogous to the exercise of calibrating a spot interest rate model (such as the Hull-White model) to observed zero-coupon bond prices.

In calibrating, it is important not to overfit (as is often done in interest rate models, alas). For instance, if one has twelve forward prices to calibrate to, it is always possible to choose a λ function that is a twelfth-order polynomial that fits the prices exactly. This is cheating, and the results of the calibration will be unstable. A very slight perturbation of the prices used to calibrate—say moving from the midpoint to the bid or ask—will lead to a very large change in the estimated λ function. Similarly, overfit calibrations vary wildly from day to day. Such problems are said to be "ill-posed." Solving them necessitates the imposition of some constraints on the function to penalize overfitting. This is called "regularization."[10]

To see this formally, note that at any time there are only a finite number of forward prices quoted in the marketplace. Call the set of available forward quotes $\mathcal{D}$. The regularization technique involves choosing a function λ that minimizes the sum of squared deviations between the forward prices implied by (8.9) for a given set of delivery dates and the prices quoted for these dates, subject to some regularization constraint. To make the problem tractable, λ is a function of load only. PJ use the H^2 norm as the regularizer:

$$R(\lambda) = \int\limits_{\ln(\widehat{X})}^{\ln(X)} \left[\lambda^2 + \left(\frac{\partial \lambda}{\partial q} \right)^2 \right] dq.$$

where X is the maximum load (given by the physical capacity of the power system) and $\ln(\widehat{X})$ is a minimum load level (power systems can be unstable if load falls too far). Then, choose a function λ to minimize:

$$\sum_{i \in \mathcal{D}} [F_i(q_t, f_{t,T}|\lambda) - \mathcal{F}_i]^2 + \kappa R(\lambda)$$

In this expression, $F_i(q_t, f_{t,T}|\lambda)$ is the solution to (8.8) for a forward contract corresponding to forward price quote $i \in \mathcal{D}$ given current load q_t and current fuel price $f_{t,T}$; note that this forward price depends on the λ function. Moreover, $\mathcal{F}_i$ is the quoted ith forward price. Finally, κ is the regularization parameter.

The regularization technique in essence penalizes overfitting. In the regularized problem, there is a trade-off between the precision with which the forward quotes are fit and the smoothness of the λ function. Note that $R(\lambda)$ is large when $|\partial \lambda / \partial q|$ is large. Thus, $R(\lambda)$ is large (small) when λ is very jagged (smooth). Choice of a regularization parameter κ determines the smoothness of the resulting fit; the bigger the value of this parameter, the greater penalty for non-smoothness, and the smoother the resulting solution.

This problem is solved using finite difference techniques. Create a valuation grid in q and τ with increments Δq and $\Delta \tau$; there are N total time steps and M total q values. An initial guess for λ is made. In the valuation grid, λ is represented as a vector, where the length of the vector is equal to M.

The estimation then proceeds by the Method of Small Parameter. Specifically, letting λ_0 denote the initial guess for the λ function, define

$$\lambda(q) = \lambda_0(q) + \sum_{j=1}^{\infty} \lambda_k(q)$$

where the λ_k are improvements to the initial guess. Similarly, define V_0 as the solution to (8.13) based on λ_0, and let

$$V = V_0 + \sum_{j=1}^{\infty} V_k$$

where the V_k are improvements to the initial guess.[11] Note that the use of the $V(.)$ function exploits the dimensionality reduction.

Consider an ε-family of market price of risk functions:

$$\lambda(q) = \lambda_0 + \sum_{j=1}^{\infty} \varepsilon^k \lambda_k(q)$$

with a corresponding representation of V:

$$V(\tau, q) = V_0(\tau, q) + \sum_{j=1}^{\infty} \varepsilon^k V_k(\tau, q).$$

Plugging these various equations into the valuation PDE and equating powers of ε implies:

$$\frac{\partial V_0}{\partial \tau} = c_0 \frac{\partial^2 V_0}{\partial q^2} + c_1[\lambda_0] \frac{\partial V_0}{\partial q} + c_0 V_0 \tag{8.10}$$

$$\frac{\partial V_1}{\partial \tau} = c_0 \frac{\partial^2 V_1}{\partial q^2} + c_1[\lambda_0] \frac{\partial V_1}{\partial q} + c_0 V_1 - \sigma_q q \lambda_1 \frac{\partial V_0}{\partial q} \tag{8.11}$$

$$\frac{\partial V_k}{\partial \tau} = c_0 \frac{\partial^2 V_k}{\partial q^2} + c_1[\lambda_0] \frac{\partial V_k}{\partial q} + c_0 V_k - \sum_{j=0}^{k} \sigma_q q \lambda_j \frac{\partial V_{k-j}}{\partial q} \tag{8.12}$$

for $k = 2, 3, \ldots$ where $c_0 = .5\sigma_f^2 \gamma(\gamma - 1)$, $c_1[\lambda_0] = q[\gamma \rho \sigma_q \sigma_f + \alpha_q(\tau, q) - \sigma_q \lambda_0(\tau, q)]$, and $c_2 = .5\sigma_q^2 q^2$. There is a set of equations (8.10)–(8.12) for each maturity date included in the analysis.

The PDE (10) is solved implicitly. Now note that it can be shown from (8.11) that in the discretized q and τ grid, a recursion relationship holds:

$$A_{n+1} V_1^{(i)}[n + 1] = V_1^{(i)}[n] + G_{n+1}^{(i)} \lambda_1 \tag{8.13}$$

where $n + 1$ indicates the time step, A_{n+1} is a tri-diagonal $(M - 2) \times (M - 2)$ matrix determined by the implicit scheme and the coefficients in the PDE, $V_1^{(i)}[n]$ is an $M - 2$ vector giving the value of V_1 at each interior load point for maturity $i \in \mathcal{D}$ at time step n, and

$$G_{n+1}^{(i)} = -.5\frac{\Delta \tau}{\Delta q} \sigma_q q \frac{\partial V_0^{(i)}(q, (n + 1)\Delta \tau)}{\partial q}$$

where the partial derivative is estimated using a central finite difference. Furthermore, $G_n^{(i)} = 0$ if $n\Delta t$ is greater than the time to maturity of forward contract $i \in \mathcal{D}$. Completing this recursion implies:

$$V_1^{(i)}[N] = [\sum_{j=1}^{N-1} (\Pi_{k=0}^{j} A_{N-j}) G_{N-j}^{(i)}] \lambda_1 \equiv \mathcal{B}^{(i)} \lambda_1 \tag{8.14}$$

Now note that the regularized objective function becomes:

$$\sum_{i \in \mathcal{D}} [V_0^{(i)} + \mathcal{B}^{(i)} \lambda_1 - \frac{\mathcal{F}_i}{f_i^{\gamma}}]^2 + \kappa R(\lambda_1) \tag{8.15}$$

where f_i is the fuel forward price with the same maturity as power forward contract i. Using the trapezoidal rule to approximate the integral in the expression for the regularizer, $R(\lambda_1)$ is quadratic in λ_1. Therefore, minimizing (8.14) with respect to λ_1 produces a set of linear equations (the first order conditions) that can be solved for λ_1.

Given this improvement, a similar method can be used to solve for λ_k, $k > 1$, based on (8.12); the main difference in the solution technique for $k = 2, 3, \ldots$ as opposed to $k = 1$ is the presence of additional forcing terms that depend on the q-derivatives of V improvements $k - 1, k - 2, \ldots, 2$. The user can choose the total number of improvements to implement, with more improvements involving greater computational cost (particularly storage).

Figure 8.2 depicts the λ function fitted to seven forward prices from PJM (June–December, 2005 deliveries) observed on June 5, 2005, based on four improvements. Note that the market price of risk function is uniformly negative. This implies that under the equivalent measure load drifts up more rapidly than under the physical measure. This shifts the density of load to the right. Given that the power price is monotonically increasing in load, this in turn implies that forward prices are upward biased; that is, the expectation under the equivalent measure exceeds the expectation under the physical measure. Note also that the absolute

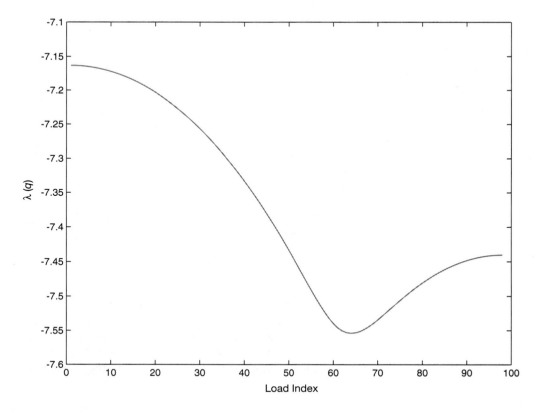

Figure 8.2 PJM market price of risk function.

value of the λ function is mainly increasing in load, which implies that upward bias should be more extreme for forwards expiring during high demand periods.

8.7   USING THE CALIBRATED MODEL TO PRICE OPTIONS

Once a λ function has been fit, it is possible to use the model to price options not utilized in the calibration. There are a variety of electricity options traded (primarily on the OTC market). Among the most common are daily strike options, monthly strike options, and spark spread options. Consider each in turn.

Daily Strike Options

A daily strike option has a payoff that depends on the price of power on a given day. Typically, these options have a payoff that depends on the price of power for delivery during peak hours of a given day.

Daily strike options can by physically settled or cash settled. For a physically settled daily strike call option, upon exercise the owner effectively receives a long position in a daily forward contract that entitles him to receive delivery of a fixed amount of power during the peak hours on that day. Upon exercise, the owner of a put establishes a shortposition in a daily forward contract. The option owner must decide to exercise prior to the beginning of the delivery period (e.g., the day before delivery).

A cash settled daily strike option can be constructed in many ways. For instance, one can have a cash settled daily strike call in which the owner is paid an amount equal to the maximum of zero or the difference between the relevant daily forward as of the same date prior to the delivery period and the strike price. As an example, the call owner's payoff (determined on Tuesday) may depend on Tuesday's forward price for delivery on Wednesday. Alternatively, a daily strike call can pay the difference between the average spot price observed on the pricing date and the strike. For instance, the daily strike call can pay the maximum of zero or the difference between the average spot price observed on Wednesday and the strike price. In a market with a centralized real-time market (such as PJM), it is eminently feasible to construct options with such a payoff structure.

I focus on daily strike options with payoffs that depend on a forward price.[12] For such an option, the payoff of a call expiring at t' with the forward contract expiring at T as the underlying is $\left(F_{t',T}(q_{t'}, f_{t',T}) - K\right)^+$ and the put payoff is $(K - F_{t',T}(q_{t'}, f_{t',T}))^+$.

Monthly Strike Options

Upon exercise, the holder of a monthly strike call receives a long position in a monthly forward contract. For instance, upon exercise at the end of June, the holder of a July monthly strike call receives a forward contract for delivery of a fixed amount of power during the peak hours of the coming July. Denoting the forward price as of exercise date t' for delivery of peak power on day j in the option month as $F_{t',j}$, the payoff to the monthly strike call is:

$$\left(\frac{\sum_{j \in \mathbf{M}} F_{t',j}}{\sum_{j \in \mathbf{M}} \delta_j} - K\right)^+$$

where $\mathbf{M}$ is the set of delivery dates in the contract month and δ_j is an indicator variable taking a value of 1 when $j \in \mathbf{M}$ and zero otherwise.

Spark Spread Options

A spark spread call option has a payoff equal to the maximum of zero or the difference between a forward price and the price of fuel multiplied by a contractually specified heat rate. The heat rate is measured in terms of megawatts (MW) per million British Thermal Units (mmBTU). The heat rate measures the efficiency of a generating plant. The marginal cost of generating power from that plant equals its heat rate multiplied by its fuel price. Therefore, a spark spread option can be viewed as an option to burn fuel to produce power because its payoff is based on the difference between the price of power and the cost of generating it at a given heat rate. For this reason, power plants are often viewed as bundles of spark spread options, although spark spread options are also traded as stand-alone financial products.

Spark spread options raise some of the same issues relating to the timing of exercise and physical settlement and cash settlement as daily strike options. Specifically, if the spark spread option must be exercised at some time t' prior to the power delivery date T, the call payoff is $(F_{t',T} - f_{t',T} H^*)^+$ where H^* is the contractually specified heat rate, which effectively determines the strike.

8.8   OPTION VALUATION METHODOLOGY

Splitting the (Finite) Difference: Daily Strike and Monthly Strike Options

Daily strike and monthly strike options are valued by solving the PDE (8.7) using a "splitting" finite difference method. This method, described in Duffy (2006), can handle non-zero correlations and is computationally efficient. The ability to handle non-zero correlations makes this method preferable to alternating direction implicit techniques.[13] The splitting method also allows use of the natural boundary conditions—most notably, the von Neumann conditions for the load boundaries, and conventional Dirichlet conditions for the fuel boundaries.

Because it is a finite difference method, the technique first involves creating a grid in time, the log fuel price, and log load; the log transform of the fuel price ensures that one of the "split" equations has constant coefficients. The time increment is δt; given the seasonality in load, it is convenient to use $\delta t = 1/365$. The log fuel price increment is $\delta \widehat{f}$, and the log load increment is δq.

As its name suggests, the splitting method works by splitting the PDE (8.7) into two parts at each time step. After making the log transformation, the first PDE portion is:

$$
rC = \frac{\partial C}{\partial t} + \frac{\partial C}{\partial q_t}[\alpha_q(q_t, t) - \sigma_q \lambda(q_t, t)]
$$

$$
+ .5\frac{\partial^2 C}{\partial q_t^2}\sigma_q^2 + .5\sigma_f \sigma_q \rho_{qf} \frac{\partial^2 C}{\partial q_t \partial \widehat{f}_{t,T}} \tag{8.16}
$$

The second PDE "split" is:

$$
0 = \frac{\partial C}{\partial t} - .5\sigma_f^2 \frac{\partial C}{\partial \widehat{f}}
$$

$$
+ .5\sigma_f^2 \frac{\partial^2 C}{\partial \widehat{f}_{t,T}^2} + .5\sigma_f \sigma_q \rho_{qf} \frac{\partial^2 C}{\partial q_t \partial \widehat{f}_{t,T}} \tag{8.17}
$$

One time step prior to expiry, (8.16) is solved using an implicit method for each different fuel price from the second lowest to the second highest, where following Yanenko (1971) the cross-partial derivative is set using an explicit approximation (i.e., based on the values of C from the time step immediately later in time). For one time step prior to expiration, the option payoff is used as the initial condition. For earlier time steps, the value of the option given by (8.17) from the previous time step is used. For each fuel price, von Neumann boundary conditions are used in the solution. For the highest and lowest fuel prices, I employ Dirichlet boundary conditions. For a put, for instance, at the highest fuel price, the value of the put is zero, whereas at the lowest fuel price, the put price is the difference between the strike price and power forward price, multiplied by the present value of $1 paid at option expiry. Given the typical high speed of mean reversion, the coefficient on the first order term in (8.16) is usually large in absolute value. Therefore, although (8.7) is a convection-diffusion equation, the convection effect is more important than is usually the case for the parabolic PDEs encounted in finance, and so it is desirable to utilize discretization approaches commonly employed for convection problems. Specifically, I use forward differencing to estimate $\partial C / \partial q$ when the coefficient is negative, and backward differencing when the reverse is true.

At each time step, the solution to (8.16) from the previous time step is used as the initial condition in the solution for (8.17), which is again solved implicitly for each log load step from the second lowest to the second highest. Dirichlet boundary conditions are used for each of these solutions. For the lowest and highest log load steps, I employ von Neumann boundary conditions.

This method is relatively computationally efficient. When the model is coded in Matlab, using daily time steps, it takes about two seconds on a 2.4 GHz pentium machine to estimate the value of an option that has a month to expiration.

For daily strike options, the payoffs are determined as follows. It is assumed that the option holder must decide to exercise the option the day prior to the power delivery date— i.e., $t' = T - \delta t$.[14] Upon exercise, for a load q and log fuel price $\widehat{f}$, the holder of the call receives a payment equal to the maximum of zero, or the difference (a) between the day-ahead forward price $F_{t',T}(q, f)$ implied by the solution to the Pirrong-Jermakyan model calibrated to the observed curve, and (b) the strike price.[15]

For monthly strike options, the delivery days in the month are first determined. For simplicity, I assume that delivery occurs during the peak hours of each business day of the month. The option is assumed to be exercisable on the business day prior to the first day of the delivery month. On this date, the Pirrong-Jermakyan model forward price for each day of the delivery month is determined for each $\widehat{f}$ and q in the grid.[16] For instance, the prices of forwards expiring on business days falling between July 1 and July 31 are determined as of the expiry date of June 30. The proceeds to the exercise of the call equal the maximum of zero, or the difference between the average of these forward prices and the option strike price.

Matlab Implementation for a Monthly Strike Option

The adjacent Matlab code presents an implementation of the splitting methodology for the valuation of a monthly strike option—the program can be modified slightly to value a daily strike option. There are several steps in the program:

- The program takes as inputs the load volatility, `sigmaq`, the fuel volatility `sigmaf`, the speed of mean reversion `mrcoef`, and a matrix of drift coefficients `new_qdrift`. The volatilities and mean reversion are scalars. `new_qdrift` is an $nq \times nt$ matrix, where nq is the number of load steps, and nt is the number of time steps. Because the load drift $\alpha(.)$ varies by load level (due to mean reversion and the dependence of the market price of risk on load) and time (due to the time-varying mean log load), there is a different drift for every log load-time point. `new_qdrift` can be determined using the techniques described in Pirrong-Jermakyan (2006), and the calibration method described previously.

- `new_qdrift` is used to create `c1(:,:)`, an $nq \times nt$ matrix of coefficients on the first order term in q in (8.7). In addition, `sigmaq` is used to create `c2(:,:)`, a matrix of coefficients on the second order term in q in (8.7), and the interest rate `r` is used to create `c0(:,1)`, the coefficients on the zero order term.

- The program also utilizes a 4×1 vector `option_date_vec` to determine the payoff relevant dates and the expiration date of the option. This vector is utilized to create an $nt \times 1$ vector consisting of zeros and ones, where ones correspond to dates that contribute to option payoff. For instance, for a monthly strike option on peak power expiring in July, the vector `monthly_strike_vec` has ones in the rows corresponding to weekdays in July. The vector `monthly_strike_dummy` is `monthly_strike_vec` divided by `sum(monthly_strike_vec)`. This is used to create an average of forward prices included in the deliverable bundle of the monthly strike option for the purpose of determining payoff and upper and lower fuel price boundary conditions.

- The core of the program is the finite difference method employed in the splitting. The program time steps from option expiration to the present date. At each time step, equation (8.16) can be discretized as follows for negative `c1`:

$$\frac{C_{i,j}^{k+.5} - C_{i,j}^{k}}{\delta t} = c1_{i,k+1} \frac{C_{i,j}^{k+.5} - C_{i-1,j}^{k+.5}}{2\delta q}$$
$$+ c2_{i,k+1} \frac{C_{i+1,j}^{k+.5} - 2C_{i,j}^{k+.5} + C_{i-1,j}^{k+.5}}{\delta q^2}$$

$$+ .5\rho\sigma_q\sigma_f \frac{C_{i+1,j+1}^k - C_{i+1,j-1}^k - C_{i-1,j+1}^k + C_{i-1,j-1}^k}{4\delta q \delta \widehat{f}}$$

$$- rC_{i,j}^{k+1}$$

where the superscript indicates the number of time steps prior to expiration at which the option price C is measured, the first subscript $2 \leq i \leq nq - 1$ indicates the point on the load grid and the second subscript $2 \leq j \leq nf - 2$ indicates the point on the fuel grid.[17] Note that the coefficients are time and load dependent as well. Further note that this expression allows determination of the value of the option at the pseudo-time step $k + .5$ based on already solved for values at time step k. Gathering terms for each time step generates an $nq - 2 \times nq - 2 \times nt - 1$ array `mlarray` such that `mlarray(:,:,k+1)*u_array(2:nq-2,k+.5)` equals `u_array(2:nq-2,k)+corr_correction`, where `u_array(:,k+.5)` is the option value at pseudo-time step $k + .5$ and the `corr_correction` term arises from the term multiplied by ρ and depends on the values from `u_array` at time step k. This system of equations can be solved through matrix inversion or (as in the code) Matlab left division to determine the option value for interior log load points at pseudo-time step $k + .5$. Applying the von Neumann boundary conditions permits determination of the option value for the highest and lowest log load points. A set of equations must be solved for each fuel price step $j = 2, \ldots, nf - 1$, so these steps are nested inside a fuel price loop (the `j1` loop). For $j = 1$ and $j = nf$, Dirichlet boundary conditions are used to determine the option value for each load step.

Once `u_array` has been determined at the pseudo-time step $k + .5$, after a log transformation, the program proceeds to the full time step $k + 1$ by discretizing (8.17) as follows:

$$\frac{C_{i,j}^{k+1} - C_{i,j}^{k+.5}}{\delta t} = -.5\sigma_f^2 \frac{C_{i,j+1}^{k+1} - C_{i,j-1}^{k+1}}{2\delta\widehat{f}} + .5\sigma_f^2 \frac{C_{i,j+1}^{k+1} - 2C_{i,j}^{k+1} + C_{i,j-1}^{k+1}}{\delta\widehat{f}^2}$$

$$+ .5\rho\sigma_q\sigma_f \frac{C_{i+1,j+1}^{k+.5} - C_{i+1,j-1}^{k+.5} - C_{i-1,j+1}^{k+.5} + C_{i-1,j-1}^{k+.5}}{4\delta q \delta \widehat{f}}$$

Gathering common terms again leads to a set of linear equations that can be solved for `u_array` at the full time step. The matrix in this set of linear equations is `mlarray_f`. A set of equations must be solved for each load step $i = 2, \ldots nq - 1$, so the equation solutions are nested inside a load loop (the `j2` loop). For each of these load steps, Dirichlet boundary conditions allow determination of `u_array` for the highest and lowest fuel prices. For $i = 1$ and $i = nq$, and for each $j = 1, \ldots nf$, I use von Neumann boundary conditions to solve for the option value. As written, the program solves for the value of a put. It then uses put-call parity to solve for the call option value.

The following is code for valuing a monthly strike option:

power_option_splitting_london.m

```
function v=power_option_splitting(vall,strike,date_vec,sigmaq,sigmaf,rho,
  qvec,new_qdrift,cptype,option_date_vec,nq,nf,r)

% THIS PROGRAM USES A SPLITTING TECHNIQUE TO SOLVE THE 2D PDE THAT VALUES A
% MONTHLY STRIKE OPTION.  THE TECHNIQUE CAN BE READILY ADAPTED TO SOLVE FOR
% THE VALUE OF A DAILY STRIKE OPTION

% THE FUNCTION TAKES INPUTS:

% nq:=number of log load points in the valuation grid
% nf:=number of log fuel points in the valuation grid
% vall:=a matrix of forward market heat rates for each date between the
%    present and option expiry.  vall is determined by solving the
%    Pirrong-Jermakyan calibration problem applied to observed power forward
%    prices and fuel prices
% qvec:=nq x 1 vector of log load points.  Each row in vall corresponds to
%    a log load point in qvec
% strike:=the monthly option strike in $/MWh
% sigmaq:=load volatility determined from historical data--see
%    Pirrong-Jermakyan (2006)
% sigmaf:=fuel volatility
% rho:=load-fuel correlation
% new_qdrift:=matrix of load drifts (in the equivalent measure)
% cptype:= option type indicator -1 for a put +1 for a call
% option_date_vec:=a 4x1 vector of dates, with the first element the
% current date, the second element the option expiration date, the third
% element the first forward delivery date included in the monthly strike
% bundle, and the last (fourth) element the last forward delivery date
% included in the bundle

ndates=size(vall,3);
nt=ndates;
nm=size(vall,2);

sigmaq2=sigmaq^2;


% determine 1st, 2nd, and 0 order load coefficients in valuation PDE

for jtc=1:nt

    c1(:,jtc)=new_qdrift(:,jtc);
    c2(:,jtc)=.5*sigmaq2*ones(nq,1);
    c0(:,jtc)=r*ones(nq,1);

end

% create al, bl, cl, and ar, br, and cr matrices

% assume daily time steps

dt=1/365;
```

```
nu1=dt/(dq);
nu2=dt/((dq^2));

ar=zeros(nq,nt-1);
br=ar;
cr=ar;

al=ar;
bl=ar;
cl=ar;

% centdiff is an indicator that equals zero when using upwind/downwind
% differencing (depending on the sign of c1) on the 1st order load term and
% equals 1 when using central differencing.  Given the magnitude of c1,
% non-central differencing typically preferable

centdiff=0;

for jta=1:nt-1

    if centdiff==0

        c1dum=(c1(:,jta)>0);
        al(:,jta)=-nu2*c2(:,jta)+nu1*(1-c1dum).*c1(:,jta);
        bl(:,jta)=1-dt*c0(:,jta)+2*nu2*c2(:,jta)+nu1*(c1dum.*c1(:,jta)-
           (1-c1dum).*c1(:,jta));

        % use cx instead of cl (c letter l) to avoid confusion with c1
        % (c numeral one)

        cx(:,jta)=-nu2*c2(:,jta)-nu1*c1dum.*c1(:,jta);

    else


    % central differences

        al(:,jta)=-nu2*c2(:,jta)+.5*nu1*c1(:,jta);
        bl(:,jta)=1-dt*c0(:,jta)+2*c2(:,jta)*nu2;
        cx(:,jta)=-nu2*c2(:,jta)-.5*c1(:,jta)*nu1;

    end

end

% fill in mlarray and mlarrayinv
% mlarray is a matrix implied by the discretization of the first (load)
% split in the valuation PDE
% this array is used to determine option values at pseudo-step

mlarray=zeros(nq-2,nq-2,nt-1);
mrarray=zeros(nq-2,nq,nt-1);

for jt1=1:nt-1
    for jqr=2:nq-3
        for jqc=1:nq-2;
```

```
            if jqc==jqr
                mlarray(jqr,jqc,jt1)=bl(jqr+1,jt1);
            end

            if jqc==jqr+1
                mlarray(jqr,jqc,jt1)=cx(jqr+1,jt1);
            end

            if jqc==jqr-1
                mlarray(jqr,jqc,jt1)=al(jqr+1,jt1);
            end

        end
    end

% fill in values of mlarray implied by load boundary conditions
% use von Neumann boundary condition implied by reflecting
% barriers at upper and lower load levels

    mlarray(1,1,jt1)=al(2,jt1)+(4/3)*bl(2,jt1);
    mlarray(1,2,jt1)=cx(2,jt1)-(1/3)*bl(2,jt1);
    mlarray(nq-2,nq-2,jt1)=(4/3)*bl(nq-1,jt1)+cx(nq-1,jt1);
    mlarray(nq-2,nq-3,jt1)=al(nq-1,jt1)-(1/3)*bl(nq-1,jt1);


end

% Define fuel grid
% use fuel prices that are well away from current fuel prices

    F_min=2;
    F_max=16;

    f_min=log(F_min);
    f_max=log(F_max);

    df=(f_max-f_min)/(nf-1);
    f=f_min:df:f_max;


% now define terms that will determine mlarray_f
% this array is used to solve for option values at the full step

A_f=-.5*(sigmaf^2)*((dt/df^2)+.5*(dt/df));
B_f=1+(sigmaf^2)*(dt/df^2);
C_f=.5*(sigmaf^2)*(-(dt/df^2)+.5*(dt/df));

% determine mlarray_f

    for jfr=1:nf-2
        for jfc=1:nf-2;

            if jfc==jfr
                mlarray_f(jfr,jfc)=B_f;
            end
```

```
            if jfc==jfr+1
                mlarray_f(jfr,jfc)=C_f;
            end

            if jfc==jfr-1
                mlarray_f(jfr,jfc)=A_f;
            end

        end
    end


% payoff matrix
% it is assumed that monthly strike option requires delivery of a bundle of
% on peak forward price with delivery during weekdays
% therefore, need a weekday indicator variable wday taking values of one
% during weekdays and zero otherwise

[wday,w]=weekday(date_vec);

% cdate:=current date
% edate:=option expiry
% fdeldate:=first delivery date in bundle
% ldeldate:=last delivery date in bundle

    cdate=option_date_vec(1);
    edate=option_date_vec(2);
    fdeldate=option_date_vec(3);
    ldeldate=option_date_vec(4);

% monthly_strike_vec:=zeros for non-delivery dates, ones for delivery dates

    monthly_strike_vec=(date_vec>=fdeldate).*(date_vec<=ldeldate).*
        (wday>1).*(wday<7);

% monthly_strike_dummy:=set of weights to be applied to each deliverable in
%    bundle to determine average price

    monthly_strike_dummy=monthly_strike_vec(2:nt)/
        sum(monthly_strike_vec(2:nt));

% jexpiry is the number of days until expiration

    jexpiry=edate-cdate+1;

% determine option payoff.  Multiply heat rate array for expiration date by
% monthly_strike_dummy to determine average heat rate.  Second dimension of
% vall is a delivery date dimension

    vpaymat=vall(:,:,jexpiry)*monthly_strike_dummy;

% rvec will be used to implement Dirichlet boundary conditions (in
% fuel dimension)
    rvec=zeros(nf-2,1);

% cross correlation term
```

```
      cross_coefficient=rho*sigmaf*sigmaq*dt/(dq*df);


% can do payoff as put or a call
% or can implement by doing payoff for put only, then using put call
% parity to value call
% desirable to use a put because don't have to worry about value as f
% goes to infinity or 0
% payoff for a put is strike minus average market heat rate for monthly
% strike bundle times fuel price for that bundle

    for jf=1:nf

        payoff(:,jf)=max(-vpaymat*exp(f(jf))+strike,0);

    end


% initialize u_array
% u_array will contain the option values for each date from the present
% to expiry
% since option value is solved for at whole and half (pseudo) time steps,
% u_array consists of 2*jexpiry-1 nq x nf matrices

    u_array=zeros(nq,nf,2*jexpiry-1);

% u_array value at expiry given by option payoff

    u_array(:,:,2*jexpiry-1)=payoff;

% begin time stepping from expiry to the present

    for jt=jexpiry-1:-1:1


% Implementation of splitting methodology
% first loop over fuel steps
% this solves at the half step in q implicitly

        for j1=2:nf-1

% corr_correction term arises from cross derivative in PDE
% use explicit approximation per Yanenko

            corr_correction=(u_array(3:nq,j1+1,2*jt+1)-
                u_array(3:nq,j1-1,2*jt+1));
            corr_correction=corr_correction+(-u_array(1:nq-2,j1+1,2*jt+1)+
                u_array(1:nq-2,j1-1,2*jt+1));
            corr_correction=.125*cross_coefficient*corr_correction;

            u_array(2:nq-1,j1,2*jt)=mlarray(:,:,jt)\
                (u_array(2:nq-1,j1,2*jt+1)+corr_correction);

% von Neumann boundary conditions

            u_array(1,j1,2*jt)=(4/3)*u_array(2,j1,2*jt)-
                (1/3)*u_array(3,j1,2*jt);
```

```
                u_array(nq,j1,2*jt)=(4/3)*u_array(nq-1,j1,2*jt)-
                  (1/3)*u_array(nq-2,j1,2*jt);

        end % end j1 loop

% fill in fuel boundaries--use Dirichlet BC

                v_bound=vall(:,:,jt)*monthly_strike_dummy;
                u_array(:,1,2*jt)=exp(-r*dt*(jexpiry-jt))*(-exp(f(1))*
                  v_bound+strike);;
                u_array(:,nf,2*jt)=0;


% now do the fuel split so loop over load steps

        for j2=2:nq-1

                rvec(nf-2,1)=0;
                rvec(1,1)=-A_f*exp(-r*dt*(jexpiry-jt))*(-exp(f(1))*
                  vall(j2,:,jt)*monthly_strike_dummy+strike);
                corr_correction=(u_array(j2+1,3:nf,2*jt)-
                  u_array(j2+1,1:nf-2,2*jt));
                corr_correction=corr_correction+(-u_array(j2-1,3:nf,2*jt)+
                  u_array(j2-1,1:nf-2,2*jt));
                corr_correction=.125*cross_coefficient*corr_correction';
                rhs_vector=u_array(j2,2:nf-1,2*jt)'+corr_correction+rvec;
                u_array(j2,2:nf-1,2*jt-1)=(mlarray_f\rhs_vector)';

% Dirichlet boundary conditions

                u_array(j2,1,2*jt-1)=-exp(-r*dt*(jexpiry-jt))*(exp(f(1))*
                  vall(j2,:,jt)*monthly_strike_dummy-strike);
                u_array(j2,nf,2*jt-1)=0;


        end % end j2 loop

% fill in values for lowest and highest loads
% use von Neumann boundary conditions


                u_array(1,:,2*jt-1)=(4/3)*u_array(2,:,2*jt-1)-
                  (1/3)*u_array(3,:,2*jt-1);
                u_array(nq,:,2*jt-1)=(4/3)*u_array(nq-1,:,2*jt-1)-
                  (1/3)*u_array(nq-2,:,2*jt-1);


    end % end jt loop

    v=zeros(nq,nf,jexpiry);

    clear u_array

% convert v if option is a put using put call parity
% only use full step values

    if cptype>0
```

```
        for jt=1:jexpiry
            for j2=1:nf

                fvec=exp(f(j2))*vall(:,:,jt)*monthly_strike_dummy;
                v(:,j2,jt)=u_array(:,j2,2*jt-1)+
                  exp(-r*dt*(jexpiry-jt))*(fvec-strike);

            end
        end

    else

        for jt=1:jexpiry

            v(:,:,jt)=u_array(:,j2,2*jt-1);

        end

    end % end cptype>0

% Now, that was easy, wasn't it?
```

Spark Spread Options

Because in the PJ model the forward price is a multiplicatively separable function of the fuel forward price and a function of load, the payoff to the spark spread call can be re-expressed as:

$$(F_{t',T} - f_{t',T}H^*)^+ = (f_{t',T}V(q_{t'}, t', T) - f_{t',T}H^*)^+$$
$$= f_{t',T}(V(q_{t'}, t', T) - H^*)^+.$$

Therefore, the payoff to the spark spread option is multiplicatively separable in load and fuel. Consequently, it is possible to utilize the PJ decomposition discussed previously to write the value of the spark spread option as another multiplicatively separable function of the current fuel forward price and current load. Specifically, denoting the spark spread call option value as $H(.)$:

$$H(q_t, f_{t,T}, t, T, H^*) = f_{t,T}\Phi(q_t, t, T, H^*).$$

The $\Phi(.)$ function can be determined using a standard implicit solver with $(V(q_{t'}, t', T) - H^*)^+$ as an initial condition.[18]

Matlab Implementation of Spark Spread Option Valuation

The spark spread option code is relatively simple, due to the dimensionality reduction. Hence, we need only create a load and time grid. The Matlab code determines the payoff for a spark spread call for each load point in the load grid for each maturity of option included in the bundle of options to be valued. This payoff is then passed to the function `fpowdirect_implicit_sparkspread_1.m`. This function also takes a matrix of load drift coefficients `drift_mat` that reflects both the $\alpha(.)$ and $\lambda(.)$ functions, load and fuel volatilities, and information related to the time and load grids. The function uses an implicit PDE solver (preferably based on one-sided differences) to determine the $\Phi(.)$ function for each maturity, at time and load step. The output of this function is measured in MMBTU per MWh. To convert the value to \$/MWh, multiply the function output by the appropriate fuel forward price. For instance, for a spark spread option expiring in July 2007, multiply the function output for that maturity by the July 2007 fuel forward price.

The following is the code for evaluating a spark spread optio. This shell calls an implicit PDE solver, fpowdirect_implicit_sparkspread_1.

spark_speed_shell.m

```
% spark spread option code uses dimensionality reduction and 1D
% implicit solver assuming pgbeta (gamma)==1.
% The solver determines the value of spark spread option in a portfolio
% of said options, the first of which expires on fdeldate and the last
% on ldeldate

% date manipulations

cdate=option_date_vec(1);
edate=option_date_vec(2);
fdeldate=option_date_vec(3);
ldeldate=option_date_vec(4);

jexpiry0=fdeldate-cdate+1;
jexpiry1=ldeldate-cdate+1;

for jm=1:jexpiry1-1

% determine the payoff to each option in the package
% vall(:,jm,jm+1) is the market forward heat rate for the forward
% maturing on day jm+1 as of day jm.  This assumes that option is
% exercised one day before the delivery date.
% Spark spread option payoff (for a call) is the difference between
% this forward price and the strike price.  vall and strike are
% measured in MMBTU per MWh.

    payoff(:,jm)=max(vall(:,jm,jm+1)-strike,0);

end % end jm payoff definition loop

% pgbeta is the coefficient on the fuel price in the power price
% equation in the PJ model

    sigmaq2=sigmaq^2;
    sigmaf2=sigmaf^2;
    pgbeta=1;

% call the implicit solver

    [v,mlarrayx]=fpowdirect_implicit_sparkspread_1(new_qdrift,sigmaq,
        sigmaq2,sigmaf,sigmaf2,rho,pgbeta,q,nq,jexpiry1,dt,dq,payoff);
```

This is the implicit solver called by the spark_speed_shell program:

fpowdirect_implicit_sparkspread_1.m

```
function [vall,mlarray]=fpowdirect_implicit_sparkspread(drift_mat,sigmaq,
    sigmaq2,sigmaf,sigmaf2,rho,pgbeta,q,nq,nt,dt,dq,pay_mat);

% this function solves the direct problem to value a portfolio of spark
% spread options.
% function returns vall, an array of option values for each maturity, each
% time step, and each load step
% to get value of spark spread option in $/MWh, multiply the elements of
% vall by the appropriate fuel forward price

% drift_mat:=nq x nt matrix of load drift coefficients
% sigmaq:=load volatility
% sigmaf:=fuel volatility
% rho:=load-fuel correlation
% pgbeta:=fuel price exponent in power price equation from PJ model; must
%    equal one in this case to esnure separability of option payoff in load
%    and fuel price
% q:=vector of log load points--this is the load grid
% nq:=number of load points in grid
% nt:=number of time steps until expiration of longest-dated option in the
%    package
% dt:=length of time step--typically 1 day=1/365 years
% dq:=log load step size
% pay_mat:=matrix of payoffs.  Each column gives a payoff for a different
%    option in the package


% create c0 c1 c2 vectors
% these are the coefficients on the first, second, and zero order terms,
% respectively, in the valuation PDE.  This takes advantage of the PJ
% dimenionality reduction that is feasible due to the separability in fuel
% and log load of the spark-spread payoff when pgbeta=1
% due to the time variation and load dependence of these coefficients, each
% is an nq x nt matrix

for jtc=1:nt

    c1(:,jtc)=pgbeta*rho*sigmaq*sigmaf*ones(nq,1)+drift_mat(:,jtc);
    c2(:,jtc)=.5*sigmaq2*ones(nq,1);
    c0(:,jtc)=.5*sigmaf2*pgbeta*(pgbeta-1)*ones(nq,1);

end

% create al, bl, cl, and ar, br, and cr matrices

nu1=dt/(dq);
nu2=dt/((dq^2));

ar=zeros(nq,nt-1);
br=ar;
cr=ar;
```

```
al=ar;
bl=ar;
cl=ar;

centdiff=0;

% user has choice to use central differences, or one-sided differences to
% given the fact that the load mean reversion coefficient is usually very
% large (in absolute value) it is typically desirable to utilize
% non-central differences

for jta=1:nt-1

    if centdiff==0

        cldum=(cl(:,jta)>0);
        al(:,jta)=-nu2*c2(:,jta)+nu1*(1-cldum).*cl(:,jta);
        bl(:,jta)=1-dt*c0(:,jta)+2*nu2*c2(:,jta)+nu1*(cldum.*cl(:,jta)-
           (1-cldum).*cl(:,jta));
        % use cx instead of cl (c letter l) to avoid confusion
        % with cl (c one)
        cx(:,jta)=-nu2*c2(:,jta)-nu1*cldum.*cl(:,jta);

    else


    % central differences

        al(:,jta)=-nu2*c2(:,jta)+.5*nu1*cl(:,jta);
        bl(:,jta)=1-dt*c0(:,jta)+2*c2(:,jta)*nu2;
        cx(:,jta)=-nu2*c2(:,jta)-.5*cl(:,jta)*nu1;

    end

end

% fill in mlarray
% value of the option at time step jt+1 times the appropriate "slice" of
% mlarray equals the value of the option at time step jt (with a greater
% time step indicating a time closer to the present/further from expiration)
% mlarray is nq-2 x nq-2 x nt-1 because the coefficients are time varying

mlarray=zeros(nq-2,nq-2,nt-1);
mrarray=zeros(nq-2,nq,nt-1);

for jt1=1:nt-1
    for jqr=2:nq-3
        for jqc=1:nq-2;

            if jqc==jqr
                mlarray(jqr,jqc,jt1)=bl(jqr+1,jt1);
            end

            if jqc==jqr+1
                mlarray(jqr,jqc,jt1)=cx(jqr+1,jt1);
            end
```

```
                    if jqc==jqr-1
                        mlarray(jqr,jqc,jt1)=al(jqr+1,jt1);
                    end

            end
        end

        % fill in boundary conditions
        % use von Neumann conditions

        mlarray(1,1,jt1)=al(2,jt1)+(4/3)*bl(2,jt1);
        mlarray(1,2,jt1)=cx(2,jt1)-(1/3)*bl(2,jt1);
        mlarray(nq-2,nq-2,jt1)=(4/3)*bl(nq-1,jt1)+cx(nq-1,jt1);
        mlarray(nq-2,nq-3,jt1)=al(nq-1,jt1)-(1/3)*bl(nq-1,jt1);

end


% now begin time stepping
% jt is the time step loop
% jm is the maturity loop

vall=zeros(nq,nt-1,nt);

for jt=nt-1:-1:1
    for jm=jt:nt-1

        if jm==jt

            v(2:nq-1,jm)=mlarray(:,:,jt)\(pay_mat(2:nq-1,jm));
        % apply VN boundary conditions
            v(1,jm)=(4/3)*v(2,jm)-(1/3)*v(3,jm);
            v(nq,jm)=(4/3)*v(nq-1,jm)-(1/3)*v(nq-2,jm);
            vall(:,jm,jt+1)=pay_mat(:,jm);

        else

            v(2:nq-1,jm)=mlarray(:,:,jt)\(v(2:nq-1,jm));
        % apply VN boundary conditions
            v(1,jm)=(4/3)*v(2,jm)-(1/3)*v(3,jm);
            v(nq,jm)=(4/3)*v(nq-1,jm)-(1/3)*v(nq-2,jm);

        end

    end

    vall(:,:,jt)=v;

end
```

8.9 RESULTS

The behavior of power options prices implied by this model is best understood through the use of figures and a focus on a few salient results. All option values in the figures are based on a calibrated PJ model. The model is calibrated using estimates of load volatility σ_q, mean reversion parameter k, and average log load $\theta_q(t)$ estimated from PJM data for January 1, 2000–May 31, 2005; see PJ (2006) for a description of the estimation methodology. The model is calibrated to PJM power forward prices (from the NYMEX ClearPort system) and natural gas forward prices for Texas Eastern Pipeline Zone M-3 observed on June 7, 2005 using the method of Pirrong-Jermakyan. The fuel volatility is the implied volatility from the at-the-money NYMEX natural gas futures options with delivery months corresponding to the maturity of the option being analyzed, as observed on June 7, 2005.

The valuation grid has 100 points in the load and fuel dimensions. The minimum fuel price is $1.00, and the maximum is $25.00. The minimum load is the smallest PJM load observed in 1999–2005, and the maximum load is the total amount of generation bid into PJM on July 15, 2004 (the date used to determine the payoff function for July forwards in the model calibration—PJM bid data are available only with a six month lag).

Figure 8.3 depicts the value of a daily strike call option expiring on July 15, 2005, measured two days prior to expiration, as a function of fuel price and load. The strike of this option is $85, which was the at-the-money strike on June 7, 2005. The horizontal plane

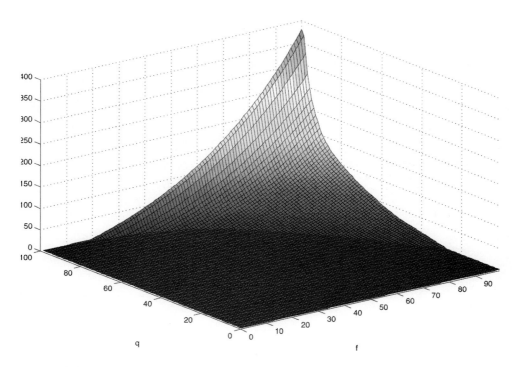

Figure 8.3 Daily strike option value—2 days to expiry.

dimensions are the fuel price f and the load q (running into the chart from front to back). The option value is increasing in fuel price and load, as would be expected. Thus, load and fuel Deltas are both positive. Note, too, that there is noticeable convexity of the option value in both f and q. That is, both load and fuel Gammas are positive. The load Gamma is noticeably large and positive for high levels of load, and for high fuel prices. This reflects (a) the convexity of the load-power price relation when time to expiry is short, and (b) the convexity of the option payoff function.

Figure 8.4 depicts the value of the same option on June 7, 2005, or approximately 38 days prior to expiry. In the figure, the positive fuel Delta and Gamma are readily apparent; the convexity in fuel price is especially evident for intermediate fuel prices (where the option is near-the-money).

However, the option value exhibits little dependence on load. In fact, the load Delta and load Gamma are effectively zero. (When one plots the option value as a function of load for a given fuel price in Matlab, the change in the option value across the range of load values is smaller than the minimum increment that can be depicted by the Matlab plotting function.) Indeed, the zeroing out of the load Delta and Gamma occurs as time maturity falls to as little as seven or eight days. Thus, despite the strong dependence of spot power prices on load, daily strike options with maturities of more than a few days exhibit virtually no dependence on load.

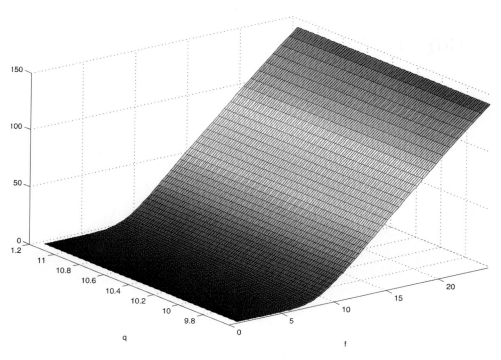

Figure 8.4 Daily strike option value—38 days to expiry.

   This phenomenon reflects the strong mean reversion in load. Due to this strong mean reversion, the distribution of load for future dates conditional on current load converges quite quickly to the unconditional load distribution. Thus, for maturities beyond a few days, variations in current load convey very little information about the distribution of load at expiry, and thus such variations have little impact on the daily strike option value.

   This analysis implies that for a week or more prior to daily strike option expiration, such options are effectively options on fuel. Until expiration nears, these options can be hedged using fuel forwards (to hedge fuel Delta) and fuel options (to hedge fuel Gamma). In the last few days before expiry, however, the option value exhibits progressively stronger dependence on load (especially when load is high), and hedging requires the use of load-sensitive claims (e.g., a forward to hedge load Delta, or another load-sensitive option to hedge load Gamma).

   The effects of load mean reversion on power option value is especially evident when one examines monthly strike options. Figure 8.5 depicts the value of a July, 2005 monthly strike call option one day prior to expiry. Even given this short maturity, there is only a slight load Delta, and virtually no load Gamma. However, the non-zero fuel Delta and Gamma are evident. The lack of load dependence reflects the fact that the payoff to the monthly strike option depends on forward prices for delivery dates that are half-a-month on average after option expiry. For all but the forward contracts maturing a few days after the monthly strike option's expiry, load has little impact on the forward price. Hence,

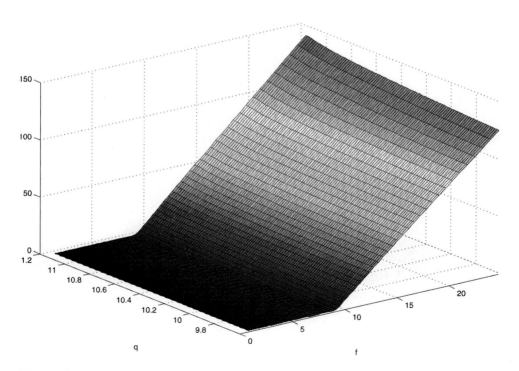

Figure 8.5 Daily strike option value—1 day to expiry.

variations in load at expiry have little effect on most of the daily forwards included in the monthly bundle.

Mean reversion also impacts option time decay. This is most evident for a spark spread option. Note that due to their multiplicative separability in load and fuel (and the separability of the forward price in these variables in the PJ framework), conditional on q spark spread option values are linear in the fuel price and hence have a fuel Gamma of zero. Thus, in contrast to what is observed for monthly and daily strike options, this implies that there is no time decay attributable to the fuel factor for a spark spread option. Any time decay for this type of option is attributable to the impact of load.

With this in mind, consider Figure 8.6, which depicts the value of $\Phi(q_t, t, T)$ for a spark spread call option with $H^* = 10$ as a function of time to expiration and load (with the load dimension running into the chart).[19] The maximum time to expiration on the chart is 55 days, and hence corresponds to a mid-August 2005 expiration date. Note that the option value is virtually constant until a few days short of expiration. Thus, there is very little time decay until very close to expiration. As the option nears expiry, however, for low loads the option value declines precipitously. Conversely, for high loads (especially very high loads), the value of the option increases dramatically.

These characteristics again reflect mean reversion in load. Well before expiry, due to mean reversion the conditional distribution of load (the only payoff relevant variable for the spark spread claim) changes virtually not at all as time passes. This contrasts with the

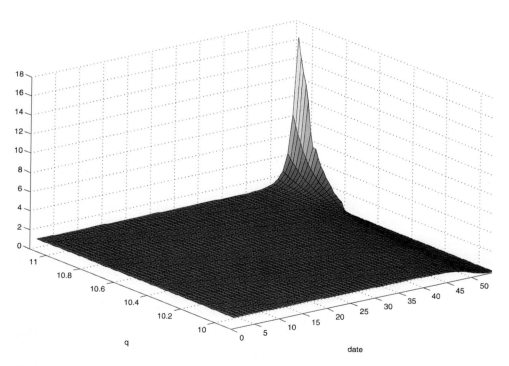

Figure 8.6 Daily strike option value—55 days to expiry.

value of an option with a payoff determined by a geometric Brownian motion (GBM), where the dispersion in the conditional distribution of the payoff-relevant variable declines monotonically as time passes. The stationarity of load translates into little time decay.

Similar influences affect time decay for daily and monthly strike options. These options exhibit time decay, but this reflects the dependence of payoffs on a GBM—the fuel price. The dispersion in payoffs declines as time passes for monthly and daily strikes due to the fall in the dispersion of fuel prices at expiry. Holding fuel price at expiry constant, the passage of time does not affect the variability in payoffs attributable to load. That is, $\partial u/\partial t$ is very close to zero when a daily strike option has more than a few days prior to expiry (regardless of the level of load), and is very close to zero immediately prior to expiry even when a monthly strike option is at-the-money.

The behavior of power options just documented should serve as a caution to using standard options models—especially those based on GBM—to value these claims. It is abundantly clear that load (or equivalently weather) and fuel prices are the major determinants of short horizon price dynamics in power. Although GBM assumes that payoff-relevant information flows evenly through time, due to mean reversion in load, the flow of payoff-relevant information is concentrated close to expiration. In essence, power options exhibit a split personality. They are effectively options on fuel until expiration nears, at which time they effectively become mainly a function of load. GBM-based models cannot handle this split personality. Jump-diffusion-type models are more capable of doing so, but as noted in §8.3, it is difficult to specify such a model that is both tractable and relatively realistic. Thus, fundamentals-based models have important virtues that make them better suited than alternative approaches to handle the inherent complexities of power contingent claims.

8.10 SUMMARY

With restructuring, electricity has become the world's largest commodity. It is also the world's most complex commodity, and this complexity has impeded the development of commodity derivatives. Markets for power contingent claims are growing, however, and so there will be a commensurately growing need for reasonable and tractable models to value them. The nature of electricity price behavior makes traditional valuation approaches based on the exogenous specification of power price movements extremely problematic. Fortunately, the transparency of fundamentals in the power market permits an alternative approach. The Pirrong-Jermakyan model described in this chapter specifies that power prices depend on key (and observable) demand and supply drivers, and derives the implications of this for the pricing of power contingent claims. The model is tractable, and can be calibrated in a theoretically grounded way to observable forward prices. Once calibrated, it can be used to price other contingent claims, including volume-sensitive claims that are important to many market participants.

The PJ model represents a good start, but it must be recognized that it has many moving parts, and that each can be improved. Moreover, work remains to be done to incorporate outages, and other power price drivers into the basic PJ framework. This is particularly important for options. Pirrong (2006a, 2006b) presents some approaches to this problem, but other methods may be feasible as well. Thus, fundamentals-based power derivative valuation modeling promises to be a very fruitful field for future research.

ENDNOTES

1. Hydro generation incorporates an element of storability into power markets.
2. The market would be incomplete even if power prices were continuous (as is possible in the model presented next) because power is non-storable. Non-storability makes it impossible to hold a hedging "position" in spot power.
3. One of the α parameters multiplies the generation outage probability vector, and can be interpreted as a measure change. The other α's cannot be interpreted in this way.
4. This characterization implicitly assumes that physical capacity is constant. The framework can be extended to allow variations in capacity due to new construction of power plants and outages.
5. The conditions are (1) there exists a "penalty function" $h(Q)$ that is convex in some interval, but is infinite outside the interval, and (2) in the absence of any control, Q would evolve as the solution to $dQ = \mu dt + \sigma dW$. The penalty function can be interpreted as the cost associated with large loads. If $Q > X$, the system may fail, resulting in huge costs. I thank Heber Farnsworth for making me aware of the Harrison-Taksar approach.
6. This is an example of a Skorokhod Equation.
7. Pirrong-Jermakyan (2006) describe in detail a process for estimating $\theta_q(t)$.
8. If there is a lower bound on load (a minimum load constraint), there exists another local time process and another Neumann-type boundary condition.
9. PJ set out two approaches—one using the bids of generators, and the other using econometric techniques—to establish this relation.
10. See Tikhonov and Arsenin (1977).
11. Remember that the forward price F is the V function multiplied by f^γ.
12. Options with payoffs that depend on a spot price present some additional challenges that are addressed in Pirrong (2006a).
13. Earlier drafts of this paper utilized a combination of quadrature and finite difference methods to value options in the (close to realistic case) where $\rho = 0$, and quadrature methods for $\rho \neq 0$.
14. This assumption can be readily modified.
15. The daily strike put payoff is defined analogously.
16. The forward is calculated using the market price of risk function calibrated to the forward curve observed on the valuation date.
17. A similar expression obtains for a positive `c1`.
18. Due to the multiplicative separability, using the transformation presented in Pirrong-Jermakyan (2005), it is possible to solve for $\Phi(.)$ even when $\rho \neq 0$.
19. The spark spread option value is extremely high when load is high close to expiration. Therefore, to highlight the lack of time decay and avoid the impact of option values for very high loads on the scaling of the figure, spark spread option values are presented only for loads that are no more than 15 percent above the mean load.

REFERENCES

[1] Barone-Adesi, G. and Gigli, A. (2002), "Electricity Derivatives," working paper, Universita della Svizzera Italiana.

[2] Bessimbinder, H. and Lemmon, M. (2002), "Equilibrium Pricing and Optimal Hedging in Electricity Forward Markets," *Journal of Finance*, 57.

[3] Duffy, D. (2006), *Finite Difference Methods in Financial Engineering: A Partial Differential Equations Approach.* John Wiley & Sons: New York.

[4] Eydeland, A. and Wolyniec, K. (2002), *Energy and Power Risk Management: New Developments in Modeling, Pricing, and Hedging.* John Wiley & Sons: New York.

[5] Geman, H. (2005), *Commodities and Commodity Derivatives: Modeling and Pricing for Agriculturals, Metals, and Energy.* Wiley Finance: West Sussex.

[6] Geman, H. and Roncoroni, A. (2006), "Understanding the Fine Structure of Electricity Prices," *Journal of Business*, 79.

[7] Harrison, M.J. and Taksar, M. (1983), "Instantaneous Control of Brownian Motion," *Mathematics of Operations Research.*

[8] Pirrong, C. (2006a), "Incorporating Outages into the Pirrong-Jermakyan Framework," working paper, University of Houston.

[9] Pirrong, C. (2006b), "The Valuation of Power Options in a Pirrong-Jermakyan Framework," working paper, University of Houston.

[10] Pirrong, C. and Jermakyan, M. (2006), "The Price of Power: The Valuation of Power and Weather Derivatives," working paper, University of Houston.

[11] Pirrong, C. (2006), "Incorporating Outages in a Pirrong-Jermakyan Model," working paper, University of Houston.

[12] Tikhinov, A. and Arsenin, V. (1977), *Solution of Ill-Posed Problems.* Halsted Press: New York.

CHAPTER 9

COMMERCIAL REAL ESTATE ASSET-BACKED SECURITIES

Tien Foo Sing

SECTIONS

9.1   INTRODUCTION

Asset securitization is a multi-stage process involving pooling together receivables or cash flows generated from real estate mortgages and other financial assets, credit enhancing them, structuring them into tradable securities, and then distributing the securities to investors via either private or public markets. These securities are known as "asset-backed securities" (ABS). Real estate and financial assets that contain securitizable cash flows include collateralized residential and commercial mortgages, real estate leases, and other non-real estate-based cash flows such as automobile loans, credit card balances, home equity credit lines, collateralized debt obligations (CDOs)/collateralized bond obligations (CBOs), equipment leases, and other loans and receivables. Securitization has been developed into an effective financial engineering technology that bridges users of funds directly with suppliers of funds via capital markets, and thus reduces high transaction costs levied by financial intermediaries in conventional bank lending.

In the U.S., the earliest form of securitization was initiated by a government sponsor agency, Government National Mortgage Association (GNMA), through its first mortgage pass-through securities in 1970. Thereafter, other quasi-government or privatized agencies such as Federal National Mortgage Association (FNMA) and Federal Home Loan Mortgage Corporation (FHLMC) followed in the 1980s with their respective securitization programs that converted real estate loan pools into securities with high credit ratings. As in the 4Q2005, real estate mortgage-backed securities grew by leaps and bounds from zero to a sizable market with a total market value of U.S.$5.9 trillion.[1] In terms of market share, mortgage-backed securities constitute 23% of the total outstanding bond market debt, as in the 4Q2005 (see Figure 9.1). Securitization of other receivables had a late start, with the first ABS backed by computer equipment leases being created in 1985. The ABS market has since then expanded enormously from a meager U.S.$0.9 billion in 1985 to U.S.$1.955 trillion in the 4Q2005. The major asset types securitized in ABS markets are shown in Figure 9.2.

This chapter aims to examine commercial real estate-backed securitization—in particular, the securitization of cash flows from commercial real estate leases. It discusses cash flows that are securitizable at different stages of the real estate life cycle, starting from development conceptualization and planning approval, construction, and then up until the disposal and/or leasing of useable floor space. The real estate securitization experience and

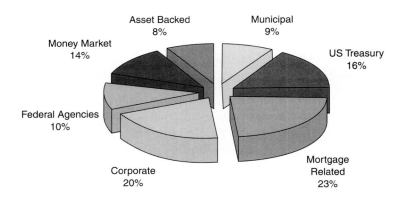

Total Outstanding Debt = US $25.3 Trillion

Sources:
U.S. Department of Treasury
Federal Reserve System
Federal National Mortgage Association
Government National Mortgage Association
Federal Home Loan Mortgage Corporation

Figure 9.1 Outstanding bond market debt as in 4Q2005. *Source: Compiled by the Bond Market Association.*

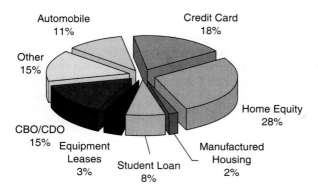

Figure 9.2 ABS outstanding by major types of credit as in 4Q200.   *Source: Compiled by the Bond Market Associations.*

development in Singapore are examined together with real-world commercial real estate-backed securitization deals structured by developers in Singapore. Pricing of these securities using swap methodology that is designed to take into default risks of the securities is also presented.

9.2   MOTIVATIONS FOR ASSET-BACKED SECURITIZATION

The securitization of U.S. mortgages in the 1970s was motivated by several factors. One of them was the interest rate ceiling imposed on deposit accounts of mortgage-lending institutions in the U.S. As a result of this interest rate ceiling, an exodus of depositors' funds from these institutions occurred when money market mutual funds and alternative investments offered higher rates than the capped deposit interest rates. Mortgage-lending institutions faced liquidity pressure when savers withdrew their deposits, while they were not able to convert the long-term mortgage obligations into cash to meet the demand by depositors. The mismatch in the duration of cash flows between the supply and demand sources, and the shortage of new capital, forced mortgage-lending institutions to cut back their lending to housing mortgages. This had adverse effects on home ownership due to escalating costs of mortgage housing loans.

The secondary market channel was created via various government and quasi-government agencies such as GNMA, FNMA, and FHLMC to help replenish capital of mortgage-lending institutions. The securitization of mortgages improves the efficiency of fund flows from supply-surplus regions to the demand-surplus regions.

The creation of the mortgage-backed securities (MBS) market in the U.S. was mainly triggered by the shortage of supply of new capital to the mortgage institutions. However, in the asset-backed securitization market, the demand side factors motivated by the needs for liquidity by owners/originators of assets have driven the changing financing structure in the traditional lending market. Securitization offers an alternative arrangement that reduces over-reliance by real estate developers on traditional financing via banks and financial intermediaries (see Figure 9.3 in the next section). In the long run, however, the paradigm shift in financing arrangement can lead to disintermediation of banks' roles, if efficiency and costs of securitization go down. While the roles of banks and lending institutions as intermediaries of capital are diminished, specialization types of fee-based services are created, which include packaging/pooling of assets, structuring of cash flows into tradable securities, credit rating and enhancement, and distributing of asset-backed securities to investors.

High concentration risks of banks and financial intermediaries in real estate financing can be mitigated, when the exposure to real estate risks are gradually shifted to secondary capital markets. Reduction in funding risks and costs can also be achieved via the securitization process, which can then be translated into lower funding costs for real estate owners, who tap into the alternative source of funding. The securitization also facilitates the removal of their assets off the balance sheet. In the process, they could realize the book values through the sale or assignment of the cash flows to a special purpose vehicle.

From institutional investors' perspective, asset-backed securities are a new class of investible asset that can provide risk diversification to their portfolio. These securities give a purer form of investment risk-return characteristics that are separated from corporate risks of the issuers/originators.

9.3 CONCEPTS OF SECURITIZING REAL ESTATE CASH FLOWS

Unlike traditional real estate financing, which is an on-the-balance sheet arrangement where long-term debt remains as a liability in the owner's book, securitization involves the outright sale of the asset to a special purpose vehicle (SPV). As shown in Figure 9.3, the long-term debt and owner equity in the liability side of the originator's book can be removed following the sale. The property value is debited, and the liability is now replaced by the claims by the ABS investors in the SPV's book. This process is known as "off-the-balance-sheet" financing.

The main objective of setting up a SPV to hold the asset is to create a bankruptcy-remote framework that will protect investors against risks associated with the owner's business operations. By segregating the securitized assets from the owner's book, investors will be entitled to a purer form of claims on income derived directly from the property. Credit rating of the ABS instruments can be assessed on the quality of the assets and their corresponding cash flows, which are independent of the owner's own financial and business risks.

The securitization technology is ubiquitous and applicable to different classes of financial assets, as long as they are able to generate streams of future cash flows. These cash flows can be financially engineered in various ways to meet capital market investors' risk-return preference. In real estate, securitization can be structured across a spectrum of cash flows over the full life-cycle of a real estate development process. The securitizable cash flows generating from the land acquisition and planning stage, to construction, and finally to the post-completion stages can be summarized in Figure 9.4. This chapter, however, focuses only on the discussion of commercial mortgages and rental cash flows from commercial properties at the post-completion stage.

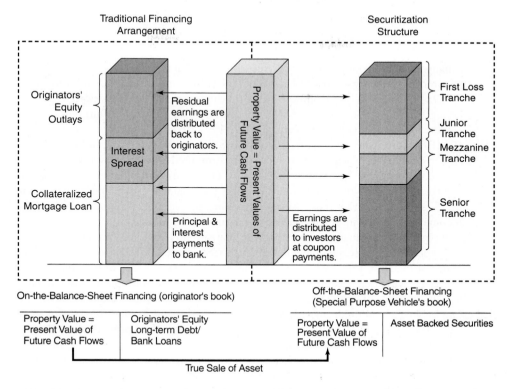

Figure 9.3 Traditional and securitization markets for real estate financing.

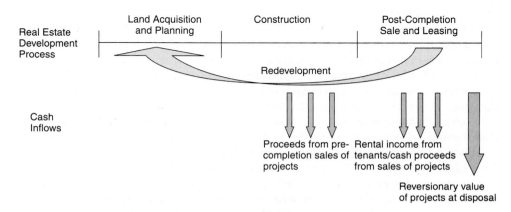

Figure 9.4 Potential source of real estate cash flows for securitization.

9.4 COMMERCIAL REAL ESTATE-BACKED SECURITIZATION (CREBS)—SINGAPORE'S EXPERIENCE

In Singapore, securitization of commercial mortgages can be traced as far back as 1986. The first commercial mortgage-backed bonds of U.S.$11.69 million (S$18.5 million)[2] were issued in 1986 by Hong Leong Holdings Limited, which pledged the legal mortgage on its Hong Leong Building located in the downtown central business district. During the boom periods in the real estate market between 1994 and 1997, 16 commercial mortgage-backed bonds (CMBB) were issued with a total value of U.S.$1.47 billion (S$2.32 billion).[3] Many of the earlier securitization deals in Singapore were structured as simple pay-through bonds backed by mortgages on single commercial assets. The securitization provides a mean for banks to take commercial real estate mortgages off their balance sheet, and reduces their exposure to real estate market risks. At the same time, they generate a new source of fee-based income through the mortgage-backed bond-structuring services.

Following the Asian financial crisis in 1997 that severely hit many Asian economies, where Singapore had no escape, many developers faced severe liquidity problems, and the book values of their asset also suffered hefty depreciation. Direct sale of the commercial real estate assets was not a feasible option for developers, because this option required them to make a huge write-off of the property value from the book. Moreover, at the time, the real estate market was in doldrums—it would have been difficult for developers/owners of commercial real estate to find interested investors to purchase their properties wholesale. Therefore, the developers/owners tapped into the expertise of investment banks in structured financing, and resorted to the securitization route as an alternative way to source for financing through the secondary market. They took the equity interests of the property off their book via an outright sale to an SPV without taking a big cut in values. The SPV, in turn, raised funds in capital markets through issuing bonds that guaranteed comparable fixed coupon yields. The first commercial real estate-backed securities (CREBS) were issued in 1999 by the Neptune Orient Line (NOL), the largest shipping line in Singapore, which involved the sale of the NOL headquarter building located at Alexandra Road for U.S.$116.91 million (S$185 million). There were altogether 10 CREBS deals arranged over a three-year period from 1999 to 2002, with an estimated U.S.$2.59 billion (S$4.1 billion) bonds issued to fund the transactions (see Table 9.1).

In most of the CREBS structured during the periods, a simple subordination structure with only two tranches of bonds—senior and junior—was adopted, and there was no other third-party guarantee and credit protection being included. Over-collateralization was also not used as credit enhancement in these deals. Buy-back options were built into the terms and conditions of sale, which allowed the developer to retain claims on the future appreciation of the asset value. The buy-back feature violated the "true" sale requirements stipulated in legislation changes made by the Monetary Authority of Singapore (MAS), the de-facto central bank of Singapore, in the circular Notice 628 on December 4, 2000. As a result, real estate assets in some CREBS have been reconsolidated into the book of CREBS sponsors.[4] With the stricter legislative changes imposed, coupled with the popularity of real estate investment trusts (REITs)following the successful listing of the first CapitaMall Trust (CMT)

Table 9.1 List of Commercial Real Estate-Backed Securitization Deals in Singapore.

Property Securitized	Property Type	Sponsor/ Owner	Bond Issued (S$ Mil.)	Special Purpose Vehicle	Underwriter	Coupon Rates		Bond Tenure	Issue Date
						Senior Bonds	Junior Bonds		
Neptune Orient Line HQ	Office	NOL	$185.00 mil.	Chenab Investments Ltd	DBS Bank	6.75%	7.25%	10-year	Mar-99
Robinson Point	Office	Birchvest Investment Pte Ltd. (DBS Land)	$193.00 mil.	Visor Limited	DBS Bank	6.00%	2%	10-year	Jul-99
Century Square Shopping Mall	Shopping Center	First Capital Corporation	$200.00 mil.	Pemberton Development Ltd	DBS Bank	N.A.	N.A.	7-year	Jun-99
268 Orchard Road	Office	RE Properties (DBS Land)	$184.00 mil.	Baronet Limited	DBS Bank	5.50%	6.50%	10-year	Sep-99
Tampines Center	Shopping Center	DBS Bank	$180.00 mil.	Tampines Assets Limited	DBS Bank	5.63%	6.00%	7-year	Dec-99
Six Battery Road	Office	Birchvest Investments Pte Ltd (DBS Land)	$878.00 mil.	Clover Holdings Limited	DBS Bank	6.00%	6.50%	10-year	Dec-99
Raffles City	Shopping Center cum Office	Raffles Holdings	$984.50 mil.	Tincel Limited	DBS Bank	5.00%	7.40%	10-year	Jun-01
Wisma Atria	Shopping Center cum Office	Al Khaleej Investment/ Wisma De	$451.00 mil.	Upperton (Aspinden) Holdings	United Overseas Bank (UOB)	4.94%	7.0% (A) & 8.85% (B)	5-year	May-02
Compass Point Shopping Center	Shopping Center	Fraser & Neave Ltd	$335.00 mil.	Sengkang Mall Limited	DBS Bank	4.88%	8.00%	10-year	Nov-02
Capital Square	Office	Keppel Land	$505.00 mil.	Queensley Holdings Limited	DBS Bank	4.50%	N.A.	7-year	Nov-02

Source: Compilation by the author

in July 2002, the CREBS structure has been replaced by the REIT vehicle as a more popular way to unlock the book values of assets of sponsoring developers.

In the early batches of CREBS, pooling of commercial mortgages and multi-layer tranching of securities were not adopted. These two features were only incorporated when listed Singapore real estate investment trusts (S-REITs) securitized mortgages on the portfolios of commercial properties. CMT utilized the CMBS structure via the SPV, Silver Maple Investment Corporation Limited (SMICL), to obtained three tranches of financing comprising S$172 million term loans and S$28 million revolving credit facilities secured on three of the retail properties in the CMT portfolio in February 2002, and S$125 million term loans on the acquisition of the IMM building in June 2003. Ascendas-REIT (A-REIT) also converted S$628.2 million mortgages secured on its 40 properties into CMBSs. Six CMBS deals have been structured as of today, which have an aggregate bond value of U.S.$1.29 billion (S$2.04 billion) at par. Details of the CMBS deals are summarized in Table 9.2.

CMBSs bring several advantages to private real estate funds, developers, REITs, the secondary real estate market, and institutional investors. For users of funds like developers

Table 9.2 List of Commercial Mortgage-Backed Securities (CMBS) Deals in Singapore

Issue Date	Duration	Number of Tranches	Issue Size (S$ Mil.)	Collateral Assets	CMBS Issuer	CRE Mortgager
Feb 26, 2002	5 years	Two tranches: One Fixed Rate Note @3.86% and one Floating Rate Notes at 0.43% above Singapore dollar swap rate#1	S$200.00	Three retail malls in CMT portfolio: Funan the IT Mall, Junction 8, Tampines Mall	Silver Maple Investment Corporation Limited	CapitaMall Trust (CMT)
Jun 26, 2003	7 years	One Floating Rate Note @ 0.62% above the U.S. dollar London Interbank Offered Rate (LIBOR)#2	S$125.00	Acquisition of IMM Building for inclusion in CMT portfolio	Silver Maple Investment Corporation Limited	CapitaMall Trust (CMT)
Feb 27, 2004	4 years	Five tranches: A, B, C, D, and E (D and E are unrated)#3	S$506.00	Three retail malls: Reivervale Mall, Lot One Shoppers Mall, Bukit Panjang Plaza	CapitaRetail Singapore Ltd	Three Single Purpose Trusts (SPTs) that hold the three assets
Mar 16, 2004	5 years	Four rated tranches: A1 to A4	S$580.00	Four office buildings, one mixed use commercial and retail complex, and two commercial carpark facilities in Singapore	Silver Loft Investment Corporation Limited	CapitaCommercial Trust (CCT)
Aug 5, 2004	5 years	One Floating Rate Note @ EUR-EURIBOR-Telerate, plus a spread of 0.33% per annum #4	S$292.70	17 properties: business park properties (6), light industrial properties (4), hi-tech industrial properties (2), and distribution and logistic centers (5)	Emerald Assets Limited	Ascendas REIT
May 12, 2005	7 years	One Floating Rate Note @ EUR-EURIBOR-Telerate plus a spread of 0.23% per annum #5	S$335.40	23 properties: logistics and distribution centers (6), hi-tech industrial properties (6), light industrial properties (10), and business and science park (1)	Emerald Assets Limited	Ascendas REIT

#1 The Fixed Rate Notes, if not redeemed by February 26, 2007, would accrue at the rate of 2.38% above the three-month Singapore Dollar Swap Rate to the final date of redemption on August 26, 2008. #2 The Floating Rate Notes, if not redeemed by June 26, 2010, will accrue interest at 2.30% above the U.S. dollar LIBOR to the final redemption date on December 26, 2011. #3 CMT subscribe to S$60 million of the junior class E-tranche of the CapitaRetail Singapore CMBS, which is expected to pay a minimum 8.2% yield. #4 The legal maturity date is February 2009. #5 The legal maturity date is November 12, 2013. & Exchange rate conversion :€$1:S$2.0329 (August 23, 2005). *Source: Compilation by the author*

and REITs, CMBSs offer an avenue for them to tap into a new supply of funds in overseas markets, especially the European money markets that have strong demand for senior-rated real estate-backed instruments. REITs can secure a stable long-term source of funding via CMBSs and hedge against interest rate fluctuations by matching their asset cash flows with coupon obligations on bonds. The cost of funding will be attractive when the spread of long-term senior bond yield over the riskless instrument is low. The savings in funding costs can also be attained by mortgage pooling, which creates economies of scale in mortgages. For the secondary real estate market and institutional investors, CMBSs add diversity to the choice of real estate asset classes with fixed income characteristics. The rating requirement and monitoring mechanism of bond markets, on the other hand, improve information efficiency in the secondary real estate market.

The models for securitizing real estate cash flows have evolved from a simple single mortgage-backed bonds structure in the 1980s and early 1990s, to ones with more complex structure in the late 1990s and early 2000s. Two streams of commercial real estate cash flows, equity and debt, are securitized. However, the tightening of the ABS rules in 2000 by the MAS has seen developers switching to REITs for securitizing equity cash flows, and then using the ABS structure. On the mortgage side, CMBSs continue to attract interest from users of funds, especially REITs, as a way to hedge against interest rate volatility. Figure 9.5 depicts securitization activities in Singapore involving commercial real estate.

In Singapore, securitization efforts thus far have mainly been undertaken and driven by the users of funds that include real estate developers, owners of commercial properties, and also S-REITs. Banks, on the other hand, still focus predominantly on loan origination, and

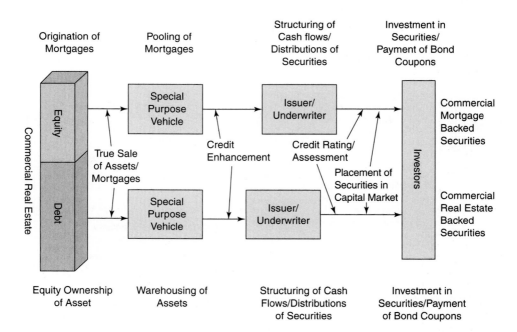

Figure 9.5 Typical commercial real estate-backed securitization in Singapore.

have been taking a less-active role, especially in mortgage pooling, tranching of cash flows, and structuring of securities. Moving ahead, we would expect the CMBS market to expand at a faster pace given the rising cost of borrowing and increased pressure on commercial banks in Singapore to meet the capital adequacy ratio (CAR) under the Basel II, which will be fully implemented in 2007.

9.5   STRUCTURE OF A TYPICAL CREBS

In the ABS transactions, a special purpose vehicle (SPV) is established with the intention to create a "bankruptcy remote" structure by separating the real estate asset off the originator's balance sheet. This structure insulates the ABS investors against the credit risks of the originator. The SPV obtains all of the ownership rights and obligations of the assets via the equitable assignment. This arrangement distinguishes it from the traditional collateralized loans and mortgage pay-through securities, where real estate assets are retained on the balance sheet of the originator. Figure 9.6 displays a diagrammatic illustration of the structure of the ABS deals.

SPV was a legal entity incorporated under the company act with the sole objective to facilitate the purchase of the securitized real estate and to issue bonds and preference shares to finance purchases. There are strict restrictions imposed on the scopes of activities

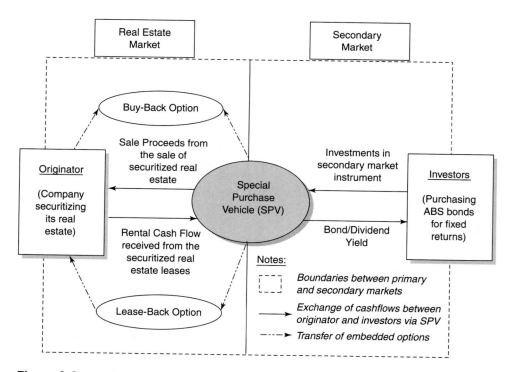

Figure 9.6 A typical structure of commercial real estate ABS. *Source: Sing, Ong and Sirmans (2003).*[5]

and operations, the appointment of independent directors, and debt issuance policy of the SPV. The ABS bonds are non-recourse debt securities. These restrictions are put in place to ensure that bankruptcy remoteness is maintained and the probability of bankruptcy of the SPV is reduced. The SPVs are restricted from incurring recourse debt, and they rely only on the cash flows generated from the securitized real estate to refund interests and principals.

In Singapore, CREBS, debts securities issued by the SPVs, were partitioned into two classes—senior bonds and junior bonds—to give different priority of claims on the cash flows accrued to the SPVs. The senior bonds with higher priority and better credit quality are distributed to investors who prefer limited credit risk through either private or public placement arrangements. Junior bonds, on the other hand, are retained by the originator or sold to firms that demand higher returns at the expense of higher risks. When the ABS bonds are redeemed, the senior bonds will be paid off first before the junior bondholders.

There has been no over-collateralization structure in the CREBS that have been issued in Singapore thus far. CREBS bonds were issued up to the market value of the commercial real estate. Credit enhancement in CREBS takes the form of leasing back and selling back options granted by the originator. The originator, as the lessee when leasing back the securitized building, will guarantee minimum cash flows that are sufficient to meet the bondholder's debt obligation. The SPV is also given a sell-back option, which gives the right to the SPV to sell back the real estate to the originator at the market price at the maturity of the bond. This ensures that the outstanding bonds can be fully redeemed at maturity.

The underwriting of the CREBS bonds by DBS bank, a reputable bank listed in Singapore, gives a positive signal to investors. With knowledge and experience in the capital markets, the financial institution is able to design different classes of securities and set offering prices that will meet different investing requirements of investors. An asset management company (servicer) was normally appointed by the SPVs to perform the day-to-day operations of the underlying property, the collection of rental incomes, or the provision of services to property tenants. Other than the routine property management function, the SPV is also required to carry out cash flow management and oversee property tenant services, monitoring underlying property conditions and reporting duties. It also ensures that the collections of rental revenues are distributed as coupon payments to the investors.

A CREBS Case by Visor Limited

In the case of CREBS issued by Visor Limited—an SPV set up by the sponsor, Birchvest Investments Private Limited, a wholly owned subsidiary of DBS Land (now CapitaLand)—a prime office building, called Robinson Point and located at 39 Robinson Road, was securitized for U.S.$121.97 million (S$193.00 million) in July 1999. Upon the transaction, the property holding company, Robinson Point Private Limited, was removed off the balance sheet of its parent company, Birchvest Investment Private Limited, the originator of the CREBS deal. The structure of the CREBS is represented in Figure 9.7.

In the sale and purchase agreement, the originator undertakes to lease back the property for a period of 10 years. Pursuant to the 10-year lease agreement, Birchvest and its parent

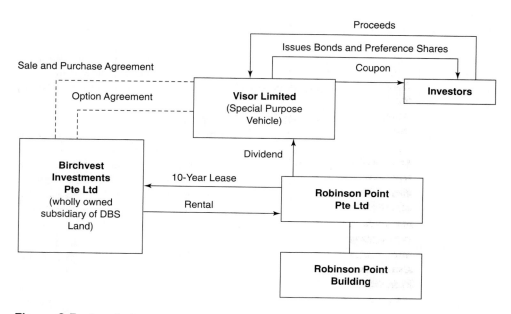

Figure 9.7 A typical structure of commercial real estate ABS. *Source: Prospectus of Visor Limited CREBS Bond Issuance.*

company guarantee to pay rents and other income that are equivalent to or exceed the interest payments to be made by Visor to the bondholders.

For Visor to fund the purchase of the prime office property, it issues U.S.$121.97 million (S$193 million) in principal of 10-year fixed-rate bonds, and 19,300 preference shares. The bonds are issued in two tranches, comprising U.S.$78.99 million (S$125 million) in principal of senior bonds and U.S.$42.97 million (S$68 million) in principal of junior bonds. The senior bonds will pay a fixed-rate interest of 2% per annum, the junior bonds will pay a fixed-rate interest of 6% per annum, and both interests are payable semi-annually in arrears.

In the transaction, there are complex buy-back and sell-back options being structured into the agreement. The originator is given call options that are exercisable after year three, but up to six months before expiration of the bond issuance, to repurchase the property. Upon exercising the buy-back option, if the market value of the property appreciates above the original purchase price of U.S.$121.97 million (S$193.00 million), bondholders will be entitled to share a percentage of the excess amount, in addition to the principal amount upon redemption of the bonds. At the same time, the SPV is also guaranteed by the originator in the form of sale-back options exercisable in the last six months leading to the bond expiration to ensure that bonds could be fully redeemed at least at par upon exercising of the option.[6]

9.6 PRICING OF CREBS

The cash flow characteristics of CREBS[7] deals in Singapore are comparable to swap contracts. Upon exercising the leaseback options, the originator pays market rents, which are analogous to a stream of floating cash flows, to the SPV in return for an exclusive right of use of the property for a specific lease period. The SPV converts these floating cash flows to fixed-rate coupons payable to the bondholders. In the swap analogies, the CREBS bondholders purchase a cash flow floor (fixed rate) from the SPV, and the originator (lessee) writes a cash flow cap (floating rate) to the SPV. The credit risks of CREBS could then be valued in a swap framework, taking into account uncertainties associated with the floating rental rate, fixed coupon rate, notional principal of CREBS, and transacted property price.

Swaps and Swaptions

A *financial swap* is a contract that facilitates the exchange of cash payments consisting of usually one fixed-rate payment and one floating-rate payment between two counterparties for a notional sum of value (see Figure 9.8). Swap contracts are highly sensitive and susceptible to credit risks: default and interest rate risks.

An option on a swap, which is known as a *swaption*, gives the holder a right to swap a floating cash flow for a fixed cash flow, or vice versa, at a specified rate, and at a particular date in the future. The plain vanilla interest rate swap contract is composed of a floor written by the fixed-rate payer and a cap written by the floating-rate payer. In an equity swap, equity investors who contemplate a decline in the equity market may enter into a swap arrangement whereby he agrees to pay equity returns (dividends and capital appreciation) for a London Interbank Offer Rate (LIBOR) or a fixed-rate return.

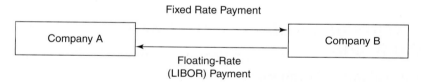

Figure 9.8 A typical interest rate swap contract.

The Cash Flow Swap Structure for CREBS

This chapter applies the default-risky swap framework to evaluate credit risks associated with the CREBS deals.[8] In the application of the proposed swap valuation models to pricing credit risks in CREBS, assumptions are made to simplify the cash flows. These assumptions, however, could be relaxed in the subsequent extension. First, the subordination structure of the bonds is removed, which thus implies that there is only one fixed-rate stream of coupon payment for bondholders. Second, the buy-back option will not be exercised by the originator prior to the expiration, such that bonds will only be fully redeemed at par value upon expiration. At the end of the bond maturity, the SPV could exercise the put option to sell back the property to the originator at a market price that is equivalent to the principal value of the bonds, and the bondholders will not share the price appreciation in the property as given in the put option agreement.[9] This assumption thus implies that the bondholders' initial principal will be redeemed at par value at maturity, and it avoids the complication of having to model the price-generating process of the property.

Given the previous assumptions, a typical CREBS transaction can thus be reduced to a simple swap of floating cash flows, in the form of rental revenues generated from leasing the real estate, for fixed-rate coupon payments passed through to bondholders. The cash flow swaps are facilitated by the SPV, which act as an intermediary, as shown in Figure 9.9. With the swap characteristics, the default-risky cash flows and associated interest rate risks in the CREBS can then be readily evaluated using the default-risky swap framework.

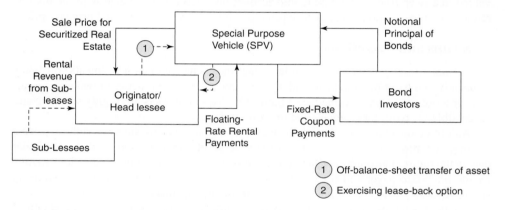

Figure 9.9 Cash flow swaps in a typical CREBS.

9.7 VALUATION OF CREBS USING A SWAP FRAMEWORK

Basic Swap Valuation Framework

Theoretically, the equilibrium swap rate is determined by equating the present values of cash flows between the fixed-rate leg and the floating-rate leg of a swap. Let the fixed swap rate be represented by $\bar{r}$ and the forward rate by $\hat{r}$. The value of a two-period fixed-for-floating default-free swap contract can be determined as follows:

$$b(1)\bar{r} + b(2)\bar{r} = b(1)\hat{r}_1 + b(2)\hat{r}_2 \tag{9.1}$$

where $b(x)$ denotes a discounted bond price (notional principal) in future periods, $x = [1, 2]$. Dividing both sides of equation (9.1) by $[b(1) + b(2)]$, the equilibrium fixed swap rate $\bar{r}$ can be estimated as a convex combination of the forward rates:

$$\bar{r} = \frac{b(1)}{b(1) + b(2)}\hat{r}_1 + \frac{b(2)}{b(1) + b(2)}\hat{r}_2 \tag{9.2}$$

In the absence of default risk, the swap valuation in equation (9.1) can be further generalized into a multi-period (N-period) swap as follows:

$$\sum_{i=1}^{N} b(i)\bar{r} = \sum_{i=1}^{N} b(i)\widehat{r}_i \tag{9.3}$$

The equilibrium fixed rate for the swap contract as in equation (9.2) can be represented by a weighted average of the forward rates $(\widehat{r}_i)$, which is given next:

$$\bar{r} = \frac{\displaystyle\sum_{i=1}^{N} b(i)\widehat{r}_i}{\displaystyle\sum_{i=1}^{N} b(i)} \tag{9.4}$$

Pricing of Credit Risks for CREBS Using the Proposed Swap Model

In the context of CREBS, the originator exercises the lease-back option, which gives him an exclusive right of use of the real estate for a period not exceeding the bond maturity. For the SPV, it charges market rents on the originator for the use of the real estate space in pursuant to the lease agreement. The rental cash flow is then converted into fixed-rate coupon payments and passed through to the bondholders. Technically, the SPV facilitates the swap of the floating cash flows received from the originator for the fixed-rate cash flows payable out to the bondholders.

In equilibrium, the fixed-rate coupons payable to the bondholders should equate the present values of the cash flows from leasing the securitized property, such that the swap value is zero in the absence of default risk. The equilibrium default-free swap value can be represented by equation (9.5), as follows:

$$\sum_{i}^{N} b(i)FRP + b(N)V_0 = \sum_{i}^{N} b(i)NRI_i + b(N)V_N \tag{9.5}$$

where FRP is the fixed-rate payment, NRI_i is the net rental income in period i, V_0 is the principal of bond issued by the SPV, and V_N is the price of securitized property at time N, which coincides with the bond maturity.

Dividing both sides of equation (9.5) by V_0, the equation could be rewritten as follows:

$$\sum_{i}^{N} b(i)\bar{r} + b(N) = \sum_{i}^{N} b(i)R_i + b(N)\delta \tag{9.6}$$

where $\bar{r}$ denotes the fixed-rate coupon for bonds, R_i denotes the floating rental return, and δ represents the ratio of real estate price over the bond principal at the maturity period.

Modeling Default Risks in the CREBS Swap

Duffie and Singleton (1997)[10] model default is an exogenous process that is defined by a hazard rate function and the loss recovery, which is a fraction of the market value of the bonds in the event of default. The defaultable bond-pricing model of Duffie and Singleton (1997) is represented as follows:

$$V\left(t\right) = E_Q\left[\exp-\left(\int_r^T R\left(s\right)ds\right)\bigg|\xi_t\right] \tag{9.7}$$

where E_Q denotes the risk-neutral expectation conditional on information available up to date t, (ξ_t), and $R(t)$ denotes a default-adjusted short rate, which is the sum of a short-term riskless interest rate and a default risk premium.

In the proposed default-risky swap model, uncertainties are added to the discount rate variables. The adjusted rental return rate (R) is the first state variable, which is assumed to follow a specific stochastic process with a mean-reverting tendency, as follows:

$$dR = \alpha\left(\mu - R\right)dt + \sigma_R R dz_1 \tag{9.8}$$

where α is the speed of rental adjustment, μ is the long-term average rental rate, σ_R^2 is the instantaneous variance coefficient for rental changes, and dz_1 is the increment of a standard Wiener process. $[\alpha\left(\mu - R\right)]$ is the drift term, which represents a mean-reverting force that pulls the rental return toward its long-term value. The use of "R," instead of the usual "$\sqrt{R}$" in the second right-hand term, indicates a normalized diffusion process that is flexible enough to capture the negative rental rates.

The second state variable is the riskless discount rate (r), which is assumed to follow the standard Cox, Ingersoll, and Ross (CIR) (1985)[11] stochastic process, represented as follows:

$$dr = \kappa\left(\theta - r\right)dt + \sigma_r\sqrt{r}dz_3 \tag{9.9}$$

where θ, κ, and σ_r are positive constants, and dz_3 is the increment of a standard Wiener process.

Based on the preceding assumptions, a default-free interest rate swap can be expressed as a portfolio of bonds, which comprises a long position in a fixed-rate (or floating-rate) bond and a short position in a floating-rate (or fixed-rate) bond. It can be evaluated as a series of forward-rate agreements (FRAs)[12] with maturities corresponding to the settlement date specified in the swap contract. For FRAs with a flat-term structure of interest rates, the fixed interest rate of the swap can be determined such that the initial value of the swap is zero. The equilibrium default-free cash flow swap can then be determined by equating the fixed-rate leg and floating-rate leg of the cash flows as follows:

$$\sum_{i=1}^{N} b_x\left(0,i\right)FRP + b_x\left(0,N\right)V_0 = \sum_{i=1}^{N} b_l\left(0,i\right)NRI_i + b_l\left(0,N\right)V_N \tag{9.10}$$

where $b_x\left(0,i\right)$ and $b_l\left(0,i\right)$ represents the discounted bond prices for the fixed-rate leg and the floating-rate leg, respectively.

Solving equation (9.10) using the classical martingale approach, which is denoted by a subscript Q, the following swap pricing equation can be derived:

$$E_Q \left\{ \sum_{i=1}^{N} FRP \exp \left[-\int_0^i r_i^c(s)\, ds \right] \middle| \xi_i \right\}$$

$$= E_Q \left\{ \sum_{i=1}^{N} NRI_i \exp \left[-\int_0^i R_i(s)\, ds \right] \middle| \xi_i \right\} \qquad (9.11)$$

where r_i^c represents the interest rate of the replacement bond, which is composed of a riskless interest rate (r_i) and a constant credit spread (h)—i.e., $[r_i^c = r_i + h]$, R_i represents the rental return rate, and ξ_i reflects the information revealed up to time i. The credit-risk spread (h) measured as the difference between the fixed coupon yield and the riskless interest rate is included to compensate the fixed-rate receiver (bondholders) against default risks. It accounts for the probability of default and the loss recovery on default.

Let $V_{NRI}(t)$ and $V_{FRP}(t)$ denote the present values of the floating- and fixed-rate payments in a CREBS deal respectively. The default-risky component of the basic "swap" pricing formula for ABS can be represented as

$$V(t) = V_{NRI}(t) - V_{FRP}(t). \qquad (9.12a)$$

$$V(t) = E_Q \left\{ \sum_{i=1}^{N} NRI_i \exp \left[-\int_0^i R_i(s)\, ds \right] \middle| \xi_i \right\} -$$

$$E_Q \left\{ \sum_{i=1}^{N} FRP \exp \left[-\int_0^i r_i^c(s)\, ds \right] \middle| \xi_i \right\} \qquad (9.12b)$$

where $V(t) < 0$ indicates that bondholders are vulnerable to the default risks of the originator. However, when $V(t) \geq 0$, the transaction will be favorable to the bondholders.

9.8 NUMERICAL ANALYSIS OF DEFAULT RISKS FOR A TYPICAL CREBS

The proposed default-risky swap model given in equations (9.11) and (9.12b) does not contain standard analytical solutions. The swap value and the equilibrium swap rate that compensate for the default-risky floating rate components could be jointly determined using the Monte Carlo simulation technique. For illustrative purposes, the proposed default-risk swap model is applied to an actual Visor CREBS case, as described in "A CREBS Case by Visor Limited." The originator Birchvest Private Limited securitizes the prime Robinson Point office building through the issuance of U.S.$121.97 million (S$193 million).

Monte Carlo Simulation Process

The stochastic discount rate processes are generated using Monte Carlo simulation technique. Discrete values of the stochastic state variables as defined in equations (9.8) and (9.9) in the reduced-form swap model are first generated. Using the Euler's discretization approach, the continuous time stochastic processes of rental return and riskless interest rates are estimated as follows:

$$\Delta R_k = \alpha \left(\mu - R_{k-1} \right) \Delta t + \sigma_R R_{k-1} \sqrt{\Delta t}\, z_1 \tag{9.13}$$

$$\Delta r_k = \kappa \left(\theta - r_{k-1} \right) \Delta t + \sigma_r \sqrt{r_{k-1} \Delta t}\, z_2 \tag{9.14}$$

The random samples z_1 and z_2 having standardized bivariate normal distributions are defined as:

$$z_1 = \varepsilon_1 \tag{9.15}$$

$$z_2 = \rho \varepsilon_1 + \varepsilon_2 \sqrt{1 - \rho^2} \tag{9.16}$$

where ρ is the correlation between the two variables in the bivariate distribution, and ε_1 and ε_2 are independently drawn from a standardized univariate normal distribution. A six-month discrete time interval is used in the simulation, $\Delta t = 0.5$.

Generating the random values for rental return, R_t, and riskless interest rates, r_t, from time zero to bond maturity, where $t = [0, k]$, following discretized stochastic processes in equations (9.13) and (9.14). The discounted payoffs for the floating-rate leg and fixed-rate leg can be calculated along the sample paths.

When the Euler methodology is used to generate discretized value for the stochastic riskless interest rate variable given in equation (9.14), the riskless interest rate path was generated from k normally distributed variates $\{\widehat{r}_0, \ldots, \widehat{r}_k\}$. The bond price is then discounted by the k-variates riskless interest rate as follows:

$$\exp \left(-\sum_{j=1}^{N} (\widehat{r}_j + h) \Delta t \right) \tag{9.17}$$

The simulation of the k-dimensional riskless interest rate path is replicated M times. Let $f^n (\Delta t)$ denote the cash flow for the bond at path n. The average present values of the risky cash flows discounted by the Monte Carlo simulated k-dimensional interest rate can be represented as follows:

$$\frac{\sum_{n=1}^{M} f^n (\Delta t) \exp \left[-\sum_{j=1}^{i} (\widehat{r}_j + h) \Delta t \right]}{M} \tag{9.18}$$

This Monte Carlo simulation process is then repeated for the risky rental (floating) cash flows.

Input Parameters

Based on a set of input parameters as summarized in Table 9.3, the default-risky swap value for the CREBS can be computed numerically using equation (9.12b). The input parameters like rental volatility (σ_R), default-free interest rate volatility (σ_r), average rental rate (μ), risk-free rate (θ), and correlations between the rental and risk-free rate (ρ) were determined ex-post, based on historical data obtained from relevant publish sources in Singapore, which include the quarterly rental index of the Urban Redevelopment Authority (URA) and the quarterly yield rates of the five-year bond of the Monetary Authority of Singapore (MAS) from 1990 to 2002.

Table 9.3 Input Assumptions for Monte Carlo Numerical Analysis

Input Parameters	Base Value
A) Historically Estimated Parameters:	
Sale price for the securitized real estate	V_0 = S$193,000,000
Initial rental rate	R_0 = 7%
Average long-term rental rate	μ = -1.31%
Annualized rental volatility	σ_R = 14.02%
Fixed-rate coupon yield	r^c = 5%
Initial (stochastic) default-free interest rate	r_0 = 3.7%
Average five-year default-free interest rate	θ = 3.78%
Default-free interest rate volatility	σ_r = 0.83%
Correlation coefficient between stochastic interest rate and rental rate	ρ = -15.9%
B) Calibrated Parameters:	
Credit spread	h = 5.3%
Speed of mean reverting of rental return	α = 8%
Speed of adjustment of riskless interest rate	κ = 40%

The two mean reverting adjustment parameters, (α and κ), and the credit spread parameter, (h), are calibrated by equilibrating the present values of two default-risky cash flows in swap equation (9.12) to zero.

Analysis of Results

Based on the preceding input parameters, Monte Carlo simulations were carried out using Matlab, where the program codes are given in the next section.[13] The results are summarized in Table 9.4. The default-risky swap value, as shown in Table 9.4, is defined as the difference between the present values of floating-rate leg cash flows and those of the fixed-rate leg cash flows discounted by the default-adjusted short rates.[14] When the value of the default-risky component of swaps is positive, the cumulative discounted present value of the floating-rate cash flows is greater than that of the fixed-rate cash flows. The rental revenues are sufficient to cover the bondholders' coupon payments. It implies that the probability of default by the floating-rate payers (the originator) is low. The larger the positive value of the default-risky swap component, the larger is the protection for the fixed-rate receivers (the bondholders) against default, which means a lower default risk. When the value of the default-risky swap component is negative, the likelihood is that rental revenues are insufficient to meet the coupon obligations. The bondholders are exposed to high default risks.

For a deterministic scenario, where the volatilities for the rental rate and the riskless interest rate are zero, the default risk premium for the swap contract was estimated at U.S.$4.68 million (S$7.4 million), which is equivalent to 3.83% of the initial securitized real estate value.

Table 9.4 Results of Monte Carlo Simulations for Discounted Swap Values

Rental Rate Volatility	Default-Free Interest Rate Volatility	Swap Value		
		U.S.$ Million#	S$ Million	(%)@
A) Deterministic Scenario:				
0%	0%	4.68	7.4	3.83%
B) Stochastic Scenario:				
10%	5%	4.33	6.85	3.55%
	10%	4.27	6.75	3.50%
	20%	4.25	6.73	3.49%
	30%	4.63	7.32	3.79%
	40%	5.11	8.09	4.19%
	50%	5.55	8.79	4.55%
20%	5%	3.41	5.4	2.80%
	10%	3.22	5.09	2.64%
	20%	3.32	5.26	2.73%
	30%	3.72	5.89	3.05%
	40%	4.26	6.74	3.49%
	50%	4.60	7.28	3.77%
30%	5%	1.70	2.69	1.39%
	10%	1.64	2.6	1.35%
	20%	1.80	2.85	1.48%
	30%	2.19	3.46	1.79%
	40%	2.57	4.07	2.11%
	50%	2.94	4.66	2.42%
40%	5%	-0.67	-1.06	-0.55%
	10%	-0.83	-1.32	-0.68%
	20%	-0.54	-0.85	-0.44%
	30%	-0.11	-0.17	-0.09%
	40%	0.13	0.2	0.10%
	50%	0.62	0.98	0.51%
50%	5%	-3.44	-5.45	-2.82%
	10%	-3.68	-5.83	-3.02%
	20%	-3.43	-5.43	-2.81%
	30%	-3.32	-5.25	-2.72%
	40%	-2.88	-4.55	-2.36%
	50%	-2.32	-3.67	-1.90%

@ Estimated swap value expressed as a percentage of the notional bond issue value (S$193 million).
# Based on the exchange rate of U.S.$1.00: S$1.5824, as indicated on 29 April 2006.

Given that the historical annualized rental volatility is approximately 14% in Singapore, the value default risky swap component will always remain at the positive region, which implies that the default risks faced by the fixed-rate receivers are properly insulated. The default-risky swap value will only dip into a negative region when the rental volatility increases above 30%.

9.9   MATLAB CODE FOR THE NUMERICAL ANALYSIS

The following Matlab code is a Monte Carlo simulation to price the commercial ABS.

exrelationdepend25.m

```
%%%%%%%%%%%%%%%%%%%%%%%%%%%%%%%%%%%%%%%%%%%%%%%%%%%%%%%%%%%%%%%%%%%%%%%%%%%%
%    Monte Carlo Simulation for CREBS valuation using the proposed swap
%    pricing model
%
%    Variable Description:
%
%    V0= the current property asset value
%    u1= the long-term average property return rate
%    a1= the speed of property return rate adjustment
%    u2= the long-term average fixed interest rate
%    a2 = the speed of risk-free interest rate adjustment
%    rho= correlation
%    nSimulations = Number of simulations used for Monte Carlo simulation
%    h= credit spread
%    More simulations increase accurancy, typically minimum 10000
%%%%%%%%%%%%%%%%%%%%%%%%%%%%%%%%%%%%%%%%%%%%%%%%%%%%%%%%%%%%%%%%%%%%%%%%%%%%
function S=exrelationdepend25(V0,u1,u2,a1,a2,r,nSimulations,rho,h)

        floatvol=0:0.05:0.5;
        fixvol=0:0.05:0.5;

        num_p=length(floatvol);
        num_r=length(fixvol);

        exchangeprice=zeros(num_p,num_r);

         for k=1:num_p
           for l=1:num_r
              cash1=0;
              cash2=0;
              sum5=0;
              sum6=0;
              for j = 1: nSimulations
                sum3=0;
                sum4=0;
                Rt=0.07;
                rt=0.037;

                for i=1:20;

                    Epsilon3 = normrnd(0,1);
                    Rt = Rt + a1*(u1-Rt)*0.5 + floatvol(k)*sqrt(0.5)*
```

```
                   Rt*Epsilon3;
                   sum3=sum3+Rt*0.5;
                   discount1=exp(-sum3);
                   sum5=sum5+discount1*Rt*V0*0.5;

                   Epsilon4 = rho * Epsilon3 + normrnd(0,1) * sqrt(1 -
                     rho ^ 2);
                   if rt<0
                       rt=0;
                   end
                   rt = rt + a2*(u2-rt)*0.5 + fixvol(l)*sqrt(0.5*rt)*
                     Epsilon4;
                   sum4=sum4+0.5*(rt+h);
                   discount2=exp(-sum4);
                   sum6=sum6+discount2*r*V0*0.5;

               end
          end
                   cash1=sum5/nSimulations;
                   cash2=sum6/nSimulations;

             exchangeprice(k,l)=cash1-cash2;
      end
   end
   S=exchangeprice;

   surf(fixvol,floatvol,exchangeprice);
   xlabel('Riskless Interest Rate Volatility');
   ylabel('Commercial Property Rent Volatility');
   zlabel('Swap Present Value');
   title('Sensitivity Measures');
   axis([0 0.5 0 0.5 -inf inf]);
   set(gca,'box','on');
```

```
>> V0=193000000;
```

If we run the simulation with the following parameters:

```
u1=-0.013;
u2=0.038;
a1=0.07;
a2=0.3;
r=0.05;
nSimulations=50000;
rho=-0.159;
h=0.053;
```

the exchange price is calculated as follows:

```
>> S=exrelationdepend25(V0,u1,u2,a1,a2,r,nSimulations,rho,h)
S = 1.0e+006 *
```

Figure 9.10 shows the present value of an asset (real-estate) swap in a one-sided default model in model A.

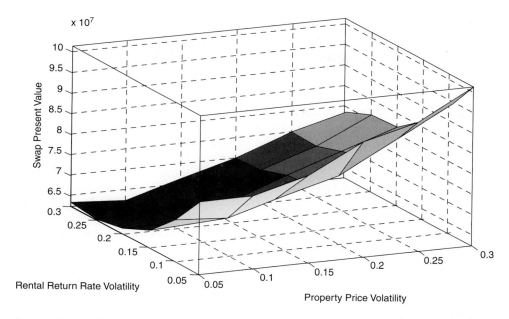

Figure 9.10 The present value of an asset (real-estate) swap in a one-sided default model in Model A.

Figure 9.11 shows the present value of a swap in the presence of bilateral default risks in model B.

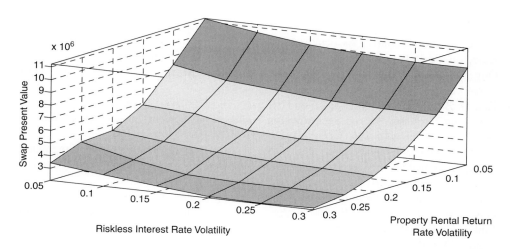

Figure 9.11 The present value of swap in the presence of bilateral default risks in model B.

9.10 SUMMARY

Unlike in the U.S., the CMBS market has expanded rapidly, with nearly every one in five commercial mortgages originated being securitized. Mortgage conduits and commercial banks are actively packaging their commercial mortgages and selling them in the capital markets as a way of injecting new operating capital. In Singapore, however, commercial banks have not been forthcoming with the idea of securitizing and disposing of their commercial mortgages. The current healthy liquidity position, the low default risks of commercial mortgages, and the reluctance of banks to sever good relationships with their corporate mortgagors offer disincentives for them to create CMBSs. The Basel II proposal on risk-based capital adequacy management by the Committee on Banking Supervision, once fully implemented in Singapore by the latest in 2007, may create urgency on commercial banks to look at securitization as a way of hedging credit risks in commercial mortgages.

For real estate fund users, CREBS and CMBS will remain as an attractive funding option, of which the potential has not been fully exploited. When the securitization technology becomes commonplace as in the equity market, disintermediation of primary mortgage providers, like commercial banks and financial institutions, may not be impossible in the future.

This chapter uses a proposed swap-pricing model to price the default-risky component of CREBS. The results show that volatilities of rental rate and riskless interest rate are two important variables in determining the value of the default risk in CREBS deals. It is important to take into consideration the dynamics of rental revenue of securitized real estate and riskless interest rates when setting the equilibrium fixed rates and floating rates in CREBS deals so as to mitigate the likelihood of default.

ENDNOTES

1. Source: The Bond Market Association.
2. Based on the exchange rate 6 of U.S.$1.00: S$1.5824 on April 29, 2006.
3. Ong, S. E., Ooi, J., and Sing, T. F. (2000), "Asset Securitization in Singapore: A Tale of Three Vehicles." *Real Estate Finance*, 17(2), pp. 47-56.
4. Fan, G. Z., Sing, T. F., Ong, S. E., and Sirmans, C. F. (2004), "Governance and Optimal Financing for Asset-Backed Securitization," *Journal of Property Investment & Finance*, Vol. 22, No. 5, pp. 414-434.
5. Sing, T.F., Ong, S.E. and Sirmans, C.F. (2003), "Asset-Backed Securitization in Singapore: Value of Embedded Buy-Back Options," *Journal of Real Estate Finance & Economics*, Vol. 27, No. 2, pp. 173-180.
6. For more details on the option features and pricing of the options, refer to Sing, T. F., Ong, S. E., and Sirmans, C. F. (2003), "Asset-Backed Securitization in Singapore: Value of Embedded Buy-Back Options," *Journal of Real Estate Finance & Economics*, Vol. 27, No. 2, pp. 173-180.
7. The default-risky swap pricing methodology is based on the following paper: Sing, T. F., Ong, S. E., Fan, G. Z., and Sirmans, C. F. (2004), "Analysis of Credit Risks in Asset-Backed Securitization Transactions in Singapore," Special issue for Maastricht-Cambridge

Symposium 2002, *Journal of Real Estate Finance & Economics*, Vol. 28, No. 2/3, pp. 235-254.

8. The swap valuation models have been proposed by Duffie and Huang (1996), Duffie and Singleton (1997), and Hübner (2001) in the following papers:

   Duffie, D. and M. Huang (1996), "Swap Rates and Credit Quality," *Journal of Finance*, 51(3), July, pp. 921-949.

   Duffie, D. and K. Singleton (1999), "Modeling Term Structures of Defaultable Bonds," *Review of Financial Studies*, 12(4), pp. 687-720.

   Hübner, G. (2001), "The Analytic Pricing of Asymmetric Defaultable Swaps," *Journal of Banking & Finance*, 25, pp. 295-316.

9. In the ABS cases, the originator will have to pay the SPV the original market price plus a percentage of capital gain when the sale-back option is exercised. This capital gains portion to be distributed back to the bondholders is omitted in this study. Its omission, however, will not significantly affect the results of the analysis.

10. Duffie, D. and Singleton, K. (1997), "An Economic Model of the Term Structure of Rate Swap Yields," *Journal of Finance*, 52(3): 1287–1321.

11. Cox, J. C., Ingersoll, J., and Ross, S. (1985), "A Theory of the Term Structure of Interest Rates," *Econometrica*, 53, pp. 385-407.

12. Forward rate agreement (FRA) is a single period bilateral agreement where one party agrees to pay or receive the difference between an agreed fixed rate (the FRA rate) and LIBOR in the future calculated on a fixed interest period.

13. The author wishes to thank Dr. Fan, Gangzhi, for his assistance in the numerical analyses using Matlab.

14. The defaulted-adjusted short rates are the sum of the risk-free rates and default risk premiums, which are consistent with the risk-neutral assumptions. Discounting the cash flows by the default-adjusted short rate will account for the probability and timing of default, as well as the loss recovery in default (*op. cit.* Duffie and Singleton, 1999).

INTEREST RATE TREE MODELING IN MATLAB

In this chapter, we provide Matlab implementations for several popular interest rate models that are used to price fixed income securities including Hull-White, Black-Derman-Toy (BDT), Black-Karasinski, and Heath-Jarrow-Morton (HJM). Matlab code for building the trees, pricing, and calculating Greek sensitivities are provided. In practice, to price interest rate derivatives, interest rate trees are calibrated to observed market data—i.e., term structure of yields and volatilities. Given the emphasis on the Matlab implementations in this chapter, details of the tree-building procedures, underlying theory, and derivations of the models are not provided. However, the reader is referred to other sources for their documentation.

In §A.1, we discuss building BDT trees and give examples to price fixed-income derivatives in Matlab. In §A.2, we discuss building Hull-White trees in Matlab. In §A.3, we build Black-Karasinski trees in Matlab and show how to view the trees with Matlabs `treeviewer`. In §A.4, we discuss HJM pricing in Matlab. In §A.5, a Matlab Excel Link example is provided to show how Excel can interface with Matlab to price coupon bonds using the HJM model. In §A.6, we provide 2-factor HJM implementation in Matlab.

A.1 BDT MODELING IN MATLAB

The idea behind the BDT model is that interest rates can move either up or down with probability $\frac{1}{2}$. The construction of the BDT tree was developed using a forward induction technique by Jamshidian (1991).[1] Jamshidian has shown that in the BDT model, the short rate level at time t has the following representation as a lognormally distributed random process:

$$r(t) = U(t)e^{(\sigma(t)z(t))} \tag{A.1}$$

Here, $z(t)$ is a standard Brownian motion, $\sigma(t)$ is the short-rate volatility at t, and $U(t)$ is the median of the distribution for $r(t)$. At each time step, $U(t)$ and $\sigma(t)$ are determined to make the model match the observed yield and volatility curves. If one assumes $\sigma(t)$ is constant, so that building the model requires only that there is a match to the yield curve, then only the median $U(t)$ need be determined. In this case, the level of the short rate at time t simplifies to:

$$r(t) = U(t)e^{(\sigma z(t))}$$

If $i = 0, \ldots, N$ is the ith time step and $j = 1, \ldots, i$ is the jth space step in the tree, we can determine the Δt-period short rate at node (i, j) from the relation

$$r_{i,j} = U(i)e^{(\sigma(i)j\sqrt{\Delta t})} \tag{A.2}$$

Initially, one assumes $U(0) = r_{0,0}$. $U(i)$ and $\sigma(i)$ can be determined with the aid of Arrow-Debrue state prices. Due to the lognormal distribution assumption of interest rates, the BDT model does not have closed-form analytical solutions for bond prices and bond options. For details of the BDT tree-building procedure, see Black, Derman, and Toy (1990), Jamshidian (1991), and Clewlow and Strickland (1999). For a BDT implementation in C++, see London (2004).

To build a BDT in Matlab, the `bdttree` function is called where `BDTTree = bdttree(VolSpec, RateSpec, TimeSpec)` creates a structure containing time and interest-rate information on a recombining tree, where the arguments are as in Table A.1.

Table A.1

Argument	Description
VolSpec	Volatility process specification. See `bdtvolspec` for information on the volatility process.
RateSpec	Interest-rate specification for the initial rate curve. See `intenvset` for information on declaring an interest-rate variable.
TimeSpec	Tree time layout specification. Defines the observation dates of the BDT tree and the `Compounding` rule for date to time mapping and price-yield formulas. See `bdttimespec` for information on the tree structure.

The following Matlab code builds a BDT tree based on a specified `VolSpec`, `RateSpec`, and `TimeSpec`.

```
load deriv.mat

Compounding = 1;
ValuationDate = '01-01-2000';
StartDate = ValuationDate;
EndDates = ['01-01-2001'; '01-01-2002'; '01-01-2003';
'01-01-2004'; '01-01-2005'];
Rates = [.05;.0575;.0625;.0675;.07];
Volatility = [.1;.095;.09;.085;.08];

RateSpec = intenvset('Compounding', Compounding,...
                     'ValuationDate', ValuationDate,...
                     'StartDates', StartDate,...
                     'EndDates', EndDates,...
                     'Rates', Rates);

BDTTimeSpec = bdttimespec(ValuationDate, EndDates, Compounding);
BDTVolSpec = bdtvolspec(ValuationDate, EndDates, Volatility);
BDTTree = bdttree(BDTVolSpec, RateSpec, BDTTimeSpec);
```

Suppose we want to price a cap using the BDT tree built where:

```
CapStrike = 0.065;
Settle = '01-Jan-2000';
Maturity = '01-Jan-2004';
CapReset = 1;
Principal = 100000;

We call the function

Price = capbybdt(BDTTree, CapStrike, Settle, Maturity, Principal)

Price =

    3.3034
```

Suppose we want to price a bond option in Matlab. The function call is as follows:

```
[Price, PriceTree] = optbndbybdt(BDTTree, OptSpec, Strike,...
    ExerciseDates, AmericanOpt, CouponRate, Settle, Maturity,...
        Period, Basis, EndMonthRule, IssueDate, FirstCouponDate,...
            LastCouponDate, StartDate, Face, Options)
```

where the arguments are as in Table A.2.

Table A.2 (continued next page)

Argument	Description
BDTTree	Forward-rate tree structure created by bdttree.
OptSpec	Number of instruments (NINST)-by-1 cell array of string values `'Call'` or `'Put'`.
Strike	European option: NINST-by-1 vector of strike price values.
	Bermuda option: NINST by number of strikes (NSTRIKES) matrix of strike price values.
	Each row is the schedule for one option. If an option has fewer than NSTRIKES exercise opportunities, the end of the row is padded with NaNs.
	For an American option: NINST-by-1 vector of strike price values for each option.
ExerciseDates	NINST-by-1 (European option) or NINST-by-NSTRIKES (Bermuda option) matrix of exercise dates. Each row is the schedule for one option. For a European option, there is only one exercise date: the option expiry date. For an American option: NINST-by-2 vector of exercise date boundaries. For each instrument, the option can be exercised on any coupon date between or including the pair of dates on that row. If only one non-NaN date is listed, or if ExerciseDates is NINST-by-1, the option can be exercised between the underlying bond Settle and the single listed exercise date.

Table A.2 (continued)

AmericanOpt	NINST-by-1 vector of flags: 0 (European/Bermuda) or 1 (American).
CouponRate	Decimal annual rate.
Settle	Settlement date. A vector of serial date numbers or date strings. Settle must be earlier than or equal to Maturity.
Maturity	Maturity date. A vector of serial date numbers or date strings.
Period	(Optional) Coupons per year of the bond. A vector of integers. Allowed values are 1, 2, 3, 4, 6, and 12. Default = 2.
Basis	(Optional) Day-count basis of the instrument. A vector of integers. 0 = actual/actual (default), 1 = 30/360 (SIA), 2 = actual/360, 3 = actual/365, 4 = 30/360 (PSA), 5 = 30 360 (ISDA), 6 = 30/360 (European), and 7 = actual/365 (Japanese).
EndMonthRule	(Optional) End-of-month rule. A vector. This rule applies only when Maturity is an end-of-month date for a month having 30 or fewer days. 0 = ignore rule, meaning that a bond's coupon payment date is always the same numerical day of the month. 1 = set rule on (default), meaning that a bond's coupon payment date is always the last actual day of the month.
IssueDate	(Optional) Date when a bond was issued.
FirstCouponDate	Date when a bond makes its first coupon payment. When FirstCouponDate and LastCouponDate are both specified, FirstCouponDate takes precedence in determining the coupon payment structure.
LastCouponDate	Last coupon date of a bond prior to the maturity date. In the absence of a specified FirstCouponDate, a specified LastCouponDate determines the coupon structure of the bond. The coupon structure of a bond is truncated at the LastCouponDate regardless of where it falls and is followed only by the bond's maturity cash flow date.
StartDate	Ignored.
Face	Face value. Default is 100.
Options	(Optional) Derivatives pricing options structure created with derivset.

The Settle date for every bond is set to the ValuationDate of the BDT tree. The bond argument Settle is ignored.

Suppose we want to value a European bond call option on a 4% coupon bond with a face value with a strike of 85 and a maturity of two years with a valuation date of January 1, 2002: Price = the fixed-income instruments. We add the underlying bond to the portfolio:

```
InstSet = instadd('Cap',CapStrike,Settle,Maturity);InstSet =
instadd(InstSet, 'Bond',0.04,'01-01-2000','01-01-2002');
InstSet = instadd(InstSet, 'OptBond',1,'Call',85,'01-01-2002',0);
instdisp(BDTSubSet)
Index Type CouponRate Settle          Maturity      Period    Basis
1     Bond 0.04       01-Jan-2000     01-Jan-2002   2         0
EndMonthRule IssueDate FirstCouponDate LastCouponDate StartDate
1            NaN       NaN             NaN            NaN
```

```
    Face
    100
Index Type Strike Settle        Maturity      CapReset Basis
2     Cap  0.06   01-Jan-2000   01-Jan-2004    1        0
    Principal
    100
Index  Type     UnderInd OptSpec Strike ExerciseDates AmericanOpt
3      OptBond  1        Call    85     01-Jan-2002   0
```

To calculate the risk measures, we call the function:

```
     [Delta Gamma Vega Price] = bdtsens(BDTTree, BDTSubSet)

Delta =

-177.8993
 207.9652
 -25.3722


Gamma =

  1.0e+003 *

    0.5004
    4.5744
    0.0720


Vega =

  -0.0002
   2.8968
  -0.0000


Price =

   96.9116
    3.3034
   13.4131
```

Delta and Gamma are calculated based on yield shifts of 100 basis points. All sensitivities are returned as dollar sensitivities. To find the per-dollar sensitivities, we divide the risk measures by their respective instrument prices, as follows:

```
  -1.8357
   2.1459
  -0.2618
```

A.2   HULL-WHITE TREES IN MATLAB

Hull and White (1994)[2] developed a general tree-building procedure to build a trinomial tree calibrated to the yield curve. Their model was an extension of the Vasick model[3]

$$dr = a(\bar{r}(t) - r)dt + \sigma dz$$

and is more commonly expressed in the form

$$dr = (\theta(t) - ar)dt + \sigma dz \qquad (A.3)$$

where $\theta(t)$ is a tree fitting parameter and a is the speed of mean reversion of interest rates.

To build a BDT tree, one uses equally spaced time steps and a binomial process with transition probabilities fixed (at $\frac{1}{2}$), allowing only the freedom to adjust the space step. In trinomial trees, we fix both the time and space steps, but we are free to choose the probabilities to ensure that the distributions of the short-rate changes over each time interval $\Delta(t)$ have the right mean and standard deviation to match the short-rate process being approximated.

Building a Hull-White tree is a two-stage procedure. The first stage in the Hull and White procedure builds a trinomial tree to approximate a short rate $x = x(t)$ modeled by an Ornstein-Uhlenbeck process:

$$dx = -axdt + \sigma dz, \quad x(0) = 0$$

For each t, $x(t)$ is distributed symmetrically about 0. Also, for small time changes Δt, if we ignore second order and higher terms in Δt, then changes in x are normally distributed with finite mean and variance. That is, $dx(t) = x(t + \Delta t) - x(t) \sim N(-ax(t)\Delta t, \sigma^2 \Delta t)$. The spacing between interest rates (used to construct the state space) on the tree, Δr, is set to

$$\Delta r = \sigma \sqrt{3 \Delta t}$$

with Δt the time step length.[4] The next stage of tree development is to displace the nodes on the x tree by $\alpha(t)$ and thereby convert the x tree to an r tree that fits the initial term structure. That is, the r tree contains the short rate $r(t) = x(t) + \alpha(t)$ at each node, so that $\alpha(t) = r(t) - x(t)$. Recall the models $dr = (\theta(t) - ar)dt + \sigma dz$ and $dx = -axdt + \sigma dz$. From these, the term $\alpha(t)$ must follow the dynamics:

$$d\alpha(t) = (\theta(t) - a\alpha(t))dt$$

For details of the Hull-White tree-building procedure, see Hull-White (1994), Hull (1997), and Clewlow and Strickland (1998). For Hull-White implementations (one and two-factors models) in C++, see London (2004).

To build a Hull-White tree in Matlab, we need to define a Hull-White volatility specification with `HWVolSpec` which accepts the valuation date, volatility dates, volatility curve, α date(s), and α curve as input parameters. The model parameters are calibrated to the volatility and α input values.

```
load deriv.mat

Compounding = 1;
ValuationDate = '01-01-2004';
StartDate = ValuationDate;
VolDates = ['12-31-2004'; '12-31-2005'; '12-31-2006'; '12-31-2007'];
VolCurve = 0.01;
AlphaDates = '01-01-2008';
AlphaCurve = 0.1;
Rates = [0.0275; 0.0312; 0.0363; 0.0415];

BKVolSpec = bkvolspec(ValuationDate, VolDates, VolCurve,... AlphaDates,
AlphaCurve);

RateSpec = intenvset('Compounding', Compounding,...
  'ValuationDate', ValuationDate,...
  'StartDates', ValuationDate,...
  'EndDates', VolDates,...
  'Rates', Rates);

HWTimeSpec = hwtimespec(ValuationDate, VolDates, Compounding);
HWTree = hwtree(HWVolSpec, RateSpec, HWTimeSpec)
```

After building a Hull-White Tree, we can use the Matlab function floorbyhw to value a floor:

```
Strike = 0.03;
Principal = 100000;
Settle = '01-Jan-2005';
Maturity = '01-Jan-2009';

Price = floorbyhw(HWTree, Strike, Settle, Maturity,1,0,Principal)

Price =

   461.59
```

It is a lot easier to use Matlab for fixed-income derivatives pricing than C++ (compare the above code to the following C++ code). Suppose we want to price a cap using Black's 1976 model in C++ and then calibrate the Hull-White model to both the yield curve and caplet volatilities. We first define Black's class:

BlackModel01.h

```
#ifndef _BLACKMODEL__
#define _BLACKMODEL__

#include <vector>
#include <math.h>
#include "StatUtility.h"

class BlackModel
{
        public:
```

```
                BlackModel() {};
                virtual ~BlackModel() {};
                std::vector<double> priceBlackCap(std::vector<double>
                  capVol, std::vector<double> PDB, std::vector<double>
                  maturity, double Rcap, double L, double tenor);
                double BlacksFormula(double f, double P, double L,
                  double Rcap,double vol, double tau, double dtau);
};

#endif
```

with method definitions:

BlackModel02.cpp

```
#include "BlackModel.h"

std::vector<double> BlackModel::priceBlackCap(std::vector<double> capVol,
  std::vector<double> PDB, std::vector<double> maturity, double Rcap,
  double L, double tenor)
{
        int i;
        std::vector<double> f;      // forward rates
        std::vector<double> R;      // yield price
        std::vector<double> capV;
        std::vector<double> P;
        std::vector<double> t;
        std::vector<double> caplet;
        double cap = 0.0;
        double faceValue = 0.0;
        double Ps = 0.0;
        double tmp = 0.0;

        std::vector<double>::iterator iter;
        faceValue = L*(1 + Rcap*tenor);

        for (iter = capVol.begin(); iter != capVol.end(); iter++)
        {
                tmp = *iter;
                capV.push_back(tmp);
        }
        for (iter = PDB.begin(); iter != PDB.end(); iter++)
        {
                tmp = *iter;
                P.push_back(tmp);
        }
        for (iter = maturity.begin(); iter != maturity.end(); iter++)
        {
                tmp = *iter;
                t.push_back(tmp);
        }
        for (i = 0; i < capVol.size(); i++)
        {
                tmp = -(1/t[i])*(log(P[i]));
                R.push_back(tmp);
```

```
                        tmp = -(1/tenor)*log(P[i+1]/P[i]);
                        f.push_back(tmp);
                }

                for (i = 0; i < capVol.size()-1; i++)
                {
                        tmp = BlacksFormula(f[i],P[i],L,Rcap,capV[i],t[i],tenor);
                        caplet.push_back(tmp);
                }

                return caplet;
}

double BlackModel::BlacksFormula(double f, double P, double L, double Rcap,
   double vol, double tau, double dtau)
{
                StatUtility util;
                double d1 = (log(f/Rcap) + ((vol*vol)/2)*tau)/(vol*sqrt(tau));
                double d2 = d1 - vol*sqrt(tau);

                return P*dtau*L*(f*util.normalCalc(d1) - Rcap*util.normalCalc(d2));
}
```

We define the cap-pricing function in the HullWhite class, which calls the *priceBlack-Cap* method of the BlackModel class:

HullWhite_priceCapHW.cpp

```
#include "HullWhite.h"
#include <numeric>

double HullWhite::priceCapHW(vector<double> mats, vector<double> vols,
   vector<double> rates, double a, double FV, double vol, double Rcap,
   double tenor, double L)
{

        int i;
        TNT::Array2D<double> B(NUM,NUM);
        double d1, d2;
        double K = L;
        double volP, a1;
        double tmp = 0.0;
        double totalsum = 0.0;
        double sum = 0.0;
        double sum1 = 0.0;
        double sum2 = 0.0;
        double tau, tau1, tau2, tau3;
        double epsilon = 0.001;
        double error = 0.0;
        double error1 = 0.0;
        double volSum2 = 0.0;
        double alpha1, alpha2 = 0;
        double d1prime, d2prime, d3prime, d4prime;
        double volPrime = 0.0, a2;
        double aprime = 0.0;
        double aPrime = 0.0;
```

```cpp
double diff = 0.0;
double SSE = 0.0;
double val = 0.0;
vector<double> P;
vector<double> model;
vector<double> market;
int cnt = 0;
int len = vols.size();

std::cout << "Hull White Cap Calibration" << endl << endl;
std::cout << "Cap Rate :  " <<  Rcap << endl;
std::cout << "Principal:  " << L << endl;
std::cout << "Face Value Bond: " << FV << endl;
std::cout << "Tenor: " << tenor << endl;

// compute pure discount bond prices
for (i = 0; i < len; i++)
{
        tmp = exp(-mats[i]*rates[i]);
        P.push_back(tmp);
}

// compute market quotes
BlackModel bm;
market = bm.priceBlackCap(vols,P,mats,Rcap,L,tenor);
val = std::accumulate(market.begin(),market.end(),0.0);

for (i = 0; i < len-1; i++)
{
   volP = sqrt((((vol*vol)/(2*a*a*a))*(1 - exp(-2*mats[i]*a))*(1 -
     exp(-a*(mats[i+1]-mats[i]))))*(1 - exp(-a*(mats[i+1]-
     mats[i])))));
   d1 = log((FV*P[i+1])/(K*P[i]))/volP + volP/2;
   d2 = d1 - volP;
   tmp = K*P[i]*util.normalCalc(-d2) - FV*P[i+1]*
     util.normalCalc(-d1);
   model.push_back(tmp);
}
sum = 0;
SSE = 0;
for (i = 0; i < len-1; i++)
{
        sum = sum + ((model[i] - market[i])/market[i])*((model[i] -
          market[i])/market[i]);
        SSE = SSE + (model[i] - market[i])*(model[i] - market[i]);
}

// Minimization routine
totalsum = sum;
alpha1 = vol;
a1 = a;
do
{
   sum1 = 0;
   sum2 = 0;
   volSum2 = 0;
   for (i = 0; i < len-2; i++)
```

```
                {
                  tau = mats[i+1] - mats[i];
                  tau1 = mats[i];
                  tau2 = mats[i+1];
                  tau3 = mats[i+1] + mats[i];
                  volP = sqrt(((alpha1*alpha1)/(2*a1*a1*a1))*(1 -
                     exp(-2*tau1*a1))*(1 - exp(-a1*(tau)))*(1 - exp(-a1*(tau))));
                  // compute d1 and d2
                  d1 = log((FV*P[i+1])/(K*P[i]))/volP + volP/2;
                  d2 = d1 - volP;
                  aprime = -3*pow(a1,-4);
                  volPrime = 0.5*(pow(volP,-0.5))*(2*alpha1/(2*a1*a1*a1))*((1 -
                     exp(-2*tau1*a1))*(1 - exp(-a1*(tau)))*(1 - exp(-a1*(tau))));
                  aPrime = 0.5*pow(volP,-0.5)*((0.5*alpha1*alpha1*pow(a1,-3)*
                     (2*tau*exp(-a1*tau) - 2*tau*exp(-2*a1*tau) +
                     2*tau1*exp(-2*tau1*a1) - 2*tau3*exp(-a1*tau3) +
                     2*tau2*exp(-2*a*tau2)) +(0.5*aprime*alpha1*alpha1)*
                     (1 - 2*exp(-a1*tau) + exp(-2*a1*tau)
                      - exp(-2*a1*tau1) + 2*exp(-a1*tau3) - exp(-2*a1*tau2))));
                  d1prime =  -((log(FV*P[i+1]/K*P[i]))/(volP*volP))*volPrime +
                     0.5*volPrime;
                  d2prime = d1prime - volPrime;
                  d3prime = -((log(FV*P[i+1]/K*P[i]))/(volP*volP))*aPrime +
                     0.5*aPrime;
                  d4prime = d3prime - aPrime;
                  sum1 = sum1 + (model[i] - market[i])/market[i];
                  volSum2 = volSum2 + (K*P[i]*util.normalCalcPrime(-d2)*
                     (-d2prime) -
                     FV*P[i+1]*util.normalCalcPrime(-d1)*(-d1prime))/market[i];
                  sum2 = sum2 + (K*P[i]*util.normalCalcPrime(-d2)*(-d4prime) -
                     FV*P[i+1]*util.normalCalcPrime(-d1)*(-d3prime))/market[i];
                }
                alpha2 = alpha1 - sum1/volSum2;
                error = alpha2 - alpha1;
                alpha1 = alpha2;

                a2 = a1 - sum1/-sum2;
                error1 = a2 - a1;
                a1 = a2;
                cnt++;
                if (cnt > 20)
                    break;
         }
    while ((error > epsilon) || (error1 > epsilon));

    if (cnt < 20)
    {
       std::cout << "Calibrated alpha = " << a1  << endl;
       std::cout << "Calibrated vol = " << alpha1 << endl;
    }
    else
            std::cout << "No Convergence for Calibration.  Try
               different values." << endl;

    return val;
}
```

We read a file that contains caplet maturities, volatilities, and yields called Cap.txt in the HullWhite folder. The main function is:

HullWhite_main.cpp

```cpp
#include <fstream>
#include <iostream>
#include <strstream>
#include "HullWhite.h"
#include "BDT.h"

void main()
{
        char buffer[SIZE_X];
        char dataBuffer[SIZE_X];
        char* str = NULL;
        const char* file = "c:\\Caplet.txt";
        vector<double> m;
        vector<double> v;
        vector<double> r;
        double mat = 0.0;
        double rate = 0.0;
        double a = 0.10;           // mean speed of reversion
        double vol = 0.10;         // volatility
        double strike = 0.055;     // exercise price
        double T = 5;              // option maturity
        double coupon = 0.0;       // bond coupon rate
        double swapMat = 5;        // swap Maturity
        double swaptionMat = 3;    // swaption maturity
        double price = 0.0;        // price of bond
        double faceValue = 106.7;  // face value of bond
        double principal = 100;    // principal amount of bond

    HullWhite hw;
        BDT bdt;

        // read from file
        ifstream fin;              // input file stream
        fin.clear();
        fin.open(file);

        if (fin.good())
        {
                while (!fin.eof())
                {
                        fin.getline(buffer,sizeof(buffer)/
                          sizeof(buffer[0]));
                        istrstream str(buffer);

                        // Get data
                        str >> dataBuffer;
                        mat = atof(dataBuffer);
                        m.push_back(mat);

                        str >> dataBuffer;
                        vol = atof(dataBuffer);
                        v.push_back(vol);
```

```
                                str >> dataBuffer;
                                rate = atof(dataBuffer);
                                r.push_back(rate);
                }
        }
    else
        std::cout << "File not good!" << "\n";

    fin.close();

    price = hw.priceCapHW(m,v,r,a,faceValue,vol,0.07,0.25,principal);
    std::cout << "Cap price = " << price << endl << endl;

    vector<double> zero;
    zero.push_back(0.055);
    zero.push_back(0.0575);
    zero.push_back(0.0600);
    zero.push_back(0.0625);
    zero.push_back(0.0650);
    zero.push_back(0.0675);
    zero.push_back(0.07);
    zero.push_back(0.0710);
    zero.push_back(0.0740);
    zero.push_back(0.0775);

    vector<double> vols;
    vols.push_back(0.06);
    vols.push_back(0.065);
    vols.push_back(0.07);
    vols.push_back(0.075);
    vols.push_back(0.08);
    vols.push_back(0.085);
    vols.push_back(0.09);
    vols.push_back(0.095);
    vols.push_back(0.10);
    vols.push_back(0.105);

    price = hw.priceDiscountBondOptionsHW(zero,10,2,vol,a,2,strike,
        'C','E');
    std::cout << "HW Discount Bond Option Price = " << price << endl;

    price = bdt.priceDiscountBondsBDT(zero,5,5,vol,strike,'C','E',
        zero[0]);
    std::cout << "BDT Discount Bond Option Price = " << price <<
        endl << endl;

    price = hw.payerSwaptionHW(zero,swapMat,swaptionMat,vol,a,strike,
        'E',coupon);
    std::cout << "HW European pay swaption price = " << price << endl;

    price = hw.payerSwaptionHW(zero,swapMat,swaptionMat,vol,a,strike,
        'A',coupon);
    std::cout << "HW American pay swaption price = " << price <<
        endl << endl;
```

```
price = hw.receiverSwaptionHW(zero,swapMat,swaptionMat,vol,a,
   strike,'E',coupon);
std::cout << "HW European recevier swaption price = " << price <<
   endl;

price = hw.receiverSwaptionHW(zero,swapMat,swaptionMat,vol,a,
   strike,'A',coupon);
std::cout << "HW American recevier swaption price = " << price <<
   endl;

}
```

The output is as follows:

```
Hull White Cap Calibration

Cap Rate: 0.07
Principal: 100
Face Value Bond: 100
Tenor: 0.25
Calibrated alpha = -0.317789
Calibrated vol = 0.0984802
Cap price = 3.48947
```

The cap price is $0.0348 per $100 of notional, so that a cap at 7% on $1,000,000 is $34,800.

A.3   BLACK-KARASINSKI TREES IN MATLAB

The Hull-White tree-building procedure can be extended to a lognormal process for the short rate which does not allow negative rates. For this reason, it is often used by practitioners. The lognormal HW or restricted Black-Karasinski (1991)[5] model can be represented as:

$$d\ln r(t) = a(\ln \bar{r} - \ln r(t))dt + \sigma dz \tag{A.4}$$

or written in its more general Black-Karasinski form:

$$d\ln r(t) = (\theta(t) - a\ln r(t))dt + \sigma dz. \tag{A.5}$$

The time-dependent term in the drift is used to calibrate the model to the initial yield curve. The time-homogenous (constant) parameters a and σ determine the volatility term structure. From (A.5), using Ito's lemma, we obtain:

$$dr(t) = r(t)\left[\theta(t) + \frac{\sigma^2}{2} - a\ln r(t)\right]dt + \sigma r(t)dz(t)$$

We can adapt the Black-Karasinski model to the two-stage methodology outlined in §A.2 to construct a short-rate tree (for computing discount bond and bond options that do not have closed-form analytical solutions). First, we set $x = \ln r$, yielding the process:

$$dx = (\theta(t) - ax)dt + \sigma dz$$

We then set $\theta(t) = 0$, so that the process becomes

$$dx = -axdt + \sigma dz$$

as before. At time 0, $x = 0$. We assume that $\Delta r = \Delta x = \sigma\sqrt{3\Delta t}$, the same as before. The tree is symmetrical with equally spaced state and time steps. The model (as well as the Hull-White model), however, can be modified to have time-dependent changes in Δr and Δt—i.e., $\Delta t_i = t_{i+1} - t_i$ and $\Delta r_i = \sigma\sqrt{3\Delta t_i}$ for each i. At node (i, j), we compute $x_{i,j} = j\Delta x$. We then need to compute the Arrow-Debreu security prices at each node (i, j) and the displacement (shift) parameters α_i at each time step $i = 1, \ldots, N$. The α_i are chosen to correctly price a $(i + 1)\Delta t$-maturity discount bond. The Δt−period interest rate at the jth node at time $i\Delta t$ becomes

$$
\begin{aligned}
r_{i,j} &= \exp(\alpha_i + x_{i,j}) \\
&= \exp(\alpha_i + j\Delta x)
\end{aligned}
\tag{A.6}
$$

For details of the Black-Karasinski tree-building procedure, see Hull (1997) and Clewlow and Strickland (1998).

To build a Black-Karsinski tree in Matlab, we need to generate a BKTree using `bktree` which takes a BKVolSpec, BKTimeSpec, and BKRateSpec:

```
Compounding = -1;
ValuationDate = '01-01-2004';
StartDate = ValuationDate;
VolDates = ['12-31-2004'; '12-31-2005'; '12-31-2006'; '12-31-2007'];
VolCurve = 0.01;
AlphaDates = '01-01-2008';
AlphaCurve = 0.1;
Rates = [0.0275; 0.0312; 0.0363; 0.0415];

BKVolSpec = bkvolspec(ValuationDate, VolDates, VolCurve,...
  AlphaDates, AlphaCurve);              RateSpec = intenvset
  ('Compounding', Compounding,...
   'ValuationDate', ValuationDate,...
   'StartDates', ValuationDate,...
   'EndDates', VolDates,...
   'Rates', Rates);
BKTimeSpec = bktimespec(ValuationDate, VolDates, Compounding);
  BKTree = bktree(BKVolSpec, RateSpec, BKTimeSpec)

BKTree =

      FinObj: 'BKFwdTree'
      VolSpec: [1x1 struct]
      TimeSpec: [1x1 struct]
      RateSpec: [1x1 struct]
      tObs: [0 0.9973 1.9973 2.9973]
      dObs: [731947 732312 732677 733042]
      CFlowT: {[4x1 double]  [3x1 double]  [2x1 double]  [3.9973]}
      Probs: {[3x1 double]  [3x3 double]  [3x5 double]}
      Connect: {[2]  [2 3 4]  [2 2 3 4 4]}
      FwdTree: {1x4 cell}
```

To view the tree, enter `treeviewer(BKTree)`. Matlab displays the tree as shown in Figure A.1. Once we have built the tree, we can price fixed-income securities like bonds and caps.

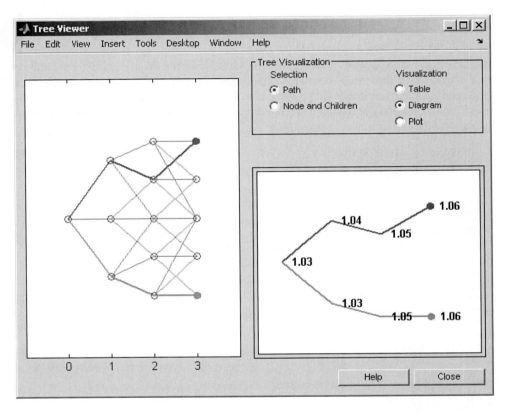

Figure A.1   Black-Karasinski tree. *Source: MathWorks, www.mathworks.com/products/ derivatives/functionlist.html.*

```
load deriv;
 BKSubSet = instselect(BKInstSet,'Type', {'Bond', 'Cap'});
 instdisp(BKSubSet)
 Index Type   CouponRate Settle        Maturity     Period    Name ...
 1     Bond   0.03       01-Jan-2004 01-Jan-2007 1            3% bond
 2     Bond   0.03       01-Jan-2004 01-Jan-2008 2            3% bond
 Index Type   Strike     Settle        Maturity     CapReset...Name ...
 3     Cap    0.04       01-Jan-2004 01-Jan-2008 1            4% Cap
 [Price, PriceTree] = bkprice(BKTree, BKSubSet);

 Price =
   98.1096
   95.6734
    2.2706
```

To view the tree, we enter `treeviewer(PriceTree, BKSubSet)` and can view prices of the instruments as shown in Figure A.2.

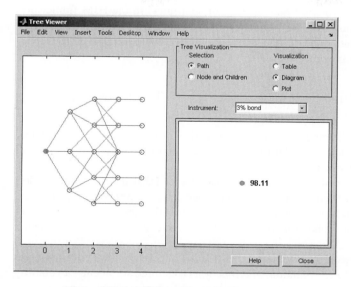

First 3% Bond (Maturity 2007)

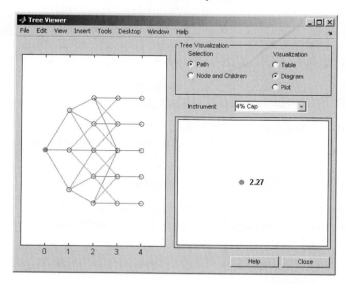

4% Cap

Figure A.2   Price of first 3% bond and 4% cap using Black-Karasinski.   *Source: MathWorks, www.mathworks.com/products/derivatives/functionlist.html.*

A.4   HJM PRICING IN MATLAB

Heath, Jarrow, and Morton (HJM) (1992)[6] developed a general framework for modeling interest rates in terms of forward rates instead of spot rates. In the HJM framework, the volatility function is allowed to be a function of the entire forward rate curve. HJM developed this assuming that under an objective measure, the evolution of $f(t, T)$, the instantaneous forward rate, is governed by

$$df(t, T) = \alpha(t, T)dt + \sum_{i=1}^{N} \sigma_i(t, Tf(t, T))dz_i(t) \qquad (A.7)$$

The volatility functions $\sigma_i(\cdot)$, being dependent on the entire forward rate curve, completely specify the forward rate model. The volatilities and correlations of the forward rates are all determined by the volatility function.

For a detailed discussion of single-factor and two-factor HJM discrete-state models (including arbitrage free restrictions on the models), see Jarrow (2002). The underlying code implementations of HJM trees built in Matlab are directly based on these discrete-state models. For C++ implementations of these HJM discrete-state models, see London (2004).

To price fixed income securities with an HJM tree in Matlab, one needs to first build an HJM tree using the `hjmtree` function. The function takes three arguments: a volatility specification (`VolSpec`), an interest-rate term structure specification (`RateSpec`), and a time specification (`TimeSpec`).

`VolSpec` is a structure that specifies the forward rate volatility process. You create `VolSpec` using either of these functions: `hjmvolspec` or `bdtvolspec`. The `hjmvolspec` function supports the specification of up to three factors. It handles these models for the volatility of the interest-rate term structure:

- Constant volatility (Ho-Lee): $\sigma(t, T) ==$`Sigma_0`
  `VolSpec = hjmvolspec('Constant', Sigma_0)`

- Stationary volatility: $\sigma(t, T) =$`Vol(T-t) = Vol(Term)`
  `VolSpec = hjmvolspec('Stationary', CurveVol, CurveTerm)`

- Exponential volatility: $\sigma(t, T) =$`Sigma_0*exp(-Lambda*(T-t))`
  `VolSpec = hjmvolspec('Exponential', Sigma_0, Lambda)`

- Vasicek, Hull-White: $\sigma(t, T) =$`Sigma_0*exp(-Decay(T-t))`
  `VolSpec = hjmvolspec('Vasicek', Sigma_0, CurveDecay, CurveTerm)`

- Nearly proportional stationary: $\sigma(t, T) =$`Prop(T-t)*`
  `max(SpotRate(t), MaxSpot)`
  `VolSpec = hjmvolspec('Proportional', CurveProp, CurveTerm, MaxSpot)`

A one-factor model assumes that the interest term structure is affected by a single source of uncertainty. Incorporating multiple factors allows you to specify different types of shifts in the shape and location of the interest-rate structure. The function `hjmvolspec` generates the structure `VolSpec`, which specifies the volatility process $\sigma(t, T)$, used in the creation of the forward rate trees. In this context, T represents the starting time of the forward rate, and t represents the observation time. The volatility process can be constructed from a combination of factors specified sequentially in the call to function that creates it. Each factor specification starts with a string specifying the name of the factor, followed by the pertinent parameters. The time values t, T, and Term are in coupon interval units specified by the Compounding input of `hjmtimespec`. For instance, if Compounding $= 2$, Term $= 1$ is a semiannual period (six months).

The `bdtvolspec` function supports only a single volatility factor. The volatility remains constant between pairs of nodes on the tree. You supply the input volatility values in a vector of decimal values.

`RateSpec` is the interest-rate specification of the initial rate curve. You create this structure with the function `intenvset`.

`[RateSpec, RateSpecOld] = intenvset(RateSpec, 'Argument1', Value1, 'Argument2', Value2,...)` creates an interest term structure (`RateSpec`) in which the input argument list is specified as argument name/argument value pairs. The argument name portion of the pair must be recognized as a valid field of the output structure `RateSpec`; the argument value portion of the pair is then assigned to its paired field.

If the optional argument `RateSpec` is specified, `intenvset` modifies an existing interest term structure `RateSpec` by changing the named argument to the specified values and recalculating the arguments dependent on the new values.

`[RateSpec, RateSpecOld] = intenvset` creates an interest term structure `RateSpec` with all fields set to `[ ]`. `intenvset` with no input or output arguments displays a list of argument names and possible values. `RateSpecOld` is a structure containing the properties of an interest-rate structure prior to the changes introduced by Table A.3. Arguments may be chosen from Table A.4 and specified in any order.

It is sufficient to type only the leading characters that uniquely identify the parameter. Case is ignored for argument names. When creating a new `RateSpec`, the set of arguments passed to `intenvset` must include `StartDates`, `EndDates`, and either `Rates` or `Disc`. Call `intenvset` with no input or output arguments to display a list of argument names and possible values.

`TimeSpec` is the tree time layout specification. You create this variable with the functions `hjmtimespec` or `bdttimespec`. It represents the mapping between level times and level dates for rate quoting. This structure indirectly determines the number of levels in the tree. The `hjmtimespec` function specifies the time structure for HJM interest-rate tree.

Table A.3

`RateSpec`	(Optional) An existing interest-rate specification structure to be changed, probably created from a previous call to `intenvset`.

Table A.4

`Compounding`	Scalar value representing the rate at which the input zero rates were compounded when annualized. Default $= 2$. This argument determines the formula for the discount factors: `Compounding`$= 1, 2, 3, 4, 6, 12$. `Disc` $= (1 + Z/F)\wedge(-T)$, where F is the compounding frequency, Z is the zero rate, and T is the time in periodic units—e.g., $T = F$ is one year. `Compounding = 365`. `Disc = ` $(1 + Z/F)\wedge(-T)$, where F is the number of days in the basis year and T is a number of days elapsed computed by basis. `Compounding = -1`. `Disc = exp(-T*Z)`, where T is time in years.
`Disc`	Number of points (NPOINTS) by number of curves (NCURVES) matrix of unit bond prices over investment intervals from `StartDates`, when the cash flow is valued, to `EndDates`, when the cash flow is received.
`Rates`	Number of points (NPOINTS) by number of curves (NCURVES) matrix of rates in decimal form. For example, 5% is 0.05 in `Rates`. `Rates` are the yields over investment intervals from `StartDates`, when the cash flow is valued, to `EndDates`, when the cash flow is received.
`EndDates`	NPOINTS-by-1 vector or scalar of serial maturity dates ending the interval to discount over.
`StartDates`	NPOINTS-by-1 vector or scalar of serial dates starting the interval to discount over. Default $=$ `ValuationDate`.
`ValuationDate`	(Optional) Scalar value in serial date number form representing the observation date of the investment horizons entered in `StartDates` and `EndDates`. Default $=$ `min(StartDates)`.
`Basis`	(Optional) Day count basis of the instrument. A vector of integers. $0 =$ actual/actual (default), $1 = 30/360$ (SIA), $2 =$ actual/360, $3 =$ actual/365, $4 = 30/360$ (PSA), $5 = 30/360$ (ISDA), $6 = 30/360$ (European), $7 =$ actual/365 (Japanese).
`EndMonthRule`	(Optional) End-of-month rule. A vector. This rule applies only when `Maturity` is an end-of-month date for a month having 30 or fewer days. $0 =$ ignore rule, meaning that a bond's coupon payment date is always the same numerical day of the month. $1 =$ set rule on (default), meaning that a bond's coupon payment date is always the last actual day of the month.

Description

`TimeSpec = hjmtimespec` sets the number of levels and node times for an HJM tree and determines the mapping between dates and time for rate quoting.

`TimeSpec` is a structure specifying the time layout for `hjmtree`. The state observation dates are `[Settle; Maturity(1:end-1)]`. Because a forward rate is stored at the last observation, the tree can value cash flows out to `Maturity`.

Syntax

```
TimeSpec = hjmtimespec(ValuationDate, Maturity, Compounding)
```

Arguments

Table A.5

ValuationDate	Scalar date marking the pricing date and first observation in the tree. Specify as serial date number or date string.
Maturity	Number of levels (depth) of the tree. A number of levels (NLEVELS)-by-1 vector of dates marking the cash flow dates of the tree. Cash flows with these maturities fall on tree nodes. Maturity should be in increasing order.
Compounding	(Optional) Scalar value representing the rate at which the input zero rates were compounded when annualized. Default $= 1$. This argument determines the formula for the discount factors: Compounding = 1, 2, 3, 4, 6, 12 Disc = (1 + Z/F)$\wedge$(-T), where F is the compounding frequency, Z is the zero rate, and T is the time in periodic units—e.g., T = F is one year. Compounding = 365 Disc = (1 + Z/F)$\wedge$(-T), where F is the number of days in the basis year and T is a number of days elapsed computed by basis. Compounding = -1 Disc = exp(-T*Z), where T is time in years.

Examples

Specify an eight-period tree with semiannual nodes (every six months). Use exponential compounding to report rates.

```
Compounding = -1;
ValuationDate = '15-Jan-1999';
Maturity = datemnth(ValuationDate, 6*(1:8)');
TimeSpec = hjmtimespec(ValuationDate, Maturity, Compounding)

TimeSpec =

         FinObj: 'HJMTimeSpec'
  ValuationDate: 730135
       Maturity: [8x1 double]
    Compounding: -1
          Basis: 0
    EndMonthRule: 1
```

Creating an HJM Volatility and Pricing Model

HJM Volatility Specification Example

Consider an example that uses a single factor—specifically, a constant-sigma factor. The constant factor specification requires only one parameter, the value of σ. In this case, the value corresponds to 0.10.

```
HJMVolSpec = hjmvolspec('Constant', 0.10)

HJMVolSpec =

FinObj: 'HJMVolSpec'
FactorModels: {'Constant'}
FactorArgs: {{1x1 cell}}
SigmaShift: 0
NumFactors: 1
NumBranch: 2
PBranch: [0.5000 0.5000]
Fact2Branch: [-1 1]
```

The NumFactors field of the VolSpec structure, VolSpec.NumFactors = 1, reveals that the number of factors used to generate VolSpec was one. The FactorModels field indicates that it is a 'Constant' factor, and the NumBranches field indicates the number of branches. As a consequence, each node of the resulting tree has two branches, one going up, and the other going down.

Consider now a two-factor volatility process made from a proportional factor and an exponential factor.

```
% Exponential factor
Sigma_0 = 0.1;
Lambda = 1;
% Proportional factor
CurveProp = [0.11765; 0.08825; 0.06865];
CurveTerm = [ 1 ; 2 ; 3 ];
% Build VolSpec
HJMVolSpec = hjmvolspec('Proportional', CurveProp, CurveTerm,...
1e6,'Exponential', Sigma_0, Lambda)

HJMVolSpec =
FinObj: 'HJMVolSpec'
FactorModels: {'Proportional' 'Exponential'}
FactorArgs: {{1x3 cell} {1x2 cell}}
SigmaShift: 0
NumFactors: 2
NumBranch: 3
PBranch: [0.2500 0.2500 0.5000]
Fact2Branch: [2x3 double]
```

The output shows that the volatility specification was generated using two factors. The tree has three branches per node. Each branch has probabilities of 0.25, 0.25, and 0.5, going from top to bottom.

To create an HJM tree, use the following:

```
Compounding = -1;
ValuationDate = '01-01-2000';
StartDate = ValuationDate;
EndDates = ['01-01-2001'; '01-01-2002'; '01-01-2003';
      '01-01-2004'; '01-01-2005'];
Rates = [.1; .11; .12; .125; .13];
Volatility = [.2; .19; .18; .17; .16];
CurveTerm = [1; 2; 3; 4; 5];

HJMVolSpec = hjmvolspec('Stationary',Volatility,CurveTerm);
   RateSpec = intenvset('Compounding', Compounding,...
                     'ValuationDate', ValuationDate,...
                     'StartDates', StartDate,...
                     'EndDates', EndDates,...
                     'Rates', Rates);
HJMTimeSpec = hjmtimespec(ValuationDate, EndDates, Compounding);
HJMTree = hjmtree(HJMVolSpec, RateSpec, HJMTimeSpec);
```

We can view the HJM tree with the Matlab statement `treeviewer(HJMTree)` shown in Figure A.3. Note how the branches grow exponentially and do not recombine. Given the exponential increase in the number of branches, it is known as a bushy tree.

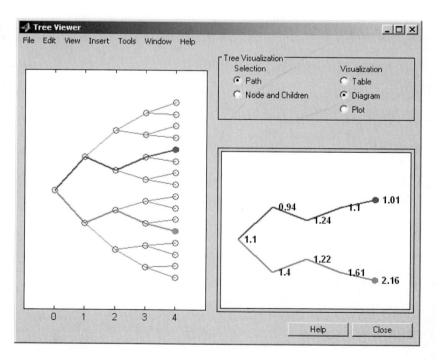

Figure   A.3   The HJM tree with the Matlab statement. *Source: MathWorks, www.mathworks.com/products/derivatives/functionlist.html.*

Now that we have built the HJM tree, we can price fixed income instruments. We first load the data set of bond and cap data.

```
HJMSubSet = instselect(HJMInstSet,'Type', {'Bond', 'Cap'});
instdisp(HJMSubSet)

Index Type CouponRate Settle       Maturity        Period Basis
EndMonthRule IssueDate FirstCouponDate LastCouponDate StartDate
Face Name    Quantity
1     Bond 0.04      01-Jan-2000    01-Jan-2003     1      NaN   NaN
NaN        NaN         NaN            NaN          NaN 4% bond 100
2     Bond 0.04      01-Jan-2000    01-Jan-2004     2      NaN   NaN
NaN        NaN         NaN            NaN          NaN 4% bond 50

Index Type Strike Settle        Maturity        CapReset Basis Principal
    Name   Quantity
3     Cap  0.03   01-Jan-2000    01-Jan-2004     1        NaN   NaN
    3% Cap 30

[Price, PriceTree] = hjmprice(HJMTree, HJMSubSet)

Price =

   79.3878
   73.0426
   45.1451


PriceTree =

    FinObj: 'HJMPriceTree'
     PBush: {1x6 cell}
    AIBush: {1x6 cell}
      tObs: [0 1 2 3 4 5]
```

```
Sigma_0 = 0.0076;
Lambda = 0.0154;

% Build VolSpec
HJMVolSpec = hjmvolspec('Exponential', Sigma_0, Lambda);
RateSpec = intenvset('Rates',0.02,'StartDates','01-Jan-2000','EndDates',
  '01-Jan-2004');

HJMVolSpec =

FinObj: 'HJMVolSpec'
FactorModels: {'Exponential'}
FactorArgs: {{1x2 cell}}
SigmaShift: 0
NumFactors: 1
NumBranch: 2
PBranch: [0.5000 0.5000]
Fact2Branch: [-1 1]
```

A.5   MATLAB EXCEL LINK EXAMPLE

We can use Matlab Excel Link to use Excel to price fixed income instruments using an HJM tree (or any other interest rate model), as shown in Figure A.4. Suppose we want to price the following instrument using Excel as a front end:

Index	Type	CouponRate	Settle	Maturity	Period	Basis
EndMonthRule	IssueDate	FirstCouponDate	LastCouponDate	StartDate	Face	Name
1	Bond 0.04		01-Jan-2000	01-Jan-2002	1	0
1	NaN	NaN	NaN	NaN	100	4% Bond
2	Bond 0.05		01-Jan-2000	01-Jan-2003	1	0
1	NaN	NaN	NaN	NaN	100	5% Bond
3	Bond 0.06		01-Jan-2000	01-Jan-2004	1	0
1	NaN	NaN	NaN	NaN	100	6% Bond

Index	Type	UnderInd	OptSpec	Strike	ExerciseDates	AmericanOpt	Name
4	OptBond	3	Call	101	01-Jan-2003	0	Option

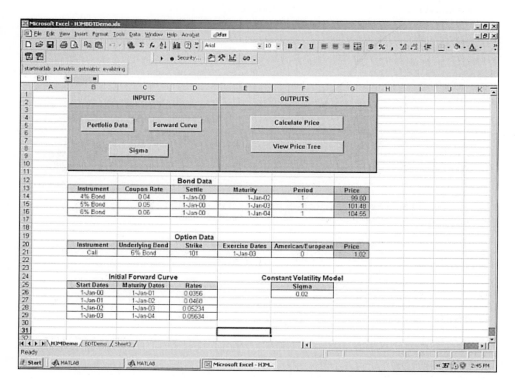

Figure A.4 Pricing fixed income instruments using an HJM tree.

The following code stores the portfolio data in Excel worksheet variables and creates
an instrument set for processing.

```
Sub PutInstData()
' Send portfolio data and build InstSet

    'Send Bond data first
    mlPutMatrix "BondName", Worksheets("HJMDemo").Range("BondName")
    mlPutMatrix "BondRate", Worksheets("HJMDemo").Range("BondRate")
    mlPutMatrix "BondSettle", Worksheets("HJMDemo").Range("BondSettle")
    mlPutMatrix "BondMaturity", Worksheets("HJMDemo").Range("BondMaturity")
    mlPutMatrix "BondPeriod", Worksheets("HJMDemo").Range("BondPeriod")

    'Send Option
    mlPutMatrix "OptType", Worksheets("HJMDemo").Range("OptType")
    mlPutMatrix "OptUndBond", Worksheets("HJMDemo").Range("OptUndBond")
    mlPutMatrix "OptionStrike", Worksheets("HJMDemo").Range("OptionStrike")
    mlPutMatrix "OptionExDates",
       Worksheets("HJMDemo").Range("OptionExDates")
    mlPutMatrix "OptionAmEu", Worksheets("HJMDemo").Range("OptionAmEu")

    'Excel Serial Date Number Form to MATLAB Serial Date Number Form
    mlevalstring "BondSettle = x2mdate(BondSettle);"
    mlevalstring "BondMaturity = x2mdate(BondMaturity);"
    mlevalstring "OptionExDates = x2mdate(OptionExDates);"

    'Create InstSet
    mlevalstring "ProcessInst"

End Sub


Sub PutFwdCurve()
 'Send the initial forward curve to MATLAB and calculate RateSpec.

    mlPutMatrix "FwdStartDates",
       Worksheets("HJMDemo").Range("FwdStartDates")
    mlPutMatrix "FwdEndDates", Worksheets("HJMDemo").Range(" FwdEndDates")
    mlPutMatrix "FwdRates", Worksheets("HJMDemo").Range("FwdRates")

    'Excel Serial Date Number Form to MATLAB Serial Date Number Form
    mlevalstring "FwdStartDates = x2mdate(FwdStartDates);"
    mlevalstring "FwdEndDates = x2mdate(FwdEndDates);"

    'mlevalstring "ProcessFwdCurve"
    mlevalstring "RateSpec = intenvset('Rates', FwdRates, 'StartDates',
       FwdStartDates, 'EndDates', FwdEndDates,'Compounding', 1);"

End Sub

Sub PutSigma()

 'Send sigma to MATLAB.
 mlPutMatrix "Sigma", Worksheets("HJMDemo").Range("Sigma")

End Sub
```

```
Sub CalculatePrices()

    Call CalculateResults(False)

    Call MLGetMatrix("PriceBond", "G14")
    Call MLGetMatrix("PriceOpt", "G21")
    MatlabRequest

End Sub

Sub ViewPriceTree()

'View the price tree
    Call CalculateResults(True)

End Sub

Sub CalculateResults(bPlot As Boolean)

    'Create TimeSpec
    mlevalstring "TimeSpec = hjmtimespec(RateSpec.ValuationDate,
      RateSpec.EndDates(1:end), RateSpec.Compounding);"
    'Create VolSpec
    mlevalstring "VolSpec = hjmvolspec('Constant', Sigma);"
    'Build tree
    mlevalstring "HJMTree = hjmtree(VolSpec,RateSpec,TimeSpec);"


    If (bPlot) Then
        'Compute price/view tree
        mlevalstring "[Price, PriceTree] = hjmprice(HJMTree, InstSet);"
        mlevalstring "treeviewer(PriceTree,InstSet);"
    Else
        'Compute price
        mlevalstring "[Price] = hjmprice(HJMTree, InstSet);"
        mlevalstring "PriceBond =Price(1:3);"
        mlevalstring "PriceOpt =Price(end);"
    End If

End Sub
```

To process the data in Matlab, the following code is called:

```
%-----------------------
% Process the bond data:
InstSet = instadd('Bond', BondRate(1), BondSettle(1), BondMaturity(1),
          BondPeriod(1));
for i=2:length(BondName)
      InstSet = instadd(InstSet, 'Bond', BondRate(i), BondSettle(i),
                  BondMaturity(i), BondPeriod(i));
end

% Process option

% First find option index
BondIndex = strmatch(OptUndBond, BondName);
```

```
% If found, add to portfolio
if ~isempty(BondIndex)
      InstSet = instadd(InstSet, 'OptBond', BondIndex, OptType,
                 OptionStrike, OptionExDates, OptionAmEu);
end

InstSet = instsetfield(InstSet, 'Index',1:4, 'FieldName', {'Name'}, ...
                'Data', {'4% Bond'; '5% Bond'; '6% Bond';'Option'
});

clear i
```

A.6   Two-Factor HJM Model Implementation in Matlab

The following is an implementation of a two-factor HJM tree to build a forward rate. We assume both factors have volatilities generated by the Vasicek exponential volatility function—i.e., $\sigma_i e^{-\lambda_i(T-t)}, i = 1, 2$. We first specify the volatility function using `hjmvolspec`.

```
VolSpec = hjmvolspec('Exponential', 0.1, 1, 'Exponential', 0.5,1)

FinObj: 'HJMVolSpec'
FactorModels: {'Exponential'  'Exponential'}
FactorArgs: {{1x2 cell}  {1x2 cell}}
SigmaShift: 0
NumFactors: 2
NumBranch: 3
PBranch: [0.2500 0.2500 0.5000]
Fact2Branch: [2x3 double]
```

We can then price fixed-income derivatives using

```
VolSpec = hjmvolspec('Exponential', 0.1, 1, 'Exponential', 0.5,1)
RateSpec = intenvset('Compounding', Compounding,...
                'ValuationDate', ValuationDate,...
                'StartDates', StartDate,...
                'EndDates', EndDates,...
                'Rates', Rates);
TimeSpec = hjmtimespec(ValuationDate, EndDates, Compounding);
HJMTree = hjmtree(VolSpec, RateSpec, TimeSpec);
[Price, PriceTree] = hjmprice(HJMTree, RateSpec, TimeSpec)
```

For a two-factor HJM implementation in C++, see London (2004).

ENDNOTES

1. Jamshidian, F. (1991), "Bond and Option Evaluation in the Gaussian Interest Rate Model." *Research in Finance* 9: 131–170.
2. Hull, J., and White, A. (1994), "Numerical Procedures for Implementing Term Structure Models I: Single Factor Models," *Journal of Derivatives*, 1: 7–16.
3. In many books and papers, the model is written in a more general form:

$$dr = (\theta(t) - r)dt + \sigma dz$$

where

$$\theta(t) = a\bar{r}(t).$$

4. This relationship between Δr and Δt is considered a good choice because it satisfies stability convergence conditions of the trinomial method, which is the same as an explicit finite difference scheme.
5. Black, F. and Karasinski, P. (1991), "Bond and Option Pricing When Short Rates Are Lognormal." *Financial Analysts Journal*, July: 52–59.
6. Heath, D., Jarrow, R., and Morton, A. (1992), "Bond Pricing and the Term Structure of Interest Rates: A New Methodology for Contingent Claims Valuation." *Econometrica*, 60(1): 77–105.

CHAPTER 7 CODE

Due to the length of the code files in Chapter 7, "Energy and Power Derivatives," the Matlab code is shown in this appendix. The code includes code to price swing options by Doerr (2003) in §7.7, maximum likelihood parameter estimation of electricity diffusion models by Xiang (2004) in §7.13, and the pricing of natural gas futures by Xu (2004) in §7.17.

FROM SECTION 7.7, SWING OPTION PRICING IN MATLAB

The following Matlab code, written by Doerr (2004), provides the implementation of the LSM algorithm for pricing swing options using upswings, downswings, and penalty functions.

find_strategy.m

```
function f = find_strategy(cf_matrix,exercises,timesteps,strikes)
%calculates strategy matrix from given cashflow matrix
strat = zeros(exercises,timesteps);
strat(:,timesteps) = strikes(timesteps)*ones(exercises,1);
for e=2:exercises
    strat(:,timesteps+1-e) = cat(1,strikes(timesteps+1-e)*
      ones(exercises+1-e,1),zeros(e-1,1));
end
num_exercise(:,1) = (cf_matrix(:,1)~=0);
for i=2:timesteps
    num_exercise(:,i) = num_exercise(:,i-1) + (cf_matrix(:,i)~=0) ;
end
for i=1:timesteps
    num = num_exercise(:,i);
    cf = cf_matrix(:,i);
    num_exercise(:,i) = num.*(cf~=0);
end
%c = cf_matrix;
%n = num_exercise;
for i=1:exercises
    for j=i:timesteps-1-exercises+i
        cf_vector = cf_matrix(:,j);
        num_vector = num_exercise(:,j);
        a = (num_vector==i);
        if norm(a)==0
            strat(i,j) = 0;
```

503

```
        else
            strat(i,j) = min(cf_vector(num_vector==i)) + strikes(j);
        end
    end
end
cf_matrix;
f = strat;
```

coinc_strat_upswing.m

```
function swi = coinc_strat_upswing(paths,timesteps,delta_t,start_value,f,
  alpha,sigma,exercises,strikes)

loops = 10;
av = 0;
sqr_av = 0;
for l=1:loops
        S = create_paths_anti(paths,timesteps,delta_t,start_value,f,
          alpha,sigma);
        all_comb = combnk(1:timesteps,exercises);
        [c dummy] = size(all_comb);
        ex = unidrnd(c,paths,1);
        ex_ind = all_comb(ex);
        for i=2:exercises
        col_vector = all_comb(:,i);
        ex_ind = cat(2,ex_ind,col_vector(ex));
        end
        for i=1:timesteps
        ex_matrix(:,i) = zeros(paths,1);
        for e=1:exercises
        ex_matrix(:,i)=ex_matrix(:,i)+(ex_ind(:,e)==i);
        end
        end
        strike = repmat(strikes,paths,1);
        payoff = max(S-strike,0);
    cf = payoff.*ex_matrix;
    sim_value = sum(sum(cf'))/paths;
    av = av + sim_value;
    sqr_av = sqr_av + sim_value*sim_value;
end
av = av/loops;
sqr_av = sqr_av/loops;
rmse = sqrt(sqr_av-av*av);
swi = [av rmse];
```

cont_values.m

```
function c = cont_values(payoff,prices,cfws)

[zeile spalte wert] = find(payoff);
[m n] = size(payoff);
red_prices = prices(payoff>0);
red_cf = cfws(payoff>0);
p = polyfit(red_prices,red_cf,2);
```

```
red_cont = polyval(p,red_prices);
cont = sparse(zeile,spalte,red_cont,m,1);
c = full(cont);
```

create_paths_anti.m

```
function cp=create_paths_anti(paths,timesteps,delta_t,start_value,f,
  alpha,sigma);
%creates paths for electricity spot prices following a one-factor
%mean-reverting process
halfpaths = floor(paths/2);
rand_num = randn([halfpaths timesteps]);
anti = -rand_num;
full_randnum = cat(1,rand_num,anti);
%var = 1/(2*alpha)*(exp(2*alpha*delta_t)-1);
vari = sigma*sigma/(2*alpha)*(1-exp(-2*alpha*delta_t));
X = full_randnum*diag(sqrt(vari));
%Y = exp(sigma*X);
Y = exp(X);
beta = ones(1,timesteps)*f^diag(1-exp(-alpha*delta_t));
A = Y*diag(beta);
P = start_value*ones(paths,1);
S = start_value*ones(paths,timesteps);
for i=1:timesteps
    P = (P.^(exp(-alpha*delta_t(i)))).*A(:,i);
    S(:,i) = P;
end
L = log(S);
%cp=[mean(L) var(L)];
cp = S;
```

strat_upswing.m

```
function swi = strat_upswing(paths,timesteps,delta_t,start_value,f,alpha,
  sigma,exercises,strikes,strat_matrix,loops)
%calculates value of swing option by applying a given strategy matrix
av = 0;
sqr_av = 0;
for l=1:loops
        S = create_paths_anti(paths,timesteps,delta_t,start_value,f,
          alpha,sigma);
        cf_matrix = zeros(paths,timesteps);
        ex_ind = zeros(paths,1);
        for i=1:timesteps
        pcs = S(:,i);
        str = strikes(i)*ones(paths,1);
        pyf = pcs - str;
        for j=1:min(i,exercises)
                r = (pcs>strat_matrix(j,i)) & (strat_matrix(j,i)~=0) &
                (ex_ind==j-1);
                cf_matrix(:,i) = cf_matrix(:,i) + r.*pyf;
        end
        ex_ind = ex_ind + (cf_matrix(:,i)>0);
        end
```

```
    val_vector = sum(cf_matrix');
    av_value = sum(val_vector)/paths;
    av = av + av_value;
    sqr_av = sqr_av + av_value*av_value;
end
av = av/loops;
sqr_av = sqr_av/loops;
rmse = sqrt(sqr_av-av*av);
swi = [av rmse];
```

ls_upswing_strat.m

```
function ls = ls_upswing_strat(paths,timesteps,delta_t,start_value,f,
  alpha,sigma,exercises,strikes)
%calculates value of a swing option using extended L+S; strategy matrix
%is calculated in addition only upswings, no penalty!!
loops = 5;
av=zeros(exercises,1);
sqr_av=zeros(exercises,1);
av_strat = zeros(exercises,timesteps);
sqr_strat = zeros(exercises,timesteps);
for s=1:loops
   S = create_paths_anti(paths,timesteps,delta_t,start_value,f,alpha,sigma);
        cashflow = zeros(paths,timesteps,exercises);
        cont = zeros(paths,exercises);
        for i = 1:timesteps
        strike = strikes(timesteps+1-i)*ones(paths,1);
        pcs = S(:,timesteps+1-i);
        pyf = max(pcs,strike)-strike;
        for e = 1:exercises
                if e >= i
                cashflow(:,timesteps+1-i,e) = pyf;
            else
                if i > 2
                cf = sum(cashflow(:,timesteps+2-i:timesteps,e)')';
                else
                cf = cashflow(:,timesteps,e);
                end
                cont(:,e) = cont_values(pyf,pcs,cf);
            end
            end
            if i>1
                cashflow = reset_cfmatrix(cashflow,pyf,cont,i,timesteps,
                  exercises);
            end
    end
    for e=1:exercises
        valvector = sum(cashflow(:,:,e)')';
        av_value(e) = sum(valvector)/paths;
        av(e) = av(e)+av_value(e);
      sqr_av(e) = sqr_av(e)+av_value(e)*av_value(e);
    end
    strat_matrix = find_strategy(cashflow(:,:,exercises),exercises,
      timesteps,strikes);
    av_strat = av_strat + strat_matrix;
    sqr_strat = sqr_strat + strat_matrix.*strat_matrix;
```

```
end
av=av/loops;
sqr_av=sqr_av/loops;
rmse=sqrt(sqr_av-av.*av);
strat = av_strat/loops;
sqr_strat = sqr_strat/loops;
rmse_strat = sqrt(sqr_strat-strat.*strat);
%ls = strat;
ls=[av rmse strat rmse_strat];
```

ls_upswing.m

```
function ls = ls_upswing(paths,timesteps,delta_t,start_value,f,alpha,sigma,
    exercises,strikes)

loops = 5;
av=zeros(exercises,1);
sqr_av=zeros(exercises,1);
for s=1:loops
    S = create_paths_anti(paths,timesteps,delta_t,start_value,f,alpha,sigma);
    cashflow = zeros(paths,timesteps,exercises);
        cont = zeros(paths,exercises);
        for i = 1:timesteps
        strike = strikes(timesteps+1-i)*ones(paths,1);
        pcs = S(:,timesteps+1-i);
        pyf = max(pcs,strike)-strike;
        for e = 1:exercises
                if e >= i
                cashflow(:,timesteps+1-i,e) = pyf;
        else
                if i > 2
                cf = sum(cashflow(:,timesteps+2-i:timesteps,e)')';
                else
                cf = cashflow(:,timesteps,e);
                end
                cont(:,e) = cont_values(pyf,pcs,cf);
        end
        end
        if i>1
                cashflow = reset_cfmatrix(cashflow,pyf,cont,i,timesteps,
                    exercises);
        end
    end
    for e=1:exercises
        valvector = sum(cashflow(:,:,e)')';
        av_value(e) = sum(valvector)/paths;
        av(e) = av(e)+av_value(e);
      sqr_av(e) = sqr_av(e)+av_value(e)*av_value(e);
    end
end
av=av/loops;
sqr_av=sqr_av/loops;
rmse=sqrt(sqr_av-av.*av);
ls=[av rmse];
```

ls_updownswing.m

```
function ls = ls_updownswing(paths,timesteps,delta_t,start_value,f,alpha,
  sigma,ups,ustrikes,downs,dstrikes)

loops = 5;
av = 0;
sqr_av = 0;
for s=1:loops
    S = create_paths_anti(paths,timesteps,delta_t,start_value,f,alpha,sigma);
    % cashflow(:,:,u,d) means u-1 upswings and d-1 downswings are
    % already exercised!!
    cashflow = zeros(paths,timesteps,ups+1,downs+1);
    cont = zeros(paths,1,ups+1,downs+1);
    % initial timestep
    pcs = S(:,timesteps);
    t = timesteps;
    upyf = max(pcs-ustrikes(t),0);
    dpyf = max(dstrikes(t)-pcs,0);
    % both upswings and downswings left
    for u=0:ups-1
        for d=0:downs
            cashflow(:,t,u+1,d+1) = max(max(upyf-penalty(u-d+1),
                dpyf-penalty(u-d-1)),-penalty(u-d));
        end
    end
    % no downswings, but still upswings left
    for u=0:ups-1
        cashflow(:,t,u+1,downs+1) = max(upyf-penalty(u+1-downs),
            -penalty(u-downs));
    end
    % no upswings, but still downswings left
    for d=0:downs-1
        cashflow(:,t,ups+1,d+1) = max(dpyf-penalty(ups-d-1),-penalty(ups-d));
    end
    % no upswings and no downswings left
    cashflow(:,t,ups+1,downs+1) = -penalty(ups-downs);
    % stepping backwards in time
    for i=2:timesteps
            i;
            pcs = S(:,timesteps+1-i);
        upyf = max(pcs-ustrikes(timesteps+1-i),0);
        dpyf = max(dstrikes(timesteps+1-i)-pcs,0);
        % calculate continuation values
        ustop = min(ups,timesteps+1-i);
        for u=0:ustop
            for d=0:min(downs,timesteps+1-i-u)
                u;
                d;
                    if i > 2
                            cf = sum(cashflow(:,timesteps+2-i:timesteps,
                                u+1,d+1)')';
                    else
                            cf = cashflow(:,timesteps,u+1,d+1);
                    end
                cont(:,1,u+1,d+1) = cont_values(upyf,pcs,cf) +
                    cont_values(dpyf,pcs,cf);
            end
```

```
        end
        cashflow = reset_cfmatrix_ud(cashflow,pcs,ustrikes(i),dstrikes(i),
           cont,i,timesteps,ups,downs);
    end
    cashflow(:,:,1,1);
    valvector = sum(cashflow(:,:,1,1)')';
        av_value = sum(valvector)/paths;
    av = av + av_value;
    sqr_av = sqr_av + av_value*av_value;
end
av=av/loops;
sqr_av=sqr_av/loops;
rmse=sqrt(sqr_av-av.*av);
ls=[av rmse];
```

reset_cfmatrix.m

```
function ncf=reset_cfmatrix(old_cfmatrix,payoff,contmatrix,timestep,
  timesteps,exercises)
% timestep is counted backwards!!
[m dummy] = size(payoff);
for e=timestep:exercises
   new_cfmatrix(:,:,e) = old_cfmatrix(:,:,e);
end
stop = min(timestep-1,exercises);
for c=1:stop
   e = stop+1-c;
   if e==1
      z = find(payoff>contmatrix(:,1));
      wert = payoff(z);
   else
      z = find(payoff+contmatrix(:,e-1)>contmatrix(:,e));
      wert = payoff(z);
   end
   for j=timesteps-timestep+2:timesteps
      old_cfvector = old_cfmatrix(:,j,e);
      red_oldcf = full(sparse(z,1,old_cfvector(z),m,1));
      if e==1
         new_cfvector = zeros(m,1);
      else
         new_cfvector = old_cfmatrix(:,j,e-1);
      end
      red_newcf = full(sparse(z,1,new_cfvector(z),m,1));
      new_cfmatrix(:,j,e) = old_cfmatrix(:,j,e)-red_oldcf+red_newcf;
   end
   new_cfmatrix(:,timesteps+1-timestep,e) = full(sparse(z,1,wert,m,1));
end
ncf = new_cfmatrix;
```

reset_cfmatrix_ud.m

```
function new = reset_cfmatrix_ud(old_cashflow,pcs,ustrike,dstrike,
  contmatrix,i,timesteps,ups,downs)
%i is timestep counted from back
```

```
[paths dummy] = size(pcs);
new_cashflow = old_cashflow;
upyf = max(pcs-ustrike,0);
dpyf = max(dstrike-pcs,0);
ustop = min(ups-1,timesteps-i);
%both upswings and downswings left
for u=0:ustop
   for d=0:min(downs-1,timesteps-i-u)
      %exercise upswing
      cont_noex = contmatrix(:,1,u+1,d+1);
      cont_ex = contmatrix(:,1,u+2,d+1);
      old_cf = cat(2,zeros(paths,1),old_cashflow(:,timesteps+2-i:timesteps,
         u+1,d+1));
      cf_ex = cat(2,zeros(paths,1),old_cashflow(:,timesteps+2-i:timesteps,
         u+2,d+1));
      ncf_up = exercise(upyf,cont_noex,cont_ex,old_cf,cf_ex);
      %exercise downswing
      cont_noex = contmatrix(:,1,u+1,d+1);
      cont_ex = contmatrix(:,1,u+1,d+2);
      old_cf = cat(2,zeros(paths,1),old_cashflow(:,timesteps+2-i:timesteps,
         u+1,d+1));
      cf_ex = cat(2,zeros(paths,1),old_cashflow(:,timesteps+2-i:timesteps,
         u+1,d+2));
      ncf_down = exercise(dpyf,cont_noex,cont_ex,old_cf,cf_ex);
      %put together up and down
      new_cashflow(:,timesteps+1-i:timesteps,u+1,d+1) =
         merge_updown(ncf_up,ncf_down,old_cf);
   end
end
%no upswings left
for d=0:min(downs-1,timesteps-i-ups)
   cont_noex = contmatrix(:,1,ups+1,d+1);
   cont_ex = contmatrix(:,1,ups+1,d+2);
   old_cf = cat(2,zeros(paths,1),old_cashflow(:,timesteps+2-i:timesteps,
      ups+1,d+1));
   cf_ex = cat(2,zeros(paths,1),old_cashflow(:,timesteps+2-i:timesteps,
      ups+1,d+2));
   new_cashflow(:,timesteps+1-i:timesteps,ups+1,d+1) = exercise(dpyf,
      cont_noex,cont_ex,old_cf,cf_ex);
end
%no downswings left
for u=0:min(ups-1,timesteps-i-downs)
   cont_noex = contmatrix(:,1,u+1,downs+1);
   cont_ex = contmatrix(:,1,u+2,downs+1);
   old_cf = cat(2,zeros(paths,1),old_cashflow(:,timesteps+2-i:timesteps,
      u+1,downs+1));
   cf_ex = cat(2,zeros(paths,1),old_cashflow(:,timesteps+2-i:timesteps,
      u+2,downs+1));
   new_cashflow(:,timesteps+1-i:timesteps,u+1,downs+1) = exercise(upyf,
      cont_noex,cont_ex,old_cf,cf_ex);
end
new = new_cashflow;
```

penalty.m

```
function p=penalty(v)

if v~=0
   p = 1000000000;
else
        p = 0;
end;
```

The main driver functions are given by:

staple_paper.m

```
function st = stapel_paper(paths)

alpha = 0.55;
sigma = 0.95;
timesteps = 7;
delta_t = [1 1 1 1 1 1 1];
f = 22.5406;
strikes = f*delta_t;
start_values = [0.1 1 5 10 15 20 25 30 40 60 100];

res=zeros(1,3);
for sta=1:11
        ind = start_values(sta);
   act_res = ls_updownswing(paths,timesteps,delta_t,start_values(sta),f,
     alpha,sigma,3,strikes,3,strikes);
   act_erg = cat(2,ind,act_res);
   res = cat(1,res,act_erg);
end
for sta=1:11
        ind = start_values(sta);
   act_res = ls_upswing(paths,timesteps,delta_t,start_values(sta),f,alpha,
     sigma,3,strikes);
   act_erg = cat(2,ind,act_res(3,:));
   res = cat(1,res,act_erg);
end
for sta=1:11
        ind = start_values(sta);
   act_res = coinc_strat_upswing(paths,timesteps,delta_t,start_values(sta),
     f,alpha,sigma,3,strikes);
   act_erg = cat(2,ind,act_res);
   res = cat(1,res,act_erg);
end

st = res;
```

staple.m

```
function st = stapel(paths,timesteps,delta_t,f,ups,downs,strikes)

%[za sa] = size(alphas);
%[zs ss] = size(start_values);
```

```
%res = zeros(exercises,1);
%for a = 1:za
%    for s = 1:zs
%        res = cat(2,res,ls_upswing(paths,timesteps,delta_t,start_values(s),
%            f,alphas(a),sigma,exercises,strikes));
%    end
%end
%st = res;

alphas = [0.05,0.5];
start_values = [0.01,1,5,10,15,20,30,40,50,60,70,80];
sigmas = [0.392];

res = zeros(1,3);
for a=1:2
    for sig=1:1
        for sta=9:12
            ind(1,1) = start_values(sta);
                ind(1,2) = alphas(a);
            act_res = ls_updownswing(paths,timesteps,delta_t,start_values(sta),
                f,alphas(a),sigmas(sig),ups,strikes,downs,strikes);
            zahl = act_res(1,1);
            act_erg = cat(2,ind,zahl);
                res = cat(1,res,act_erg);
        end
    end
end

for a=1:2
    for sig=1:1
        for sta=9:12
            ind(1,1) = start_values(sta);
                ind(1,2) = alphas(a);
            act_res = ls_updownswing_p2(paths,timesteps,delta_t,
                start_values(sta),f,alphas(a),sigmas(sig),ups,strikes,
                downs,strikes);
            zahl = act_res(1,1);
            act_erg = cat(2,ind,zahl);
                res = cat(1,res,act_erg);
        end
        end
end

st = res;
```

From Section 7.13, Parameter Estimation in Matlab

The following Matlab code, written by Lei Xiong and Anthony Ware, estimates the model parameters using the maximum likelihood methodology from Xiong (2004) given in the previous section. The market data Xiong and Ware used to calibrate and estimate the model parameters (stored in the array and used in the functions) is from the Alberta Nordic Pool (but not provided).

Before doing the estimation, the data needs to be deseasonalized:

fixdata.m

```
% This is a utility function to help prepare the
% data, for example by detrending, or in the case of hourly electricity
% data, removing average daily fluctuations. It also offers the choice
% to randomize the data in order to compensate for quantisation effects
% should the user wish to do so
% datafile: the name of the data
% makerandom: randomization factor (0 means no randomization).
% deseasonalize: 1 if you want to get rid of seasonal factors
% y: rearranged logarithm of spot price
% Dt: annualized time step
%    e.g. 1/365 for daily gas data, 1/252 for daily oil data
% new_mdata: it is empty if no forward price is supplied.
%    Otherwise, it is arranged in 5 columns. The first is the
%    market date (t), the second is the delivery start date(T),
%    the third is the delivery end date (T+M), the fourth is
%    the forward price, and the fifth is the spot price for
%    that day.

function [y,Dt] = fixdata(datafile,makerandom,deseasonalize)

new_mdata = [];

switch datafile
 case 'pooltest'
        load pooltest
        N = length(p);
        p1 = p(:,1); p1 = p1(:);
        %p1 = randomize(p1,makerandom);
        Ndays = floor(N/24);
         N = Ndays*24;
        p1 = reshape(p1(1:N),24,Ndays);
        p1 = log(p1);
        s = [];
        if deseasonalize
        s = mean(p1,2);
            y = p1 - repmat(s,1,Ndays);
        else
            y=p1;
        end
        Dt = 1/(24*365);
        p1 = y(:);
        p(:,1) = p1;
        y = p;
 case 'onpeak'
        load onpeak
        p = log(onpeak);
        y = p(:);
        Dt = 1/365;
```

```
case 'offpeak'
        load offpeak
        p = log(offpeak);
        y = p(:);
        Dt = 1/365;
case 'paverage'
        load paverage
        p = avep;
        p = log(p);
        y = p(:);
        Dt = 1/365;
end
```

initheta.m

```
% This function gets the initial transformed theta (see "transtheta")
% together with the initial theta.
% y : the data you deal with
% Nseason:
%     -1: with no trend and no seasonal factor
%             0: with trend but no seasonal factor
%       1: with trend and one seasonal factor
%          (with a seasonal cycle as a year)
%       2: with trend and two seasonal factors
%          (with a seasonal cycle as half a year)
%       3: with trend and three seasonal factors
%          (with a seasonal cycle as a quarter)
% getdist:

%       1: the jump component has exponentially distributed
%          absolute value of jump size with a sign of the jump
%          determined by a Bernoulli variable.
%       2: the jump component is log-normal.
% Ttheta0: transformed initial theta
% theta0: initial theta

function [Ttheta0,theta0] = inittheta(y,getdummy,getdist)

if nargin < 2,
  Nseason = -1;
end

if nargin < 3,
  getdist = 1;
end

B = y(:,2)-y(:,1);
C = [-y(:,1) ones(size(y(:,1)))];
x = lsqlin(C,B);
thetapart = zeros(1,6);
thetapart(2) = x(2)/x(1);
thetapart(1) = x(1);
thetapart(3) = norm(C*x-B)^2/(size(y,1));
datadiff = y(:,2)-y(:,1);
```

```
switch getdist
  case 1
    thetapart(4) = 0.45;
    thetapart(5) = 0.45;
    thetapart(6) = mean(abs(datadiff));
  case 2
    upind = find(datadiff>0);
    downind = find(datadiff<0);
    thetapart(4) = 0.5;
    thetapart(5) = mean(datadiff(upind));
    thetapart(6) = 0.5;
thetapart = [thetapart -mean(datadiff(downind))];
end

switch getdummy
  case 'n'
    theta0 = thetapart;
  case 'y'
    theta0 = [thetapart,thetapart(2)];
end

Ttheta0 = transtheta(theta0,1,getdist);
```

GeeV.m

```
function [gv,N,R,fftT,Tgrad] = GeeV(Ttheta,fftT,getdist)
% This function helps to compute the integral in the density function by
% fast Fourier transform algorithm, called by function "LogExponential"
% Ttheta: the transformed theta
% fftT: is the interval of FFT
% gv: result obtained from the FFT computation
% N: the number of points of FFT computation
% R: the range of the the integration
% Tgrad: the gradient matrix w.r.t `Ttheta'

dt = 1;
dograd = (nargout>4);
TOL = 1e-5;
Nmax = 2^13;
% the allowed maximum value of N
theta = transtheta(Ttheta,-1,getdist,dt);
k = theta(1);
% k is kappa, the coeffecient of mean reversion
a = theta(2);
% a is alpha, long term mean of logged the price
sigma2 = theta(3);
% sigma^2 volitility, var(dp_t)
w = theta(4);
% omega, poisson arrival rate
psi = theta(5); % sign of the jump, it's a Bernoulli's parameter 0<psi<1
r = theta(6);
% r is gamma, the magnitude of jump.
if  any(imag(Ttheta)) | any(isinf(Ttheta))|k==0
  gv = []; N = [];  R = []; fftT = [];  Tgrad = [];
  return
end
```

```
% ----------------find a suitable value for R--------------------------
R2 = 10;
expR2 = (-(R2*sigma2/(4*k))*(1-exp(-2*k)) + (w/(2*k))* ...
    log((1+(r^2)*R2*exp(-2*k))./(1+(r^2)*R2)));
count = 0;
while expR2 > log(TOL);
count = count+1;
R2 = 2*R2 ;
expR2 = (-(R2*sigma2/(4*k))*(1-exp(-2*k)) + (w/(2*k))* ...
        log((1+(r^2)*R2*exp(-2*k))./(1+(r^2)*R2)));
end


R = sqrt(R2);
%----------------find a suitable value for fftT and N ----------------
N = 2 ^ ceil( 1+log2( R*fftT/pi ) );
fftT = N*pi/(2*R);
isNtoobig = 0;
if log2(N)> 18
  %disp(['N too large; R2=',num2str(R2),'; k=',num2str(k),'; s2=',
  %num2str(sigma2)]);
isNtoobig = 1;
gv = []; N = [];  R = []; fftT = [];  Tgrad = [];
    return
end
doagain = 1;
while doagain==1
    ds = 2*R/N;
    ss = linspace(-R,R-ds,N);
    ss = ss([(N/2)+1:N,1:N/2]);
    A1 = -((ss.^2)*sigma2/(4*k))*(1-exp(-2*k));
    A2 = (1i*w*(1-2*psi)/(k))*(atan(ss*exp(-k)*r)-atan(ss*r));
    A3 = (w/(2*k))*log((1+(ss.^2)*exp(-2*k)*(r^2))./(1+(ss.^2)*(r^2)));
    h = exp(A1+A2+A3);     % see formula 26 in the document
    g1 = (1/(2*pi))*ds*fft(h);
    g=[g1((N/2+1):end),g1(1:N/2+1)];
    gv = real(g);

  if max(abs(gv(1)))<TOL*max(gv)
    doagain=0;
  else

   N = 2*N; fftT = 2*fftT;


   if log2(N)>18
     %disp(['N too large; R2=',num2str(R2),'; k=',num2str(k),'; s2=',
     %num2str(sigma2)]);
     isNtoobig = 1;
     gv = []; N = [];  R = []; fftT = [];  Tgrad = [];
     return
   end
  end
end

[tmp,i]=max(gv);
if i==1
```

```
      gv = []; N = [];  R = []; fftT = [];  Tgrad = [];
      return
end
errest = abs(mean(gv([i-1,i+1])-gv(i)));

while errest > TOL*gv(i) & N<Nmax
    N = 2*N;
    R = 2*R;
    ds = 2*R/N;
    ss = linspace(-R,R-ds,N);
    ss = ss([(N/2)+1:end,1:N/2]);
    A1 = -((ss.^2)*sigma2/(4*k))*(1-exp(-2*k));
    A2 = (1i*w*(1-2*psi)/(k))*(atan(ss*exp(-k)*r)-atan(ss*r));
    A3 = (w/(2*k))*log((1+(ss.^2)*exp(-2*k)*(r^2))./(1+(ss.^2)*(r^2)));
    h = exp(A1+A2+A3);
    % h = h(s).
    g1 = (1/(2*pi))*ds*fft(h);
    g=[g1((N/2+1):end),g1(1:N/2+1)];
    gv = real(g);
    [tmp,i]=max(gv);
    errest = abs(mean(gv([i-1,i+1])-gv(i)));
end

%-----------------Evaluate the gradient-----------------------------------
if dograd
    % to compute gradient we'll take the fft of  s.*h, (s.^2).*h,
    % (atan(...)...).*h
    % ds/pi = R/(N*pi) = 1/fftT and this is the mean of z!
    % f_{j}(theta) = g(t,theta) = 1/2\pi \int^{\infty}_{\infty} Q(s,\theta)...
    % exp(-1i*s*t) ds and t= (y_{j} -a) -(y_{j-1}-a)*exp(-k)
    % evaluate gradient

  if k~=0|w~=0
    A1k = -A1/k - (ss.^2)*sigma2*exp(-2*k)/(2*k);
    A2k = -A2/k - 1i*w*(1-2*psi)*r*exp(-k)*ss./(k*(1+r^2*ss.^2*exp(-2*k)));
    A3k = -A3/k -w*r^2*ss.^2*exp(-2*k)./(k*(1+r^2*ss.^2*exp(-2*k)));
    fk2 = (1/(2*pi))*fft((A1k+A2k+A3k).*h)*ds;
    fs2 = (1/(2*pi))*fft(ss.^2.*h)*ds;
    A2w = A2/w;
    A3w = A3/w;
    fw = (1/(2*pi))*fft((A2w+A3w).*h)*ds;

    %derivative respect to psi
    A2psi = -(2*1i*w/k)*(atan(ss*exp(-k)*r)-atan(ss*r));
    fpsi = (1/(2*pi))*fft(A2psi.*h)*ds;
    fs1 = -1i*(1/(2*pi))*fft(ss.*h)*ds;

    %derivative respect to gamma
    A2r = 1i*w*(1-2*psi)/k*(exp(-k)*ss./(1+r^2*ss.^2*exp(-2*k))-ss./
      (1+r^2*ss.^2));
    A3r = w/k*(r*exp(-2*k)*ss.^2./(1+r^2*ss.^2*exp(-2*k))-r*ss.^2./
      (1+r^2*ss.^2));
    fr = (1/(2*pi))*fft((A2r+A3r).*h)*ds;
    gradtmp1 = [fs1; fk2; fs2; fw; fpsi; fr];
    gradtmp2 = [gradtmp1(:,(N/2+1):end), gradtmp1(:,(1:N/2+1))];
    Tgrad =real(gradtmp2);
  else
```

```
       Tgrad =[];
       return
     end
else
   Tgrad =[];
```

LogExponential.m

```
function [MinLLhood,Tgradient,gv,N,R,fftT] = LogExponential(Ttheta,p,
   getdist,getdummy,pdummy)
%Get the negative likelihood value for the Log-Exponential Jump

% Ttheta: the transformed theta
% y: rearranged data y_t, y(:,1) = y_t, y(:,2) = y_t+1
% getdist: represents the distribution type, shall be `1'
% Dt: the annualized time step
% onoffind: the index of on-peak or off-peak data
% MinLLhood: minus loglikelihood at the solution
% Tgradient: the gradient of the function at `Ttheta'
% gv: result obtained from the FFT computation
% N: the number of points of FFT computation
% R: the range of the the integration
% fftT: the interval of FFT computation

if nargin<5, pdummy = []; end
n = length(p)-1;
dt =1;
dograd = (nargout>1);
NofTh = length(Ttheta);
MinLLhood = 0; Tgradient = [];

theta = transtheta(Ttheta,-1,getdist);
if  any(imag(Ttheta)) | any(isinf(Ttheta))
    MinLLhood = 1e6; gv = []; N = []; R = []; fftT = [];   Tgradient =
       1e-6*ones(NofTh,1);
    return
end

k = theta(1);
a = theta(2);
sigma2 = theta(3);
w = theta(4);
psi = theta(5);
r = theta(6);

%---------- Set up some values for the seasonal factors----------

ft = 0;
ft1 = 0 ;% ft is used to adjust the drift by considering the
         % seasonal factors

if strcmp(getdummy,'y') % if the length of theta is larger than 6, we have
                        % included the seasonal factors
        a2 = theta(7);
    if ~isempty(pdummy)
```

```
%           ft1 = -a*pdummy(1:end-1,1) - a2*pdummy(1:end-1,2);
%             ft = (-a*pdummy(2:end,1) - a2*pdummy(2:end,2)) - exp(-k)*ft1;
            ft1 = -a*pdummy(2:end,1) - a2*pdummy(2:end,2);
            ft = (-a*pdummy(2:end,1) - a2*pdummy(2:end,2)) - exp(-k)*ft1;
        else
            ft1 = -a*p(1:end-1,2) - a2*p(1:end-1,3);
            ft = (-a*p(2:end,2) - a2*p(2:end,3)) - exp(-k)*ft1;
        end
        t_i_s = (p(2:end,1)) - exp(-k)*(p(1:end-1,1))+ft    ;
    else
        t_i_s = (p(2:end,1)-a) - exp(-k)*(p(1:end-1,1)-a)    ;
    end
fftT = 2*max(  abs( t_i_s ));
%------------------------Compute the minus-loglikelihood from FFT---------
 % fftT is the interval of FFT computation
if dograd
    [gv,N,R,fftT,Tgrad] = GeeV(Ttheta,fftT,getdist);
else
    [gv,N,R,fftT] = GeeV(Ttheta,fftT,getdist);
end

if isempty(gv)
    MinLLhood = 1e6; gv = []; N = []; R = []; fftT = []; Tgradient =
        1e-6*ones(NofTh,1);
    return
end

  % the values at which we really want.
t_j_s = linspace(-fftT,fftT,N+1);

if isreal(t_i_s) ~=1 | isnan(gv)
    MinLLhood = 1e6; gv = []; N = []; R = []; fftT = []; Tgradient =
        1e-6*ones(NofTh,1);
    return
else
    fis = interp1(t_j_s,gv,t_i_s,'linear',0);
    if any(fis<=0)
        MinLLhood = 1e6; gv = []; N = []; R = []; fftT = [];  Tgradient =
            1e-6*ones(NofTh,1);
        return
    else
        MinLLhood = -sum(log(fis)); Tgradient = 1e-6*ones(NofTh,1);

        %-------------------------- Evaluate the Tgradient----------.
        if dograd
            temp = zeros(n,6);
            Tgradient = 1e-6*ones(NofTh,1);
            for i = 1:6
                temp(:,i) = interp1(t_j_s,Tgrad(i,:),t_i_s,'linear',0);
            end

            Tk = exp(-k)*(p(1:end-1,1)-a);
            fT = temp(:,1);
            fk = fT.*Tk + temp(:,2);% Dg/Dk = (P_{j-1}-a)*exp(-k) *
                                    % gt + gk ; k denotes kappa;
            fa = fT.*(exp(-k)-1);
            fsigma2 = 1/(4*k)*(exp(-2*k)-1)*temp(:,3);
```

```
            fw = temp(:,4);
            fpsi = temp(:,5);
            fr = temp(:,6);
            gsigma2 = fsigma2*sigma2;
            fk = fk*k;
            gw = fw*w;
            gr = fr*r;
            gpsi = fpsi*0.5*(1-tanh(Ttheta(5))^2);
            gradtemp = [fk,fa ,gsigma2,gw,gpsi,gr];

            %~~~~~~~~~~~~~~~~ the following is the Tgradient with respect to
            %~~~~~~~~~~~~~~~~ seasonal factors---beta, eta
            if strcmp(getdummy,'y') % if the length of theta is larger
                                    % than 6, we have included the seasonal
                                    % factors
                if ~isempty(pdummy)
%                       fa = fT.*(exp(-k)*pdummy(1:end-1,1) -
%                         pdummy(2:end,1));
%                       fa2 = fT.*(exp(-k)*pdummy(1:end-1,2) -
%                         pdummy(2:end,2));
%                      Tk = exp(-k)*(p(1:end-1,1) - a*pdummy(1:end-1,1) -
%                        a2* pdummy(1:end-1,2));
                        fa = fT.*(exp(-k)*pdummy(2:end,1) - pdummy(2:end,1));
                        fa2 = fT.*(exp(-k)*pdummy(2:end,2) - pdummy(2:end,2));
                       Tk = exp(-k)*(p(1:end-1,1) - a*pdummy(2:end,1) -
                         a2* pdummy(2:end,2));
                else
                    fa = fT.*(exp(-k)*p(1:end-1,2) - p(2:end,2));
                    fa2 = fT.*(exp(-k)*p(1:end-1,3) - p(2:end,3));
                    Tk = exp(-k)*(p(1:end-1,1) - a*p(1:end-1,2) -
                      a2* p(1:end-1,3));
                end
                fk = fT.*Tk + temp(:,2);% Dg/Dk = (P_{j-1}-a)*exp(-k) *
                                        % gt + gk ; k denotes kappa;
                fk = fk*k;
                gradtemp = [fk, fa, gradtemp(:,3:end), fa2];
            end

            for i = 1:NofTh
                Tgradient(i) = -sum(gradtemp(:,i)./fis); % D_{\theta}L =
                                                         % sum (D_{\theta}
                                                         % fi/fi)
            end

        end
    end
end
```

DoEst.m

```
function [Ttheta,MinLLhood,flag,Tgrad,hess] = DoEst(Ttheta0,y,getdist,
  getdummy,pdummy)
% This function is used to get the estimates
```

```
% Ttheta0: starting transformed theta
% y: rearranged data y_t, y(:,1) = y_t, y(:,2) = y_t+1
% getdist: represents the distribution type
% Dt: the annualized time step
% onoffind: the index of on-peak or off-peak data
% Ttheta: the transformed theta
% MinLLhood: minus loglikelihood at the solution
% flag: the exit condition
%    > 0 The function converged to a solution theta;
%    = 0 The maximum number of function evaluations
%        or iterations was exceeded;
%    < 0 The function did not converge to a solution.
% Tgrad: the gradient of the objective function at `Ttheta'
% hess: the value of the Hessian of the objective function
%        at the solution

%Note I changed the tolx from 1e-10 to 1e-6
if nargin<3, getdist = 1;    end

if nargin<5, pdummy =[];    end
Display = 'iter';
  Npoints = 30;

if length(y)>1500
    LargeScale = 'on';
else
    LargeScale = 'off';
end
switch getdist
    case 1
        %            distype = 'LogExponential';
        distype = 'Logdensity';
    case 2
        distype = 'DbExponential';
        %     case 3
        %            distype = 'Logdensity';
end

%----------------------------First Try----------------------------------
iternum = 20; % the number of iteration
j = 0;
theta0 = [0.1094   -0.2577    0.0202    0.7669    0.5344    0.2401];
Ttheta0 = transtheta(theta0,1);
opt = optimset('maxfunevals',2000,'tolx',1e-6,'maxiter',iternum, ...
    'gradobj','off','largescale',LargeScale,'display',Display);
[Ttheta, MinLLhood, flag1, output, Tgrad, THess] = fminunc(distype,Ttheta0,
  opt,y,getdist,getdummy,pdummy);
i = 0;
theta = transtheta(Ttheta,-1,getdist);
if flag1 ==1
    switch getdummy
        case 'n'
            if getdist == 1
                transfactor = diag(1./[theta(1),1,theta(3),theta(4),0.5*
                    (1-tanh(Ttheta(5))^2,theta(6)]);
            else
                transfactor = diag(1./[theta(1),1,theta(3),theta(4),
```

```
                        theta(5),theta(6),theta(7)]);
              end
        case 'y'
            if getdist == 1
                transfactor = diag(1./[theta(1),1,theta(3),theta(4),0.5*
                  (1-tanh(Ttheta(5))^2),theta(6),1]);
            else
                transfactor = diag(1./[theta(1),1,theta(3),theta(4),
                  theta(5),theta(6),theta(7),1]);
            end
    end
    [TthetaP,maxmllhd,hess] = findpeak(Ttheta,Npoints,THess,distype,y,
      getdist,getdummy,pdummy);
    if maxmllhd <= (-MinLLhood)
        % -MinLLhood is the maximum of likelihood
        flag = flag1;
        return
    end
end
flag = 0;
while  flag<=0 | i<5
    %---------Keep restarting the optimization from last guess----------
    Ntry = 5 ;% Number of restarting times
    while ( flag<=0 ) & j<Ntry
        opt = optimset('GradObj','off', 'maxiter',iternum,'DiffMinChange',
           1e-10,'tolx',1e-6,'largescale',LargeScale,'display',Display,
             'tolfun',1e-7);
        TthetaP = Ttheta*1.005;
        [Ttheta, MinLLhood, flag, output, Tgrad, THess] = fminunc(distype,
           TthetaP,opt,y,getdist,getdummy,pdummy);
        j = j+1;
    end

    if strcmp(LargeScale,'on'), LargeScale = 'off'; else LargeScale =
      'on'; end
    j = 0;
    Ntry = 5; % Number of restarting times
    while ( flag<=0 ) & j<Ntry
        opt = optimset('GradObj','off', 'maxiter',iternum,'DiffMinChange',
           1e-10,'tolx',1e-6,'largescale',LargeScale,'display',Display,
            'tolfun',1e-7);
        TthetaP = Ttheta*1.005;
        [Ttheta, MinLLhood, flag, output, Tgrad, THess] =
           fminunc(distype,TthetaP,opt,y,getdist,getdummy,pdummy);
        j = j+1;
    end

    % -----Keep trying to get the highest points in every slice--------

    [TthetaP,maxmllhd,hess] = findpeak(Ttheta,Npoints,THess,distype,y,
      getdist,getdummy,pdummy); % TthetaP is the Ttheta w.r.t the peak
                               % of those slices

    if maxmllhd <= (-MinLLhood)       % -MinLLhood is the maximum of
                                      % likelihood
        return
    else
```

```
            [Ttheta, MinLLhood, flag,output,Tgrad,THess] = fminunc(distype,
                TthetaP,opt,y,getdist,getdummy,pdummy);
        end

        i = i+1;
end
```

findpeak.m

```
function [TthetaP,maxmllhd,hess] = findpeak(Ttheta,Npoints,THess,distype,y,
    getdist,getdummy,pdummy)
%   this function find the peak from slices
%   Npoints is the number of points in one slices
%   TthetaP is the Ttheta w.r.t the peak of those slices

NofTh = length(Ttheta); % the length of theta
llkhds = ones(Npoints,NofTh);
thetaplot = zeros(Npoints,NofTh);
Z = 1.96; % 95 percent confidence
theta = transtheta(Ttheta,-1,getdist);

%~~~~~~~Get the Hessian for untransformed theta~~~~~~~~
switch getdummy
    case 'n'
        if getdist == 1
            transfactor = diag(1./[theta(1),1,theta(3),theta(4),
                0.5*(1-tanh(Ttheta(5))^2),theta(6)]);
        else
            transfactor = diag(1./[theta(1),1,theta(3),theta(4),
                theta(5),theta(6),theta(7)]);
        end
    case 'y'
        if getdist == 1
            transfactor = diag(1./[theta(1),1,theta(3),theta(4),
                0.5*(1-tanh(Ttheta(5))^2),theta(6),1]);
        else
            transfactor = diag(1./[theta(1),1,theta(3),theta(4),
                theta(5),theta(6),theta(7),1]);
        end
end

hess = transfactor * THess * transfactor;
stder = (sqrt(diag(inv(hess))'));
lb = theta - Z*stder;
ub = theta + Z*stder;

for tt = 1:NofTh
    thetatemp = ones(Npoints,1)*theta;
    thetaincrease = linspace(lb(tt),ub(tt),Npoints)';
    thetatemp(:,tt) = thetaincrease;   %thetaincrease records the
                                       %increasement for every parameter
    Tthetatemp = transtheta(thetatemp,1,getdist);
    thetaplot(:,tt) = thetatemp(:,tt);
    for j = 1:Npoints
```

```
        llkhds(j,tt) = -feval(distype,Tthetatemp(j,:),y,getdist,
          getdummy,pdummy);
     end
end

% Get the highest points for each slice
ymax = zeros(NofTh,2);
for tt = 1:NofTh
    [ymax(tt,1),ymax(tt,2)] = max(llkhds(:,tt));
end

% Get the maximum of the highest points for all slices
[maxmllhd,indmax] = max(ymax(:,1));
maxtt = ymax(indmax,2); % maxtt is the index of the max row, form 1-Npoints,
                        % theta(indmax) needs to be changed

thetatemp = ones(Npoints,1)*theta;
thetaincrease = linspace(lb(indmax),ub(indmax),Npoints)';
thetatemp(:,indmax) = thetaincrease;   %thetaincrease records the
                                       %increasement for every parameter
Tthetatemp = transtheta(thetatemp,1,getdist);
TthetaP = Tthetatemp(maxtt,:);
```

FROM SECTION 7.17, NATURAL GAS PRICING IN MATLAB

The key Matlab code, written by James Xu (2004), for the pricing of natural gas futures using real-time gas data is given next.

estimateRData.m

```
clear; close all;
load gasTD_19920102_19991230.mat
ind=[];
for i = 1:length(tTDFS(:,2))
    if tTDFS(i,1)==tTDFS(i,2)
        ind=[ind;i];
    end
end
tTDFS(ind,2)=tTDFS(ind,2)+1;

type = 'A';
FWDtype = 'org';

Ntheta = 12;
NthetaX = 7;
period = 251;

[X1,ft1,RAtheta1,VsqdiffF,flag,output] = XRAthetafromtTDFS(tTDFS,NthetaX,
  Ntheta,period,FWDtype,type);
disp(RAtheta1)

thetaX0 = ones(1,NthetaX) * 0.1;
```

```
opt = optimset('maxfunevals',2e5,'tolx',1e-10,'maxiter',3000,'gradobj',
   'off','largescale','on','display','iter');

[thetaX1,Vasq1,flag1,output1] = fminsearch(@allsquares1,thetaX0,opt,
   X1,period,type);
[asq1,thetaXend1,sigmat1] = allsquares1(thetaX1,X1,period,type);
theta_est = [thetaXend1(1:NthetaX), RAtheta1(NthetaX+1:end)];
RAtheta_est = [RAtheta1(1:2),thetaXend1(3:NthetaX),
   RAtheta1(NthetaX+1:end)];

disp([theta_est;RAtheta_est])

%
% drawXLft;

L1 = theta_est(2);
figure(7);
hold off
plot(S)
hold on
plot(ft1+L1,'r')
%legend('X', 'estimated L');
title('S and f(t)+L');
hold off

tTDFSX = tTDFS;

dataname = strcat('allRData_',FWDtype,'_',type);
eval(['save ' dataname]);
```

allsquares1.m

```
function [asq,thetaXend,sigmat] = allsquares1(thetaX,X,period,type)

NthetaX = length(thetaX);
t = 1:length(X);

c = thetaX(3);
sigmat = exp(c*ones(size(t)));
if NthetaX>3
    Npsgm = (NthetaX-3)/2; % number of periods in sigma(t);
    lambda = thetaX(4:3+Npsgm);
    omega = thetaX(4+Npsgm:NthetaX);
    for k = 1:Npsgm
        sgtmp = lambda(k)*cos((2*pi*k*t)/period)+
          omega(k)*sin((2*pi*k*t)/period);
        sigmat = sigmat.*exp(sgtmp);
    end
end

switch type
    case 'A'
        sgx = (sigmat(1:end-1).^2);
    case 'B'
        sgx = (sigmat(1:end-1).^2).*X(1:end-1);
```

```
      case 'C'
          sgx = (sigmat(1:end-1).^2).*(X(1:end-1).^2);
end

B = sum((X(1:end-1).^2)./sgx);
C = sum((-X(1:end-1))./sgx);
D = sum((X(2:end)-X(1:end-1)).*X(1:end-1)./sgx);
E = sum(1./sgx);
F = sum((X(1:end-1)-X(2:end))./sgx);

alpha = (D*E-C*F)/(C^2-B*E);
L = -B/C - D/(C*alpha);

Bt = (alpha*(L-X(1:end-1))+X(1:end-1)-X(2:end));
Dc = sum(1-(Bt.^2)./sgx);
Dlambda = 0;
Domega = 0;
if NthetaX>3
    Dlambda = zeros(1,Npsgm);
    Domega = zeros(1,Npsgm);
    for k = 1:Npsgm
        Dlambda(k) = sum((1-(Bt.^2)./sgx).*(cos(2*pi*k*t(1:end-1)/period)));
        Domega(k) = sum((1-(Bt.^2)./sgx).*(sin(2*pi*k*t(1:end-1)/period)));
    end
end

asq = Dc^2 + norm(Dlambda)^2 + norm(Domega)^2;
thetaXend = thetaX;
thetaXend(1) = alpha;
thetaXend(2) = L;
```

XRAthetafrontTDFS.m

```
function [X,ft,RAtheta,VsqdiffF,flag,output] = XRAthetafromtTDFS(tTDFS,
  NthetaX,Ntheta,period,FWDtype,type)
% compute L and RAtheta from tTDFS matrix-data-file.

noft = length(unique(tTDFS(:,1))); % length of t
nofFTi = size(tTDFS,1)/noft; % number of Forwards for 1 fixed t
tt = reshape(tTDFS(:,1),nofFTi,noft);
TT = reshape(tTDFS(:,2),nofFTi,noft);
TTD = reshape(tTDFS(:,3),nofFTi,noft);
FF = reshape(tTDFS(:,4),nofFTi,noft);
SS = reshape(tTDFS(:,5),nofFTi,noft);

iternum = 1000; % the number of iteration
opt = optimset('maxfunevals',2e5,'tolx',1e-10,'maxiter',iternum,'gradobj',
  'on','largescale','on','display','iter');
RAtheta0 = initRAtheta(SS,NthetaX,Ntheta);
% RAtheta0 = [0.0110   -0.0237   -0.0141    0.0498    0.0004    0.0006
%    0.8765 0.0002    0.1500    0.0600    0.0100   -0.0500   -0.0301
%   -0.0121];
[RAtheta,VsqdiffF,flag,output] = fminsearch(@sqdiffF,RAtheta0,opt,
  NthetaX,tt,TT,TTD,FF,SS,period,FWDtype,type);
```

```
Ntry = 4 ;% Number of restarting times
j = 0;
while flag <=0 & j<Ntry
    RAtheta = RAtheta*1.05;
    [RAtheta,VsqdiffF,flag,output] = fminsearch(@sqdiffF,RAtheta,opt,
      NthetaX,tt,TT,TTD,FF,SS,period,FWDtype,type);
    j = j+1;
end


[sqdF,X,ft] = sqdiffF(RAtheta,NthetaX,tt,TT,TTD,FF,SS,period,FWDtype,type);


function RAtheta0 = initRAtheta(SS,NthetaX,Ntheta);
RAtheta0 = [0.0100   zeros(1,NthetaX-1)   0.05*ones(1,Ntheta-NthetaX)]*1.5;
%   RAtheta0 = [ 0.0110    2.3000    -2.5000    0.4000    0.1000    -0.2000
%    -0.0700    -0.0001 0.1500    0.0600    0.0500    -0.0300]*1.5;
```

To initialize the data and initial parameter estimates, the following code is used.

```
function RAtheta0 = initRAtheta(SS,NthetaX,Ntheta);
RAtheta0 = [0.0100 zeros(1,NthetaX-1) 0.05*ones(1,Ntheta-NthetaX)]*1.5;
%   RAtheta0 = [ 0.0110    2.3000    -2.5000    0.4000    0.1000  -0.2000
    -0.0700    -0.0001 0.1500    0.0600    0.0500    -0.0300]*1.5;
%%%%%%%%%%%%%%%%%%%%%%%%%%%%%%%%%%%%%%%%%%%%%%%%%%%%%%%%%%%%%%%%%%%%%%%

%%%%%%%%%%%%%%%%%%%%%%%%%%%%%%%%%%%%%%%%%%%%%%%%%%%%%%%%%%%%%%%%%%%%%%%
% draw results
type = 'C';
FWDtype = 'org';
dataname = strcat('allRData_',FWDtype,'_',type);
eval(['load ' dataname]);

ft1 = ft1(1:length(X1));
sigmat1 = sigmat1(1:length(X1));

alpha = theta_est(1);
L = theta_est(2);
c = theta_est(3);
lambda1 = theta_est(4);
lambda2 = theta_est(5);
omega1 = theta_est(6);
omega2 = theta_est(7);
b = theta_est(8);
beta1 = theta_est(9);
beta2 = theta_est(10);
eta1 = theta_est(11);
eta2 = theta_est(12);

n = length(S);
X = S-ft1;
Xt = X(1:end-1);
Xtp = X(2:end);
switch type
    case 'A'
        sgx = sigmat1(1:end-1);
```

```
    case 'B'
        sgx = sigmat1(1:end-1).*sqrt(Xt);
    case 'C'
        sgx = sigmat1(1:end-1).*Xt;
end

M = 30; % rows of grids
N = 16; % columns of grids


fig = figure(10);
scz = get(0,'screensize');
figsize = [scz(1)+130,scz(2)+60,scz(3)-260,scz(4)-160];
set(fig,'position',figsize);

hold off;
dx = (alpha*(L-Xt)+Xt-Xtp)./sgx;

yy = 2; xx = 1;
subpp = subplotposition(M,N,yy,xx);
subplot(M,N,subpp);
axis off;
text(1,1,'A)','fontsize',12);

yy = 1:6; xx = 3:8;
subpp = subplotposition(M,N,yy,xx);
subplot(M,N,subpp);
[Nx,Px] = hist(dx,0.025*n);
hist(dx,0.025*n);
lim = max(abs(Px)*1.05);
xlim = [-lim, lim];
set(gca,'xlim',xlim)
h = findobj(gca,'Type','patch');
set(h,'FaceColor','w')
hold on;
a = linspace(-lim,lim,100);
b = 1/(sqrt(2*pi))*exp(-(a.^2)/(2));
c = b*n*(Px(2)-Px(1));
plot(a,c,'linewidth',2)
hold off;

yy = 2; xx = 9;
subpp = subplotposition(M,N,yy,xx);
subplot(M,N,subpp);
axis off;
text(1,1,'B)','fontsize',12);

yy = 1:6; xx = 11:16;
subpp = subplotposition(M,N,yy,xx);
subplot(M,N,subpp);
qqplot(dx);
xlim = [-3.7, 3.7];
ylim = [-9, 9];
set(gca,'xlim',xlim,'ylim',ylim);
title('')
xlabel('')
ylabel('')
```

```
yy = 12; xx = 1;
subpp = subplotposition(M,N,yy,xx);
subplot(M,N,subpp);
axis off;
text(1,1,'C)','fontsize',12);

% switch type
%      case 'A'
%            rateb = [0.8, 0.15,   0.03, 0.3, 1.5, 0.6, 3.0,    0,0,0,0,0];
%      case 'B'
%            rateb = [0.8, 0.1,    0.02, 0.3, 1.5, 0.6, 3.0,    0,0,0,0,0];
%      case 'C'
%            rateb = [0.8, 0.2,    0.02, 0.3, 1.5, 0.6, 4.0,    0,0,0,0,0];
% end
% lb = theta_est - abs(theta_est).*rateb;
% ub = theta_est + abs(theta_est).*rateb;

switch type
    case 'A'
        stderr = [0.0046    0.0788    0.0151    0.0209    0.0241
0.0223    0.0210  0  0  0  0  0 ];
    case 'B'
        stderr = [0.0043    0.0858    0.0144    0.0242    0.0238
0.0242    0.0239  0  0  0  0  0];
    case 'C'
        stderr = [0.0043    0.0900    0.0127    0.0227    0.0210
0.0252    0.0201  0  0  0  0  0];
end
lb = theta_est - stderr;
ub = theta_est + stderr;

Npoints = 16;
drawslices(theta_est,NthetaX,lb,ub,t,S,ft1,period,Npoints,M,N,type)

Nsim = 250;
[simS,simX,simft,simsigmat,ts]=SimSX(S(1),theta_est,NthetaX,1,length(S),
  Nsim,period,type);

yy = 17; xx = 1;
subpp = subplotposition(M,N,yy,xx);
subplot(M,N,subpp);
axis off;
text(1,1,'D)','fontsize',12);

yy = 16:19; xx = 3:16;
subpp = subplotposition(M,N,yy,xx);
subplot(M,N,subpp);
[haxes,hline1,hline2] = plotyy(ts,ft1,ts,sigmat1);
axes(haxes(1))
ylabel('f(t)')
set(gca,'xlim',[1,length(S)+50])
axes(haxes(2))
ylabel('sigma(t)')
set(gca,'xlim',[1,length(S)+50])
set(hline2,'LineStyle','--')
%        legend('sigmat1',0);
```

```
%          legend('ft',0);
hold off;

yy = 24; xx = 1;
subpp = subplotposition(M,N,yy,xx);
subplot(M,N,subpp);
axis off;
text(1,1,'E)','fontsize',12);

sortS = sort(simS);
simS_05p = sortS(ceil(size(simS,1)*0.05),:);
simS_95p = sortS(floor(size(simS,1)*0.95),:);
yy = 23:30; xx = 3:16;
subpp = subplotposition(M,N,yy,xx);
subplot(M,N,subpp);
plot(ts,S,'r','linewidth',1.5);
hold on;
plot(ts,simS(2,:),'b');
plot(ts,simS_05p,'g-.')
plot(ts,simS_95p,'m:');
xlabel('t');
ylabel('Price');
legend('real spot prices','1 path of simulation','5% percentile','95%
  percentile',2);
title('real spot prices vs. simulated spot price');
ylim = [0, max([simS(2,:),S])+0.3];
set(gca,'xlim',[1,length(S)+50],'ylim',ylim);
hold off;

% text(200,300,'hello')

set(gcf, 'PaperPositionMode', 'manual');
set(gcf, 'PaperUnits', 'inches');
set(gcf, 'PaperPosition', [0.3 1 8.5 7.5]);
```

minusloglkhood.m

```
function [mllhd,fis] = minusloglkhood(theta,NthetaX,t,S,ft,period,type)

Ntheta = length(theta);
X = S-ft;
t = t(:)';
t = t(1:end-1);
X = X(:)';

Xtp = X(2:end);
Xt = X(1:end-1);

alpha = theta(1);
L = theta(2);
c = theta(3);
sigmat = exp(c*ones(size(t)));
if NthetaX>3
    Npsgm = (NthetaX-3)/2; % number of periods in sigma(t);
    lambda = theta(4:3+Npsgm);
```

```
        omega = theta(4+Npsgm:NthetaX);
        for k = 1:Npsgm
            sgtmp = lambda(k)*cos((2*pi*k*t)/period)+
                omega(k)*sin((2*pi*k*t)/period);
            sigmat = sigmat.*exp(sgtmp);
        end
end

switch type
    case 'A'
        H1t = ones(size(Xt));
    case 'B'
        H1t = sqrt(Xt);
    case 'C'
        H1t = Xt;
end

A1 = log(sqrt(2*pi)*sigmat.*H1t);
A2 = ((alpha*(L-Xt)+Xt-Xtp).^2)./(2*(sigmat.^2).*(H1t.^2));

logfis = -A1-A2;

mllhd = -sum(logfis);
```

forwardcurve.m

```
function [Ftis,ftiTis] = forwardcurve(RAtheta,NthetaX,Sti,ti,Tis,TDis,
   period,FWDtype,type)
% This function simulate forward price from given Spot price and L

Ntheta = length(RAtheta);

alpha1 = RAtheta(1);
L1 = RAtheta(2);

Tis = Tis(:)';
ft = zeros(1,max(max(Tis)));
if Ntheta > NthetaX % if the length of theta is larger than 4, we have
                    % included the seasonal factors
    t_of_ft = 1:max(max(Tis));
    b = RAtheta(NthetaX+1);
    ft = b*t_of_ft;
    if FWDtype == 'int'
        int_ft_TTTTD = 0.5*b*(Tis+TDis);
    end
    Npft = (Ntheta-NthetaX-1)/2;
    if Npft ~= 0
        beta = RAtheta(NthetaX+2:Ntheta-Npft);
        eta = RAtheta(Ntheta-Npft+1:end);
        for i = 1:Npft
            Pi = 2*pi*i/period;
            ftmp = beta(i)*cos(Pi*t_of_ft)+eta(i)*sin(Pi*t_of_ft);
            ft = ftmp + ft;
            if FWDtype == 'int'
```

```
                int_ft_TTTTD = int_ft_TTTTD + beta(i)*(sin(Pi*TDis)-
                    sin(Pi*Tis))./(Pi*(TDis-Tis))...
                                    + eta(i)*(cos(Pi*Tis)-
                                      cos(Pi*TDis))./(Pi*(TDis-Tis));
            end
        end
    end
end
ft = ft(:)';

switch type
    case {'A','B','C'}
        fti = ft(ti);
        fTis = zeros(size(Tis)); fTis(:) = ft(Tis); fTis = fTis(:)';
        if FWDtype == 'int'
            Aa = (exp(alpha1*(ti-Tis))-exp(alpha1*(ti-TDis)))./
                (alpha1*(TDis-Tis));
            Ftis = int_ft_TTTTD + L1+ (Sti-L1-fti).*Aa;
        else
            Ftis =   (L1+fTis) + (Sti-L1-fti).*exp(alpha1*(ti-Tis));
        end
end

ftiTis = [fti,fTis];

factor = 0;
Ftis = Ftis.*(1+factor*randn(size(Ftis))); % randomized Forward price,
                                           % controlled by 'factor'
```

sqdiffF.m
```
function [sqdF,X,ft] = sqdiffF(RAtheta,NthetaX,tt,TT,TTD,FF,SS,period,
  FWDtype,type)
% Compute the sum of squares of the differences between
% real Forward prices and those given by F(alpha1,mu1,t,T,S).
% We get the 'L1', 'alpha1' and 'mu1' via minimizing 'sqdF'.
% All the input arguments tt,TT,FF and SS are matrices, e.g., 12-by-500

Ntheta = length(RAtheta);

switch type
    case {'A','B','C'}

        alpha1 = RAtheta(1);
        L1 = RAtheta(2);

        ft = zeros(1,max(max(TT)));
        if Ntheta > NthetaX % if the length of theta is larger than that
                            % about X, we have included the seasonal
                            % factors
            t_of_ft = 1:max(max(TT));
            b = RAtheta(NthetaX+1);
            ft = b*t_of_ft;
            if FWDtype == 'int'
                int_ft_TTTTD = 0.5*b*(TT+TTD);
```

```
                 end
                 Npft = (Ntheta-NthetaX-1)/2;
                 if Npft ~= 0
                     beta = RAtheta(NthetaX+2:Ntheta-Npft);
                     eta = RAtheta(Ntheta-Npft+1:end);
                     for i = 1:Npft
                         Pi = 2*pi*i/period;
                         ftmp = beta(i)*cos(Pi*t_of_ft)+eta(i)*sin(Pi*t_of_ft);
                         ft = ftmp + ft;
                         if FWDtype == 'int'
                             int_ft_TTTTD = int_ft_TTTTD + beta(i)*(sin(Pi*TTD)-
                                 sin(Pi*TT))./(Pi*(TTD-TT))...
                                             + eta(i)*(cos(Pi*TT)-
                                               cos(Pi*TTD))./(Pi*(TTD-TT));
                         end
                     end
                 end
         end

         fftt = zeros(size(tt)); fftt(:) = ft(tt);
         ffTT = zeros(size(tt)); ffTT(:) = ft(TT);
         if FWDtype == 'int'
             Aa = (exp(alpha1*(tt-TT))-exp(alpha1*(tt-TTD)))./
               (alpha1*(TTD-TT));
             FF2 = int_ft_TTTTD + L1+ (SS-L1-fftt).*Aa; % FF2 is the
                                                        % recomputed FF
                                                        % from given but
                                                        % unreal RAtheta
         else
             FF2 = (L1+ffTT) + (SS-L1-fftt).*exp(alpha1*(tt-TT));
         end

         sqdF = sum(sum((FF-FF2).^2));

         XX = SS-fftt;
         X = XX(1,:);
end
```

SimFWDmat.m

```
function tTDFSX = SimFWDmat(RAtheta_sim,NthetaX,S,X,tt,TT,TTD,period,
  FWDtype,type)
% This function simulate forward price from given Spot price
% almu1_sim is the given risk-neutralized parameter containing alpha1 and
% mu1 and seasonal factors
% tt is start time, TT is the beginning of delivery time, TTD is the end
% of delivery time.

Ntheta = length(RAtheta_sim);

alpha1 = RAtheta_sim(1);
L1 = RAtheta_sim(2);

ft = zeros(1,max(max(TT)));
if Ntheta > NthetaX % if the length of theta is larger than 4, we have
                    % included the seasonal factors
```

```
    t_of_ft = 1:max(max(TT));
    b = RAtheta_sim(NthetaX+1);
    ft = b*t_of_ft;
    if FWDtype == 'int'
        int_ft_TTTTD = 0.5*b*(TT+TTD);
    end
    Npft = (Ntheta-NthetaX-1)/2;
    if Npft ~= 0
        beta = RAtheta_sim(NthetaX+2:Ntheta-Npft);
        eta = RAtheta_sim(Ntheta-Npft+1:end);
        for i = 1:Npft
            Pi = 2*pi*i/period;
            ftmp = beta(i)*cos(Pi*t_of_ft)+eta(i)*sin(Pi*t_of_ft);
            ft = ftmp + ft;
            if FWDtype == 'int'
                int_ft_TTTTD = int_ft_TTTTD + beta(i)*(sin(Pi*TTD)-
                    sin(Pi*TT))./(Pi*(TTD-TT))...
                                        + eta(i)*(cos(Pi*TT)-
                                          cos(Pi*TTD))./(Pi*(TTD-TT));
            end
        end
    end
end
ft = ft(:)';

tTDFSX(:,1) = tt(:);
tTDFSX(:,2) = TT(:);
tTDFSX(:,3) = TTD(:);

len = length(tt);
SS = zeros(len,1);
XX = zeros(len,1);

i = 1; j = 1;
SS(i) = S(j);
XX(i) = X(j);

for i = 2:len
    if tt(i)==tt(i-1)
        SS(i) = SS(i-1);
        XX(i) = XX(i-1);
    else
        j = j+1;
        SS(i) = S(j);
        XX(i) = X(j);
    end
end

tTDFSX(:,5) = SS;
tTDFSX(:,6) = XX;

switch type
    case {'A','B','C'}
        fftt = zeros(size(tt)); fftt(:) = ft(tt);
        ffTT = zeros(size(tt)); ffTT(:) = ft(TT);
        if FWDtype == 'int'
            Aa = (exp(alpha1*(tt-TT))-exp(alpha1*(tt-TTD)))./
```

```
                    (alpha1*(TTD-TT));
            Fprice = int_ft_TTTTD + L1+ (SS-L1-fftt).*Aa;
        else
            Fprice =  (L1+ffTT) + (SS-L1-fftt).*exp(alpha1*(tt-TT));
        end

end

factor = 0;
tTDFSX(:,4) = Fprice.*(1+factor*(1-2*rand(size(Fprice))))); % randomized
                                                            % Forward price,
                                                            % controlled by
                                                            % 'factor'
```

allestimate.m

```
ntimes = 50;

type = 'C';
alltheta_est = zeros(ntimes,24);

for i = 1:ntimes

    SimAllData;
    estimate;
    alltheta_est(i,1:12) = theta_est;
    alltheta_est(i,13:24) = RAtheta_est;

end

save allestimate_C theta_sim RAtheta_sim alltheta_est
```

drawPrices

```
load gasTD_19920102_19991230.mat
S(end+1) = S(end);
SS = reshape(S,251,8);
SS = SS';
% plot(1:251,SS(1:8,:),'g--');
% hold on;
% subplot(1,2,1)
figure(3);
hold off;
plot(mean(SS(1:8,:)),'b','LineWidth',2)

title('natural gas spot average daily prices over 8 years')
axis([0,260,1.7,2.7]);
xlabel('time (day)')
ylabel('price (dollors per MMBTU)')
hold off;
%
%
% DATESTR(729895,2)
load novagasmonthly
```

```
dn = datenum(1997,12,30);
ind = find(mdata(:,1)==dn);
fp = mdata(ind,4)';
delivdate = mdata(ind,2)';
% subplot(1,2,2)
figure(4);
plot(delivdate,fp);
title('natural gas futures prices')
axis([dn-50,max(mdata(ind,2))+50,2,2.7]);
xlabel('delivery time (mm/dd/yy)')
ylabel('price (dollors per MMBTU)')

xtick = [dn, delivdate(11),delivdate(23),delivdate(35)];
xticklabel = {'01/01/98','01/01/99','01/01/00','01/01/01'};
set(gca,'xtick',xtick, 'XTickLabel',xticklabel)

% load gasTD_19920102_19991230.mat
% fig3 = figure(3)
% plot(S)
% title('AECO gas prices')
% xlabel('time  (days)')
% ylabel('price (dollors per MMBTU)')
% xlim = [0,2100];
% set(gca,'xlim',xlim);
```

est1fMR.m

```
function [alpha, L, sigma] = est1fMR(S,type)

switch type
    case 'A'
        A = ones(size(S));
        A = A(1:end-1);
    case 'B'
        A = sqrt(S(1:end-1));
    case 'C'
        A = S(1:end-1);
end

St = S(1:end-1);
Stp = S(2:end);

B = sum((St.^2)./(A.^2));
C = sum((-St)./(A.^2));
D = sum((St.*(Stp-St))./(A.^2));
E = -sum(C);
F = sum(-1./(A.^2));
G = sum((Stp-St)./(A.^2));

alpha = (D*F-C*G)/(C*E-B*F);
L = -B/C - D/(C*alpha);
sigma = sqrt(mean(((alpha*(St-L)+(Stp-St)).^2)./(A.^2)));

% x = S(1:end-1); y = S(2:end);
% p = polyfit(x,y,1);
```

```
% z = p(1)*x + p(2);
% alpha = 1-p(1);
% L = p(2)/alpha;
% switch type
%     case 'A'
%           sigma = std(y-z);
%     case 'B'
%           sigma = std((y-z)./sqrt(x));
% end
```

SimFWDtTD.m
```
function [tt,TT,TTD,ttTTTTD] = SimFWDtTD(t,n,m,Tdiff,DelivLen)
% n is the number of T for 1 t
% m is the number of trading days in 1 month, usually being 30 here
% Tdiff is the difference of 2 succesive T's
% DelivLen is the length of delivery period

t = t(:)';
tt = repmat(t,n,1);

nofT = n + ceil(length(t)/m) + 3; % nofT is the number of all T's. To make
                                  % sure there are enough number of T's,
                                  % we add 3 up to it.

T0 = t(1)+Tdiff;
Ts = T0:Tdiff:(T0+nofT*Tdiff);
Ts = Ts + cumsum(round(rand(size(Ts)))); % Tdiff sometimes is 30,
                                         % sometimes is 31.

Ts = Ts(:);

TT = zeros(size(tt));
for i = 1:size(tt,2)
    ind = find(Ts>tt(1,i));
    ind = ind(1:n);
    TT(:,i) = Ts(ind);
end
tt = tt(:);
TT = TT(:);

TTD = TT+DelivLen;

ttTTTTD = [tt,TT,TTD];
```

SimSX.m
```
function [S,X,ft,sigmat,t]=SimSX(S0,theta,NthetaX,t0,TEnd,N,period,type)
% to get 2 matrices containing S's, X's and L's simulation respectively.
% S0 is the initial value of S
% N is the number of simulation paths
% t0 is the beginning of the time, TEnd is end
% the time length of every simulation is TEnd-t0+1
% dt is the time-step
% theta = [alpha, L, c, lambda..., omega..., b, beta..., eta...]
```

```
dt = 1;
t = t0:TEnd;

Ntheta = length(theta);

alpha = theta(1);
L = theta(2);
c = theta(3);
sigmat = exp(c*ones(size(t)));
if NthetaX>3
    Npsgm = (NthetaX-3)/2; % number of periods in sigma(t);
    lambda = theta(4:3+Npsgm);
    omega = theta(4+Npsgm:NthetaX);
    for k = 1:Npsgm
        sgtmp = lambda(k)*cos((2*pi*k*t)/period)+omega(k)*
          sin((2*pi*k*t)/period);
        sigmat = sigmat.*exp(sgtmp);
    end
end

ft = 0;
if Ntheta>NthetaX % if the length of theta is larger than that about X,
                  % we have included the seasonal factors
    b = theta(NthetaX+1);
    ft = b*t;
    Npft = (Ntheta-NthetaX-1)/2;
    if Npft ~= 0
        beta = theta(NthetaX+2:Ntheta-Npft);
        eta = theta(Ntheta-Npft+1:end);
        for i = 1:Npft
            ftmp = beta(i)*cos((2*pi*i*t)/period)+eta(i)*
              sin((2*pi*i*t)/period);
            ft = ftmp +ft;
        end
    end
    ft = ft(:)';
end

M = TEnd-t0+1; % column of the S matrix
X = zeros(N,M);

X(:,1) = S0 - ft(1);
W1=randn(N,M);

switch type
    case 'A'
        for j=2:M
            X(:,j) = X(:,j-1) + alpha*dt*(L-X(:,j-1)) +
              sigmat(j-1)*(dt^0.5)*W1(:,j-1);
        end
    case 'B'
        for j=2:M
            X(:,j) = X(:,j-1) + alpha*dt*(L-X(:,j-1)) +
              sigmat(j-1)*(dt^0.5)*sqrt(X(:,j-1)).*W1(:,j-1);
        end
    case 'C'
```

```
            for j=2:M
                X(:,j) = X(:,j-1) + alpha*dt*(L-X(:,j-1)) +
                    sigmat(j-1)*(dt^0.5)*X(:,j-1).*W1(:,j-1);
            end
end

S = X + repmat(ft,N,1);
```

forwardmatch.m

```
% ss = input('====Do you want to see how the expectation of the simulated
%   spot price match the forward curve?(y/n) ','s');
% if strcmp(ss,'y')
scz = get(0,'screensize');
figsize = [scz(1)+130,scz(2)+60,scz(3)-260,scz(4)-160];
% maxF = max(tTDFSXL(:,4));
% minF = min(tTDFSXL(:,4));
fig = figure(8);
set(fig,'position',figsize);

loop1 = 0;
t1 = 1;
while 1
    while 1
        if loop1~=1
            getdate = input(['====Please input a number within ',
                num2str(t(1)),'~',num2str(t(end)),': '],'s');
        else
            getdate = '0';
            t1 = t1+1;
            pause(0.3);
        end

        if isempty(getdate)
            t1=t1+1;
        elseif getdate=='0'
            loop1 = 1;
        else
            t1 = str2num(getdate);
        end

        [ti,Tis,TDis,Sti,Ftis] = DataFilter(tTDFSX,t1);
        if isempty(ti)
            if loop1==1, return; end
            disp('There is no forwards w.r.t. the number you input.
                Choose again, please.');
        else
            break;
        end
    end
%       if isempty(getdate), break; end

    %%%%%%%%%%%%%%%%%%%%%%%%%%%%%%%%%%%%%%%%%%%%%%%%%%% sim %%%%%%%%%%%%%%%%%
    N = 500;
    [Stis,Xtis,ftis,sigmatis,tis]=SimSX(Sti,RAtheta_est,NthetaX,ti,
```

```
    Tis(end),N,period,type);

sortS = sort(Stis);
simS_05p = sortS(ceil(size(Stis,1)*0.05),:);
simS_95p = sortS(floor(size(Stis,1)*0.95),:);

tiTis = [ti,Tis];
StiFtis = [Sti,Ftis];

subplot(30,1,[1,6]);
hold off
[haxes,hline1,hline2] = plotyy(tis,ftis,tis,sigmatis);
%        set(gca,'xtick',tT,'xticklabel',tT);
axes(haxes(1))
ylabel('f(t) (dollars)')
xlabel('time t (days)');
set(gca,'xtick',tiTis,'xticklabel',tiTis-tiTis(1));
axes(haxes(2))
ylabel('sigma(t)')
set(gca,'xtick',tiTis,'xticklabel',tiTis-tiTis(1));
set(hline2,'LineStyle','--')
title('f(t) and sigma(t)')

subplot(30,1,22:30);
hold off
plot(tiTis,StiFtis,'bo');
hold on;
% plot(tis,Stis(2,:),'k');
% plot(tis,simS_05p,'g-.')
% plot(tis,simS_95p,'m:');
plot(tiTis,StiFtis,'b','linewidth',1.5);
plot(tis,mean(Stis),'r');
set(gca,'xtick',tiTis,'xticklabel',tiTis-tiTis(1));
xlabel('time t (days)');
ylabel('Price (dollars)');
%        legend('One path of spot price simulation','5% percentile',
%        '95% percentile','Forward curve','Mean of spot price
%        simulations',0);
title('Expectation of simulated spot prices vs. the real
  futures curve');
hold off;

%%%%%%%%%%%%%%%%%%%%%%%%%%%%%%%%%%%%%%%%%% formula %%%%%%%%%%%%%%%%%%%%%%
[myFtis,ftiTis] = forwardcurve(RAtheta_est,NthetaX,Sti,ti,Tis,TDis,
  period,FWDtype,type);

subplot(30,1,10:18);
hold off

tiTis = [ti,Tis];
StiFtis = [Sti,Ftis];
StimyFtis = [Sti,myFtis];
plot(tiTis,StiFtis,'bo');
hold on;
plot(tiTis,StiFtis,'b','linewidth',1.5);
plot(tiTis,StimyFtis,'ro');
plot(tiTis,StimyFtis,'r');
```

```
%            ylim = [minF,maxF];
%            ylim = [ylim(1)-eps,ylim(end)+eps];
    set(gca,'xtick',tiTis,'xticklabel',tiTis-tiTis(1));
    xlabel('time t (days)');
    ylabel('Price (dollars)');
%        legend('One path of spot price simulation','5% percentile',
%        '95% percentile','Forward curve','Mean of spot price
%        simulations',0);
    title('Futures curve from formula vs. the real forward curve');
    hold off;

    set(gcf, 'PaperPositionMode', 'manual');
    set(gcf, 'PaperUnits', 'inches');
    set(gcf, 'PaperPosition', [0.2 1.5 7 7.3]);

end

% end
```

```
% Compute the cumulative Normal distribution in terms of the error function.
function y = N1(x);
  y = (1+erf(x/sqrt(2)))/2;

% Compute the inverse cumulative Normal distribution in terms of the
% error function
function y = N1inv(x);
  y = sqrt(2)*erfinv(2*x-1);
```

REFERENCES

CHAPTER 1

Audley, D., Chin, R., and Ramamuthy, S. (2002), "Term Structure Modeling," in *Interest Rate, Term Structure, and Valuation Modeling*. Edited by Fabozzi, F., John Wiley & Sons, Inc.

Chicago Board of Trade (2001), "Hedging a Fixed-Income Portfolio with Swap Futures," CBOT Interest Rate Swap Complex Series. *http://www.cbot.com/cbot/pub/page1/1,3248,1060,00.html.*

Fabozzi, F. and Mann, S. (Editors) (2001), *The Handbook of Fixed-Income Securities*. McGraw-Hill: New York, NY.

Fabozzi, F. (2002), *Interest Rate, Term Structure, and Valuation Modeling*. John Wiley & Sons, Inc.

Hull, J. (2005), *Fundamentals of Futures and Options Markets*. Prentice Hall.

James, J. and Webber, N. (2000), *Interest Rate Modeling*. John Wiley & Sons: Chichester, UK.

Jarrow, R. and Turbull, S. (2000), *Derivative Securities, 2nd ed.* South-Western Publishers: Cincinnati, Ohio.

Johnson, S.R. (2002), "Futures on Debt Positions," Williams School of Business, Xavier University, working paper. *http://www.academ.xu.edu/johnson/.*

Johnson, S.R. (2002), "Hedging Debt Positions with Futures and Options," Williams School of Business, Xavier University, working paper.

Johnson, S.R. (2004), *Bond Evaluation, Selection, and Management*. Blackwell Publishing.

Piennar, R. and Choudry, M. (2002), "Fitting the Term Structure of Interest Rates Using the Cubic Spline Methodology," in *Interest Rate, Term Structure, and Valuation Modeling*. Wiley & Sons, Inc., 157–185.

Strumeyer, G. (2005), *Investing in Fixed Income Securities: Understanding the Bond Market*. Wiley & Sons: Hoboken, NJ.

Waggoner, D. (1997), "Spline Methods for Extracting Interest Rate Curves from Coupon Bond Prices," working paper 97–10, Federal Reserve Bank of Atlanta.

CHAPTER 2

Bouyè, E., Durrleman, V., Nikeghbali, A., Riboulet, G., and Roncalli, T. (2000), "Copulas for Finance: A Reading Guide and Some Applications," Groupe de Reserche Operationnelle, Credit Lynonnais, Paris, working paper.

Drouet Mari, D. and Kotz, S. (2001), *Correlation and Dependence*. Imperial College Press, London.

Embrechts, P., Lindskog, F., & McNeil, A. (2001), "Modelling Dependence with Copulas and Application to Risk Management," ETH Zurich, Department of Mathematics, working paper.

Galiani, S. (2003), "Copula Functions and Their Applications in Pricing and Risk Managing Multiname Credit Derivative Products," Masters Thesis, King's College, London.

Hull, J. and White, A. (2005), "The Perfect Copula," University of Toronto, working paper.

Joe, H. (1997), *Multivariate Models and Dependence Concepts*. Chapman and Hall, London.

Joe, H. and Xu, J.J. (1996), "The Estimation Method of Inference Function for Margins for Multivariate Models," Dept. of Statistics, University of British Columbia, technical report, 1966.

Johnson, N.L. and Kotz, S. (1972), *Distribution in Statistics: Continuous Multivariate Distributions*. John Wiley & Sons, Inc.: New York.

Li, D. (1999), "On Default Correlation: A Copula Function Approach," The RiskMetrics Group, working paper, no. 99/07.

Lindskog, F., McNeil, A., and Schmock, U. (2001), "Kendall's Tau for Elliptical Distributions," ETH Zurich, Department of Mathematics, working paper.

Mashal, R. and Naldi, M. (2002), "Generalizing Asset Dependency: Application to Credit Derivatives Pricing," Quantitative Credit Research Quarterly, Lehman Brothers Inc., working paper.

Mashal, R. and Zeevi, A. (2002), "Beyond Correlation: Extreme Co-Movements Between Financial Assets," working paper, Columbia Graduate School of Business.

Meneguzzo, D. and Vecchiato, W. (2002), "Copula Sensitivity in Collateralized Debt Obligations and Basket Default Pricing and Risk Monitoring," Risk Management Dept., Intesa Bank, Mila, working paper.

Scaillet, O. (2000), "Nonparametric estimation of copulas for time series," IRES, working paper.

Schonbucher, P. and Schubert, D. (2001), "Copula-dependent default risk in intensity models," Department of Statistics, University of Bonn, working paper.

CHAPTER 3

Archer, W. and Ling, D. (1995), "The Effect of Alternative Interest Rate Processes on the Value of Mortgage-Backed Securities," *Journal of Housing Research*, 6: 2, 285–314.

Bandic, I. (2002), "Pricing Mortgage-Backed Securities and Collateralized Mortgage Obligations," University of British Columbia, working paper.

Boudoukh, J., Richardson, M., Stanton, R., and Whitelaw, R. (1995), "A New Strategy for Dynamically Hedging Mortgage-Backed Securities," working paper.

Boudoukh, J., Richardson, M., Stanton, R., and Whitelaw, R. (1998), "The Pricing and Hedging of Mortgage-Backed Securities: A Multivariate Density Estimation Approach," working paper.

Boudoukh, J., Richardson, M., Stanton, R., and Whitelaw, R. (2003), "The Valuation and Hedging of Deferred Commission Asset-Backed Securities," working paper.

Chatterjee, S. (1999), "The ARM Prepayment Model," *Quantitative Perspectives*. Andrew Davidson & Co., February.

Chatterjee, S. (2005), "Fixed-Rate Home Equity Loan Prepayment Model," *Quantitative Perspectives*. Andrew Davidson & Co., September.

Fabozzi, F., Richard, S., and Horwitz, D. (2002), "Monte Carlo Simulation/OAS Approach to Valuing Residential Real Estate-Backed Securities," in *Interest Rate, Term Structure, and Valuation Modeling*. Edited by Fabozzi, F., John Wiley & Sons, 443–468.

Gauseel, N. and Tamine, J. (2004), "Valuation of Mortgage-Backed Securities: From Optimality to Reality," Societe Generale Asset Management, working paper.

Johnson, S.R. (2002), "Analysis of Mortgage-Backed Securities: Monte Carlo Simulation Cash Flow Analysis," Xavier University, Williams School of Business. *http://www.academ. xu.edu/johnson/*.

Johnson, S.R. (2002), "Mortgage-Backed Securities," Xavier University, Williams School of Business. *http://www.academ.xu.edu/johnson/*.

Kalotay, A., Yang, D., and Fabozzi, F. (1991), "An Option-Theoretic Prepayment Model for Mortgages and Mortgage-Backed Securities," Andrew Kalotay Associates, Inc., working paper.

Kalotay, A., Yang, D., and Fabozzi, F. (1991), "When to Refinance: An Option-Based Approach," Andrew Kalotay Associates, Inc., working paper.

Kariya, T. and Kobayashi, M. (2000), "Pricing Mortgage-Backed Securities: A Model Describing the Burnout Effect," *Asia-Pacific Financial Markets*, 7, 189–204.

Kariya, T., Ushiyama, F., and Pliska, S. (2002), "A 3-Factor Valuation Model for Mortgage-Backed Securities (MBS)," working paper, April.

McConnell, J., and Singh, M. (1994), "Rational Prepayments and the Valuation of Collateralized Mortgage Obligations." *Journal of Finance*, 49, 891–921.

Obazee, P. (2002), "Understanding the Building Blocks for OAS Models," in *Interest Rate, Term Structure, and Valuation Modeling*. Edited by Fabozzi, F., John Wiley & Sons, 338–339.

Pliska, S. (2005), "Mortgage Valuation and Optimal Refinancing," Department of Finance, University of Illinois at Chicago, working paper.

Roll, R. and Scott, R. (1989), "Modeling Prepayments on Fixed-Rate Mortgage-Backed Securities," *Journal of Portfolio Management*, Spring, 73–82.

Sing, T.F., Ong, S.E., Fan, G., and Sirmans, C.F. (2001), "Cash Flow Swaps in Asset-Backed Securitization Transactions," Department of Real Estate, National University of Singapore, working paper.

Spahr, R. and Sunderman, M. (1991), "The Effect of Prepayment Modeling in Pricing Mortgage-Backed Securities," *Journal of Housing Research*, 3: 2, 381–399.

Stern, H. (2000), "ARM Home Equity Loan Prepayment Loan," *Quantitative Perspectives*. Andrew Davidson & Co., working paper.

Surkov, V. (2004), "Valuation of Mortgage-Backed Securities in a Distributed Environment," University of Toronto, Masters Thesis.

Titman, S., and Torous, W. (1989), Valuing Commercial Mortgages: An Empirical Investigation of the Contingent Claims Approach to Valuing Risky Debt. *Journal of Finance*, 44, 354–373.

CHAPTER 4

Bluhm, C., Overbeck, L., and Wagner, C. (2003), *An Introduction to Credit Risk Modeling*. Chapman & Hall/CRC.

Boscher, H. and Ward, I. (2002), "Long or short in CDOs," *RISK Magazine*, June, 135–129.

Credit Suisse First Boston (1997), *CreditRisk+—A Credit Risk Framework*.

Duffie, D. and Garleanu, N. (2001), "Risk and Valuation of Collateralized Debt Obligations." *Financial Analysts Journal* (January/February), 41–59.

Galiani, S. (2003), "Copula Functions and Their Applications in Pricing and Risk Managing Multiname Credit Derivative Products," Masters Thesis, King's College, London.

Gibson, M. (2004), "Understanding the Risk of Synthetic CDOs." Trading Risk Analysis Section, Division of Research and Statistics, Federal Reserve Board, working paper.

Goodman, L. (2002), "Synthetic CDOs: An Introduction." *Journal of Derivatives*, (Spring), 60–72.

Gregory, J. and Laurent, J. (2002), "Basket Default Swaps, CDOs, and Factor Copulas," working paper.

Gupton, M., Finger, C., and Bhatia, M. (1997), CreditMetrics—Technical Document. Risk Management Research, Morgan Guaranty Trust Company.

Hull, J., and White, A. (2004), "Valuation of a CDO and an nth to Default CDS without Monte Carlo Simulation," Rotman School of Management, University of Toronto, working paper.

Isla, L. (2003), "European CDOs: Review and Outlook," *Structured Credit Research*, Lehman Brothers, April.

Lehnert, N., Altrock, F., Rachev, S., Truck, S., and Wilch, A. (2005), "Implied Correlation in CDO Tranches," preprint.

Li, D. (2000), "On default correlation: a copula function approach." *Journal of Fixed Income* (March), 115–118.

Li, D. and Liang, M. (2005), CDO^2 Pricing Using Gaussian Mixture Model with Transformation of Loss Distribution, Barclays Capital, Quantitative Analytics, Global Credit Derivatives, working paper.

McGinty, L, and Ahuluwalia, R. (2004), A Relative Value Framework for Credit Correlation. Credit Derivatives Strategy, JP Morgan.

Merton, R. (1974), "On the Pricing of Corporate Debt: The Risk Structure of Interest Rates." *Journal of Finance*, 29, 449–470.

Picone, D. (2003) "Collateralized Debt Obligations." City University Business School, London and Royal Bank of Scotland, working paper.

Schmidt, W. and Ward, I. (2002), "Pricing Default Basket," *RISK Magazine*, January, 111–114.

Schonbucher, P. (2003), *Credit Derivatives Pricing Models: Models, Pricing, and Implementation*. John Wiley & Sons: Chichester, UK.

Tavakoli, J. (2003), *Collateralized Debt Obligations and Structured Finance: New Developments in Cash and Synthetic Securitization*. John Wiley & Sons, Hoboken, NJ.

Vasicek, O. (1987), "Probability of loss on loan portfolio." Moody's KMV (can be downloaded at *http://www.moodyskmv.com/research/whitepaper/Probability_of_Loss_on_Loan_Portfolio.pdf*), working paper.

Willemann, S. (2004), "An evaluation of the base correlation framework for synthetic cdos," working paper.

CHAPTER 5

Bluhm, C., Overbeck, L., and Wagner, C. (2003), *An Introduction to Credit Risk Modeling*. Chapman and Hall/CRC Financial Mathematics Series, Boca Raton.

Chen, R. and Sopranzetti, B. (2002), "The Valuation of Default-Triggered Credit Derivatives," Rutgers Business School, working paper.

Das, S., Freed, L., Geng, G., and Kapadia, N. (2002), "Correlated Default Risk," working paper.

Duffie, D. and Singleton, K. (1999), "Modeling Term Structures of Defaultable Bonds," *Review of Financial Studies*, 12(4), 687–720.

Galiani, S. (2003), "Copula Functions and Their Applications in Pricing and Risk Managing Multiname Credit Derivative Products," Masters Thesis, King's College, London.

Gregory, J. and Laurent, J. (2002), "Basket Default Swaps, CDOs, and Factor Copulas," working paper.

Houweling, P. and Vorst, T. (2002), "An Empirical Comparison of Default Swap Pricing Models," Erasmus University Rotterdam, working paper.

Hull, J, Predescu, M., and White, A. (2003), "The Relationship Between Credit Default Swap Spreads, Bond Yields, and Credit Rating Announcements," Rotman School of Management, University of Toronto, working paper.

Lando, D. (1998). "On Cox processes and credit risk securities," Department of Operations Research, University of Copenhagen, working paper.

Li, D. (1998), "Constructing a Credit Curve," in *Credit Risk, a RISK Special Report*, November, 40–44.

Mashal, R. and Naldi, M. (2002), "Pricing Multiname Credit Derivatives: A Heavy-Tailed Approach," *Quantitative Credit Research Quarterly*, Lehman Brothers, working paper.

Merton, R. (1973), "Theory of Rational Option Pricing." *Bell Journal of Economics and Management Science* 4: 141–183.

Naldi, M. (2001), "Basket Default Swaps and the Credit Cycle," *Quantitative Credit Research Quarterly*, Lehman Brothers, June.

O'Kane. D. (2001), "Credit Derivatives Explained: Market, Products, and Regulations," *Structure Credit Research*, Lehman Brothers, March.

O'Kane, D. and Turnbull, S. (2003), "Valuation of Credit Default Swaps," *Fixed Income Quantitative Credit Research*, Lehman Brothers, April.

Romano, C. (2002), "Calibrating and Simulating Copula Functions: An Application to the Italian Stock Market," CIDEM, working paper.

Schmidt, W. and Ward, I. (2002), "Pricing Default Basket," *RISK Magazine*, January, 111–114.

Schonbucher, P.J. (2003), *Credit Derivatives Pricing Models: Models, Pricing, and Implementation.* John Wiley & Sons: Chichester, UK.

Zheng, C.K. (1999), "Default Implied Volatility for Credit Spread," Morgan Stanley, working paper.

CHAPTER 6

Alaton, P., Djehiche, B., and Sillberger, D (2000), "On Modeling and Pricing Weather Derivatives," working paper.

Basawa, I. And P. Rao (1980), *Statistical Inference for Stochastic Processes*, Academic Press, New York.

Benth, F. and Šaltytė-Benth, J. (2005), "The Volatility of Temperature and Pricing of Weather Derivatives," University of Oslo, March.

Campbell, S. and Diebold, F. (2002), "Weather Forecasting for Weather Derivatives," reprint, December.

Cao, M., Li, A., and Wei, J. (2003), "Weather Derivatives: A New Class of Financial Instruments," University of Toronto, Rotman School of Management.

Dornier, F. and Queruel, M. (2000). "Caution to the Wind." *Risk, Energy, and Power Risk Management*, August.

Engle, R. (1982). "Autoregressive Conditional Heteroskedasticity with Estimates of the Variance of the United Kingdom Inflation." *Econometrica*, 50.

Jewson, S. and Caballero, R. (2003), "The Use of Weather Forecasts in the Pricing of Weather Derivatives," Meteorological Applications, 1–13.

Jovin, E. (1998), "Advances on the Weather Front (An Overview of the U.S. Weather Derivatives Market, Global Energy Risk)," 212(9), pg. S4 (2).

Kaminski, V. (1998), "Pricing Weather Derivatives (Global Energy Risk)." *Electrical World*, 212(9), pg. S4 (2)

Platen, E. and West, J. (2004), "Fair Pricing of Weather Derivatives." University of Technology Sydney, 1–27, July.

Roustant, O., Laurent, J., Bay, X., and Carraro, L. (2003), "A Bootstrap Approach to the Price Uncertainty of Weather Derivatives," working paper.

Zeng, L. (2000), "Pricing Weather Derivatives." *Journal of Risk Finance*, 72–78, Spring.

CHAPTER 7

Barlow, M., Gusev, Y., and Lai, M. "Parameter Estimation of Multifactor Models in Power Markets," preprint.

Barone-Adesi, G. and Gigli, A. (2002), "Electricity Derivatives." Institute of Finance-USI, Italy, unpublished working paper, 1–15.

Carmona, R. and Touzi, N. (2003), "Optimal Multiple Stopping and Valuation of Swing Options," working paper, May.

Chacko, G. and Viceria, G. (2001). "Spectral GMM Estimation of Continuous-time Processes," Graduate School of Business Administration, Harvard University, Tech. Report.

Clement, D. and P. Protter (2002), "An Analysis of a Least Squares Regression Method for American Option Pricing," *Finance and Stochastics*, 6, 449–471.

Clewlow, L. and Strickland, C. (2000), *Energy Derivatives: Pricing and Risk Management*. Lacima Publications.

Deng, S. (1999), "Stochastic Models of Energy Commodity Prices and Their Applications: Mean-Reversion with Jumps and Spikes," Georgia Institute of Technology, working paper.

Doerr, U. (2003), "Valuation of Swing Options and Exercise and Examination of Exercise Strategies by Monte Carlo Techniques," Masters Thesis, Christ Church College. University of Oxford, September.

Duffie, D., Pan, J., and Singleton, K. (2000), "Transform Analysis and Asset Pricing for Affine Jump-Diffusions." *Econometrica*, 68, 1343–1376.

Energy Information Administration (2002), "Derivatives and Risk Management in the Petroleum, Natural Gas, and Electricity Industries," U.S. Department of Energy, Washington D.C., October, 1–87.

Eydeland, A. and Geman, H. (1999), "Fundamentals of Electricity Derivatives, in: Energy Modelling & the Management of Uncertainty," *Risk Publications*, London, 35–43.

Gibson, R. and Schwartz, E. (1990), "Stochastic Convenience Yield and the Pricing of Oil Contingent Claims." *Journal of Finance*, 45: 3, July, 959–976.

Goto, M. and Karolyi, G. A. (2003), "Understanding Electricity Price Volatility Within and Across Markets," The Central Research Institute of Electric Power Industry in Japan and the Dice Center for Financial Economics, Tech. Report, 2003.

Jaillet, P., Ronn, E., and Tompaidis, S. (2004), "Valuation of Commodity-Based Swing Options," *Management Science*, Vol. 50, No. 7, 909–921.

Kaminski, V. (1997), "The Challenge of Pricing and Risk Managing Electricity Derivatives, in: The US Power Market," *Risk Publications*, London, 149–171.

Keppo, J. (2004), "Pricing of Electricity Swing Options," *Journal of Derivatives*, Vol. 11, 26–43.

Lari-Lavassani, A., Sadeghi, A., and Ware, T. (2001), "Modeling and Implementing Mean Reverting Price Processes in Energy Markets." Electronic Publications of the International Energy Credit Association.

Longstaff, F. and Schwartz, E. (2001), "Valuing American Options by Simulation: A Simple Least-Squares Approach," *Review of Financial Studies*, 14, 113–147.

Lucia, J. and Schwartz, E. (2001), "Electricity Prices and Power Derivatives: Evidence from the Nordic Power Exchange." University of Valencia, working paper.

Matyas, L. (1999). *Generalized Method of Moments Estimation*, Cambridge.

Meyer, J. (2004), "Valuation of Energy Derivatives with Monte Carlo," Masters Thesis, Christ Church College. University of Oxford, September.

Pilipovic, D. (1998), "Energy Risk: Valuing and Managing Energy Derivatives," preprint.

Pindyk, R. (1999), "The Long-Run Evolution of Energy Prices," Massachusetts Institute of Technology, unpublished working paper.

Pindyk, R. (2003), "Volatility in Natural Gas and Oil Markets," Massachusetts Institute of Technology, working paper, June.

Schwartz, E. (1997), "The Stochastic Behavior of Commodity Prices: Implications for Valuation and Hedging." *Journal of Finance*, 53 (3), July, 923–973.

Stoft, S., Belden, T., Goldman, C., and Pickle, S. (1998), "Primer on Electricity Futures and Other Derivatives." Environmental Energy Technologies Division, Berkeley National Laboratory, University of California-Berkeley.

Villaplana, P. (2002), "Pricing Power Derivatives: A Two-Factor Approach Jump-Diffusion Approach." University of Pompeu Fabra, Barcelona, Spain, working paper.

Xiong, L. (2004), "Stochastic Models for Electricity Prices in Alberta," Masters Thesis, Department of Mathematics and Statistics, University of Calgary, September.

Xu, Z. (2004), "Stochastic Models for Gas Prices," Masters Thesis, Department of Mathematics and Statistics, University of Calgary, August.

Chapter 8

Barone-Adesi, G. and Gigli, A. (2002), "Electricity Derivatives," working paper, Universita della Svizzera Italiana.

Bessimbinder, H. and Lemmon, M. (2002), "Equilibrium Pricing and Optimal Hedging in Electricity Forward Markets," *Journal of Finance*, 57.

Duffy, D. (2006), *Finite Difference Methods in Financial Engineering: A Partial Differential Equations Approach*. John Wiley & Sons: New York.

Eydeland, A. and Wolyniec, K. (2002), *Energy and Power Risk Management: New Developments in Modeling, Pricing, and Hedging*. John Wiley & Sons: New York.

Geman, H. (2005), *Commodities and Commodity Derivatives: Modeling and Pricing for Agriculturals, Metals, and Energy*. Wiley Finance: West Sussex.

Geman, H. and Roncoroni, A. (2006), "Understanding the Fine Structure of Electricity Prices," *Journal of Business*, 79.

Harrison, M.J. and Taksar, M. (1983), "Instantaneous Control of Brownian Motion," *Mathematics of Operations Research*.

Pirrong, C. (2006a), "Incorporating Outages into the Pirrong-Jermakyan Framework," working paper, University of Houston.

Pirrong, C. (2006b), "The Valuation of Power Options in a Pirrong-Jermakyan Framework," working paper, University of Houston.

Pirrong, C. and Jermakyan, M. (2006), "The Price of Power: The Valuation of Power and Weather Derivatives," working paper, University of Houston.

Pirrong, C. (2006), "Incorporating Outages in a Pirrong-Jermakyan Model," working paper, University of Houston.

Tikhinov, A. and Arsenin, V. (1977), *Solution of Ill-Posed Problems*. Halsted Press: New York.

CHAPTER 9

Duffie, D. and M. Huang (1996), "Swap Rates and Credit Quality," *Journal of Finance*, 51(3), July, 921–949.

Duffie, D. and Singleton, K. (1997), "An Econometric Model of the Term Structure of Interest Rate Swap Yields," *Journal of Finance*, 52(3): 1287–1321.

Fan, G., Sing, T., Ong, S.E., and Sirmans, C. (2004), "Governance and Optimal Financing for Asset-Backed Securitization," *Journal of Property Investment & Finance*, Vol. 22, No. 5, 414–434.

Ong, S. and Sing, T. (2000), "Asset Securitization in Singapore: A Tale of Three Vehicles," *Real Estate Finance*, 17(2), 47–56.

Sing, T., Ong, S., and Sirmans, C. (2003), "Asset-Backed Securitization in Singapore: Value of Embedded Buy-Back Options," *Journal of Real Estate Finance & Economics*, Vol. 27, No. 2, 173–180.

Sing, T.F., Ong, S.E., Fan G.Z., and Sirmans, C.F. (2004), "Analysis of Credit Risks in Asset-Backed Securitization Transactions in Singapore." Special issue for Maastricht-Cambridge Symposium 2002, *Journal of Real Estate Finance & Economics*, Vol. 28, No. 2/3, 235–254.

APPENDIX A

Black, F. and Karasinski, P. (1991), "Bond and Option Pricing When Short Rates Are Lognormal." *Financial Analysts Journal*, July: 52–59.

Heath, D., Jarrow, R., and Morton, A. (1992), "Bond Pricing and the Term Structure of Interest Rates: A New Methodology for Contingent Claims Valuation." *Econometrica*, 60(1): 77–105.

Hull, J. and White, A. (1994), "Numerical Procedures for Implementing Term Structure Models I: Single-Factor Models." *Journal of Derivatives*, 1: 21–32.

Jamshidian, F. (1991). "Bond and Option Evaluation in the Gaussian Interest Rate Model." *Research in Finance* 9: 131–170

INDEX

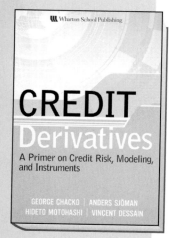

CREDIT DERIVATIVES
A Primer on Credit Risk, Modeling, and Instruments
George Chacko, Anders Sjoman, Hideto Motohashi, and Vincent Dessain

The credit risk market is the fastest growing financial market in the world, attracting everyone from hedge funds to banks and insurance companies. Increasingly, professionals in corporate finance need to understand the workings of the credit risk market in order to successfully manage risk in their own organizations; in addition, some wish to move into the field on a full-time basis. Most books in the field, however, are either too academic for working professionals, or written for those who already possess extensive experience in the area. *Credit Derivatives* fills the gap, explaining the credit risk market clearly and simply, in language any working financial professional can understand. Harvard Business School faculty member George C. Chacko and his colleagues begin by explaining the underlying principles surrounding credit risk. Next, they systematically present today's leading methods and instruments for managing it. The authors introduce total return swaps, credit spread options, credit linked notes, and other instruments, demonstrating how each of them can be used to isolate risk and sell it to someone willing to accept it.

ISBN 0131467441 ■ © 2006 ■ 272 pp. ■ $69.99 USA ■ $86.99 CAN

UNDERSTANDING ARBITRAGE
An Intuitive Approach to Financial Analysis
Randall Billingsley

Arbitrage is central both to corporate risk management and to a wide range of investment strategies. Thousands of financial executives, managers, and sophisticated investors want to understand it, but most books on arbitrage are far too abstract and technical to serve their needs. Billingsley addresses this untapped market with the first accessible and realistic guide to the concepts and modern practice of arbitrage. It relies on intuition, not advanced math: readers will find basic algebra sufficient to understand it and begin using its methods. The author starts with a lucid introduction to the fundamentals of arbitrage, including the Laws of One Price and One Expected Return. Using realistic examples, he shows how to identify assets and portfolios ripe for exploitation: mispriced commodities, securities, misvalued currencies; interest rate differences; and more. You'll learn how to establish relative prices between underlying stock, puts, calls, and 'riskless' securities like Treasury bills — and how these techniques support derivatives pricing and hedging. Billingsley then illuminates options pricing, the heart of modern risk management and financial engineering. He concludes with an accessible introduction to the Nobel-winning Modigliani-Miller theory, and its use in analyzing capital structure.

ISBN 0131470205 ■ © 2006 ■ 224 pp. ■ $39.99 USA ■ $49.99 CAN

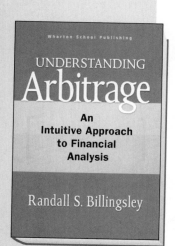